PASS THE 65™

A PLAIN ENGLISH EXPLANATION TO HELP YOU PASS THE SERIES 65 EXAM

ROBERT M. WALKER

MW00356319

Copyright © 2015 Sure Fire Publications, LLC.

NASAA Statements of Policy and Model Rules reprinted with permission.

FINRA rules and definitions from the FINRA manual reprinted with permission from FINRA; ©2015 Financial Industry Regulatory Authority (FINRA).

MSRB General Rules reprinted with permission from MSRB.

All rights reserved. No part of this book may be reproduced or transmitted in any form or by any means whatsoever, including photocopying, recording or by any information storage and retrieval system, without written permission from the publisher. Contact Sure Fire Publications, LLC.® at 1106 Lathrop Avenue, Forest Park, IL 60130-2228 (855) 392-6227

Although the author and publisher have made every effort to ensure that this book is as accurate and comprehensive as possible, they shall have no liability with respect to loss or damage stemming from use of its contents.

To ease readability, the author and publisher have not necessarily noted registered trade or service marks every time a company is mentioned. However, we acknowledge the rights and ownership that come with trade and service mark registration. If you have an objection to our use of a registered trade name without a registration symbol, please let us know and we will add the symbol or remove the name in the next edition.

www.examzone.com

Pass the 65™, 1st Edition ISBN-13 978-0-9831411-1-2

Library of Congress Control Number (LCCN) 2015901701

Publisher: Sure Fire Publications, LLC.® Forest Park, IL

Printed in the U.S.A.

Table of Contents

CHAPTER 1: Economic Factors & Business Information   *15*

    BASIC ECONOMIC CONCEPTS   15

    INFLATION, DEFLATION   15

    INTEREST RATES   17

    ECONOMIC INDICATORS   19

    FINANCIAL REPORTING   27

    TYPES OF RISK   37

    QUANTITATIVE METHODS   45

CHAPTER 2: Investment Vehicles   *59*

    TYPES AND CHARACTERISTICS OF EQUITY SECURITIES   59

    PREFERRED STOCK   67

    TYPES AND CHARACTERISTICS OF FIXED-INCOME SECURITIES   72

    METHODS USED TO DETERMINE THE VALUE OF FIXED-INCOME SECURITIES   94

    TYPES AND CHARACTERISTICS OF CASH AND CASH EQUIVALENTS   98

    POOLED INVESTMENT VEHICLES   102

    INSURANCE-BASED PRODUCTS   129

    TYPES AND CHARACTERISTICS OF DERIVATIVE SECURITIES   142

CHAPTER 3: Client Investment Recommendations & Strategies   *185*

    TYPE OF CLIENT   185

    CLIENT PROFILE   191

    CLIENT INVESTMENT RECOMMENDATIONS AND STRATEGIES   193

    PORTFOLIO MANAGEMENT STYLES & STRATEGIES   204

    PORTFOLIO MANAGEMENT TECHNIQUES   215

    PERFORMANCE MEASURES   218

    POSSIBLE CALCULATIONS ON YOUR EXAM   226

    TAX CONSIDERATIONS   227

    RETIREMENT PLANS   251

    SPECIAL TYPES OF ACCOUNTS: SAVING FOR EDUCATION   258

    ERISA ISSUES   260

    TRADING SECURITIES   264

    MARGIN   276

CHAPTER 4: Laws, Regulations, and Guidelines, Including Prohibition on Unethical Business Practices   *298*

    THE SECURITIES INDUSTRY   298

    ETHICAL PRACTICES AND FIDUCIARY OBLIGATIONS   301

STATE AND FEDERAL SECURITIES ACTS _____ 374

Glossary _____ *419*

Expanded Table of Contents

CHAPTER 1: Economic Factors & Business Information _____ *15*

BASIC ECONOMIC CONCEPTS _____ 15

INFLATION, DEFLATION _____ 15

INTEREST RATES _____ 17
  YIELD CURVES _____ 17
  YIELD SPREAD _____ 18

PRACTICE _____ 18

ECONOMIC INDICATORS _____ 19
  VALUE OF US DOLLAR, BALANCE OF TRADE, BALANCE OF PAYMENTS _____ 21
  BUSINESS CYCLES _____ 23
  FISCAL AND MONETARY POLICY _____ 24

PRACTICE _____ 26

FINANCIAL REPORTING _____ 27
  INCOME STATEMENT _____ 27
    ➤   EPS, P/E, and Profitability _____ 30
  CASH FLOW _____ 31
  BALANCE SHEET _____ 33
    ➤   Assets _____ 33
    ➤   Liabilities _____ 34
    ➤   Stockholders' Equity/Net Worth _____ 35
    Liquidity Measurements: Working Capital, Current Ratio, Quick Ratio, etc. _____ 35
  FOOTNOTES _____ 37
  TOP-DOWN AND BOTTOM-UP _____ 37

TYPES OF RISK _____ 37
  SYSTEMATIC RISKS _____ 38
    ➤   Market Risk _____ 38
    ➤   Natural Event Risk _____ 39
    ➤   Interest Rate Risk _____ 39
    Duration _____ 39
    ➤   Purchasing Power Risk _____ 40
    ➤   Call Risk _____ 40
    ➤   Reinvestment Risk _____ 41
    ➤   Prepayment Risk _____ 41
    ➤   Currency Exchange Risk _____ 42
    ➤   Political Risk _____ 42
  UN-SYSTEMATIC RISK _____ 42
    ➤   Business Risk _____ 42
    ➤   Legislative or "Regulatory" Risk _____ 43
    ➤   Credit/Default Risk _____ 43
    ➤   Liquidity Risk _____ 43
    ➤   Opportunity Cost _____ 43

PRACTICE _____ 44

QUANTITATIVE METHODS _____ 45

TIME VALUE OF MONEY _____ 45
   ➤ Future Value _____ 45
   ➤ Present Value _____ 47
   ➤ Internal Rate of Return and Net Present Value _____ 47
DESCRIPTIVE STATISTICS AND RISK MEASUREMENTS _____ 48
   ➤ Measures of Central Tendency _____ 49
   ➤ Standard Deviation _____ 49
   ➤ Sharpe Ratio _____ 51
   ➤ Beta _____ 51
   ➤ Alpha _____ 51
   ➤ R-Squared _____ 52

Chapter 1 Quiz _____ 52

CHAPTER 2: Investment Vehicles _____ 59
TYPES AND CHARACTERISTICS OF EQUITY SECURITIES _____ 59
  COMMON STOCK _____ 59
   ➤ Authorized, Issued, Treasury, Outstanding _____ 60
   ➤ Rights, Privileges of Common Stock Ownership _____ 61
   Dividends _____ 62
     > Regular Way Settlement _____ 62

PRACTICE _____ 63
     > Stock Splits, Stock Dividends _____ 64
   ➤ What Is a Share of Common Stock? _____ 65
   ➤ Rights, Warrants _____ 66
   ➤ ADRS _____ 67

PREFERRED STOCK _____ 67
  YIELD, TOTAL RETURN _____ 70
  FINAL THOUGHT _____ 71

PRACTICE _____ 71

TYPES AND CHARACTERISTICS OF FIXED-INCOME SECURITIES _____ 72
  RETIRING THE DEBT _____ 73
  BOND CERTIFICATES _____ 73
  QUOTES _____ 74
  NOTATION _____ 74
  RISKS TO BONDHOLDERS _____ 75
  CORPORATE BONDS _____ 75
   ➤ Liquidation Priority _____ 76
   ➤ Sinking Fund _____ 77
   ➤ Callable and Convertible _____ 77

PRACTICE _____ 78
  CREDIT RATINGS: MOODY'S, S&P & FITCH _____ 80
  US GOVERNMENT SECURITIES _____ 81
   ➤ T-Bills _____ 81
   ➤ T-Notes, T-Bonds _____ 82
   ➤ Strips _____ 83
   ➤ Treasury Receipts _____ 83
   ➤ TIPS _____ 83
   ➤ I-Bonds _____ 84
  GOVERNMENT AGENCY SECURITIES _____ 84

FOREIGN BONDS 86

MUNICIPAL SECURITIES 87

    ➢   General Obligation Bonds 88

    ➢   Revenue Bonds 88

    ➢   Secondary Market 90

PRACTICE **91**

    ➢   THE MSRB 92

CMOS, CDOS 92

METHODS USED TO DETERMINE THE VALUE OF FIXED-INCOME SECURITIES ____ **94**

RATES, YIELDS, PRICES 94

    ➢   Discount Bonds 94

    Current Yield 94

    Yield to Maturity 95

    Yield to Call 95

    ➢   Premium Bonds 95

    Current Yield 96

    Yield to Maturity 96

    Yield to Call 96

CONVERTIBLE SECURITIES 97

TYPES AND CHARACTERISTICS OF CASH AND CASH EQUIVALENTS _____ **98**

T-Bills 98

Bankers' Acceptances 98

Commercial Paper 99

Repurchase Agreements 99

Tax-Exempt Municipal Notes 100

Certificates of Deposit (CDs) 100

    ➢   Brokered CDs 100

    ➢   Negotiable/Jumbo CDs 101

    ➢   Demand Deposits 101

PRACTICE **101**

POOLED INVESTMENT VEHICLES **102**

INVESTMENT COMPANIES 102

    ➢   Advantages of Mutual Fund Investing 103

    ➢   Types of Mutual Funds 105

    Equity Funds 105

    Bond Funds 106

    Money Market Funds 107

    Specialty Funds 107

    ➢   Comparisons of Mutual Funds 108

    ➢   Sales Charges and Expenses 110

    A-, B-, and C-Shares 110

    Reducing the Sales Charge 113

        >   Breakpoints 113

        >   Letter of Intent 113

        >   Rights of Accumulation 114

        >   Combination Privilege 114

        >   Conversion/Exchange Privilege 115

    ➢   Structure and Operation of the Mutual Fund Company 115

    Board of Directors 115

Investment Adviser 115

Custodian 116

Transfer Agent 116

Underwriters/Distributors/Wholesalers 116

➢ Closed-End Funds 116

➢ Unit Investment Trusts 117

➢ Face-Amount Certificate Companies 118

➢ ETFS 118

REITS 120

ALTERNATIVE INVESTMENTS 121

➢ Direct Participation Programs (Limited Partnerships) 121

Suitability 122

Purpose of the Program 122

Investing in DPPs 124

Cash Flow and Income 125

Recourse Debt 127

➢ Hedge Funds 128

➢ Private Equity Funds 128

INSURANCE-BASED PRODUCTS **129**

Features of Annuities 129

Buying Annuities 132

Receiving Payments (Settlement Options) 133

➢ The Separate Account 134

Accumulation and Annuity Units 135

> AIR and Annuity Units 136

LIFE INSURANCE 137

➢ Permanent vs. Temporary Insurance 137

Variable Policies 138

➢ Policy Loans 140

➢ Settlement Options 140

➢ Needs Analysis 141

TYPES AND CHARACTERISTICS OF DERIVATIVE SECURITIES **142**

OPTIONS 142

➢ Calls 144

PRACTICE **144**

The Premium 145

> Time and Intrinsic Value 146

Breakeven, Max Gain, Max Loss 147

> Buyers 147

> Sellers 148

Gains and Losses 148

➢ The T-chart 149

➢ Exercise, Trade, Expire 150

PRACTICE **151**

➢ The Terminology: Synonyms 152

➢ Puts 153

Time and Intrinsic Value 154

PRACTICE **155**

Max Gain, Max Loss, Breakeven 155

PRACTICE _____ 157
  ➤ Strategy _____ 158
  ➤ Hedging (Risk Modification Techniques) _____ 159
    Hedging Long Positions _____ 159
      > Protection _____ 159
      > Max Gain, Max Loss, Breakeven _____ 160
      > Increasing Overall Return _____ 161
    Hedging Short Positions _____ 162
      > Protection _____ 162
      > Max Gain, Max Loss, Breakeven _____ 163
      > Increasing Overall Return _____ 163

PRACTICE _____ 164
    Index Options, CBOE VIX _____ 165
  FUTURES _____ 166
  FORWARDS _____ 168

PRACTICE _____ 168

Chapter 2 Quiz _____ 173

CHAPTER 3: Client Investment Recommendations & Strategies _____ 185

TYPE OF CLIENT _____ 185
  SOLE PROPRIETOR _____ 185
  PARTNERSHIPS _____ 186
    ➤ General Partnership _____ 186
    ➤ Limited Partnership _____ 186
  LLC (LIMITED LIABILITY COMPANY) _____ 187
  CORPORATIONS _____ 189
    ➤ S-Corporations _____ 189
    ➤ C-Corporations _____ 190

CLIENT PROFILE _____ 191

Client investment recommendations and strategies _____ 193
  Investment Objectives, Time Horizon, Risk Tolerance _____ 193
  Client Recommendations _____ 196

Portfolio management styles & strategies _____ 204
  VALUATION RATIOS _____ 204
    ➤ Price-to-Earnings Ratio _____ 204
    ➤ Price-to-Book Ratio _____ 204
    ➤ Price-to-Sales, Price-to-Cash Ratios _____ 204
  Market Capitalization (Market Cap) _____ 205
  GROWTH INVESTING _____ 205
  VALUE INVESTING _____ 206
  ACTIVE VS. PASSIVE MANAGEMENT _____ 207
  TECHNICAL ANALYSIS _____ 207
    ➤ Charts and Patterns _____ 207
    ➤ Advance-Decline Ratio _____ 209
    ➤ Volume _____ 210
    ➤ Market momentum and sentiment _____ 210
    ➤ Moving Average _____ 210
    ➤ Theories _____ 211

PRACTICE _____ **211**
BUY AND HOLD _____ 212
CAPM _____ 213
MODERN PORTFOLIO THEORY _____ 213
EFFICIENT MARKET HYPOTHESIS _____ 214

PORTFOLIO MANAGEMENT TECHNIQUES _____ **215**
ASSET ALLOCATION _____ 215
DIVERSIFICATION _____ 216
SECTOR ROTATING _____ 217
DOLLAR COST AVERAGING _____ 217

PRACTICE _____ **218**

PERFORMANCE MEASURES _____ **218**
HOLDING PERIOD AND ANNUALIZED RETURN _____ 219
YIELD _____ 219
YIELD VS. TOTAL RETURN _____ 220
INFLATION-ADJUSTED OR "REAL" RETURN _____ 221
AFTER-TAX RETURN _____ 222
TAX-EQUIVALENT YIELD _____ 222
RISK-ADJUSTED RETURN _____ 223
TIME-WEIGHTED, DOLLAR-WEIGHTED RETURN _____ 223
EXPECTED RETURN _____ 224
BENCHMARKS _____ 225
➤   Weighting _____ 225

POSSIBLE CALCULATIONS ON YOUR EXAM _____ **226**
Mortgage Payments _____ 226
Withdrawal Rates _____ 226

TAX CONSIDERATIONS _____ **227**
PORTFOLIO INCOME _____ 228
➤   Dividends _____ 228
Bond Interest _____ 229
➤   Taxation of municipal securities _____ 230
CAPITAL GAINS _____ 231
➤   Cost Basis _____ 231
➤   Proceeds _____ 232
➤   Holding Period _____ 232
Capital Losses _____ 232
➤   Offsetting Gains with Losses _____ 233
➤   Wash Sale Rules _____ 234
Unrealized Capital Gains _____ 235
Capital Gain or Loss on a primary residence _____ 235
MUTUAL FUND INCOME DISTRIBUTIONS _____ 236
➤   Capital Gains in Mutual Funds _____ 237
Distributions to Shareholders _____ 237
Shareholder Sales _____ 237
➤   Unrealized Gains _____ 237
➤   Cost Basis on Reinvestments _____ 238
Taxation of Annuities _____ 238
➤   Accumulation Period _____ 238
72(t) and Substantially Equal Periodic Payments _____ 239
Loans _____ 239

1035 Exchanges 239
➤   Annuity Period 240
Taxation of Life Insurance 240
TAXATION OF OPTIONS 241
➤   Expiration 241
➤   Close 241
➤   Exercise 241
➤   Leaps 242
TRANSFERRED SECURITIES 242
➤   Inherited Securities 242
➤   Gifted Securities 243
➤   Tax-deductible Charitable Donations 243
ESTATES 243
GIFTS 245
➤   Gift Splitting 246
TRUSTS 246
➤   Revocable, Irrevocable 247
➤   Tax Liability 247
➤   Simple vs. Complex 248
➤   Charitable Trusts 248
DISCLAIMING AN INHERITANCE 248
AMT 249
PROGRESSIVE, REGRESSIVE 249
TYPES OF INCOME 250
CORPORATE TAXES 250

PRACTICE 251

RETIREMENT PLANS 251
INDIVIDUAL RETIREMENT PLANS 252
➤   Traditional 252
Penalties 252
➤   Roth 253
Converting a Traditional to a Roth IRA 253
Income Limits 253
➤   Investment Restrictions 254
➤   Rollovers and Transfers 254
RETIREMENT PLANS OFFERED THROUGH AN EMPLOYER 255
➤   Defined Contribution Plans 255
➤   Defined Benefit Plans 257

SPECIAL TYPES OF ACCOUNTS: SAVING FOR EDUCATION 258
529 Savings Plan 258
Prepaid Tuition 259
Coverdell Education Savings Account 259
Calculating Educational Funding Needs 260

ERISA ISSUES 260
Fiduciaries 260
Safe Harbor, 404(c) 261
Company Stock 263

TRADING SECURITIES 264
FIRST MARKET – NYSE AND REGIONAL EXCHANGES 264

	➢ Consolidated Tape	265
	➢ Trading Curbs, Halts	266
OVER-THE-COUNTER		268
	➢ NASDAQ	269
	➢ Non-NASDAQ	269
THIRD MARKET		269
FOURTH MARKET		270
SELLING SHORT		270
	➢ Regulation SHO	271
BOND TRADING		272
TYPES OF ORDERS		273
	➢ Market Order	273
	➢ Limit Order	273
	➢ Stop Order	274
	➢ Further Details	275

PRACTICE — 275

MARGIN — 276

REG T	277
RUNNING THE NUMBERS	278
MINIMUM MAINTENANCE	280
SHORT POSITIONS	281
COMBINED EQUITY	282
MARGINABLE SECURITIES, ACCOUNTS	283

Chapter 3 Quiz — 283

CHAPTER 4: Laws, Regulations, and Guidelines, Including Prohibition on Unethical Business Practices — *298*

THE SECURITIES INDUSTRY — 298

ETHICAL PRACTICES AND FIDUCIARY OBLIGATIONS — 301

BUSINESS PRACTICES FOR INVESTMENT ADVISERS AND IARS		301
	➢ Fraud	302
	➢ Conflicts of Interest	304
Acting as Principal		305
Agency Cross Transaction		306
Additional Compensation for Directed Brokerage		307
12b-1 Fees		307
Holds a Position in the Security Recommended		308
Trade Allocations		308
Disclose or Abstain		309
Compensation Based on Capital Gains, Appreciation		309
Assignment of Contract		310
Notification of Change in Partnership Structure		311
	➢ Custody of Client Assets	311
	➢ Disclosing Identity, Affairs of Clients	314
	➢ Advertisements	314
	➢ Use of Solicitors	321
	➢ Use of Reports	321
	➢ Misleading Names	321
	➢ Code of Ethics	322
	➢ NASAA Model Rule on Business Practices for Advisers	324

Plain English Explanation _____ 329
Uniform Prudent Investor Act _____ 334
BUSINESS PRACTICES – BROKER-DEALERS AND AGENTS _____ 334
   Plain-English Explanation _____ 340
MORE NASAA CONCERNS _____ 345
   ➤ Research Reports _____ 345
   ➤ Using the Internet _____ 345
   ➤ Holding Seminars _____ 346
REGISTRATION OF PERSONS - INVESTMENT ADVISERS AND IARS ___ 347
   ➤ FEDERAL COVERED ADVISERS _____ 349
   Notice Filings _____ 349
   Withdrawal from Federal Registration_____ 350
   ➤ Disclosure Brochure _____ 350
   ➤ Wrap-Fee Programs _____ 353
   ➤ State Registration _____ 353
   Record Keeping _____ 354
   ➤ Investment Adviser Exclusions _____ 356
   ➤ Investment Adviser Exemptions _____ 358
NSMIA _____ 359
SEC RELEASE IA-1092 _____ 360
FLOW CHARTS _____ 362
BROKER-DEALER AND AGENT REGISTRATION REQUIREMENTS _____ 363
   ➤ Registration Procedure _____ 365
   ➤ Record Keeping Requirements _____ 366
   ➤ Net Capital Requirements _____ 367
   ➤ Renewals and Other Registration Specifics _____ 367
Defining Our Terms _____ 368
Exclusions and Exemptions for Persons _____ 370
   ➤ Not a Broker-Dealer _____ 370
   ➤ Exemptions _____ 371
   ➤ Agents _____ 372
   Exemptions _____ 373
STATE AND FEDERAL SECURITIES ACTS _____ 374
About the Financial Industry Regulatory Authority _____ 374
UNIFORM SECURITIES ACT _____ 375
   ➤ Administrative Provisions _____ 376
   Administrative Orders _____ 378
      > Punitive Orders _____ 378
      > Non-punitive Orders _____ 380
   ➤ Criminal Penalties _____ 381
   ➤ Civil Liabilities _____ 381
   ➤ Securities _____ 382
   Registering Securities _____ 384
      > Administrative Stop Orders _____ 385
   Methods of Registration_____ 386
      > Coordination _____ 386
      > Registration by Filing _____ 387
      > Qualification _____ 388
   Exempt Securities _____ 389
   Federal Covered Securities _____ 390

Exempt Transactions _____ 392

Offers and Sales _____ 394

Not Offers _____ 394

D-O-A _____ 395

FEDERAL SECURITIES ACTS _____ 396

➢ Securities Act of 1933 _____ 396

Exempt Securities _____ 397

Exempt Transactions _____ 398

SECURITIES EXCHANGE ACT OF 1934 _____ 399

TRUST INDENTURE ACT OF 1939 _____ 399

INVESTMENT COMPANY ACT OF 1940 _____ 400

INVESTMENT ADVISERS ACT OF 1940 _____ 401

INSIDER TRADING & SECURITIES FRAUD ENFORCEMENT ACT OF 1988 (ITSFEA) _____ 402

Chapter 4 Quiz_____ 402

*Glossary*_____ *419*

CHAPTER 1: Economic Factors & Business Information

BASIC ECONOMIC CONCEPTS

Even though I started investing at least a decade later than I should have, I am proud to report that I now have enough money in my retirement accounts to see some light at the end of the tunnel. If I keep funding the accounts and investing wisely, I could shave several years off my working life. On the other hand, if I get too lazy to make contributions, or if I invest those contributions foolishly, I could end up adding several years to my career, whether I want to or not.

What about you—will you be able to stop working someday? Even if you keep working, wouldn't it be nice to know you didn't have to at some point? Maybe you are already saving and planning through a 401(k), IRA, or other retirement account. If so, your financial future is subject to factors such as inflation, interest rates, recessions, corporate profits, and credit ratings.

Let's start with inflation.

INFLATION, DEFLATION

Some of my ancestors came to Chicago long before American banks were insured by the FDIC and never really trusted the idea of putting their hard-earned money in a bank that could collapse without warning. Several of my uncles and aunts would make purchases for washers & dryers or even used cars by simply pulling out a coffee can from a secret hiding place and grabbing a stack of twenty-dollar bills.

Unfortunately, if you put your extra cash in a coffee can, prices are probably rising throughout the economy. That means you are losing **purchasing power** as your money just sits there. Of course, it makes no sense to subject your cash to fire, theft, rodents, or flood, but even when you park your money in an FDIC-insured bank deposit, you usually find that the low rates of interest the bank pays do not keep pace with **inflation**. It might look as if you're earning more dollars, but because of inflation those dollars can't buy as much as they used to.

Inflation is a loss of purchasing power due to an overall rise in price levels. Your dollar used to buy a dozen eggs, for example. Now it buys only eleven, because the price of eggs has risen. What do you do now if you still need a dozen eggs? You spend more of your money. What if you don't have any more money? That's the problem with inflation. If your bank CD is paying you 2% while prices are rising 3%, you are losing ground. Your **inflation-adjusted** or **real rate of return** would be negative-1% in that case.

Inflation is sometimes described as "the result of too many dollars chasing a limited supply of goods and services." What would happen if they ran out of beer during the third inning at the old ballpark and then somebody stood up and announced he'd be happy to sell a cold six-pack to the highest bidder? How high would the price of cold beer rise on a hot August afternoon with thirty thousand thirsty fans bidding for such a tight supply?

That's *inflation*. At first maybe consumers will free up some money for gasoline by cutting back on snack chips. Maybe they can pay the power bill if the whole family agrees to brown-bag their lunch for a few months. While it's always nice to see American families pull together like that, the fact is we don't like to see the snack chip company or the local restaurants lose revenue and resort to laying off workers.

A loss of purchasing power for consumers is a fairly obvious economic problem, but sometimes economists worry about the opposite scenario: **deflation**. While inflation can make things too expensive for consumers to buy, deflation can make things ever cheaper. With deflation at work profit margins at businesses will be crushed, as they pay last month's prices for raw materials and then struggle to sell their finished goods at next month's cheaper prices. That's assuming they can sell anything to anyone—would you rush out to buy something today if you knew it would be cheaper tomorrow? Wouldn't we all be tempted to put off our purchases indefinitely, waiting for the prices of cell phones, clothing, and automobiles to drop in our favor? That would lead to lay-offs. And then those workers would have less money to spend and less confidence in their ability to buy anything on credit.

About two-thirds of the American economy is driven by consumer spending, so if consumers aren't spending, that's a problem. Therefore, the Federal Reserve Board's **Federal Open Market Committee (FOMC)** is forever monitoring and manipulating short-term interest rates in an attempt to find the right economic temperature—not too hot, not too cold. An inflation rate of about 2–3% is generally considered ideal, although it isn't as if there's a magic button they can push to adjust the economy.

Inflation/deflation is measured by the **CPI**, or **Consumer Price Index**, usually expressed as a percent of change from the previous month and from the same month the year prior. In other words, the CPI for October expresses the % the index rose or fell from September of this year and compared to October of last year. The CPI measures the trend for pricing of consumer goods and services, including food, beverages, housing, transportation, apparel, etc. Social security and retirement benefits are often tied to the CPI in that beneficiaries receive a cost of living adjustment based on the index. Occasionally, that cost of living adjustment factors in deflation, and beneficiaries receive smaller checks.

To eliminate two volatile/seasonal items from the index, economists focus on the index tracking "all items less food and energy," frequently referred to as **core inflation**. Because an oil spill or weather event could send the price of energy or food into a shock, economists like to separate out these items from the items that the Federal Open Market Committee is more able to control through their monetary policy.

Economists also monitor the **PPI**, or **Producer Price Index**. If producers are paying higher prices for materials, they will end up passing that on to consumers as much as possible. Perhaps you've seen the price of breakfast cereals jump dramatically. Did the demand for Corn Flakes or Special K suddenly force the $4 box of cereal up to $5.99? Probably not—it's just that the price of corn, sugar, rice, etc., has shot up recently and the increased cost is being passed on to consumers. Unfortunately, cereal producers will eventually hit the point where they can't pass on increased costs to consumers, and then their corporate profits will sag, and they will start laying people off, setting off a whole wave of bad economic news concerning a drop in consumer confidence, personal income levels, and employment rates. As we'll soon see, if the CPI and PPI are revealing inflation, the FOMC will raise interest rates to let some air out of the tires. If prices start to collapse we can end up with deflation, so "the Fed" will pump some air back into the tires by lowering interest rates.

Okay. So what are interest rates?

INTEREST RATES

If you need $50,000 to start a restaurant, chances are you have to borrow the money. The $50,000 you need to borrow is the **principal** amount of the loan. The extra money that you pay to borrow this principal is what we call **interest rates**. When there's a lot of money to be lent out, lenders will drop their rates in order to get you to borrow. When money is tight, however, lenders can charge higher rates. One way corporations borrow money is by selling bonds to investors, who act as lenders. How much should the corporate borrower pay the buyers of the bonds?

How about zero? Zero percent financing sounds tempting to a borrower; unfortunately, the buyers of debt securities demand compensation. They're the lenders of the money, and they demand the best interest rate they can receive in return for lending their hard-earned cash. So, bond issuers pay investors exactly what they have to pay them and not one basis point more. Interest rates, then, are really the result of constant spoken and unspoken negotiations going on between providers of capital (lenders) and those who would like to get their hands on some of it. If a corporation could get by with paying zero percent in order to borrow money through a bond issue, they would. Since they can't do that, they offer investors only as much as they have to in order to obtain the loan.

The exam may ask you to define or recognize the following interest rates:

- **Discount rate**: the rate banks have to pay when borrowing from the Federal Reserve.
- **Fed funds rate**: the rate banks charge each other for overnight loans in excess of $1 million. Considered the most volatile rate, subject to daily change.
- **Broker call loan rate**: the rate broker-dealers pay when borrowing on behalf of their margin customers.
- **Prime rate**: the rate that the most creditworthy corporate customers pay when borrowing through unsecured loans.

YIELD CURVES

Municipal bonds are usually issued under a serial maturity, which means that a little bit of the principal will be returned every year, until the whole issue is paid off. Investors who buy bonds maturing in 2025 will generally demand a higher yield than those getting their principal back in 2017. The longer your money is at risk, the more of a reward you demand, right? If a friend wanted to borrow $1,000 for one month, you'd probably do it interest-free. What if they wanted to take three years to pay you back? You could get some interest on a thousand dollars by buying a bank CD, which carries no risk, right? So, if somebody's going to put your money at risk for an extended period of time, you demand a reward in the form of an interest payment.

Same with bonds. If your bond matures in 2026 when mine matures in 2018, isn't your money at risk for 8 more years? That's why your bond would be offered at a higher yield than mine. If I buy a bond yielding 3.65%, yours would probably be offered at more like 3.99%. The extra 34 basis points is your extra reward for taking on extra risk.

This is how it works under a normal **yield curve**, where long-term bonds yield more than short-term bonds. Guess what, sometimes that yield curve gets inverted. Suddenly, the rule flies out the window, and folks are getting higher yields on short-term bonds than on long-term bonds. The cause of this is generally a peak in interest rates. When bond investors feel that interest rates have gone as high as they're going to go, they all clamor to lock in the high interest rates for the longest period of time. In a rush of activity, they sell off their short-term bonds in order to hurry up and buy long-term bonds at the best interest rate they're likely to see for a long time. Well, if everybody's selling off short-term bonds, the price drops [and the yield increases]. And if they're all buying up long-term bonds, the price increases [and the yield drops]. That causes the yield curve to invert, a situation that usually corrects itself very quickly.

NOTE: the curve sloping upward is a "normal yield curve," in which as the term to maturity increases, so does the yield. The curve sloping downward is an "inverted yield curve," a fairly rare situation where short-term debt securities yield more than long-term.

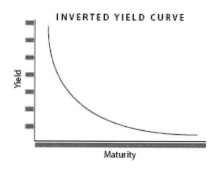

YIELD SPREAD

Yield curves are based on the term to maturity of debt securities. The **yield spread** is based on credit quality, as it considers the difference in yields between high-rated and low-rated bonds. If investors are demanding a much greater yield on low-rated bonds than on high-rated bonds, that's a negative indicator for the economy. Basically, it means investors are nervous about issuers' ability to repay. If investors don't demand a much higher yield on the low-rated bonds, that means in general they are confident about issuers' ability to repay, which is a positive indicator. So, when the "yield spread narrows," there is much reason to rejoice, while, on the other hand, when the yield spread widens, there could be trouble up ahead. If the 10-year US Treasury Note currently yields 3%, while 10-year junk bonds are yielding 8%, the spread or "risk premium" is 5 percentage points. Investors are demanding, in other words, a "risk premium" of 5 extra percentage points (500 basis points) of yield in order to buy the riskier bonds. If the T-Note is yielding 2% while high-yield bonds are yielding 5%, the yield spread has narrowed to just three percentage points. And, as we just saw, that implies more confidence on the part of bond investors.

PRACTICE

1. Inflation can also be thought of as:

    A. Capital appreciation

    B. Capital depreciation

C. A loss of purchasing power

D. An interest rate

2. The Consumer Price Index is used to:

A. Predict the direction of long-term interest rates

B. Measure inflation

C. Determine short-term financing rates

D. Establish intermediate-term rates on international business loans

3. Which of the following best expresses the Federal Reserve Board's role in shaping economic policy?

A. They establish long-term interest rates used by mortgage lenders

B. They negotiate more attractive interest rates for low-income home purchasers

C. Through monetary policy they raise and lower short-term interest rates

D. They write tax policy

(ANSWERS)

1. **C,** inflation is a loss of purchasing power.

2. **B,** the CPI measures inflation/deflation.

3. **C,** the Fed can control short-term rates, but has little control over long-term rates such as mortgage rates.

ECONOMIC INDICATORS

Gross Domestic Product (GDP) measures the total output of an economy. It's an estimate of the total value of all goods and services produced and purchased over a three-month period. If the GDP number comes in at 3%, that means that the economy grew at an annual rate of 3% over the financial quarter. If GDP is −2%, the economy is shrinking at an annual rate of −2%. A **recession** is defined as two consecutive financial quarters of declining GDP, up to six quarters (18 months). After that, if the economy is still declining, it is said to be in a **depression**. If the GDP is positive two quarters in a row, the economy is said to be in a period of **expansion**.

The Fed monitors many **economic indicators** to try and determine whether inflation is threatening the economy, or whether the Fed needs to provide some economic stimulus to a sagging economy. The exam might bring up **employment indicators**. As you might guess, employment indicators are based on employment. The following indicators tell us how many people are working and how much compensation they're receiving. If people aren't working, that signals an economic slowdown, and the Fed might have to lend a hand by lowering interest rates to free up money in the economy. If too many people are working, that signals inflation, and the Fed might have to step in by raising interest rates.

- Average Weekly New Claims for Unemployment Insurance: if people are showing up for unemployment insurance at a higher rate, that's negative. If the number of new claims drops, that means economic activity is picking up—positive.
- Unemployment Rate (Non-farm Payroll): also called "payroll employment." Includes full-time and part-time workers, whether they're permanent or temporary employees. Tracks how many people are working in the private sector. Released monthly. Called "non-farm" because it doesn't measure seasonal agricultural jobs, which skew the numbers.
- Employment Cost Index (ECI): measures the growth of wages and benefits (compensation) because if wages are rising really fast, inflation can't be far behind. Quarterly figure.

A **leading indicator** shows up before something happens and is used to predict. A **coincident indicator** tells us where we are right about now, and a **lagging indicator** gives us data about where we've just been, confirming a trend.

Leading (predict changes in the economy):

- the average weekly hours worked by manufacturing workers
- the average number of initial applications for unemployment insurance
- the amount of manufacturers' new orders for consumer goods and materials
- the speed of delivery of new merchandise to vendors from suppliers
- the amount of new orders for capital goods (equipment used to make products) unrelated to defense
- the amount of new building permits for residential buildings
- the S&P 500 stock index
- the inflation-adjusted monetary supply (M2)
- the spread between long and short interest rates
- consumer confidence
- bond yields

Coincident (current state of the economy):

- the number of employees on non-agricultural payrolls
- industrial production
- manufacturing and trade sales
- personal income levels
- Lagging (confirm trends, do not predict):
- the value of outstanding commercial and industrial loans
- the change in the Consumer Price Index for services from the previous month
- the change in labor cost per unit of labor output
- inventories
- the ratio of consumer credit outstanding to personal income
- the average prime rate charged by banks

- length/duration of unemployment

In the following table we're showing what the main indicators would tend to reveal to an economist. For example, if the "S&P 500" is "Up," that means the economy could be headed for an expansion, and when the "S&P 500" is "Down," the economy could be headed for a contraction. The "Fed" typically intervenes to "smooth out" the otherwise rough patches in the economy, so if they see "inflationary signals," they might start tightening credit/raising interest rates. If they see "deflationary signals," they might provide economic stimulus by loosening credit/lowering interest rates.

INFLATIONARY/EXPANDING	DEFLATIONARY/CONTRACTING
S&P 500 Up	S&P 500 Down
Building Permits Up	Building Permits Down
# of Manufacturing Workers Up	# of Manufacturing Workers Down
Unemployment Claims Down	Unemployment Claims Up
Consumer Confidence Up	Consumer Confidence Down
Manufacturers' New Orders Up	Manufacturers' New Orders Down
Capital Goods Spending Up	Capital Goods Spending Down
Personal Income Up	Personal Income Down
Manufacturing & Trade Sales Up	Manufacturing & Trade Sales Down
Payroll Employment Up	Payroll Employment Down
Inventory Levels Down	Inventory Levels Up
Duration of Unemployment Down	Duration of Unemployment Up

VALUE OF US DOLLAR, BALANCE OF TRADE, BALANCE OF PAYMENTS

Believe it or not, as recently as the early 1970s the value of the United States dollar was tied to a specific weight of gold. I mean, if you really wanted to, you could require the federal government to give you a specific weight of gold for each dollar you turned in. As a Forbes subscriber, I have read dozens of impassioned calls by Steve Forbes to return to this anachronistic "gold standard" system that forced the federal government to hold and secure enough gold to account for all currency then in circulation. When a country ties its currency either to a commodity such as gold, or to another currency, they are using a **fixed exchange rate** system. Many nations currently tie their currency to the US dollar, in fact, which is, again, a type of fixed exchange rate system for those nations.

Like most world currencies, the US Dollar's value is today determined by a free-market, supply-and-demand system known as a **floating-rate currency** system. How does a dollar compare to the yen, or the Euro in terms of its **exchange rate**? That is a question whose answer can change every day of the week, depending on many factors. Primarily, the exchange rate between the dollar and another currency is determined by the supply and demand for the currencies and the amounts held in foreign reserves. Is the US suddenly the place to invest? If so, the value of the dollar will rise, and vice versa. Although the values could be wildly different by the time you read these words, the current exchange rate for the Euro is 1 Euro = 1.15 Dollars and the current exchange rate for the Yen is 1 Yen = .01 Dollars, or one penny. If the exam shows an exchange rate, understand that if the rate between Euro and Dollar became 1 Euro = 1.45 Dollars, we could say either that the Euro strengthened or that the US dollar weakened. It now takes 30 cents more to equal the same Euro, in other words.

Imports and exports are directly affected by the value of the American dollar relative to foreign currencies. As our dollar strengthens, our exports become less attractive to consumers in other countries, whose weak currency can't buy our expensive stuff. When our dollar *weakens*, our exports are *more* attractive because suddenly their strong currencies can buy lots of our relatively cheap stuff. Likewise, a strong dollar makes foreign travel less expensive for Americans, whereas a weak dollar makes foreign travel more expensive. It's just a way of asking how much of their stuff our dollar can buy. So, if the exchange rate for Euro to Dollar goes from 1 Euro = 1.15 Dollars to 1 Euro = 1.45 Dollars, that could help Americans export to European nations, whose currency can now go farther when buying American goods. Florida could see even more European tourists enjoying long vacations this season.

The **balance of trade** number tracks money in and money out of the economy for imports and exports. If we export more to a country than we import from it, we have a **trade surplus** with that nation. If we import more from a country than we export to it, we have a **trade deficit** with that nation. The exam could refer to the difference between a country's exports and imports as their **current account**. Therefore, if a country imports more than it exports, it runs a current account deficit and a current account surplus when it exports more than it imports. Also note that by "exports" and "imports" we include goods and services. So, whether the U-S-of-A is still manufacturing and exporting lots of finished goods or not, we definitely export a lot of services in terms of legal, accounting, investment banking, professional consulting, etc. Know also that if the US has a trade deficit with China, that means that China is holding a lot of our currency—that's how they pay for all those imports from us. We never want anyone to dump large quantities of our currency all at once and devalue it drastically in an act of retaliation or a sudden lack of confidence. That, of course, makes relations with China or other such trading partners very tricky at times.

The strength of the dollar and trade deficits constantly work towards an equilibrium. If a weak dollar increases foreign demand for American-made goods, that increased demand for American-made goods will also increase the demand for dollars, making them stronger. And then it will be harder to export to foreign buyers. On the other hand, if a strong dollar hurts exports, the lack of foreign demand for American-made goods will also eventually drive down the value of the dollar, which—as we saw—should eventually increase the attractiveness of our exports.

Interest rates also help determine the value of our currency. When interest rates in the United States are much higher than interest rates abroad, the demand for US assets will increase the demand for the dollars needed to buy them (e.g., bank accounts, stocks, bonds, and real estate), and increase the value of the dollar compared to foreign currencies. On the other hand, if interest rates in the United States are lower than interest rates abroad, the demand for foreign assets will likely strengthen and the demand for US assets will likely weaken. This will cause the demand for foreign currencies to strengthen, leading to a depreciation of the dollar compared to foreign currencies.

So, if we had a trade deficit with the European Union, would a strong dollar or a weak dollar help to bring us back to a surplus? Well, if we were already importing more from the EU than we were exporting, we would want to make our exports more attractive to the Europeans and our imports from the EU less attractive to Americans, which would happen as the dollar weakens. The dollar weakening is another way of saying the other currency is strengthening, remember. And, yes, the exam likes to confuse test-takers over inherently confusing concepts like that. Remember that time is on your side—slow down the tricky questions and break them down carefully. That's half the battle at the testing center.

In any case, the **balance of payments** statistic tracks all money coming in versus going out of the economy. So, it counts both imports vs. exports and also investments and other financial transactions. If more money is coming in than going out, we have a surplus. If more money is going out than coming in, we have a deficit. If a test question says that foreigners are paying off loans to American banks, this could lead to a balance of payments surplus for the US, for example. Or, the exam might want you to say something like, "a balance of payments deficit is financed by capital inflows from foreign investors." As I write these words, China is basically financing our balance of payments deficit by buying up huge quantities of dollar-denominated US Treasury Securities. If they ever decide to dump the things all at once, look out—bond prices would plummet, meaning interest rates would skyrocket.

The value of the dollar compared to another currency also comes into play when an investor buys an **ADR**. We look at ADRs in Chapter 2; for now, just know that you can buy shares of Toyota or Nokia, for example, as ADRs (**American Depository Receipts**), priced in American dollars. This way, you don't have to figure out how much you just paid for a stock priced at 176.453 yen. However, the relative values of the dollar to the yen will come into play, especially when it comes time to pay dividends. When the underlying stock pays the dividend in the foreign currency, the foreign currency received by the bank will need to be converted to US dollars. If the US dollar is strong, the foreign currency will purchase or convert to fewer US dollars for the holder of the ADR. As a result, the dividend received by the holder of the ADR is lower. So, a *weak* dollar would actually be beneficial to the holder of an ADR, since the dividend paid would convert to *more* US dollars.

BUSINESS CYCLES

As I mentioned, Gross Domestic Product (GDP) for the US measures the total output of the American economy. It's the total value of all goods and services being produced and provided by workers stationed here in the good old U-S-of-A. If GDP is increasing, the economy is growing. If GDP is declining, so is the economy. The American economy rides a continuous roller coaster known as the **business cycle**. As it moves through the unpredictable business cycle, the economy expands, hits a peak, contracts, hits bottom, and then comes back up again. The phases are: **expansion, peak, contraction,** and **trough**. If the GDP is positive two quarters back-to-back, we are in an expansionary phase. Two consecutive quarters of economic decline means we're in a contraction. A contraction lasting from 2 to 6 quarters (6 to 18 months) is called a **recession**. If it persists longer than that, the economy is in the more rare state of **depression.**

Stocks of companies operating in some industries are more dependent on this business cycle than others. So-called **cyclical stocks** do about as well as the overall economy. They tend to perform very well during an expansion but very poorly during a contraction. Cyclical industries include: heavy equipment, steel, automotive, durable goods (washer & dryer, refrigerator, etc.), travel, and aerospace. Real-world examples would include companies such as Caterpillar, John Deere, GM, Ford, and GE.

On the other hand, other industries can survive economic contractions more easily and are, therefore, called **defensive** or "non-cyclical." These industries include: food, clothing, pharmaceuticals, healthcare, alcohol and tobacco. Don't be too quick to draw conclusions on a test question, though. We said "food" is a defensive industry, but the test could say "restaurants." That's not what we mean—we mean groceries and food supply companies. Restaurants get clobbered in a recession, as they are one of the first items consumers reduce or eliminate entirely from their budget. Clothing is a defensive industry, but we don't mean "designer clothing," which people would cut back on in a recession. We mean the basics, like underwear, socks, T-shirts, and flip-flops.

If convinced a recession is just ahead an investor should purchase defensive stocks. People will, after all, keep buying razor blades, groceries, medicine, beer, snack chips and other essentials regardless of the current economic climate. If an expansion/recovery appears to be just around the corner, an investor should purchase cyclical stocks, like automobile and trucking/logistics companies. How does the investor know when the recessions and recoveries are about to appear? He doesn't, but hey, the stock market is always at least partly about speculation. As we'll see in Chapter 3, some investors study overall economic trends to make investments along these lines; some investors buy stocks based only on the behavior of that stock in the marketplace; still other investors refuse to pick investments but, rather, allocate percentages of their portfolio to this or that type of stock.

Also, we keep mentioning the more commonly used GDP, but the exam may ask about **GNP (Gross National Product),** too. Gross National Product for the US would count the production of US workers stationed here as well as working overseas for American companies. It would not count the production of, say, Japanese citizens working at a Mitsubishi plant in Mississippi. Gross *Domestic* Product counts what is produced domestically, by both US workers and foreigners working here in the United States (even for foreign-owned companies like Toyota and Mitsubishi). So, GNP tells us how much American workers are producing wherever they're stationed, while GDP tells us what is produced here in America, whoever is doing that work.

FISCAL AND MONETARY POLICY

Whatever information economists are tracking, policy makers can use either **fiscal policy** or **monetary policy** to manage the economy based on what they see—or think they see. Fiscal policy is what the President and Congress do: tax and spend. Followers of John Maynard Keynes are called "Keynesians" and recommend that fiscal policy be used to increase aggregate (overall) demand. To stimulate the economy, just cut taxes and increase government spending. Lower taxes leave more money for Americans to spend and invest, fueling the economy. If the government is spending more on interstate highway construction, this means a lot more folks are going to be hired for construction crews. Or maybe the federal government orders military transport vehicles from a unit of GM. If so, GM will order a lot more parts from suppliers and hire more workers, who would make and spend more money to push the economy along.

On the other hand, if we need to cool things down, followers of Keynesian economics suggest that the federal government increase taxes and cut spending. Higher taxes leave less money for Americans to spend and invest, and decreased spending puts less government money into companies like GM, who, in turn, spend less money with their suppliers and on salaries.

Monetarists (e.g., Federal Reserve Board), on the other hand, feel that controlling the money supply is the key to managing the economy. As we said, the cost of money equals its "interest rate." If there's too much demand and too little supply, the cost of money goes up. That slows down the economy and fights inflation. If there's too little demand and too much supply, the cost of money goes down. That helps to stimulate the economy and pump some air back into a deflated economy.

Wait, money has a cost? I thought I paid the cost of things *with* money. Sure, but if I want to start a business or buy a house, I need money. How much do I have to pay to borrow this money?

That's the interest rate—the cost of borrowing money.

So, how can the money supply be influenced? Through monetary policy, enacted by the Federal Reserve Board. The Federal Reserve Board (The Fed) requires that member banks keep a certain percentage of their customer deposits in reserve. This is called, not surprisingly, the **reserve requirement**. If the Fed raises the reserve requirement, banks have less money to lend out to folks trying to buy homes and start businesses. So if the economy is overheating, the Federal Reserve Board could raise the reserve requirement in order to cool things down, and if the economy is sluggish, they could lower the requirement in order to make more money available to fuel the economy.

The Fed's FOMC can also use **open market operations** to either buy US Treasury securities or sell US Treasury securities on the secondary market. If they want to cool things down by raising interest rates, they can sell Treasuries on the open market to depress their price and, thereby, increase their yield. If they want to fuel a sluggish economy by lowering interest rates, they can buy Treasury securities, thereby driving up their price, which is the same thing as pushing down their yield. Yields and rates are the same thing, remember. It is the price of debt securities that moves in an inverse relationship to rates/yields.

When people say the FOMC is raising short-term interest rates by 25 basis points, they're talking about the **discount rate**, which is the rate the Federal Reserve Board charges banks that borrow directly from the FRB. If banks have to pay more to borrow, you can imagine that they will in turn charge their customers more to borrow from them. So, if the Fed wants to raise interest rates, they just raise the discount rate and let the banking system take it from there. Remember that the Federal Reserve Board does not set tax policy—they enact monetary policy. And, typically, they only influence short-term interest rates, although if circumstances require it, they can also influence longer-term rates reflected by Treasury Notes and Treasury Bonds, discussed more in Chapter 2.

So, think of the Federal Reserve Board/FOMC as a sort of pit crew trying to perform tune-ups on an economy that never actually pulls over for a pit stop. If the economy starts going too fast, they let some air out of the tires by raising the reserve requirement, raising the discount rate, and selling Treasury securities. If the economy starts to slow down, they pump some air into the tires by lowering the reserve requirement, lowering the discount rate, and buying Treasuries.

MONETARY POLICY	RESERVE REQUIREMENT	DISCOUNT RATE	OPEN MARKET
Fight Inflation – Tight $	Increase	Increase	Sell Treasuries
Stimulate Economy – Loose $	Decrease	Decrease	Buy Treasuries

MONETARY POLICY	RESERVE REQUIREMENT	DISCOUNT RATE	OPEN MARKET
FISCAL POLICY	**TAXATION**	**GOVERNMENT SPENDING**	
Fight Inflation	Increase	Decrease	
Stimulate Economy	Decrease	Increase	

PRACTICE

1. Which of the following is a leading indicator?

    A. Inventory

    B. Corporate profits

    C. Average weekly hours worked by manufacturing employees

    D. Prime rate

2. An economic slump would be associated with which of the following?

    A. Rising unemployment, inflation, rising interest rates

    B. Falling unemployment, inflation, rising interest rates

    C. Rising unemployment, falling GDP, falling interest rates

    D. Falling unemployment, deflation, rising GDP

3. Which of the following is considered a lagging indicator?

    A. S&P 500 index

    B. Building permits

    C. Claims for unemployment

    D. Inventory levels

(ANSWERS)

1. **C,** average hours worked by manufacturing employees, building permits, and the stock market are well-known leading indicators.

2. **C,** in an economic slump, interest rates would drop as people are being laid off and the demand for capital decreases as businesses cut back on financing equipment, inventory, construction projects, etc.

3. **D,** inventory and "duration of unemployment" are well-known lagging indicators. The others are leading indicators

FINANCIAL REPORTING

Many profitable American businesses are privately owned. Five Guys Burgers & Fries and Toys 'R' Us, for example, are well-known companies, but we would have to estimate their revenue and profits, since private companies don't have to report their financial results to the public. By comparison, if we want to know the revenue and net income after tax for Starbucks or Microsoft, we can go to the SEC's **EDGAR** site and pull up the companies' most recent quarterly or annual reports. It's not that Five Guys and Toys 'R' Us don't have income statements, balance sheets, and statements of cash flows. They simply don't have to make those **financial statements** public. The companies have not taken money from the general public; therefore, they get to keep their financials private. If you think about it, how many business owners want to publicize all their mistakes and risks of disaster up ahead? Not many, which is why only those ready to do so should consider an IPO. If you complete your IPO, you become a reporting company. Going forward, you'll have to err on the side of caution and disclose everything you can think of that might be material to an investor.

Fundamental analysts study a public company's products and services, their competitors, their industry space, and the financial reports in their 10Q and 10K filings. Whether you buy a bond or a share of stock, the security is only as solid as the company who issued it, so a fundamental analyst wants a detailed picture of the company behind the stocks and bonds available to investors. The company can only pay the interest on their bonds if they have enough revenue to cover it. The preferred stockholders will only get paid if the profits are dependable, and the common stock will only rise over the long term if the profits at the company rise.

INCOME STATEMENT

The place to check the company's revenue, expenses, and profit is the **income statement**. We'll be looking at another financial statement called the **balance sheet**, and it may help to remember the inherent difference between the two statements, which are each put out by the same company. The balance sheet is a snapshot of the company's financial strength at a particular point in time. The income statement shows the results of the company's operations over a particular *period* of time. So, if you want to see how solid a company's finances are, check the balance sheet. If you want to see how profitable a company was this year, look at their income statement.

A public company probably had to register its securities with the SEC under the **Securities Act of 1933**. That same company almost certainly is then a reporting company required to file reports with the **SEC** under the **Securities Exchange Act of 1934**. This allows the shareholders and bondholders who invested in these public companies to see what kind of financial condition (balance sheet) their company is in and whether the sales and profits are increasing, decreasing, or flattening out (income statement). As usual, there are different terms used for the same thing here. An income statement can also be referred to as a "statement of earnings" or "statement of operations," while the balance sheet is often referred to as the "statement of financial condition." Whatever we call it, although the reports are primarily for shareholders, this information is available to anyone who wants to see it. That includes the company's competitors, which is another reason many companies stay private.

If you go to your favorite financial website or search on a particular company's "10-K" or "annual shareholder report," you can see both the balance sheet and the income statement for companies such as Microsoft, Oracle, or Starbucks. For now, though, let's start small. Let's say you're an 11-year-old kid again, and you have launched a lemonade stand for the summer. Each glass of lemonade sells for $1. The dollars you take in this summer can be called **sales** or **revenue**. You sell 10,000 glasses of lemonade, so your sales/revenue is exactly $10,000. Sales/revenue is the top line of the income statement. In some businesses there are a lot of returns, refunds, and discounts. Retailers, for example, often report their **net revenue** or **net operating revenue,** which is simply their revenue *after* all the returns, refunds, and discounts have been accounted for.

In any case, your lemonade stand didn't do any discounting or experience any returns, so your revenue is what it is. However, as "Mr. Wonderful" of Shark Tank fame frequently reminds entrepreneurs, $10,000 in revenue is not the same thing as $10,000 of profit. That lemonade you sold was produced by a combination of the following ingredients: purified water, fresh lemons, lemon juice, sugar, and ice. Those are the goods you bought to make the product you sold, which is why the money you spent on them is called the **cost of goods sold**. Many companies list these items under "cost of revenue." Either way, you also have to serve your product in environmentally friendly cups, which cost $1,000, on top of the $2,000 paid for the ingredients. So, now your $10,000 in revenue is down to $7,000 after subtracting the $3,000 for "cost of goods sold." The $7,000 is known as your **gross profit.**

Revenue – Cost of Goods Sold = Gross Profit

Gross profit is an amount of money. **Gross margin** is a percentage found by dividing gross profit back into revenue:

Gross Profit / Revenue = Gross Margin

Your $7,000 of gross profit compared to/divided by your revenue of $10,000 equals an amazing gross margin of 70%. Not many businesses enjoy 70% gross margins, but, either way, we're not done subtracting yet. Like all businesses, you have **operating expenses** to cover. Operating expenses are the expenses not directly associated with the production of the company's products. For example, no matter what they produce or provide businesses generally incur the following expenses: office rent, administrative salaries, office supplies, entertainment costs, travel costs, etc. You have a handful of operating expenses with your lemonade stand, as well. While you worked the stand yourself most of the time, you had to hire your older sister a few hours each week, too. Her $500 paycheck represents an operating expense to you. There are other operating expenses, including the advertising you do by putting up signs at both ends of the block and running a classified ad in the local paper. Your advertising expense was $500 over the summer. Operating expenses are often referred to as "SG&A" for **"selling, general, and administrative"** expenses. At a manufacturing company, the labor of the workers on the production floor would generally be part of cost of goods sold, since that labor goes directly into the cost of the finished product. The so-called "white collar workers" out in the cozy offices sending emails and making phone calls would be part of "selling, general, and administrative" expenses.

Even though you're just an 11-year-old kid, you decided not to slap a piece of cardboard on a stick with the words "Cold Lemonade – $1." Instead, you got the boy next door to build you a stand for $200, and that is a different type of expense. See, you're going to be in business for the next five years, and you'll be using that stand each summer. So, you subtract 1/5 of that $200 on your income statement each year. Instead of subtracting $200 all at once, you only subtract $40 to "depreciate" this vital asset. Even though you spent the money all up front, next year you will also subtract $40 as a

depreciation expense on your income statement. You will do that five times until you have depreciated the cost of the stand to zero. To depreciate an asset means to spread its cost over its approximate useful life. A manufacturing company would not expense a $10 million piece of equipment out on the shop floor the way they would expense the paper and toner used up in the office. The latter are consumed and expensed all at once while the equipment is slowly subtracted/written down on the income statement to spread the cost over its estimated useful life. Also, tangible assets are depreciated, while intangible assets are **amortized**. In either case, an asset's cost is being spread over its estimated useful life by taking a series of charges on the income statement through these non-cash expenses called either depreciation or amortization.

There are other assets subject to depreciation at your lemonade stand. You had to buy several large thermoses, a couple of blenders, a cooler, a little money drawer, a calculator, and a copy of QuickBooks™. These fixed assets all work out to $300, which you depreciate over three years, subtracting another $100 this year.

So, after subtracting the cost of the ingredients, the cups, the labor, the advertising, and the depreciation of assets, you're left with $5,860 of **operating profit** or **operating income** or even **operating earnings** to make sure it has three names. Whatever we call this amount, when we compare it to the $10,000 in revenue, we see that your operating profit of $5,860 represents an **operating margin** of 58.6%.

> *Operating Income / Revenue = Operating Margin*

Another name for "operating profit" is "**EBIT**," or "earnings before interest and taxes." EBIT is a company's revenue minus all expenses other than interest and taxes. From the income statement, EBIT is the line we arrive at once we've taken revenue and subtracted cost of goods sold plus all operating expenses.

Companies that issue bonds need to cover the interest payments, so bond analysts often compare the EBIT to the annual interest expense to arrive at the "**times interest earned**." If a company has $3 million in "EBIT" and $1 million in interest payments to cover, their "times interest earned" is 3-to-1. In other words, the interest expense is earned three times over, which represents a cushion to the bondholders.

Similar calculations derived from the income statement include "EBT," which is "earnings before taxes," and **EBITDA,** which stands for "earnings before interest, taxes, depreciation, and amortization." EBITDA takes revenue and subtracts the cost of goods sold plus the basic operating expenses of running the business. It leaves off the fancier subtractions for interest, taxes, depreciation and amortization. Analysts often consider EBITDA for companies with a lot of fixed assets subject to depreciation. Such companies may show a loss on their income statement due largely to depreciation and financing connected to those fixed assets, but when viewed through EBITDA may look more impressive. For example, although a consulting firm might be able to show a profit the first year or two, a restaurant or manufacturing company might have to invest so much in their property and equipment that profits are five years into the future. Looking at just the company's EBITDA, however, analysts might see that the company is generating some rather impressive amounts of cash.

Regardless, we are not all the way to the bottom line yet. We have accounted for cost of goods sold, operating expenses, and depreciation. But there are still interest payments and taxes to account for before arriving at the company's net income or loss for the reporting period. Your mom had to spot you some credit to buy your first batch of ingredients and other essentials and, unfortunately, she actually charges you interest on the loan. On the plus side, you get to deduct that interest before figuring your taxable income, just as homeowners deduct the interest paid on their mortgages. So, you subtract the $20 of interest, and your taxable income is $5,840, called your **pre-tax profit**. Dividing that into your revenue of $10,000, we see that you have a **pre-tax margin** of 58.4%. Your taxes work out to $40, and after paying those, you have a **net profit**, or **net income after tax**, of $5,800.

Net profit is an amount of money. **Net profit margin** is a percentage showing how much of your revenue falls to the bottom line of the income statement. If you divide your net profit of $5,800 into your revenue of $10,000, you see that you have an astounding 58% **net margin**.

> *Net Income / Revenue = Net Profit Margin*

Lucky for you, you have no shareholders making claims on those profits. All you have to do is pay your mom back and pay her on time. As with any business using "leverage" rather than "equity financing," the profits are all yours.

> ➢ EPS, P/E, and Profitability

To understand how it works at large public companies, let's pretend that you *do* have shareholders in your lemonade stand. You just reported net income of $5,800. If you had raised your capital by issuing stock, you would have been issuing "shares," right?

Well, it's time to start sharing. Who gets dividends first? Preferred stockholders. If you pay a preferred dividend of $800, that leaves exactly $5,000 of "**earnings available to common**." If your company has $5,000 in earnings available to common with 1,000 shares of common stock outstanding, that represents $5 of **earnings per share** (EPS). Each share of stock is attached to $5 of profit, in other words.

> *Earnings per Share = Earnings Available to Common / Shares Outstanding*

We could apply a more stringent test that assumes all convertible securities (bonds, preferred stock, or warrants) are actually turned into common stock all at once. When these investors convert to common stock, your $5,000 in earnings could end up being divided among more shares. If your company ended up with 1,250 shares outstanding after conversion, your **diluted earnings per share** would be only $4.

Now that we have our earnings per share, we can also find out how much gets paid out in dividends. Not surprisingly, we call this the **dividend payout ratio**. This just takes the annual dividends paid and divides it by the earnings per share (EPS). Your company has earnings-per-share (EPS) of $5. If you paid out $1 in common dividends, you paid out 20% of your earnings, which is called your "dividend payout ratio."

Publicly traded stocks trade at various "multiples" such as the **price-to-earnings ratio**. The P/E ratio compares the market price of the stock to the earnings per share. Growth stocks trade at high P/E ratios, while those trading at low P/E ratios are considered value stocks.

In any case, let's review your privately held lemonade stand's income statement:

Revenue	$10,000
Cost of Goods Sold	− $3,000
SG&A Expenses	− $1,000
Depreciation, Amortization	− $140
OPERATING INCOME	**$5,860**
Interest Expense	− $20
PRE-TAX INCOME	**$5,840**
Taxes	− $40
NET INCOME after tax	**$5,800**

The numbers above show us that for every $1 your lemonade stand brings in, you keep 58 cents. That concept can be referred to as your **net margin,** profit margin ratio, or even your margin-of-profit ratio. When expressed as a formula, a company's profit margin ratio equals:

Net Income / Revenue (or "net sales")

Remember that the term "**net**" **sales** refers to the fact that there are often returns and refunds involved with selling product. These are subtracted from gross sales to arrive at the figure for net sales. Net margin shows how efficiently a company can extract profits from each dollar of sales/revenue. Both common and preferred stockholders, which we will look at in a future chapter, are interested in these profits, so a company's profit margin ratio is of special interest to them. One of the most profitable public companies I can think of off the top of my head trades under the stock symbol MSFT. This company typically reports net profit margins in the mid to high-20-percent range. SBUX, on the other hand, comes in at more like 8 or 9%. Both are leaders in their industry group, it's just that software enjoys higher margins than restaurants.

CASH FLOW

As we saw when discussing fancy terms such as EBITDA, some subtractions on the income statement do not involve an outlay of cold, hard cash. Depreciation and amortization spread an asset's historical cost over an estimated useful life, but no cash is actually being spent when we record the expense on the income statement.

Therefore, since there's a difference between an accounting entry called "depreciation" and actual cash being spent, analysts ignore intangible expenses like that when focusing on **cash flow**, which is simply how much cash is being generated (or consumed) by a company. One way to estimate cash flow is to take the net income from the income statement and then add back two non-cash charges: depreciation and amortization. Your lemonade stand doesn't have a lot of depreciation and amortization going on, but companies that invest in expensive factories, warehouses, and equipment can show quite different figures for net income on the one hand and cash flow from operations on the other. When they add back all the depreciation that reduced their net income, their cash flow is a much higher amount.

But, there's no need to estimate, since in the corporation's 10-K, we also find a separate **statement of cash flows** that shows how much cash has been generated or used up by the business over the reporting period. You might think that would be the same thing as the net income on the income statement, but that's not the case. Accounting methods usually have the company booking revenue/sales before any cash has been exchanged; the statement of cash flows eliminates this sort of distortion, as well as intangible "expenses" like depreciation/amortization. A good fundamental analyst knows that some companies have been known to book "profits" when they're really not generating enough cash to stay afloat.

The statement of cash flows is separated into three distinct ways in which a company can generate (or exhaust) their precious cash: cash flows from operating activities, cash flows from investing activities, and cash flows from financing activities. **Cash flows from operating activities** are what that phrase sounds like: the company generated or exhausted this much cash through their core operations. For example, Starbucks generates most of its cash by operating thousands of successful coffee shops, but it can also generate cash through investing activities and through financing activities. Most shareholders in SBUX would probably care most about the cash the company generates through its operations—I mean, they're not an investment company or a finance company, right? Cash flow from operations shows us the net income from the income statement, adds back depreciation/amortization, and then records the changes in working capital (from the balance sheet). After dealing with the change in the line items under current assets and current liabilities (working capital), the company can then calculate and report the net cash provided/used by operating activities.

Cash flow from investing activities indicates how much cash was used or generated, usually from investing in capital equipment, and to some extent buying and selling securities, e.g. US Treasuries. Capital equipment ("capex") can be thought of as all the hard, tangible stuff that brick-and-mortar companies have to invest in (buying a printing press, remodeling existing stores, building new stores, etc.). If a company is like MSFT or ORCL, they might go on a business buying binge, which would be reflected in their cash used for acquisitions. Big increases in this number could indicate that the company is making strategic acquisitions of former competitors, or it could mean that they're generating too much of their returns by buying up smaller fish as opposed to operating successfully.

Cash flow from financing activities is the cash generated/used through basically any activity involving the shareholders (owners) or bondholders (creditors) of the company. If stock is issued, cash is generated, while if the company engages in share buyback programs, cash is used up. If a company issues bonds, cash is generated, while when it finally redeems or calls those bonds, cash is used up. Also, when the company pays out dividends to shareholders, it's pretty easy to see where that cash is ending up, right? Young, growing companies often issue a lot of stock to finance their operations. That may be fine, but new stock issues will dilute the value of the existing shareholders' equity. More mature companies, with plenty of cash on hand, often buy back their shares to make each existing share more valuable. Either way, we could track these activities under this section of the statement of cash flows.

Heads up: the terms "cash flows from investing activities" and "cash flows from financing activities" could be potentially confusing. Remember that if a company buys Government securities or shares of a public company on the open market, we'd see that under "cash flows from investing activities." And, if the company <u>invests</u> in a printing press, that's under cash flows from investing activities, too—no matter how much "sense" it might make to think of that as a "financing" activity. No, cash flow from financing activities includes the cash generated by issuing stocks or bonds and the cash flow exhausted buying back stock and/or retiring bonds.

In any case, back to your little pretend lemonade stand. Maybe next summer the local Starbucks will begin to feel the pressure of your competitive beverage business and offer you "seven times cash flow" to buy you out and make you go away. Or, if you were a public company, analysts would compare your stock price to your cash flow, calling it "price-to-cash flow," or **price-to-cash** for those in a hurry. As we'll see, a stock's market price can be compared to the earnings (**price-to-earnings**), the book value (**price-to-book**), the sales (**price-to-sales**), or the cash flow (**price-to-cash**). The market price of the stock is being quoted all throughout the day. The earnings, sales, and cash flow can all be pulled from the income statement and/or the statement of cash flows. And the book value can be determined from the next financial statement, the balance sheet.

BALANCE SHEET

If you were applying for a loan, the lender would want to know two very important things: how much money do you make, and what kind of collateral do you have? You could submit your statement of cash flow showing all your sources of income minus expenses. But the lender would also like to see what kind of **assets** you're holding minus your **liabilities**. Your lemonade stand might need to borrow money in order to expand someday. If so, the bank would want to see your balance sheet when you apply. The basic formula for the balance sheet is expressed as:

Assets = Liabilities + Stockholders' Equity

or

Assets – Liabilities = Stockholder's Equity

Assets represent what a company owns. Liabilities represent what a company owes. You take what a company owns, subtract what it owes, and that's the **net worth** of the company. Another name for net worth is **stockholders' equity**, which implies that the stockholders are the owners of the company, so what we want to know is: what is that ownership actually worth?

➢ Assets

Assets are divided into three types. The first type is **current assets**. Current assets represent cash and anything that could be converted to cash in the short-term: **cash & equivalents, accounts receivable, inventory**. Cash is cash, and it's a good thing. "Equivalents" are money market instruments earning some interest, which is also a good thing. If they mature in the very-near term, commercial paper, bankers' acceptances, repurchase agreements, and T-Bills are considered "cash equivalents" here on the balance sheet.

From your profits at the lemonade stand, you very wisely deposited $560 into a savings account at the end of the summer, as you know how important it is to have some cash on hand for expenses and investments into the business. File that under "cash." Accounts receivable is what customers owe the company. You were nice enough to sell two of your best friends lemonade on credit throughout the summer, and they ran up a tab of $40 between them. You fully intend to be paid for those sales in the near-term, so you list that payment as an asset (money coming IN).

Inventory is the stuff the company makes and plans to sell (convert to cash) just as soon as possible. When temperatures dropped suddenly and the cold rain started up in late August, you were left holding a rather large quantity of lemons, sugar, etc. You very creatively made up as much lemonade as possible and turned it into popsicles. Next season, you intend to sell that inventory for $40, making the inventory a current asset.

Ah, but what if the inventory develops a hideous flavor sitting in a deep freezer all winter and spring? That's always something to keep in mind when assigning a value to—or trusting the value of—a company's inventory. As we'll see, the **quick ratio** excludes inventory from current assets for that very reason—the company might not be able to sell the stuff sitting in storage. But, for now, let's assume you will sell it and list its value as a current asset called inventory.

The second type, **fixed assets,** include office buildings, factories, equipment, furniture, etc. This is the stuff a company uses as opposed to putting directly into its finished products. Fixed assets could all be converted into cash, but this stuff was not purchased in order to be sold; it was purchased in order to generate revenue: printing presses, industrial control systems, fleet of delivery vans, etc. A large corporation would list the value of the real estate, as well as the value of the assembly line equipment, as well as the furniture and even the artwork hanging on the walls of the visitor lobby under fixed assets. They get depreciated over time, so the company's balance sheet usually reflects the original cost of the equipment and then shows how much value has been depreciated (written down) at this point. For your lemonade stand, we said that the stand itself, plus some very basic capital equipment including blenders, ice trays, software, etc., totaled $500. We depreciated $140 of that on your income statement, so we're showing the original cost of $500 and then subtracting the "accumulated depreciation" at this point to show that the net book value is now $360.

Then there are **intangible assets**. Intangible assets include patents, trademarks, and **goodwill**. When a company acquires another company, they usually pay more than just the value of the fixed assets. They're paying for the brand-identity, the customer base, etc. So, that excess paid above the hard, tangible value of assets you can touch and see is called "goodwill." Let's face it, your lemonade stand has no intangible assets at this point, but if you ever purchase the goodwill of a rival lemonade stand up the street, we would list that intangible asset here. Then, we would add all three types of assets and call the sum your **total assets**.

Your lemonade stand has very little inventory, but many manufacturing companies, car dealers, and supermarkets live and die by how effectively they manage their inventory. To measure this effectiveness analysts look at a company's **inventory turnover ratio**. This formula provides a link between the income statement and the balance sheet. To calculate it, we take the cost of goods sold from the income statement and divide that amount by the average inventory over the period. It is a ratio because it shows how many "times" inventory is turned over during the reporting period. If the turnover rate is too slow, that company is not deploying its capital effectively.

➤ Liabilities

On the other side of the balance sheet equation we find liabilities, which represent what a company owes. Anything that has to be paid out in the short term is a **current liability**. **Accounts payable, accrued wages,** and **accrued taxes** all represent bills the company has to pay currently, which is why they're called current liabilities. Your mom picked up a few batches of ingredients over the summer and put them on her credit card. Just as soon as she remembers doing so, you fully intend to pay her back the $60, listed under accounts payable. And, you still owe your sister $100, which is listed under accrued wages.

The principal amount of a loan or a bond that has to be paid more than a year out is a **long-term liability**. You still owe your mother $240 in principal, which is why it's listed under long-term liabilities. Add the current and the long-term liabilities together and you have **total liabilities** of $400.

> Stockholders' Equity/Net Worth

Stockholders' Equity is sometimes called Shareholders' Equity or "net worth." Whatever we call it, remember that equity equals ownership, and the stockholders own a percentage of the company. What is that ownership worth at the time the balance sheet is printed? That's stockholders' equity. Companies place the total par value of their preferred stock under this heading. Common stock is assigned a par value of, say, $1, so if a company has 1,000,000 shares of common stock, they would list the par value as $1,000,000 and place it under stockholders' equity. If investors bought the stock in the IPO at $11, that represents a surplus of $10 above the par value, so the company would list **paid-in surplus** of $10,000,000, as well. And then any earnings that have been retained are listed as **retained earnings**. Why did you only retain $600 this year? Because you know that a business that involves very little capital equipment, very little financing, and very little recurring costs can afford to pay out big distributions to the owners. As the sole owner, you cut yourself a $5,200 dividend check on September 1st and smiled all the way to the bank.

Analysts measure the hard, tangible asset value associated with a share of common stock, and this concept is known as the **book value per share**. To calculate it, take the stockholders' equity minus the preferred shares, divided by the shares outstanding. Value investors love to buy stocks trading at a low multiple to book value. If they can buy the stock at or below book value, even better.

In order to judge how effectively a company generates profits from its shareholders' investment into the company analysts calculate the company's **return on equity**. The return on equity (ROE) shows how much in profits each dollar of common stockholder's equity generates for the company. As with many measures of a company's financial health, this one combines a line from the income statement with a line from the balance sheet. The formula is:

Net Income / Shareholders' Equity

Usually, "return on equity" relates only to common stock. Therefore, the preferred dividend is excluded from net income before comparing what's left to shareholder's equity. For more precision, some analysts use the term "return on common equity" to clarify that preferred stock is not being considered for this calculation.

Liquidity Measurements: Working Capital, Current Ratio, Quick Ratio, etc.

Bondholders are very concerned about a company's **asset coverage** of the bonds and the safety of their promised income stream. We looked at the safety of income on the income statement. Now let's see how the balance sheet reveals the asset coverage of the bonds.

Current assets represent what a company owns. Current liabilities represent what a company owes. Hopefully, the company owns more than it owes. If not, it has a "burn rate" showing how quickly it could go bankrupt. Fundamental analysts take current assets and subtract current liabilities in order to measure **working capital** (sometimes called "net working capital"). This is a measure of how able a company is to finance current operations. We're talking about short-term **liquidity** here. When a company's short-term liabilities exceed its current assets, that company is in danger of getting behind in payments to suppliers and interest payments to creditors. On the other hand, if a company's current assets exceed its current liabilities by a healthy amount, this company is in a strong position to fund current operations, just as your lemonade operation would be if you had $1,000 in total bills and $4,000 in the bank.

Working Capital = Current Assets − Current Liabilities

Your lemonade stand shows current assets of $640 and current liabilities of $160. Your working capital is, therefore, the difference of $480. Working capital is an amount of money. Analysts also express current assets and current liabilities as a ratio, known as the **current ratio**. Instead of subtracting $160 from $640, we would say that $640, divided by (over) $160, gives you a current ratio of 4 to 1. Basically, for every $1 of short-term debt, you have $4 of liquid assets to cover it. Not bad.

Current Ratio = Current Assets / Current Liabilities

Inventory is a current asset along with accounts receivable and cash & equivalents. But, inventory is not always a liquid asset. When we subtract inventory from current assets, we arrive at our **quick assets**. Quick assets include assets easily converted to cash: cash and marketable securities plus accounts receivable.

Looking at the quick assets of a company, analysts apply a more stringent test, known as the **quick ratio** or the **acid test**. The "i" in the words "quick" and "acid" reminds us that "inventory" is subtracted from current assets before we compare them to current liabilities. Why do that? Again, those frozen lemonade pops might go bad in storage, or simply might not strike your customers' fancy next summer. So, in case you didn't sell your inventory, what would your short-term financial condition look like then? We would deduct the $40 of inventory from your $640 of current assets first, and then compare that $600 to the $160 of current liabilities. At this point we would still see a ratio of 3.75 to 1 for your quick ratio. For every $1 of short-term debt, you have $3.75 to cover it, even if the inventory completely spoils.

Current ratio, quick ratio, the acid test, and working capital measure short-term liquidity. A company's ability to meet current interest payments would be reflected from a look at these concerns. The company's ability to repay the principal and avoid bankruptcy is reflected through a longer-term look at the balance sheet. For a picture of the company's long-term **solvency** analysts calculate the **debt-to-equity ratio**. The debt-to-equity ratio shows us how leveraged the company is. It gives analysts an idea as to how much money was raised through borrowing/leverage compared to the money raised by selling ownership/equity stakes. The formula is:

Total Liabilities divided by Shareholders' Equity

The higher the ratio, the more leveraged the company is. Another formula that is frequently used for the same purpose is called the **debt ratio**, which compares the total debt of the company to its total assets. Again, the higher this number/ratio, the more leveraged the company is. The formula is:

Still another ratio that shows bondholders the risk of default is the **bond ratio**. This formula shows the percentage of the company's capitalization that comes from the issuance of bonds with maturities greater than one year. To calculate the bond ratio analysts take the value of the company's long-term debt and divide that by the long-term debt plus shareholder's equity. This shows what percentage the bonds make of the company's total capitalization. Except for utility companies, a bond ratio above 33% is generally considered a high amount of leverage.

We looked at "book value per share" for common stock. Similarly, analysts often calculate an issuer's **net asset value per bond** to see how much in tangible assets is associated with each bond issued. To calculate this number we take the net tangible assets of the company (not goodwill and other intangible assets) and divide that by the number of bonds issued by the company.

In a later chapter we'll see that ratings agencies including Moody's Investor Services and S&P use the concerns discussed above when assigning a credit rating to an issue of debt securities.

FOOTNOTES

In a company's shareholder reports, the financial statements are accompanied by **footnotes** that help clarify the numbers. For example, what does the company mean by "equivalents" in its "cash and equivalents" line item—debt securities with six months to maturity? Three months? How/when does a company recognize "revenue"? Is it when the company ships pies to a distributor, or only when somebody has actually paid for the product? Also, unusual revenue events or charges need to be explained so that investors don't get the wrong idea about its long-term impact.

Whenever the numbers in a financial statement require further clarification, the footnotes section is used to provide it. A **10-K** or **annual shareholder report,** for example, will present the consolidated financial statements and then follow up with "notes to consolidated financial statements" that help clarify all the numbers presented from the balance sheet, income statement, and statement of cash flow.

TOP-DOWN AND BOTTOM-UP

The terms **top-down analysis** and **bottom-up analysis** relate to different types of fundamental analysts. If a fundamental analyst starts with the overall-economy view and then tries to figure out which industries and which companies in that industry will benefit or lose out on upcoming economic trends, he's using "top-down analysis." If the analyst starts at the granular level like what we did with the lemonade stand, that is known as "bottom-up analysis."

TYPES OF RISK

The first risk to consider when investing your capital is called **capital risk**. Not surprisingly, this is the risk that you could lose your invested capital. If you buy US Treasury Bonds, you won't really have to face capital risk, but if you buy corporate bonds or common stock, you will always face this basic risk of losing some or all of your invested principal.

One of the best ways to brush up on investment risks is to read through the first pages of a mutual fund prospectus. I'm looking at the prospectus for a growth fund myself at the moment. It declares that its investment goal is "growth of capital," and then goes on to say that "dividend income, if any, will be incidental to this goal." In other words, the fund invests in growth stocks, but some companies that are expected to grow will also pay dividends, and this fund does not mind cashing the checks. It's just that the dividends have nothing to do with the fund's reasons for investing in the stock—it's the growth or capital appreciation that they're after. The "principal strategy" tells me that the fund focuses on companies with $10 billion or more of market value (market cap) and uses fundamental analysis to determine which companies show strength in terms of earnings, revenue, profit margins, etc.

SYSTEMATIC RISKS

The next section of the prospectus is called "important risks," and it lists investment risks such as:

Stock market risk, or the risk that the price of securities held by the Fund will fall due to various conditions or circumstances which may be unpredictable.

> Market Risk

The exam might refer to the above "stock market risk" as "market risk." **Market risk** is a type of **systematic risk,** which means it affects securities across the board, as opposed to an **unsystematic risk,** which affects only particular issuers or industry sectors. Market risk is the risk that an investment will lose its value due to an overall market decline. As the prospectus says, the circumstances may be unpredictable. For example, no one can predict the next war or where the next tsunami, hurricane, or nuclear disaster will hit, but when events like that take place, they can have a devastating effect on the overall market. Whether they panic because of war, weather, or whatever, the fact is that when investors panic, stock prices plummet. We might think of stock market risk as the fact that even though the company might be doing just fine, your stock investment in that company could plummet just because the overall stock market plummets due to a market panic. Human behavior is what ultimately determines stock prices, and if you've read your history, you know that human behavior can get a little volatile from time to time.

The S&P 500 index is generally used to represent the "overall market," so what can an investor do to combat overall market risk? He can make a little side bet against the overall market by purchasing puts on a **broad-based index** such as the **S&P 500.** Or, he can sell the **ETFs (exchange traded funds)** that track a broad-based index short. Now, if the market rises, his stocks make money. If the market drops, his little side bet against the overall market makes money. To bet the other way is called **hedging** or **risk modification techniques.** So, if you own a broad spectrum of the overall market, you can buy puts or sell calls on the S&P 500 index, or you can sell Spiders™ short. That way, you can make a little money whether the overall market goes up or down, and—best of all—you can sleep at night. Also, remember that **diversification** will NOT help reduce overall market risk. If the overall market is going down, it doesn't matter how many different stocks you own; they're all going down. That's why you'd have to hedge by betting against the overall market to protect yourself.

Each of the 500 stocks in the S&P 500 would also have a **beta** or **beta coefficient.** Beta is a risk measurement that tells us how volatile the individual stock is compared to the overall market. Beta measures market risk, indicating what a particular stock will likely do if the overall market moves a certain amount up or down. For example, if MSFT has a beta of .8, it goes up and down only 80% as much as the overall market as measured by the S&P 500. If the S&P 500 rises 10%, MSFT goes up only 8%, and when the S&P 500 drops 10%, MSFT drops only 8%. If SBUX has a beta of 1.3, it is 30% more volatile than the overall market—or 1.3 times as volatile, whichever clicks for you. If the S&P drops 4%, SBUX drops 5.2%, and so on. A stock with a beta of 1 is in line with the overall market in terms of volatility. Note that a stock with a beta of less than 1 is simply less volatile than the overall stock market. Stocks in general are volatile, so that investment could still scare the heck out of many investors.

> Natural Event Risk

Natural event risk is fairly self-explanatory, as it refers to the fact that a tsunami, earthquake, hurricane, etc., could have a devastating effect on a country's economy, and possibly the economy of an entire area such as Europe or Southeast Asia. A recent annual report from Starbucks mentions a "global pandemic" as a major risk to the price of the stock, something I would not have thought of. In other words, if disease sweeps the globe or any part of it, public gathering places are going to be shut down, people will be too sick to pick coffee beans, and transportation routes may be closed to prevent the spread of illness. None of that would have anything to do with the taste of Starbucks coffee or the management skills of the company.

Unfortunately, it's not easy to place natural event risk exclusively in the systematic or unsystematic risk category. While a tsunami would have a negative impact on the markets overall, there are many weather-related events that hit certain sectors or issuers in particular, making it an unsystematic risk. For example, food and energy producers are affected by weather events that might not impact other industries. And, there are some industries that do very well after a flood or band of thunderstorms— mold remediation, construction, hazardous waste removal, etc. As always, read the question carefully.

> Interest Rate Risk

The prospectus I'm looking at covers several of the family's funds. In the bond fund prospectus, I see that the important risks include:

Risk that the value of the securities the Fund holds will fall as a result of changes in interest rates.

What the prospectus is talking about is **interest rate risk**. Interest rate risk is the risk that interest rates will rise, sending the value of bonds down. This risk is more severe the longer the term to maturity. When rates go up, all bond prices fall, but the long-term bonds suffer the most. So, a 30-year government bond has no default risk, but carries more interest rate risk than a 10-year corporate bond. The reason we see short-term and intermediate-term bond funds is because many investors want to reduce interest rate risk. Maybe they will need this money in just a few years, so they can't risk a drop in market value due to a sudden rise in interest rates. They will probably sacrifice the higher yield offered by a long-term bond fund, but they will sleep better knowing that rising rates won't be quite as devastating to short-term bonds. In other words, if your daughter is just 8 years old, the bonds in her 529 educational savings account can be 10 years to maturity or so, but if she's 16, the bonds need to be maturing in just a few years. Never buy bonds that mature outside the time frame of your investor's anticipated holding period.

Remember that interest rate risk is systematic because it has nothing to do with the particular issuer of the bond. Interest rate risk is all about the bond's market price sensitivity to a sudden rise in interest rates. The longer the term on the bond, the greater the interest rate risk.

Duration

The interest rate risk of a particular bond can be expressed as the bond's **duration**. Duration predicts how a small change in interest rates would affect the bond's market price. The longer/higher a bond's duration, the more sensitive it is to a change in interest rates. So, when interest rates go up, they smack the prices of bonds with long/high durations down much harder than those with lower durations.

If the duration of a bond is 10, we can conclude that if interest rates rose 1%, the bond's market price would drop by 10%. Remember: the lower the coupon and the longer the maturity, the higher/greater the duration. And the greater the duration, the more susceptible the bond's price is to interest rate spikes.

For interest-paying bonds, the duration is always less than the years to maturity. For example, if the maturity is 10 years, the duration has to be less than 10 for a coupon bond. But, for zero coupon bonds, the duration *is* the maturity. Surprisingly, the mathematical formula for duration is very helpful in understanding the concept, but it's just so intense that I decided not to include it in the book. If you really want to spend 15 minutes crunching the numbers, do a Google search and have at it. You'll quickly see why the longer you have to wait for your money, the riskier it is for you, although some of you may not actually need a complex math formula to convince you of that. You may have already had the pleasure of lending too much money to the wrong "friend." In case the question on the exam is only asking for a definition, tell it that duration "equals the weighted average of a bond's cash flows." The longer the investor has to wait for his cash flows, the higher the formula weights that and increases the duration.

> Purchasing Power Risk

Purchasing power risk is sometimes called **inflation risk** and even constant dollar risk to make sure it has three names. If inflation erodes the value of money, an investor's fixed return simply can't buy what it used to. Fixed-income investments carry purchasing power or inflation risk, which is why investors often try to beat inflation by investing in common stock. The ride might be a wild one in the stock market, but the reward is that we should be able to grow faster than the rate of inflation, whereas a fixed-income payment is *fixed*. Retirees living solely on fixed incomes are more susceptible to inflation or purchasing power risk than people still in the workforce, since salaries tend to rise with inflation. The longer the retiree has to live on a fixed income, the more susceptible she is to inflation risk. Unfortunately, common stock is often too volatile for investors with shorter time horizons and high needs for liquidity. The solution is often to put the majority of a retiree's money into short-term bonds and money market instruments, with a small percentage in large-cap stock, equity income, or growth & income funds. That way, the dependable income stream from the short-term debt securities will cover the living expenses, while the smaller piece devoted to conservative stock investments will likely provide some protection of purchasing power. Not to mention that blue chip stocks almost by definition pay dividends, and dividends tend to increase over time. So, putting a reasonable percentage of a retiree's money into blue chip stocks is not necessarily "risky," as might have been thought in the past. In fact, Modern Portfolio Theory suggests that by adding some conservative stocks to a bond portfolio, one may actually reduce overall volatility. Volatility and risk are synonymous these days, so try not to write off any of the major asset classes if you can help it. Blue chip stocks can balance out a primarily fixed-income portfolio, just like fixed-income securities balance out a stock portfolio.

> Call Risk

The bond fund prospectus on my desk also warns of **call risk**, or "the risk that a bond might be called during a period of declining interest rates." Most municipal and corporate bonds are **callable**, meaning that when interest rates drop, corporate and municipal bond issuers will borrow new money at today's lower rate and use it to pay off the current bondholders much sooner than they expected. The problems for the current bondholders are that, first, the bond price stops rising in the secondary market once everyone knows the exact call price that will be received. And, second, what do they do with the money they just received from the issuer? Reinvest it, right? And, where are interest rates now? Down—so they probably take the proceeds from a 9% bond and turn it into a 6% payment going forward. Hmm—you used to get $90 per year; now you can look forward to $60. Couldn't you protect yourself by buying non-callable bonds? Sure—and they'll offer you lower rates than what they pay on callable bonds. As they say, there is no free lunch. Also, notice that call risk is essentially the same thing as prepayment risk; it's just that prepayment risk is related specifically to mortgage-backed securities while call risk refers to bonds and preferred stock.

> Reinvestment Risk

Remember that bonds paying regular interest checks force investors—if they don't just spend the money—to reinvest into new bonds every few months or so. What kind of rates/yields will debt securities be offering when they go to reinvest the coupon payments? Nobody knows, which is why it's a risk, called **reinvestment risk**. It's very annoying to take a 9% interest payment and reinvest it at 3%, but it does happen. To avoid reinvestment risk, buy a debt security that gives you nothing to reinvest along the way: zero coupons, i.e., Treasury STRIPS.

So, even though bond investing is less risky than stock investing, notice how bondholders can get hit coming and going. If it's a corporate bond—and plenty of municipal securities—you could end up getting stiffed (credit risk). Whether it's a corporate, municipal, or even a US Treasury bond, when rates go up, the price of your bond gets knocked down (interest rate risk). If rates go down, callable bonds are called (call risk), and the party's over, and with non-callable bonds you still have to reinvest the interest checks every six months at a lower rate going forward (reinvestment risk). And, even if none of the above happens, inflation could inch its way up, making those coupon payments less and less valuable (purchasing power risk).

Oh, well. If you want fixed income, you take on these risks to varying degrees, depending on which bond you buy and when you buy it. So, am I saying that nobody ever wins by purchasing bonds?

No. Can you think of a situation where buying bonds could turn out to be profitable? What if you purchased 30-year, non-callable bonds right when interest rates were sky-high and getting ready to drop? Wouldn't that make your purchase price extremely cheap (rates high/price low) and, then, suddenly the market price would shoot to the moon as interest rates started to fall, the faster the better?

How are you going to know when rates have peaked? No idea, but if you figure it out, please text me at your earliest convenience.

> Prepayment Risk

Prepayment risk is basically the form of call risk that comes with owning a mortgage-backed security. A homeowner with a mortgage will typically take advantage of a sudden drop in interest rates by refinancing. Therefore, if an investor holds **mortgage-backed securities** like those issued by GNMA, FNMA, or FHLMC (Ginnie, Fannie, Freddie), that investor will take a hit if interest rates drop suddenly and all the principal is returned sooner than expected. This is called **prepayment risk**. When the investor receives the principal sooner than expected, she typically ends up reinvesting it into similar mortgage-backed securities and receiving a lower rate of interest going forward, while the homeowners in the pool of mortgages, on the other hand, are enjoying *paying* lower interest rates going forward. Since GNMA (Ginnie Mae) securities are guaranteed by the US Treasury, their main risk is this prepayment risk.

Also, since most countries use a different currency from the American dollar, **currency exchange risk** is also part of the package when investing in foreign markets, emerging or otherwise. The value of the American dollar relative to foreign currencies, then, is a risk to both international and emerging markets investors. So, even if it's a **developed market**, such as Japan, if you're investing internationally into Japanese stocks, the value of the yen versus the dollar presents foreign exchange or currency risk. If you're investing in China, you have that risk, plus the political risk of investing in companies operating in an immature capitalist system likely to suffer many fits and starts before all the kinks are worked out.

➤ Political Risk

The American business climate and financial markets are pretty darned dependable, especially when compared to, say, Syria. Of course, we might occasionally want to raise the bar a little bit, but you get the point. Remember that **political risk** is part of the package if you want to invest in **emerging markets**. An emerging market is a country or region where the financial markets are immature and unpredictable. They're not fully developed, a little awkward, a bit volatile, basically like teenagers—bright future, but some days you really aren't sure if they're going to make it. If you own stocks and bonds in companies operating and trading in undeveloped economies, lots of fits and starts can make the ride a wild one—what happens if the Chinese government gets tired of capitalism and nationalizes/seizes the companies whose shares you used to own? Total loss. Or maybe the transition from communism to "capitalism" doesn't go so well, and suddenly the whole country is shut down with riots in the streets and government tanks rolling in. When this type of thing happens, emerging market investments naturally are affected, and not in a good way. By definition, an investor facing this sort of political risk is also facing currency exchange risk, among all the other risks that may be presented as part of the investment package.

UN-SYSTEMATIC RISK

Un-systematic risk relates to a particular issuer or industry space, as opposed to the overall market or to all long-term bonds, for example. **Diversification** of a portfolio reduces these risks by spreading them out among stocks of many different issuers operating in different industry sectors. Modern Portfolio Theory states that this type of risk is "diversifiable" and that investors should not expect to be compensated for taking on non- or un-systematic risks. They should only expect to be compensated for taking on systematic risk.

➤ Business Risk

Buying stock in any company presents **business risk**. Business risk includes the risk of competition or the "risk of **obsolescence**," which is the risk that a company's products/services suddenly become obsolete. Historically, long-term shareholders in 8-track player and electric typewriter companies may have experienced the pains of this type of investment risk. Nowadays, one could almost picture how movie theaters could become a thing of the past, so investing in a movie theater chain carries more "risk of obsolescence" than investing in a company that manufactures underwear or shoes. The risk of poor management, of better competitors, or of products/services becoming obsolete are all part of business risk. In other words, the stock you own is only as solid as the businesses who issued it. So, you also need to diversify your portfolio so that it's not all subject to the same type of business risk. Airlines, retailers, and financial services companies, for example, would all face different business risks.

➤ Legislative or "Regulatory" Risk

Legislative or **regulatory risk** means that if laws change, certain securities could be negatively affected. If the federal government suddenly announced that all car makers will have to get 75 mpg for all large SUVs and pickup trucks by the following year, this would probably knock down the value of certain stocks and bonds. Or, what if an investor bought a portfolio of tax-exempt municipal bonds, and then Congress decided to eliminate the exemption for municipal bond interest—investors would dump their municipal bonds, forcing the market prices down suddenly.

Different industries are subject to different regulatory risks, so perhaps if I diversify my stocks and bonds among many different industries, this will protect me from legislative risk somewhat.

➤ Credit/Default Risk

Credit risk is the risk that the issuer of a bond will be unable to pay interest and/or return principal to the bondholders. US Treasury securities have little or no default risk, but some municipal securities and most corporate bonds carry default/credit risk to a large degree. Even if the issuer never misses a payment, if S&P and Moody's downgrade their credit score, the market value of the bonds could also plummet.

➤ Liquidity Risk

Marketability or liquidity is the ability to quickly turn an investment into cash and at a fair price. Money market securities are easy to buy and sell at a fair price; municipal bonds, DPPs (limited partnerships), and thinly traded stocks are not. How much money could you make on your house if you absolutely had to sell it by tomorrow? Might have to drop your asking price pretty severely, unless there were, like, 10 buyers pounding on your door for an opportunity to put in a bid, right? So, thinly traded securities have **liquidity/marketability risk** compared to securities with more active secondary markets. When a stock gets kicked off NASDAQ and lands in that purgatory known as the OTC Bulletin Board, it starts to trade in a less liquid market. That means you don't get nearly as good a price when you sell or when you buy.

➤ Opportunity Cost

If you pass up an investment opportunity to make 5%, your **opportunity cost** is 5%, and you need to do better than 5% with the opportunity you choose instead. If you could have made 5% and you end up making 7% with another investment, you made 2% better than your opportunity cost.

INVESTMENT RISK	SIGNIFICANCE	NOTES	
Systematic	Affect the overall market	"Non-diversifiable"	Diversification won't help; investor must "hedge"
Un-systematic	Affect particular stocks only	Diversifiable	Buy many stocks in many industries
Market	Markets panic due to war, weather events, etc.	Measured by Beta	Hedge with options, futures, ETFs, etc.

INVESTMENT RISK	SIGNIFICANCE	NOTES	
Business	How strong is the issuer?	Competition, obsolescence	Diversify your holdings
Political	Emerging markets, e.g., China, Vietnam	Unstable political-economic systems	Don't confuse with "legislative risk"
Legislative/ Regulatory	Changes to laws/regulations	Tax code changes EPA requirements, OSHA mandates	Could have negative effect on stock or bond price
Currency	Value of dollar	ADRs, international and global investing	Weak dollar makes ADR more valuable
Interest Rate	Rates up/Market price down	Long-term bonds most susceptible, measured by "duration"	Preferred stock is rate-sensitive, too
Credit, Default	Issuer could fail	Downgrade in credit rating lowers value of bond	Low bond values = high-yield
Purchasing Power	Inflation erodes buying power	Fixed-income presents purchasing power risk	Live and die by the CPI
Reinvestment Risk	Investing at varying rates of interest	If rates down, investor goes forward at lower rate	Zero-coupons avoid this risk
Liquidity Risk	Trying to sell when there are few or no buyers	Esoteric securities, partnerships, hedge fund investments are illiquid	Thinly traded stocks less liquid
Opportunity Cost	What you give up to invest elsewhere	If you give up a 5% T-Bond investment, 5% is your opportunity cost	Try to do better than 5%

PRACTICE

1. A 10-year zero-coupon Treasury bond is most susceptible to which of the following?

 A. Credit risk

B. Reinvestment risk

C. Liquidity risk

D. Purchasing power risk

2. Non-systematic risks (e.g., legislative) are best reduced through:

    A. Hedging strategies

    B. Diversification

    C. Buy and hold

    D. Equity options

(ANSWERS)

1. **D,** There is no income to reinvest. The US Treasury Department's credit is excellent, but fixed-income securities are generally poor at protecting purchasing power.

2. **B,** Diversify to protect against un-systematic risk. Hedging strategies are associated with systematic risk on the exam.

QUANTITATIVE METHODS

TIME VALUE OF MONEY

The **time value of money** means that a dollar can always earn some rate of interest in a savings account, CD, or T-Bill, so any amount of money is worth more the sooner it is received. We're about to look at **future value** and **present value**, where we will see that money that's earning 5% year after year grows magically into a large pile of cash due to "compounded returns" and the more frequently the principal compounds, the better. For now, let's just look at what happens in one year.

If you invest $100 today at 5% interest, you will have $105 in one year. We call that $105 the future value of the $100. It is calculated by simply multiplying $100 by 1.05. The number 1.05 represents that you will end up with 105% of what you started with—the $100 plus 5%. On the other hand, $100 received one year from now is worth only $95.24 today. Instead of multiplying $100 by 1.05 to calculate its future value, simply divide the $100 by 1.05 to find its present value. $100 divided by 1.05 = $95.24. In other words, if you invest $95.24 at 5% for one year, you'll end up with $100 at the end of the year. You can double-check that by taking $95.24 times 1.05 and getting back to $100. If the exam makes you calculate either future value or present value, I recommend double-checking your math.

➢ Future Value

Of course, it's hard to get excited over the fact that $100 invested at 5% for one year takes the investment all the way up to $105. But, if you're patient and leave it in there a few years, it can grow quite nicely, even at just 5%. To see how large the investment would become, multiply $100 by 1.05, then multiply that by 1.05, and so on for every year you leave it in the account. These are **compound returns**, and through the magic of **compound interest** we see that $100 times 1.05 leaves us with $105 after year one. If we multiply that by 1.05, we have $110.25 after year two. Multiply that by 1.05, and we have $115.76 after year three, $121.55 after year four, and $127.62 after year five. So, the future value of $100 invested for five years at 5% compounded interest is $127.62. If that still doesn't impress you, add zeros to your initial investment: $10,000 becomes $12,762 after five years, or $100,000 becomes $127,628 after five years, and so on.

The exam could say that a company's profits are $1 per share—if they grow 7% per year for 5 years, what will the earnings per share be at the end of the period? Just multiply the $1 by 1.07 five times in a row to get your answer. Or, the 25-cent dividend compounds at 6% for five years, and so on.

The formula for future value can be expressed a few different ways. One way is:

$$FV = Principal \times (1 + r)t$$

Math is a language, and that is just the mathematical way to represent what we were doing by multiplying an investment by 1.05 for 5% or 1.10 for 10%, and so on. In this formula, "r" means "rate of return" and "t" means "time." Remember, our returns are compounded. So if you get 10% the first year, you'll have more money earning 10% the next year, and so on. Even if it's the same 10% rate of return, it's always 10% of a bigger number. So, if we expect to get 10% each year over a 5-year period, we would say that the FV (future value) of a dollar invested today will be $1 x (1.10)5. 1.10 is just the "1" plus 10%. The investment will multiply itself by 1.10 five times in a row. And remember that the "5" doesn't mean to multiply by 5. It means to multiply the 1.10 by itself five times. The exponent "5" means "to the fifth power."

So what we're doing in our example is multiplying our invested dollar by 1.10 five times in a row. The dollar would be worth $1.61 at the end of five years, and you can add as many zeroes as your client is willing to invest. $100,000 now would be worth $161,000 then (give or take). One million bucks now equals about $1.61 million in five years. At a ten percent return. Which is not guaranteed, you might mention to your client.

Another way the formula can be written is:

$$Pn = PO (1 + r)n$$

"Pn" now stands for the future value of the investment. The little "n" is just the number of years the portfolio will be compounding. P0 is the original investment or original amount. So, it's really the same idea and formula expressed differently.

We just looked at a magical portfolio that compounds conveniently once per year, right on schedule. Well, if we had an investment that compounded more frequently—every six months, quarter, or month—that would be known technically as a "really good thing." So tell the exam that the more frequently an investment compounds, the better that is for the investor.

Also remember that when an investor buys a bond paying 5%, he receives 5% *simple* interest. That means the issuer pays 5% of the same $1,000 principal each year. If a corporate bond paid compound interest, it would work like our compound returns above. In that case, a 5% bond would pay (but doesn't) $50 the first year, but then 5% of $1,050 the next year, and 5% of $1,102.50 the next, and so on. Which would be great, but the reality is that the issuer pays 5% <u>simple</u> interest on a bond. If you hold a bond for five years paying 5% simple interest, you get your $1,000 back plus total interest payments of $250. So compound interest pays interest on the principal plus the accumulated interest on that principal, while simple interest pays a rate applied only to the principal. Bank CDs pay compounded rates of interest. Unfortunately, the rates of interest are so low and the terms so short that one barely notices a difference between simple and compound interest on those safe-money products. So, where would an investor find a 5% compounded rate of return? There might not be any security guaranteeing that rate, but a diversified bond portfolio could easily return that much or more over the investor's holding period through reinvestments of interest payments.

XYZ common stock currently pays a dividend of 44 cents annually. If the dividend is increased by 6% per year for five years, what will the dividend be at the end of this period?

Answer: just take 44 cents and multiply it by 1.06 five times in a row. The "1.06" is just a numeric way of saying that the dividend will be 100% of what it was plus six percent. At the end of the period, it will be…59 cents.

> Present Value

Future value answers this question: if I invest this much money and get this rate of return for this period of time, what will my money be worth in the future? **Present value** answers this question: if I need this much money in the future and can get this rate of return for this period of time, how much money do I have to put in now, in the present? Maybe you need a certain amount of money to put your child through college. Given a particular rate of return, how much do you need to invest today to get there? That's present value. I already sneaked it in when I said that $100 received in one year is worth only $95.24 today, since I could invest $95.24 right now at 5% and turn it into $100 in just one year.

The formula for Present Value is:

$$PV = FV / (1 + r)t$$

So, for Future Value, we said that $100,000 invested today at 10% would be worth $161,000 in five years. Well, what if your client said she needed exactly $190,000 in five years—how much must she invest at 10% to get there? Start with $190,000 and DIVIDE by 1.10 five times in a row. The investor needs to put in $117,975 in the present to end up with $190,000 at the end of her holding period. Not that we should tell her to expect 10% compounded returns for five years; just illustrating how these formulas work for the exam.

One of your clients requires $200,000 in 7 years. If your client invests the money at 4% compound interest, how much needs to be invested to achieve the goal?

Answer: again, we move in the opposite direction that we moved for Future Value. Take the $200,000 and divide it by 1.04 seven times. $151,983, give or take.

> Internal Rate of Return and Net Present Value

Whenever a business is considering the opportunity to invest in a new call center, printing press, or other cash-generating asset, they first need to determine whether the investment will produce enough cash to not just cover the cost of borrowing the capital, but also to make a profit. In other words, they need to calculate the **Net Present Value (NPV)** of the expected cash flows for the project. To do this, they "discount" the cash flows by a required rate of return called the **internal rate of return**. Internal rate of return can be defined as "the discount rate that makes the net present value of the cash flows equal to zero." That sounds fancy, but it really just means that the investment will look attractive if it can generate any positive cash flow above our required rate of return.

Think of net present value (NPV) as the difference—positive or negative—between the present values of an investment's cash inflows and its cash outflows. If the net present value is negative, the project should be rejected as not financially feasible. A negative NPV means that it costs more to borrow the money than it's worth given the cash flows expected from the investment/project. If the net present value is positive, on the other hand, the investment may be attractive, since the cash inflows outweigh the outflows/costs associated with generating it.

Financial analysts working with these concepts are performing **discounted cash flow analysis**. The basic question that this methodology tries to answer is, "how much cash can we generate from this investment adjusted for the time value of money?" Why adjust for the time value of money? Because, a company could always just park excess cash in a very safe place and receive X amount on that cash; if they're going to, instead, aggressively invest that cash back into the business, they need to get a higher internal rate of return than what they could get parking the cash in T-Bills or bank CDs. If the company can't find any internal projects that provide a higher internal rate of return than what they can get in the securities markets, they might just invest their capital in the securities markets.

Of course, whether they're trying to calculate the cash flows generated by investing in, say, preferred stock of a public company or investing it internally into, say, a call center in Des Moines, Iowa, the company using discounted cash flow analysis always faces certain challenges:

- Small changes in inputs/assumptions can lead to large changes in results
- Estimating future cash flows is inherently imprecise

DESCRIPTIVE STATISTICS AND RISK MEASUREMENTS

Many people think of "risk" as the chance of losing money, but risk is generally defined these days in terms of the wild fluctuations of value that an investment experiences. Why is that so important? Well, during the accumulation phase of your retirement savings plan, you can withstand some of this fluctuating value. But, once you retire, if you're liquidating shares of your mutual funds to generate cash to withdraw, you can be getting crushed during bear markets for stocks or bonds. If one month the account is worth $300,000 and the next only $265,000, that's way too much volatility for a retiree living off the account. Not that younger people should just shrug off big fluctuations in value, either.

Risk can be measured through "descriptive statistics" including both "measures of central tendency" such as the mean, median, and mode, and "measures of variability or dispersion," such as standard deviation. Measures of central tendency present a summary of a set of data and give investors an idea of what a typical return might be for a stock, bond, or mutual fund investment. The "mode" is the most common number in the set of data—maybe the portfolio returns 2% frequently, and that becomes the "mode." The "median" is the halfway point or "middle value," meaning that half the numbers are below this number, and half the numbers are above. Then there is the "mean," which is the average of the numbers. You may have read about the "average annual income" in your area and also the "median income." Those two numbers are not the same thing. The average annual income would be figured by adding up everybody's income and dividing by that number of people. The median income tells us where the middle point of all the incomes would be, where half are below and half above this number. Another name for "mean" is "arithmetic mean," and I am just about certain that you will see this term on your exam. Unfortunately, the test question writer can then hassle you with the difference between an "arithmetic mean" and a "geometric mean," which means I have to drill down on this difference without putting you to sleep somehow. Here goes: if we calculated an "arithmetic mean," we would be figuring a simple average that could be misleading for purposes of measuring investment returns. For example, if you put $10,000 into your brokerage account and had the following returns, what would your account be worth at the end of the third year?

10,000
9,000
7,200
9360

Year 1: −10%

$$3\sqrt{.9 \times .8 \times 1.3}$$

Year 2: −20%

Year 3: +30%

If we try to take a simple "arithmetic mean" or average of −10, −20, and +30%, it might seem that the account should be back at $10,000. But, in fact, the account would be worth only $9,360. When the value dropped 10%, the account went to $9,000. When it lost 20%, it dropped to $7,200. If that account rises 30%, we're only back to $9,360. So, in order to avoid this mistake, we would need to find the so-called "geometric mean," rather than the "arithmetic mean." If the exam expects you to calculate a geometric mean, the answer is "$9,360."

> Measures of Central Tendency

In any case "measures of central tendency" include the mean, median, and mode, and they all, essentially, give us a "central tendency" for the results of an investment over a past period. On the other hand, when we discuss **standard deviation**, we will be looking at how much variability there is among an investment's returns. Therefore, a test question writer can refer to standard deviation not as a "measure of central tendency" but as a "measure of variability" or a "measure of dispersion." Through the perspective of standard deviation, an investment whose results are "all over the road" is "risky," whether the surprises are on the plus or the minus side. Seriously.

In any case, a piece of data that resides far from the "central tendency" of a set of numbers is called an outlier. If an investment has had an unusually high or low return in one year, that will skew the mean much more than it will the mode or median. In a set of results where there is an "outlier," statisticians prefer to use the median over the other two m-words. When there are no outliers, the arithmetic mean is the best measure of central tendency. Either way, if you're talking to your client about the unusual 75% loss his account sustained this year, I'm not sure I'd refer to it as an "outlier." Guess it depends on the client.

Since we're having so much fun, let's go ahead and give our math-loving readers a treat and crunch some actual numbers here. Let's say that the returns for a portfolio over the past 9 years were: 5, 6, 5, 7, 6, 8, 9, 15, 5. The mode is the most common value of 5. The median is 6 because there are four values above and below that number. The mean is just the average of the nine numbers, 7.33%. And the returns are all positive because it's just a little pretend example.

> Standard Deviation

So, measures of central tendency give us an idea of what the typical returns have been for a particular investment, while a "measure of variability/dispersion" tells us how far away from that average an investment's returns can be. Perhaps it will be clearer if I use English. Many years ago I bought shares of ORCL for $15, and immediately the market showed me how smart that was. The stock immediately dropped to $14, $13, $12, and so on, even wavering in the $5 range for a while, as if it were taunting me. In spite of my friends' advice to just take my losses, I held on to what I'd bought, and at this point my investment is up about 250%. Then again, the returns deviated drastically along the way—up 80% one year, down 66% another. We can measure how frightfully my annual returns on ORCL deviated from their own average and call it standard deviation. We do this by taking the value of the investment at the end of each period and then find the average return. Then, we go back and see how much these returns deviated (varied) from that average. Since my returns have been all over the road, the "standard deviation" of the investment is very high. So, in terms of volatility, the investment looks pretty terrible, even though it is, after all, up 250%.

Standard deviation measures how much an investment deviates from its average return. Or, we could say that standard deviation measures the dispersion of a data set from its arithmetic mean. However we define it, standard deviation is understood in percentage terms, so a standard deviation of 5 means the investment typically deviates 5 percentage points above and below its average return. If the average return is 10% and the standard deviation is 5, tell the exam that the likely range of return outcomes is from 5% to 15%. Actually, that's what happens within "one standard deviation," which tells us what happens about 2/3 (68%) of the time. What happens about 95% of the time? Those returns lie within "two standard deviations." So, if the average return is 10 and the standard deviation is 5, two-thirds of the time the returns are within 5% and 15% (–5 and +5 from the mean); about 95% of the time the returns are within 0 and 20% (–10 and +10 from the mean). And, in virtually all cases (99.7% of the time), the returns in our data set will be within three standard deviations, which would put virtually all of our annual returns within –5% on the low end and 25% on the high end. What about that other .3%? What happens there? Well, those are the years that can really smart, which is why prudent investors don't trust their computer models too much.

As always, the exam can test a concept from many angles, so if you get a test question showing a table of numbers, understand that the set of numbers that hover more closely together is showing you a lower standard deviation. In other words, if the monthly returns for one stock were 3%, 5%, and 6%, that would represent a much lower standard deviation—less volatility—than a stock whose returns were –4%, 7%, and 17%. If a mutual fund gained 1% every month, its standard deviation would be zero, since every month it did the same thing—went up by 1%. Maybe you're wondering what the fund's standard deviation would be if it steadily lost 1% each month. Also zero. So, while it's nice to have a low standard deviation, this is not to be confused with making money.

A portfolio's expected return is 6%, with a standard deviation of 4. Therefore, the portfolio will most likely show returns between…?

Answer: just subtract and add 4 to 6%. The likely range of outcomes is between 2% and 10%. And, if the question asked what the range would be 95% of the time, add and subtract 8 to get from –2% all the way up to 14%.

The exam may just ask you to identify which portfolio is the riskiest and/or has the highest standard deviation in a way that lets you eyeball your way to the answer. That's what we're hoping. Maybe it will say that one portfolio had a high return of 8% and a low of –10%, while another had a high of 4% and a low of –8%. Obviously, the second one has a lower standard deviation. It didn't go up as high or down as low. Similarly, an equity income mutual fund usually doesn't go up or down as much as a growth fund, so its standard deviation is lower, regardless of which fund has a higher total return. Another name for this simplified form of standard deviation is **range**.

Just in case the exam expects you to know the math behind standard deviation, here goes. If our portfolio had a high of 8% and a low of –10%, what was the average or the mean return? Just take –10 plus 8 divided by two to get the average. The average or mean is –1%. If you're more of a visual person, imagine moving 9 spaces from either –10 or 8 on an imaginary number line—where do you end up?

Negative one percent. As we said, we now look at how far the returns were from that average. Positive 8% is 9 away from –1% and –10% is also 9 away from –1%. Since it's math, we now square both of those numbers. 9 squared = 81 and 9 squared = 81. We add those two 81s to get 162. Then, we divide 162 by (n–1) where "n" equals the number of values in our little data set. Since there are only two numbers, we divide 162 by (2–1), which is, of course, just 162. In case that wasn't enough steps, we now have to hit the little square root button on the calculator, and our answer is approximately 12.73. Yes standard deviation is also defined as "the square root of variance." So, 12.73 is the standard deviation of this portfolio. A portfolio with a standard deviation of, say, 9.2, then would be considered less risky.

> Sharpe Ratio

The **Sharpe ratio** uses standard deviation to determine if an investor is getting enough return for the risk he's taking. The exam might say that the Sharpe ratio measures the excess return per unit of risk. Mathematically, it would be the actual return you get minus the "riskless rate of return," divided by the standard deviation.

Seriously. So, the Sharpe ratio measures **risk-adjusted returns**. And, the higher the number, the better. Also, the **riskless rate of return** that we use as a comparison to what we're actually getting is the yield on 3-month T-Bills. So, if an investment gets a 10% return when the yield on 3-month T-Bills was 5%, we're down to 5% of excess return. If the standard deviation is 5, we would divide 5 by 5 for a Sharpe ratio of 1. Notice how if the standard deviation had been 10, that Sharpe ratio would have been a lower number. Which is bad. The higher the Sharpe ratio, the better the investor is being compensated for the risk he's taking. That could be confusing—a high standard deviation is a red flag, but a high Sharpe ratio is a good thing.

> Beta

We discussed beta when looking at market risk, but let's go ahead and do a quick recap here. If you click on the overview of a stock at your favorite financial website, chances are you'll see the **beta**, which is an investment's tendency to go up and down compared to the overall market. We use the S&P 500 as the measure of the "overall market" and then track how much the stock or portfolio moved compared to that index. So a beta of "1" means a security moves exactly in step with the overall market (S&P 500). A beta of more than 1 implies that the stock is more volatile than the overall market, while a beta of less than 1 implies that the stock is less volatile than the overall market. The exam might want you to say that a stock with a beta of more than 1 (1.5, for example) will out-perform the market when stock prices rise but under-perform the market when stock prices fall. Or, we could reverse that if the beta were less than 1, right? A stock with a low beta could be said to "under-perform a bull market and out-perform a bear market."

If ABC common stock has a beta coefficient of .5, what would occur if the S&P dropped by 10%?

Answer: the stock would drop by 5%. The ".5" tells you the stock moves half as much as the overall market.

> Alpha

So, if a portfolio has an expected return of 8%, it will always return at least 8%. Except when it doesn't. If the expected return is 8%, but we only get a 6% return, we could call that "negative alpha," which sounds much better than "missed it by two." The portfolio manager apparently didn't do as well as he or she should have. However, if the portfolio manager took a portfolio with an expected return of 8% and actually got a 10% return, that excess return could be referred to as "positive alpha." Portfolio managers who get excess returns or show positive alpha are said to be adding value with their money management skills. Those who consistently show "negative alpha" are eventually shown the door. You will often see hedge funds/alternative investments described in terms of "alpha-driven" results, meaning that this portfolio's performance is almost entirely dependent on the skills of the portfolio manager, not on the movement of the overall market.

Another way to define **alpha** is to say that it compares an investment's risk-adjusted results to a benchmark. The exam may point out that the two most commonly used risk-adjusted return measurements are the Sharpe ratio and alpha. The exam may point out all kinds of stuff.

> R-Squared

R-squared is a statistical measurement that tries to explain how much of a portfolio's movement is explained by the movement in the benchmark index. For a fixed-income portfolio, T-Bills can serve as a benchmark. For stocks, the S&P 500 provides a useful benchmark. The values are from 0 to 100. If the R-squared value is 100, that means that 100% of the movement is explained by the movement of the benchmark index. A lower value (under 75, say) would indicate that the portfolio does not move in line with the index. Since index funds are so cheap to own, some investors don't like to pay for active portfolio management if the portfolio acts just like an index. So a lower R-squared value could be viewed as a sign that the portfolio manager is not just playing golf, mirroring an index, and charging unnecessary fees for active management.

CHAPTER 1 QUIZ
19 Questions

1. During a period of low interest rates in the United States relative to other countries, you would expect the value of the dollar to

    A. Remain unchanged

    B. Drop due to decreased demand for dollars

    C. Rise due to decreased demand for dollars

    D. Drop due to increased demand for dollars

2. Rising unemployment and falling personal incomes would most likely lead the Federal Reserve to do which of the following?

    A. Purchase US Treasury securities

    B. Decrease income tax rates

    C. Increase reserve requirements

    D. Increase discount rate

3. Which of the following is an accurate statement concerning a corporation's financial statements?

    A. Profitability is shown only on the balance sheet

    B. Assets and liabilities are shown on the income statement

C. The balance sheet shows income and expenses over the reporting period

D. The income statement shows the results of operations over a reporting period

4. An investor concerned about an economic contraction up ahead would be best advised to purchase common stock of issuers in which of the following industry groups?

A. Restaurants

B. Soft drinks

C. Automotive Parts

D. Heavy Equipment

5. During a period of high interest rates in the United States relative to other countries, you would expect the value of the dollar to:

A. Drop, thereby aiding US exports to foreign buyers

B. Rise, thereby aiding US exports to foreign buyers

C. Rise due to high demand for dollar-denominated debt securities

D. Drop due to excessive demand for dollars

6. Which of the following risks is considered "un-systematic"?

A. Purchasing power

B. Legislative

C. Interest rate

D. Reinvestment

7. Which of the following types of investment risk would affect the largest number of industries and companies listed for trading on an exchange?

A. Political

B. Foreign Exchange

C. Obsolescence

D. Inflation

8. Devaluation of the US dollar would NOT be expected to

$\$ \downarrow \Rightarrow E \uparrow, I \downarrow$

A. Decrease American exports

B. Increase American exports

C. Decrease imports into America from foreign sources

D. Increase the value of a dividend paid to an American holding an ADR

9. Which of the following items is/are found on a corporation's income statement?

   A. Cash and equivalents

   B. Depreciation

   C. Accounts payable

   D. Goodwill

10. If a fundamental analyst says that a company she is following has a strong balance sheet, you would expect the company to have:

   A. A large amount of bonds relative to shareholder's equity

   B. A large amount of intangible assets relative to long-term liabilities

   C. A large amount of cash equivalents relative to current liabilities

   D. A large amount of current liabilities relative to current assets

11. Which of the following is a leading indicator?

   A. Personal income

   B. Corporate profits

   C. Savings

   D. Building permits

12. Which of the following accurately describes "inflation"?

   A. The result of too many dollars chasing a limited supply of goods and services

   B. The inverse of interest rates

   C. Credit risk

   D. The risk of improper diversification of assets

13. In a set of portfolio returns for a 10-year period, there is one year with a negative result that is far outside the typical returns. In this case, the preferred measure of central tendency to use would be the:

54

A. Mean

B. Median

C. Mode

D. Standard deviation

14. Which of the following betas would indicate that the stock is expected to outperform a bull market and underperform a bear market?

A. .9

B. 1.4

C. .8

D. 1.0

15. The price-to-earnings ratio for a common stock is best defined as:

A. The net profitability of the issuing corporation

B. The earnings of the company compared to net interest costs

C. The enthusiasm investors have for a company's profits

D. The hard, tangible book value compared to the stock's market price

16. If interest rates are expected to rise over the next several years, what would be the effect on the present value of $11,555 to be received in five years?

A. It would decrease the present value

$I\uparrow \longrightarrow PV\downarrow$

B. It would have no effect

C. It would increase the present value

D. It would make the cash flows equal to less than zero

17. A public corporation has just lost one of its major customers representing 1/3 of revenue. If the next quarterly report is not due for 3 weeks, the corporation would file at this time:

A. No report

B. A 10-K

C. A 10-Q

D. An 8-K

18. In a public company's annual report (10-K) management presents the balance sheet, the income statement, and the statement of cash flows. Footnotes would follow these statements for what reason?

    A. Only if a majority of the board rules they are required under the Securities Exchange Act of 1934

    B. To clarify the valuation of inventory or to explain a one-time, non-recurring charge to income

    C. Only as permitted under the Securities Act of 1933

    D. To predict growth in either revenue or net income outside normal parameters

19. What does "standard deviation" have to do with?

    A. The dispersion/variability of an investment's results

    B. Credit/default risk

    C. Systematic risk

    D. It is a measure of central tendency

(ANSWERS TO CHAPTER 1 REVIEW QUIZ)
1. ANSWER: B

WHY: low interest rates would not attract foreign investment into US Treasury securities, so as the demand for dollars decreases, so would the value of the dollar.

2. ANSWER: A

WHY: the "Fed" would need to provide stimulus through a "loose money" policy if people are losing their jobs and making less money. The Fed cannot set tax rates.

3. ANSWER: D

WHY: assets and liabilities are recorded on the balance sheet. The results of operations over the reporting period are shown on the income statement—revenue, net income, profit margins.

4. ANSWER: B

WHY: during an economic slump consumers can most likely be depended on to buy soft drinks. On the other hand, consumers will likely cut back on restaurant spending and shopping for new cars, and businesses will generally reduce their spending on heavy equipment, during a contraction.

5. ANSWER: C

WHY: if foreign investors can park their cash in US Treasury securities paying high yields, they will. This increased demand for dollars will raise their relative value, which will hurt—not aid—exports.

6. ANSWER: B

WHY: changes in legislation or regulations are usually specific to a particular industry rather than system-wide. For example, a law requiring increased fuel efficiency in automobiles would hit the automobile industry without necessarily impacting other sectors. This is why diversification among industry sectors is important.

7. ANSWER: D

WHY: inflation would impact all fixed-income securities first, and then stocks across the board. The other risks are specific to certain types of investments. For example, a laptop computer maker has more obsolescence risk than a company that builds homes. Foreign exchange risk is presented by American Depository Receipts and international funds, but these can be a small part of a diversified portfolio to minimize foreign exchange risk. Same for political risk—if the investor limits her exposure to emerging markets, this un-systematic risk can also be minimized through diversification.

8. ANSWER: A

WHY: a devalued dollar would increase, not decrease, America's ability to export to foreign customers.

9. ANSWER: B

WHY: depreciation is an expense on the income statement. While it is also reflected on the balance sheet where fixed assets are listed, the other three answer choices are only balance sheet items.

10. ANSWER: C

WHY: a company with a lot of cash equivalents relative to current liabilities probably has a lot of working capital, and a strong current and quick ratio.

11. ANSWER: D

WHY: the building permits are taken out BEFORE the homes are built—leading indicator.

12. ANSWER: A

WHY: when demand outpaces supply, inflation can occur. Inflation and interest rates move together, not inversely.

13. ANSWER: B

WHY: whenever there is an outlier in a set of data, the median tends to give a more accurate picture than the mean.

14. ANSWER: B

WHY: a stock with a beta of > 1 will outperform a bull market but underperform a bear market. In other words, it will go up higher and down lower than the overall market.

15. ANSWER: C

WHY: the P/E ratio shows us how popular a company's profitability is at the moment, showing how much investors will pay for the profits and expectation of future growth in profits.

16. ANSWER: A

WHY: if you're not sure on a question like this, try running calculations. Find the present value of $11,555 received in 5 years if rates are at 3% and then at 6%. You'll see that if rates are at 6%, the present value decreases.

17. ANSWER: D

WHY: this is a material event that needs to be promptly disclosed, on a Form 8-K.

18. ANSWER: B

WHY: one-time or non-recurring charges to revenue or sales increases need to be explained in the footnotes. The company's management can't allow investors to get overly excited by one big infusion of cash that is unlikely to repeat, so if the company profited by, for example, selling off equipment, that should be explained. Similarly, if an accounting change makes the inventory appear suddenly under- or over-valued, that should also be explained. The numbers presented in the consolidated financial statements often require further clarification, which is what the footnotes section is for.

19. ANSWER: A

WHY: standard deviation is the opposite of a measure of "central tendency." Rather than showing the typical result, it shows how far away from its own average return an investment's results could be. For example, a money market mutual fund has virtually no standard deviation since the share price remains at $1. A growth fund, however, might have an average return of 12% over 10 years, with some of those years going up as high as +39% and down as low as –40%. The growth fund's returns would be more variable, more widely dispersed and unpredictable.

CHAPTER 2: Investment Vehicles

Now that you have a better understanding of economic factors and investment risks you can better understand how they affect the investment vehicles available to your clients. Investment vehicles must be matched appropriately with the needs and profile of each client. Some investors want a predictable stream of income from their investment. For example, maybe they loan a corporation $100,000 and receive $4,000 a year in interest payments for 10 years. That 4% **yield** is nice, but at the end of the term, the investor will only get back $100,000, and we already know that inflation will have reduced the purchasing power of that money over 10 years. Other investors will give up a steady stream of income (yield) in order to reach for **growth** or **capital appreciation**. Rather than lending money to a corporation, these **equity** investors prefer to buy **common stock** in the company. This way, if the company becomes more valuable, so do the shares of common stock the investor owns. Common stock is an ownership stake in a public company. If you want to loan, buy a bond. If you want to own, buy stock instead.

TYPES AND CHARACTERISTICS OF EQUITY SECURITIES

COMMON STOCK

Fans of the *Shark Tank* have seen early-stage venture capitalists offer deals to entrepreneurs coming in with business ideas ranging from ingenious to insane. Very seldom does a "shark" act like a banker and merely lend money to a business. Rather, these aggressive investors seek an equity stake in early-stage companies. The sharks are not fixed-income investors. The sharks are early-stage investors in common stock, staking a claim on the company's profits long before the company ever thinks about doing an IPO.

Common stock represents an owner's claim on the profits of the company. It does not give the investor a stated rate of return. If you receive 60 cents per share of common stock as a dividend this year, you might or might not receive that much next year. In fact, the company might stop paying dividends entirely if it hits a rough patch. And, some companies—like Berkshire Hathaway—never pay dividends. But that's okay. Some investors are looking for the share price to go up over time, which is called capital appreciation or growth. Both the market value of and the income provided by common stock are totally speculative, but common stock also has unlimited potential gain. That unlimited upside potential is what makes common stock such an attractive investment, even if it could also drop 50-75-even 100% very quickly.

Then again, even if you lose 100% on one investment, another common stock investment could more than make up for that over time. While I do have one 100% loss in my 15 years of equity investing, just one holding of PCLN in one of three accounts has more than made up for that. Not many stocks will go up 4,200% the way PCLN has for me, but when that happens, you do learn to live with the occasional strike-out along the way. While that percentage will change by the time you read this, note that my cost basis on the stock is . . . $21 a share. See "stock quote: PCLN." Bwahaha.

Common stock is easy to transfer to another party, as it can be sold, donated, gifted, or inherited. The issuer of the stock hires a firm (usually a bank) to keep track of all those transfers of ownership, and they're called the **transfer agent**. The transfer agent keeps the ownership records of the company's stock. With maybe 50 million shares of Microsoft trading daily, imagine how much those ownership records change each day! The transfer agent deals with issuing and validating stock and bond certificates, recording name changes when investors sell their certificates, and re-issuing lost, stolen, or destroyed certificates. If there's a problem with the ownership records of the security, contact the transfer agent. They can validate the ownership and re-issue certificates, as the case may be. And, usually for a fee.

Just to make sure the transfer agent is on the ball, the corporation also hires another outside firm—typically a bank—and we refer to this party as the **registrar**. The registrar audits the transfer agent, just to make sure that all the ownership records are accurate.

> Authorized, Issued, Treasury, Outstanding

Authorized shares represent the number of shares a company has authorized itself to issue to the public through the documents that guide the corporation, the by-laws and the corporate charter. Let's say a company is authorized to issue 1,000,000 shares of common stock, according to the charter. When they first sell shares to the public during their IPO, they probably won't issue all of them the first time out. The number they actually issue would be known quite simply as **issued** shares. This corporation could issue 1 million, but they only issue 500,000. Therefore, there are 500,000 issued shares.

For various reasons, the corporation might decide to buy back some of those shares that are out in the secondary market. These shares, which were issued but repurchased, are called **treasury stock**. Since it's sort of locked up in a vault, it has no voting rights and pays no dividends. If this corporation had issued 500,000 shares and then purchased 100,000 for the treasury, they would have how many shares left outstanding?

400,000 **shares outstanding**. So, just take "issued" and subtract "treasury" to get the number of shares "outstanding."

$$
\begin{array}{rl}
500,000 & \text{Issued} \\
-\quad 100,000 & \text{Treasury} \\
\hline
400,000 & \text{Outstanding}
\end{array}
$$

When we talk about a company's **earnings per share (EPS)**, we're only talking about the **outstanding shares**, which are also the only shares that get to vote. That's why the company can boost its earnings per share (EPS) by repurchasing their outstanding stock on the secondary market. Even if the company's total profit/earnings stayed the same, the earnings *per share* would rise if the company were reducing the number of outstanding shares. For example, if the company earned $1 million, that would be an earnings per share of $2 if there were 500,000 shares outstanding. However, after the company buys back 100,000 shares for the treasury, that same $1 million profit would be $2.50 of earnings per share. Right? Buying back shares is similar to cutting a big pizza into fewer slices—each one is bigger for those at the table.

> Rights, Privileges of Common Stock Ownership

Owners of common stock enjoy several important rights. Unlike other securities holders of the company, common stockholders get to vote for any major issue that could affect their status as a proportional owner of the corporation. Things like stock splits, mergers and acquisitions, board of director elections, and changes of business objectives all require shareholder approval at the annual or any special meetings called to take a vote on a big issue.

But, one thing shareholders never get to vote on is whether a dividend is paid and, if so, how much it should be. Letting shareholders propose and vote on dividends would be like letting your kids propose and approve their own allowance.

Shareholders vote their shares. If you own 100 shares of common stock, you have 100 votes to cast. Let's say there are three seats up for election on the Board of Directors. There are two ways that your votes could be cast for the election. Under **statutory voting**, you can only cast the number of shares you own for any one seat. So, you could cast up to 100 votes for any one seat, representing a total of 300 votes for three seats. Under cumulative voting, you could take those 300 votes and split them up any way you wanted among the three candidates. You could even cast all 300 votes for one candidate and give nothing to the others. That's why the exam might want you to say that **cumulative voting** gives a benefit to the small/minority shareholders. In other words, if we can manage to get a candidate on the slate who will look out for us small shareholders, we can all cast all of our votes for her. The big guys will still get their way with the other candidates, but this gives us a fighting chance every once in a while. And remember that "the big guys," including pension funds and mutual funds, may have millions of shares (votes) versus our couple of hundred votes. Oh well. That's how it works— one vote per share, not per shareholder.

Beyond voting, common stockholders also have the right to inspect the corporation's financials through quarterly (10-Q) and annual (10-K) reports, just to see how the corporation is spending the shareholders' money and running the show up there at headquarters. Shareholders may also see the list of stockholders and the minutes of shareholder meetings.

Common stockholders have what the test may call a "pre-emptive right" to maintain their percentage of ownership. In other words, if the company wants to raise more money in the future by selling more common stock, existing shareholders would get a chance to buy their percentage of the upcoming issue. If not, their ownership would be diluted.

Should a corporation go belly-up and have to be liquidated, common stockholders get in line for their piece of the proceeds. Unfortunately, they are last in line. They are behind all the creditors, including bondholders, and also behind preferred stockholders.

But, at least they are in line, and if there are any residuals left, they get to make their claim on those assets. That's known as a **residual claim** on assets, by the way, because they don't like to get real creative with the language in this industry. The test could also refer to common stock as the most "junior" security, since all other securities represent senior claims.

Shareholders have **limited liability**, which means they are shielded from the debts of the company and lawsuits filed against it. I'm not sure why they bring this up—it's not like the bondholders *are* liable, just something the exam might mention. Limited liability is a good news–bad news thing. The bad news is when you buy common stock, you can lose all your money. The good news is that when you buy common stock, you can only lose all your money.

Rather than a stated rate of return, common stock owners receive a claim on earnings and dividends. Some of the profits/earnings are reinvested into the business, which tends to make the share price rise. Some of the profits might be paid out as dividends, so let's take a look at that.

Dividends

Did you know that a cash dividend is only paid if the **Board of Directors** of the corporation decides to pay it? That's right, if a corporation doesn't declare a dividend, the dividend doesn't get paid. End of story. But, if they do declare a dividend, here's how it works. The day that the Board declares the dividend is known as the **declaration date**. The board decides when they'll pay the dividend, too, and we call that the **payable date**. The board also sets the deadline for being an owner of stock if you want this dividend, and we call that the **record date** because an investor has to be the "owner of record" as of that date to receive the dividend. Now, since an investor has to be the owner of record as of the record date to receive the dividend, there will come a day when it's too late for investors to buy the stock and also get the dividend.

Why?

> Regular Way Settlement

Stock transactions don't "settle" until the third business day following the **trade date**, which means you might put in your purchase order to buy 1,000 shares of Frank & Emma's on a Monday, but you aren't the official owner until that transaction settles on Thursday. Your broker-dealer has to send payment to the seller's broker-dealer, who has to deliver the 1,000 shares. Both sides have to agree that the terms of the transaction have been met, and the whole thing has settled between the buyer and seller. This process takes three business days and is known as **regular way settlement**, or "T + 3," where the "T" stands for Trade Date. Assuming there are no holidays, a trade taking place on Monday would settle on Thursday, while a trade on Tuesday would settle on Friday. So, if an investor has to be the owner of record on the record date, and it takes three business days for the buyer to become the new owner, wouldn't she have to buy the stock at least three business days prior to the record date? Yes.

On the other hand, if she buys it just two business days before the record date, her trade won't settle in time. We call that day the **ex-date** or **ex-dividend date**, because starting on that day investors who buy the stock will not receive the dividend. On the ex-date, it's too late. Why? Because the trades won't settle in time, and the purchasers won't be the owners of record (with the transfer agent) as of the record date.

The regulators set the ex-date, as a function of "regular way" or "T + 3" settlement. The ex-date is two business days before the record date. So, the Board of Directors sets the payable and record date, while the exchange regulators establish the ex-dividend date based on the record date.

Because investors don't qualify for the dividend starting with the ex-date, the amount of the dividend is taken right out of the stock price when trading begins on the ex-date. If the dividend to be paid is 70 cents, and the stock is set to open at $20 on the ex-date, it would open at 19.30, and any orders to buy the stock below the current market price will be reduced by that same amount.

Here is an example of a real-world press release from a few years ago announcing an upcoming dividend:

> **Equity Office declares first quarter common dividend**
>
> Mar 16, 2005-- Equity Office Properties Trust (EOP), a publicly held office building owner and manager, has announced that its Board of Trustees has declared a first quarter cash dividend in the amount of $.50 per common share. The dividend will be paid on Friday 15 April 2005, to common shareholders of record at the close of business on Thursday 31 March 2005.

So, March 16th is the Declaration Date. The Payable Date is April 15th. The Record Date is Thursday, March 31st. The article doesn't mention the Ex-Date (because that's not established by the company), but we can figure that it must be...right, Tuesday, March 29th. If you bought the stock on Tuesday, your trade wouldn't settle until Friday, April 1st, which means the seller's name would be on the list of shareholders at the close of business on Thursday, March 31st.

Quick note: EOP is a REIT, and the "T" in "REIT" stands for "trust." That's why the press release refers to the board as the "Board of Trustees." EOP is a Real Estate Investment Trust, but the stock works like any other stock. It simply pays a nice dividend. As we'll see later, REITs are just shares of stock that tend to pay nice dividend yields. If you owned 1,000 shares of EOP as of the record date, what would you receive?

A check for $500. So, if the dividend stays the same or increases in Q2, Q3, and Q4, you'll collect at least $2,000 just for sitting on your shares of EOP this year. Ever heard that the rich get richer? This is partly why.

It also brings up a testable point as to how a dividend can be paid. A dividend can be paid in the following ways:

- Cash (which means they cut you a check)
- Stock (more shares of stock)
- Shares of a subsidiary
- Product (extremely rare)

Cash dividends are taxable, while stock dividends are not.

PRACTICE

1. An investor purchases common stock on a Thursday. Under regular way settlement, the transaction will settle:

    A. Friday

    B. Monday

    C. Tuesday

D. Wednesday

2. The Board of Directors declared a dividend on Monday, March 1st. If the record date is Tuesday, March 16th, the ex-dividend date is:

    A. Monday, March 15th

    B. Friday, March 12th

    C. Thursday, March 18th

    D. Tuesday, March 23rd

3. Which of the following is/are true concerning treasury stock?

    A. Has been issued and repurchased by the company

    B. Reduces the number of outstanding shares

    C. Tends to raise EPS

    D. All of these choices

(ANSWERS)

1. **C,** Thursday is the trade date or the "T" in "T + 3." T + 1 is Friday, T + 2 is Monday, and T + 3 is Tuesday.

2. **B,** go back two business days.

3. **D,** they buy it back to leave fewer shares outstanding; therefore, the same total earnings/profits of the company are divided among fewer shares for a higher EPS.

> Stock Splits, Stock Dividends

If you and a friend each ordered a personal-size pizza, you could cut yours in half while she cut hers into 8 little slices. Would your friend have received more pizza by cutting the slices smaller and having more of them than you did?

Absolutely not.

It's exactly the same thing with stock splits or stock dividends. Even when the investor ends up with more shares, the total value of his investment is unchanged. They can cut the big pie, in other words, however they want—he still has the same amount of pie. If he had 100 shares at $10 before, that was worth $1,000. No matter how many shares he has after the split or the dividend, the total value is still just $1,000. So, when a corporation does a 2:1 stock split, the investor would have twice as many shares. What would the price per-share be?

Half as much. The investor has $1,000 worth of stock both before and after the split. He used to have 100 shares worth $10 each. Now he has 200 shares worth $5 each. A thousand bucks, either way. The earnings pie has simply been cut into more slices which are, by definition, smaller.

A stock *dividend* would work the same way in terms of more shares/lower price. If an investor receives a 20% stock dividend, that's 20% more shares of stock, but the total value of the investment is the same. It's just divided among more shares. So an investor with 200 shares of XYZ common stock @40 would have $8,000 of XYZ stock. If XYZ declared a 20% stock dividend, she would then have 240 shares. Her $8,000 would be divided among 240 shares, with a per-share price of $33.33. Companies that are still in a growth phase are more likely to pay stock dividends (vs. cash dividends) than more established companies, who are more likely to pay cash dividends compared to small, growing companies.

Stock splits and stock dividends leave the investment's overall value the same. The investor simply has more shares at a lower price, which means her **cost basis** in the stock changes. 100 shares @50 might become 125 shares @40. Just keep track of your cost basis so that when you sell someday you can tell the IRS how much of a **capital gain** or loss you realized on the stock. But whether you have 100 shares @50 or 125 shares @40, you've paid $5,000 for a certain percentage of ownership. And, we'll deal with concerns such as "cost basis" and "capital gains" in more detail in the Taxation section of Chapter 3.

No matter how they slice the earnings pie, you own the same percentage before and after the stock split or stock dividend. They've made the shares smaller and "cheaper," but you have more of them. A "forward split" means you end up with more shares. A 2:1, 3:2, or 5:4 split would be a forward split that pushes the share price down.

Sometimes companies have the opposite problem. Their share price is so low that the big, institutional investors (pension funds, mutual funds, insurance companies) won't touch it. These entities usually won't buy a stock trading below $5, so if our company's stock is trading for $1, we might need to increase that price. One way to do it would be to become a more competitive, profitable company and let the increased profits take the share price up.

A much faster way would be to complete a 1:10 reverse stock split instead.

If the test question says that JoAnne owns 100 shares of ABCD @$1, we might find ABCD doing a reverse split of 1:10. That means for every 10 shares she owns now, she'll end up with only one really big share. She'll have 10 shares when it's all over, in other words. If the shares were trading for $1 before the split and everybody now has shares that are 10 times bigger, the share price magically becomes $10 a share. JoAnne now owns 10 ABCD @$10.

ABCD is a $10 stock, just like that! Doesn't the stock represent the same % ownership, though? Sure, but human beings are funny creatures—many of them will just think the stock has gone up due to profits. Just remember that whether the exam is talking about a stock dividend, a forward split, or a reverse split, the investor's cost basis changes because the share price changes. But no change in *value* actually occurs.

Finally, remember that shareholders vote on stock splits, whether forward (5:4, 2:1, 3:2) or reverse (1:7, 1:10, etc.). Shareholders do not vote on dividends, period.

➢ What Is a Share of Common Stock?

Before we move on, let's make sure we understand exactly what a share of stock is. When you buy a company's common stock, you simply own a percentage of the company. What are all owners interested in? Profits, called *earnings.* The bottom line. You start your own business for one main reason—to earn a profit. You buy a <u>share</u> of somebody else's business for the same reason—to <u>share</u>

in the profits. So, you only buy a share of common stock if you think the company will earn a profit, increase that profit, and, eventually, pay some of that profit out to you as a dividend. That's all there is to it—if you want to <u>share</u> in the earnings/profits of the company, buy some *shares* of common stock.

What if there aren't any earnings?

Then, you bought the wrong stock. Unlike starting a business that goes sour, however, you can usually sell your stock for some price on the secondary market, get back some of your money, and move on with your life.

> Rights, Warrants

As we mentioned, one of the rights common stockholders enjoy is the right to maintain their proportionate ownership in the corporation. We call this a **pre-emptive right** because the existing shareholders get to say yes or no to their proportion of the new shares before the new shareholders get a chance to buy any. Otherwise, if you owned 5% of the company, you'd end up owning less than 5% of it after they sold the new shares to everyone *but* you. That situation could be called **dilution of equity,** which is never a good thing for common stockholders.

For every share owned, an investor receives what's known as a **right**. A right is an equity-type security with a very short life span. It works like a coupon, allowing the current shareholders the chance to purchase the stock below the market price—called the subscription price. If a stock is trading at $20, maybe the existing shareholders can take two rights plus $18 to buy a new share. Those rights act as coupons that give the current shareholders two dollars off the market price. So, the investors can use the rights, sell them, or let them expire in a drawer somewhere, like most coupons.

Warrants have absolutely nothing to do with rights except that they both have stated purchase prices for the issuer's common stock. Unlike a right, a **warrant** is a long-term equity security. If you own a warrant, you own is the opportunity to purchase a company's stock at a pre-determined price. If you have a warrant that lets you buy XYZ for $30 per share, then you can buy a certain number of shares at that price whenever you feel it makes sense to do so, like when XYZ is trading for a lot more than $30 per share. When issued, the price stated on the warrant is above the current market price of the stock. It usually takes a long time for a stock's price to go above the price stated on the warrant, assuming that ever happens at all. But, they're good for a long time, typically somewhere between two and ten years.

Warrants are often included with a bond offering. As we'll see in a few pages, corporations pay interest to borrow money through bonds. If they attach warrants, they can "sweeten" the deal a little and maybe get investors to accept a lower interest payment. Why would you take 4% when your buddy gets 6% on his bond? Doesn't he make $60 a year, while you only make $40? Yes. But if the company's common stock rises, he'll still be making $60 a year, while you could make a huge profit through those warrants. If you have warrants to buy 1,000 shares @30 and those shares rise to $50, are you going to fret about that $20 a year your buddy made? Not when you just made about $20,000, right?

By the way, the warrants are not "attached" as in glued to the bond certificates—they are just thrown in as part of the deal and can be traded separately if the investor so choses.

> ADRS

"ADR" stands for **American Depository Receipt**, and like many of the abbreviations you'll need to know for the exam, this one means exactly what it says. It's a <u>receipt</u> issued to somebody in <u>America</u> against shares of foreign stock held on <u>deposit</u> in a foreign branch of an American bank. The investor buys shares of a Japanese corporation's stock, only the shares are held in a bank in Japan, which issues a receipt to the investor in America. The receipt is what is traded in America. It pays dividends, maybe, but they are paid in the foreign currency and then have to be converted into US dollars, which is why ADR owners are subject to currency risk. Also, if the stock is worth a certain number of yen on the Japanese markets, that won't work out to as many US dollars when our dollar is strong, although it would work out to more American dollars if our dollar is weak.

The financial institution that creates the ADR is called a "depositary." The ADR is created under an agreement between the foreign issuer of the shares, the depositary, and the ADR owners. The depositary maintains a register of the ADR holders, although most investors would have their shares held by their broker-dealer as the nominal owner. The deposit agreement can extend voting rights to the holders of ADRs, but this is not the way it normally works. Rather, assume that the owner of an ADR does not have the right to vote. If the deposit agreement does give voting rights to the ADR holders, the ADR holders would have to instruct the institution how to vote by a certain deadline. The depositary institution is the holder of record for the underlying foreign shares, but they typically do not vote these shares. Their role is to create the ADR and maintain a register of the owners while they, themselves, oversee custody of the underlying foreign shares.

PREFERRED STOCK

A common stock investor might receive dividends, but the dividend is not stated by the company on the stock certificate. In fact, the company may never get around to paying a dividend on their common stock at all. Common stock investors are generally interested in growth or capital appreciation more than income. That means they want to buy the stock low and watch it increase in market price over time. On the other hand, income investors who want to buy a corporation's stock would likely want to buy the company's **preferred stock**. Preferred stock always receives dividends before owners of common stock can be paid. It also gets preferential treatment over common stock if the company has to be forcibly liquidated to pay creditors through a bankruptcy proceeding. And, unlike common stock, the preferred stock dividend is printed right on the stock certificate. Only occasionally does a member of the *Shark Tank* offer a deal that refers to "first-money out," which is a way of referring to a preferred stock position. If an investor wants the highest claim on a company's profits and wants his income stream defined, he needs to buy preferred stock.

The par value for preferred stock could be $25, $100, or some other amount. Whatever it is, the stated dividend is a percentage of the par value. If the par value is $100, then six percent preferred stock would pay 6% of $100 per share, or $6 per share per year. Three percent preferred stock would pay a dividend of 3% of the par value each year. A few years ago Berkshire Hathaway was buying $5 billion positions of preferred stock in struggling financial companies offering 10% stated dividends. That would be $500 million of income per year, which is partly why I hold a fairly large position in Berkshire Hathaway as of this writing. They seem to get a lot of sweet deals like this presented to them.

Preferred stock is expected to pay the stated dividend, but dividends still have to be declared by the Board of Directors, and dividends come out of profits. Preferred stockholders aren't creditors.

They're just proportional owners who like to receive dividends. If the board doesn't declare a dividend, do you know how much an owner of a 6% **straight preferred stock** would receive?

Nothing. However, if the investor owned **cumulative preferred stock**, that might be different. He wouldn't necessarily get the dividend now, but the company would have to make up the missed dividend in future years before it could pay dividends to any other stockholders. If the company missed the six bucks this year and wanted to pay all shareholders dividends next year, cumulative preferred stockholders would have to get their $12 before anybody else saw a dime.

This 6% works more like a maximum than a minimum. If an investor wants the chance to earn more than the stated 6%, he'd have to buy **participating preferred stock**. Generally, if the issuer increases the dividend paid to common stockholders, they will also raise the dividend paid to participating preferred stockholders. If the test wants to talk kind of funny, your question might have an answer such as "the return on straight preferred stock is fixed as to the minimum and as to the maximum," while a question with participating preferred stock as the answer might say something like "the return on participating preferred stock is fixed as to the minimum but not as to the maximum." The latter is just a more formal way of saying, "Unlike all the other types of preferred stock, the dividend on participating preferred stock might be increased."

Adjustable-rate preferred stock has a rate of return that is tied to another rate, typically the rate paid on US Treasury Bills or "T-Bills." If T-Bill rates rise, so does the rate paid on the adjustable-rate preferred stock, and vice versa. Because the rate adjusts, the price remains stable. Also, a question might not be so specific as to mention "T-Bill rates" or "3-month T-Bill yields." Rather, it could just say that adjustable-rate preferred stock is tied to "prevailing interest rates."

Be ready to adjust your thinking at the testing center, something we'll help you with once you start using our practice questions at www.passthe65.com or www.examzone.com.

Corporate issuers often get tired of paying preferred stockholders a high dividend rate when a new group of investors would accept a lower rate now that the interest-rate environment has changed. While most types of preferred stock go on for "perpetuity," **callable preferred stock** may be retired early at the issuer's discretion. If you had purchased 5.5% preferred stock a few years ago and then interest rates went down so that new investors would accept, say, 3%, the issuer would likely issue a new batch of 3% preferred stock to new investors and use some of the proceeds to pay you and all the expensive 5.5% preferred stockholders off. When you bought the callable preferred stock, the call price and the first possible date were named, so if interest rates go down at that point, the issuer might buy back the callable preferred stock, forcing you to reinvest at lower rates. This problem is known as "call risk," as we saw when discussing investment risks. Call risk, in other words, affects both bond holders and owners of preferred stock, if their securities are callable. Because it can be retired early, callable preferred stock tends to pay the highest dividend rate of all types of preferred stock.

Unlike all other types of preferred stock, **convertible preferred stock** is not just a fixed-income security. Rather it is an income-and-growth investment. This unique type of preferred stock lets an investor exchange one share of preferred stock for a certain number of common shares. It works much like a warrant here, where the investor starts out on the fixed-income side, but also captures any upside on the common stock. Say the convertible preferred stock is convertible into 10 shares of common stock. If so, the convertible preferred stock is usually worth whatever 10 shares of common stock are worth. If the common stock rises, so does the convertible preferred stock it's tied to. If the common stock rises to $14, we would expect the convertible preferred stock to trade at around $140. If it trades at exactly $140, it trades at **parity** to the common stock, the exam might say.

Remember that the market price of preferred stock is very sensitive to changes in interest rates. If a security has a fixed payment, the market compares that fixed payment to current interest rates, and these rates can change dramatically. Current interest rates represent what investors could receive if they bought low-risk debt securities. If low-risk debt securities are paying 4%, and your preferred stock pays you a fixed 6%, how do you feel about your preferred stock's yield? Pretty good, right? In fact, you feel so good about it that if somebody wanted to buy it from you, they'd have to pay a higher price.

On the other hand, if interest rates shoot up to 10%, suddenly your 6% preferred stock doesn't look so good. In that case the market price would drop. Not the par value—par value is etched in stone. It's the market price that fluctuates.

Market prices adjust for interest rates: rates up/prices down, rates down/prices up. Well, as we mentioned, if the rate adjusts along with the T-Bill rate, the price doesn't need to move. But for other types of preferred stock, the price moves in the opposite direction of interest rates, just like bond prices. That's because the value is really determined by a comparison of the fixed rate of return to current interest rates. Your exam might point out that both bonds and preferred stocks are "interest-rate sensitive" investments.

But, if we add another variable, now the security's price isn't so sensitive to interest rates. Convertible preferred stock has a value tied to interest rates, like other preferred stock, but its value is also tied to the value of the common stock into which it can be converted. If rates are up, preferred stock prices drop. But if you're holding a convertible preferred stock while the common stock is skyrocketing, the price of the preferred stock would skyrocket right along with it. Remember, it's worth a fixed number of common shares. If the value of the common stock goes up, so does the value of the convertible preferred stock it's tied to. So, the exam might want you to know that convertible preferred stock is less sensitive to interest rates than other types of preferred stock.

Remember that unlike a bond, preferred stock generally does not have a **maturity date**, and unlike common stock, usually does not give the owner voting rights. Two specific cases where preferred stock *does* get to vote are: 1) the corporation defaults on the dividend payment a certain number of times and 2) the corporation wants to issue preferred stock of equal or senior status.

A test question might ask if a company's preferred stock trades in "sympathy" or in conjunction with their common stock. As a general rule, the answer is no. If a company's profits rise, their common stock value usually rises, too, while nothing would happen to the preferred stock because of this. The exception is convertible preferred stock, but, again, as a general rule the company's preferred stock price (straight, cumulative, callable) is related to interest rates and credit quality. Their increased profits or common stock price have nothing to do with the value of their preferred stock.

Let's wrap up by looking at similarities and differences between common and preferred stock.

SIMILARITIES	DIFFERENCES
dividends must be declared by the board of	preferred stock is a fixed-income security paying

SIMILARITIES	DIFFERENCES
directors in order to be paid	a stated rate of return
both are equity securities	preferred stock has a higher claim on dividends and on assets in a bankruptcy
	common stock has voting rights and pre-emptive rights

YIELD, TOTAL RETURN

There are only two ways to make money on stocks. 1, the stock price goes up. 2, the stock pays a dividend. If I'm looking only for the share price to go up, I'm a "growth investor." If I'm solely interested in the dividends, I'm an "income investor." If I want both growth and income, guess what kind of investor I am?

Would you believe "growth and income"?

But, really, that's the only way to make money on stocks. Therefore, measuring the investor's return on equity securities really comes down to those two concerns: **capital appreciation** (growth) and dividends (income). If you buy a stock at $10, and a year later it's worth $20, that's a capital appreciation of 100%. If the stock pays $2 in annual dividends and costs $200 on the open market, that's a yield of 1%. **Yield** asks how much an investor receives in income compared to what he pays for the security.

> *Annual Dividend Divided By Market Price = Dividend Yield*

The test may give you a "quarterly dividend" in the question. If so, remember that there are four financial quarters per year, so a quarterly dividend of 30 cents might need to be considered an annual dividend of $1.20, depending on how the question is written.

Another concept is **total return**. Here, we add the dividend received plus the capital growth/appreciation on the security. In other words, if you buy a stock for $10 and the market price rises to $12, you have $2 of capital appreciation (sometimes called a "paper gain" or an **unrealized gain** just to make sure it has three separate names). If the stock pays $1 in dividends, you're basically "up $3" on a $10 investment.

That's a total return of "3 outa' 10" or 30%. Financial services representatives must be careful when quoting "yield" or "total return" to investors. If a customer receives a 5% dividend yield on a common stock investment, a registered representative might want to talk only about that and ignore the fact that the market price is down, say, 20%, and the total return is negative. The registered representative should give the customer the whole picture to avoid misleading her, right?

FINAL THOUGHT

In order to do your job effectively you have to know many facts that are generally accurate and also know when they *don't* apply. For example, it is true that preferred stock generally provides income while common stock is purchased primarily for growth, but, there are many common stocks that also pay dependable dividends. As I write these words, I hold several stocks that provide better yields than US Treasury Notes and bank CDs. Software companies are not known for dividends, and yet Microsoft pays out about 1/3 of their net income to the shareholders as I write this, which is an extremely generous dividend payout. Preferred stock is generally just a fixed-income security, but, again, convertible preferred stock throws that general rule out the window.

Test candidates often bemoan the fact that their exam is "tricky," but, in fact, it's their industry that is tricky. There are few black-and-white statements that one can make without getting in trouble with clients and the regulators. So, learn the general features of, say, common and preferred stock, but continue to remember all the nuances involved. Common stock is *usually* purchased for growth while preferred stock is *usually* purchased for income, but we could also find some common stocks paying higher yields than preferred stocks and some convertible preferred stocks that provided all kinds of growth to the investor after also providing income. So, as always, resist jumping to conclusions on both the exam and in your career.

PRACTICE

1. Which of the following represents the least expensive common stock?

    A. Market price – $10, earnings per share: $.40 $P/E = 25$

    B. Market price – $15, earnings per share: $.75   20

    C. Market price – $95, earnings per share: $5.00   19

    D. Market price – $100, earnings per share: $4.00   25

2. An issuer's transfer agent would perform all the following tasks except:

    A. Canceling old certificates

    B. Recording transfers of ownership

    C. Transferring funds among client accounts

    D. Validating torn, mutilated certificates

3. An investor who owns which of the following securities might receive more than the stated rate of return?

    A. Common stock

    B. Cumulative preferred

    C. Participating preferred

D. All of the above

4. XXX convertible preferred stock (par value $100) can be converted into XXX common stock at $10. If XXX common is currently trading at $14.50, what is the parity price for XXX convertible preferred stock?

 A. $104.50

B. $145.00

C. $1,450

D. Not enough information provided in the question

(ANSWERS)

1. **C,** the lowest P/E ratio is the cheapest stock, regardless of the market price. The P/E of 19 is the cheapest stock. The other stocks trade at P/E ratios of 25 (A), 20 (B), and 25 (D).

2. **C,** the transfer agent deals with certificates and the names of those who own them.

3. **D,** cumulative preferred stock might be making up for arrearages; participating preferred often raises the dividend. The stated return on common stock is zero, so any dividend paid would be more than the stated rate.

4. **B,** 10 shares times the CMV of $14.50 = $145

TYPES AND CHARACTERISTICS OF FIXED-INCOME SECURITIES

As we've seen, some investors are willing to tolerate the ups and downs of the stock market, hoping to be compensated with long-term growth. Other investors prefer a stated rate of return or fixed-income stream. For obvious reasons, we call them **fixed-income** investors. Some fixed-income investors buy preferred stock, but, more likely, they buy **debt securities** called **bonds.** Corporate bonds represent loans *from* investors *to* a corporation. Investors buy the bonds, and the corporation then pays them interest on the loan every six months and promises to return the principal amount at the end of the term along with the final interest payment. The bonds/loans are liquid, meaning that the lenders can sell the bonds to other investors if they need to convert to cash.

A corporation issuing bonds is said to be using **leverage,** a term that means to use borrowed money. Issuers use leverage when issuing bonds. Investors use leverage when opening margin accounts, which we'll explain later in Chapter 3.

As with preferred stock, a bond has a specific value known as the **par value** or **principal** amount. Since it's printed on the face of the certificate, it is also called the "face amount" of the bond. Bonds have a par value of $1,000 and, occasionally, $5,000. This is the amount an investor will receive with the very last interest payment from the issuer. You might think of this as the investor "getting his original money back." Up to that point, the investor has only been receiving interest payments against the money he loaned to the corporation by purchasing their bond certificates. Note that most mortgages are amortized so that each payment is a mix of both interest and principal, while a bond pays only interest until the very end, at which point it delivers (investors hope) all the principal with the final interest payment.

So the bond certificate has "$1,000" printed on the face, along with the interest rate the issuer will pay the investor every year. This interest rate could be referred to as the **coupon rate** or **nominal yield**. The nominal yield is named right there on the certificate. It can also be referred to as the "coupon rate" because bonds used to come with coupons that investors would present when it came time to claim their interest checks. They would present these interest coupons twice a year, because that's how often most bonds pay interest—semi-annually. So, the interest rate a bondholder receives is a stated, known thing. That's a big difference from common stock, where you simply own a piece of a company and hope that company becomes more valuable. If you buy a 5% bond, you get 5% of $1,000 every year, which is $50 per year. Nominal yield is a known, stated thing. Whether they are spending the interest payments or reinvesting them toward compound returns, fixed-income investors have something in common: their income is fixed.

RETIRING THE DEBT

A bond has a maturity date that represents the date when the issuer will pay the last interest check and the principal. At that point, it's all over—the debt has been paid in full, just like when you pay off your car, student loan, house, etc. This can be referred to as "maturity" or **redemption**. As we saw with "yield to call," many bonds are repurchased by the issuer at a set price if interest rates drop. So, a bond might not make it to the maturity date because it might be called early.

Also, sometimes the issuer will simply make an offer to repurchase your bonds at a certain price. You can accept or reject the offer, known as a **tender offer**. You would "tender your bonds" to the issuer for payment, and that would retire the debt. Or, you could just hang onto them, unlike with a call. When a bond is called, remember, it's all over.

BOND CERTIFICATES

There are four different forms that a bond can take in terms of the certificate itself. In the olden days, bonds were issued as "bearer bonds," which meant that whoever "bore" or had possession of the bond was assumed to be the owner. No owner name at all on the certificate; it just said "pay to the bearer," so whoever bore the bond received the principal at maturity. In order to receive the interest, investors holding bearer bonds used to clip coupons attached to the bond certificate every six months. There was no name on the interest coupon, either, so the IRS had no way of tracking the principal or the interest income. And you know how much that irritates the IRS. So, bonds haven't been issued in bearer form since the early '80s—that doesn't mean they don't exist. A few are still floating out there on the market, so you have to know about them for the test. Just remember: no name on certificate, no name on payment coupons.

Bonds also used to be **registered as to principal only**. That meant that we had a name on the bond certificate—the person who would receive the principal amount at maturity. But, again, with the silly little unnamed interest coupons. Therefore, only the principal was registered, thus the name "registered as to principal only." See, these vocabulary terms often mean exactly what they say…except when they don't.

Anyway, the bond market got smart in the early 1980s and started registering both pieces of the **debt service**. Now, the issuer has the name of the owner [principal] and automatically cuts a check every six months for the interest. We call these bonds fully registered, because both pieces of the debt service (interest, principal) are registered.

Book entry/journal entry bonds are still fully registered. It's just that it's done on computer, rather than on paper. The investor keeps the trade confirmation as proof of ownership, but we still have an owner name on computer, and we automatically cut interest checks to the registered owner. Book entry/journal entry is how virtually all securities are issued these days. But, since bonds often have 30-year maturities, there are still investors out there with bond certificates in their safe-deposit box.

QUOTES

Bonds are quoted either in terms of their price, or their yield. Since the coupon rate or nominal yield doesn't change, if you give me the price, I can figure the yield. And, if you give me the yield, I can figure the price. This process is known as "interpolation," by the way, which is just a fancy word for converting bond yields into bond prices, and vice versa. If we're talking about a bond's price, we're talking about bond points. A **bond point** is worth $10. You'll need to memorize that for the test. So, if a bond is selling at "98," that means it's selling for 98 bond points. With each point worth $10, a bond selling for 98 bond points is trading for $980. A bond trading at 102 would be selling for $1,020. Although fractions have been eliminated from stock and options pricing, they are still very much alive in the world of bond pricing. If a bond point is worth $10, how much is 1/2 a bond point worth? Five dollars, right? A quarter-point would be worth $2.50, right? An eighth is $1.25, and so on. Therefore, if you see a bond priced at 102 3/8, how much does the bond cost in dollars and cents? Well, "102" puts the price at $1,020, and 3/8 of $10 is $3.75. So, a bond trading at 102 3/8 costs $1,023.75.

102 [$1,020] + 3/8 [$3.75] = $1,023.75

If we're talking about **basis points**, we're talking about a bond's yield. Yield to maturity, to be exact. If I say that a bond with an 8% coupon just traded on a 7.92 basis, I'm telling you that the price went up above par, pushing the yield to maturity down to 7.92%. In other words, the price pushed the yield to maturity to a particular percentage, or number of "basis points." A basis point is the smallest increment of change in a bond's yield. When the media talks about the Fed easing interest rates by fifty basis points, they're talking about 1/2 of 1 percent. We would write 1% as .01, right? Well, basis points use a 4-digit display system, so .01 is written as:

.0 1 0 0.

Then, we read that figure as "100 basis points." Two percent would be 200 basis points. One-half of one percent would be written as .0050 or "50 basis points." So, a bond trading at a 7.92 basis means that the YTM is 7.92% or 792 basis points. An easy way to work with basis points is to remember that all the single-digit percentages are expressed in hundreds. 400 basis points just means 4%. Anything less than 100 basis points is less than 1%. So 30 basis points is only .3 of 1%.

Fascinating, isn't it?

NOTATION

The exam might want to see the look on your face when they make you read the following:

10M XYZ 8s debentures of '19, callable @103 in '16

Huh?

Well "10M" means $10,000 par value or 10 bonds. XYZ is the issuing corporation, and they pay "8s" or 8% in interest each year. The little "s" means you get the $80 in two semi-annual payments of $40 each. Remember that—a test question might ask how much the investor receives at maturity on this bond. The answer is $1,040. Remember that interest is always paid retroactively, meaning for the previous 6 months. So, when the bond matures, you get your final interest payment (for the previous 6 months) plus the principal/par value of $1,000. This investor owns 10 bonds, so she would receive $10,400 at maturity in 2019.

Assuming we make it that far—remember, if interest rates drop in 2016, the company can buy back the bonds for $1,030 each, end of story. That's what "callable at 103 in '16" means.

RISKS TO BONDHOLDERS

We already discussed investment risks, but let's go ahead and review the types of risks most bonds present to investors:

- **Credit/default risk**: the risk that the issuer will miss interest payments or be unable to return the principal to investors. US Treasury securities lack this risk—but that's the *only* investment risk they lack.
- **Interest rate risk**: the risk that interest rates will rise, knocking bond market prices down. This is most severe on longer-term bonds.
- **Purchasing power risk**: because the income paid on a bond is fixed, there is always the risk that inflation will erode the value of the coupon/interest payment to the investor.
- **Call risk**: the risk that when interest rates drop, issuers will buy back/redeem their bonds early, eliminating the upward swing we just looked at on the bond see-saw. This forces bond investors to reinvest at lower rates going forward when they buy new bonds with the proceeds of the call. Not all bonds are callable, but those that are have this risk.
- **Reinvestment risk**: this is partly the last line under "call risk," but also refers to the fact that every six months a fixed-income investor will reinvest interest payments into new bonds; when she does so, she will reinvest at lower rates if interest rates/yields have dropped compared to the stated interest rate on the existing bond in her portfolio.
- **Market risk**: the risk that investors will panic and trample your bond's market price in a stampede for the exits.

CORPORATE BONDS

How big is the market for corporate bonds? According to NAIC Capital Markets Weekly (www.naic.org), "The total US corporate bond universe currently outstanding amounts to $3.8 trillion, 76% of which were investment grade and 24% of which were high-yield, or 'speculative' grade."

That's a lot of outstanding bonds, wouldn't you say? What if they all default? Not likely? But what if too many of them default, and how do we determine what "too many" might be when we're talking about almost $4 *trillion* of debt obligations backed up mostly by promises from American corporations?

To protect bondholders, Congress passed the **Trust Indenture Act of 1939**. If a corporation wants to sell $5,000,000 or more worth of bonds that mature outside of one year, they have to do it under a contract or "indenture" with a trustee, who will enforce the terms of the indenture to the benefit of the bondholders. In other words, if the issuer stiffs the bondholders, the trustee/trust company can get a bankruptcy court to forcibly sell off the assets of the company so that bondholders can recover some of their hard-earned money.

Remember that a corporate bond pays a fixed rate of interest to the investor, and that bond interest has to be paid, unlike a dividend on common or preferred stock that is paid only if the board of directors declares it. We'll see that a bondholder usually doesn't suffer as much price volatility as a stock investor. But, unlike the owner of common stock, bondholders don't get to vote on the things we looked at in the preceding chapter—they're not owners, remember; they're loaners. The only time bondholders get to vote is if the corporation goes into bankruptcy. Creditors will be offered various little scenarios by the corporation who can't actually pay them, and the bondholders will get to vote on these terms. In other words, the only time bondholders get to vote is when disaster strikes.

Since bankruptcy is always a concern, corporations often secure the bonds by pledging specific assets like airplanes, government securities, or real estate. Would you believe we call these **secured bonds**? For a secured bond the issuer pledges title of the assets to the trustee, who just might end up selling them off if the issuer gets behind on its interest payments. Investors who buy bonds attached to specific collateral are secured creditors, the first to get paid should the company go belly up. If the collateral used is real estate, we call it a **mortgage bond**. If the collateral is securities, we call it a **collateral trust certificate**. And if the collateral is equipment, such as airplanes or railroad cars, we call it an **equipment trust certificate**. Since these bonds are the most secure, they offer the lowest coupon payment, too. Remember, if you take a small risk, you usually only get a small reward. Unfortunately, that doesn't mean that taking a bigger risk will pay off, either, but let's keep moving.

Most corporate bonds are backed by a promise known as the "full faith and credit" of the issuer. That's why we might want to see what S&P and Moody's have to say about a particular issuer's full faith and credit. If the credit is AAA, we probably won't be offered a huge coupon payment. But if the issuer is rated right at the cut-off point of BBB (Baa for Moody's), then we might demand a bigger pay-off in exchange for buying bonds from an issuer just one notch above junk status. Regardless of the rating, if we buy a bond backed simply by the full faith and credit of an issuer, we are buying a **debenture**. Debenture holders are general creditors and get paid after secured bondholders. Therefore, debentures pay a higher coupon than secured bonds, since they carry more risk.

"Sub" means "below," as in "submarine" for "below the water," or "subterranean" for "below the ground." **Subordinated debentures** are below debentures when it comes to liquidating a company and paying out money to the bondholders. Since these bonds are riskier, they pay a higher coupon than debentures.

If all the bondholders have been paid and there's still money left over (it could happen, right?), then we start talking about paying out some money to stockholders. Preferred stockholders get preference, so we pay them first, and common stock is always last in line.

> Liquidation Priority

So, if a company goes belly up, investors will make claims on whatever assets the company still has in the following order of priority:

1. Secured creditors
2. Debentures/general creditors
3. Subordinated debentures

4. Preferred stock
5. Common stock

Also note that I didn't say everybody above gets his money back, or even that he gets *any* money back. Those are *claims* on corporate assets. Common stock usually receives nothing, and even the unsecured bondholders may be lucky to get back $80 or $90 per bond. It all depends on how the bankruptcy court process works out.

Speaking of bankruptcy, remember that an **income bond** only pays income if the company has income. It's usually issued by a company coming out of bankruptcy and usually offers a high coupon, just in case it ever gets around to making a payment. The re-organized company gets some breathing room from the creditors and maybe this breathing room will help it finally get its act together long enough to start paying interest on its "income" or "adjustment" bonds.

➤ Sinking Fund

In any case, since the issuing corporation has to return the principal value of the bond at some point, they usually establish what's known as a **sinking fund**. If you actually held your interest-only mortgage 30 years, maybe your spouse would one day have to gently remind you, "Now, remember to add the $300,000 to this month's interest check, honey. Time to pay the principal back." Since that's how corporations pay back the principal (all at once), they set some money aside in escrow, which means they park it in safe, dependable US Treasury securities. With this sinking fund established, the company would be able to return the principal, make a "tender offer" where they offer to buy back the investors' bonds, or complete a "call." Having this money set aside sure can't hurt the old rating with S&P and Moody's either, right?

➤ Callable and Convertible

A bond issued in the year 2020 might be callable starting in the year 2025 at 104, meaning that in the year 2025 the issuer can retire the debt by giving each bondholder a check for $1,040 plus any accrued interest.

When might they want to call a bond? When interest rates have fallen. Isn't that when homeowners refinance their loans? Just like homeowners do, when rates go down, bond issuers start to think maybe the outstanding debt could be replaced with brand-new, much cheaper debt. If interest rates fall to 6%, they reason, let's issue new debt at 6% and use part of the proceeds to retire the outstanding debt we're currently paying 8% on.

Replacing one bond issue with another is called **refunding**. It tends to happen when interest rates fall. It allows the issuer to issue less-expensive debt and use part of the proceeds to retire more-expensive debt.

It's not such a great deal for the bondholders, though. What can they do with the proceeds of the call? Reinvest them. At what rate? A lower rate. This is a form of reinvestment risk. Upon reinvestment the bondholders will get a lower rate of return, since interest rates have now fallen. And, what happens to bond prices as rates decline? They go up, only they stop going up the day the issuer announces that the bonds will be called, meaning the bondholder doesn't get the full appreciation in price he would have otherwise gotten. Once the issuer says the bonds will be called, the market knows the exact price that the bonds are now worth—bondholders can probably take a slight haircut and sell to other investors, or wait for the call and receive the full price from the issuer. Either way, the big capital gain the investor was dreaming of when rates started dropping is over. Not going to happen.

So, since the bondholder takes on this call risk, callable bonds yield more than non-callable bonds. As always, if you want something good from the corporation, they take something away. Just like we saw in the section on equity securities—if the preferred stock is convertible, you get a lower dividend rate. If the bond comes with a warrant, you get a lower yield on the bond.

Then, there are **convertible bonds**, which—like convertible preferred stock—can be converted into a certain number of shares of the issuer's common stock. Bonds have a par value of $1,000, so the investor applies the $1,000 of par value toward purchasing the company's stock at a pre-determined price. When a convertible bond is issued, it is given a conversion price. If the conversion price is $40, this means that the bond is convertible into common stock at $40. In other words, the investor can use the par value of her bond towards the purchase of the company's common stock at a set price of $40. Bonds have a par value of $1,000, so if she applies that $1,000 toward the purchase of stock at $40 per share, how many shares would she be able to buy? 25 shares, right? $1,000 of par value divided by $40 per share of common stock tells us that each bond can be converted into 25 shares of common stock. In other words, the two securities trade at a 25:1 relationship, since the big one (bond) can be turned into 25 of the little ones (stock). The company sets the conversion price; they have no control over where their common stock trades on the open market, right? If the price goes up, the value of the convertible bonds goes up. Just like if the price goes down, that drags down the market value of the bonds.

So how much is this particular bond worth at any given moment? It's worth whatever 25 shares of the common stock are worth at that moment, give or take. Just take the par value of the convertible bond and divide it by the conversion price to find out how many shares of common stock the bond could be converted into.

PRACTICE

1. MMY Corporation has convertible debentures that can be exchanged for shares of MMY common stock at a set price of $40. If MMY common is currently trading at $57, what is the parity price of the MMY convertible debentures?

    A. $1,017

    B. $1,425

    C. $1,000

    D. $1,765

2. Which TWO of the following are associated with falling interest rates?

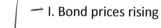

I. Bond prices rising

II. Bond prices falling

III. Coupon rates rising

IV. Coupon rates falling

    A. I, III

B. I, IV

C. II, III

D. II, IV

3. Which of the following bonds is most susceptible to a call?

A. 6% nominal, matures in 2017, callable @103

 B. 6% nominal, matures in 2017, callable @par

C. 9% nominal, matures in 2020, callable @par

D. 9% nominal, matures in 2020, callable @103

4. If a company is liquidated, the following parties will make claims in which order of priority?

I. Preferred stockholders

II. Secured bondholders

III. Subordinated debenture owners

IV. Common stockholders

A. I, II, III, IV

B. II, I, III, IV

C. II, III, I, IV

D. I, II, IV, III

5. All of the following would increase the market price of an outstanding bond except:

A. Interest rates fall

 I↓ → P↑

B. S&P upgrades the credit rating

C. Moody's upgrades the credit rating

D. The company undergoes a reverse stock split

(ANSWERS)

1. **B,** "convertible at 40" means 1 bond can be exchanged for 25 shares. If each share is now worth $57, 25 of them are worth $1,425. Parity.

2. **B,** bond prices refer to bonds trading on the secondary market. As rates on new bonds fall, the market prices of existing bonds rise. Rates down, price up—commit that to memory. Coupon rates

ARE interest rates, so if the exam says that rates are falling, it is also saying that coupon rates on new bonds are falling. Which, again, makes the bonds already out there on the secondary market look more attractive.

3. **C,** if you held these four mortgages, which one would you refinance first? The one with the highest interest rate—9%. Which 9% mortgage should you refinance first, the one you can pay off at par, or the one you can pay off with a $30 per bond penalty? Right?

4. **C,** pay the secured creditors, then the general creditors (debentures), then the SUB-ordinated creditors. If there's still money left—and I'm not sure why there would be—give PREFERENCE to preferred. Common is last—that's why it's called "common."

5. **D,** stock splits don't really achieve much of anything except to change the per-share-price of the stock.

CREDIT RATINGS: MOODY'S, S&P & FITCH

There's nothing worse than lending a corporation money and then finding out they are not going to pay you back as it turns out. This is known as a "default," and it's the worst thing that can happen to a bond holder's investment.

How likely is it that a bond will go into default? It isn't going to happen on a United States Treasury security. It might happen on <u>some</u> municipal securities. But when you get into the category of corporate bonds, you see that it happens more than you'd like, especially when the economy contracts suddenly.

Luckily, Moody's, S&P, and Fitch assign bond ratings designed to help you gauge the likelihood of default. Remember that this is all that the bond rating agencies are talking about, the risk of default. They aren't making any recommendations with these ratings. The highest quality issuers have AAA/Aaa (S&P/Moody's) ratings. The **investment grade** issues go from AAA/Aaa down to BBB/Baa. And below that, things get more and more interesting—yields increase as safety decreases.

Standard & Poor's (& Fitch)	Moody's
AAA	Aaa
AA	Aa
A	A
BBB	Baa

BELOW THIS IS JUNK, NON-INVESTMENT GRADE,
HIGH-YIELD, SPECULATIVE

BB	Ba
B	B

So, credit quality is the highest on the AAA/Aaa-rated bonds. As credit quality drops, default risk rises. Therefore, investors expect to be compensated for the added risk by receiving a higher yield on their investment. High yield and low quality go hand in hand, just as low yield and high quality do. How does a bond become "high yield" or "junk"? One way is that a brand new issue of low-rated bonds offers high coupon rates to get investors interested in lending the money. The other way is that existing bonds trade at lower and lower prices as people get nervous about a possible default. As the price drops, the yield increases.

We already saw that interest rates going up can knock down the market price of a bond holder's investment. Now we're saying that credit ratings can also knock that market price down. In the first case, the risk applies to bonds across the board—rates up, prices down. On the other hand, when a bond's credit rating is reduced, that is a risk you faced specific to that particular issuer or maybe the industry space the issuer occupies. The first risk, in other words, is systematic while the second is unsystematic.

How often do bonds default? Not very often. To put it in perspective, here is the recent history of default rates on high-yield corporate bonds—we're talking just about the junk bonds here. "The default rate in 2009 reached 13.7% before declining to 1.3% in 2010, as the economy began to recover, due in part to government initiatives and a general improvement in credit trends. Note this amount is significantly lower than the 16.4% default rate that occurred during the last financial downturn in 2002 (www.naic.org)."

I noticed that the rate of default for investment-grade bonds was not even mentioned—it's that low. In my never-ending quest to make this book even more interesting I also discovered that the main investment of insurance companies is typically corporate bonds. Insurance companies, in other words, can issue bonds to finance their operations, and they can also invest in bonds issued by other corporations. Investment-grade corporate bonds appear to be an ideal place for insurance companies to invest the net premiums paid on products like fixed annuities. According to the website cited above, 92% of those corporate bonds held by insurance companies are investment-grade. Apparently, insurance companies are not that interested in losing billions of dollars in the bond market right about the time the next hurricane hits.

US GOVERNMENT SECURITIES

We said the rate of default on high-yield corporate bonds has ranged in recent years from about 1% to 13%. Well, the rate of default on US Treasury securities is 0%, going all the way back to the George Washington Administration. If you buy a bill, note, or bond issued by the United States Treasury, you do not have to worry about **default risk**. You are going to get your money back. You just aren't going to get rich in the process. In fact, you usually need to be rich already to get excited about US Government debt. These things are for capital preservation, and the only folks with lots of capital to preserve long-term are rich, by definition. Working stiffs need to save up for retirement through common stock or equity mutual funds. The less daring will save up by investing through corporate bonds or bond mutual funds. But if one already has millions of dollars, the goal might become preserving that money as opposed to risking it trying to get bigger returns.

T-Bills, T-Notes, T-Bonds, STRIPS, and TIPS are all securities that can be traded on the secondary market, what we call "negotiable" securities. Other Treasury products—I-Bonds, Series EE Bonds, and Series HH Bonds—are not "negotiable," meaning they can't be traded/sold to other investors.

➢ T-Bills

US Treasury Bills pay back the face amount at maturity, and investors, therefore, hope to buy them at the deepest discount possible. If the T-Bill pays out $1,000, you'd rather get it for $950 than $965, right? In the first case you make $50 interest; in the second case you make only $35. That's why the BID *looks* higher than the ASK for T-Bills trading on the secondary market. The bid is the discount that buyers are trying to get; the ask price/yield is the discount the sellers are willing to give up.

So, the quote might look like this:

3.0%   2.75%

In other words, the buyers want a 3% discount; the sellers are only willing to give up a 2.75% discount from the par value.

These bills mature in one year or less (4 weeks, 13 weeks, 26 weeks, 52 weeks), so there are no coupon payments. They work kind of like short-term "zero coupon" bonds, where the difference between the discounted purchase price and the face amount is the investor's return. T-Bills are offered in minimum denominations of $100 and, like all Treasuries, T-Bills are issued in **book entry**/journal entry form. The maturities available change from time to time. Currently (as you can see at www.treasurydirect.gov) the available maturities are 4 weeks, 3 months, 6 months, and extremely short-term "cash management bills." That website, by the way, offers a great primer on bills, notes, bonds, etc. As you'll see, T-Bills are auctioned every Monday by the **Federal Reserve Board**. The big institutions put in "competitive tenders," trying to buy the bills for the lowest possible price. A small investor puts in a "non-competitive" tender that will be filled, since he is not trying to lowball the United States Treasury. Yes, a large bank will probably get a better price on T-Bills today, but they also might not get their bid filled at all.

The website mentioned above provides the perfect bullet list on US Treasury Bills, so let's just take a look at that:

Key Facts

- Bills are sold at a discount. The **discount rate** is determined at auction.
- Bills pay interest only at maturity. The interest is equal to the face value minus the purchase price.
- The minimum purchase (face amount) is $100.
- Bills are auctioned every week.
- Bills are issued in electronic form.
- You can hold a bill until it matures or sell it before it matures.
- In a single auction, an investor can buy up to $5 million in bills by non-competitive bidding or up to 35% of the initial offering amount by competitive bidding.

➢ T-Notes, T-Bonds

T-Bills are great for the short-term, but investors may get tired of receiving low yields, and yields that may fluctuate every time they buy a new T-Bill. If the investor wants to receive interest payments and receive a particular yield for several years, US Treasury Notes and US Treasury Bonds are available. T-Notes are offered with 2- to 10-year maturities. T-Bonds mature in 30 years. These both make semi-annual interest payments, and are both quoted in 32nds, with each "32nd" worth exactly $.3125.

- The yield on a note or bond is determined at auction.
- Notes and bonds are sold in increments of $100. The minimum purchase is $100.
- Notes and bonds are issued in electronic form.
- You can hold a note or bond until it matures or sell it before it matures.
- In a single auction, an investor can buy up to $5 million in notes or bonds by non-competitive bidding or up to 35% of the initial offering amount by competitive bidding.

➢ Strips

The Treasury Department can also take T-Notes and T-Bonds and "strip" them into their various interest and principal components. Once they strip the securities into components, they can sell interest-only or principal-only **zero coupon bonds** to investors. We call these **STRIPS**, an acronym that stands for the "separate trading of registered interest and principal of securities." If an investor needs to send kids to college and wants to lock in a yield long-term without having to reinvest interest payments along the way, put him into STRIPS. This way, he'll pay a known amount and receive a known amount on a future date. He won't get rich, necessarily, but he won't lose the kids' college fund trading debit call spreads, either.

➢ Treasury Receipts

Broker-dealers sell the same basic product, only they call them **treasury receipts**. For both receipts and STRIPS, remember that they are purchased at a discount and mature at the face value. And remember that the STRIPS is guaranteed by Uncle Sam, while a Treasury Receipt is not.

➢ TIPS

As if government securities weren't safe enough in terms of default risk, the Treasury department also protects investors from inflation by issuing **TIPS**. The **Treasury Inflation-Protected Securities** adjust for inflation, meaning that if inflation rises, you receive more money, and when it falls, you receive less. Inflation is measured through the Consumer Price Index (CPI), which tracks the basic things that consumers buy. If the (fixed) coupon rate on the security is 3%, suddenly the investor could be receiving 3% of, say, $1,030 to reflect inflation/rising consumer prices. If the economy is experiencing falling prices (the CPI is negative), the principal amount of the TIPS could be lower than $1,000 when calculating the semi-annual interest payment. Even if the principal amount used to calculate an interest payment could be less than $1,000, the TIPS will pay out the $1,000 face amount at maturity, period. So, there is no default risk and no purchasing power/inflation risk on a TIPS. Basically, if you can find a safer security than a TIPS, buy it.

An investor purchases an inflation-protected Treasury note (TIPS) with a coupon rate of 3%. Inflation in the first year is 4%. Therefore:

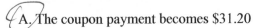

A. The coupon payment becomes $31.20

B. The principal becomes $1,030

C. The coupon payment becomes $40

D. The principal amount becomes $1,070

Answer: A. The rate of inflation is 4%, so the principal becomes 4% larger. Multiply the principal of $1,000 by 1.04 to get the new principal amount of $1,040. Then multiply that principal by 3%, and the new annual coupon payment is $31.20.

> ➢ I-Bonds

Like all the other Government Securities above, TIPS are "negotiable securities," meaning you can sell them to other investors on the secondary market. I-bonds, on the other hand, are "non-negotiable," meaning there is no secondary market for them. An investor buys the I-bond from the US Government and can only sell it by redeeming it to the US Government for payment. In other words, they're not securities; they're merely "savings bonds." An I-bond is a savings bond issued by the US Treasury, which means it's absolutely safe and also exempt from state and local income taxes. An I-bond pays a guaranteed rate that is fixed but also pays more interest income when inflation rises. The semi-annual inflation rate announced in May is the change between the CPI (inflation) figures from the preceding September and March; the inflation rate announced in November is the change between the CPI figures from the preceding March and September. So, since they adjust the interest income to levels of inflation, there's no default risk and no real purchasing power risk, either. There are also tax advantages. First, the interest isn't paid out; it's added to the value of the bond. You can, therefore, defer the taxes until you cash in the bond. And, if you use the proceeds for qualified education costs in the same calendar year that you redeem the bonds, the interest is tax-free. The investor does not even have to declare that the I-bonds will be used for educational purposes when she buys them. As long as she uses the proceeds in the same year she redeems the bonds—and meets the other requirements of the Education Savings Bond Program—the interest is tax-free.

GOVERNMENT AGENCY SECURITIES

The US Government also has agencies that issue debt securities to finance their operations. Investors are often attracted to this category because the securities are relatively safe but also offer yields that are higher than on comparable T-Bills, T-Notes, and T-Bonds. Part of the reason for the higher yields is that Government agency securities are not direct obligations of the US Government, unless we're talking specifically about "Ginnie Mae." That's right, securities issued by "Fannie Mae" and "Freddie Mac" are not direct obligations, while securities issued by "Ginnie Mae" *are* backed by the full faith and credit of the United States Treasury. Either way, Fannie Mae (**Federal National Mortgage Association**), Freddie Mac (**Federal Home Loan Mortgage Corporation**) and Ginnie Mae (**Government National Mortgage Association**) all issue mortgage-backed securities.

Fannie Mae and Freddie Mac provide liquidity for mortgages, meaning that lenders can make a mortgage to a homeowner and then sell the mortgage to Fannie or Freddie. This allows the lender to take the proceeds and make more mortgages to more homeowners. In fact, you may have been alerted that "Fannie Mae" or "Freddie Mac" has purchased your mortgage at some point. Why? Well, a big pool of mortgages can be packaged together by a financial institution and then turned into mortgage-backed securities that are sold to investors. If an investor buys a mortgage-backed security, she receives a monthly check representing both interest and principal being paid by the homeowners whose mortgages are now in the pool. When will all the principal on these mortgages be paid off?

Nobody knows for sure, which is why the securities all carry **prepayment risk**. Prepayment risk is the risk that interest rates will drop, folks will pay off their mortgages by refinancing at a lower rate, and investors will get their money back sooner than they wanted it, reinvesting it at a lower rate going forward. On the other hand, if interest rates start to rise, investors may experience **extension risk**, as homeowners take longer to pay off the principal, since, by definition, there aren't any great refinancing activities available when rates are even higher than what homeowners are currently paying. So, an investor who owns mortgage-backed securities issued by Fannie, Freddie, or Ginnie really owns an undivided or proportional interest in a big pool of mortgages. Rather than *paying* monthly interest and principal, these investors are *receiving* most of the monthly interest and principal being paid off by the homeowners in the pool, with the creator of the product taking a few basis points for its trouble, of course.

Ginnie Mae (GNMA) is the only one of the three that is backed by the full faith and credit of the US Government, which insures all the mortgages in the pool. Fannie Mae (**FNMA**) and Freddie Mac (**FHLMC**) are public companies, so you can buy stock in them, especially if you're a high-risk investor. There is no stock in Ginnie Mae because it's not a company. Fannie and Freddie are also referred to as **government-sponsored enterprises**, which Freddie Mac explains on its website as "a shareholder-owned company created by Congress to serve a public purpose." That's exactly right, of course, so even if you've heard that the US Government has "bailed out" Fannie and Freddie, remember that Fannie and Freddie are both still just shareholder-owned companies, with the US Treasury now the biggest and highest-ranking shareholder. Turns out, the US Treasury likes to buy senior convertible preferred shares in these instances. That way, after they pump in a few hundred billion dollars in exchange for senior convertible preferred shares, the US Treasury can determine if and when any dividends get paid on the many different issues of preferred and common stock, and if the companies finally get their acts together, the US Treasury can sell the convertible securities at a profit, and "return it to the taxpayers."

That's the plan, anyway. In any event, please remember that GNMA has always been a direct obligation of the US Government, while Fannie Mae and Freddie Mac have never been direct obligations. Buying common stock, preferred stock, or debt securities issued by FNMA or FHLMC sounds like a high-risk proposition to me, which is why I have taken a pass and intend to well into the future.

Ginnie Mae pass-through securities are generally sold with a minimum par value of $25,000, so the investor would be required to invest at least $25,000 unless interest rates had recently shot upwards, forcing the price down on the secondary market.

I would expect the exam to stick more to the Ginnie, Fannie, and Freddie side of things, but it could also mention a few others. With that in mind, please note that other government-sponsored enterprises—not direct obligations of the US Government—include:

- Federal Farm Credit Banks (FFCBs)
- Federal Home Loan Banks (FHLBs)
- Student Loan Marketing Association (SLMA)

These "GSEs," or "**Government-Sponsored Enterprises**" are publicly chartered by Congress but privately owned by shareholders. The GSE raises money by letting a selling group of dealers offer its securities to investors, with the proceeds then loaned to a bank, which, in turn, makes loans to individuals including farmers, homeowners, and students. **The Federal Farm Credit Banks** provide funds for Banks for Cooperatives, Intermediate Credit Banks, and Federal Land Banks by issuing both short-term discount notes and interest-bearing bonds with both short- and long-term maturities. These enterprises help farmers stay in business, a goal that the US Government obviously (and rightfully) considers an important one. The Federal Home Loan Banks (there are 12 of them) help to provide liquidity for savings and loan (S & L) institutions. Like the Federal Farm Credit Banks, the

Federal Home Loan Banks issue both short-term discount notes and also interest-paying bonds of various maturities. Finally, the **Student Loan Marketing Association** (SLMA) or "Sallie Mae" provides liquidity to institutions making student loans. Sallie Mae purchases both uninsured loans and loans insured under the Guaranteed Student Loan Program (GSLP).

In all cases, remember that only Ginnie Mae (GNMA) is a direct obligation of the US Government. All other securities issued by "government-sponsored enterprises" are considered relatively safe, but still not directly backed by the United States Treasury's full faith and credit. The interest that investors earn on the securities discussed in this section is assumed to be taxable by the federal, state, and local governments.

FOREIGN BONDS

Some investors choose to purchase bonds issued outside the US, which typically offer higher yields. Does that imply that international investing is riskier? Absolutely. If you want absolute **safety**, you sacrifice yield. If you want high yield, you sacrifice safety. Investing in foreign bonds is risky, but there is a big difference between a **developed market** and an **emerging market**. In general, the following countries enjoy securities markets and economies that are considered developed: US, Canada, European Union countries, Australia, New Zealand, and Japan. Emerging markets would include everyone else, though South Korea and Singapore are much more advanced than China, India, and other "emerging" nations. If you purchase bonds issued and traded in emerging markets, you're investing in regions characterized by low per capita incomes, primitive securities markets, and/or economies that are not fully industrialized. In other words, there is a promising future, but it hasn't actually shown up yet.

Whether the foreign market is considered developed or emerging, investors have to deal with currency risk. If your bond pays interest and principal in yen or bot, you have to convert that to US dollars. Therefore, if the dollar is strong, you get fewer dollars. Luckily, not all foreign bonds pay interest and principal in foreign currencies. Your exam might bring up the difference between "US Pay Bonds" and "Foreign Pay Bonds." If your bond pays you in US dollars, currency risk is eliminated, but if it pays in another currency (foreign pay bond), then you, obviously, do have **currency exchange risk**. Types of so-called "US Pay Bonds" include "Eurodollar bonds," which are issued and traded outside the US but are denominated in US dollars. Another type is called the "Yankee bond," which allows foreign issuers to borrow money in the US marketplace. Eurodollar bonds are not registered with the SEC and cannot be sold to US investors until a certain number of days after being issued. Yankee bonds, on the other hand, are registered with the SEC.

We already looked at **political risk**, which is associated with emerging markets. And, there are "operational risks" when investing in foreign markets, especially emerging markets. That just means that the securities markets are less liquid/efficient, and usually carry much higher transaction costs. In the US we can assume that "government" bonds are *much* safer than bonds issued by US *corporations,* but I'm not sure I would make that assumption in foreign markets, where governments have been known to default.

The term **sovereign debt** refers to bonds issued by a national government payable in a foreign currency. Sovereign debt is generally and not surprisingly a riskier investment when issued by a develop-ing nation, and a safer investment when issued by a develop-ed nation. The stability of the government is, obviously, a key factor in determining the credit risk, as is their propensity to pay back loans.

Brady bonds are issued by the governments of emerging markets, usually in Latin America. Brady bonds are typically collateralized by US Treasury securities, making these debt securities much safer than they seem on the surface. This attracts more buyers, keeping yields down and allowing the issuers to pay off their debts at reasonable rates.

MUNICIPAL SECURITIES

Across the street from my office a large brick industrial building used to block our view of the Eisenhower Expressway. The building was supposed to be turned into a major condominium and townhouse development before the bottom fell out of the real estate market. Unfortunately, the developers borrowed $15 million but sold only one condominium, sending the property into foreclosure. So the park district, whose land presses right up against the foreclosed property, decided to buy the property out of foreclosure from the bank and then turn it into more recreational space for the kids of Forest Park.

The park district needed $6 million to complete their project; therefore, they raised that amount by issuing **municipal bonds**. In a recent election, a majority of Forest Parkers including yours truly voted to allow the park district to raise our property taxes slightly in order to create the funds needed to pay off a $6 million bond issue. The bonds have already been issued, the property purchased from the bank, and the massive structure torn completely down. Since the bonds were backed by property taxes, they are known as **general obligation** bonds.

The bonds were offered by a group of broker-dealers who formed a temporary **syndicate** just long enough to get the bonds sold to investors, give the park district its $6 million, and keep a percentage as their profit or **spread**. Going forward, most investors will probably just hold the bonds until maturity, collecting tax-exempt interest checks every six months along the way. Meanwhile, some investors may want to turn those bonds into cash before maturity; if so, their broker-dealer will either find a buyer on the secondary market and charge a **commission** to complete the sale, or the firm will buy the bonds themselves and make a **markdown** when acting in a **principal** capacity.

For me, all it takes to see the connection between this municipal securities section and the so-called "real world" is to walk 15 steps to the front window and look at the gaping hole where the following "Roos Building" used to block the expressway.

➢ General Obligation Bonds

The phrase **general obligation** means that the municipality is legally obligated to pay the **debt service** (interest and principal) on the bonds issued. GOs are backed by the **full faith and credit** of the municipality. Where does a municipality get the money they'll need to pay off the bonds? If necessary, they'll dip into all the sources of general revenue available to a city or state or park district, like sales taxes, income taxes, parking fees, property taxes, fishing licenses, marriage licenses, whatever. And, if they have to, they'll even raise taxes in order to pay the debt service on a general obligation bond.

General obligation bonds are backed by the full taxing power of the issuer, and that's why GOs require voter approval. As I said, my fellow Forest Parkers and I had to approve a $6 million bond issue before the park district could do the borrowing and back up the loan with our increased property taxes. States get most of their revenue from sales and income taxes, while local governments rely on property taxes.

Since local governments (cities, park districts, school districts) get a major chunk of their revenue from property taxes, a GO bond will be associated with property taxes. A fancy term for property taxes is **ad valorem**. A municipality might assess property at 50% of its market value. So, a home with a market value of $500,000 would have an **assessed value** of only half that, or $250,000. As a homeowner, you take the assessed value of your home and multiply it by a rate known as the **millage rate** to find your tax bill.

Some municipalities limit the number of mills that can be levied against property. If so, they might end up issuing **limited tax bonds**, which means property tax rates can only go so high to pay the debt service on a particular GO. School districts are often limited as to how high property taxes can go to support their bonds, while other governmental units have no such limits. So if you see limited tax bonds, associate the term with GOs. The test might use the initials LTGO for "limited tax general obligation" bonds. That's what it says on the outline, anyway.

Whenever the issuer's full faith and credit backs the bonds, we refer to the bonds as "general obligations." There is a peculiar type of municipal bond that is backed by that full faith and credit but also by the revenues generated at the facility being built with the bond proceeds. These bonds are called **double-barreled bonds**. For example, a hospital is something that all residents of a municipality can benefit from, which is why the county or state might put its full faith and credit behind the bond issue. However, hospitals also generate revenues, which can be used to pay debt service. In this case, the issuer has two sources of revenue to pay debt service, which is why we call it a double-barreled bond. Anything backed by the issuer's full faith and credit as well as revenues is called a double-barreled bond. Since the full faith and credit of the issuer backs the issue, we consider this to be a GO.

➢ Revenue Bonds

Rather than putting the full faith and credit of the issuer behind it, a revenue bond identifies a specific source of revenue, and only that revenue can be used to pay the interest and principal on the bond. Have you ever driven on a toll-way? What did you drop in the basket? A **user fee**, right? Well, that money you put in the toll basket helped to pay the debt service on the revenue bond issued to build the toll-way. If money problems arise, the issuer won't raise property taxes. They'll raise the tolls, the user fees/user charges. You don't like the higher tolls? Use the freeway. But, homeowners aren't affected one way or another since their property taxes cannot be used to pay off revenue bonds—only your generous quarters or E-Z Pass account can be used for that. Facilities that could generate enough revenue to pay off the bonds include airports, convention centers, golf courses, and sports stadiums.

Since we don't have property tax on the table, the municipal government doesn't need any type of voter approval to issue a revenue bond. So you never want to associate "voter approval" with a revenue bond. That belongs under the "GO" heading.

There are other ways that a municipality could identify specific sources of revenue for a bond issue. For example, if the residents of a county wanted their roads paved, the county could add a special tax on gasoline throughout the county and let motorists pay for the new roads each time they fill up their tanks. This **special tax** will be used to pay the debt service on the revenue bonds, which are issued to raise the money required to pave the roads. That's an example of a **special tax bond**, a type of revenue bond. Any tax that is not a property or sales tax is considered a special tax, including special taxes on business licenses, excise taxes, and taxes on gasoline, tobacco, hotel/motel, bottled water, and alcohol. The exam might even refer to these as "sin taxes" if it's feeling especially judgmental on testing day.

There are also **special assessment bonds**. Say that a wealthy subdivision in your community experiences problems with their sidewalks. The concrete is chipped, threatening the property values of the homes in the exclusive subdivision. The residents want the municipality to fix the sidewalks. The municipality says, okay, as long as you pay a special assessment on your property, since you're the only ones who'll benefit from this improvement. That special assessment will be the revenue used to pay the debt service on a special assessment bond, which is issued to raise the money to fix the sidewalks.

Isn't it a neat process? They identify a future source of revenue, like tolls, park entrance fees, or special taxes on gasoline. Then, since they need all that money right now, they issue debt securities against this new source of revenue they're creating. They take the proceeds from selling the debt securities and get the project built. Then those revenues they identified come in, and they use them to pay the interest and, eventually, the principal due to investors who bought the bonds.

Cities like Chicago and New York have public housing projects, which are under HUD, a unit of the federal government. Municipalities issue **PHA (Public Housing Authority)** or **NHA (New Housing Authority) bonds** to raise money for housing projects. The debt service is backed by the rental payments, which are in turn backed by contributions from Uncle Sam. PHAs and NHAs are considered the safest revenue bond because of this guaranteed contribution from the federal government. Sometimes they are referred to as "Section 8" bonds because everything needs at least three names in this business. Note that they are not double-barreled bonds, because it's not the issuer's full faith and credit backing the things.

Industrial Development Revenue bonds are used to build or acquire facilities that a municipal government will then lease to a corporation. These **IDRs** carry the same credit rating as the corporation occupying the facility. The issuing municipality does not back the debt service in any way. Again, the debt service will be paid only from lease payments made by a corporation, so it's the corporation that backs the debt service. As you know, corporations have been known to go belly-up occasionally. If they're the ones backing up the debt service, you can imagine what happens when they themselves no longer have any assets behind them.

Ouch. And if it happens, the issuer won't be there to bail out the bondholders.

A special type of revenue bond is known as a **moral obligation bond**. While revenue bonds are only serviced by specific sources of revenue, a moral obligation bond provides for the possibility of the issuer going to the legislature and convincing them to honor the "moral obligation" to pay off the debt service. This is a moral obligation, not a legal one, and it would take legislative action to get the money authorized.

➢ Secondary Market

Municipal bonds do trade in the secondary market, but not as actively as corporate stocks and bonds or Treasury bonds. If a school district raises $2,000,000 by issuing bonds, how many bonds are there to trade?

2,000 if the denominations are $1,000, and just 400 if the denominations are $5,000. In other words, there's very little liquidity in some of these issues. That's why a municipal bond dealer will usually only provide *either* a bid or an offer price. If you want to buy a municipal bond, the dealer will quote you an offer price; if you want to unload a municipal bond, the dealer will give you a bid. If you like the dealer's price, you have a deal. If not, storm out of the showroom and wait for the inevitable phone call explaining the amazing discount that was just approved four seconds ago by the sales manager.

Sometimes a broker-dealer will have a customer come in trying to liquidate some municipal bond no one at the office has ever heard of. The broker-dealer will submit a "bids wanted" to see what various municipal bond dealers will pay for the customer's funky municipal bond. If the customer wanted to buy a funky municipal bond no one's ever heard of, the firm could send out an "offers wanted" to see how much the various dealers would charge for the bonds.

Since most municipal securities are issued under a serial maturity with different yields for different maturity years, quotes are usually given in terms of yield to maturity. If the municipal bond dealer says "it's offered at 5.60," that means he'll sell the bond at a price that makes the yield to maturity 5.6%. That was a **firm quote**, by the way, meaning the dealer will do the deal at that price. Had he said, "looks like the offer is around 5.60," that would have been a **nominal quote**. He's just sharing information there, but if he gives a firm quote, he has to honor it. Municipal securities dealers who publish quotes can only publish firm quotes. The nominal quotes are between the dealer and an interested party. Sometimes we'll call these "workable indications." The nice little old lady sitting in the broker-dealer's office wants to liquidate 1,000 bonds issued 20 years ago by a small school district in rural South Dakota. The broker-dealer calls a municipal bond dealer asking for a workable indication or a "likely bid" the dealer would pay for the bonds. The language used by the municipal securities dealer would be vague, with phrases such as the following attached to his nominal quote:

"It looks like..."

"Subject to..."

"Last I saw..."

"It's around..."

When we get down to doing the deal, the dealer will then give a firm quote, but right now they're just feeling the situation out.

Since most municipal securities usually don't trade actively, time isn't as critical as it is when trading stocks. Therefore, dealers sometimes give "out firm" quotes. Maybe the dealer will give you a firm quote that's good for the next hour. However, if somebody else calls, he'll call you back and give you five minutes to make up your mind.

The test will probably bring up the term **broker's broker**. A broker's broker executes securities transactions exclusively with other broker-dealers and not with public investors. Broker's brokers generally do not take inventory positions in securities. Rather, they execute transactions in municipal securities for firms who are not active in that side of the business. An example of a broker's broker is the firm Cantor Fitzgerald. They provide a wire service through which dealers who want to put a block of bonds out for bids can see what buyers will pay, without divulging the identity of the seller. Buyers who subscribe to the service can put in their bids, and at the end of the day the broker's broker will notify the sellers of the high bid. If the seller accepts, the broker's broker informs the high bidder that the bid was accepted, congratulations. The broker's broker charges the seller a fee, pretty much as they do on eBay.

Municipal securities transactions are reported by dealers through an electronic reporting system known as "**RTRS**" for "**Real-Time Transaction Reporting System**." The sell-side of the transaction has 15 minutes to report the trade in terms of volume and price. Delaying such reports, or failing to report transactions, deprives the marketplace of important information and is, therefore, a major violation of industry rules. This is true whether reporting trades in municipal securities or in any type of securities trading anywhere.

PRACTICE

1. Which of the following is associated with the secondary market?

      A. Notice of Sale

      B. Broker's Broker

      C. Bond Counsel

      D. Bond Buyer

2. All of the following deal with the primary market except:

      A. Quotes

      B. Notice of Sale

      C. Legal Opinion

      D. Bond Counsel

(ANSWERS)

1. **B,** broker's brokers help municipal dealers buy and sell on the secondary market.

2. **A,** on the primary market, bonds are sold at the public offering price—bonds are only quoted when trading among investors in the secondary market.

➢ THE MSRB

The SEC is the ultimate securities regulator and is part of the federal government. National securities **exchanges** and associations such as FINRA, CBOE, etc., are "self-regulatory organizations" or "SROs." The SRO that regulates municipal securities firms is the MSRB, which stands for the "Municipal Securities Rulemaking Board." This organization has lots to say about how municipal securities dealers do business. They have nothing to say about the issuers. They have no power over an issuer like California or New York City. They have all kinds of power over the broker-dealers and bank dealers who do municipal securities business with them.

But, although they write the rules for broker-dealers and bank dealers, the MSRB has no enforcement division. Therefore, FINRA enforces MSRB rules for broker-dealers, while various banking regulators (FDIC, Comptroller of the Currency, FRB) enforce MSRB rules for bank dealers.

CMOS, CDOS

CMOs or **collateralized mortgage obligations** are derivative securities and are inherently complex products. Generally, a financial institution takes either a pool of mortgages or a pool of mortgage-backed securities issued by GNMA, FNMA, or FHLMC and creates a CMO. The CMO offers various classes of bonds called **tranches**. The tranches are bonds that offer different rates of interest, repayment schedules, and levels of priority for principal repayment. Investors can choose the yield, maturity structure, and risk level that best suits them. Let's look at a very simple example of a "plain vanilla" CMO product. The investors in the CMO are divided up into three tranches: A, B, and C. Each tranche differs in the order that it receives principal payments, but it receives interest payments as long as it is not completely paid off. Class A investors are paid out the principal first with prepayments and repayments until they are paid off. Then class B investors are paid off, followed by class C investors. In a situation like this, class A investors bear most of the prepayment risk, while class C investors bear the least.

CMOs are usually rated AAA, so default risk is not a major concern. You just never know if you'll get your money back sooner [rates fall] or later [rates rise]. As we saw in Chapter 1, the risk of receiving your principal sooner than expected is called **prepayment risk**, which is associated with falling interest rates. The risk of receiving your principal later than expected is called **extension risk**, and is associated with rising interest rates. Two specific types of CMOs are called **PACs** and **TACs**. A "PAC" is a **planned amortization class**, while a "TAC" is a **targeted amortization class**. Since there is a "plan" with the PAC, the exam might say that it protects the investor more against prepayment and extension risk. A TAC does offer some protection against prepayment risk but not extension risk. In either case, there is a "support class" created to protect against prepayments—if the principal is repaid more quickly than expected, it goes into a support class. For the PAC, if interest rates rise and principal is being repaid more slowly, money will be transferred from the support class to protect that PAC owner against extension risk. This would not happen for the owner of a TAC. If the exam is in an especially bad mood the day you take it, it might even bring up the methods of estimating prepayment rates on CMOs. One method is called the "average life" method in which CMOs are compared to other types of fixed-income securities, with an average maturity calculated for each tranche. The "**PSA model**" estimates the speed of prepayments against a benchmark. If the "PSA" is 100, that means that prepayment rates will remain stable. If the PSA is greater than 100, prepayments are expected to speed up. If the PSA is less than 100, prepayments are expected to slow down.

Beyond the PAC and TAC, the exam might mention the **Z-tranche**, which is basically a zero coupon bond inside the CMO that returns principal (and, therefore, accrued interest) only after all the other tranches have been paid off/retired. And, there are "principal only" and "interest only" securities which are pretty much what they sound like. The principal and the interest are separated so that principal-only investors are concerned with how quickly they receive the principal—the *faster* the better. Interest-only investors enjoy a higher yield when prepayments slow down and a lower yield when prepayments speed up. That is because interest payments are based on the remaining principal amount on the loans—as that principal declines, so does the amount of interest paid by homeowners and received by the interest-only investors in the CMO. The faster that principal declines, the lower the yield to the investor; the longer it takes homeowners to pay off the principal, the *higher* the yield to the investor.

CMOs are not extremely liquid and are often too complex to be suitable for many investors. Registered representatives should get the customer's signature on a suitability statement when selling these products. Also, advertising and sales literature on CMOs must be filed with FINRA ten days *before* its first use, subject to any revisions that FINRA demands before the firm uses the piece. The communication must refer to the securities as "collateralized mortgage obligations" and not some other name, and CMOs cannot be compared to *any* other product, since they are totally unique. The following disclosure statement has to appear in an advertisement for a CMO:

The yield and average life shown above consider prepayment assumptions that may or may not be met. Changes in payments may significantly affect yield and average life. Please contact your representative for information on CMOs and how they react to different market conditions.

FINRA has even gone so far as to offer a standardized CMO print advertisement that broker-dealers can use, but even if the firm uses that format, they still have to submit the ad to FINRA prior to first use. Broker-dealers have to offer educational material about the features of CMOs to customers that must include:

- A discussion of the characteristics and risks of CMOs. This would include: how changing interest rates may affect prepayment rates and the average life of the security, tax considerations, credit risk, minimum investments, liquidity, and transactions costs.
- A discussion of the structure of a CMO. This would include the different types of structures, tranches, and risks associated with each type of security. It is also important to explain to a client that two CMOs with the same underlying collateral may have different prepayment risk and different interest-rate risk.
- A discussion that explains the relationship between mortgage loans and mortgage securities.
- A glossary of terms applicable to mortgage-backed securities.

The exam might also bring up a product that is exactly the same as a CMO only completely different—the **CDO** or **collateralized debt obligation**. A CDO is also sold in tranches, and each tranche has its own maturity and particular risks. The difference is that CDOs are not based on mortgages. Rather, they are based on pools of various debt securities, loans, etc. Due to their complexity and risks, CDOs are typically suitable only for sophisticated or institutional investors.

METHODS USED TO DETERMINE THE VALUE OF FIXED-INCOME SECURITIES

RATES, YIELDS, PRICES

Interest rates represent what new bonds have to pay in order to attract investors. But, bonds are issued with a fixed interest rate (like a fixed mortgage). If the bond is an 8% bond, it will always be an 8% bond, and it will always pay 8% of the par value every year no matter who owns it at the time or how much she paid for the thing.

So, please, remember that if a bond pays a nominal yield of 8%, it will always pay 8% of par or $80 per $1,000 per year. Whenever interest rates change, they will change the bond's market price. When rates on new bonds go up, the existing bond's price will go down, since new bonds would be issued with higher nominal yields suddenly. When rates go down, the existing bond's price will go up, since new bonds would be issued with lower nominal yields suddenly.

And yields move right along with interest rates, like this:

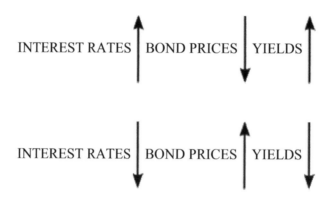

> Discount Bonds

Remember, even though a bond has a par value of $1,000, we don't necessarily expect the bond to trade at $1,000 in the open market. A bond's price fluctuates, and the main reason has to do with interest rates.

If a bondholder has a bond that pays a nominal yield of 8%, what is the bond worth when interest rates in general climb to 10%? Not as much. If you had something that paid you 8%, when you knew you could be receiving more like 10%, how would you feel about the bond?

Not too good. But, when interest rates fall to 6%, suddenly that 8% bond looks better.

Current Yield

When we take a bond's price into consideration, we're looking at a concept known as **current yield**. Current yield (CY) takes the annual interest paid by the bond to an investor and divides it by what an investor would have to pay for the bond.

Current Yield = Annual Interest divided by the Market Price

Current yield equals how much you get compared to what you paid to get it.

$80/$800 gives us a current yield of 10%. So, the nominal yield is still 8%, but the bond trades at a price that makes the current yield 10%, to keep the yield in line with current interest rates. So, if interest rates go up to 10%, suddenly, this bond that pays only 8% isn't worth as much, right? The only motivation for buying this 8% bond sitting out on the open market would be if an investor could get it at a **discount**. And, if she can get the $80 that the bond pays in annual interest for just $800, isn't she really getting 10% on her money? That's why we say her current yield is equal to 10%, higher than the nominal yield that never, ever changes.

If you see a current yield higher than the coupon rate, you know you're looking at a **discount bond**, which is any bond trading for less than the par value. An 8% bond with a 10% current yield, for example, has to be a discount bond. The only way to make a bond's yield rise is to push its price down, after all.

Yield to Maturity

Yield to maturity is the theoretical return an investor gets if she holds the bond all the way to maturity. At maturity, an investor receives the par value, which is $1,000. If the investor puts down only $800 to buy the bond and receives $1,000 when the bond matures, she receives more at maturity than she paid for the bond. That's why her yield to maturity is higher than *both* the nominal and current yield. She gets all the coupon payments, plus an extra $200 when the bond matures. If you see a yield to maturity that is higher than the coupon rate, you're looking at a discount bond. For example, a 4% nominal yield trading at a 5.50 yield to maturity—or **basis**—is a discount bond. The yield to maturity would also be higher than the current yield so that it goes in this order from lowest to highest yield for this bond: nominal, current, then yield to maturity.

Another way the test could define yield to maturity is, "the discount rate at which the sum of all future cash flows from the bond is equal to the price of the bond."

Yield to Call

Like homeowners, sometimes issuers get tired of making interest payments that seem too high. That's why some bonds are issued as **callable**, meaning that after a certain time period the issuer can buy the bonds back from investors at a stated price. A bond that matures in 10 or 20 years is often callable in just 5 years. Since the investor who bought a bond for less than par is going to make money when the principal of $1,000 is returned, do you suppose he'd rather make his profit sooner or later?

Sooner, right? When you're making money, you want to make it as fast as possible. That's why **yield to call** is the highest of all for a discount bond.

➢ Premium Bonds

Of course, whatever can go up can also go down. What happens when interest rates fall? Bond prices rise. If you owned this 8% bond and saw that interest rates have just fallen to 6%, how would you feel about your bond?

Pretty good, right? After all, it pays 2% more than new debt is paying. Do you want to sell it? Not really. But you might sell it to me if I paid you a premium. A **premium bond** is any bond trading for more than par value.

If I paid you $1,200, you might be willing to sell it. From my perspective, I see that new debt is only going to pay 6%, which is too low for my needs. Even though I have to pay more than par for your 8% bond, it will all work out if I can get all those interest payments at a higher-than-prevailing rate.

Current Yield

So, we've just pushed the price of the bond up as interest rates went down. Dividing our $80 of annual interest by the $1,200 we put down for the bond gives us a current yield of just 6.7%. That's lower than the coupon rate, which is why the current yield is below our coupon rate/nominal yield. Whenever you see a coupon of 8% and current yield of 6.7% (or anything lower than that 8% printed on the bond), you know you're looking at a premium bond. Remember, the coupon rate/nominal yield doesn't change. Therefore, the only way to get the yield lower than the coupon rate is to pay more than par for the bond. Just like the only way to get the yield higher than the coupon rate is to pay less than par for the bond.

Yield to Maturity

Now, when this investor's bond matures, how much does she get back from the issuer? Only $1,000. So, she put down $1,200 and will only get back $1,000 at maturity. Pretty easy to see why her Yield to Maturity goes down.

Yield to Call

Remember when we decided that a person who buys a bond at a discount wants the bond to return the principal amount sooner rather than later? Well, if you pay more than the par value for a bond, you're going to lose some money when the bond returns your principal. So, if you're going to lose money, do you want to do it quickly, or spread it out over time, collecting the higher-than-prevailing-rate interest payments in the meantime?

That's why a person who purchases a bond at a premium will have a lower yield to call than yield to maturity. He's going to lose money in either case, so he'd prefer to lose it over 10 or 20 years (maturity) rather than just a few years (call).

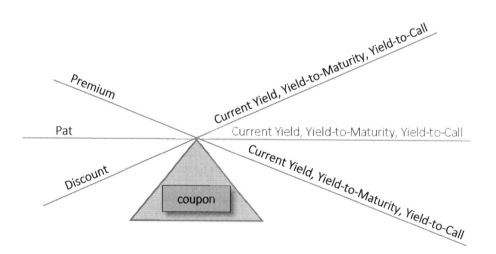

So, yield to call is the lowest yield for a bond purchased at a premium.

CONVERTIBLE SECURITIES

We looked at the concept of convertible securities both under convertible preferred stock and convertible bonds. Let's take a moment to examine the calculations involved. If a convertible corporate bond is convertible "@$40," we could also say it is convertible into 25 shares, since $1,000 would go exactly that far when purchasing stock priced at $40 a share.

> *Par/Conversion price = # common shares*
>
> *1,000/40 = 25 shares*

Going forward, then, how much is the bond worth? That depends—how much are 25 shares of the common stock worth at the moment? Since the bond could always be converted into 25 shares, it basically has to be worth whatever 25 shares of the common stock are worth—at least. When the bond trades for exactly what the 25 shares are worth, we call this relationship **parity**, which is just a fancy word for "same" or "equal." Since one's price depends on the other, the two should have a price that is at "parity." At least—I say "at least" because the bond is worth that number of shares AND all the future interest payments it will make. So "parity" is basically like a floor price that the convertible bond should never drop below, regardless of what interest rates are doing.

If an IXR Corporation bond is convertible into 25 shares of IXR common stock, and IXR stock is trading @50, what is the bond's price at parity?

25 X $50 = $1,250. And, if the common stock went up to $60 a share, the bond would be worth 25 times that number, right? 25 X $60 = $1,500.

Some convertible securities have to be converted to the issuer's common stock—mandatory or forced convertibles. More likely, a convertible bond *may* be converted to common stock by the investor. When would the investor choose to convert if it were entirely up to her? Only when there is some advantage in doing so. If the bond we looked at trades for $1,250 when the underlying stock trades for $50, there is no advantage in converting. The investor has already realized a 25% paper gain on the bond due to the increase in the stock price if the bond is trading for $1,250. If, however, the stock were trading at $50 and the bond were worth only $1,200 on the secondary market, suddenly, the prices are out of whack. Rather than parity, we see a disparity, in fact. In other words, an "arbitrage" opportunity would exist, allowing quick moving investors to sell short 25 shares of the stock for $50 a share and then buy them back for just $1,200 (not the full $1,250) by purchasing the convertible bonds.

For a real-world example of an institutional investor trading convertible securities examine the Calamos Convertible Fund, symbol CCVIX.

There are convertible bonds offering potential upside to fixed-income investors. There are also convertible preferred stocks that do the same thing for those willing to go with an equity security for their fixed-income stream. If a test question says the preferred stock is "convertible at $20," or "convertible at $10," just ask how far the par value would go when being used to buy common stock at that set price. Convertible preferred stock is like a gift certificate worth $100 (or whatever the par value is) toward the purchase of/conversion to common stock at a set price. If the par value is $100, and the preferred stock is "convertible at $10," that is just another way of saying that one share of preferred stock can become 10 shares of common stock at any point, so it should be worth that much no matter how high interest rates go. If the common stock trades @11, the preferred stock trades

@110 if trading at parity. So, if the common stock rises to $15 a share, and the preferred stock that converts to it is trading for just $125, there is another "arbitrage opportunity" making it opportune to convert.

Another time to convert would be if the stock price rises and the bond is getting close to maturity. At maturity, a bond is worth the par value, so if the stock price is currently taking the market price up to $1,250, the only way to capture that for sure is to convert it to the common stock, which has no maturity date.

Of course, the investor could also just go about his daily life without worrying about arbitrage opportunities, knowing he's getting a fixed-income stream plus the upside if the company's common stock rises. Whether he converts or not, when the market price of the convertible security rises, that is a good thing for the investor.

TYPES AND CHARACTERISTICS OF CASH AND CASH EQUIVALENTS

Debt securities maturing in greater than one year are sometimes called **funded debt. Money market securities**, on the other hand, are debt securities maturing in one year or less. They are considered to be safe, liquid investments. The exam may refer to money market securities as "cash equivalents" because, basically, they are just as good as cash. Better actually, because unlike cash sitting in a drawer somewhere, money market instruments are earning interest. It's not necessarily a high *rate* of interest, but at least you're putting your cash to work and you're not risking it in the stock market, where anything can happen, or the bond market, where interest rates could rise and knock down the value of your holdings. Of course, the problem with investing too much of your money into cash equivalents is that you will miss out on the big growth opportunities that arise when the stock or bond markets decide to go off on a run. As we saw in Chapter 1, this is called opportunity cost. Also, cash equivalents generally do not keep pace with inflation, leaving the investor with purchasing power risk.

T-BILLS

With a T-Bill, remember that the "T" stands for "Treasury," and T-Bills are guaranteed by the United States Treasury. Bank CDs usually yield about the same as T-Bills, but the bank's FDIC insurance stops at $250,000 per account. T-Bills, on the other hand, are simply guaranteed no matter how large the denomination. Any given Monday T-Bills are available by auction from as small as $100 par value to as large as $5 million. No matter how big your bill, it's fully insured/guaranteed by the US Treasury.

BANKERS' ACCEPTANCES

A **bankers' acceptance** is a short-term credit investment created by a non-financial company and guaranteed by a bank as to payment. "BAs" are traded at discounts to face value in the secondary market. These instruments are commonly used in international transactions, and the exam might associate them with "importing and exporting." As with a T-Bill, bankers' acceptances are so short-term that it would make no sense to send interest checks to the buyer. Instead, these short-term debt securities are purchased at a discount from their face value. The difference between what you pay and what you receive *is* your interest income. The "BA" or "bankers' acceptance" is backed both by a bank's full faith and credit and the goods being purchased by the importer. I'm not sure you need to know this to answer test questions, but this is how the BA is created. First, a computer manufacturer in California imports computer parts from a Japanese company but—like most Americans—is not in the mood to, like, pay. So, the California company issues a "time draft" to the Japanese company, which is really a post-dated check that is good on a future date and backed up by their bank's line of credit. The Japanese company can now sit on this time draft until the due date and receive the full amount. Or, if they get antsy, they can cash it immediately at their bank at a slight discount. If they do the latter, the Japanese bank would then have a "bankers' acceptance" guaranteed by the American company's bank and the computer parts purchased by the American importer. The Japanese bank can either wait until the due date or sell the thing on the secondary market at a discount.

COMMERCIAL PAPER

Normally people have to pay much higher interest rates to borrow long-term as opposed to borrowing short-term. But, in order to build major items such as an $800 million factory, a company generally bites the bullet, issues long-term bonds (funded debt), and pays the lenders back slowly, in the same way that you are probably currently paying off the mortgage on your house. But if Microsoft needs a mere $50 million to tide them over for a few months, they would probably prefer to borrow it short-term at the lowest possible interest rate. If so, they issue a piece of **commercial paper** with a $50 million face amount, selling it to a **money market mutual fund** for, say, $49.8 million. Again, the difference between the discounted price and the face amount *is* the interest earned by the investor. Commercial paper is generally issued only by corporations with high credit ratings from S&P, Moody's, or Fitch. Unfortunately, each of the three ratings agencies uses different nomenclature, so I have decided not to tell you about the P-1 down to P-3 ratings issued by Moody's, let alone the A1 down to A3 ratings issued by S&P or the F1 down to F3 ratings issued by Fitch. Do know that a rating below any of those "3's" would be considered speculative commercial paper and would, therefore, not be found in the typical money market mutual fund portfolio. Some large corporations issue their commercial paper directly to the lenders/investors, which may be mutual funds, pension funds, etc. The industry cleverly calls this "directly placed commercial paper." Would you, therefore, believe that when corporations use commercial paper dealers to sell to the investor, the industry refers to this as "dealer-placed commercial paper"? Either way, retail investors typically get their commercial paper exposure when they buy money market mutual funds as opposed to, say, fronting Microsoft $3 million until a week from next Tuesday.

REPURCHASE AGREEMENTS

Large financial institutions borrow money at low interest rates over the short term by taking your money and paying whatever a savings account or CD currently offers. They then lend your money out to someone else long-term at a higher interest rate. As long as they're able to borrow at a lower rate from you than they lend it at to someone else, they're fine. But this business model also puts them at risk in terms of fluctuating interest rates. Think of the flat and inverted yield curves we looked at, or even a positive yield curve with only a tiny spread between short-term and long-term interest rates. These interest rate environments are no good for bankers, who live by the time-tested motto: borrow at three, lend at six, golf at three. If they suddenly have to pay high interest rates to borrow short-term while they're earning lower and lower rates when they lend the money out long-term, that's got to hurt. In order to shield themselves from interest-rate risk over the short-term, large financial institutions engage in **repurchase agreements** and **reverse repurchase agreements**. Basically, one party sells the other party government securities today with the agreement to repurchase them at a set price in the near future. The difference between what you pay today and what you receive in the near future would be your fixed rate of return over that time frame should you agree to take the other side of the transaction. For the party of the transaction doing the selling to raise the cash, this would be a repurchase agreement. To the party on the other side, who starts out as the buyer, the agreement would be known as a reverse repurchase agreement. Although definitely part of the money market, repurchase agreements (repos) are more of a private arrangement than a security that gets bought and sold. There is really no secondary market for these transactions.

TAX-EXEMPT MUNICIPAL NOTES

Cities, counties, school districts, etc., can borrow money long-term by issuing municipal bonds, and they can borrow short-term by issuing notes. "Anticipation notes" are very common, and their name tells you exactly what's going on: there is money coming into the city's coffers in the near future, but there are some bills due *right now.* For example, property taxes are collected twice a year. If the city wants some of that money now, they can issue a tax anticipation note, or TAN. If it's backed up by revenues—from sewer and water services, for example—it's a revenue anticipation note, or RAN. If the note is backed up by both taxes and revenues, they call it a tax and revenue anticipation note, or TRAN. But my personal favorite of these short-term municipal notes has to be the bond anticipation note, or BAN. In this case, the issuer borrows money from somebody now and backs it up with part of the money they're going to borrow in the near future when they issue more bonds.

Seriously.

The interest paid on these municipal notes is lower than the nominal rates paid on a corporation's commercial paper, but that's okay—the interest paid is also tax-exempt at the federal level. So, if an investor or an institution is looking for safety, liquidity, and dependable, tax-exempt interest over the short-term, they purchase these anticipation notes directly or through a tax-exempt money market mutual fund.

CERTIFICATES OF DEPOSIT (CDS)

In order to earn a higher interest rate than what their bank offers on savings or checking accounts, many bank customers put relatively large amounts of money into **certificates of deposit** or **CDs**. These are basically long-term deposits that pay higher rates of interest if the depositor agrees to leave the funds untouched for a while. Bank CDs are insured by the FDIC just like other bank deposits, so this is about as safe as "safe money" gets. As you might imagine, the yields on these government-insured deposits are also rather meager. Then again, for the liquid part of one's portfolio, bank CDs are often perfect. The drawbacks have to do with the fact that they are long-term deposits, not securities. If the individual wants her money out now to cover a roof replacement she will be penalized and probably lose all or most of the interest she was going to make. Bank CDs are not bonds to be traded on the secondary market. CDs don't do much to protect purchasing power, either, but they are great at maintaining an investor's needs for liquidity and capital preservation. The rate of interest offered is compounded; however, it's hard to see a big difference between that and simple interest when the rate is low and the term to maturity so short.

> ➢ Brokered CDs

As opposed to just walking into a local bank and accepting the yields they're currently offering on their certificates of deposit, investors who purchase brokered CDs open their portfolio up to yields offered by banks all across the country. A brokered CD account would also provide liquidity for the investor since he could ask the broker/registered representative to sell the CD on the secondary market as opposed to taking an early withdrawal penalty from a bank. Assuming the CDs are all FDIC insured (up to $250,000), investors can put a substantial amount of money into brokered CD accounts and receive FDIC insurance on each individual certificate of deposit in the portfolio. All without opening up accounts at dozens of different banks to avoid exceeding the $250,000 FDIC coverage. Of course, there are fees, and these work pretty much like brokered mortgages—the interest rate you receive is a little bit less favorable after the broker takes his cut.

Although most CDs are short-term, there are also long-term certificates of deposit with maturities as long as perhaps 20 years. Although brokered CDs can be a great option for many investors, some investors have been shafted by brokers who put them into 20-year CDs which then led to large losses when the investors needed their cash. As one might imagine, these long-term CDs may have limited or even no liquidity and investors can actually lose money by selling these things on the secondary market. Also, the interest payments on long-term CDs are often complex and explained in fine print few investors understand. Broker-dealers and registered representatives selling these long-term CDs need to be sure that investors understand how these products differ from traditional bank CDs and must disclose all potential risks. Higher yields on the one hand, but the secondary market for the products might not be as liquid as one would hope—suddenly, rather than sacrificing the interest on a bank CD, the individual could actually lose principal. I don't know about you, but "losing money" and "CDs" really don't go together in my mind. The regulators tend to have similar difficulty squaring the two in their own.

> Negotiable/Jumbo CDs

Some people like to step outside the realm of FDIC insurance and purchase **jumbo** or **negotiable** CDs. The denominations here are often several millions of dollars. Therefore, jumbo CDs are usually not insured by the FDIC but are, rather, backed by the issuing bank. That makes their yields higher. Also, if you've ever pulled out of a bank CD early, you know how painful that can be. With a jumbo CD you have a negotiable/marketable security that you can sell to someone else. That's what the word "negotiable" means—tradable. If you still have one of those archaic things known as a "checkbook," you'll notice your checks are "non-negotiable." They're just bank drafts—not tradable or marketable instruments. Well, a "negotiable CD" is a tradable, marketable instrument as opposed to just a long-term deposit at a bank.

> Demand Deposits

A CD is a "term deposit" made under an agreement to keep the funds put in over a certain time frame. On the other hand, a **demand deposit** is a deposit at a bank in which the funds can be withdrawn at any time. The majority of such "demand deposits" are simply checking and savings accounts. As you probably know, these accounts pay rates of interest that are so subtle as to be nearly imperceptible. Financial institutions have to make funds available in demand deposit accounts within a set period of time, and the bank or other institution must inform customers clearly of their policy on availability of funds. The exam might bring up any of these points on demand deposits:

- No maturity period
- Payable on demand
- Usually interest-bearing
- No limit on withdrawals or transfers
- No eligibility requirements

PRACTICE

1. All of the following pay interest subject to state taxes except:

    A. GNMA

B. FNMA

C. Municipal securities

D. T-Bills

2. Which of the following CMOs leaves the investor with the most prepayment risk?

A. PAC

B. TAC

C. ZAC

D. MAC

3. Securities typically found in a money market mutual fund portfolio do NOT include which of the following?

A. US Treasury bonds

B. Negotiable certificates of deposit

C. Commercial paper

D. Bankers' acceptances

(ANSWERS)

1. **D,** the states can't tax Treasury securities. The federal government doesn't tax most municipal securities, but the states can do what they want there. GNMA, FNMA, and FHLMC are subject to tax at all levels.

2. **B,** a TAC has a "target," while a PAC has a "plan." The other two are fictitious.

3. **A,** T-Bonds are long-term securities. Money market mutual funds hold short-term debt securities.

POOLED INVESTMENT VEHICLES

INVESTMENT COMPANIES

Some investors never buy particular stocks or bonds. Rather, their exposure to stocks and bonds comes through packaged products called mutual funds or **investment company products**. The best known of all investment company products is the **open-end fund**, but there are also **closed-end funds**, and **unit investment trusts (UITs)** out there. Your exam knows that a Series 65 license does not allow the test-taker to sell mutual funds for compensation, but a Series 65 licensee could be managing a mutual fund portfolio, or advising people to steer clear of mutual funds and let his company manage their portfolio instead. Either way, the regulators expect Series 65 candidates to know quite a bit about the products commonly called "mutual funds."

A share of stock is an ownership stake in a company. A preferred stock or a corporate bond is an obligation of a company to pay a stated rate of return to a fixed-income investor. Many investors, however, don't want to pick companies to own or loan money to. Instead, they choose to invest through packaged products that contain securities selected and managed by professional investors. As I said, the best known packaged product is the open-end mutual fund. Chances are most readers own a few of these in their retirement or educational savings accounts. If you're familiar with names including Fidelity, Vanguard, Janus, or the American Funds, you are familiar with mutual fund companies.

A mutual fund is an investment portfolio managed by a registered investment adviser. The portfolio will serve up as many shares as investors want to buy any day the markets are open. Buying and selling the shares is easy, and it happens between the investors and the fund itself. There is no secondary market trading with open-end mutual fund shares. Investors send in money to buy shares of the big portfolio. The fund then uses the money to buy stocks and bonds that everybody in the fund owns little pieces of. When an investor sends in, say, $10,000, the portfolio gets bigger, but it also gets cut up into more shares. That way each share stays the same size when investors are buying or selling them from/to the fund. The only way for the shares to get bigger is for the portfolio to grow, which happens when securities in the fund go up in value and when they pay income to the portfolio. That, of course, is how it works for an investor buying a few stocks and bonds on his own. Any day he logs into his brokerage account, he will see that his account is either up or down by some amount of money and some percentage. If the market value of the securities went up, or if the securities received interest or dividend payments, the portfolio value will be up that day. If the market prices have dropped—or dropped by more than any income received—the opposite will be true.

Now, couldn't an investor bypass the mutual fund and just buy stocks and bonds in whatever companies or governments he chooses? Sure, but most people refuse to change the oil in their car—why would they suddenly become do-it-yourselfers with six- and seven-figure retirement accounts? It takes a lot of work to decide which stocks or bonds to purchase. Also, if you only have $400 to invest, you can't take a meaningful position in any company's stock, and even if you tried, you'd end up owning just *one* company's stock. Common stock can drop to zero in a hurry, so you'd never put all your money in just one or two stocks. As we discussed earlier, **diversification** would protect against this **unsystematic risk**, and mutual funds own stocks and bonds from many different issuers, usually in different market sectors. Plus, the portfolio is run by professionals who know when it's time to rebalance the portfolio as sure as the crew at Jiffy Lube knows when it's time to rotate your tires.

Also, the term "mutual fund" is sort of an accepted nickname, not a legal term. Generally, when we say "mutual fund," we mean "open-end investment company share." As we'll see, there are also "closed-end investment company shares" that could-be-but-usually-are-not-called "mutual funds." As you've noticed, things go by many different names in this industry. We could call your investment in a growth fund through Fidelity or Janus an "open-end investment company share," an investment in a "management company," a "mutual fund," or a "pooled investment vehicle," depending on where we wanted to put the emphasis or what kind of mood we were in.

➢ Advantages of Mutual Fund Investing

The exam may bring up some advantages of mutual fund investing over picking stocks and bonds individually:

- Investment decisions made by a professional portfolio manager

- Ease of diversification
- Ability to liquidate a portion of the investment without losing diversification
- Simplified tax information (1099s make tax prep easier)
- Simplified record keeping (rather than getting 150 annual reports from 150 companies, you get two reports per year from one mutual fund)
- Ease of purchase and redemption of securities
- Automatic reinvestments of capital gains and income distributions at **net asset value (NAV)**
- Safekeeping of portfolio securities
- Ease of account inquiry

The first point is probably the main reason people buy mutual funds. They have no knowledge of the securities markets and they have even less interest in learning. Let a professional portfolio manager—often an entire *team* of portfolio managers—decide what to buy and when to buy or sell it. As we mentioned, it's tough to have your own diversified portfolio in individual stocks and bonds because a few hundred or thousand dollars will only buy a few shares of stock or a few bonds issued by just a few companies. On the other hand, a mutual fund would usually hold stock in, say, 100 or more companies, and their bond portfolios are also diversified. Therefore, even with the smallest amount of money accepted by the fund, the investor is immediately diversified. The exam may call this the "undivided interest concept." That just means that your $500 owns a piece of all the securities in the portfolio, just as the rich guy's $1 million does. Yes, you own a much smaller piece, but you're also just as diversified as the rich guy is. You both own your percentage of everything inside the portfolio.

Notice that another bullet point said, "Ability to liquidate a portion of the investment without losing diversification." That's actually a bigger deal than it might seem. See, if you invest the way I do, you own 100 shares of IBM, MSFT, and GM, maybe. Now, what are you going to do if you need $5,000 to cover an emergency? If you sell a few shares of each holding, you'll pay three separate commissions. And, if you sell all 100 shares of just one stock, your diversification is seriously reduced. With a mutual fund, you redeem a certain number of shares and remain just as diversified as you were before the sale. And, you can usually redeem/sell your shares without getting hit up for any fees.

What exactly do we mean by "diversification"? Mutual funds can diversify their holdings by:

- Industries
- Types of investment instruments
- Variety of securities issuers
- Geographic areas

If it's a stock fund, it is basically a growth fund, an income fund, or some combination thereof. No matter what the objective, the fund will usually purchase stocks from issuers across many different industries. In a mutual fund prospectus you'll often find a pie chart that shows what percentage of assets is tied up in a particular industry. Maybe it's 3% in telecommunications, 10% retail, 1.7% healthcare, etc. That way if it's a lousy year for telecommunications or retail, the fund won't get crushed like a small investor who owns stock in just a few companies, each one representing a major chunk of his portfolio. A bond fund can be diversified among investment interests. That means they buy debentures, secured bonds, convertible bonds, zero coupons, mortgage-backed securities, and even a few money market instruments to be on the safe side. Even if the fund did not spread their investments across many different industries (telecom, pharmaceutical, retail, etc.) and chose, instead, to focus on just a few industries, they would still purchase securities from a variety of issuers. So, if they like retail, they can still buy stock in a variety of companies—Walmart, Target, Sears, Nordstrom, Home Depot, etc. And, since any geographic area could be hit by an economic slump, a tropical storm, or both, most funds will spread their holdings among different geographic areas. I mean, the Pacific Rim countries sure look promising, but I don't want all my holdings in companies from Japan, Taiwan, and Singapore.

The Investment Company Act of 1940 defines a **diversified fund** like so:

> *"Diversified company" means a management company which meets the following requirements: At least 75 per centum of the value of its total assets is represented by cash and cash items (including receivables), Government securities, securities of other investment companies, and other securities for the purposes of this calculation limited in respect of any one issuer to an amount not greater in value than 5 per centum of the value of the total assets of such management company and to not more than 10 per centum of the outstanding voting securities of such issuer.*

So, how does the "Act of 1940" then define a **non-diversified company**?

> *"Non-diversified company" means any management company other than a diversified company.*

That just means that if the fund wants to promote itself as being "diversified," it has to meet the definition—for 75% of the fund's assets, no more than 5% of assets are in any one company, and it doesn't own more than 10% of any company's outstanding shares. If it doesn't feel like meeting the definition, it will have to refer to itself as a "non-diversified fund," which could end up scaring some investors off.

Many students seem miffed that I don't buy a lot of mutual funds, myself. That's because I like to own pieces of particular companies of my own choosing and am willing to do a little research myself. Unfortunately, I also end up getting proxy (voting) materials and annual reports from, like, 20 different companies, and keeping track of all the dividends I've received from the various sources is slightly annoying. With a mutual fund, I'd get one **1099-DIV** that would keep track of all the dividends and capital gains distributions, and I'd also get just one semi-annual report and one annual report from the fund.

➢ Types of Mutual Funds

Equity Funds

The primary focus of **equity funds** is to invest in equity securities—a.k.a., common stock. Within equity funds, we find different objectives. **Growth funds** invest in companies that appear likely to grow their profits faster than competitors and/or the overall stock market. These stocks usually cost a lot compared to the profits that they might or might not have at this point. As we've seen, the comparison of the stock price to the earnings of the company is called the "**price-to-earnings ratio**" or price-to-earnings "multiple." The **p/e** or **price-to-earnings ratio** compares the stock price to the earnings each share represents. If you're willing to pay high price-to-earnings multiples, you're a growth investor.

What if you prefer to buy stocks trading at low price-to-earnings ratios? You're a "value investor." **Value funds** seek companies trading for less than the portfolio managers decide they're actually worth. The exam might say that value funds buy stock in established companies that are currently out of favor. Since the share price is depressed while the dividend keeps getting paid, value stocks tend to have high dividend yields. Therefore, they are considered more conservative than growth funds.

What if you just can't make up your mind between a growth fund and a value fund? Luckily, there are funds that blend both styles of investing, and the industry calls these **blend funds**. In other words, no matter how creative the portfolio managers might get, they end up being either a growth fund, a value fund, or a blend of both styles.

If your investor's objective is to receive income from equities, the industry would be happy to sell her an **equity income fund**. These funds buy stocks that provide dependable dividend income. Receiving dividends tends to reduce the volatility of an investment, so equity income funds are lower risk than equity growth funds.

What if you can't decide between a mutual fund family's growth funds and its income funds? Chances are, you'll choose their "growth and income fund." A growth and income fund buys stocks in companies expected to grow their profits and also in companies that pay dependable, respectable dividends. Since we've added the income component, growth & income funds would have lower volatility than growth funds. So, from highest to lowest volatility, we would find growth, then growth & income, and then equity income funds.

Balanced funds are in a lower volatility category than growth, growth & income, and equity income funds. Why? Because a balanced fund keeps a large percentage of its assets in both the stock and the bond markets, and diversifies heavily among both asset classes. The bond market is not as volatile as the stock market, so if the fund devotes, say, 30% or more to the bond market, this will reduce the price fluctuation/volatility of the fund. What percentage is devoted to the stock and to the bond markets? Read the prospectus, as this is a policy set by the particular fund's board of directors.

Bond Funds

Stock is not for everybody. Even if an investor wants to own equity mutual funds, chances are you'll still put a percentage of her hard-earned money into bond funds, as well. A rule-of-thumb is that whatever your age is, that's the percentage that you should put into fixed-income. So, which type of fixed-income (bond) funds should the investor purchase? If the investor is not in a high tax bracket or is investing in an IRA, 401(k), etc., we'll be recommending taxable bond funds—corporate and US Government bonds, in other words. The investor's time horizon will determine if we should purchase short-term, intermediate-term, or long-term bond funds. Her risk tolerance will tell us if she needs the absolute safety of US Treasury funds or is willing to reach for higher returns with high-yield corporate bond funds. If the investor is in a taxable account and wants to earn interest exempt from federal income tax, we put her into a tax-exempt bond fund, which purchases municipal bonds. If the investor is in a high-tax state such as Maryland, Virginia, or California, we can sell her the "Tax-Exempt Fund of Maryland," Virginia, or California. Now, the dividends she receives will be exempt from both federal and state income taxes. But, we're not done just because we put her into a tax-exempt bond fund. How much of a yield does she want and how much risk can she withstand? If she's willing to roll the dice, we can put her into the "High-Yield Tax-Exempt Fund." If her risk tolerance is lower, we'll buy funds that stick primarily to investment-grade municipal bonds.

Money Market Funds

We've also seen that an investor's need for liquidity tells us how much to park in the safe, liquid money market. There are both taxable and tax-exempt money market mutual funds. The tax-exempt money market funds buy short-term obligations of states, counties, cities, school districts, etc. They pay *really* low rates of interest, but since it's tax-free, rich folks still come out ahead. We're talking about TANs, RANs, BANs, etc.

Specialty Funds

Specialty/specialized funds do what their name implies—they specialize in their approach to investing. Some funds specialize in a particular industry, some in geographic regions, some in writing covered calls, etc. You can buy the Latin America, the Europe, or the Pacific Rim fund. You would then hope that those regions don't go into a major economic slump or suffer a natural disaster. See, when the fund concentrates heavily in a particular industry or geographic region, it generally takes on more volatility. Most equity funds hold stocks in many different industries. On the other hand, there are **sector funds** that do exactly as their name implies—focus on particular industry sectors. If you buy a "growth fund," so far you have no idea which industries the so-called "growth companies" compete in. On the other hand, if you buy the Pharmaceuticals Fund, the Financial Services Fund, or the Healthcare Fund, you know in which industry space the companies operate. Concentrating in just one sector is the very definition of aggressive investing. Investment results would almost have to be unpredictable at best. So, make sure the investor has a long anticipated holding period and high risk tolerance before recommending sector funds in a test question.

There are **asset allocation** funds for conservative investors. I've seen definitions that say that asset allocation funds are another name for balanced funds, and I'm not sure how I could argue with that. I mean, if a balanced fund invests a percentage in equity and a percentage in debt, how is that different from an asset allocation fund, which invests a percentage in equity and a percentage in debt?

Both international and **global funds** appeal to investors who want to participate in markets not confined to the US. The difference between the two is that an **international fund** invests in companies located anywhere but the US, while a global fund would invest in companies located and doing business anywhere in the world, including the US. Remember that when you move away from the US, you take on more political/social risk as well as currency exchange risk.

Could you take a guess as to what a precious metals fund would invest in? I thought so. Typically, a gold, silver, or copper fund would be made of common stock in the mining companies, as they tend to open up the mines only when the prices of these precious metals are high.

What if you don't believe that portfolio managers are likely to beat an index such as the S&P 500 over the long-term? First of all, you're in good company with plenty of evidence to support your notion. Secondly, if you can't beat the S&P 500 index, join it. Just buy an **index fund** that tracks an index as opposed to a fund trying to trade individual stocks. An index is just an artificially grouped basket of stocks. Why are there 30 stocks in the **Dow Jones Industrial Average**, and why are the 30 particular stocks that are in there in there?

Because the Dow Jones publishing company says so. Same for the S&P 500. S&P decided that these 500 stocks make up an index, so there you have it. Investors buy index funds because there are no sales charges and very low expenses. Since there's virtually no trading going on, the **management fees** should be—and typically are—very low. So, for a no-brainer, low-cost option, you can put your money into an index and expect to do about as well as that index, no better, no worse. I have a big part of my Health Savings Account in the S&P MidCap 400, and about 1/3 of my SIMPLE IRA in the S&P 500. I actually went the ETF route, but the difference is minimal since I do no trading of any kind. Either way, one gets an unmanaged index and low management fees.

The goal of an index fund is to mimic the performance of the underlying index as closely as possible. Since it can't do that 100%, the amount by which the index fund fails to track the index is called its **tracking error.**

> ➢ Comparisons of Mutual Funds

Once we decide that the investor wants to invest in a growth fund or a value fund, how do we go about comparing one growth or value fund to another? The mutual fund prospectus would be a good place to go. In this disclosure document we will find the fund's investment objectives and style. Do they focus on companies valued at $5 billion and above? $1 billion and below? Do they use fundamental analysis, poring over income statements and balance sheets, possibly meeting with senior management of the companies whose stock they hold? During the dot-com craze I think I remember a mutual fund company advertising that their analysts counted fiber optic cable for a company whose stock they held. That would certainly be a fundamental analyst's approach to investing. Some funds rely on technical analysis—charts, patterns, trends, etc. Is a company's dividend payout ratio important when selecting investments for the portfolio, or is the fund really only looking at the growth potential? Is this a small cap, mid-cap, or large cap fund, and how is the fund defining "small, mid, and large cap"? There are also investment policies disclosed in the prospectus. Maybe the fund is telling you that it may invest up to 10% of its assets in securities of issuers outside the United States and Canada and not included in the S&P 500. Or, that they allow themselves to invest 20% of their assets in lower-quality debt securities rated below BB/Ba by S&P and Moody's, or even in debt securities no one has *ever* actually rated. If that sounds too risky for the investor, well, that's why we're disclosing it here in the prospectus before we ever think about taking his or her money.

The prospectus provides information on the party managing the portfolio. We call that party the **investment adviser** or the portfolio manager. Often, it's a team approach, so we can see the names of the individual portfolio counselors and how much experience they have doing this sort of thing. The prospectus I happen to be looking at now has a team of eight managers, and their experience in the industry ranges from 18 to 40 years.

One of the most misunderstood aspects of mutual fund investing has to do with the fees and expenses. You'll often hear people say, "No, I don't pay any expenses on my mutual funds—they're all no-*load.*" Actually, whether the fund is "no load" or not, all funds charge operating expenses. You might not get a bill for your share of the expenses, but the fund takes out enough money from the portfolio to cover their expenses, whether this happens to be a "no load" fund or one that charges either front- or back-end sales charges. Sales charges are one thing; expenses are another. Not all funds have sales charges, but all funds have operating expenses.

In the prospectus the investor can see how much of her check is going toward the sales charge, and how much of the dollars she then invests will be eaten up by ongoing operating expenses. The section that details the fees and expenses of the fund has been entitled "Fees and expenses of the fund" in the prospectus sitting on my desk at the moment. If two growth funds have similar 10-year track records but one has expenses of 1.5% while the other charges just .90%, this could certainly be the tiebreaker. Expense ratios, in other words, are important factors when determining your investment into a particular fund.

A mutual fund's **turnover ratio** tells us how actively the portfolio managers trade the portfolio securities. A turnover rate of 20 or 30% is considered a buy-and-hold strategy, while a turnover ratio greater than 100% indicates a fund that does a lot of buying and selling.

How well does the fund perform? The prospectus will show you **total return**, usually as a bar chart and a table of numbers. Since I'm looking at a growth fund prospectus, the red bars are often very long and pointing in both upward and downward directions. Over the past 10 years, the fund has gone up as high as 45% and down as much as 22%. As we said, investing in growth stocks requires a higher risk tolerance and a longer time horizon. There was a 3-year period here where the fund averaged returns of *negative* 9%. That's why this would not be an account from which an investor should expect to make withdrawals/sales—a growth fund is for an investor with a long time horizon, as these results make pretty clear.

What is total return? As usual, it's much simpler than you might assume. The point of buying a mutual fund share is that it might go up in value. The mutual fund will usually also pay out dividends from all those stocks and bonds they hold in the portfolio. And, at the end of the year if they took more profits than losses while trading their stocks and bonds, they will distribute a capital gain to shareholders. Total return takes all three of those things and compares it to where the fund started. If the fund started out with a "net asset value" or "NAV" of $10 and finished the year at $11 per share, that's $1 of "capital appreciation." If the fund also paid a dividend of 50 cents per share and a $1 capital gains distribution, we would add that $1.50 to the capital appreciation of $1 for a total of $2.50 of good stuff. Comparing that $2.50 to where we started—$10—gives us a total return of 25%. How likely is it that a fund could have a total return of 25%? The prospectus I happen to be looking at reports that the portfolio returned 26%, 31%, and 45% during the first three years in the last 10-year period. So, naturally, it had a similar return the next three years, right? No, after that, it was anybody's guess: positive 7%, then negative 12%, followed by negative 22%. Which means the following year was probably even worse, right? No. The next year the fund had a total return of nearly 33% in a positive direction. Now we see why the prospectus says that "past results are not predictive of future results." Yeah. I guess not.

See, mutual funds are not short-term investments, especially not equity funds. You need a long time horizon, as the prospectus for this growth fund tells you on the very first page. Nobody knows what will happen this year or next. We can show you the returns over 1, 5, and 10 years and let you be the judge. But no one can tell you which funds will go up this year, let alone which funds will go up the most. If they could do that, why would they need their day job?

As we've seen, taxation always plays a part on an investor's returns, so the prospectus will also show results after taxes have been figured in. Of course, this is a little tricky, as we see from the caveat in the prospectus on my desk:

Your actual after-tax returns depend on your individual tax situation and likely will differ from the results shown below. In addition, after-tax returns may not be relevant if you hold your fund shares through a tax-deferred arrangement, such as a 401(k) plan, IRA, or 529 Savings Plan.

Long before the investment adviser starts investing investor dollars, remember that it costs money to market mutual fund shares to investors. To cover the costs of printing sales literature and compensating sales people, some mutual funds charge **sales charges** that are basically cover charges investors pay to get in the front door. If the **net asset value (NAV)** of our aggressive growth fund is $9.50, we might actually charge people $10.00 for a stock worth $9.50 and call the difference of 50 cents a sales charge.

If the mutual fund is sponsored/underwritten/distributed by a broker-dealer, there will be a sales charge on purchases or redemptions of the fund. This sales charge covers the distribution expenses of printing and mailing out sales literature and prospectuses, advertising the fund, compensating sales people and still leaves a nice profit for the **distributor** of the fund. Notice how distribution expenses are not related to investing the portfolio—the investment adviser, the board of directors, the custodian, the transfer agent, the board of directors, and even the lawyers and accountants all get paid out of the portfolio's income. Sales charges are one-time events taken out of an investor's check when he buys or sells his shares.

How much of a sales charge will the investor pay? 5.5% is not uncommon for small investments. The maximum allowed sales charge is 8.5%, though I can't imagine anyone actually paying that much to get into a mutual fund these days. In any case, if a mutual fund charges a maximum sales charge of 5.5%, that means that when the investor cuts her check, 5.5% of it goes to the distributor and the broker-dealer who sold her the fund. Only the other 94.5% goes into the mutual fund for investment purposes.

So, if the NAV is $9.45 but the **public offering price** or "POP" is $10.00, the difference of 55 cents is the sales charge. How big is that sales charge? It is exactly 5.5% of the investor's $10 check. There are few calculations on the Series 65 exam, but you could be expected to know that the sales charge as a percentage equals:

(POP minus NAV) divided by the POP

If we plug our numbers into that formula, we see that $10 minus $9.45 is 55 cents. 55 cents divided by the POP of $10 equals 5.5%.

A-, B-, and C-Shares

I'm not sure the exam drills down hard on A-, B-, and, C-shares, but they are on the outline, and they are inherently confusing. So, I'm going to take my time explaining this stuff. See, a mutual fund that adds a sales charge can get the sales charge from investors either when they buy or when they sell their shares of the fund. "A"-shares charge a **front-end load** when the investor acquires them. "B"-shares charge a **back-end load** when the investor sells them. For a "B"-share, the investor pays the NAV, but she will leave a percentage behind when she sells. The percentage usually starts to decline in the second year, and after several years (6 to 8), the back-end load goes away completely—effectively, the "B"-shares are converted to "A"-shares. "B"-shares are associated with **contingent deferred sales charges**. Break down those words. The sales charge is deferred until the investor sells, and the amount of the load is contingent upon when the investor sells. For a test question on the proceeds of a B-share redemption, just take the NAV and deduct the appropriate percentage from the investor's proceeds. If the NAV is $10, the investor receives the $10, minus the percentage the fund keeps on the back end. So, if she sells 100 shares and there is a 2% back-end sales charge, she gets $1,000 minus $20, or $980 out the door.

So, since the back-end or deferred sales charge eventually goes away, as long as the investor isn't going to sell her shares for, say, seven years, she should purchase B-shares, right?

Wouldn't it be great if things were *ever* that simple in the world of investing? See, we've been acting as if distribution expenses are covered only by sales charges, either on the front-end (**A-shares**) or back-end (**B-shares**). Turns out, distribution expenses are also covered by the **12b-1 fee**. What?

Yes, a "12b-1" fee *also* covers distribution costs, and these things will put money in your pocket if you begin to sell mutual funds with a Series 6 or Series 7 license. You've heard about so-called **no-load funds**, but you may not have gotten the whole story. A no-load fund can still charge a 12b-1 fee, as long as it doesn't exceed .25% of the fund's assets. Every quarter, when they take money out to cover expenses, these so-called "no load funds" can also take an amount not to exceed 25 basis points—one-quarter of 1%.

Even though 12b-1 fees are associated with no-load funds, loaded funds also charge 12b-1 fees. So, again, should the investor buy the A-share or the B-share? The choice has to do with this 12b-1 fee. The A-shares for our aggressive growth fund might charge a load as high as 5.5% on the front end, but the 12b-1 fee we tack on will often be .25%, while the B-shares will pay a 12b-1 fee of, say, 1.00%. That complicates things, doesn't it? While the person who bought the B-shares is waiting for that contingent deferred sales charge schedule to hit zero, he's paying an extra .75% every year in expenses. .75% times seven years is an extra 5.25%. Yeah, but still, the A-shares start out with a maximum of 5.5% upfront sales charge, so the B-shares are still better.

Oh, if things were only that simple. See, this 12b-1 fee is a percentage. As an investor's assets are growing over time, that .75% is also taking more *money* from him, even if it's a flat percentage— almost like the reverse of compounded interest. We're probably going beyond the depth of the exam, but if you invest $10,000 into a fund, the first year's 12b-1 fee would be $75.00. If your investment grows to $11,000, the 12b-1 fee is going to be $82.50 next year. If the assets in your account are eventually $13,000, the extra .75% in 12b-1 fees equals $97.50.

And, as we'll soon see, 5.5% would probably be the *maximum* sales charge on the A-shares. If the investor puts in more money, she can reduce the sales charge to 3 or even 2%, which is why long-term investors with a decent amount of money should almost always buy the A-shares. In fact, investors with $1 million or more will find that funds with sales charges waive those charges for investments of that size. Does that hurt you, the salesperson? No—you want the 12b-1 fee. And .25% of $1 million is $2,500 in 12b-1 fees, an amount that will grow as the investor's account value grows.

Just to make the decision harder, there are also **C-shares**, which usually don't charge an upfront load but do carry a 1% 12b-1 fee. The level 1% 12b-1 fee (which is so much higher than the .25% allowed for a "no load" fund) is where we got the clever **level load** nickname, by the way.

So, which type of share should an investor buy? Although I think this concept is a little too subjective (like what makes something "small cap" versus "mid cap"), I'd recommend the following answers:

- Long-term investor with $50,000+ to invest – A-shares
- Long-term investor with small amount to invest – B-shares
- Short-term investor with up to $500,000 to invest – C-shares

The difference in expenses between A-shares on one hand and B- and C-shares on the other has to do with the 12b-1 fee. Clearly any fund with A-, B-, or C-shares is not even trying to present itself as no-load; any "no-load" fund family by definition does not have A-, B-, or C-shares. But, a no-load fund from, say, Fidelity or Vanguard, can charge a 12b-1 fee as long as it remains no more than .25% of the fund's average net assets.

Okay, fine. Either way, the 12b-1 fee is just one expense. The fund also charges a management fee to cover the cost of the investment adviser serving as portfolio manager. That fee would be the same for all investors across the board and would have to be a separate line item. A mutual fund can't bury their management fees under the 12b-1 fees or sales charges. Sales charges and 12b-1 fees cover distribution costs. The management fee covers portfolio management—the fund has to keep the two separate. The next item in the expenses table of the prospectus would be "other expenses." To see what the dollar amounts are, check the **statement of additional information** or **SAI**. For example, I recently glanced at the SAI for the American Balanced Fund and saw that the investment adviser took in about $123 million managing the portfolio for the previous year—nice work, especially as this is only one of maybe 50 mutual funds they manage. The transfer agent got something like $30 million, which also isn't bad in my humble opinion.

When you add the management fee, the 12b-1 fee, and the "other expenses" fee, you have the **expense ratio** for the fund. Well—you have the expense ratio when you take those expenses and divide them by the assets of the fund. For the A-shares, maybe the expense ratio is .70%. But, the expense ratio for the B- and C-shares could be 1.45%, due to that extra .75% 12b-1 fee. A mutual fund expense ratio shows how efficiently the fund is administered—how much in expenses they rack up compared to the assets being managed on behalf of investors.

If the investor purchases a B-share, she pays the NAV or "net asset value." Only if/when she sells would the fund take a sales charge from her. If the investor purchases the A-shares, she pays more than the NAV. That extra that she pays is the sales charge, as we said. When you add the sales charge to the NAV, you get the public offering price (POP). So, another formula the exam could throw at you is:

NAV + the Sales Charge = the POP

It looks so much more intimidating as a formula. All we're saying is that if the NAV is $9.45 and the Sales Charge is 55 cents, the POP is $10.00. Or, they could really mess with you and ask you to *determine* the amount of the sales charge. That formula would be:

POP - the NAV = the Sales Charge

Which, again, looks much more intimidating as a formula. All we're saying is that if the POP is $10 and the NAV is $9.45, the Sales Charge must be 55 cents. As we saw earlier, that sales charge would be 5.5%, since the public offering price of $10 has a sales charge built into it representing exactly 5.5%. That's the percentage that goes to the distributors of the fund, leaving the other 94.5% for the investor to, you know, invest.

So, how and when is this net asset value (NAV) figured? At the end of each day that the markets are open. Mutual funds use **forward pricing**. That means that if you take my check for $10,000 at 11 a.m., you won't know how many shares I'll end up buying just yet. The fund will refigure the NAV when trading closes that day, and then put my $10,000 into the fund at the NAV they come up with then. Same thing for a seller. A seller "redeems" her shares to the fund. When she turns in a **redemption** order at 1 p.m. she won't know the exact dollar amount of her check because the NAV won't be determined until after the markets close at 4 p.m. Eastern.

The NAV is nothing more than the value of one share of the portfolio. The assets of the portfolio would be the value of the securities plus any cash they've generated minus any liabilities. Where did the liabilities come from? The fund might borrow to handle redemptions—they don't always want to sell off stocks and bonds to pay investors ready to sell their shares, so they borrow some money. If the fund has $10,000,000 in assets and $550,000 in liabilities, the net assets of the fund would be $9,450,000. If there are 1 million shares, the NAV per share is $9.45. Investors will receive $9.45 per share if they redeem their A-shares today, but they'll pay a POP higher than that if they're buying. Buyers of the B-shares will pay $9.45, but those redeeming/selling their shares will receive $9.45 per share minus whatever percentage they leave behind to the contingent deferred sales charge.

Just to keep everything nice and simple.

Reducing the Sales Charge

Although A-shares charge a front-end load, investors can reduce that sales charge by employing various methods laid out in the prospectus. And, as a registered representative, you would be required to help the customer utilize any and all of these methods.

> Breakpoints

In general, the more you want to buy, the better the price. Doesn't a small box of Cap'n Crunch™ at the convenience store cost a lot more per ounce than a shrink-wrapped pack of 4 oversized boxes from Costco? Same with mutual funds. If you want to invest $1,000, you're going to pay a higher sales charge percentage than if you want to invest $100,000. For mutual funds, investors are rewarded with breakpoints. Let's say that the L & H Fund had the following sales charge schedule:

INVESTMENT	SALES CHARGE
< $50,000	5.5%
$50,000 – $99,999	5.0%
$100,000 – $149,999	4.0%
$150,000 – $199,999	3.0%

That means that an investor who buys $100,000 worth of the fund will pay a much lower sales charge than an investor who invests $20,000. In other words, less of her money will be deducted from her check when she invests. A breakpoint means that at this <u>point</u> the fund will give you this <u>break</u>. A lower sales charge means that an investor's money ends up buying more shares. For mutual funds, we don't pick the number of shares we want; we send in a certain amount of money and see how many shares our money buys us. With a lower sales charge, money will buy more shares. Keep in mind that fractional shares are common. For example, $1,000 would buy 12.5 shares if the POP were $80.

> Letter of Intent

So, what if we didn't have the $100,000 needed to qualify for that breakpoint? We could write a **letter of intent** explaining to the mutual fund our intention to invest $100,000 in the fund over the next 13 months. Now, as we send in our money, say, $5,000 at a time, the fund applies the lower 4% sales charge, as if we'd already invested the full amount. The lower sales charge means we end up buying more shares, right? So, guess what the fund does? It holds those extra shares in a safe place, just in case we fail to invest that $100,000 we intended to. If we don't live up to our letter of intent, no big deal. We just don't get those extra shares. In other words, the higher sales charge applies to the money actually invested.

Also, that letter of intent could be backdated up to 90 calendar days in order to cover a previous purchase. If an investor bought $3,000 of the L & H fund on March 10, he might decide in early June that he should write a letter of intent to invest $50,000 over 13 months. He could backdate the letter to March 10 to include the previous investment and would then have 13 months from that date to invest the remaining $47,000.

Breakpoints are available to individuals, husbands & wives, parents & minor child in a **custodial account**, corporations, partnerships, etc. So, if the mom puts in $30,000 and also puts in $20,000 for her minor child's UGMA account, that's a $50,000 investment in terms of achieving a breakpoint. The child cannot be an adult; he must be a minor. Corporations and other businesses qualify for breakpoints. About the only folks who don't qualify for breakpoints are investment clubs.

Another important consideration for breakpoints is that a sales rep can never encourage an investor to invest a lower amount of money in order to keep him from obtaining a lower sales charge offered at the next breakpoint. That's called **breakpoint selling** and is a violation of FINRA rules. Likewise, if a rep fails to point out to an investor that a few more dollars invested would qualify for a breakpoint, that's just as bad as actively encouraging him to stay below the next breakpoint. Remember, sales reps (broker-dealers) get part of the sales charge. It would definitely be to their advantage to get the higher sales charge. Unfortunately, they have to keep their clients' interests in mind, too.

Yes, they take all the fun out of this business.

> ### Rights of Accumulation

If an investor's fund shares appreciate up to a breakpoint, the investor will receive a lower sales charge on additional purchases. In other words, when an investor is trying to reach a breakpoint, new money and account accumulation are counted the same way. So, if an investor's shares have appreciated to, say, $42,000 and the investor wanted to invest another $9,000, the entire purchase would qualify for the breakpoint that starts at $50,000. In other words, the $42,000 of value plus an additional $9,000 would take the investor past the $50,000 needed to qualify for the 5% sales charge.

This is known as **rights of accumulation**. Please note that this has *nothing* to do with a letter of intent. If you write a letter of intent to invest $100,000, you'll need to invest $100,000 of new dollars into the fund to get the breakpoint you're intending to get. Rights of accumulation means that you could save money on future purchases, based on the value of your account.

> ### Combination Privilege

Most "funds" are part of a "family" of funds. Many of these fund families will let you combine your purchase in their Income Fund with, say, their Index or Growth Fund in order to figure a breakpoint. They call this, very cleverly, a **combination privilege**. So, if the individual invests $20,000 in the Income Fund and $30,000 in the Growth Fund, that's considered a $50,000 investment in the family of funds, and that's the number they'd use to figure the breakpoint.

Just trying to keep everybody in our happy family.

> Conversion/Exchange Privilege

The fund might also offer a **conversion/exchange privilege**. This privilege allows investors to sell shares of, say, the L & H Growth Fund, in order to buy shares of the L & H Income Fund at the NAV, rather than the higher POP. If we didn't do that, the investor might get mad enough to leave our happy family, since there would be no immediate benefit to his staying with us. I mean, if he's going to be charged the POP, why not look for a new family with a growth fund that might actually, you know, grow?

Remember, however, that buying the new shares at the NAV is nice for the investor, but the IRS still considers the sale a taxable event. So if you get a test question on the tax treatment, tell the exam that all gains or losses are recognized on the date of the sale.

➢ Structure and Operation of the Mutual Fund Company

So far we've been looking at a mutual fund in terms of an investment product. Now, let's take a look at a mutual fund as a company—who performs which functions at, say, the Growth Fund of America™?

Board of Directors

A mutual fund has a **board of directors** that oversees operations of the fund or family of funds. The board's responsibilities include:

- establish investment policy
- select and oversee the investment adviser, transfer agent, custodian
- establish dividends and capital gains policy
- approve 12b-1 plans

Remember, the board of directors does not manage the portfolio; it manages the company. The shareholders of the fund elect and re-elect the board members. Shareholders also vote their shares to approve the investment adviser's contract and 12b-1 fees. Policy decisions would include the percentage of junk or non-rated bonds that may be held by the portfolio, or the percentage of stocks in companies not operating in North America and/or contained in the S&P 500.

Investment Adviser

Each fund has an **investment adviser**, whose job is to manage the fund's investments according to its stated objectives. For example, Capital Research and Management Company is the investment adviser to/for the American Funds. At this level an investment adviser is a company, and this company has portfolio managers registered as investment adviser representatives.

Shareholders and the board vote to hire/retain investment advisers, who are paid a percentage of the fund's net assets. That's why they try so hard. The more valuable the fund, the more they get paid. Their fee is typically the largest expense to a mutual fund. Investment advisers have to advise the fund (select the investments) in keeping with federal securities and tax law. They must also base their investment decisions on careful research of economic/financial trends rather than on hot stock tips from their bartender. Since everything needs at least two names, the investment adviser is also called the "portfolio manager."

Custodian

The fund also keeps its securities and cash under the control of a **custodian**. Keeping track of all the dividends received from common and preferred stock held in the portfolio, interest payments from the bonds and money market instruments owned by the fund, purchases and sales made by the adviser, etc., is a big job, and the custodian performs it. The exam might say that the custodian is responsible for the payable/receivable functions involved when the portfolio buys and sells securities. That means they release the money and receive the securities purchased, and they accept the money and deliver the securities sold by the portfolio manager.

Transfer Agent

The **transfer agent** is incredibly busy. This is the party that issues new shares to buyers and cancels the shares that sellers redeem. Most of these shares are simply electronic files (book entry), but it still takes a lot of work to "issue" and "redeem" them. While the custodian receives dividends and interest payments from the portfolio securities, it is the transfer agent that distributes income to the investors. The transfer agent acts as a customer service rep for the fund and often sends out those semi-annual and annual reports that investors have to receive. As we just saw, investors can purchase and redeem shares directly with the transfer agent, should their registered representative be too busy or unreachable.

Underwriters/Distributors/Wholesalers

Loaded funds are sponsored by underwriters, who bear the costs of distributing the fund up front and then get compensated by the sales charge that they either earn themselves or split with the broker-dealers who make the sales. Underwriters (a.k.a. "wholesalers," "distributors," or "sponsors") also prepare sales literature for the fund, since they're the ones who will be selling the shares, either directly to the public or through a network of broker-dealers. If a fund distributes itself, it usually covers the distribution costs through a 12b-1 fee, as we mentioned. The fund can call itself "no load" as long as the 12b-1 fee does not exceed .25% of net assets.

These are the methods of distribution for mutual fund shares:

- Fund/to underwriter/to dealer/to investor (assume sales charge here, a nice big one, probably)
- Fund/to underwriter/to investor (underwriter cuts out the other middleman but still gets a sales charge)
- Fund/to investor (no-load funds, which can charge 12b-1 fees no larger than .25% of assets, deducted quarterly)

➢ Closed-End Funds

The third type of investment company defined by the Investment Company Act of 1940 is the **management company**. Within this category, we find both open-end funds and closed-end funds. So far, we've been talking about the open-end funds. Let's say a few words on the closed-end variety at this point. Both types of investments are portfolios run by investment advisers. So, both the open-end and closed-end fund industry is hugely important to the investment advisory industry. The main difference between the two "management companies" is that **open-end fund** companies continually issue and redeem shares, while **closed-end fund** shares trade on the secondary market.

Unlike closed-end funds, open-end funds don't do an IPO and then force shareholders to trade the fixed number of shares back and forth. Rather, they issue new shares every time somebody wants to buy them, and they let the shareholders sell back/redeem the shares whenever they put in a redemption order.

On the other hand, closed-end funds do an initial offering, at which point there is a fixed number of shares. What if you want to sell your closed-end fund this afternoon? You trade it the same way you trade any other share of stock. How much will you receive? Whatever a buyer is willing to pay. These things can trade at a discount to their NAV, or at a premium. It just depends on the supply and demand for these shares, and since this is such a small part of the secondary market, the pricing is less than efficient. Therefore, if the test question says that the NAV is $9.45 with the POP at $9.00, something's up, right? You can't buy an open-end fund at a discount. As we saw, the cheapest you can buy the shares is at the NAV. So, if the shares are selling below NAV, they have to be shares of a closed-end fund.

However, that doesn't mean that closed-end funds *always* trade at a discount. If people really want your shares, they might pay a premium. So, we're not saying that closed-end funds always trade at a discount to their NAV; we're saying that *only* the closed-end fund could do that. Only the closed-end fund shares are traded between investors.

And, since closed-end shares trade the same way that GE or MSFT shares trade, investors can both purchase them on margin and sell them short. As we discuss elsewhere, "selling short" involves borrowing shares from a broker-dealer and selling them, with the obligation to buy them back and replace them later. If the price falls, you buy low after you already sold high. If the price goes up on you, you're in trouble.

Another difference between open- and closed-end funds is that you would purchase, say, 100 shares of the closed-end fund and pay whatever that costs. For an open-end fund, you would just cut a check for, say, $1,000, and see how many shares you end up with next time they figure the NAV. In almost all cases, you'll get "full and fractional shares" with an open-end fund, which means that $100 would turn into 12.5 shares if the POP were $8.00. That little "point-5" of a share is the fractional share. For a closed-end fund, you would either buy 12 shares or 13 shares, not 12.5.

The exam might also bring up the fact that open-end funds only issue common stock to investors. That's right—even if it's a bond fund, the investor isn't buying bonds in the mutual fund company. The investor is buying a percentage of the bond portfolio—the ownership stake in that portfolio is common stock. A closed-end fund can use leverage by issuing bonds to investors—I mean, borrowing their money and paying them back a rate of interest. They can also issue preferred stock and even common stock with greater/lesser voting rights.

The investment objectives between an open-end and a closed-end fund could be exactly the same. There are closed-end corporate bond funds, tax-exempt bond funds, aggressive growth funds, etc. Nuveen Investments (www.nuveen.com) is the largest issuer of closed-end municipal bond funds. Why would you want those versus the open-end variety? Well, what happens to your yield when the price of the bond drops—it goes up, right? So, if you can buy somebody's closed-end bond fund at a discount, you just goosed your yield a little bit. What about when you want to sell your shares? Well, let's hope they're trading at a premium by then. If not, welcome to the NFL.

> Unit Investment Trusts

We've looked at one type of investment company, the "management company" category that includes open- and closed-end funds. **Unit Investment Trusts** are another type of investment company. The

Investment Company Act of 1940 defines a Unit Investment Trust (UIT) as: an investment company which (A) is organized under a trust indenture, contract of custodianship or agency, or similar instrument, (B) does not have a board of directors, and (C) issues only redeemable securities, each of which represents an undivided interest in a unit of specified securities; but does not include a voting trust.

The lack of the board of directors is a testable point. Also, UITs select, but don't actively manage, the securities in the trust; therefore, no management fees are charged. There is no investment adviser at all, in fact. The exam might refer to a UIT as a "supervised, unmanaged investment company," because while the portfolio is supervised by a trustee, the securities in it are not managed/traded the way most open- and closed-end funds would actively manage (management company) their assets. Running the trust does involve fees for bookkeeping, trustee fees, administrative fees, etc., but—again—no management fees are charged. When the shares are purchased an upfront sales charge is often added, or a deferred sales charge is imposed if and when the unit holder redeems.

Similar to a closed-end fund, a fixed/finite number of shares are offered to investors on the primary market. But, unlike a closed-end fund, unit investment trust interests are redeemable. Also, unlike both open- and closed-end funds, unit investment trusts have a termination date, which means what it sounds like. On that date, everything is liquidated, unit holders are paid out, and that's that.

A UIT, like an open- or closed-end fund, could be referred to as a "pooled investment" on your exam. The "shares of beneficial interest" are also redeemable, meaning the investor can present them to the trust and receive the fair market value, as opposed to selling them for whatever price a buyer will offer on the secondary market.

> Face-Amount Certificate Companies

The Investment Company Act of 1940 defines a face-amount certificate company as:

an investment company which is engaged or proposes to engage in the business of issuing face-amount certificates of the installment type, or which has been engaged in such business and has any such certificate outstanding

Think of a face-amount certificate as a debt security in which the certificate is purchased at a discount and redeemed at a future date for the higher face amount.

> ETFS

An **ETF** is an **exchange-traded fund**. Why did they name it that? Because it is a fund that trades on an exchange and this is not an industry brimming with creative types. An ETF is typically an index fund that trades throughout the day among investors. That means that if an investor wants to do as well as a particular index, she can track that index with an exchange-traded fund (ETF). To track the S&P 500, she can buy the "Spider," which is so named because it is an "SPDR" or "Standard & Poor's Depository Receipt." Of course, she could already have been doing that with Vanguard's S&P 500 open-end index fund. But, that is a boring old open-end fund, and how does an investor buy or sell those shares? Directly from the open-end fund. No matter what time of day, if we put in a redemption order, we all receive the same NAV at the next calculated price—forward pricing. So, if the S&P 500 drops 80 points in the morning and rises 150 points by mid-afternoon, there is no way for us to buy low and then sell high.

But with the ETF version investors can buy and sell their shares as often as they want to. They can try to buy when the index drops and sell when it rises. Unlike the open-end versions, these ETFs can be bought on margin and can be sold short for those who enjoy high-risk investment strategies. The test might say that ETFs facilitate "intra-day trading," which just means that you can buy and sell these things as many times as you want throughout the day. An ETF is organized as a UIT (unit investment trust), or in some cases an open-end fund, but, still, these shares trade back and forth among investors. I could maybe explain that more fully, but you've surely suffered enough at this point.

So, are the ETFs cheaper than the open-end index fund versions? Depends how you do it. If you were only going to invest $500, the open-end fund by Vanguard would be cheaper. By the way, I don't work for Vanguard. I'm just using them because they have a low expense ratio, and their S&P 500 index fund is the biggest fund in America. Anyway, you wouldn't pay a sales charge and the expenses are only .18% (18 basis points) at the time of this writing. The ETF has an expense ratio of only .11% (11 basis points). But, since the ETF version (Spider) is a stock, you would pay a commission to buy it, just as you would pay to buy shares of GE, Walmart, etc. So, if you invested $500 into the ETF and paid a $10 commission, that commission would work out to be 2% (200 basis points), which is much higher, and that's before we factor in the expenses. On the other hand, if you're investing a larger amount, such as $100,000, the same $10 commission is now 1 basis point (.0001) versus the 18 basis points (.0018) for the open-end index fund's operating expenses. So, I think it's safe to say that for a small amount of money—as usual—the open-end mutual fund is a great option. For larger amounts of money, though, the ETF might be cheaper, assuming the investor is paying low commissions.

As with the open-end index funds, ETFs offer diversification. For a rather small amount of money, an investor can own a little piece of, say, 500 different stocks with the SPDR, or 100 stocks with the QQQ. It is also easy to implement asset allocation strategies with ETFs. An investor can find ETFs that track all kinds of different indexes (small cap, value, growth, blue chip, long-term bonds, etc.). If an investor wanted to be 80% long-term bonds and 20% small-cap stock, that goal could be achieved with just two low-cost ETFs. This point is not necessarily a comparison to the open-end index funds, which would offer the same advantage. Rather, it is a comparison to purchasing individual bonds or small cap stocks. In order to spread the risk among many bonds and small cap stocks, an investor would have to spend large sums of money. With an ETF (as with the open-end index funds) diversification can be achieved immediately with a much smaller investment.

The exam may point out that there are some tax advantages with ETFs. That is because an investor can turn her ETF into what's known as "creation units," rather than actually selling anything. See, even though ETFs aren't redeemable for cash, the investor can basically exchange them for the underlying security, which is called a "creation unit." Another tax advantage would be the same as the open-end index fund variety—there is virtually no selling of shares within the portfolio, so there are few capital gains distributions. An ETF such as the SPDR (SPY) or Mid-Cap SPDR (MDY) would be appropriate for most investors with a time horizon and risk tolerance suitable for stock (equity) investing in general. But not every ETF is the same. Due to their popularity, ETFs have spawned new versions that make the regulators nervous. FINRA has put out a notice to member firms that "inverse" or "leveraged" ETFs may not be suitable for many investors. Therefore, firms need to be very diligent when recommending these particular versions of exchange-traded funds. FINRA is perfectly clear when they write:

Leveraged ETFs seek to deliver multiples of the performance of the index or benchmark they track. Some leveraged ETFs are "inverse" or "short" funds, meaning that they seek to deliver the opposite of the performance of the index or benchmark they track.

Right there, I'm getting nervous for retail investors—will they understand that when a leveraged ETF loses the bet, it loses *big time*. Will they understand that when the rest of their friends are cheering about the "market being up lately," they should not be cheering along with them? If not, educate them carefully and understand the higher risks yourself if you're going to recommend them to investors. Again, FINRA says it perfectly clearly when they write:

While the customer-specific suitability analysis depends on the investor's particular circumstances, inverse and leveraged ETFs typically are not suitable for retail investors who plan to hold them for more than one trading session, particularly in volatile markets.

The main testable points concerning ETFs would seem to be:

- Organized as Unit Investment Trusts (UITs)
- Trade like shares of stock, intra-day
- Investors pay a commission rather than a sales charge
- Shares can be bought on margin, sold short
- ETFs have low expense ratios
- ETFs are convenient for investors seeking diversification/asset allocation
- ETFs are very low cost when purchased in larger quantities
- Indexes include small cap, mid-cap, large cap, growth, value, S&P 500, Dow Jones, NASDAQ, even fixed-income
- Offer certain tax advantages

REITS

Investing in real estate has many advantages and disadvantages. The advantages are that property values often appreciate over time and that real estate provides nice diversification to a securities portfolio, since usually real estate and the stock market are not correlated. The disadvantages include the fact that real estate costs a lot of money, and it isn't liquid. It often takes months or even years to get a house sold, or sold for a decent price, so the lack of **liquidity** keeps many investors from buying real estate, especially commercial real estate (shopping malls, skyscrapers, factories, etc.).

Which is where **REITs** come in. **A Real Estate Investment Trust** (REIT) is a company that owns a portfolio of properties and sells shares to investors. You could buy into REITs that own apartment buildings, office buildings, shopping centers, hotels, convention centers, self-storage units, timber—you name it. This way you can participate in real estate without having to be rich, and you can sell your shares as easily as you can sell shares of other publicly traded stock. REITs, then, are just equity securities that give the investor an ownership stake in a trust that owns real estate. They do not pass through losses (only real estate *partnerships* do that), they pay out high dividend yields provided the company makes a profit, but the dividend is taxed at your ordinary income rate, not the kinder, gentler rate on **qualified dividends**.

The type of REIT I just described is called an **equity REIT**. The exam could also mention a different type of REIT that provides financing for real estate projects as opposed to just buying up and managing properties. These are called **mortgage REITs** and they provide financing as well as buy up mortgages and mortgage-backed securities. Some REITs do a little of both, and are called, fittingly, **Hybrid REITs.**

Not all REITS are publicly traded. If an investor buys a privately-held REIT, he has made an investment like he DPPs or limited partnership interests we will look at later in this chapter.

ALTERNATIVE INVESTMENTS

Liquidity is the ability to cash in an investment without taking a big loss just to turn it into cash. Stocks that trade on national exchanges are usually easy to liquidate at a moment's notice and at a fair price. Then again, stocks trading on national exchanges are usually in companies that have already experienced quite a bit of growth. What if you wanted to get in on the ground floor and invest in less-developed companies that could become the next Facebook or Twitter? To do that, investors with an appetite for risk coupled with a low need or liquidity seek **alternative investments** such as direct participation programs and private equity funds.

➢   Direct Participation Programs (Limited Partnerships)

The basic characteristic of a **Direct Participation Program (DPP)** is that rather than paying taxes as a business, the owners of the business all take a share of the income or net loss on their own personal income taxes. The owners who provide most of the money to the business are the **limited partners**, meaning their liability is limited to their investment. If they put up $100,000, then $100,000 is all they could ever lose as passive investors in the partnership. To maintain their limited liability status (which means they can't be sued for personal assets) they have to stay out of day-to-day management of the business. Day-to-day management is up to the **general partner**. The general partner either runs the show himself or appoints someone to do it. Either way, it's his responsibility to get the thing managed. If he's the manager, he can also be compensated for his efforts through a salary. While the LPs provide most of the capital, the GP (general partner) must have at least a 1% financial interest in the partnership. The GP can enter into legally binding contracts on behalf of the partnership and has the authority to buy and sell property. The general partner has unlimited liability. His fiduciary responsibility to the limited partners means he cannot:

- compete with the partnership
- borrow money from the partnership
- sell property to the partnership
- commingle personal assets with partnership assets

The GP can't compete with the partnership through some other business venture and also can't charge some bogus "no compete" payment, since they can't compete anyway. Also, while the GP can't borrow money from the partnership, he/they could provide a loan to the partnership at prevailing interest rates.

Limited partners definitely stay out of day-to-day management decisions, but because of **partnership democracy** they do get to vote on the big issues like suing the GP for fraud or negligence, or dissolving the partnership. Why would they sue the GP? Maybe the oil & gas program turns out to be a big scam in which the guy is using partners' money to fund a gambling habit or a high-rolling lifestyle. Maybe the GP misleads the LPs about the problems and risks of the partnership, causing them to lose money—if they're American limited partners, trust me, they'll find a reason to sue. This is why the GP usually forms a corporation or an LLC to protect his personal assets. As we discuss elsewhere, those structures separate the individual human being from the corporate or LLC structure.

Through partnership democracy, the LPs also get regular financial reports, what the exam could refer to as "the right to copy certain partnership records." So, if you're talking about deciding which assets should be sold, the LPs don't get to decide that. If you're talking about changing the partnership from a baseball team to a soccer team, now the LPs get to vote. Similarly, common stockholders don't get to decide on every day-to-day issue that pops up at corporate headquarters, but if the corporation wants to change business objectives or buy another company, the stockholders get to vote. If the exam asks if LPs can make loans to the partnership, the answer is yes. In other words, some of the capital LPs provide to the partnership can be through debt securities paying a reasonable rate of interest. If you're in business for yourself, you may have fronted some cash to your business and then had the business pay you a rate of interest on the "promissory note." Same idea here.

Suitability

These partnerships or DPPs must have economic viability. They can't just be money-losing schemes devised by wealthy folks to do nothing but provide net losses and tax shelter. If the IRS suspects the thing never had a chance to make money, they can deem it an abusive tax shelter and go after everyone connected to the program with the full force of the IRS: audits, penalties, interest, seizure of assets, etc.

So, economic viability is the first consideration for a potential investor—only recommend a DPP investment if the program has a chance of making money someday. The second consideration would be tax benefits. If investors have a lot of **passive income**, they can use **passive losses** from DPPs to offset them for tax purposes. On the other hand, if they *don't* have any passive income to offset, don't recommend a program based on the tax shelter it provides, since they would not be able to benefit from that feature.

The last thing the investor apparently needs is liquidity because, basically, there isn't any. You buy an interest in a limited partnership—it's yours. Don't think you're going to be calling your broker a few weeks later to sell—there is no secondary market for these securities. You buy in as a limited partner and you become a direct participant in the business. A passive participant, but you are directly participating in the gains and losses. That's why they call them direct participation programs. You don't *actively* participate in the business, which is why you receive passive—not earned—income. But you *directly* participate in the business's net income or net loss.

Purpose of the Program

So what do these partnerships do? For test purposes, they seem to be either in the oil and natural gas business or real estate. The exam wants you to know which programs are the riskiest and which are the safest. Well, if you're talking about oil, which is riskier: drilling for oil, or selling oil that's already coming out of the ground? Obviously, drilling for oil is riskier, since most folks who drill for oil never actually find any. **Exploratory programs** for oil and gas are the riskiest programs and, therefore, carry the highest return potential.

Sometimes folks drill for oil in an area where oil has already been found. It's still risky, but a lot less risky than exploratory programs. They call these **developmental programs** because the investors plan to develop an area that geological engineers are convinced has oil and gas underground. They're less risky than exploratory with a lower return potential.

The safest program just buys existing production. They call these **income programs**. They have immediate cash flow and are, therefore, the safest programs with the lowest potential reward.

In real estate, which is riskier, buying raw land or buying an apartment complex already filled with renters? The first option provides no income and is also much riskier. **Raw land** is purely speculative and is, therefore, the riskiest type of real estate DPP. You buy a chunk of land betting that an airport will be built nearby in the next five years. If you're right, the land skyrockets in value. If you're not, it doesn't. And, you receive no income or tax benefits on raw land as you sit waiting for its value to go up.

New construction programs are aggressive programs, but once the projects are completed the townhouses or condominiums can be sold for large capital gains. So they're a little safer than raw land and probably provide a lower reward potential.

Existing properties is sort of like the income program for oil. The business is already flowing; let's buy in. Immediate cash flow. We can examine the financials and know what we're getting into here. Lower risk, lower reward.

Tax credits are the benefit for **government-assisted housing** programs. That means that if the partnership builds, acquires, or rehabs a government-assisted housing project, it will benefit from tax credits, and possibly from subsidy payments from the federal government. Remember that a tax credit is always better than a tax deduction. Just to make sure, let's compare a $100,000 tax deduction to a $100,000 tax credit:

DEDUCTION	CREDIT
$1,000,000 Income	$1,000,000 Income
– $100,000 Deduction	x .30 30% tax rate
$900,000 Net Income	$300,000 Tax
x .30 30% tax rate	– $100,000 CREDIT
$270,000 Tax Owed	$200,000 Tax Owed

Notice how a deduction is subtracted from the top line—revenue. For a credit, you figure the amount of tax you were going to have to pay, and then apply the credit dollar-for-dollar against that amount.

Another common type of limited partnership is the **equipment leasing program.** These partnerships typically lease equipment that other companies do not want to actually own. For example, computers, transportation equipment, construction equipment, etc., might not be cost-effective for the users to own; therefore, it makes more sense to simply lease such equipment from an equipment leasing program.

There are definitely risks involved when investing in limited partnerships. First, the venture might go belly up. Second, the IRS might determine that the partnership is really just an abusive tax shelter, set up to generate deductions without ever intending to be economically viable. A DPP may be considered abusive if it's based on a false assumption or if the partnership overstated property values in order to take large depreciation deductions. If that happens, the IRS can suddenly disallow deductions that the partners previously claimed, causing investors to pay back taxes *plus* interest and penalties on the back taxes. If a registered representative recommended the investment, he sure hopes it can be deemed a suitable recommendation at that point. If not, there are always disciplinary complaints and arbitration claims that the customer could file against him, both of which would end up in the BrokerCheck system at www.finra.org if things turn out bad for the broker.

The general partner is also known as the **sponsor** of the program. In some cases, the sponsor will do a private placement in which he sells to investors directly. In other cases, the sponsor will hire an underwriting firm to line up investors. If your investor wants to buy into a DPP, he fills out the **subscription agreement** and attaches his check. By signing the agreement, your customer (the LP) attests to his net worth and indicates that he understands all the risks involved. Only when the General Partner (GP) signs the agreement does he become a limited partner (LP). When selling the partnership interests, the syndicator/sponsor can take a "syndication fee" of 10%. So, for a $100,000 partnership interest, a syndication fee of $10,000 could be taken.

Most of these interests are sold through private placements. As we'll see in the chapter on issuing securities, private placements are generally sold only to accredited investors, so the LPs will disclose their income and net worth on the subscription agreement, or at least attest to the fact that they meet the requirements. Some interests are sold through public offerings. Either way, investors get disclosure of the risks involved, as they do for any new investment that is not specifically excused from the registration requirements of the Securities Act of 1933. If the partnership assets are disclosed, we call it a **specified program**. If the assets are not disclosed, we call it a **blind pool offering**. Maybe the partnership is going to wildcat/speculate on some oil patches—they don't necessarily want anyone else to know where they think the oil is located. Or, if it's raw land, maybe they don't want others to know which area they think is the next hot market. If so, the limited partnership interests may be offered through a blind pool offering. Can you imagine a riskier investment than turning your money over to a sponsor who isn't even telling you where the assets of the partnership are located or what they are? Me neither.

FINRA now requires firms offering DPPs (and unlisted/non-traded REITs) to provide some specific disclosure about liquidity. If the GP running the program that's being offered has done, say, 10 previous partnership deals, in how many of them were people *actually* able to sell their interests if they wanted to by the target date laid out in the offering document? Two times? Three times? FINRA isn't saying that meeting the target date for investors to liquidate/sell is always imperative, but they're saying investors should have an idea of how liquid their investment might *actually* be. A member firm may be receiving these liquidity stats from the sponsor of the program, and FINRA says they can just rely on his numbers unless they have reason to believe he's fudging.

No, they don't actually use the word *fudging*.

Sharing arrangements will also be laid out in the offering document, so the LP knows how he and the GP will share expenses and income. Let's do a quick bullet list here:

- overriding royalty interest: this would give the sponsor no responsibility for costs, only a share of the royalty stream when oil/gas is sold
- functional allocation: General Partner bears the capitalized costs (oil rig, other equipment) while LPs bear the deductible expenses (intangible drilling costs like labor and geological surveys)
- reversionary working interest: LPs bear all the costs and the GP doesn't get a share of income until all of those costs have been recovered
- disproportionate working interest: the GP receives a disproportionate share of income and bears very little of the costs

The GP has already filed the **certificate of limited partnership** with the state. This is a public document that provides the following information:

- Name and address of partnership
- Description of the partnership's business
- Life span of the partnership
- Conditions for assignment/transfer of limited partnership interests to others
- Conditions for dissolving the partnership
- Conditions for admitting new partners
- Projected date for return of capital (if one is determined)

The **partnership agreement** is signed by all partners and is the foundation for the partnership. In this agreement we would find the following information:

- business purpose of the partnership
- terms and conditions—e.g., required capital commitments now and in future
- powers and limitations of the GP's authority

This document binds the partnership and authorizes the GP to run the business. It's a private document, for partners' eyes only. If the partnership is liquidated, either because it went belly-up or because it's time to pull the plug, interested parties would be paid off in the following order:

1. Secured creditors
2. Other creditors
3. Limited partners
4. General partners

Notice that the General Partner has unlimited liability, a fiduciary responsibility to the limited partners, and is also the last one to get paid should the whole thing go belly up?

Oh well. That's the nature of being the GP. Lotta risk, lotta reward.

Cash Flow and Income

Since we're running numbers, make sure you know the difference between the Cash Flow statement and the **Income Statement**.

Let's say a limited partner in a real estate partnership takes the following share of income and expenses from operations:

Rental income:	$50,000
Operating expenses:	$20,000
Interest expense:	$25,000
Depreciation:	$20,000

So, the Income Statement (P & L) looks like this:

$50,000	Income
-20,000	Expenses
-25,000	Interest
-20,000	Depreciation
-$15,000	Income

The limited partner, assuming he had sufficient passive income to offset, could deduct $15,000 for purposes of tax relief.

But, if we're talking about "cash flow" we add back that non-cash subtraction called "depreciation." Why? Well, depreciation is not an actual outlay of cash. If you buy a printing press for $1 million and it has a useful life of 10 years, you would subtract 1/10 of its value or $100,000 each year on your income statement. Since you're not actually paying out $100,000 in cash each year, you would add that back when figuring "cash flow," just to keep things nice and simple.

So, if we add back the "depreciation" of $20,000, we'd see a positive cash flow of $5,000. In case the exam gets really nasty the day you take it, tell it that we figure cash flow by adding back depreciation.

With that loss of (–$15,000) from his share of the income and expenses, the investor can offset other passive income that he might have from other partnerships or from owning rental properties. Only *passive* income, though—not portfolio or earned income. The test might point out that real estate investment trusts (REITs), another type of "pooled investment vehicle," do *not* pass through losses. But, remember, real estate limited partnerships do pass through losses to the partners, which is what the partners are often hoping for, especially in the early years. At some point, though, income from the partnership will start to exceed the fancy little deductions we've been discussing. This is known as the **crossover point**, should the exam decide to go there.

Let's make sure you understand depreciation/depletion. These are just accounting entries that allow partnerships to write down the cost of equipment and other assets over time. If a chair costs the business $100 and has a useful life of 10 years, they'll write down $10 of its cost each year for 10 years. If the partnership leases equipment, they'll depreciate the cost of that equipment a little bit every year. If they have to buy an oil rig, same thing. Depletion is for natural resources only. As you take oil out of the ground and sell it, you get to take a "depletion allowance" for every barrel of oil sold. It's just a method of cost recovery. If you can remember that depreciation is for equipment and depletion is only for natural resources, you'll probably be good to go. Also, raw land is not depreciated. Raw land should do the opposite—appreciate, right? If not, raw land does absolutely nothing for the owner. There is no tax shelter provided while sitting on raw land.

The exam might bring up **depreciation recapture**. When an asset that has been used for depreciation expenses is then sold, the IRS typically recaptures some of the benefit through a tax called, yes, "depreciation recapture." So, while the depreciation of an apartment building provided tax shelter to the partners in the past, now some of that benefit is recaptured when the asset is sold for a gain.

Recourse Debt

If a limited partner signs a "recourse note," that means that the creditors/lenders have recourse to go after his personal assets if the partnership defaults and the collateral is insufficient to cover the balance owed. If the LP buys a limited partnership interest for $100,000 and signs a recourse note for which he is responsible for $50,000, his cost basis in the investment is now $150,000, since that is the amount he can lose.

Of course, if it's a non-recourse note, then the creditors have no recourse to go after the individual investors if the collateral is insufficient to cover their losses on the loan. So, recourse debt adds to cost basis, while non-recourse debt does not.

PROGRAM	RISK/REWARD	TAX BENEFITS	OBJECTIVE
Raw Land	High	None	Capital Appreciation
Oil Exploration	High	Depreciation	Capital Appreciation, Tax Shelter
New Construction	Moderate-High	Tax Shelter initially	Capital Appreciation, Tax Shelter
Oil-Developmental	Moderate-High	Depreciation	Capital Appreciation, Tax Shelter
Existing Real Estate	Moderate	Depreciation	Income, Tax Shelter
Oil Production/Income	Moderate	Depletion, Depreciation	Income, Tax Shelter

Direct participation programs also get involved with agricultural programs, cattle programs, and sports teams—to name just a few. I happen to have tutored someone who is good friends with a limited partner in the Chicago White Sox. I'm not an attorney or an accountant, but I'm reasonably certain that an LP interest in the White Sox is all about a share of the INCOME and not the tax benefits. I know for sure that if you invest in a hedge fund—also structured as a limited partnership—you are only looking for capital appreciation. Most entities that want flow-through of income/loss to the owners and protection for personal assets set up LLCs (limited liability companies) these days, but that doesn't mean that limited partnerships have gone away. Not by a long shot. Many of their former tax benefits were taken away a while back, but they still provide tax shelter in many cases and often provide huge capital gains (or losses) to the limited partners. Also a "DPP" does not have to be formed as a limited partnership. Here is how FINRA defines the term "direct participation program":

…a program which provides for flow-through tax consequences regardless of the structure of the legal entity or vehicle for distribution including, but not limited to, oil and gas programs, real estate programs, agricultural programs, cattle programs, condominium securities, Subchapter S corporate offerings and all other programs of a similar nature, regardless of the industry represented by the program, or any combination thereof.

> Hedge Funds

In general, hedge funds are only open to institutions and to individuals called "accredited investors." We'll look at these **accredited investors** when we discuss Reg D private placements under the Securities Act of 1933. There, too, the well-moneyed accredited investor can do things the average Joe and JoAnne cannot, but we'll save that for another section. An accredited investor has over $1 million in net worth outside his primary residence or makes > $200,000 per year. If it's a married couple, the assets held jointly count toward that $1 million figure, or the annual income needs to be > $300,000, just to make sure you have even more numbers to learn for your exam.

Why does the investor need to be rich? Because these hedge funds use some very high-risk strategies including short selling, currency bets, risky options plays, etc. If you're an average Joe and JoAnne, it wouldn't be cool to let you risk all of your investment capital on such high-risk investing. On the other hand, if you're a rich individual or a big institution, chances are your hedge fund investment is just a percentage of the capital you invest. So, if you lose $1 million, chances are you have several more million where that came from.

A typical arrangement for a hedge fund is to have a limited number of investors form a private investment partnership. The fund typically charges 2% of assets as a management fee and extracts the first 20% of all capital gains. Then, they start thinking about their investors (we hope). Once you buy, there's a good chance you will not be able to sell your investment for at least one year, even if it sucks. Rather than trying to beat an index such as the DJIA, hedge funds generally go for "absolute positive investment performance"—usually 8% or so—regardless of what the overall market is doing.

Now, just to keep everything nice and simple, although a **non-accredited purchaser** cannot invest directly in a hedge fund, there are mutual funds called "funds of hedge funds," which she can invest in. As the name implies, these mutual funds would have investments in several different hedge funds. In most cases, the investor would not be able to redeem her investment, since hedge funds are illiquid (they don't trade among investors). Also, these investments would involve high expenses, since there would be the usual expenses of the mutual fund, on top of the high expenses of the hedge funds the mutual fund invests in.

So, other than the fact that they're really expensive, very risky, and make it really tough for the investor to liquidate her position, they're a great investment. The main testable points on hedge funds would seem to be:

- Open to sophisticated, accredited investors with high net worth
- Illiquid—usually can't be sold for at least one year
- Employ riskier, more diverse strategies
- Charge high management fees and usually 20% of all gains
- Non-accredited investors can buy mutual funds that invest in hedge funds

> Private Equity Funds

Similar to a hedge fund, a **private equity fund** is structured as a limited partnership and is open only to sophisticated investors, as it is not liquid and generally takes on much greater risk than an open- or closed-end mutual fund. As the name implies, private equity groups invest in securities that are not publicly traded. They will often approach a public company and cut a deal to buy all the common stock plus maybe a premium, taking the company private. After they appoint some better managers and board members, improve the profits at the acquired company, and get some good media buzz, maybe they then approach investment bankers to do another IPO so the owners can cash in as investors clamor for the stock. Private equity funds are typically set up for a period of time, maybe 10 years. After that, investors receive their money back from the general partner who set up the fund, plus—we hope—a profit.

INSURANCE-BASED PRODUCTS

FEATURES OF ANNUITIES

An **annuity** is an investment sold by an insurance company that either promises a minimum rate of return to the investor or allows the investor to allocate payments to various mutual fund-type accounts that invest in the stock and bond markets. These products offer regular payments for the rest of the annuitant's life, but owners of annuities can instead take money out as lump sums or random withdrawals on the back end. Annuities are part of the retirement plans of many individuals, and they can either be part of the "safe-money" piece or can provide plenty of exposure to the stock and bond markets.

The three main types of annuities are fixed, indexed, and variable. That's actually only two types, since an **indexed annuity** *is* a **fixed annuity**, but it has many features that make it completely different from a plain-old fixed annuity. A fixed annuity promises a minimum rate of return to the investor in exchange for one big payment into the contract or several periodic payments. The **purchase payments** are allocated to the insurance company's own **general account,** so the rate of return is "guaranteed." But, that just means it's backed by the claims-paying ability of the insurance company's general account. Before turning over your hard-earned money to an insurance company, expecting them to pay it back to you slowly, you should check their **AM Best** rating and their history of paying claims.

A fixed annuity would be suitable for someone who wants a "safe money" investment that is more dependable than anything in the stock or bond markets, something that promises to make dependable payments for the rest of his life, no matter how long he ends up living. The fixed annuity offers peace of mind if not a high rate of return. What does the investor want—peace of mind or high rate of return? Sorry, this is an either-or thing.

An interesting type of fixed annuity is the **equity-indexed annuity**. With this product, the investor receives a guaranteed minimum rate of return. But, he/she receives a higher rate of return when an index—usually the S&P 500—has a good year. Do they receive the full upside, as if they owned an S&P 500 index fund? No, and that should be made clear by the sales representative. Equity indexed annuities have a **participation rate**. A participation rate of 70% means that the contract only gets credited with 70% of the increase in the S&P 500. If the index goes up 10%, the contract makes only 7%. Except when it doesn't. The contracts also have a cap placed on the maximum increase for any year, regardless of what the stock market does. So with a participation rate of 70% and a cap of 6%, what happens if the S&P goes up 30%? Well, 70% of that would be 21%; however, if you're capped at 6%, then 6% is all the contract value will rise that year. As you can see, indexed annuities are really all about the downside protection, which is why a securities license is not required to sell fixed annuities, equity-indexed or otherwise.

If the individual buys a **deferred annuity**—whether the return is fixed or variable—that means his money is tied up, for maybe 10 years. During this **surrender period** he would lose money to the annuity company if he took his money back out. In other words, this is not for investors who have high liquidity needs. Rather, as with direct participation programs and other alternative investments, it's for the money they don't plan to touch any time soon. Not only is there a **surrender charge** on a deferred annuity, but the investor will have tax problems if he is under age 59½. So, the following should be disclosed to the investor buying any deferred annuity:

- Surrender periods cause investors who sell early to pay surrender penalties
- Early withdrawals subject to 10% penalty tax
- And if he's buying an indexed annuity, also disclose that:
- There is a participation rate placed on how much upside the investor earns when the stock market index rises
- There is often a cap on how much the account value can increase annually

A fixed annuity (including the indexed annuity) is an insurance contract where somebody puts money into the contract, and the insurance company promises to pay the money back, plus a certain rate of return and keep making monthly payments for as long as the annuitant is alive. A **variable annuity** doesn't promise a particular rate of return, which is where they get the "variable" part. Since investors are investing in little mutual fund–type accounts of their choosing, maybe they'll end up doing much better than the modest rate that the fixed annuity guarantees. In other words, in a variable annuity, the annuitant bears the investment risk rather than having the insurance company promise a certain rate of return. In exchange for bearing the risks we've looked at in the stock and bond markets, the variable annuitant gets the opportunity to do much better than he would have in a fixed annuity.

Could he do worse? Sure, but what does he want? If he wants a guarantee, he buys a fixed annuity where the insurance company guarantees a certain rate of return. Now he lives with "purchasing power risk," because if the annuity promises 2%, that's not going to be sufficient with inflation rising at 4%. If he wants to protect his purchasing power by investing in the stock market, he buys a variable annuity, but now he takes on all the investment risks we've discussed.

Variable annuities use mutual fund accounts as their investment options, but we don't call variable annuities "mutual funds." We call the investment options that would otherwise be called "mutual funds **"subaccounts."** Salespeople must go out of their way to avoid confusing customers into thinking an annuity *is* a mutual fund. It is not a mutual fund. Mutual funds aren't subject to early withdrawal penalties from the issuer or the IRS. Mutual funds don't offer a death benefit or add expenses to cover it. On the other hand, mutual funds are not tax-deferred accounts. A mutual fund held in a regular old taxable account will subject investors to taxation every year. The dividend and capital gains distributions are taxable, and if the investor redeems some shares for a gain, that's also taxable for the year it occurs. This tax burden reduces the principal in the account each year, which is a major drag on long-term returns. A variable annuity, however, is really a retirement plan where you get to keep all the dividends and capital gains in the account, adding to your principal, and compounding your returns forever and ever and ever.

Whoa, sorry. Not forever. You get to defer taxation until you take the money out, which is usually at retirement. Your money grows much faster when it's not being taxed for 10, 20, maybe 30 years, but every dance reaches the point where you have to pay the fiddler. It's been a fun dance, for sure, but the reality is that you will pay ordinary income tax rates on the earnings you've been shielding from the hungry hands of the IRS all these years—if and when you decide to get your own hands on the money. Ordinary income rates, remember. If you're in the 35% tax bracket, the gains coming out of your variable annuity are taxed at that rate. So, tax deferral is a big advantage, and there are other advantages to the complex packaged product known as an "annuity." I'm looking at a handy brochure that compares mutual funds and variable annuities. The company, which sells both, is pointing out that no matter how diligently you save for retirement, you could end up outliving your nest egg.

Unless you buy an annuity, that is. An annuity comes with a **mortality guarantee**, which means that once you go into the pay-out phase, you will receive monthly payments as long as you are alive (a mortal). Of course, the fixed annuity tells you what the check will be worth at a minimum, while the variable annuity—well, it varies, people. In the variable annuity, the annuitant will get a check each month, but it could be mighty meager if the markets aren't doing particularly well.

A fixed annuity is really just an insurance product providing peace of mind and tax deferral. A variable annuity functions like a mutual fund investment that grows tax-deferred, and offers some peace of mind. See, whether it's fixed or variable, the insurance company offers a **death benefit** that promises to pay a beneficiary at least the amount of money invested by the annuitant during his or her life—period.

Insurance companies sell peace of mind. Both the mortality guarantee and the death benefit—even on *variable* annuities—help a lot of investors sleep better. Pretty tough to put a price tag on that. For maximum peace of mind, individuals should buy a fixed or indexed annuity. For some peace of mind and the chance to invest in the stock and bond markets, individuals should consider a variable annuity. A variable annuity offers the investment choices that you'd get from a family of mutual funds (growth, value, high-yield bonds, etc.), the tax deferral you'd get from an IRA or 401(k) plan, plus a death benefit similar to what you'd get from a life insurance policy. A fixed annuity—or indexed annuity—offers the tax deferral, the death benefit, and a dependable stream of minimum payments, even if you live to 115.

Interestingly, in a life insurance policy, the mortality risk to the insurance company is that somebody will put in $10,000 and die the next year, forcing the company to pay out hundreds of thousands, maybe a million. In an annuity, their mortality risk is that the annuitant will end up living to 115. The insurance company makes a mortality guarantee, which promises to pay the annuitant each month for the rest of her life. But, they cover their risk with a fee, called a mortality risk fee. An insurance company has the risk that their expenses will rise. They promise to keep expenses level, but they charge an expense risk fee to cover their risk. In fact, usually the two are combined and referred to as a "mortality and expense risk fee," or "M & E" for those in the real world who love to abbreviate. Variable annuities use mutual fund–type accounts as investment vehicles, but they add charges in excess of what those mutual funds charge investors—all the guarantees offered in the annuity contract can easily add an extra 1% to annual expenses, which can really add up over 20 or 30 years.

While holding a deferred annuity, the individual can **surrender** the contract for its "surrender value." But, watch out here. The first several years typically comprise your **surrender period**. During that time if you decide to cash in the annuity, you will get hit with a **surrender charge**, which is often called a "contingent deferred sales charge" just as we discuss elsewhere in connection with mutual fund B-shares. Yes, many annuities allow people to withdraw 10% of the contract value per year, but anything beyond that is subject to some nasty surrender charges. These surrender charges start out pretty high—say 8% or higher—which is one reason that deferred annuities are long-term investments. Don't be pitching a deferred annuity to a senior citizen, who might need to access a big chunk of her money for an emergency. You need to be pretty sure the individual can leave the money alone for at least as long as the surrender period.

When the individual purchases the annuity, the following are deducted from the check:

- Sales charge (if they have a front-end load)
- Administrative fee

- State premium tax

Most annuities use the contingent deferred sales charge called the "surrender period," but some are still sold with front-end sales charges. Either way, there is a premium tax and administrative fees taken out of the check.

In a variable annuity the individual then allocates what's left of his **purchase payment** to the various subaccounts, the little mutual fund portfolios. Maybe 20% goes into the conservative income subaccount, 20% into the growth subaccount and 60% to the high-yield long-term bond subaccount. From the money invested there are plenty of fees that will be deducted. We have all the operating expenses we saw for mutual funds: management fee, 12b-1 fee, other expenses. And, we also have the "mortality and expense risk fee" charged for the annuity features.

What is the maximum that an insurance company can charge for sales charges and expenses? The current regulations just say that the charges and expenses have to be "reasonable."

Seriously.

With a bonus annuity the annuity company may offer to enhance the buyer's premium by contributing an additional 1 to 5% of what he/she puts in. Of course, this comes with a price. First, there are fees attached and, second, the surrender period is longer. Third, if the investor surrenders the contract early, the bonus disappears. Remember that an investor will get penalized by the annuity company with a "surrender charge" if they pull all their money out early. For "bonus annuities" that period where the investor could get penalized is longer.

Bonus annuities are not suitable for everyone. Variable annuities in general are not good for short-term investment goals, since the surrender charge will be applied during the first 7 years or so. Should you switch a customer into a bonus annuity? Maybe. But, remember, even though the annuitant can avoid taxes through a 1035 exchange, when she exchanges the annuity, her surrender period starts all over again. And, yes, the securities regulators will bust you if it looks like you did the switch just to make a nice commission, forcing the investor to start the surrender period all over again. In general, investors should maximize their 401(k) and other retirement plans before considering annuities. Annuities are ideal for those who have maxed out those plans, since the annuity allows investors to contribute as much as they would like.

BUYING ANNUITIES

The categories of fixed, indexed, and variable annuities refer to the way payments will be calculated on the way out. In terms of buying annuities, the two major types are "immediate" and "deferred." These terms refer to how soon the contract holder wants to begin receiving payments—now, or later? These are retirement plans, remember, so you do need to be 59½ to avoid penalties. Therefore, some customers might want or need to wait 20 or 30 years before receiving payments. If so, they purchase a **deferred annuity**, because "deferred" means "I'll do it later," the way some readers may have "deferred" their study process a few weeks—or months—before buckling down.

The tax deferral is nice, but if the individual is already, say, 68, she may want to retire now and start receiving payments immediately. As you can probably guess, we call that an **immediate annuity**. While there are immediate *variable* annuities, it just makes more sense somehow to buy the fixed *immediate* annuity. Why? Well, the whole point of buying an immediate annuity is to know that—no matter what happens to social security and your 401(k) account—there is a solid insurance company contractually obligated to make a payment of at least X amount for as long as you live. An immediate *variable* annuity would work out well only if the investments did—while there would be some minimal payment guaranteed, it would be meager. An immediate fixed annuity does not offer a high rate of return, but it does provide peace of mind to investors in retirement. Many financial planners would suggest that at least some of their clients' retirement money be sitting in a fixed immediate annuity—maybe just enough to provide a monthly payment covering all monthly expenses. Figuring withdrawal rates from retirement accounts is very tricky, so having a payment of X amount from a solid insurance company could really smooth out the bumps.

Customers can buy annuities either with one big payment or several smaller payments. The first method is called "single premium" or "single payment." The second method is called "periodic payment." If an investor has a large chunk of money, she can put it in an annuity, where it can grow tax-deferred. If she's putting in a big single premium, she can choose either to wait (defer) or to begin receiving annuity payments immediately. She has to be 59½ years old to annuitize, but if she's old enough, she can begin the pay-out phase immediately. That's called a **single-payment immediate annuity**. Maybe she's only 42, though, and wants to let the money grow another 20 years before taking it out. That's called a **single-payment deferred annuity** (SPDA).

Many investors put money into the annuity during the accumulation phase (pay-in) gradually, over time. That's called "periodic payment," and if they aren't done paying in yet, you can bet the insurance company isn't going to start paying out. So, if you're talking about a "periodic payment" plan, the only way to do it is through a **periodic *deferred* annuity**. There is no such thing as a "Periodic Immediate Annuity" since no insurance company I'm aware of would let me start sending in $100 a month while they go ahead and start sending me $110.

To review, then, there are three methods of purchasing annuities:

- Single-Payment Deferred Annuity
- Periodic-Payment Deferred Annuity
- Single-Payment Immediate Annuity

Again, understand that variable annuities use mutual funds (called subaccounts) as the investment vehicles in the plan. But, annuities add both features and extra expenses for the investor on top of all the investment-related expenses. Tax deferral is nice. So are the death benefit and the annuity payment that goes on as long as the individual lives. But, that stuff also adds maybe 1.0–1.5% per year in expenses to the investor. You can either slide that fact past your investor or fully disclose it. Depends on whether you want your name up on FINRA's website or not.

RECEIVING PAYMENTS (SETTLEMENT OPTIONS)

So, some investors make periodic payments into the contract while others make just one big payment. Either way, when the individual gets ready to annuitize the contract, he tells the insurance company which payout option he's choosing. And, he is not able to change this decision—he makes the decision and lives with it. Or, maybe more accurately, dies with it. Essentially, what's going on at this point in the contract is that the individual is about to make a bet with the insurance company as to how long he will end up living.

Seriously. And, as in Las Vegas, the house has a major advantage here. The actuaries can estimate how long any individual is likely to live plus or minus X number of years. They can then calculate a rate of payout on the fixed and indexed annuities that all but guarantees the insurance company will come out way ahead—ever visited the Allstate or State Farm campuses? Larger than most universities. Anyway, in case we haven't made this clear, even though the fixed annuity promises a certain minimum payment for the rest of your life, if you die in a couple years, they keep the balance of your account.

Seriously. Same thing for a variable annuity, but it's probably not as surprising on the variable side. But, either way, if the individual throws the switch to receive payments and chooses **life only** or **straight life** he'll typically receive the largest monthly payout. Why? Because the insurance company sets those payments and the insurance company knows better than he does when he's going to die. Not the exact day or the exact method, of course, but they can estimate it with amazing precision. Since the insurance/annuity company only has to make payments for as long as he lives, the payments are typically the largest for a "life only" or "straight life" annuity settlement option. How does the individual win the "bet"? By living a lot longer than the actuarial tables would predict. Not a bad motivation for exercising and eating right, huh? If this option seems too risky, the individual can choose a "unit refund life annuity." This way he is guaranteed a certain number of payments even if he does get hit by the proverbial bus. If he dies before receiving them, his beneficiary receives the balance of payments.

So, does the annuitant have family or a charity she wants to be sure receives the balance of her payments? If not, why not go with the life only/straight life option—tell the insurance company to pay her as much as possible for as long as she lives. If she dies—well, what does she care if State Farm or Northwestern Mutual comes out ahead? If she does have family, friends, or a charity that she'd like to name as a beneficiary, she can choose a **period certain** settlement option. In that case, the insurance company has to do what the name implies—make payments for a certain period of time. To either her or the named beneficiaries. For older investors, this option typically leads to a lower monthly payment, since the insurance company will now be on the hook for several years even if the annuitant conveniently expires early. If it's a 20-year period certain payout, the payments have to be made to the beneficiary for the rest of that period, even if the annuitant dies after the first month or two. The annuitant could also choose **life with period certain**, and now we'd have a complicated either-or scenario with the insurance company. With this option the company will make payments for the greater of his life *or* a certain period of time, such as 20 years. If he dies after 2 years, the company makes payments to his beneficiary for the rest of the term. And if he lives longer than 20 years, they just keep on making payments until he finally expires. Please read that sentence again, because it seems that no one ever believes me when I say that if the annuitant chooses a 20-year life-with-period-certain settlement option and inconveniently lives 23 years, the insurance company makes payments for 23 years. When he dies, no more payments.

Finally, the **joint with last survivor** option would typically provide the smallest monthly check because the company is obligated to make payments as long as either the annuitant or the survivors are still alive. The contract can be set up to pay the annuitant while he's alive and then pay the beneficiaries until the last beneficiary expires. Or, it can start paying the annuitant *and* the beneficiary until both have finally, you know. Covering two persons' mortality risks (the risk that they'll live an inconveniently long time) is an expensive proposition to the insurance company, so these monthly checks are typically smaller than either period certain or life-only settlement options.

> The Separate Account

Let's discuss the difference between guaranteed insurance products and variable products. An insurance company is one of the finest business models ever constructed. See, no one person can take the risk of dying at age 32 and leaving the family with an unpaid mortgage, a bunch of other bills, and a sudden loss of income, not to mention the maybe $15,000 it takes just for a funeral these days. But, an insurance company can take the risk that a certain number of individuals will die prematurely by insuring a huge number of individuals and then using the very precise laws of probability over large numbers that tell them how many individuals will die each year with only a small margin of error. Once they've taken the insurance premiums that individuals pay, they then invest what's left after covering expenses and invest it very wisely in the real estate, fixed-income, and stock markets. They have just as much data on these markets, so they can use the laws of probability again to figure out that if they take this much risk here, they can count on earning this much return over here within only a small margin of error.

And, of course, insurance companies are very conservative investors. That's what allows them to crunch a bunch of numbers and know with reasonable certainty that they will never have to pay so many death benefits in one year that their investments are totally wiped out. This conservative investment account that guarantees the payout on whole life, term life, and fixed annuities is called the **general account**. In other words, the general account is for the insurance company's investments.

They then created an account that is separate from the general account and, believe it or not, decided to name it the **separate account**. It's really a mutual fund family that offers tax deferral, but we don't call it a mutual fund, even though it's also covered by and registered under the same Investment Company Act of 1940. The Investment Company Act of 1940 defines a separate account like so:

"Separate account" means an account established and maintained by an insurance company pursuant to the laws of any State or territory of the United States, or of Canada or any province thereof, under which income, gains and losses, whether or not realized, from assets allocated to such account, are, in accordance with the applicable contract, credited to or charged against such account without regard to other income, gains, or losses of the insurance company.

When your purchase payments for a fixed annuity or whole life insurance policy are invested into the general account, you are guaranteed a certain rate of return. When your purchase payments are invested into the separate account for **variable annuities** and **variable life insurance**, welcome to the stock and bond markets, where anything can happen.

From the perspective of the nice couple sitting across from you at the table, it all looks pretty much the same. You were talking about the Platinum Equity Income Fund a few minutes ago—now that you've switched to your variable annuity spiel, we're still seeing the same Platinum Equity Income Fund. What's up with that? It's the same darned fund, but if you buy it within a variable annuity contract, we call it a **subaccount**, just to keep everything nice and simple. Actually, there's a good reason to avoid calling subaccounts "mutual funds." If the investor thinks he's in a "mutual fund," he might think he can take out his money whenever he wants. He also might not realize that he's paying an extra 1.0–1.5% a year to place the annuity wrapper around the "mutual fund" investments. So, be careful with the language out there once you get licensed, people.

Accumulation and Annuity Units

There are only two phases of a variable annuity—the **accumulation period** and the **annuity period**. If insurance companies talked like actual humans, they would call it the "pay-in" and the "pay-out" phase. An individual making periodic payments into the contract, or one who made one big payment and is now just deferring the payout phase, is in the accumulation phase, holding **accumulation units**. When he throws the switch to start receiving payments, the insurance company will convert those accumulation units to **annuity units**. Remember that in a fixed annuity, the annuitant knows the minimum monthly payment he can expect. A variable annuity, on the other hand, will pay out the fluctuating value of those annuity units. And, although the value of annuity units fluctuates in a variable annuity during the payout phase, the *number* of those annuity units is fixed. To calculate the first payment for a variable annuity, the insurance company uses the following:

- Age of the annuitant
- Account value
- Gender
- Settlement option

Remember that health is not a factor—you don't receive money based on a health exam here. This is also why an annuity cannot suddenly be turned into a life insurance policy, even though it can definitely work in the other direction, as we'll discuss elsewhere.

> AIR and Annuity Units

As we said, once the number of annuity units has been determined, we say that the number of annuity units is fixed. So, for example, maybe every month he'll be paid the value of 100 annuity units.

Trouble is, he has no idea how big that monthly check is going to be, since nobody knows what 100 annuity units will be worth month-to-month, just like nobody knows what mutual fund shares will be worth month-to-month. Remember the "fixed-shares systematic withdrawal plan" from a mutual fund? We said that the fund will redeem a fixed number of shares and pay you whatever they happened to be worth. Again, the units really are mutual fund shares; we just can't call them that. During the pay-in phase, we call the shares **accumulation units**. During the pay-out phase, we call them **annuity units**, just to keep things nice and simple.

So, how much is an annuity unit worth every month? All depends on the investment performance of the separate account compared to the expectations of its performance.

Seriously.

AIR

If the separate account returns are better than the assumed rate, the units increase in value. If the account returns are exactly as expected, the unit value stays the same. And if the account returns are lower than expected, the unit value drops from the month before. It's all based on the **Assumed Interest Rate (AIR)** that the annuitant and annuity company agree to use. If the **AIR** is 5%, that just means the separate account investments are expected to grow each month at an annualized rate of 5%. If the account actually gets a 6% annualized rate of return one month, the individual's check gets bigger. (Remember, during the payout phase, the investor is paid the value of his fixed number of annuity units, so to say that the annuity units have increased in value is the same as saying the individual's check gets bigger.) If the account gets the anticipated 5% return next month, that's the same as AIR and the check will stay the same. And if the account gets only a 4% return the following month, the check will go down.

Don't let the exam trick you on this concept. If the AIR is 5%, here is how it would work:

Actual Return:	5%	7%	6%	5%	4%

Check: $1,020 $1,035 $1,045 $1,045 $1,030

When the account gets a 7% return, the account gets much bigger. So when it gets only a 6% return the following month, that's 6% of a bigger account, and is 1% more than we expected to get. So, just compare the actual return with the AIR. If the actual return is bigger, so is the monthly check. If it's smaller, so is the monthly check. If the actual return is the same as the AIR, the check stays the same.

LIFE INSURANCE

I've always felt that it would be awfully rude of me to die without insurance and leave family and friends footing the bill for my funeral. That's why I basically "rent" insurance coverage through something called **term life insurance**. It's very cheap, but it's only good for a certain term—maybe it's a 5-, 10-, or 20-year term. The individual pays premiums in exchange for a guaranteed **death benefit** payable to a **beneficiary** if **the insured** dies during that period. If the insured does not die during that period, the policy expires. If the **policyholder/policyowner** wants to renew, he can, but he's older now and more costly to insure. In other words, his premiums will go up, even though the death benefit will stay the same, because he's older and more likely to have some medical condition that raises his rates, too, or even that prevents him from being offered the insurance at all. So, as with all products, there are pluses and minuses. Term insurance is cheap and offers nice protection, but it does not build any cash value and has to be renewed at higher and higher rates, just like renting an apartment.

Now would be a good time to note the language used in insurance:

- **Policyholder**: the owner of the policy, responsible for paying premiums
- **Insured**: the person whose life is insured by the policy, usually the policyholder
- **Beneficiary**: the party that receives the death benefit upon death of the insured
- **Death benefit**: the amount payable to the beneficiary upon death of the insured, minus any unpaid premiums or loan balances
- **Cash value**: a value in the policy account that can be partially withdrawn or borrowed against

So, let's say that Joe Smith buys an insurance policy with a $100,000 death benefit payable to his wife. He's the policyholder and the insured. If he dies, the death benefit of $100,000 is paid to the beneficiary, his wife. As we'll see, most insurance also builds up cash value, which can be withdrawn or borrowed while Joe is still alive (note that term insurance does not build up this cash value, which is also why it's relatively inexpensive).

> Permanent vs. Temporary Insurance

As with housing, some people prefer to rent insurance for a term, and some prefer to buy it. Some feel that if you're going to be putting money aside, you might as well end up with something to show for it, so they purchase permanent insurance. The most common type of permanent insurance is called **whole life insurance**. The premiums are much higher than on the term insurance you sort of "rent," but insurance companies will guarantee a minimum cash value, and you can also pretty well plan for an even better cash value than that. This way it works to protect your beneficiaries if you die unexpectedly and also acts as a savings vehicle where the cash value grows tax-deferred. Maybe at age 55 you decide to borrow $50,000 of the cash value for *whatever* reason. Could come in really handy, yes?

One other thing to remember: to renew a term policy means you pay a higher premium. Premiums are "level" in a whole life policy, meaning they don't go up. You lock in your rate for your whole life.

So, term is "cheap," but after a few years you have no cash value. And, to keep it going, you'd have to pay more for the same benefit. Reminds me of how I spent five years paying "cheap" rent to a landlord. It was definitely lower than a mortgage payment would have been on a similar-sized house. But at the end of this 5-year term, I had forked over 40 g's to the landlord and was left with nothing but the opportunity to renew my lease at a higher rate. I covered myself with a roof for five years, and at the end of the five years I owned absolutely no part of that roof—not even one cracked, loose shingle.

Whole life insurance is more like buying the house, which is exactly what I did after five years of renting. I had to come up with a down payment, and my monthly mortgage is now $200 more per month than my rent was. The upside is that at the end of five years, I'll have some equity in the house that I can tap into for a loan maybe (kind of like cash value in an insurance policy that I can borrow against some day). Just like with a whole life policy, I'll be getting at least something back for all those payments I've made over the years. And the time will come when the full value is all paid up and mine.

So, whole life insurance involves premiums that are higher than those for term life insurance, but you end up with something even if you stop paying into the policy. There is a guaranteed cash value, whereas term leaves you with nothing. The death benefit is guaranteed (as it is on a term policy), too, so whole life insurance is a very popular product for people who want to protect their families and also use the policy as a savings vehicle, where all that increase in cash value grows tax-deferred.

If the exam asks which type of client should purchase term insurance, I would look for a young, single parent, maybe, or someone who absolutely has to protect the kids from a sudden loss of income and wants to do it as cheaply as possible.

Nothing is simple in either the securities or insurance industry. Since some clients crave flexibility, the industry bent over backwards to come up with a flexible form of permanent insurance called **universal life insurance**. Think "flexibility" when you see the words "universal life insurance." The death benefit and, therefore, the premiums can be adjusted by the client. They can be increased to buy more coverage or decreased to back off on the coverage and save some money. If the cash value is sufficient, premiums can actually stop being paid by the client and start being covered by the cash value. The cash value grows at a minimum, guaranteed rate, just like on traditional whole life policies, and if the general account does particularly well, the cash value goes up from there. As mentioned, at some point the policyholder may decide to withdraw part of the cash value, or may usually borrow up to 90% of it.

VARIABLE POLICIES

So, whether it's term, traditional whole life, or universal life insurance, we're talking strictly about insurance products. Death benefits and cash values (term has no cash value) are guaranteed by the insurance company, who invests the net premiums (what's left after deducting expenses, taxes, etc.) into their general account. Once you start attaching cash value and death benefits to the ups and downs of a separate account, however, you have created a new product that is both an insurance policy and a security. Opens a whole new market for the company, but it also means that those who sell them need both an insurance and a securities license.

Whole life and term life insurance policies tell clients exactly how much they will pay out upon death. So, in term and whole life policies, the investment risk is borne totally by the insurance company through their "general account," which is, more or less, a pile of cash and securities as tall as Mount Everest.

Well, with **variable life insurance**, the death benefit—as well as the cash value—fluctuates just like it does in a variable annuity. That's what they mean by "variable." It all varies, based on the investment performance of the separate account. The separate account, as we discussed under variable annuities, is made up of subaccounts. The investor chooses from these little quasi-mutual funds that are trying to meet different investment objectives: growth, long-term bonds, short-term Treasuries, etc. He can even choose to invest some of the premiums into a fixed account, just to play it safe, and he can switch between the subaccounts as his investment needs change without a tax problem. This stuff all grows tax-deferred, remember.

The cash value is tied to account performance, period. So if the test question says that the separate account grew, it doesn't matter by how much. The cash value increases when the separate account increases. But death benefit is tied to actual performance versus AIR, just like an annuity unit in a variable annuity. So if the AIR is 6% and the account gets a 4% return, the cash value will increase due to the positive return, but the death benefit will decrease since the account returned less than AIR.

Variable Life Insurance (VLI) policies will pay out the cash value/surrender value whenever the policyholder decides to cash in the policy. Now, there's no way to know what the value might be at the time of surrender. If the little subaccounts have performed well, the cash value might be better than expected. But if the market has been brutal, the cash value could go all the way down to zero. Probably not, but it could happen.

A minimum or fixed death benefit is guaranteed, however. Some refer to it as the "floor." No matter what the market does, the insurance company guarantees a minimum death benefit that could only be reduced or depleted by failure to pay premiums or taking out loans against the policy. Remember that any guaranteed payments are covered by the insurance company's general account. So, the minimum death benefit is guaranteed, and the policyholder also has the chance of enjoying an increased death benefit, depending on how well the little subaccounts (inside the separate account) do. As we said, that's tied to AIR, so if the market is kind, the death benefit increases, but if the market is unkind, it could, theoretically, drag the death benefit all the way down to the floor.

As with variable annuities, after the money's been allocated to the little subaccounts of the separate account, the insurance company charges regular fees, just like they do in variable annuities:

- mortality risk fee
- expense risk fee
- investment management fees

The value of the subaccounts and, therefore, the cash value are calculated daily. The death benefit is calculated annually. If the separate account has several below-AIR months, it will take several above-AIR months after that before the customer's death benefit starts to increase.

Remember that flexibility we discussed that separates traditional whole life from universal life? Well, it probably isn't too surprising that somebody eventually married that benefit to variable life to get **Variable Universal Life Insurance**. With VUL we have the death benefit and cash value tied to the separate account (variable), plus we have the flexible premium thing (universal) going on. Regular old variable life is called "scheduled premium." That means the insurance company puts your premium payments on a schedule, and you better stick to it. Variable Universal or Universal Variable Life policies are funded as "flexible premium." That means the client may or may not have to send in a check. With a VUL policy, the customer has to maintain enough cash value and death benefit to keep the policy in force. If the separate account rocks, no money has to roll in from the customer. If the separate account rolls over and dies, look out. Since that's a little scary, some VULs come with minimum guaranteed death benefits.

Variable Universal Life can get to be a sort of complicated product, and as with anything you sell, before you do so, make darn sure you understand all the ins and outs. And talking to a firm specialist or old-timer might not hurt, either, on this or any other product that's new to you. A good question is always, "Worst-case scenario, what could go wrong?"

The advantages of variable life over whole life insurance include the ability to invest some of the premiums into the stock market, which has historically enjoyed relatively high average returns and done very well at beating inflation. A robust investment market can increase the cash value and death benefit, often faster than the rate of inflation. A traditional whole life policy, on the other hand, that promised to pay $50,000 when it was purchased in 1964 represented a lot of money then. But if it pays that $50,000 out in 2014, the $50,000 doesn't go very far, due to inflation.

➢ Policy Loans

Variable policies make 75% of the cash value available to the customer as a loan after three years. Guess what, though?—they charge interest on that loan, just as they do on a whole life policy. If the loan is not repaid, that reduces both the cash value and the death benefit of the policy. And, if the customer takes out a big loan and then the separate account tanks, he'll have to put some money back in to bring the cash value back to a sufficient level, or risk having the policy lapse. Don't worry, though. Some people take out a loan with absolutely no intention of repaying it. They simply don't need as much death benefit at this point, so why not have some fun with the money right now?

➢ Settlement Options

The policyholder can choose from many options concerning the method of payment to the beneficiary. These are called "settlement options." The "lump-sum" method is self-explanatory. "Fixed-period" means that the insurance company will invest the proceeds of the policy into an interest-bearing account and then make equal payments at regular intervals for a fixed period. The payments include principal and interest. How much are the payments? That depends on the size of the principal, the interest rate earned by the insurance company, and the length of time involved in this fixed period.

The "fixed-amount" settlement option has the insurance company invest the proceeds from the policy and pay the beneficiary a fixed amount of money at regular intervals until both the principal and interest are gone. The amount received is fixed, but the period over which the beneficiary receives payments varies.

So, for "fixed-period" versus "fixed-amount," the decision comes down to this: do you want to receive an uncertain amount of money for a fixed period of time, or do you want to receive a fixed amount of money for an uncertain period of time? In other words, do you want to be paid something like $25,000 for exactly three years (fixed-period)? Or, would you prefer being paid exactly $25,000 for about three years (fixed-amount)?

In a "life-income" settlement option, the proceeds are annuitized. That means the insurance company provides the beneficiary with a guaranteed income for the rest of his/her life. Just like with annuities, the beneficiary's age expectancy is taken into account to determine the monthly payout, along with the size of the death benefit and the type of payout selected.

There is also an "interest-only" settlement option, whereby the insurance company keeps the proceeds from the policy and invests them, promising the beneficiary a guaranteed minimum rate of interest. The beneficiary might get more than the minimum, or not, and may receive the payments annually, semiannually, quarterly, or monthly. He/she also has the right to withdraw all the principal if he/she gets antsy, or to change settlement options.

Exchanges

Since these variable policies are a little confusing to some, the company has to give the policyholder at least two years (24 months) to switch back to traditional whole life without having to provide proof of insurability. The new whole life policy will have the same issue date as the original variable policy.

If you buy a variable life policy, you have the opportunity to exchange it for a different policy *even if issued by a different company*. You don't have to pay taxes since you aren't taking the cash value and, like, going on a fly-fishing trip to Alaska. You just cash in one policy and exchange it, tax-free, for another insurance policy. Or, believe it or not, you can even exchange a life policy for an annuity. You can't turn an annuity into a life policy, though.

This tax-free exchange is called a **1035 exchange**.

When selling variable insurance policies, the rep needs to remember that these are insurance policies first and foremost. You can discuss the benefits of investing in the subaccounts, but you can't present these insurance policies primarily as investment vehicles. Primarily, they're to be sold for the death benefit. They also offer the opportunity to invest in the separate account's little subaccounts, but they're not to be pitched primarily as investment vehicles.

Four federal acts are involved with variable life insurance and variable annuities. The Securities Act of 1933 covers variable life insurance (and annuities). These products must be registered with the SEC and sold with a prospectus. Even though the company that issues these contracts is an insurance company, the subdivision that sells the securities products has to be a broker-dealer registered under the Securities Exchange Act of 1934. The separate account is defined as an investment company under the Investment Company Act of 1940 and is either registered as a UIT or an Open-End Fund as defined under that act. The "money manager" or "investment adviser" has to register under the Investment Advisers Act of 1940.

And, at the state level, both securities and insurance regulators are watching these products and those who sell them, too.

➢ Needs Analysis

The exam will likely bring up the term **needs analysis,** which is the process of determining how much life insurance protection one needs based on expenses, debts, etc. To perform a needs analysis the insurance agent gathers information on current income and living expenses, plus credit card, student loan, and mortgage debt, and final expenses for funeral, probate, etc. Only by running these numbers, times an estimated inflation rate, can we accurately determine how much life insurance to buy in order to make sure all debts are paid off and that survivors have enough money to allow them to do X, Y, or Z after a breadwinner passes on.

TYPES AND CHARACTERISTICS OF DERIVATIVE SECURITIES

OPTIONS

Options are not so difficult to understand once you understand the basic concepts. Let's use a very brief story to explain how it all works in the most basic terms.

A guy steps into a tavern. He sits down at the last open stool and slaps a stack of twenties on the bar, just loud enough to get the bartender's attention. The bartender looks up from the pitcher of pale ale she's pouring.

"Just a sec'," she says, afraid to take her eyes off the thick head of foam gathering at the top.

"No hurry," the guy says, although it's clear he's not in the mood to wait.

Bartender finally comes up and takes his order. Bourbon and Pepsi. Not Coke—Coke's for losers. He wants *Pepsi* with his bourbon, okay?

The bartender shrugs and mutters something as she mixes him his drink.

Three guys sitting to his right take the bait.

"You don't like Coke, huh, buddy?" says the dark-haired guy in the wrinkled shirt.

"Nope," the guy says. "Don't like the drink, don't like the stock."

"What, you're a trader?" the blond dude with the big shoulders says, wiping foam from his mustache.

"Just a guy who says Coke is headed where it belongs—in the toilet."

The three friends all lift their chins as if connected by an invisible string pulled by the loud-talking, Coke-hating newcomer.

"That's a bold statement," the dark-haired guy says. "My dad drove a route for Coke twenty years by the way."

"Good for him," the guy says. "Used to be a decent company—that's history, though. I say Coke is a dog, and I'll bet anybody at this bar it won't go above twenty-five bucks a share the rest of the year."

He says the last part loud enough to get everyone's attention. Even the jukebox seems to quiet down at this point.

"Oh yeah?" somebody shouts from a corner booth. "I'll take that bet."

"Me, too!" somebody cries from over by the pool tables.

Pretty soon the guy has over a dozen loud-talking, well-lubed happy hour customers standing in line to bet the cocky newcomer that Coca-Cola common stock will, without a doubt, rise above $25 a share at some point between today (March 1) and the rest of the year.

How do they make this bet? The guy breaks out a stack of cocktail napkins and on each one he writes the following:

Anybody who thinks Coca-Cola stock will rise above $25 a share has to pay the guy $300. Guy ends up collecting $300 from 15 different customers, walking out with $4,500 in premiums.

What's his risk as he steps onto the rainy sidewalk outside?

Unlimited. See, no matter how high Coca-Cola common stock goes between today and the 3rd Friday of December, this guy would have to sell it to any holder of the cocktail napkin for $25 a share. Theoretically, his risk is unlimited, since there's no limit to how much he'd have to pay to get the stock.

What if the stock never makes it above $25 in the next 9 months? That's what he's hoping! If it never makes it above $25, nobody will ever <u>call</u> him and demand to buy the stock for $25. In short, he'll walk away with the $4,500 in premiums, laughing at all the suckers at the bar who bet the wrong way.

What the guy sold everybody at the bar was a Coca-Cola Dec 25 call @3. As the writer of that option, he granted any buyer willing to pay $300 the right to buy 100 shares of Coca-Cola common stock for $25 per share anytime between today and the end of the contract. When would the person holding that option want to use or exercise it?

Only if Coca-Cola were actually worth more than $25 a share. In fact, since they each paid $3 a share for this right, Coca-Cola will have to rise above $28—their breakeven point—before it ever becomes worth the trouble of exercising the call. I mean, they *could* exercise it, but why bother?

Either way, the guy who sold/wrote the calls gets the $4,500 in premiums. If Coke never makes it above $25, he'll never have to lift a finger. Just smile as the calls expire on the third Friday of December.

Think of a call option as a bet between a buyer and a seller. The buyer says the price of something is going up. The seller disagrees. Rather than argue about it all day, they put their money where their mouths are by buying and selling call options.

The buyer pays the seller a **premium**. Because he pays some money, he gets the right to buy 100 shares of a particular stock for a particular price within a particular time frame. If the buyer has the right to buy the stock, the seller has the obligation to sell the stock to the buyer at the already agreed upon price, if the buyer chooses to exercise that right.

Buyers have rights. Sellers have obligations.

The buyer pays a premium, and he receives the right to buy a particular stock at a particular price. That particular price is known as the **strike price** or **exercise price**.

➢ Calls

A "MSFT Aug 70" **call** gives the call buyer the <u>right to buy MSFT common stock for $70</u> at any time up to the **expiration date** in August. If the stock goes up to $90 before expiration, the owner of the call could still buy the stock for $70. If MSFT went up to $190, the call owner could still buy it at the strike price of $70. So you can probably see why call buyers make money when the underlying stock goes up in value.

That's right. Call buyers are betting that the stock's market price will go up above the strike price. That's why they're called "bulls." Bull = up. If you hold an Aug 70 call, that means you're "bullish" on the stock and would like to see the underlying stock go UP above 70. How far above?

As far as possible. The higher it goes, the more valuable your call becomes. Wouldn't you love to buy a stock priced at $190 for only $70?

That's what call buyers are hoping to do.

So for a call, just compare the strike price to the stock's market price. Whenever the underlying stock trades above the strike price of the call, the call is said to be **in-the-money**. A MSFT Aug 70 call would be in-the-money as soon as MSFT began to trade above $70 a share. If MSFT were trading at $80 a share, the Aug 70 call would be in-the-money by exactly $10. Notice how we are not referring to a particular buyer or seller when we say a call is in-the-money. One problem with buying options is that you might end up paying, say, $5 a share and even though the call does go in-the-money by $3 a share, you lose that difference. We'll talk about buyers' gains and losses in a minute; for now understand that any time the market price is higher than the strike price, the call is in-the-money. Period.

PRACTICE

1. A MSFT Jun 50 call is in-the-money when MSFT trades at which of the following prices?

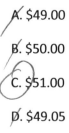

A. $49.00

B. $50.00

C. $51.00

D. $49.05

2. How far is a MSFT Jan 90 call in-the-money with MSFT trading at $85?

    A. $5

    B. $90

    C. $87.50

    D. None of these choices

3. How far are the IBM Aug 70 calls in-the-money if IBM trades at $77?

    A. $77

    B. $7

    C. $0

    D. None of these choices

(ANSWERS)

1. **C,** there is really no way to miss that question. Only one price is above $50.

2. **D,** would you pay $90 for an $85 stock? If so, please give me a call ASAP so we can set up some trading opportunities for you.

3. **B,** take the market price minus the strike price.

The Premium

The money you pay for your life or auto insurance policy is called a "premium." That's also what we call the money paid and received for an option; in fact, as you'll see with hedging, options can be used as insurance policies to protect against the risk of owning securities.

How much does an investor have to pay in premiums for an option?

Depends. Option **premiums** really just represent the probability that a buyer could win. If the premium is cheap, it's a long-shot bet. If the premium is expensive, the bet is probably already working in favor of the buyer with time left for things to get even better. As with everything else, you get what you pay for when trading options. For example, if MSFT common stock now trades for $28 a share, the right to buy it next month for $40 is all but worthless, while the right to buy it for $30 has some chance of working out for the buyer and would, therefore, trade at a higher premium. The right to buy the stock for $30 through next month is also not worth as much as the right to buy it for $30 through the next three or four months, right? The premiums would show that this is exactly right; for call options, the premiums rise as the strike prices drop, and as time goes out. I know that sounds strange, but you need to accept the fact that if today were St. Patrick's Day, a MSFT Mar 20 call is worth more than a MSFT Mar 25 call, but a MSFT May 20 call is worth more than both. Why? The right to buy MSFT for $20 is worth more than the right to pay $25…and the right to do so for two extra months is worth even more.

There are only two types of value that an option can possess: **intrinsic value** and **time value**. For calls, intrinsic value is another way of stating how much higher the stock price is compared to the strike price of the call. If the underlying stock is trading at $75, the MSFT Aug 70 call is how far in-the-money? Five dollars. The stock price is above the call's strike price by $5; therefore, the call has intrinsic value of five dollars. That just means that an investor could save $5 by owning that call and using it to buy the underlying stock.

But, if the stock is trading below the strike price, the option is out-of-the-money. With MSFT trading at $65, the Aug 70 call would have absolutely no intrinsic value. So, if there is a premium to be paid for this "out-of-the-money" call, it's only because there's plenty of time for things to improve. In other words, if the option doesn't expire for another three months, speculators might decide that the stock could easily climb more than 5 points in that time period. If so, the market will attach time value to the call. Time value simply means that the option could become more valuable given the amount of time still left before expiration.

Whenever a call is at- or out-of-the-money, the premium represents time value. Whenever a call is in-the-money, you can find the time value attached to it by subtracting intrinsic value from the premium. Let's say MSFT is trading at $72, and the Aug 70 calls are selling for a premium of $5. That means the call is in-the-money by $2 ($72 market vs. 70 strike price), yet an investor has to pay a premium of $5. So, where is that extra three dollars coming from?

Time value. If there is still plenty of time on the option, speculators might gladly pay an extra $3, even if the stock is only above the strike price by $2 at this point.

	PREMIUM	5
−	INTRINSIC VALUE	− 2
	TIME VALUE	3

So for calls, intrinsic value is a way of stating how much higher the stock price is than the strike price. Time value equals whatever is left in the premium above that number.

What if MSFT were trading at $69 with the MSFT Aug 70 calls @5—how much time value would that represent?

	PREMIUM	5
−	INTRINSIC VALUE	− 0
	TIME VALUE	5

All time value. In other words, with the stock trading at only $69, the right to buy it at $70 has NO intrinsic value. (If you disagree, please call us at your earliest convenience; we have some options we'd like to sell you here in friendly Chicago, IL.) In fact, if the stock were trading right at the strike price of 70, there would still be no intrinsic value to the MSFT Aug 70 call, right? If you want to buy a $70 stock for $70, do you need to buy an option?

No.

You only buy the call because you want to end up buying the stock for LESS than it's currently trading, which will happen if the stock moves above the strike price.

So, if you pay $5 for a MSFT Aug 70 call with the stock trading at $70 (at-the-money) or below (out-of-the-money), you're paying purely for the time value on the option.

Breakeven, Max Gain, Max Loss

So far we've been talking about the option itself. If we're looking at the options *investor*, we have to remember that he won't begin to profit until the stock starts trading above the strike price by an amount greater than what he paid for the call. If an investor paid $5 for an Aug 70 call, he will only start making money when the stock goes above $75. So, he breaks even (BE) at $75 and begins to profit above $75.

Strike Price	+	Premium	=	Breakeven
70	+	5	=	75

Another way to remember the **breakeven** on a call is to "Call UP from the Strike Price." If you see a test question about the breakeven for an investor who buys a MSFT Aug 70 call @5, just add the $5 premium to the strike price of 70 to get a BE of $75. Or "call up" from 70 by the premium of five.

What about the guy who sells the MSFT Aug 70 call @5. Where does that investor break even?

Same place:

Strike price plus premium.

That might be tough to accept at first. To be honest, it would be much easier if you did just accept it, but perhaps you're an inquiring mind who just has to know.

So here goes. See, if the stock goes up five bucks to $75, the buyer's 70 call is worth $5 (intrinsic value). He could then sell it for exactly what he paid and be "even." The seller, however, sold the option for $5 and could now (to avoid being exercised) buy it back for its intrinsic value of $5, leaving him even. In other words, the breakeven point is where the buyer and seller "tie." Nobody's made anything, but nobody's lost anything.

And, if you don't quite understand that, just remember that the breakeven on a call is the same for the buyer and the seller: strike price + premium.

The Series 65 will ask you to figure the breakeven point, the maximum gain, and the maximum loss for either the buyer or the seller of the call. Those are all hypothetical situations. See, sometimes you calculate what actually happened for an options investor; sometimes you figure out what *could* happen. If the test is talking about breakeven, maximum gain, or maximum loss, it is asking you to look at what could happen. This is how it works for calls:

> Buyers

The maximum loss is the premium they pay. Why? Because buyers can only lose whatever they pay for the option, end of story. There are no "loser fees," in other words.

To find the breakeven point add the premium to the strike price. A MSFT Aug 70 call @5 would have a breakeven point of $75. Strike price of 70 + premium of 5 = 75.

There is no limit to the call buyer's maximum gain. How high can the price of the underlying stock go before expiration?

Nobody knows. That's why the buyer's maximum gain is unlimited. His purchase price is fixed as the "strike price." The sell price is unlimited; it's wherever the market takes the stock, with no limit on the upside.

> Sellers

What's the most that the seller can win on this call option?

Sellers can only make the premium. Always. So, the seller's maximum gain is the premium.

The breakeven point is the same for buyers and sellers: strike price + premium, end of story.

The call seller's maximum loss is unlimited. If the buyer has an unlimited maximum gain, what do you suppose the seller's maximum loss is?

That's right, unlimited. His sale price is fixed at the "strike price." His purchase price is wherever the market takes the stock, which could be as high as infinity.

More, even.

We're not saying it will happen; we're saying it could happen.

Remember that whatever the buyer can win, that's what the seller can lose. Whatever the buyer can lose, that's all the seller can win. Buyers and sellers break even at the same place.

CALL BUYER	CALL SELLER
Max Loss = Premium	Max Gain = Premium
Max Gain = Unlimited	Max Loss = Unlimited
Breakeven = Strike Price + Premium	Breakeven = Strike Price + Premium

Gains and Losses

Before we move forward, let's remember that options go in-the-money or out-of-the-money. People don't do that. People have gains and losses, based on how much they paid for an option versus how much they received for the option. So, terms such as time value, intrinsic value, in-the-money, out-of-the-money, and at-the-money refer only to options. Terms such as gains, losses, and breakeven refer to the options investor. Like this:

THE OPTION	THE INVESTOR

Time value	Gains
Intrinsic value	Losses
In-the-money, out-, at-the-money	Breakeven

> ➤ The T-chart

When the exam wants you to tell it whether an investor ends up with a gain or a loss, and exactly how much he or she gained or lost, approach the problem step-by-step. These are essentially bookkeeping questions, where you track everything the investor paid and everything he/she received. This might seem complicated, but luckily you have a tool that can help called a "T-chart."

$ Out	$ In

The T-chart helps you track debits and credits. Whenever you buy or go long, you have a debit (Dr). Whenever you sell or go short, you have a credit (Cr). So debits are for the money going out of the account; credits are for money that comes into the account. If you end up with more money coming in than going out, you have a gain. If you end up with more money out than in, you have a loss. The rest simply involves running the numbers.

So let's start running.

Here's a possible Series 65 question:

An investor with no other positions buys an XYZ Jun 50 call @4 when the underlying instrument upon which the derivative is based is trading at 52. If the stock is trading at $52 at expiration and the investor closes his position for the intrinsic value, what is the investor's gain or loss?

A. $1,000 loss

B. $100 loss

C. $200 gain

D. $200 loss

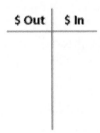

First, draw a T-chart and use the labels you prefer: – and +, "$ out" and "$ in," "Dr" and "Cr," whatever works for you:

Okay. When the investor buys the call for $4, that's money out, so let's place "4" in the debit column.

The next part looks tricky but really isn't. The phrase "at expiration" means the last day of trading. At this point, all time value has evaporated. Since the option will soon expire, it is only worth the in-the-money amount. The intrinsic value. At expiration, an option either has intrinsic value, or it is worthless. So, what is the intrinsic value of the Jun 50 call when the stock is trading at $52? Two dollars. So, at expiration, the Jun 50 call would be worth exactly $2. In this question the investor is closing his position for the intrinsic value. If he bought to open the contract, he sells it to close. When he sells the call for its intrinsic value of $2, this represents a credit, right? When you buy something, money comes out of your wallet. When you sell something, money comes into your wallet. Same for an options investor.

All right. So, if $4 went OUT of his account, and only $2 came back INTO his account, he ends up with a loss of how much? Two dollars. An option covers 100 shares, so just multiply $2 by 100 to get a total loss of $200.

The answer to the question is "D," a $200 loss.

See? It's really not that hard. You just have to do it step by step. Many students get into trouble by trying to arrive at the answer all at once. Doesn't work that way for options. You have to weed through all the information thrown at you and break the problem down into steps. These options questions might look like math questions, but really they're just testing your ability to organize information. If you need two numbers, they'll be sure and give you five or six. They're testing your ability to separate relevant information from irrelevant, and then sort all the information into neat, usable steps. Just remember the basics, watch out for traps, and let the T-chart sort everything out for you.

➤ Exercise, Trade, Expire

Notice how in the question, the investor bought an option and sold it. That's called trading options, where you'll see terms such as "opening" and "closing." No stock is involved in that case. But, if the investor decides to **exercise** the option, now stock does change hands. Sometimes options are opened and closed; sometimes they are exercised; and sometimes they **expire** worthless. So, when figuring gains and losses for questions like the ones above, remember that only three things can happen once an option contract has been opened:

- Exercise
- Close Position
- Expire

If the call goes in-the-money, the investor could choose to exercise it. That means he buys stock at the strike price and sells it immediately at the current market price. If so, you'll be entering both the strike price (Debit) and the market price (Credit) into your T-chart—just make sure you place the numbers in the correct columns. The investor could also close his position for the intrinsic value. To calculate intrinsic value, just compare the higher market price to the strike price and place the difference in your T-chart. To close the position, remember that if he bought to open, he sells the option to close. If he sold to open, he buys the option back to close. And, finally, the option could expire worthless—put a zero in the T-chart to signify expiration. The exam questions will give clues as to which of the three events has occurred. Just make sure you read the question carefully so you'll know what the exam expects. In terms of expiration, know that ordinary options expire in 9 months or sooner. There are also long-term options called **LEAPS**, and these have much longer shelf lives—12 to 39 months. So, if you think it's hard to predict where Google common stock will close a week from next Friday, how about buying a LEAPS contract that allows you to predict where it will close 38 months from next Friday?

Sounds like a bit of a leap, doesn't it? Because of the extra time on the contracts, LEAPS premiums are much higher than they are on similar ordinary options.

An American style option can be traded throughout each trading day and even exercised before the contract expires. That means that if you hold a MSFT May 30 call, you can exercise it in April, March, February, etc., if the common stock rises above $30 per share. All equity options are American style. They can be exercised early if the buyer wants to do that. Non-equity options, however, can be either American style or European style. A European style option can be traded throughout each trading day, but it can only be exercised at expiration. Many students remember it this way: "A is for anytime" and "E is for expiration only."

PRACTICE

1. Joe Schmoe is long an XYZ Dec 50 call @2.50. On the third Friday of December, XYZ is trading @56 and Joe closes the contract for its intrinsic value. What is the result?

    A. Gain of $250

    B. Loss of $250

    C. Gain of $350

    D. Loss of $350

2. Joe Schmoe buys an ABC Apr 85 call @3.25. With ABC trading @89.50, Joe exercises the call and immediately sells the stock for a:

    A. Loss of $125

    B. Gain of $125

    C. Loss of $50

    D. Gain of $450

3. Joe Schmoe sells an XYZ Jun 50 call @3.75. With XYZ @51, Joe closes the contract for its intrinsic value, realizing a:

A. Loss of $375

B. Gain of $375

C. Gain of $275

D. Loss of $1,000

(ANSWERS)

1. **C,** use the T-chart. He pays the premium of $250, so put that in the debit column. When he closes the contract, he sells it, so he takes in the intrinsic value of $6 per share or $600 total. $250 out – $600 in. That's a gain of $350.

2. **B,** use the T-chart again. Step one, he pays $3.25, so put that in the debit column. When he exercises the call he has the "right to buy stock at the Strike Price," so put the strike price in the buy/debit column, too. Now you have $3.25 per share and $85 per share in the debit column. He sells the stock for $89.50, so put that in the credit column. With $88.25 in the debit column and $89.50 in the credit column, he gains the difference of $1.25 or $125 total.

3. **C,** all sales go in the credit column, so put $3.75 per share in the credit column. He buys it back to close, and it's worth exactly $1 per share when he does. He makes the difference between $3.75 and $1 per share, or $275 total.

> The Terminology: Synonyms

It would be a lot easier if we could just refer to the two parties in the options contract as the buyer and the seller. Unfortunately, we have other ways of referring to each. The exam might talk about the buyer of an option, or it might refer to him as being "long the option." Or, maybe he is referred to as the owner or the "holder" of the option.

It's all the same thing.

To sell an option is to write an option. If you sell an option, you are said to be "short" the option.

All means the same thing. Why would they use the word "hold" instead of "buy" or "own"? Think back to our guy in the tavern. When he sold the little cocktail napkins, the buyers were now holding the option in their hands. And, we call the seller the "writer," because, as you remember, our guy in the tavern literally wrote the terms of the contract on each cocktail napkin.

Buyer-holder-owner.

Seller-writer.

Why would we call the buyer "long" and the seller "short"?

Because it blows people's minds and, therefore, makes them confused and us the experts.

Long = buy. Short = sell.

BUYER	SELLER
Long	Short
Holder	Writer
Owner	

So far, we've been talking about calls, which give investors the right to buy stock. Let's take a look at **puts** now, which give investors the right to sell stock at the strike price before expiration.

➢   Puts

If we clipped the following coupon from the newspaper, what would it allow us to do?

That coupon represents an IXR Oct 40 put. As the holder/owner/buyer of this put we have the right to sell IXR stock for $40.

What if IXR is only worth $2?

Awesome! We get to sell the stock for $40 at any time before the end of trading on Friday, October 20, even if it's worth only two bucks on the open market. In fact, even if it's worth zero, we can still sell it for the $40 strike price.

That's how a **put** works. A put buyer gets the right to sell IXR at the strike price before the contract expires. No matter how low IXR goes, the holder of an Oct 40 put has the right to sell 100 shares of IXR for $40 each before the end of trading on the third Friday of October.

Who buys puts? Investors who think a stock is about to drop in price. Bears. Bear = down. (Bulls point UP, like the horns on a Bull. Bears point DOWN, like the claws on a Bear, or just remember "bear down.")

Strange as it seems, as the stock price drops below the strike price, the value of the put goes up.

Think of it like this—if a stock is now at $20, wouldn't you like to sell it to somebody for $40? If you were ready to exercise the put, you could just buy the stock for $20, then immediately sell it to the put writer for $40. That would involve exercising the put. As we saw with calls, though, options investors don't always exercise their options, but, rather, close the positions for their intrinsic value. If they take in more than they spend, they end up with a profit. And if they spend more than they take in, they don't.

For puts, intrinsic value is the amount of money that a put's strike price is above the market price, which is another way of saying that the market price has fallen below the strike price. An October 40 put has how much intrinsic value when the underlying stock trades at $20?

$20. Wouldn't you love to sell something worth only $20 for $40?

Talk about putting it to somebody, huh? The owner of a put profits when he can sell higher than the market price. He needs the stock price to go down, below the strike price. That's when he profits, when the stock is losing value. Sounds illegal, perhaps, but it's not. In fact, it's a beautiful opportunity to make money as a stock loses money.

So puts go in-the-money when the market price of the stock drops below the strike price. And, if you've already noticed that buying puts is very similar to selling stock short, I really like your chances of passing this exam the first time. Not that I'm particularly worried about those who didn't see that. In any case, let's take a second to look at how the two strategies are the same, and how they're different:

BUYING A PUT	SELLING STOCK SHORT
Bearish (profits when stock goes down)	Bearish (profits when stock goes down)
Limited loss (just the premium paid)	UN-limited loss
Less of a capital commitment	More capital, plus margin interest
Loses time value quickly	Stock can drop slowly, still profitable

Time and Intrinsic Value

IXR Oct 40 put @5 with IXR trading at $38

	PREMIUM	5
−	INTRINSIC VALUE	− 2
	TIME VALUE	3

IXR Oct 40 put @5 with IXR trading at $40

Premium of $5 minus intrinsic value of $0 = time value of $5.

	PREMIUM	5
−	INTRINSIC VALUE	− 0

So, in the first case, the put has $2 of intrinsic value, since it would allow the buyer to sell the stock for $2 more than it's worth. The premium costs $5, so the additional $3 is time value. In the second case, the put has zero intrinsic value, since nobody needs the right to sell at $40 when the stock is at $40. So, the $5 premium is ALL time value.

PRACTICE

1. A MSFT Jun 65 put @3 has how much intrinsic value with MSFT @65?

    A. $3

    B. $2

    C. $65

     D. 0

2. An IBM Mar 75 put @3 has how much time value with IBM @74?

    A. $1

    B. $3

     C. $2

    D. None of these choices

(ANSWERS)

1. **D,** the right to sell a $65 stock at $65 has no intrinsic value. The premium represents pure speculation or "time value."

2. **C,** there is $1 of intrinsic value, since the $74 stock can be sold for $75. The rest of the premium ($2) equals its "time value."

Max Gain, Max Loss, Breakeven

There are exactly two things you can do with stock: buy it, or sell it. How do you make money? By buying low and selling high. When you buy an option, you're hoping to buy the stock low and sell it high, which you can do with either a call or a put. If you buy a call, you're picking your buy price—hopefully, the market price will go above that, so you can buy the stock low (strike price) and sell it high (market price). If you buy a put, you're picking your sell price—hopefully, the market price will go below that, so you can buy the stock low (market price) and sell it high (strike price).

Okay. So you can see why a bearish investor might buy puts.

Why would anyone sell them?

Back to our tavern. It's Monday after that third Friday in December, and our hero is back at the bar buying all the call buyers cheap beer just so they'll stick around long enough for him to rub it in.

Yes, unfortunately, for everyone but the seller/writer of the calls, Coca-Cola only made it to $22, and the calls all expired worthless. So, with the $4,500 still in his pocket, the guy is in a pretty good mood. He's in such a good mood that he can't keep himself from not only trashing Coca-Cola but talking up his favored Pepsi. Pepsi is such an awesome stock, he swears, that it couldn't possibly fall below $70 a share in the next nine months. He's so confident his favorite stock won't fall below $70 that he'll take a bet with anyone who says the stock is a loser. You have to pay him three hundred dollars to make the bet, but it gives you the right to sell him 100 shares of Pepsi for $70, no matter how low it goes in the next nine months. Even if the stock drops to ZERO dollars, you can make him pay you $70 a share.

The 15 losers look at each other and decide the temptation is just too great. They imagine how much fun it will be to see the dude's face when they all make him give them $70 a share for a worthless stock. What if they're wrong? Then, just like before, they lose part or all of their premium. But that's all they can lose, too.

How much can our Pepsi-loving dude make? Same as before—just the premium. That's all the seller of an option can ever make. In fact, if you can remember that any time somebody starts with a credit in their T-chart, that's ALL they can ever make (maximum gain), you will save yourself lots of frustration and probably snag a few more test questions.

How much can he lose on this Pepsi put?

The good news for him as the writer/seller/short dude of a put (as opposed to a call) is that his maximum loss is NOT unlimited. In fact, you won't see the word "unlimited" associated with puts. A stock can only go down to zero, which caps the maximum loss for the seller and the maximum gain for the buyer. If this guy collects $3 a share ($300 total) granting the right to sell him stock at $70 per share, the worst that could happen is that he'd pay $70 for a stock worth zero and would have only collected $3 per share. A maximum loss of $67 per share, and it could only happen if PepsiCo, like, went out of business in the next nine months. Which could never happen, unless it did.

So, like before, the guy lines up the same 15 buyers and takes $300 from each one. He takes out a cocktail napkin for each buyer and writes:

So, after finishing his drink and buying the house another round, the guy walks out with $4,500 and

the obligation to buy Pepsi for $70 a share, no matter what it's actually worth at the time. Oh well. He's confident that the stock will remain at $70 or above. If so, those Pepsi puts will end up just as worthless as the Coke calls did.

So, the buyer and seller of a put have the following maximum gain, maximum loss, and breakeven:

BUYER	SELLER
Max Loss = Premium	Max Gain = Premium
BE = SP - Premium	BE = SP - Premium
Max Gain = BE down to zero	Max Loss = BE down to zero

PRACTICE

1. IBM is trading at $93. Which of the following options would, therefore, command the highest premium?

    A. IBM Aug 90 call

    B. IBM Oct 90 call

    C. IBM Aug 95 put

    D. IBM Nov 100 put

2. Which position exposes the investor to the greatest risk?

    A. Long XYZ Mar 80 call @3

    B. Long XYZ Mar 85 put @4

    C. Short XYZ Mar 80 put @2

    D. Short XYZ Mar 20 put @2

3. Paula Padilla purchases a put for $300. Three hundred dollars represents:

    A. The price per share

    B. Paula's maximum gain

    C. Paula's maximum loss

    D. Paul's breakeven

4. An investor buys an ABC Apr 45 put @2.50. With ABC trading @41, he exercises his put for a:

    A. Loss of $250

157

B. Gain of $250

C. Gain of $150

D. Loss of $4,500

5. An investor sells an ABC Apr 45 put @2.50. Which of the following stock prices would prove the most profitable for the put writer?

A. $44

B. $43

C. $42

D. $45

(ANSWERS)

1. **D,** the option with the most intrinsic value ($7) AND the most time would have to be the most expensive, right?

2. **C,** the most risk is always on the short/sell/write side of the contract. Which put has a bigger maximum loss? The first one has a max loss of $78, which is much more than the max loss of $18 in choice D.

3. **C,** Paula, like any put buyer, or ANY buyer of anything, can only lose what she pays.

4. **C,** he pays $2.50 per share for the put and pays $41 for the stock. $43.50 in the debit column. He has the "right to sell stock at Strike Price," so put the $45 in the credit column. The difference of $1.50 per share or $150 total is his gain.

5. **D,** when you sell/write/short an option, you want it to expire worthless. Only the price of $45 would cause the option to expire worthless. The other three prices would leave intrinsic value on the contract, which the seller never wants to see at expiration. If you sell something, you want to walk away and never pay another dime. That happens if the thing expires at-the-money or out-of-the money. At which point it's worthless.

➤ Strategy

Too many exam candidates assume that options questions on the Series 65 involve only number crunching. In fact, a large portion involve no numbers but only recommendations as to what an investor should do given the facts presented in the question. For example, let's say that you are convinced MSFT common stock is going nowhere or possibly down over the next few months. Would you buy a call, buy a put, sell a call, or sell a put?

Step one—remember that if you think a stock is going nowhere, you do not want to buy an option, period. When you buy an option, you lay your money down, and the underlying instrument has to MOVE at least that much in your favor before you can even think about a profit. Only SELLERS profit when a stock or other underlying instrument fails to move. So, should you sell a call or sell a put? The situation says you think the stock might go…down. So you are neutral and/or bearish. The answer is—sell a call on MSFT. If the stock sits still or goes down, you win.

If you think a stock is going to sit still or possibly rise, you sell a put. Collect the premium, and then keep most or all of it if the stock does what you anticipate.

You only buy an option, remember, if you think the stock is about to move. Buy a call if you think the stock is about to rise, and buy a put if you think the stock is about to drop.

➢ Hedging (Risk Modification Techniques)

If you buy stock, you're betting that it's going up. If it doesn't go up, or—worse—if it goes down, you lose. If you sell a stock short, you're betting that it's going down. If it goes up, you lose. Maybe the problem with both strategies, then, is that the investor is betting all one way. What he could do, instead, is hedge his bet. To **hedge** a stock position means to "bet the other way, too." If you bet your buddy that the Atlanta Falcons will win the Super Bowl this year, you can also bet another buddy that they won't. To "hedge your bets" you could bet $100 that the Falcons would win and $45 that they won't. This way, you can't have a total loss, since the Falcons will either win or lose the game. Unfortunately, you also can't win as much, right? If the Falcons win, you could have made $100, but you'll have to give the other buddy $45 of it now. But, this way if the Falcons do not win the Super Bowl, at least you get $45 from the second buddy, losing only $55 total, while you could have lost $100 with just one bet in one direction.

The word "hedge" is based on the way people grow hedges to establish the boundaries on their property. Your property is your stock—with a hedge, you can establish the boundaries in terms of what you're willing to lose. Notice how hedging questions *always* involve a stock position. Without a stock position, there is nothing to hedge.

Hedging Long Positions

Let's say one of your favorite stocks looks like it's about to do a belly flop. What should you do about it? Sell the stock? Yes. You could sell the stock, but that's a drastic measure, especially when it's also possible that the stock will rally, and you'd sure hate to miss out if it did. If you've ever taken a 50% profit on a stock, only to watch it go up 300% from there, you know exactly what I'm talking about.

So, instead of taking a drastic measure, maybe you could buy an option that names a selling price for your stock. Let's see, which option gives an investor the right to sell stock at a particular price?

A put. So, if you thought one of your stocks might drop sharply, you could buy a put, giving you the right to sell your stock at the put's strike price, regardless of how low it actually goes.

> Protection

It's like a homeowner's insurance policy. If you own a home, you buy insurance against fire. Doesn't mean you're hoping your house burns down, but, if it does, aren't you glad you paid your premium? Buying puts against stock you own is a form of insurance. Insuring your downside, you might say. In Series Sevenland we call it "protection."

A question might look like this:

Jimmy Joe purchases 100 shares of QSTX for $50 a share. Mr. Joe is bullish on QSTX for the long-term but is nervous about a possible downturn. To hedge his risk and get the best protection, which of the following strategies would you recommend?

> A. sell a call

> B. buy a call

> C. sell a put

> D. buy a put

Okay, first of all, when we say "hedge," all we mean is "bet the other way." If an investor buys stock, he is bullish, or betting the price will go up. To hedge, he'd have to take a bearish position, betting that the stock might go down. There are two "bearish" positions he can take in order to bet the other way or "hedge." He could sell a call, but if the test wanted you to recommend that strategy, the question would have said something about "increasing income" or "increasing yield."

And this one doesn't. This one gives you the key phrase:

> *"...and get the best protection..."*

Whenever you see the word "protection," remember that the investor has to BUY an option. If an investor is long stock, he would buy (or go "long") a put for protection.

> ### Max Gain, Max Loss, Breakeven

Let's see how the protection might work for Mr. Jimmy Joe. Let's say he bought that stock for $50 and paid $3 for an Oct 45 put. That Oct 45 put gives him the right to sell the stock for $45, regardless of how low the stock actually drops. Downside insurance for a premium of $3. With a "deductible" of how much? $5 per share (buy stock at $50; right to sell for a loss of only $5 per share). It really is a $500 deductible insurance policy good through the third Friday of October. Just like a car owner, who can handle the first $500, after that, damaged or destroyed property is passed off to the other side of the contract, who probably isn't too happy about having to cut a check but hey that's life.

When the test asks you about the investor's breakeven point, be careful. It is NOT "strike price minus premium." That only works for a single put option—if there is a stock position, the investor does not want the stock to drop. Just like the homeowner who pays a premium to insure his house, this investor would rather not have to use the insurance. Right? If you have to use your insurance, something bad just happened. It's a lot better because of the insurance, but your car or house is now totaled, just as your stock could be wiped out in the stock market equivalent of a tropical storm or hurricane. The insurance just gives somebody the ability to sleep at night, knowing that he can replace his property for a fair price should calamity strike.

So, what he wants is for his stock to go UP. And, since he paid $3 to protect his $50 stock, how much ground does the stock have to gain before he breaks even?

Exactly. It has to go up to $53. Remember, he doesn't want to use this put; he's just hedging his risk, buying temporary portfolio insurance. Insuring his downside. He paid three for the put; the stock has to make three bucks a share before he breaks even.

So, the investor breaks even at the stock cost plus the price of the premium.

Might be easier to just use a T-chart. Put the price of the stock and the price of the put in the T-chart, and you'll see why the breakeven becomes 53. Wouldn't the stock have to rise to $53, so we could put that number in the credit column and make the T-chart "even"? You can always find the breakeven on a hedged position just by entering the stock price and the premium on the correct side of the T-chart. If it's a buy or a "long" position, place that number on the debit side. If it's a sell or a "short" position, place that number on the credit side. Then just ask yourself what number would make both sides equal.

What's the maximum gain for this investor, who owns stock and a put to protect his downside? Well, how high could his stock rise? It's unlimited, right? So his maximum gain is still unlimited.

What about his maximum loss? Easy. When he bought the stock at $50, what was the most he could have lost? All of it—fifty bucks. If the stock went to zero, he would have had no protection. But, in the question he has purchased a sale price of $45 by purchasing the Oct 45 put. If that stock collapses to zero now, he can sell it for $45. Looking at his T-chart, we would place "45" in the credit column, since that's the amount of money he would get for selling his stock at the strike price.

So, what's his maximum loss? Well, under the worst scenario $53 went out, $45 came back in. The most this investor could lose is $8 per share, or a total of $800.

He's not happy about losing $800, but he's probably giddy over not losing $5000.

That's what we mean by "protection." If my basement floods next summer, ruining the furnace, washer, dryer and water heater, I have to absorb the first $1,000 (my deductible) and then State Farm would cover the rest of the damage up to a maximum of $5,000. Only costs me a premium of $85 a year to be able to sleep even when I hear the thunder a few miles away. Will I be happy as I wade through the mess in my bathrobe and soggy slippers? No. But I'll be a lot happier than any of my neighbors who chose to take on all the risk themselves, even if they did save a few hundred bucks on premiums. I could have reduced the deductible to $500, just like a stock investor could purchase a put with a strike price closer to his purchase price, but in both cases the premium would be…higher.

And you were afraid options might turn out to be dull. Hah!

> Increasing Overall Return

So, Mr. Jimmy Joe paid for protection. However, the question might have looked like this:

Barbara Bean purchases 100 shares of QSTX for $50 a share. Barbara is bullish on QSTX for the long-term but is afraid it may trade sideways in the short-term. To hedge her risk and increase income, which of the following strategies would you recommend?

 A. sell a call

B. buy a call

C. sell a put

D. buy a put

Well, as we saw, you don't increase your income by buying a put. When you buy something, money comes out of your wallet. In this case, Barbara Bean has to sell an option. What's the only bearish option she could sell?

A call. Call sellers are bearish. Or, bearish-neutral. If the stock goes "sideways," the call will expire in Barbara's favor. Since Barbara already owns the stock, this would be a **covered call**. Let's say she bought the stock at $50, then writes a Sep 60 call at $3. If the stock shoots up to the moon, what would happen? This investor would be forced to honor her obligation to sell the stock at the strike price of $60. Well, she only paid $50 for the stock, so she just made ten bucks there. And, she took in $3 for writing the call. So, she made $13, which represents her maximum gain.

Max gain = (stock cost vs. strike price) + premium

Her maximum loss is much larger than the investor who bought the put in the preceding question. In this case the investor has not purchased a sale price for her stock. All she did was take in a premium of $3. That is the extent of her downside insurance. She paid $50 for the stock and took in $3 for the call. So, when the stock falls to $47 she has "broken even." And, if you prefer to use the T-chart, place the 50 that she paid for the stock in the debit column and the 3 that she received for selling the call in the credit column. What number would balance both sides? 47.

Now that Barbara has broken even at $47, what's to prevent her from losing everything from that point down to zero?

Right, nothing at all. So $47 is her maximum loss. Breakeven down to zero.

Notice the difference between Long Stock–Long a Put and Long Stock–Short a Call. When an investor goes long stock–long a put, she leaves her upside totally unimpeded. Her maximum gain remains "unlimited." And, her maximum loss is usually much smaller than the writer of the covered call. Only problem is she has to pay some money. Covered call writers get limited downside protection and also cap their upside. But, they also get to take in some money.

Okay, so that's half of it. In both cases so far, the investor started out owning or "long" on the stock. The exam could also ask you what an investor who has sold stock short should do in order to hedge his risk.

Hedging Short Positions

Since they sell something they'll eventually have to buy back, short sellers are hoping the stock's price goes down. Short sellers have heard all about "buy low–sell high." They just prefer to do it the other way around: Sell high; buy back low. So if an investor sells a stock short for $50, he hopes it will drop to maybe $1 or $2 a share. If the stock goes up instead, what's his risk?

That the stock could go above $50—forever. Unlimited loss potential. Remember, he still has to buy this stock back, and he definitely doesn't want to buy it back for more than he first sold it for. Which option gives an investor the right to buy stock at the strike price?

Calls.

> Protection

If this investor wants protection, he'll have to buy a call.

The test question could look like this:

An investor sells short 100 shares of ABC at $50. In order to protect against an increase in price, which of the following strategies would you recommend?

    A. buy a put

    B. sell a put

    C. sell a call

    D. buy a call

The answer is "D," buy a call. Again the word "protection" means the investor has to buy an option. If he is concerned about his purchase price, he buys a call, which gives him the right to purchase stock at a strike price. Maybe he's willing to risk having to repurchase the stock at $55 but not a penny higher. Therefore, he buys a Sep 55 call for $2. Using our T-chart, where would we plug in the numbers?

> Max Gain, Max Loss, Breakeven

Well, if he shorts (sells) the stock at $50, that's a credit, right? So, let's place $50 in the credit column. He paid $2 for the call, so that's "2" in the debit column.

Okay, where does this investor break even, then? $48, right? 50 in the credit column, 2 in the debit column, so 48 would make things even.

And if you prefer to analyze the position, start with step one—look at the stock position. He shorted the stock at $50, which means he wants it to go down. If he paid $2 for the option, doesn't the stock have to work his way by exactly $2 before he breaks even?

You bet it does. So when the stock goes down to $48, this investor breaks even. Is there anything to prevent him from making everything from that point down to zero? No. So $48 is his maximum gain, too. Breakeven down to zero.

What about his maximum loss? Well, let's say disaster strikes. The stock skyrockets to $120 a share. Does he have to buy it back at that price in order to "cover his short"? No. At what price could he buy back the stock?

The strike price of $55. That was the protection he bought. And, if he exercised his call, his T-chart would show that $50 came in when he sold short, while $57 came out (when he bought the stock at $55 after buying the call at $2). That's a loss, but it's only a loss of $7, which isn't too bad considering how risky it is to sell a security short.

So if a short seller needs protection, he buys a call. It's the same thing as long stock–long a put, only upside down.

> Increasing Overall Return

Now, let's look at the mirror image of the covered call. Say this same short seller wanted to hedge his bet while also increasing income. If he starts out bearish, he hedges with a bullish position. To increase income, he'll have to sell a position. Only bullish position he can sell is a put. So, he ends up short the stock and also short a put. In other words, he sells the stock short and also sells a put on that underlying stock. If the stock gets put to him, presumably he'll use those shares to cover his short stock position.

163

50

If he shorts the stock at $50 and sells a Jun 40 put @ 3, where would he break even? Well, short sellers want to see the stock go down. However, since he took in $3, he can let his stock position work against him by $3. This investor breaks even at $53.

Right? That's what selling an option does for a hedger; it offsets the potential loss by the amount of premium collected. And, your T-chart tells you that $50 came in when he sold the stock short, plus $3 that came in for selling the put. So 53 is the breakeven point.

What's the most he can lose? Well, how high could the stock jump? Unlimited. Does he have the right to buy the stock back at a particular price? No. So, his maximum loss is unlimited.

Like the covered call writer, he has also capped his "upside" or his maximum gain. His upside is down, remember. When the stock goes down to zero, does he get to buy it back at zero?

Not after writing that put option. The investor who bought the Jun 40 put is going to make him buy the stock for $40. Now the investor realizes his maximum gain. Sold the stock at $50, bought it back at $40. That's a gain of $10. He also took in $3 for writing the put. So, his maximum gain is $13. Stock price vs. Strike price + Premium.

PRACTICE

1. An investor who owns stock would receive best protection if she:

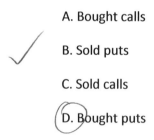

    A. Bought calls

    B. Sold puts

    C. Sold calls

    D. Bought puts

2. An investor who owns stock wants to hedge and increase his income. What should he do?

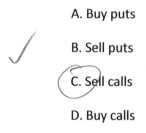

    A. Buy puts

    B. Sell puts

    C. Sell calls

    D. Buy calls

3. An investor who has a short stock position would get best protection by:

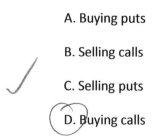

    A. Buying puts

    B. Selling calls

    C. Selling puts

    D. Buying calls

4. An investor with a short stock position wants to hedge and increase his overall yield/return. She should:

A. Buy calls

B. Buy puts

C. Sell puts

D. Sell calls

5. What is the maximum loss for the following position?

Long 100 shares XYZ @60

Buy 1 XYZ Apr 60 put at 3.35

Answer: ___ $335 ___

−6000

−335

6. What is the maximum loss for the following position?

Long 100 shares XYZ @60

Sell 1 XYZ Apr 75 call at 3.85

Answer: ___ $5615 ___

−6000

20

40

(ANSWERS)

1. **D,** to "protect," you buy an option. If you're long stock, you hedge by betting the other way—buy a put.

2. **C,** to increase income/yield, you have to sell an option. Its "arrow" has to be pointed the other way. Long stock—sell a call.

3. **D,** to "protect," you buy an option. If you're short stock, you hedge by betting the other way—buy a call.

4. **C,** to increase income/yield you have to sell an option. Its "arrow" has to be pointed the other way. Short stock—short a put.

5. **$335,** if you buy at 60 and can sell at 60, you can't lose on the stock. You can only lose the premium in this case. It's like a "zero deductible" insurance policy.

6. **$5,615,** if that stock goes to zero, the only thing working in the investor's favor is the premium. If you lose $6,000 on a stock but took in $385, you lost your maximum of $5,615.

Index Options, CBOE VIX

We just looked at how an investor with a stock position can hedge the risk of holding that stock by purchasing puts for protection or selling calls for some protection and increased overall return. Many investors, however, hold so many positions, and these positions match up so closely to a particular stock market index, that their risk is systematic—the risk that the overall market will drop.

We saw that diversifying a portfolio does not protect an investor from this kind of risk. Luckily, there are index options on the major indexes (S&P 500, NASDAQ, DOW, etc.) allowing investors to protect against market risk by purchasing puts or by selling calls. Index options do not involve the delivery of stock upon exercise. Rather, everything is based on points and dollar amounts. When an index option is exercised, the seller delivers the amount that the option is in-the-money in cash to the buyer. Exercise values are as of the close of trading, so early exercise is risky.

An exam question might ask how an investor can protect himself against an overall market drop. One way is to buy puts on the S&P 500 index. Or, if he holds a technology index, he needs to find options on an appropriate technology index.

Beyond using index options to hedge, investors can use index futures (S&P minis), and they can also sell short the ETFs that track the appropriate index. If an investor has a portfolio of stocks that match up to the S&P 500, he can make some money if that index drops after selling the SPY short. By using some of his capital to bet against the overall market, he has reduced his exposure to the systematic risk called market risk.

Perhaps you have heard of the so-called "investor fear gauge" or "volatility index" known as the VIX. The proper name for this index is the **Chicago Board Options Exchange Market Volatility Index**. As the CBOE website explains: The CBOE Volatility Index® (VIX®) is a key measure of market expectations of near-term volatility conveyed by S&P 500 stock index option prices. Since its introduction in 1993, VIX has been considered by many to be the world's premier barometer of investor sentiment and market volatility. Several investors expressed interest in trading instruments related to the market's expectation of future volatility, and so VIX futures were introduced in 2004, and VIX options were introduced in 2006." On another section of the website, we see that, "The New VIX uses options on the S&P 500 Index, which is the primary U.S. stock market benchmark. The original VIX was based on S&P 100 Index (OEX) option prices."

As the website goes on to explain, the S&P 500 and the VIX move opposite of each other, though not at a perfect 1-to-1 relationship. Rather, about 80% of the time one closes up when the other drops and vice versa. Although it is sometimes called the "fear index" or "fear gauge," a high value for the VIX is not necessarily bearish for the stock market. This is because expected market volatility over the next 30 days could be pointed in either a bullish or bearish direction. The highest VIX readings occur when investors overall anticipate large price moves in either direction. A low VIX value would imply that investors expect little movement in the overall stock market.

FUTURES

Like an options contract, a **futures contract** is a binding agreement between two parties that lets the holder buy or sell something for a set price, with delivery occurring at a specified future date. Just like a MSFT Nov 35 call would let the holder of the contract buy 100 shares of MSFT common stock for $3,500 total, a futures contract would let the holder buy so many bushels of corn or soybeans for a set price no matter what the actual market price might be in the future. My cousin Joe over in Bureau County doesn't just wait to harvest his 1,000 acres of corn and beans in the fall and then see how much he can get for it. He's already sold some corn and soybean futures to buyers who want to lock in a purchase price now for delivery, say, next November or December. My cousin, this way, can lock in a minimum price he'll receive for some of his corn and beans in case crop prices end up plummeting by the time he harvests them. And the buyers (ADM, ethanol producers, General Mills, etc.) can lock in a maximum purchase price on some of the grain they need to buy in the near future. What if Cousin Joe sells most of his soybean crop today for $8 a bushel and then soybeans climb to $15 a bushel by the time he harvests them? No problem. In fact, he'll actually make some money, having already bought some soybean futures right after he sold some contracts to the grain buyers. You can make (or lose) money betting in either direction on the future price of corn, soybeans, wheat, sugar, cocoa, pork bellies, cattle, etc.

Futures contracts are standardized by the exchange where they trade. As I write this, I see that the standard terms of coffee futures involve 37,500 pounds of coffee per contract with expiration months in March, May, July, September, and December. Corn futures contracts cover 5,000 bushels each, expressed as a price per-bushel with a minimum "tick size" of ¼ of 1 cent per bushel. So, if a farmer is producing corn, and Kellogg's needs to make Corn Flakes, the farmer can sell some of his crop even before it's harvested, and the cereal maker can lock in a maximum price for corn set for delivery as of a certain month. In these cases the commodity is actually delivered at expiration of the contract. Many speculators, however, simply buy and sell contracts, the same way that options traders do.

Notice how these commodity futures contracts allow both parties to minimize their risk. Of course, that's hypothetically what the options markets allow both parties to do, yet people long ago figured out ways to lose money speculating on those derivatives, too. That's because futures are used not just by the folks who actually buy and sell the underlying commodity but also by folks who just like to speculate. Yes, otherwise perfectly sane adults will occasionally decide to open up a futures trading account and in their spare time start developing strong opinions concerning the near-term price of cocoa, sugar, soybeans, or light sweet crude.

Not that there's anything wrong with that, of course. These days the underlying instrument is not just the raw materials/commodities used to produce other products. Stock indexes, interest rates, currencies, and other financially based instruments are used to create **financial futures**. For example, rather than trading S&P 500 index options, a speculator could trade the S&P 500 futures contracts, e.g., the E-Mini S&P and the E-Mini NASDAQ-100. Or, he could speculate on interest rate movements or foreign currency values.

Remember that options are paid in full; if you buy 3 ORCL Oct 40 calls @2, you have to pay the full $600 upfront (3 times the $200 represented by the "@2"). Not so with futures. The futures exchange requires both parties to put up an initial amount of cash, called either margin or a performance bond—usually between 5 and 15% of the contract value. Then, since the futures price will change daily, the difference in the strike price and the daily futures price is settled daily also. See, if you buy those ORCL Oct 40 calls for $2 a share, you don't actually lose anything right now if they start trading for, say, $1 a share. I mean, it stinks, but until the contract expires, it's just a "paper loss" when you're trading options. On the other hand, with futures the exchange will pull money out of one party's margin account and put it into the other's so that each party has the appropriate daily loss or profit. If the margin account goes below a certain value, a margin call is made and the account owner has to deposit more margin to keep the game going. This process of recalculating values daily is known as marking to market, just as it's called in a margin account for stocks and bonds.

With some contracts the seller delivers the underlying asset to the buyer on the delivery date. For example, my cousin Joe in Bureau County delivers 50,000 bushels of corn to the buyer of 10 contracts. Or, if it's a cash-settled futures contract, then cash is simply transferred from the trader who lost to the trader who won.

As with options, futures can be traded/closed out prior to expiration of the contract. Speculators, obviously, just want to make money trading the contracts. Few people want truckloads of sugar, cocoa, or soybean oil.

FORWARDS

A **forward** is like a futures contract in that it is a derivative that specifies a price for something for delivery at a specified future date. However, a forward is not traded on an exchange and, therefore, does not have the money flowing in and out of either party's margin account due to marking to market. Also, forward contracts are not standardized the way options and futures contracts are standardized by the exchanges on which they trade. On the options and futures exchanges, we find clearinghouses, which act as a buffer between every buyer and seller. I mean—how do you know for sure the other side can actually deliver 100,000 shares of ORCL or a million barrels of light sweet crude? You don't, but luckily the options and futures exchanges have all the buyers and sellers going through clearinghouses, which guarantee the performance of every contract, period. So, forwards are really little side deals between two parties. How do you know the other side is good for the contract if there's no exchange enforcing margin requirements, settlement dates, and guaranteeing that all contracts are good? That's the **counter-party risk** that forwards present to both sides of the contract. On a regulated exchange, options and futures traders do not have to worry about the financial strength of the other side of the contract. The advantage of trading in forwards is the flexibility they allow both sides of the contract—the expiration date, the size of the contract, the terms of the contract, etc., are up to the two parties as opposed to the standardized contracts available on the commodity futures and options exchanges. Some companies have a very specific need for a particular type of derivative that may not be offered on the options or futures exchanges. If that is the case, they may want to structure a private derivative contract with another party called a "forward."

PRACTICE

1. Which type of option may be exercised at any point up to expiration?

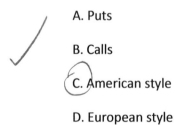

    A. Puts

    B. Calls

    C. American style

    D. European style

2. All of the following are considered "derivatives" except for:

    A. LEAPS

    B. Futures

    C. Forwards

    D. REITs

3. Futures, forwards and options share which of the following characteristics?

    A. Trade on standardized, regulated exchanges

B. Involve daily margin calls

C. Buyers and sellers are buffered by clearinghouses

D. Allow speculators to bet for or against short-term price movements

4. Which of the following explains what occurs when the owner of a put exercises the contract?

A. The owner delivers shares in exchange for 100 times the strike price   50

B. The writer delivers shares in exchange for 100 times the strike price

C. The owner delivers cash equal to 100 times the strike price

D. The owner delivers an option to sell 100 shares for the strike price

(ANSWERS)

1. **C** – both options can be traded whenever the markets are open, but European style may only be exercised at expiration.

2. **D** – REITs are pooled investment vehicles in which each shareholder owns an undivided interest in a portfolio of operating real estate, e.g. apartment buildings or office properties. The others mentioned are derivatives.

3. **D** – forwards are not traded on exchanges and, therefore, do not involve clearinghouses or daily margin requirements/calls. Options trading also does not involve daily margin calls, not for the buyer of the contract, especially. All three derivatives allow speculators to bet that short-term prices are going up or down (or going nowhere).

4. **A** – upon exercise a put buyer sells shares at the strike price, and there are 100 shares per contract.

INVESTMENT VEHICE	FEATURES	RISKS	TAX IMPLICATIONS	LOW/MED/HIGH RISK
Common stock	Claim on earnings/dividends Voting rights Pre-emptive rights Unlimited gain	Market Business Legislative	Dividends taxable Capital gains taxable	High
Preferred stock	Fixed-Income	Interest-rate	Dividends taxable	Low-Med

INVESTMENT VEHICE	FEATURES	RISKS	TAX IMPLICATIONS	LOW/MED/HIGH RISK
	No voting rights No pre-emptive rights	risk Credit risk Reinvestment risk	Capital gains taxable	
ADRs	Common stock in foreign companies Purchased in US $s Traded on American markets	All risks of common stock PLUS, currency exchange risk	Dividends taxable Capital gains taxable Foreign Gov't could tax Investor receives credit for US taxes	High
REITs	Stock in operating real estate portfolio High dividend yields	All risks of common stock	Dividends are ordinary (not qualified) Capital gains taxable	High
Corporate Bonds	A loan to a corporation Receive interest-only, principal with last payment	Interest rate Credit Reinvestment Call Inflation	Interest taxable as ordinary income all three levels Capital gains taxable	Med
Municipal Bonds	A loan to a state, city, school district, park district, etc. Tax-exempt interest	Interest rate Credit Reinvestment Call	Interest exempt at federal and (maybe) state level Capital gains taxable	Low-Med

170

INVESTMENT VEHICE	FEATURES	RISKS	TAX IMPLICATIONS	LOW/MED/HIGH RISK
		Inflation Legislative		
Treasuries	A loan to the US Government Guaranteed interest, principal	No credit risk All *other* risks to bondholders	Interest taxable at federal level Capital gains taxable all levels	Low
Zero Coupons	Bought at discount, mature at par No reinvestment risk	Interest Rate Credit Inflation Liquidity	Tax on annual accretion	Depends on issuer
Money Market Securities	Short-term debt securities High liquidity	Purchasing Power Risk/Inflation Risk	Taxable all levels (unless T-Bills or Muni)	Low
Mortgage-Backed Securities	Interests in a pool of mortgages Monthly income and principal	Prepayment Reinvestment Credit (not GNMA) Inflation	Taxable all levels	Low-Med
CMOs	Debt securities based on pools of mortgage-backed securities or mortgages	Complexity Illiquidity Interest Rate Reinvestment	Taxable at all levels	Med

INVESTMENT VEHICE	FEATURES	RISKS	TAX IMPLICATIONS	LOW/MED/HIGH RISK
Options	Derivatives based on stock, indexes, currencies, etc.	Capital risk	Gains/losses generally short-term	High
Non-qualified Variable Annuities	Insurance-and-Securities Product

No limits on income or contributions | Risks to stock and bond investors, depending on subaccount choices | Tax-deferred earnings

Earnings taxed as ordinary income

No RMDs | Med-High depending on subaccount allocations |
| Fixed Annuities | Insurance Product

No limits on income or contributions

No RMDs | Purchasing Power Risk | Tax-deferred earnings

Earnings taxed as ordinary income

No RMDs | Low—obligation of insurance company |
| Variable Life Insurance | Cash Value and Death Benefit tied to subaccount performance

Insurance-and-Securities Product | Risks to stock and bond investors depending on subaccount choices | Tax-deferred growth of cash value

Death benefit not taxable to beneficiary | Med-High depending on subaccount choices |
| DPPs/Limited Partnerships | Tax Shelter

Illiquid investments

Net worth requirements | Depends on program

Legislative risk (tax code)

Liquidity | Tax Shelter if investor has passive income | High |
| Unit Investment Trusts | Portfolio of preferred stock or bonds | Interest rate

Credit

Reinvestment | Distributions taxed as bond interest or preferred stock dividends | Medium-High |

INVESTMENT VEHICE	FEATURES	RISKS	TAX IMPLICATIONS	LOW/MED/HIGH RISK
	Non-managed Redeemable	Call Inflation		
Exchange Traded Funds (typically)	Trade-able Non-Managed Purchased on Margin Sold Short Low Expenses	Depends on index	Tax-efficient	Depends on index
High-Yield/Junk Bonds	Credit quality of issuer in doubt High yields Capital Appreciation	All risks to bondholders Increased credit risk and volatility	Depends on issuer: corporate or municipal	Medium
Warrants	Right to buy issuer's stock at set price long-term Often attached to bond or preferred stock offering	Same risks as to holder of common stock Liquidity risk Time	Price-per-share added to cost basis when exercised to buy stock	High

©Pass the Test, Inc.

CHAPTER 2 QUIZ

31 questions

1. If a client requires semi-annual interest payments, her registered representative would most likely recommend:

  A. REITs

    B. STRIPS

 C. Junk bonds

D. T-Bills

2. If a corporation has issued different types of preferred stock, which of the following types would likely offer the lowest dividend rate?

A. Callable

B. Convertible

C. Cumulative

D. Straight

3. A change in interest rates would LEAST affect the market price of which security below?

A. Cumulative preferred stock

B. Callable preferred stock

C. Participating preferred stock

D. Convertible preferred stock

4. Which of the following is a true statement concerning annuities?

A. Deferred annuities are suitable for investors with high liquidity needs

B. Immediate annuities are suitable for investors who require tax-exempt income

C. Indexed annuities offer more downside protection than variable annuities

D. Indexed annuities offer more upside potential than variable annuities

5. Which of the following bonds is trading at the deepest discount?

A. 8% coupon, 8.50 yield to maturity

B. 8% coupon, 7.05 yield to maturity

C. 8% coupon, 8.10 yield to maturity

D. 8% coupon, 9.50 yield to maturity

6. Which of the following is associated with decreasing interest rates?

A. Decreasing bond yields

B. Increasing bond yields

C. Decreasing bond prices

D. Increasing default rates

7. You could inform a client that which of the following is guaranteed against default by the US Treasury?

A. FNMA (Fannie Mae)

B. Treasury Receipt

C. GNMA (Ginnie Mae)

D. Technically, no securities are guaranteed

8. A "pooled investment vehicle" would NOT be represented by which of the following?

A. Limited Partnership

B. Closed-end fund

C. Preferred stock

D. Unit Investment Trust

9. Which of the following are money market securities?

A. Rights

B. T-Bills

C. ADRs

D. UITs

10. An investor sells a put option for a premium of $2 per share. If the exercise price is $75 and the underlying security rises to only $76, the investor would realize a:

A. $200 gain

B. $100 gain

C. $100 loss

D. $200 loss

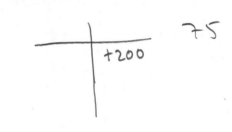

11. Which of the following is an accurate statement concerning preferred stock?

A. it is a debt security, similar to the issuer's bonds

B. it is a fixed-income equity security

C. it trades in sympathy with the issuer's common stock

D. it pays a stated rate of interest to the investor

12. High dividend yields are most associated with which of the following?

A. ADRs

B. REITs

C. Broad-Based Stock Index ETFs

D. Small Cap Growth stocks

13. If Aunt Myra wants to invest in a supervised, un-managed portfolio of fixed-income securities, she would most likely be interested in:

A. Real Estate Investment Trusts

B. Unit Investment Trusts

C. Equipment Trust Certificates

D. Investment-Grade Open-End Bond Funds

14. Common and preferred stock are similar in that:

A. Both are primarily growth investments

B. They have equal voting rights

C. Dividends are paid only if declared by the board of directors

D. Dividends are paid from any surplus interest payments to creditors

15. How do US Treasury securities relate to the so-called "yield curve"?

A. T-Notes typically yield more than both T-Bills and T-Bonds, except when there is a humped yield curve

B. T-Bonds yield less than T-Bills when the yield curve inverts

C. There is no relation, as the yield curve is comprised of corporate bonds

D. T-Bonds yield less than T-Bills in a normal or positive yield curve

16. A callable bond would be especially unattractive to investors in an environment of:

A. High inflation

B. Rising interest rates

C. Falling interest rates

D. Stable interest rates

17. Under the Investment Company Act of 1940, which of the following is not a "management company"?

A. Continuously Offered Closed-End Fund

B. Non-Diversified Closed-End Fund

C. Diversified Open-End Fund

D. Unit Investment Trust

18. Which of the following charges is taken one time from the investor's payment as opposed to deducted from fund assets going forward?

A. Sales charges

B. Transfer Agent fees

C. Management fees

D. 12b-1 fees

19. Derivative securities do NOT include:

A. Equity straddles

B. Equity spreads

C. UITs

D. forwards

20. Which of the following is a true statement of the differences between general obligation and revenue bonds?

A. General obligation bonds pay tax-free interest to institutional investors

B. Revenue bonds typically offer a higher yield to investors

C. General obligation bonds pay tax-free interest to the investor

D. Revenue bonds pay tax-free interest to the investor

21. When trying to explain Net Asset Value of a mutual fund and/or the unit value of a Unit Investment Trust, an investor would best be told:

A. Both values are fixed by the portfolio manager

B. Both values represent the liquidation value of a pooled investment vehicle interest

C. NAV is the market price paid for open-end mutual fund shares

D. The unit value of a UIT does not change due to changes in securities' values

22. An investor most concerned about purchasing power risk would LEAST likely invest in:

A. Convertible preferred stock

B. Small cap equity funds

C. Investment-grade bond funds

D. TIPS

23. If a speculator would like to purchase an equity option that can be exercised early, he should purchase which of the following?

A. European style

B. American style

C. Warrant

D. Index option

24. If an investor seeks semi-annual interest payments she should consider:

A. US Treasury Bills

B. Collateralized Mortgage Obligations

C. US Treasury Notes

D. Fannie Mae preferred stock

25. Which of the following are derivative securities purchased on margin?

A. Commodity futures

B. Equity options

C. Forwards

D. All choices listed

26. A difference between closed-end funds and open-end funds is that closed-end funds

   A. Are managed actively

   B. Are purchased only on the primary market

   C. Trade according to stated investment objectives

   D. Trade on the secondary market

27. An investor seeking both income and growth should invest in which of the following?

   A. growth stock

   B. Investment-grade bonds

   C. junk bonds

   D. bank CDs

28. An investor owns an equity indexed annuity with a 75% participation rate and a cap of 9%. If the S&P 500 rises 20%, the contract value would increase by how much according to these terms?

   A. 20%

   B. 15%

   C. 11%

   D. 9%

29. Scott Scottsdale is a married man with two young children. His insurance agent is showing him an illustration of premiums and cash values for an equal death benefit of whole life and variable life insurance issued by the same company. If you were allowed to see this illustration, you would find that which of the following is accurate?

   A. The premiums for the variable life policy would be lower

   B. The whole life policy involves a scheduled premium, while the variable life insurance premium is flexible

   C. The whole life policy offers an estimated cash value only, while the variable life insurance offers a cash value that is not allowed to vary beyond established parameters

   D. The premiums would be equal given an equal amount of insurance

30. What happens to the market price of XYZ common stock when the board of directors declares a cash dividend of $1-per-share?

A. There is essentially no effect

B. The share price rises by $1

C. The share price rises by some percentage of the dividend

D. On the ex-dividend date the share price drops by $1

31. Which of the following would increase the market price of XYZ common stock?

A. The board of directors and shareholders approve a 1:7 split

B. The board of directors declares a 12% stock dividend

C. The board of directors declares a cash dividend of $1.27-per-share

D. The board of directors and shareholders approve a 3:1 split

(ANSWERS TO CHAPTER 2 QUIZ)
1. ANSWER: C

WHY: a REIT pays dividends, and usually quarterly. A STRIP is a zero-coupon bond, meaning it pays no interest until maturity. A T-Bill is bought at a discount to face value—no interest payments there, either. The answer "junk bonds" might make you a little nervous, but it also happens to be the only answer that can work here. Don't expect the right answers to be what you expect—just make sure they work.

2. ANSWER: B

WHY: if the preferred stock is convertible to common stock, the investor has a big advantage in terms of potential growth; therefore, the investor has to accept a lower dividend rate from the issuer.

3. ANSWER: D

WHY: the other types of preferred stock are tied only to interest rates and credit quality. Convertible preferred stock has that going on but also has a value tied to a completely different factor—the price of the issuer's common stock. Therefore, interest rate moves are not as important to this type of preferred stock's market value. In fact, if the common stock is rising, interest rates are not that important at all.

4. ANSWER: C

WHY: indexed annuities pay a guaranteed minimum rate of return when the stock market has a bad year, which does not happen in a variable annuity. On the other hand, variable annuities offer the full upside of the stock market in a good year, while indexed annuities have participation rates and caps that limit the upside to the investor. Deferred annuities are for investors with low or no liquidity needs, and there is no reason to associate "tax-exempt income" with an annuity.

5. ANSWER: D

WHY: a bond with an 8% nominal yield/coupon rate will always pay out 8% of the par value each year to the investor holding it. However, bonds have market prices that move around in response to interest rate moves, and those market prices change the yields at which the bonds trade on the secondary market. If a bond is trading at a yield that is much higher than the named/nominal yield, the price must be much...lower than par. There is no other way to push yield up—price must go down.

6. ANSWER: A

WHY: rates and yields are the same thing; price moves the other way. As for choice D, if rates are low, issuers could refinance at more favorable terms—possibly avoiding default, right?

7. ANSWER: C

WHY: The Government National Mortgage Association (GNMA) issues debt securities fully guaranteed by the US Treasury. FNMA is a shareholder-owned company. A Treasury Receipt is a product created by a broker-dealer.

8. ANSWER: C

WHY: preferred stock is a form of direct ownership in a company. The other investments here are packaged products put together by financial firms looking to make management fees, syndication fees, etc., for pooling the investment capital of many investors together to form a "pooled investment vehicle."

9. ANSWER: B

WHY: a money market security has to be a debt security, first, and then has to mature in one year or less.

10. ANSWER: A

WHY: the put would expire in this case, so the seller can just enjoy the $200-per-contract premium he collected. The word "only" was meant to mislead you—it implies that the stock needed to rise by a certain amount; in fact, if it had stayed right at $75, the outcome would have been the same. The outcome would have been the same had the stock risen $10 or $50, too. Right? When one sells a put, one just needs the buyer to lose. The buyer loses if the stock never drops below the strike price.

11. ANSWER: B

WHY: the value of a company's preferred stock has no relationship to the value of the common stock. . . unless the preferred stock happens to be convertible. Owners are paid a stated dividend rate, assuming the company makes a profit and the Board of Directors declares the dividend. A bond represents a debt security whose interest must be paid.

12. ANSWER: B

WHY: REITs pay out 90% of their net income, which is a significantly higher payout rate than even the most generous public companies. The phrase "ADR" tells us nothing except the company is foreign with a big presence here in the US Small cap growth stocks often pay no dividends at all—if the companies make a profit, the boards of directors typically decide to reinvest the money into more expansion.

13. ANSWER: B

WHY: the question defines a UIT—a portfolio supervised by a trustee but not managed by an investment adviser. A REIT is a share of stock. An equipment trust certificate is a type of secured corporate bond. And the bond fund is a different type of investment company—a management company.

14. ANSWER: C

WHY: even though preferred stock has a higher claim on earnings/dividends, if there are no earnings, the board might decide to cut or suspend the dividend payment even to the preferred shareholders. Preferred stock is primarily an income investment (except for convertible preferred), and common stock has voting rights, while preferred stock typically does not.

15. ANSWER: B

WHY: normally, we expect long-term T-Bonds to yield more than short-term T-Bills since investors will pay less money for the long-term bonds, which present more interest rate and inflation risk. Therefore, if the yield curve is inverted/upside down, we would see just the opposite of this normal situation.

16. ANSWER: C

WHY: the question is really asking, "When do issuers call bonds?" Same time homeowners try to refinance their debt—when rates are going down.

17. ANSWER: D

WHY: no matter how many adjectives we add, open-end and closed-end funds are management companies. UITs and face-amount certificates are the other two types of Investment Company.

18. ANSWER: A

WHY: a sales charge would be a one-time charge taken out of an investor's check when she buys or sells her shares. The others listed are deductions that the fund makes to cover operating expenses—on an ongoing basis.

19. ANSWER: C

WHY: a UIT is an investment company product in which the investor owns a share of the portfolio. The other products listed derive their value from some underlying instrument—if this thing goes here, then this contract shall be worth this amount.

20. ANSWER: B

WHY: since the revenue bond is only as solid as the project it financed, it tends to offer a higher yield than a GO bond backed by the issuer's ability to raise taxes.

21. ANSWER: B

WHY: the value of a mutual fund or UIT is definitely subject to fluctuation. The current unit value is what the investor would receive if she needed to liquidate.

22. ANSWER: C

WHY: fixed-income securities are not great at protecting purchasing power, but at least the TIPS will pay out more when inflation rises. The best place to be for purchasing power protection is the stock market.

23. ANSWER: B

WHY: American-style options can be exercised anytime up to expiration of the contract. While European-style options (index, foreign currency) can be traded whenever the markets are opened, they are only exercised on the expiration day.

24. ANSWER: C

WHY: T-Notes and T-Bonds pay semiannual interest. T-Bills are bought at a discount. CMOs make monthly interest payments and then return principal all at once. Preferred stock pays dividends, not interest.

25. ANSWER: A

WHY: commodity futures involve daily margin calls. Equity options are paid in full. Forwards are private arrangements between two parties.

26. ANSWER: D

WHY: open-end funds do not trade among investors; rather, they are redeemed or sold back to the issuer.

27. ANSWER: C

WHY: high-yield or "junk" bonds not only provide high rates of income but also offer capital appreciation when the bond's market price improves and/or the bond matures at face value.

28. ANSWER: D

WHY: 75% of the 20% increase is 15%…but the contract can only go up 9% in a given year.

29. ANSWER: A

WHY: if the individual is willing to bear the risk that the cash value and death benefit can drop due to an ugly stock and/or bond market, the premium charged by the insurance company is lower compared to what they charge to guarantee the cash value and death benefit. Both policies involve premiums that would be fixed at a certain amount.

30. ANSWER: D

WHY: on the ex-date it's too late to buy the stock and get the dividend; therefore, you don't pay for the dividend on that day, either.

31. ANSWER: A

WHY: if everybody agrees to have fewer shares (1:7 split), the market price of those shares rises. Stock dividends and forward stock splits (3:1) push the share price down, and a cash dividend at least temporarily pushes the market price down, as well.

CHAPTER 3: Client Investment Recommendations & Strategies

TYPE OF CLIENT

Some of your clients will be human beings, and others will be businesses. Let's start with the **sole proprietor**, which is a human being *and* a business.

SOLE PROPRIETOR

If you're a handyman or a hair stylist, you typically have to pay for state and municipal licenses, so you might not want to also pay an attorney to set up a corporation or other business structure for you. Therefore, it might be tempting to just run your business as a sole proprietor. Unlike setting up a corporation or other business structure, setting up a sole proprietorship doesn't require much in terms of time and expense. The advantages of opening your business as a sole proprietorship include:

- Faster, easier, cheaper setup (corporations require setup fees, and often attorneys)
- Easy tax preparation (1040)
- Income flows directly to the owner (no separate income tax on the business)

The trouble with being in business as a sole proprietor is that you remain personally liable for the debts and lawsuits against the business. In other words, you have not created a separate legal entity. You and the business are one and the same. If the sole proprietorship called Harry's Red Hots accidentally sells 1,000 tainted hot dogs that send swarms of sick people to the emergency room, Harry is in a whole lot of trouble. All the lawsuits will be filed against Harry personally. Or, if Harry simply hits a slow patch, the creditors who used to spot him buns, hot dogs, mustard, and relish are going to come after him personally for all the unpaid bills. Even if he has insurance, once the insurance is exhausted, the angry parties move directly to Harry, not to some corporate structure that would have added a layer of defense. So, the disadvantages of owning a business as a sole proprietor include:

- Personal liability (no separate legal entity), (big disadvantage)
- Harder to obtain loans or attract investment capital due to lower financial controls (financial statements and minutes not required)

Since a sole proprietor is an individual who owns a business that often operates on a shoestring budget, as an investor he or she has a large need for liquidity. In other words, sole proprietors should not be tying up the majority of their money in emerging market funds, hedge funds, small-cap growth stocks, mutual fund B-shares or variable annuities with steep surrender charges, etc. They should probably not even tie up too much capital in long-term bonds that are tough to exit at a fair price when interest rates are rising. Short-term debt securities will provide a regular, even if small, stream of interest and a stable principal, which will help the sole proprietor deal with seasonal slowdowns, industry slumps, leaky roofs, etc. Depending on their risk tolerance, maybe they could invest 70–80% of their money in debt securities with 2-year and shorter maturities, with 20–30% in large-cap value or large-cap growth stocks. That way, as their liquidity needs are being met, their capital also has a chance of growing over the long term, which could come in very handy when they want to expand or retire. Not that they shouldn't have retirement accounts for the latter purpose, which may well be handled quite differently from the funds we've been discussing. But more on that later.

PARTNERSHIPS

As Robert Kiyosaki explains in his book the *Cashflow Quadrant: Rich Dad's Guide to Financial Freedom*, there is a big difference between being a self-employed professional and owning a business. Many business owners are really just cantankerous codgers who don't play well with other people. So they "go into business for themselves" and run everything as a sole proprietorship in which they control every aspect and answer to no one. We just looked at some pros and cons of that business structure.

Another approach is to take on a partner—maybe several partners. What we're talking about here, of course, is a **partnership**. In a partnership, the income and expenses of the business flow through directly to the owners. The business entity itself, in other words, is not taxed. The percentage of profits and losses flowing through to each of the owners is stated in the partnership agreement. Does the partnership create a separate entity that shields the owners from liabilities of the business? That depends on the type of partnership it is.

➢ General Partnership

The main difference between general and limited partnerships has to do with liability. In a **general partnership**, two or more persons own the business jointly and are still subject to creditors and lawsuits personally, just like our man Harry of Harry's Red Hots. Unless otherwise stated in the agreement, the general partners control the business jointly, equally, with one vote each. Therefore, if three college friends want to open a restaurant and maintain 33.3% ownership each, a general partnership may be the way to go. Of course, all three are personally liable should someone get food poisoning at the restaurant, or trip over a loose piece of carpet, etc.

Either way, a general partnership is like a sole proprietorship with more than one owner. The owners agree to be in business together. They do not shield themselves personally from debts or liabilities of the business. But the income and expenses do flow through directly to the partners rather than being taxable to the business, and there are more people to split up the work load and hold each other accountable.

➢ Limited Partnership

We looked at limited partnership interests in Chapter 2 because they are often offered as investment vehicles by certain broker-dealers. But, you and a few other business people could also just form your own limited partnership if the general partnership did not meet your needs. Unfortunately, to form a **limited partnership**, there still has to be at least one **general partner** (GP), who, as we just saw, has personal liability for debts and lawsuits associated with the business. But a limited partnership then has **limited partners** (LPs) who maintain **limited liability** status, meaning they can only lose what they invest into the business. By "invest into the business," I mean the money they put in as well as any debts that they personally guarantee. A debt that a limited partner signs his name to may be called a **recourse note** on the exam, meaning that creditors have legal recourse, or the ability to come after him for the amount he guaranteed personally. A **non-recourse note**, then, would mean that the creditors have no recourse to collect this debt out of the investor's personal assets beyond any collateral that might have been pledged. Maybe a test question will ask what a partnership's cost basis is equal to, with the right answer something like "it equals the capital he contributes initially plus the capital he agrees to contribute in the future."

A limited partner is very interested in maintaining limited liability status. To maintain the shield of protection, one thing that limited partners must do is stay out of day-to-day management decisions. Nevertheless, the LPs do get to vote on the big issues of the partnership through something called **partnership democracy**. Partnership democracy would be used to allow the LPs to have a voice on a limited number of items, such as:

- Dissolving the partnership
- Suing the GP for negligence, breach of fiduciary duty, and other major irritations
- Inspecting certain records

The LPs can get involved with the above without jeopardizing their limited liability status, but not much else. When you're an LP, it's generally best to lay low.

The General Partner has a "fiduciary relationship" to the LPs, which means that the GP must put the LPs' needs first. In legal terms, the GP's fiduciary duty is "two-pronged," meaning he has a duty of loyalty and a duty of good faith. His duty of loyalty means he can't compete with the partnership. His duty of good faith means he has to do whatever he possibly can to run the business successfully and in accordance with the LPs' best interests. The GP can end up getting sued by the LPs if it becomes clear that he is not meeting his duty to the limited partners, through negligence or even outright fraud. If the GP is a lousy businessman who is really just using the partnership as a front for a bunch of personal expenses or gambling activities, that is not going to sit well with the LPs. Or the courts, now that I think about it.

Since the GP has unlimited liability, the general partner is often a corporation rather than a natural person (human being). The corporate structure, as we'll see, provides a layer of protection that would be totally lacking otherwise. Finally, when the limited partnership is liquidated, the senior creditors are paid first, then the unsecured creditors. The next priority is the limited partners, with the general partner last in line. If someone ever asks if you want to be a general partner, give it some hard thought.

The advantages of the limited partnership structure include:

- Flow-through of income and expenses directly to the partners
- Limited partners have limited liability

The disadvantages of the limited partnership structure include:

- General partner has unlimited liability
- Distribution of profits not as flexible as within an LLC

LLC (LIMITED LIABILITY COMPANY)

A **limited liability company** (LLC) is a type of business ownership in which the owners are called "members" and the ones who also manage the business are called "managing members." In a minute, we will see that the S-corp. is limited to 100 shareholders, while the LLC has no limit on the number of members, who can be individuals, corporations, or even other LLCs. In fact, Pass the Test, Inc. is an S-corp. and also a member of the LLC entitled Pass the Test Management Group, LLC. There's also this guy known as Robert Walker somewhere behind both the S-corp. and the LLC, but the point is, there are three separate entities here. If the S-corp. or the LLC get sued, Robert Walker's assets are not at risk. At least, that's what my lawyers tell me.

The owners of an LLC are personally protected from the debts of and lawsuits against the company, including being sued for their own negligence in operating the business, which is nice. Looking at our LLC's **operating agreement,** I see that about the only way the other members could come after me personally is if I caused them damages due to outright fraud/deceit. And I'm basically a very honest guy.

Advantages of setting up an LLC include:

- Limited liability
- More flexible profit distributions (compared to most partnerships)
- No minutes (meetings not required, as opposed to corporations)
- Avoids double taxation of income (gives owners "flow-through")

The exam could bring up the fact that to be structured as an LLC rather than a corporation, the LLC needs to avoid two of four corporate attributes. Two of four. Remember that. That means that it needs to avoid two of the following characteristics associated with *corporations*:

- Perpetual life
- Centralized management
- Limited liability
- Freely transferable assets

It's almost impossible to avoid the centralized management, since there have to be managing members of the LLC. It's also tough to avoid limited liability as a *limited liability* company. So, how do they avoid the perpetual life and freely transferable assets associated with corporations? Unlike a corporation, an LLC often has a limited life. For example, when the LLC is set up, perhaps it has a triggering event after which the business is dissolved—when the last townhouse is sold, or when the movie goes into distribution, maybe. Or, there could even be a fixed date upon which a private investment LLC dissolves, returning cash to the members. Regarding the "freely transferable assets," the members have to agree that they won't sell their interests except according to a certain strict set of rules. For example, if you want to sell your interest to a stranger, the other members might have the right to buy the interest first to prevent that from happening, because who wants to suddenly be in business with a stranger? (Such an agreement or right might be known as a "right of first refusal.") Without such a rule, if one of the members got himself into debt, the other members might discover they were in business suddenly with the guy's bookie, who wanted to collect the debt through the seized profit interest in his hand. Though, come to think of it, much to the bookie's frustration, the other members could vote *not* to distribute profits, and thereby thwart his evil plans.

In any case, the disadvantages of setting up an LLC include:

- Limited life
- Harder to attract financing (creditors don't like the idea explained above)
- More complexity than sole proprietorship (paperwork, set-up fees)

To set up a limited liability company, the business would file its articles of organization with the Secretary of State (or similar office in the state) and pay the filing fees. The owners would also typically draft and sign an operating agreement. Similar to corporate bylaws or partnership agreements, these operating agreements spell out important points about ownership, responsibilities, and the distribution of profits.

CORPORATIONS

The limited liability company provides protection to the owners against claims on their personal assets. Corporations do the same, although they require a little bit more work in terms of having meetings and keeping the minutes of shareholder and board of director meetings.

➤ S-Corporations

The **S-Corporation (S-corp.)** is a very popular form of business ownership. The S-corporation offers protection against debts and lawsuits compared to running the business as a sole proprietor. The income and expenses pass directly to the owners (flow-through), so it's like a partnership or limited liability company in that sense. In other words, it avoids being taxed as a business entity, even as it provides that separate legal structure known as a corporation for the protection of the owners' personal assets. The advantages of using the S-corporation structure include:

- No corporate tax (the entity is not taxed itself)
- Liability protection (compared to sole proprietor)
- Write-offs (early losses can offset personal income of the owners)

Of course, there are also disadvantages to the S-corp., including:

- One class of stock
- 100 shareholders maximum
- Corporate meetings and minutes required

If your business is hoping to attract venture capital, the VC firms will not like the S-corporation structure with its direct flow-through of income and expenses and the limit of 100 shareholders. Also, all stock has equal voting rights and claims on profits, tying the hands of the financiers. And, even if it is a good idea, many business owners hate having to hold an annual board of directors meeting and an annual shareholders meeting, especially if shareholders and board members have to travel from all over to attend.

Oh well. If you want to create a business structure that offers some protection against debts and lawsuits and still avoid the double taxation of income, the S-corp.. is an attractive option. To start an S-corp., the business would file its articles of incorporation with the Secretary of State's office, usually by going through an attorney who does that sort of thing for a living. Again, the cost of establishing a corporation is what keeps many business owners owning things as sole proprietorships. More details on S-corps include:

- The corporation can have no more than 100 shareholders with a husband and wife counting as one shareholder.
- Shareholders can be individuals, estates, and certain trusts.
- Shareholders must be American residents.
- The S-corp. must be a domestic company in any state.

> C-Corporations

The **C-corporation (C-Corp.)** is the traditional corporate structure. When we were talking about common stock in General Electric, Microsoft, Oracle, etc., we were talking about C-corporations. This means that Microsoft is a separate legal entity that is taxed as a corporation—the profits do not flow directly through to large shareholders like Mr. Gates or even small shareholders like me. The corporation gets taxed on all those billions of dollars it makes year after year. Then, when the shareholders receive dividends on the stock, they are also taxed on that income.

C-corporations also have to hold annual shareholder and board of director meetings, and keep the minutes for those snooze-fests. Don't assume that C-corporations are simply S-corporations who wanted more than 100 shareholders. Many small companies are structured as C-corporations even if there are just a few shareholders.

TYPE	ADVANTAGES	DISADVANTAGES	TAXATION	PERSONAL LIABILITY
Sole proprietor	Fast, cheap setup No meetings	Personal liability	Personal income	Yes
General partnership	Flow-through of income, expenses	Personal liability	Flow-through to owners	Yes
Limited partnership	Flow-through of income, expenses	Must have one general partner, with unlimited liability	Flow-through to owners	Not for limited partners
LLC	Flow-through of income, expenses	Not good for attracting VC	Flow-through to owners	No, not even for negligence while running business
S-corp.	Flow-through of income, expenses	Annual meetings Not good for attracting VC one class of stock	Flow-through to owners	No
C-corp	Attracting capital	Double taxation of income Annual meetings	Taxed as business entity	No, not even for negligence while running business

190

CLIENT PROFILE

Whether you are a financial planner or a securities agent, before helping someone invest in securities you must gather key financial information including:

- Income sources
- Current expenditures
- Discretionary income
- Assets
- Tax bracket

To determine how much the individual has to invest, we need to look at his income statement or statement of cash flow. A personal income/cash flow statement might look like this:

Monthly Income	
Salary	$7,000
Investment Income	$1,000
Other Income	$500
Total Monthly Income	$8,500

Monthly Expenditures	
Taxes	$2,000
Mortgage Payment	$2,000
Living Expenses	$2,000
Insurance Premiums	$300
Loan Payments	$200
Travel/Entertainment	$300
Other Expenses	$200
Total Monthly Expenses	$7,000
Monthly Capital for Investing	$1,500

So, a client with the above income statement has **discretionary income** or excess **cash flow** of $1,500. Those are just fancy terms for "what he has left after paying the bills." If he has a long time horizon of, say, 10+ years, the money could go into stock mutual funds investing for growth. If he has a lower tolerance for wide fluctuations of yearly performance, he might choose growth & income, equity income, or balanced funds. And, if his time horizon is shorter, he might stay out of the stock market entirely and invest, instead, in short- or intermediate-term bond funds.

Now, I'm not sure if the exam wants to talk about an investor's "cash flow" as a synonym for "discretionary income," or if it wants to split hairs on the difference between an individual's income statement and statement of cash flow. Just in case it does want to split hairs, let's quickly discuss the differences. Let's say an individual is repaying a loan, and let's say he makes total payments of $15,000 on that loan this year. If $5,000 of that is interest and $10,000 is a reduction of principal, only the $5,000 will show up on the income statement as an expense. The cash flow statement would show us the other $10,000 that went towards the principal.

Of course, taxes always play a part in an investment strategy. If your client is in a high **marginal tax bracket**, you may want to recommend municipal bonds, which generally pay interest that is tax-exempt at the federal level. A high-tax-bracket client probably doesn't want to do a lot of short-term trading, either, since any gain taken within the space of a year will be taxed at the short-term capital gains rate (which equals his marginal tax rate). He also might want to buy stocks that pay qualified dividends rather than REITs or royalty trusts, which will force him to pay his ordinary/marginal rate on the dividends. Or, maybe he could put the REITs and royalty trusts into a retirement plan that allows the dividends to grow tax-deferred until withdrawn, when he is in a lower tax bracket. In other words, different clients will require different recommendations and strategies.

A business has both an income statement and a balance sheet. So do your clients. Remember that assets represent what somebody owns, while liabilities represent what he owes. The difference between what somebody owns and what he owes is known as his financial **net worth**. The way I think of it is that generally the income statement shows how well someone is living, while the balance sheet shows how much wealth he is building along the way.

A client's assets would include the value of his home, automobiles, personal possessions, investments, savings, and checking accounts. Liabilities would include mortgages and other loan balances, credit-card balances, and, perhaps, debit balances in margin accounts.

A personal balance sheet might look like this:

Assets	
House	$400,000
Automobiles	$30,000
Personal possessions	$15,000
Stocks and Bonds	$100,000
Keogh Plan	$80,000
IRA	$20,000
Checking	$5,000
Savings Account	$5,000

Money Market	$5,000
Total Assets	$660,000

Liabilities	
Mortgage	$250,000
Auto Loans	$10,000
Credit Card Balances	$15,000
Total Liabilities	$275,000
Net Worth	$385,000

When we looked at corporate balance sheets in Chapter 1, we mentioned that analysts look only at a company's "quick assets" rather than including the hard-to-liquidate assets such as plant and equipment in some of their calculations, e.g. the "quick ratio." Similarly for individuals, since some assets are difficult to liquidate, we might exclude those items (house, limited partnerships, rental property) in order to calculate **liquid net worth**. If a client has high total net worth but low liquid net worth, an investment adviser or securities agent might steer the client toward more liquid investments, like short-term debt versus a long-term zero coupon bond, or heavily traded stocks and bonds as opposed to some funky issue trading on the Non-Nasdaq OTC market.

Watch out for a tricky test question that says that JoAnne Johnson recently took $5,000 out of her savings account and paid down her mortgage or credit card debt by $5,000—how much did that increase her net worth?

Not one penny. If you remove a $5,000 asset in order to remove a $5,000 liability, your net worth is unchanged. JoAnne's net worth will only rise if the value of her assets rises—the house appreciates, the value of the investments inside her IRA increases, etc. To check that, simply look at our balance sheet again and see what would happen to net worth if you removed the $5,000 in savings in order to remove $5,000 of the mortgage balance. Does the net worth change? What if the value of the house increased by $20,000? Now the net worth goes up by $20,000, right?

While gathering information on a client's assets, you're also uncovering his current securities holdings. Many investors have a huge percentage of their portfolio tied up in one company's stock—their employer's. If a client has too much money concentrated in just one stock, an adviser might advise him to sell some of that holding in order to diversify. Other clients will already be diversified, which is just as important to determine before recommending investments. If they already hold 20 large-cap stocks, you probably don't want to recommend that they put the rest of their discretionary income into Dow Jones Index funds, which would be sort of redundant.

CLIENT INVESTMENT RECOMMENDATIONS AND STRATEGIES

INVESTMENT OBJECTIVES, TIME HORIZON, RISK TOLERANCE
So, now that you've opened an account for your client you want to help her allocate her money to various investment vehicles. First, what are her **investment objectives**? Investment objectives include:

capital preservation, income, growth & income, growth, and speculation. If the individual is in her 30s and setting up a retirement account, she probably needs growth to build up her financial net worth before reaching retirement age. If she's already in retirement, she probably needs income. If she's in her 50's and wants to retire in 10-12 years, she might be looking for both **growth & income,** which some firms consider one objective. An investment in a mutual fund by that name might be suitable, as might investments in blue chip or large-cap value stocks.

Some firms separate growth from **aggressive growth** as an investment objective. Some firms view growth as one objective that investors pursue with varying degrees of aggressiveness. Either way, aggressive growth investments include international funds, sector funds (healthcare, telecommunications, financial services, etc.) and emerging market funds (China, India, Brazil, etc.). For **speculation,** there are options and futures, and most investors should limit their exposure to these derivatives to a small % of their portfolio—basically, whatever amount they are allowed to lose without having to tell their wives.

If you're "saving up for retirement," that generally means you need **capital appreciation,** right? On the other hand, some folks are already rich, and they just want to preserve their capital (**capital preservation**). Investors can buy US Treasury securities all on their own, without commissions. But, many chose instead to invest in US Treasury mutual funds. Even though the fund is not guaranteed, the securities the fund owns are, remember. So, it is an investment on the safer side of things, but while Treasury securities are guaranteed against default, a mutual fund is just a mutual fund.

Knowing the investor's objective is important, but it has to be tempered by the **time horizon** before you start recommending investments. In general the longer the time horizon the more volatility the investor can withstand. If you have a three-year time horizon, you need to stay almost completely out of the stock market and invest instead in high-quality bonds with short terms to maturity. If you're in for the long haul, on the other hand, who cares what happens this year? It's what happens over a 20- or 30-year period that matters. With dividends reinvested, the S&P 500 has historically gained about 10% annually on average, which means your money would double approximately every 7 years. Sure, the index can drop 30% one year and 20% the next, but we're not keeping score every year. It's where we go over the long haul that counts. A good way to see the real-world application of risk as it relates to time horizon would be to pull out the prospectus for a growth fund and see if you can spot any two- or three-year periods where the bar charts are pointing the wrong way. Then compare those horrible short-term periods to the 10-year return, which is probably decent no matter which growth fund you're looking at. That's why the prospectus will remind folks that they "may lose money by investing in the fund" and that "the likelihood of loss is greater the shorter the holding period." See how important "time horizon" is?

Younger investors saving for retirement have a long time horizon, so they can withstand more ups and downs along the road. On the other hand, when you're 69 years old, you probably need some income and maybe not so much volatility in your investing life. So the farther from retirement she is, the more likely your investor will be buying stock. The closer she gets to retirement, the less stock she needs and the more bonds/income investments she should be buying. In fact, you may have noticed that many mutual fund companies are taking *all* of the work out of retirement planning for investors, and offering **target funds.** Here, the investor picks a mutual fund with a target date close to her own retirement date. If she's currently in her mid-40s, maybe she picks the Target 2040 Fund. If she's in her mid-60s, maybe it's the Target 2020 Fund. For the Target 2040, we'd see that the fund is invested more in the stock market and less in the bond market than the Target 2020 fund. In other words, the fund automatically changes the allocation from mostly stock to mostly bonds as we get closer and closer to the target date. The same thing happens in an age-based portfolio used in a 529 Plan. When your child is a baby, the allocation is probably 90% stock, 10% fixed-income. As your child gets older, the portfolio gets more conservative, just as many readers have done over the years.

An investor might have the primary objective of growth or even aggressive growth. He might also have a time horizon of 10+ years. However, if he doesn't have the **risk tolerance** required of the stock market, we have to keep him out of stocks. Remember that risk tolerance has to do with not only the financial resources, but also the psychological ability to sustain wide fluctuations in market value, as well as the occasional loss of principal that really irks some people. The terms "risk-averse," "conservative," and "low risk tolerance" all mean the same thing—these investors will not tolerate big market drops. They invest in fixed annuities, US Treasuries, and investment-grade bonds. In order to invest in sector funds or emerging market funds the investor needs a high risk tolerance. Moderate risk tolerance would likely match up with balanced funds, equity income funds, and conservative bond funds.

Let's put the three factors together: investment objectives, time horizon, and risk tolerance. If we know that the investor in the suitability question seeks growth, we then have to know his time horizon and risk tolerance. If he's a 32-year-old in an IRA account, his time horizon is long-term. Unless he can't sleep at night knowing the account balance fluctuates, you would almost *have* to recommend growth funds. His risk tolerance would tell us whether to use small-cap, mid-cap, or large-cap growth funds—the higher the risk tolerance the smaller the "cap." Or, maybe we get even more aggressive with emerging market and sector funds. If the investor is 60 years old and living on a defined benefit pension income, she might need to invest in common stock to protect her purchasing power. If so, her time horizon is long, but her risk tolerance is probably only moderate or moderate-low. So, we'd probably find a conservative stock fund—maybe a growth & income, equity income, or large-cap value fund.

If an investor seeks income primarily, we need to know her time horizon and risk tolerance. We don't buy bonds that mature beyond her anticipated holding period. If she has a 10-year time horizon, we need bonds that mature in 10 years or sooner. Buying 7-year bonds for someone with a 10-year holding period is not a problem, while going the other way typically is. In any case, the investor's risk tolerance will tell us if we can maximize her income with high-yield bonds, or if we should be smart and buy investment-grade bond funds instead. If she needs tax-exempt income, we put some of her money into municipal bond funds. For capital preservation nothing beats US Treasury or GNMA securities. Money market mutual funds are safe—though not guaranteed by the US Government or anyone else—but they pay low yields. Money market mutual funds are for people who want to not only preserve capital but also make frequent withdrawals from the account. See, even though your money is safer in a 30-year Treasury bond than in a money market mutual fund, the big difference is that the market price of your T-Bond fluctuates (rates up, price down), while the money market mutual fund stays at $1 per share.

Seriously. So if **liquidity** is a major concern, the money market mutual fund is actually better than T-Bonds, T-Notes, and even T-Bills, all of which have to be sold at whatever price. With the money market mutual fund you can write checks, and the fund company will redeem the right number of shares to cover it.

Total liquidity. Then again, that total liquidity comes at a price. While there are no ongoing fees to hold Treasury Notes (and no commissions to buy them directly from the US Treasury), money market mutual funds usually have annual expenses of about 75 basis points. That might not sound like much until you recall that these "investments" only earn short-term interest rates. If the fund is earning 1%, when you're paying .75%, your liquidity is causing you to miss out on much higher returns offered in the bond and stock markets. That is known as "opportunity cost," as I mentioned.

The questionnaire that the client fills out when opening an account with your firm will try to gauge what is more important—going for large returns or maintaining a stable principal? Earning a high level of income or making sure he gets his money back from the investment? Does he need to withdraw a large portion of his portfolio at a moment's notice? If so, put that portion in money market securities and short-term bonds. Here is an over-simplified chart that will help you at least begin sorting out the major investment options according to risk tolerance.

AGGRESSIVE	Emerging Markets
	International/Global
	Small-cap (growth or value)
	Sector funds
MODERATE – HIGH	Mid-, Large-cap Growth
	Growth & Income
MODERATE – LOW	Balanced, Equity Income
	Large-cap Value
LOW	Investment-Grade Bonds
VERY LOW	Treasuries, Money Market

CLIENT RECOMMENDATIONS

In order to work with some of the preceding information let's look at 10 different case studies and see what we would recommend for each investor. As in the real world of investing, none of this is scientific. But, if we follow basic industry guidelines, we can match the questions on your exam closely enough to get you prepared.

Our first investor is a divorced 71-year-old man who recently sold a small landscaping business for $300,000 after capital gains taxes. Although he loved to work 12-hour days for decades, those days are behind him now. This customer does not trust the stock market and also remembers that his father lost a bunch of money in bonds back in the late '70s. This $300,000 is the money your customer plans to live on as a supplement to social security. His house has a mortgage balance of $25,000 and his living expenses are reasonable, although he will need a new automobile in the next few years and both a roof replacement and a new water heater for his 30-year-old house.

- INVESTMENT OBJECTIVES: capital preservation, income
- TIME HORIZON/LIQUIDITY: long-term, high liquidity needs
- RISK TOLERANCE: low

This investor is clearly not interested in risking a loss of his investment principal. If you make aggressive recommendations to him, it's not just a bad idea, but also a potential arbitration or civil court proceeding.

Which is bad. Remember, if capital preservation is the main objective, your recommendation has to address that first and foremost—anything that conflicts with that goal is to be rejected. US Treasury securities provide capital preservation, so we'll either buy them directly or through a mutual fund. Easy enough.

His next objective is income. Do US Treasury securities provide income? Yes. Are they liquid? Yes, but if he anticipates frequent withdrawals from the account, we'd have to avoid long-term T-Bonds and stick to the more liquid 2-year US Treasury notes or even US Treasury bills, which have maturities of just a few weeks. Depending on the four answer choices in the suitability question, we might even end up choosing a money market mutual fund here. Why not? That's a safe place to park his money, it does provide income, and it is completely liquid.

What we can eliminate for this investor: equity funds, high-yield bond funds, municipal bond funds, and long-term bond funds. The municipal bond funds aren't risky, but if we see nothing about the investor's needs for tax-exempt income, we can't recommend them.

What we might recommend for this investor: T-Bills, short-term T-Notes, investment-grade bonds/bond funds with shorter maturities, money market mutual funds.

Our next investor is a 53-year-old school teacher who got a little too enthusiastic running half-marathons in her 40s and now lacks the energy to teach on her feet all day. She does not want to start taking withdrawals from her 403(b) account before age 59 but is ready to switch to part-time teaching now or perhaps even an administrative support position for the next 5–7 years, both of which would pay half or less of her current salary.

- INVESTMENT OBJECTIVES: income, capital preservation
- TIME HORIZON/LIQUIDITY: 5–7 years, moderate liquidity
- RISK TOLERANCE: moderate

This investor needs income, so I'm already thinking of bonds or bond mutual funds. Preferred stock might work, too, but my bias is with the bonds and bond funds. Remember that bond interest has to be paid while preferred stock dividends are paid if the board of directors declares them out of profits/net income. The investor's secondary objective is capital preservation, so I don't like junk bonds, obviously. I also don't see "capital appreciation" or growth as an objective, so why bring up stocks here? All we really have to do for this investor is recommend investment-grade bonds or bond funds that match her 5–7-year time horizon. So, if I see an intermediate-term investment-grade bond fund as an answer choice, I like that one a lot. Right?

What we can eliminate for this investor: growth stock and growth stock funds, high-yield bonds, money market mutual funds (yields are too low given her moderate liquidity needs).

What we might recommend for this investor: intermediate-term investment-grade bonds and bond funds. A balanced fund would also work. Most balanced funds invest as if the investors are all conservative and in need of income. Still, they put such a big % in the stock market, and I don't see where this investor is telling us she needs to be in equities at all. Remember—it's HER money. If she's happy in the bond market, and you're earning commissions or advisory fees, why stick your neck out? Make your case, but meeting the client's needs sometimes means doing what she wants to do regardless of what you would like her to do. Few parents can get their kids to do what they would like them to do—why would we expect adults we barely know to be totally compliant with our wishes?

Our third investor is the mother of our second investor, and is also a school teacher. Only this investor is a *retired* teacher. Her teacher's pension allows her to pay bills, but she also finds herself having to "do without" more often than she would like. Age 73, she remembers the rampant inflation of the 1970s and is afraid that her pension checks might not keep up with the price of groceries, gas, electric, clothing, etc.

- INVESTMENT OBJECTIVES: purchasing power protection
- TIME HORIZON/LIQUIDITY: long-term, moderate liquidity needs
- RISK TOLERANCE: moderate

First, remember that growth, capital appreciation, and purchasing power protection all mean the same thing, and they all point to the stock market. Don't all retirees need income investments? Not if they're already receiving a fixed income, right? A teacher's pension is a fixed-income stream—a fixed annuity, really. And, like most fixed annuities, this thing may or may not keep up with the rising cost of living. So, we need to be in the stock market. And many of the stocks we like here are going to end up paying dividends. But, that is not necessarily what we're after. I mean, it's a good sign that a company can pay a dividend—means they earn regular profits, which is sort of important in business. But, what we need here is growth or capital appreciation. And, we need to get it without getting too aggressive. In other words, this is an extremely easy recommendation to make. We want conservative growth funds or large-cap growth stocks/funds—whatever the exam calls them. A diversified, professionally managed portfolio of large-cap stocks would be ideal. Maybe the right answer choice will be something like "50% domestic large-cap stock fund, 50% international large-cap stock fund." That seems aggressive, but with her pension providing the fixed-income piece, this sort of allocation will address her purchasing power concerns without getting too crazy.

What we can eliminate for this investor: small cap funds, aggressive growth investments in general, bonds and bond funds, money market mutual funds.

What we might recommend for this investor: large cap growth stock or funds, blue chip stock or funds.

Our fourth investor is a 64-year-old man who retired last year with a modest pension benefit and a small Traditional IRA account that he does not want to touch until he's required to—at age 70½. This investor recently sold a five-bedroom house in an affluent neighborhood and bought a relatively inexpensive condominium near the shopping, restaurants, and theater district of the college town in which he was born and raised. He has been drawing down the proceeds of the sale (even after the purchase of the condo) and now has approximately $400,000 left to invest with you. This investor is in excellent physical shape and plans to spend the next several years hiking the Appalachian Trail, kayaking the Boundary Waters, snorkeling in Costa Rica, etc. Since he has no plans to take a part-time job, the investor needs income to fund the travel he plans to do over the next several years. He does not need to make withdrawals of "principal" from this account, but he does plan to spend every dollar of income that he earns from whatever investments you and he choose. And, he knows that his living expenses will likely rise over time and he, therefore, needs his principal to keep up with the rising cost of living.

- INVESTMENT OBJECTIVES: high income, capital appreciation
- TIME HORIZON/LIQUIDITY: long-term, low liquidity needs
- RISK TOLERANCE: moderate-high

If this investor wants high income, we have to start in the bond market. Since his risk tolerance and time horizon are appropriate, we might recommend a high-yield bond fund. Chances are we don't want to pick individual "junk" or "high-yield" bonds, since each individual issue is somewhat susceptible to default; however, a well-managed and well-diversified mutual fund with a proven track record should be able to maximize the portfolio's income and minimize the rate of default. If the bonds mature at par, or at least rise in market value as the issuer's financial health improves, there will be capital appreciation.

Or, the exam question might give an allocation like this: 50% high-yield bonds, 50% stocks. That would work for me. Or, even 25% high-yield bonds, 25% investment-grade bonds, 50% stocks. If the best answer choice appeared to be "REITs," I could also live with that—they are known for high income and, as stocks, they do offer capital appreciation. However, that makes me nervous since REITs pay dividends, meaning the company has to make a profit to pay them. Bond interest, on the other hand, is a legal obligation that has to be paid just like your mortgage and credit card bills have to be paid.

Our fifth investor has a 13-year-old daughter who is an excellent student dreaming of one day attending Dartmouth, Yale, or Duke. This investor has a 529 Plan opened for her daughter's education, but so far only $10,000 has gone into the account, with the investments currently worth only $7,255.43 after some bad market years and the regular expenses of the plan. She knows she needs to build up the balance of the account but would be more comfortable reinvesting regular income checks from her investments as opposed to waiting for some promise of "capital appreciation" entirely. She has some confidence in the stock and bond markets. She also knows they are both unpredictable and should, therefore, never be used as a reserve or spending account..

- INVESTMENT OBJECTIVES: capital appreciation/growth, income
- TIME HORIZON/LIQUIDITY: 5–10 years, low liquidity needs
- RISK TOLERANCE: moderate

Since capital appreciation is the primary objective, we have to look at stocks or equity mutual funds for this investor. But, since she also has a secondary objective of income, we don't buy pure growth funds; we buy "growth & income" funds. Or, maybe the answer is something like "70% stocks, 30% bonds." That seems to work. A large-cap value fund would be appropriate, also. In fact, there are many potential answer choices that could work for this investor—just make sure you put the capital appreciation first, and the income second.

What we can eliminate for this investor: bonds and bond funds, money market mutual funds.

What we might recommend for this investor: growth & income funds, stock index funds, blue chip equity funds. Equity income and balanced funds are pretty close as recommendations, but those funds would put income first, while a growth & income fund, believe it or not, puts growth first. An answer choice of "60% stock, 40% bonds" would also work. Again, there are many possible answers to an investor like this one. As always, weed out the answer choices that don't work first.

Our sixth investor is 59 years old and wants to retire at age 70. His Traditional IRA account is not well-funded and has not achieved much capital appreciation over the years. In fact, your team revealed that over the 30 years the account has been open, his contributions have equaled $50,000, with the account currently worth only $44,000. In other words, he has gotten a tax *deduction* on the contributions, but, so far, no tax *deferral.*

Oh well, a lot of customers will have a litany of complaints about their investment experience so far, but hindsight is 20/20. What matters now is the future. If the investor wants to retire in 10 years, with his account currently worth just $44,000, how can you help him? Does he have any real estate, annuities, or savings bonds to enhance his "net worth"? Unfortunately, no. Beyond a half dozen really cool and highly collectible electric guitars, the sum total of his "nest egg" is the $44,000 sitting in an IRA account. And, he has been seriously considering just taking out that money, buying a Harley, and touring the country until he runs out of gas, money, and gumption.

- INVESTMENT OBJECTIVES: capital appreciation/growth
- TIME HORIZON/LIQUIDITY: 10+ years, low liquidity needs
- RISK TOLERANCE: moderate

Before we worry about the investment vehicle first we need to convince this investor of the dire need to make his maximum IRA contribution each year until the IRS says he can't do it—which is only about 10 years away. Currently, he can contribute $6,500 a year as long as he has at least that much earned income. That number will likely rise a bit over the next 10 years, and your investment team needs to run some future value calculations to see how that amount of contributions plus a reasonable amount of growth can get him to an account large enough to help him in retirement. Frankly, though, I have my doubts—$44,000?

Anyway, once we get him on a regular monthly direct-deposit plan for his Traditional IRA account, we need to pick investment options. It seems clear that this investor will be in an equity fund, or a mix of equity funds. Also, these equity funds will be neither too aggressive nor too conservative for him. If I see an answer choice like "Mid-Cap Growth" or "Large Cap Growth," I'm really tempted to choose it. An answer choice like "S&P 500 Index Fund" would also not be wrong. Basically, this guy is just a growth investor who doesn't want to get crazy chasing overvalued and overhyped stocks. Still, choosing a conservative stock fund makes me a little cranky, too, since his account balance is going to be useless in retirement if it doesn't grow significantly through capital appreciation and regular contributions.

If the investor had a fixed annuity or a pension income to supplement this account, then we could be more aggressive with the stock picks. But, since we aren't finding any of that good stuff, we're in a tough spot. It's kind of like when you're late for an appointment: do you decide to speed or play it safe? If you speed and get by with it, you win. However, if you get caught speeding, you not only miss your goal of making the appointment, but also lose a bunch of money. Could you face this investor as he hands you a shopping cart at the local Walmart after talking him into some international aggressive growth fund that loses 70% of its value?

Me, neither. If the answer choices include mutual funds, we want growth funds that are neither too aggressive nor too conservative. If the choices are asset allocations, we might go with 80% stock, 20% bonds.

What we can eliminate for this investor: bonds and bond funds, money market mutual funds, aggressive growth investments (emerging markets, sector funds, etc.) small cap growth funds, conservative stock funds, balanced funds, equity income funds.

What we might recommend for this investor: large cap growth fund, blue chip equity fund, stock market index fund.

Our seventh investor is a 48-year-old woman who works in marketing for a successful mid-sized manufacturing company. Like most people her age, she has had to save for retirement mostly on her own. The company where she works offers a 401(k) plan, but they only match up to 5% of her salary, and her salary is only $53,000. Retirement seems a long way off, but she has a vague idea that she'd like to retire before she's 70. Her 401(k) plan balance is currently $127,415.19. She feels she cannot retire on less than $500,000, even if she makes a capital gain when selling her house and downsizing someday.

- INVESTMENT OBJECTIVES: capital appreciation/growth
- TIME HORIZON/LIQUIDITY: 20+ years, low liquidity needs
- RISK TOLERANCE: high

Again, even before we pick the investment vehicles, this investor should understand that regardless of how stingy her employer is her 401(k) account will allow her to contribute more than three times what she could contribute to a Traditional IRA account. Now, while she could definitely maximize her 401(k) contributions and also maximize her Traditional IRA with tax-deductible contributions, I don't see that she has that much money to sock away for retirement. She needs to make a reasonable contribution into her 401(k) account—as much as she can afford to.

As far as where to put those contributions, this investor will be in stocks or stock/equity mutual funds. This time, however, we want more aggressive investments. Small cap growth stocks or funds would be an ideal choice. Other correct recommendations might include sector funds, international funds, and global funds. Most stock index funds would also work—S&P Mid-Cap 400 or the Russell 2000, for example, would both be good answer choices.

What we can eliminate for this investor: bonds and bond funds, money market mutual funds, conservative stock funds, balanced funds, equity income funds.

What we might recommend for this investor: small cap growth stock/funds, stock index funds, sector funds, international funds.

Note: some texts would consider sector, international, and global funds to be "aggressive growth" vs. plain-ole "growth," but we don't know what an actual test question will look like. This investor is either a growth investor with a high risk tolerance or "an aggressive growth investor," in my book. Since nothing indicates she needs safety or liquidity, I would not rule out any stock investment as "too aggressive" here.

Our eighth investor makes a lot of money, and has a lot of money. Then again, what's "a lot of money"? To me, $3 million of investable assets ought to do it, but for this investor there is, apparently, never enough. Since his late 20s he has been making at least six figures, and since his late 30s the thought of making a mere "six figures" has given him the willies. Then again, while his average income over any 10-year period has been pretty good, there always seem to be those 3- and even 5-year periods where the income drops much more than he admits to himself or his drinking buddies. This investor is 57 years old and is not interested so much in retiring as in knowing that he *could* retire any time he wants to. He has $1.5 million to invest with you. He has a small mortgage balance, two vacation properties, and approximately $100,000 in checking and savings that he is *not* interested in investing with you. His retirement accounts total about $900,000, and he plans to keep maximizing the SEP-IRA he participates in as a salesman for a small software company. His father lived to age 93 and his grandfather to age 91. He does not plan to slow down or retire for at least 10 years.

- INVESTMENT OBJECTIVES: retirement income
- TIME HORIZON/LIQUIDITY: long-term, low liquidity needs
- RISK TOLERANCE: low

This investor seems like a prime candidate for a fixed annuity. If he already has close to $1 million in his retirement accounts, and plans to keep funding them a while, why not put $1.5 million into a fixed annuity that promises to pay a minimum amount each month once he throws the switch, no matter how long he lives? He's afraid that he never has enough money, and his father and grandfather lived long lives—I'd say he needs the annuity to assure he won't completely run out of money no matter how long he himself manages to live. If he were going to retire now, we'd choose an immediate annuity. Since he won't retire for at least 10 years, a deferred annuity works; he will not be hit with a surrender charge since he won't need to touch the money and there will also be no tax penalties that way.

If we saw statements about a fear of losing purchasing power/inflation, we might choose a variable annuity instead. That way, he could put some money in the stock market subaccounts and the rest in safer subaccounts, maybe. But with this investor's up-and-down income coupled with his fear of running out of money and his father's and grandfather's longevity, I think a question presenting this set of facts would be screaming out for a fixed annuity on at least a large chunk of the investor's money. Just make sure he keeps maximizing his other retirement options, and that he really doesn't need to touch the money for a while, and you can go ahead and recommend a deferred fixed or deferred indexed annuity. Knowing he'll get a minimum payment each month for the rest of his life will buy this investor a lot of sleep.

What we can eliminate for this investor: just about everything. I don't see a big need for current income or a huge need for capital appreciation/growth. He isn't complaining about high taxes, so we don't need to look at municipal bond funds or direct participation programs.

What we might recommend for this investor: fixed annuity or equity indexed annuity from an insurance company with a high claims-paying ability (AM Best Rating).

Investor Number Nine is a 75-year-old widow with a financial net worth of $5 million. Her income sources include rental income from a few real estate LLC interests she inherited from her husband, plus the IRA account now worth $1.2 million after she inherited and combined her husband's IRA with her own. She takes the required minimum distribution from the IRA each year, but that falls far short of funding her rather expensive lifestyle. Because she likes to shop, eat out, attend the theater, and decorate her townhouse, this investor needs income. However, since her annual income is close to $1 million, she ends up losing over 1/3 of that to the federal government and close to 5% to her state government. This investor is slightly concerned about a loss of purchasing power, though receiving income from her investments is clearly the main objective.

- INVESTMENT OBJECTIVES: tax-exempt income, purchasing power protection
- TIME HORIZON/LIQUIDITY: intermediate-to-long-term, low liquidity needs
- RISK TOLERANCE: low

This one seems pretty straightforward. The lion's share of this investor's income is taxed at the top two marginal tax rates. Since she needs income that is tax-exempt, we will recommend municipal bonds. We can either buy them a la carte or as a packaged set. If she's truly in a high-tax state, there may be an open- or closed-end fund designed for residents of that state. For example, if she lives in Maryland, there will be municipal bond funds for residents of that state. The income dividends they generate would, therefore, be exempt from both federal and state income taxes for this investor. Now, to deal with her concern over inflation/loss of purchasing power, we can put a small percentage of her account into a conservative equity fund, possibly a low-cost S&P 500 Index fund.

What we can eliminate for this investor: aggressive investments, a large concentration in growth stocks/growth funds, taxable bonds (corporate or US Treasury).

What we might recommend for this investor: municipal bonds primarily issued inside her state of residence or municipal bond funds designed for investors residing in her state.

Our tenth and final investor, a widow, has an annual income of $95,000, her mortgage is paid off, and she does not like to shop or eat out. She is 68 years old and lives comfortably on bond interest and dividend checks from a handful of stocks her husband picked decades ago. She works part-time, earning approximately $10,000 a year. She would like to continue to fund a tax-deferred account whose balance can pass directly to her only granddaughter upon her death.

- INVESTMENT OBJECTIVES: tax-deferral, estate planning
- TIME HORIZON/LIQUIDITY: long-term, low liquidity needs
- RISK TOLERANCE: moderate to high

It might seem strange to put her risk tolerance at "moderate to high," but why not?

She is already living comfortably on her investment income. She just wants to keep putting some money away that will grow tax-deferred for a rainy day, and whatever she doesn't spend in her lifetime will pass to her granddaughter. The Roth IRA is the answer here, most likely. The investor has earned income, enough to maximize her annual Roth IRA contribution. In a few years, she would have to stop putting money into a Traditional IRA, which is, again, why we're looking for a Roth IRA. The next-best answer would likely be an annuity. As with a Roth, she never has to take the money out, and can name the granddaughter the beneficiary of the account. Since the investor doesn't need to live on the Roth IRA, I don't mind the fact that if it's a new account, she needs to wait 5 years to make any withdrawals. As long as she doesn't need to touch the money for a bit longer, I can even live with the surrender period on a deferred annuity.

What we can eliminate for this investor: income investments, since she already has bond interest and cash dividends a-plenty. High-risk equities can be eliminated because nothing tells us she has an appetite for risk or is trying to keep up with purchasing power.

What we might recommend for this investor: Roth IRA, annuity.

PORTFOLIO MANAGEMENT STYLES & STRATEGIES

There are many ways to figure out a fair value for common stock. Fundamental analysts usually compare the market price of the stock to something directly related to its value—earnings, book value, sales, or cash flow, for example. Technical analysts on the stock price itself rather than on the company that issued it. Still other investors avoid picking individual stocks and bonds entirely, using the efficient frontier and other mathematically based approaches to investing.

VALUATION RATIOS

When an investor compares the market price of a stock to the earnings-per-share or book value, he is looking at a **valuation ratio**. For our purposes, a "ratio" is just one number compared to another number. We can track a baseball player's ratio of hits to strikeouts, where the higher the number, the higher the paycheck. The exam center will track your ratio of right to wrong answers, and you will need to keep that ratio at 3 to 1 or higher to be on the safe side. You might also notice that a ratio is just another way of talking about percentages. A 3-to-1 right-to-wrong answer ratio is just a different way of saying 75%, or 3 out of 4. A 4-to-1 ratio would be 80%, or 4 out of 5, and so on.

> ➤ Price-to-Earnings Ratio

When we're evaluating common stock, we compare the <u>price</u> of the stock to the <u>earnings</u> per share to see if the stock is attractively priced. This is called the price-to-earnings ratio for exactly that reason. The higher the number, the more expensive the stock is. A share of common stock is a share of the company's earnings. So, the question is, how much are people willing to pay for those earnings? If a stock trades for $25 on the secondary market when the earnings per share = $1, the stock trades for 25 times the earnings, or a "P/E ratio" of 25:1. The exam might want you to say that the price-to-earnings ratio "indicates how much investors value a company's profits as expressed through the market price of the stock." In other words, how much are investors willing to pay for a share of the company's profits? Are they willing to pay ten times the earnings? Twenty times the earnings? One hundred times the earnings? Stocks trading at high multiples are **growth stocks**, while those trading at low multiples are **value stocks**. Growth stocks involve more volatility than value stocks because much of their price is supported by enthusiasm rather than tangible measures such as book value.

> ➤ Price-to-Book Ratio

We found the earnings of the company on the income statement. We can figure the **book value** on the balance sheet. If a company had to be liquidated, the equipment, factory, real estate, etc., would be sold at auction and the proceeds would be paid first to the creditors, then to the preferred stockholders. The amount that would be left for each share of common stock is the **book value per share**. Think of this as the hard, tangible value of a share of common stock. If the book value of a share of stock is $6, and the stock now trades for $30, it is trading at a **price-to-book ratio** of 5. When you view a profile of a common stock, you usually see both the P/E and price-to-book ratios. This helps you determine if the stock is trading at a high or low multiple. As we've said before and intend to say again, stocks that trade at lower valuation ratios are called "value" stocks, while those trading at higher valuation ratios are called "growth" stocks.

> ➤ Price-to-Sales, Price-to-Cash Ratios

It isn't just that growth investors will buy stocks trading at high price-to-earnings ratios; many growth investors will buy stocks in companies that have no earnings at all. If the company has no earnings, it really isn't worth talking about the "P/E" ratio, which is "N/A" for "not applicable." For a company with no earnings/profits, it is more practical to compare the market price of the stock to the sales the company makes (**price-to-sales**). Notice how this ties in with the income statement—earnings represent the bottom line; sales represent the top line. Or, for companies not making a profit, many analysts pay closest attention to the price of the stock compared to the cash flow generated per-share. This is called, not surprisingly, **price-to-cash.**

In other words, analysts will compare the market price of the stock to *something*. If the company has actual profits and a strong balance sheet, they can compare the stock price to the earnings and the book value. If the company is still losing money as the sales are growing, they can compare the market price to the sales or cash flow per share.

The exam might also want you to know that some analysts prefer using price-to-sales even if the company *is* profitable. As many famous companies have demonstrated, it is very easy to manipulate earnings with creative accounting, but sales/revenue represents a number that is very hard to fudge. It is the top line of the income statement, remember, so it hasn't been filtered through all the subtractions for cost of goods sold, operating expenses, depreciation, amortization, or interest.

MARKET CAPITALIZATION (MARKET CAP)

As a general rule, small-cap stocks are riskier than mid-cap stocks, which, in turn, are riskier than large-cap stocks. "Cap" is a way of abbreviating "capitalization" or **market capitalization**. A company's "market cap" is their total number of outstanding shares times today's closing price on the stock. That's it. **Market cap** is simply the total value of all the outstanding shares. If that's a "small" number, we call it a "small-cap" stock. A stock with a market capitalization under $1 billion is usually considered small-cap. So, if a company has 10 million shares outstanding, and the shares close @$25 today, the market capitalization is simply $250 million, which is under a billion, which makes it a small-cap stock. Mid-cap would be up to $10 billion, and above that is the "large-cap" world of IBM, Microsoft, GE, etc. If you find that another textbook uses different numbers, this is not surprising. It would only be surprising if any three sources agreed on these numbers, so the test will likely go easy on us rather than expecting us to guess where "most people" set the cutoffs for small/mid/large-cap.

Rather than memorizing dollar amounts, know the concept of "market cap" and remember that small-cap = higher risk/reward, while large-cap = lower risk/reward. Also, the stocks that are smaller than small-cap—can you guess what we call them?

Micro-cap. These stocks frequently trade on the less liquid and less regulated OTC equities markets. Because of the small number of shares and the relative obscurity of the companies, these stock issues are more prone to manipulation. Recently, the SEC suspended trading in 17 different micro-cap stocks for reasons including that one issuer had not filed any annual (10-K) or quarterly (10-Q) reports in over two years. Who cares, you might think. Here's the problem: if a stock is trading without any public information supporting its price, that by definition is a speculative scheme that needs to be shut down before thousands of people lose their life savings chasing a dream based on nothing but greed and hot air. But, we'll discuss the regulatory angle in more depth elsewhere.

GROWTH INVESTING

Growth stocks trade at high P/E and price-to-book ratios. Many are still making revenue on the top line of the income statement but losing money on the bottom line because of all the expenses. Others are just this-far away from profitability. There's a lot of hope and speculation built into the share price of a growth stock. Remember, the higher the P/E ratio, the more speculative and volatile the stock. When a stock is trading at, say, 35 times the earnings, every earnings announcement has the ability to send the stock into a freefall or into a run-up. As an investor in KKD, this explains each earnings announcement over the past several years.

If you invest in a stock because you think it will grow faster than other stocks or the market overall, you call this thing a growth stock and consider yourself a **growth investor**. You usually pay dearly for any earnings the company might or might not have at this point. But you're convinced this is the next Coca-Cola or Microsoft, so you're willing to pay a premium for the bright future. Since that future hasn't shown up yet, much of the price you pay for a so-called "growth stock" is propped up by speculation. If the company reports disappointing earnings one quarter, the stock price could drop painfully.

But that's growth investing. Lots of ups and downs. A growth investor will deal with the frequent strikeouts in order to enjoy a few home runs along the way. He just needs a long time horizon and the ability to withstand large fluctuations in the value of his investments.

VALUE INVESTING

Value investors buy **value stocks**—stocks trading at low price-to-earnings or price-to-book ratios. A value investor tries to purchase stocks in out-of-favor corporations trading for less than they should be. For example, when GM has their CEO testifying before Congress over badly handled recalls, many traders will dump shares of GM, while value investors might decide to buy shares at currently depressed prices.. Companies that put together growth and value indexes would explain the mathematical criteria for determining which stocks go into the growth index and which go into the value index. Wherever they set the cutoff point, the growth index will have stocks trading at high multiples, while the value index will have stocks trading at lower multiples.

Value stocks would typically have higher dividend yields, too, especially if we compared large-cap value stocks to large-cap growth. Why? Large-cap companies are more likely to pay dividends to their shareholders now that their businesses are running relatively predictably. If their market price drops, suddenly the dividend yield will increase. The board of directors does not usually want to cut that dividend, so the decreasing market price by definition will raise the dividend yield. I, myself, bought 100 shares of MSFT at a dividend yield of 2.7% a few years ago. When US Treasuries were yielding around 1%, that really seemed attractive, especially as the amount of that dividend will almost certainly rise between now and my retirement date. It's not a growth stock; there is no chance the market price will double or triple anytime soon, but if purchased at a good price, a value investment like this can provide a decent long-term return through dividends and—we hope—share price appreciation. Dividends can also be invested into more shares, which pay more dividends to buy more shares, and so on. That is known as "compounded returns," and it is really the whole point of investing long-term in the stock market.

So, both growth and value investors hope the share price increases, of course. But, growth investors like to buy expensive stocks that are expected to rise even more in the future, while value investors like to buy stocks currently in trouble but worth more than the market realizes. If they were real estate investors, growth investors would buy the brand new townhouses going up in the hot, new part of town, while value investors would buy foreclosed properties and rehab them for a profit or rent them out long-term for an attractive yield.

ACTIVE VS. PASSIVE MANAGEMENT

Growth and value are terms that refer to types of stock. The terms active and passive refer to investment approaches. If you seek out particular stocks (or bonds), you are an **active** manager. If you simply buy "growth" or "value" index funds, you are a **passive** manager. Let the words talk to you: is the investor actively determining that one particular investment is more attractive than another? If so, that's "active portfolio management." Now, who uses active management styles—fundamental or technical analysts?

Both. You could determine that ORCL is a better investment right now than MSFT by looking at the fundamentals (balance sheet, income statement), or you could look at technical indicators including charts, the 200-day moving average, or short interest. Either way, if you're coming down on the side of one stock versus another, you're using active stock selection or active portfolio management.

A passive management style usually involves the use of indexes rather than trying to pick one investment over another. You could buy a "growth index fund" or a "value index fund," which is actually choosing a style, but you would never try to pick one growth or value stock over another. Using this passive indexing strategy, you will pay lower expenses, because these funds aren't doing a lot of trading and, therefore, don't have to extract big management fees. Also, if you never want to be beaten by an index, you can join it, right? Have you ever paid big management fees and sales charges for an actively managed "small-cap" fund that can't even beat a "small-cap index" like the Russell 2000? Doesn't that kind of tick you off? If so, just buy the index fund. It will neither beat nor lose to the index (by much), and will cost you less in any event.

TECHNICAL ANALYSIS

Fundamental analysts look at the company who issued the common stock. **Technical analysts**, on the other hand, study the behavior of the stock itself as it trades on the secondary market. Technical analysts don't want to hear about how a company's products have been selling or who the new CEO might happen to be. They want to know how the shares of the company's *stock* have been trading in terms of market price and **volume** levels. The exam might call what technical analysts study **stock market data**.

> Charts and Patterns

Many people feel that in terms of stock prices, history tends to repeat itself. Therefore, many technical traders make decisions on whether to buy or sell by looking at charts of a stock's market price over a certain period of time. These days, **chartists** can review the price patterns over 200 days, 30 days, one day, five minutes, what have you. The idea is that by watching the chart pattern start to develop, the trader using charts can predict where the stock is headed next.

A very popular type of chart is the candlestick chart. Each "candlestick" is a little vertical bar that indicates the opening price, the high price, the low price, and the closing price for the stock. At the left of the chart, we see what the "candle period" is, whether weekly, monthly, etc. Below the pricing information the chart also shows volume for the shares traded.

Reading the patterns that develop from such charts is part art and part science—just like fundamental analysis. The key is to find a **trendline**, defined as "local highs and local lows forming a straight line." In other words, a trendline allows us to step back from the trees in order to see the forest. Rather than obsessing over yesterday's high, low and close, a trendline shows us the bigger picture in terms of whether the price of the stock is generally moving upward, downward, or sideways. A basic premise of trendlines is that stock prices tend to bounce upward from a lower limit called **support** and also bounce downward off a higher limit called **resistance**, like this:

This means that whenever the stock goes up, it meets resistance, when all the sellers step in to depress the price, and whenever it falls, it finds support, where the buyers step in to bid the price back up again. A stock's arrival at the resistance threshold is often referred to as the market being **overbought**, and its fall to the support price is called an **oversold** market. A trader following charts might consistently try to buy close to support and sell as soon as it nears resistance. Or, maybe he waits until the stock breaks through resistance before buying it, reasoning that if it hits a **breakout** it will keep running up. Breakouts occurring on high volume—in either direction—are considered especially significant.

If the trendline's support and resistance lines run parallel, this pattern is referred to as a channel. If the parallel lines are going up, you're looking at a "channel up" pattern, and at a "channel down" pattern if the parallel lines are going down. If the lines are horizontal, the pattern is simply a "channel."

A trader using channel patterns tries to predict where the stock is about to go. If he sees a "channel up" pattern start to form, he's going to start buying the stock and probably ride it until he sees that things are about to turn around.

Parallel support and resistance lines form channel patterns. On the other hand, when the support and resistance lines start to converge, the pattern is called a wedge. A "rising wedge" pattern is considered a bearish signal. The rising wedge starts out wide at the bottom and then narrows as prices rise but the range gets smaller, with the lines squeezing together toward the top. A "falling wedge" pattern starts out wide at the top and then narrows as prices full with the range becoming smaller. A falling wedge is considered a bullish signal, a sign that the downtrend is about to turn the other way.

Insert graphics of channels and wedges.

Speaking of which, a **"head and shoulders"** price pattern on a chart also signals the reversal of a trend. A "head and shoulders" top pattern is characterized by a prior uptrend and then three distinct highs for the stock. A head and shoulders "top" indicates the bull trend is about to end, a **bearish** signal.

This is a head-and-shoulders top formation:

The stock makes a high represented as the left peak or "shoulder." It falls back and then really goes on a tear—the middle peak is called the "head." The stock then falls to the horizontal support line and makes one more big push. Unfortunately, the right shoulder is not as high as either the head or the left shoulder, which means the uptrend is about to end. So, when you see that right shoulder beginning to form, you're supposed to conclude that the stock price is headed for a big drop.

A head-and-shoulders top indicates the reversal of an uptrend and is a bearish indicator. A head-and-shoulders bottom or an **inverted head-and-shoulders** pattern, on the other hand, indicates the reversal of a downtrend and is a **bullish** indicator.

If a stock is trading in a narrow range between support and resistance, it is consolidating. A chart of a stock in **consolidation** appears to be moving sideways, like this:

The exam might talk about consolidation as the place where sophisticated investors (mutual funds, pension funds, etc.) are getting into or out of the stock. Since these institutional traders are presumed to be the experts, when we see them buying, it must mean the stock is going up, and when we see them selling, it must mean the stock is heading down. At this accumulation or distribution point, the price is, apparently, about to make a huge break on the up or down side. Consolidation and a "channel" pattern would be two ways of referring to the same phenomenon.

Other well-known chart patterns include the cup, the saucer, and the inverted saucer pattern. The cup pattern is a curved trendline. It usually starts to form just below resistance. The line curves downward as the closing prices drop, but then the line curves upward as prices rise. As the full curve is just about completed at the resistance line, many technical traders feel there is a high probability of a breakout. A cup pattern is formed over a few weeks. If the curve develops more slowly, chartists refer to the pattern as a "saucer" or a "rounding bottom." Either way, with a rounded bottom to its shape, this chart pattern indicates that the stock or index's level is about to rise. It is, in other words, a bullish indicator.

Well, as with the head-and-shoulders pattern, we could flip the saucer over and called it an "inverted saucer pattern." Here, with the curve flipped over, technical traders should conclude the stock's price is about to drop; the uptrend is about to end. Another name for this pattern is the "rounded top" pattern.

Whether it's an inverted or a regular-ole saucer pattern, the reason for the curve is a gradual shift from bearish-to-bullish or from bullish-to-bearish sentiment.

Insert graphics of cup, saucer, etc.

➤ Advance-Decline Ratio

Technical analysts look to see how many stocks advance versus how many stocks decline. The name for this statistic is the **advance-decline ratio**. If advancers outnumber decliners by 2:1, that means that twice as many stocks finished up in market price as down that day. And if decliners outnumber advancers 2:1, that means that twice as many stocks went down that day as up. Maybe a technical analyst sees that advancers have outpaced decliners for several days and decides to go with the trend. Or, maybe he's a contrarian and figures that if advancers have been outpacing decliners consistently, that trend has to reverse itself soon because of other reasons. Again, notice how he's analyzing the overall movement of <u>stocks</u>, while the fundamental analyst would be focusing on the fundamentals of the <u>companies</u> underlying those stocks.

> ➢ Volume

Volume is also of interest to the technical analyst. Volume indicates the total number of shares traded on, say, the NYSE, NASDAQ, or the regional exchanges in Chicago, Philadelphia, Boston, etc. Analysts expect stock prices to move on increasing volume. They would tend to place more significance on the fact that stock prices increased minutely on decreasing volume. Often, that situation is considered a reversal of a bullish trend, which is, of course, a bearish signal. It just means that the bull market is running out of steam—stock prices barely went up, and there was nowhere near as much trading going on.

> ➢ Market momentum and sentiment

Market momentum is the ability of the market to sustain up or downswings in price. This concept combines both price changes and volume of trading. If a stock's price increases with large trading volumes, the momentum is much higher than if the share price rises on lower volume. The higher the momentum, the more likely the direction of the stock price will be sustained. Momentum is an "anticipatory indicator" used to predict price changes. Many technical analysts use stochastics to measure the momentum of stocks and stock indexes.

Market sentiment is a judgment of the mood or tone of a market. Markets are generally either bullish (going up) or bearish (going down). One way to gauge market sentiment is through the put/call ratio. We will look at puts and calls in depth in our chapter on Options. For now, understand that if an investor is worried about his stock dropping, he needs to "hedge" or protect his stock by buying puts. On the other hand, if he has bet against the market, he needs to hedge by purchasing calls. Therefore, technical analysts track the ratio of puts to calls and call this statistic the "put/call ratio" or "puts-to-calls." The ratio is > 1 if the volume of puts exceeds the volume for calls. When fewer puts are being traded than calls, the ratio is < 1. When the ratio is trading at relatively high levels, this is taken as an indication of bearish sentiment. Why? People must be worried about their stocks dropping, as evidenced by all the puts they've purchased to protect against that. When the ratio is trading at relatively low levels, this is taken as an indication of bullish sentiment.

Options are all about volatility. The more volatile/unpredictable a stock's price, the more one has to pay for options tied to that stock. Therefore, technical analysts are often interested in tracking option volatility. There are two types of volatility here—historical and implied. Historical volatility takes the daily price changes over a year for the underlying stock and finds the "standard deviation" showing if the stock is subject to wild price swings or, rather, trades more predictably. Implied volatility looks at the price of the options tied to a stock (or index of stocks) and determines what the market implies about the volatility of the stock up ahead.

> ➢ Moving Average

A technical analyst looking at the put/call ratio would also factor in a **moving average** to make more sense of the information. A moving average simply replaces the oldest piece of data with the newest on a rolling basis. In baseball, if we say that someone is batting .286, that's over the whole season. A moving average would tell us how he's been hitting lately, and show graphically whether he's generally in a slump or on a hot streak. In other words, it would help us spot a trend. So, rather than focusing too hard on yesterday's or this week's closing price for a stock, we can use the moving average to see where the stock has been closing on average over the past so-many days.

The **200-day moving average** is probably the most commonly used. A technical analyst can track the 200-day moving average for a particular stock or for a particular index. He can also see what percentage of stocks have been closing above or below their 200-day moving average to get a feel for whether it's a bull or bear market. If a high percentage have been closing above their 200-day average, this is taken as a bullish indicator and vice versa for a low percentage.

Some technical traders assume that the movement of security index futures tied to the S&P 500, the Dow, etc., that happens before the market opens can predict the direction of the stock market. Therefore, if a customer has a large stock position to sell, he may be advised to wait until the market has opened and traded a while before placing a sell order, depending on the direction of the index futures. Most technical traders use the data on index futures to predict only the direction of the market in the very short-term.

➢   Theories

The technical analyst knows how smart he is. So much smarter than the small-time investor, in fact, that all he has to do is track what **odd-lot** investors are doing and bet the other way. If odd-lotters are buying, he sells. If odd-lotters are selling, he buys. Why? Because folks who can only afford an odd lot (<100 shares) of stock at a time always buy too high and sell too low. This is known as the **odd-lot theory**.

The **short interest theory** has to do with how many open short sales are out there. Now, as we'll see later, short sellers profit when a stock's price drops, but this theory also recognizes that short sellers eventually have to cover or buy back the shares that they borrowed to sell in the first place. So, if there are a lot of uncovered or "open" short positions out there, they might all suddenly be forced to buy the stock in a hurry. That would create buying pressure that could drive up the stock's price, which is why a large number of open short positions is a *bullish* indicator. Today I notice that the percentage of Starbucks shares sold short is about 5%, while the percentage of Krispy Kreme shares that have been sold short is about 33%. A technical analyst might conclude that Krispy Kreme is set for a rally, based on the high percentage of short-sellers, who will have to buy the stock back eventually, possibly all at the same time.

PRACTICE

1. A head-and-shoulders bottom formation is a

I. bearish indicator

II. bullish indicator

III. reversal of an uptrend

IV. reversal of a downtrend

       A. I, IV

        B. II, IV

       C. I, III

       D. II, III

2. The 200-day moving average is

A. a contrarian indicator

B. helpful in spotting trends

C. a primary tool of fundamental analysis

D. used primarily in interest rate analysis

(ANSWERS)

1. B, the head-and-shoulders pattern is always a reversal on the exam. If the reversal is at the bottom, the downtrend must be ending, with a bull market up ahead.

2. B, associate the moving average with "trends" and "technical analysts."

FUNDAMENTAL ANALYSIS	TECHNICAL ANALYSIS
Financial Statements, e.g., balance sheet, income statement	Market Data
Revenue	Advance/Decline
Net Income	Moving Average
Profits, Profit Margins	Support/Resistance
Price-to-earnings, Price-to-book	52-week High/low
Working Capital	Price and Volume Levels
Qualitative judgments on the business	Market Sentiment, Momentum
Current Ratio, Quick Ratio	Short Interest
Debt-to-Equity or Debt Ratio	Charts, Patterns
Dividend Payout Ratio	Puts/Calls, Stochastics

BUY AND HOLD

Whether I'm a growth, value, passive, or active manager, I could use **buy and hold** as a portfolio management strategy. What this approach involves is buying and then holding.

Seriously. The buy and hold approach results in lower transaction costs, because you aren't trading and generating commissions/markups. Rather you are buying, and then holding.

Plus, you avoid getting taxed on a ton of short-term capital gains. So there's some potentially confusing overlap there with passive management. Both can lead to lower transaction costs and fewer short-term capital gains. The subtle difference would be as follows. A passive investor buys index funds because of the low management fees and to ride along with the rising tide that lifts all indexes; however, he may well be constantly trading his ETFs and generating his own transaction costs (commissions, markups) and, possibly, short-term capital gains. He's "passive" in the sense that he doesn't pick one stock over another, but he's sort of missing the point by actively trading these indexes like any other share of stock. A "buy and hold" investor using index funds would buy them and then...*hold* them. Sounds boring, but consider how it worked for, say, the original investors in Coca-Cola. And their kids. And their grandkids. And their great-grandkids.

CAPM

The **Capital Asset Pricing Model** (CAPM) is one way to calculate expected return. It is very similar to the Sharpe ratio, but used for different purposes. The Sharpe ratio calculates what already happened and calls it your "risk-adjusted return," while CAPM calculates/predicts expected return based on some math we're about to look at. Both concepts use the idea that an investor could just put her money into a "riskless rate of return," so if she's going to put it into something risky, she demands a potential reward that is much larger than that riskless rate of return—a so-called "risk premium." The formula works like this. If the risk-free rate is 3%, the beta of the stock is 2, and the expected market return over the period is 10%, then the stock is expected to return 17%. To calculate that, you would simply take the risk-free rate and add that to the expected return minus that risk-free rate times the beta.

I'm sorry, I actually enjoyed writing that. You're right—I should get out more. But even though the formula looks a little wild, it actually does communicate a very basic and important concept. The calculation is saying that the expected return on a stock is equal to the risk-free return you could get on 3-month T-Bills plus the potential return on the stock that is over and above the risk-free rate. The numbers above were crunched like this: $(3\% + 2 (10\% - 3\%))$. That's 3%, plus the sum of (20% minus 6%). 3% plus 14% equals the expected return of 17%. And, it shows that investors expect to be compensated both for the time value of money and the risk of investing in stocks.

Again, the Sharpe ratio and CAPM both talk about the riskless rate of return. But CAPM calculates an expected return, while the Sharpe ratio adjusts actual returns for the risk the portfolio experienced. Notice how these approaches are purely mathematical, while fundamental analysis involves both a quantitative and qualitative examination of a company. A trader using CAPM and the Sharpe ratio is more interested in how a stock or a portfolio is behaving and is likely to behave in the future. Fundamental analysts are interested in determining which *companies* are likely to perform well in the future.

MODERN PORTFOLIO THEORY

In the old days, investors would consider the risk of any one security. **Modern Portfolio Theory,** on the other hand, looks at how a particular investment affects the risk/reward ratio of the entire portfolio. It also assumes that investors are risk-averse, no matter what they tell you. Since investors don't like risk, we could say that they would prefer to make, for example, 10% returns through the least risky path, or that, given a particular level of risk, they want to get the highest possible return. Using an entirely mathematical/statistical approach to investing, Modern Portfolio Theorists construct "optimal portfolios," which means that the investor is likely to get the highest possible return given the amount of risk/volatility that he is willing to bear. If we reverse the words, we get **portfolio**

optimization, which has to do with a graph called an **efficient frontier**. What is considered key is the unique mix of securities in a portfolio. There are many portfolios that fall along this efficient frontier, so which one is better for the investor? It depends on the amount of volatility the investor can handle, and what potential return he thinks he will settle for. Portfolios are constructed of a percentage mix of equity, bonds, and cash, and these various mixes can, theoretically—based on historical data—determine the amount of risk, and the likely return. Long story short, whichever risk-reward profile the investor chooses, we just want to make sure the portfolio lies along (not behind) the efficient frontier. The portfolios that lie on the lower left part of the curve are the most efficient for the low-risk–low-reward investors, while the portfolios that lie along the upper right part of the curve are the most efficient for the high-risk–high-reward investors.

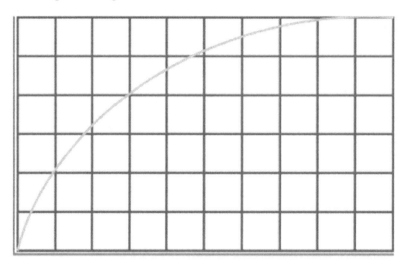

Modern Portfolio Theory is a mathematical approach to investment selection. It is interested in calculating the risk-reward nature of a portfolio by measuring expected returns, standard deviations, and correlations. Rather than thinking like a fundamental analyst that 1,000 shares of ORCL should rise next year when the company reports higher profits, Modern Portfolio Theory would, instead, calculate the likely return of a portfolio based on mathematical probabilities. Technical analysis would also be of no use to this crowd. Whether using financial statements or stock charts, to a modern portfolio theorist, either investor is actively and foolishly selecting securities.

EFFICIENT MARKET HYPOTHESIS

The idea that active portfolio management is the wrong approach is even more bluntly stated by the **efficient market hypothesis**. The efficient market hypothesis grew out of a Ph.D. dissertation by Eugene Fama. This school of thought assumes that at any given time in a liquid market all information about a security is already "priced in," making the current market price an accurate estimate of any security's intrinsic value. Because all security prices accurately reflect their intrinsic value, attempts to outperform the overall market are based on luck rather than skill.

Efficient Market Hypothesis can actually be further broken down into three separate forms: weak, semi-strong, and strong. The **weak form** of Efficient Market Hypothesis (EMH) assumes that current stock prices already represent all currently available market information. It contends that past price and volume data (technical analysis) have no relationship to the future direction of security prices. Because such technical information is considered irrelevant, weak form concludes that excess returns cannot be achieved using technical analysis. However, the weak form is the only one that states some types of fundamental analysis can produce market-beating returns.

214

The **semi-strong form** of EMH assumes that current stock prices adjust immediately to all new information released to the public—e.g. quarterly earnings announcements or news of a merger/acquisition. The semi-strong form states that security prices have already factored in all available market and non-market public information. Therefore, excess returns cannot be achieved using fundamental analysis—or technical analysis.

The **strong form** of EMH assumes that current stock prices fully reflect all public and private (insider) information. It contends that market, non-market and inside information is all factored into security prices and that no one could possibly have a monopoly on the information that drives the future direction of securities prices in a liquid market. The strong form of EMH assumes a perfectly efficient market and concludes that excess returns are impossible to achieve consistently.

The book that really threw the spotlight on the efficient market hypothesis and the general idea that stock-picking is not likely to beat a passively selected index is called *A Random Walk Down Wall Street* by Burton Malkiel. The **random walk theory** implies that actively picking stocks is about as effective as a random walk through the stock page of the newspaper. Note to readers born after 1990: newspapers used to print stock quotes; people would check them the next day, then maybe call their broker and ask him where the market was for the stock. I swear. Anyway, in the short-term, stock price movements are random and, therefore, random stock selection would be no worse than active stock picking, and would also save the investor all kinds of transaction costs and short-term capital gains, to boot. And, somewhat depressingly for professionals in this industry, there is plenty of evidence to support this notion. Actively managed mutual funds seldom do better than an unmanaged index, and the longer the time period, the less likely it is that any active stock picker can beat an unmanaged index of similar stocks. When you factor in short-term capital gains and commissions, it becomes nearly impossible for an active trader to consistently beat an index. And, if you can't beat the index, join it by purchasing an index fund or ETF.

PORTFOLIO MANAGEMENT TECHNIQUES

No matter how an investor arrives at the decision to invest in X, Y, or Z, he still has to manage those assets using various portfolio management techniques. In other words, there is a difference between picking stocks and managing a portfolio of stocks.

ASSET ALLOCATION

Asset allocation has become an accepted tenet of investing. It is also how those "optimal portfolios" are constructed for the efficient frontier investors. Virtually no one 50 years old (except the guy writing this sentence) is 100% invested in equities, or even 100% in fixed-income. The rule of thumb has been that an investor should limit his equity exposure to 100 minus his age. If he's 47, he should have no more than 53% of his portfolio allocated to equities. These days, with age expectancies getting longer, some folks are now saying to increase the equity exposure to 120 minus the investor's age, which would give the 47-year-old a maximum of 73% for equities. Obviously, this rule of thumb is just a little bit arbitrary and unscientific, although it is based on a solid premise—portfolios that use asset allocation drive over the bumps in the markets much better than those concentrated too heavily on one asset class. In general, investors in their 50s will have a little less than half their portfolio allocated to stock/equities and a little more than half devoted to fixed-income and money market/cash. Within those basic asset classes, the equity portion could be divided by market cap and growth/value/blend, international vs. domestic, and industry sectors. The fixed-income piece could be divided by term to maturity, credit quality, and types of issuers.

For example, after an investor answers a series of questions through a secure area of your firm's website, maybe your computer models return the following allocation:

- Equity – 40%
  - o 20% Large-Cap Value
  - o 20% Small-Cap Growth
- Fixed-Income – 50%
  - o 20% High-Yield
  - o 20% Investment-Grade, Taxable
  - o 10% High-Yield, Tax-Exempt
- Cash – 10%

If you present that allocation as a full-color pie chart, you can imagine that most investors will begin to relax and feel that someone who knows what he is doing is about to take charge of their investments. And, of course, most investors will end up doing a whole lot better using a registered investment adviser to allocate and manage their portfolio, as opposed to watching some guy on TV and winging it.

Whatever the asset allocation is, naturally, the portfolio manager will have to tweak things from time to time to **rebalance** the portfolio back to its intended mix. He could actively rebalance the portfolio if he weren't a believer in efficient markets—if he thought he could spot an opportunity in, say, mid-cap growth stocks, he could change the allocation based on that assumption. That's called **tactical asset allocation,** which is basically another name for market timing. But, if he does believe in efficient markets, he would maintain his clients in a certain rigid mix of equity, debt, and money market securities based on age and risk tolerance. That's called **strategic asset allocation,** which is associated with age-based portfolios used to fund education and retirement goals. To maintain the strategic mix of asset classes the investor will need to sell some of the assets that have appreciated in order to add to the ones that have gone down and now represent a smaller % of the portfolio (rebalancing). Maybe they do this quarterly, twice a year, or annually. If they do it too often, the transaction costs and short-term capital gains could easily outweigh any assumed benefits of the portfolio management technique.

DIVERSIFICATION

Another accepted tenet of prudent investing is called **diversification**. As we see when discussing the Uniform Prudent Investor Act, a fiduciary is expected to diversify the assets of a trust, except in those rare cases where it would be more beneficial and prudent not to. A diversified portfolio of stocks would not contain all technology or pharmaceutical companies, for example. If there were a number of oil company stocks, they would be diversified between domestic and international companies, producers of oil and refiners of oil. They would not all be small cap or large cap. A bond portfolio would not be all triple-A-rated or all junk, but would instead be diversified throughout different maturities, credit quality, and issuers that don't all come from the same industry.

Asset allocation and diversification are somewhat related portfolio management techniques. Where they differ is that asset allocation puts set percentages of capital into various types of stocks, bonds, and cash to achieve strategic goals in regards to risk and reward. Within those allocations, we use diversification to balance the risk of one investment with the characteristics of another. So, 20%

large-cap growth, 20% mid-cap growth, 30% small-cap growth, and 30% long-term bond is an asset allocation. Drill down into the "20% large-cap growth" category, and the various companies owned would come from different industries in order to maintain diversification.

We saw earlier that unsystematic risk can be reduced through diversification, while systematic risks cannot. In other words, investors reduce their legislative risk by purchasing securities issued by companies in different industry spaces. In order to reduce overall market risk—which is systematic—investors would use options, futures, or ETFs in order to hedge.

SECTOR ROTATING

Some portfolio managers try to anticipate which sectors are about to rise and which are about to fall. The object then becomes to sell the sectors that are about to drop and buy the ones that are about to rise. Not surprisingly, this technique is called **sector rotating**. Deciding which sectors to "underweight" and which to "overweight" could be done through fundamental or technical analysis. If a particular industry space seems set for an expansion due to economic forces, that analyst is using fundamental analysis and probably top-down analysis, as well. Another trader may decide to sell pharmaceuticals when they are "overbought" and invest in telecommunications because they appear to be "oversold" at this point. That would be technical analysis. Either way, the technique would be known as sector rotating or sector rotation.

DOLLAR COST AVERAGING

Investors often put a fixed dollar amount into securities on a regular schedule. Since stocks, bonds, and mutual funds fluctuate in price, investors using the **dollar cost averaging** technique end up buying fewer shares when they're expensive and more of their shares when they're temporarily (we hope) cheap. The test might point out that an investor's average cost is lower than the average share price...which is because of what I just said. To illustrate it clearly, though, we need a story problem. So here goes: Melody automatically invests $1,000 into a mutual fund each month. Over the past three months the Net Asset Value was $50, $40, and $25. Therefore, her average cost per share is what amount? Explanation: okay, for some reason this sort of question drives my tutoring clients absolutely nuts. But, as I tell them, you just have to figure out how many shares she bought with her total dollars invested. She invested $3,000—how many shares did she buy?

All we have to do here is draw out some sort of chart on our scratch paper. Maybe something like this:

	SHARE PRICE	# OF SHARES
Jan: $1,000	$50	
Feb: $1,000	$40	
Mar: $1,000	$25	

Okay, in January, her $1,000 bought her 20 shares. In February, her $1,000 bought her 25 shares, and in March her $1,000 bought her 40 shares. Therefore, her $3,000 in total acquired 85 shares. What is the average cost per share? Whatever $3,000 divided by 85 shares equals—about $35.29.

You know, those tutoring clients are right—this question is sort of a pain. And, I'm betting the question would also present the average share price as one of the false answers, because most people want to get through a question like this as fast as possible—adding up three numbers and dividing by three will allow you to get the question done very quickly but also very wrong. The average cost is not $38.33. That would simply be the average of the three share prices, and that would only be relevant if the investor were buying, say, 100 shares of stock each month. But that is not what happens when dollar cost averaging. Here, it's not the number of shares that is fixed—it's the dollar amount. By definition, the number of shares acquired each time varies.

The average-cost method is often used by investors to figure their cost basis when selling securities for capital gains/capital losses.

PRACTICE

1. Which investor below would be interested in buying shares of ABC at or below their estimated book value per share?

   A. Fundamental analyst

   B. Technical analyst

   C. Growth investor

   D. Value investor

2. The most common risk-adjusted return measurement is the

   A. Sharpe ratio

   B. CAPM

   C. Beta

   D. Standard deviation

(ANSWERS)

1. **D,** value investors would love to buy a stock near the book value, or even at a small multiple to the book value.

2. **A,** the Sharpe ratio is the most commonly used risk-adjusted return measurement

PERFORMANCE MEASURES

There are many ways to measure the performance of my investment account over the years. I could measure the average annual rate of return. I could adjust my returns for inflation, for taxes, or for the risk I've taken along the way. I tend not to calculate such things, but, trust me, the industry you are entering is all about these measurements of performance. The good news is according to the exam outline your test will only ask questions on half the material we are about to explore in this section. The bad news is we have no idea which half.

HOLDING PERIOD AND ANNUALIZED RETURN

If it takes you three years to achieve a 9% return, your **holding period return** is 9%. In other words, who cares how long it took to get 9%? You got 9% over your holding period. Some people think of their holding period return as their "total profit," the percentage gain on your invested principal regardless of how long it took to make it.

To measure your return on an "annualized basis," take the 9% holding period return and divide it by the three years it took to get it. And in this way you discover you've only had a 3% **annualized rate of return**. Sometimes it's more fun to take the return you get in one month and then multiply it by 12 to get your annualized rate of return from that direction. Get a 10% return in one month and suddenly you're thinking of it as a 120% annualized rate of return.

Now, remember, of course, you make a return that is actually represented by a certain number of dollars—if you make $200, you make $200. What we're doing here is measuring that return in terms of a percentage. What can I tell you? It's the financial services industry; they're obsessed with percentages. And the percentages are usually best expressed on an annual basis. So if it took more than one year to get a return, divide the percent return by the number of years. 9% over 3 years is a 3% yearly (annualized) return. A 5% return over 6 months would give you a 10% annualized return, since there are 12 months per year, right? There are two 6-month periods each year, so double that 5% if you're calculating annualized rates of return. If the exam wants to see you sweat—and, trust me, it does—it will say the return was 10% over 18 months. Luckily, 18 months is 1.5 years, so divide the 10% by 1.5, and you'll see that the annualized rate of return is 6.7%. Or, divide the 10% by 18 and then multiply that by 12. Or, pick "C" and try to nail the next 10 questions in a row. There are many ways to approach a Series 65 exam question—all I can do is make suggestions. And harass you with the following practice question:

An investment's market value decreases from $10 to $8.50 over Q1. The investment's annualized rate of return is...?

$$\frac{-1.5}{10}$$

Answer: if the market price drops from $10 to $8.50, take that $1.50 divided by the original $10. The investment just dropped 15% over one quarter. Since there are four quarters per year, multiply the 15% by four and tell the exam the return is a negative 60% annualized. Also notice that we can say "divided by" or "compared to" when we work with these calculations. When I compare something to something else, I usually just divide the first number by the second. Or, if I'm feeling especially punchy, I might divide the second number by the first. But these little ratios and calculations are usually just comparing one number to another number. Don't let them intimidate you.

YIELD

As we saw when looking at debt/fixed-income securities, one of the easiest concepts in investing is **yield**. Think of the word "yield" as "get." What do I "get" for holding an investment? Common stocks that pay dividends have a yield, as do preferred stocks, but let's look at yield in terms of bonds, since their income is dependable and predictable. The interest rate that a bond pays is called the **nominal yield** because "nom" means named, and this rate of return is named right on the bond. Remember, if you buy a $1,000 bond at par from the issuer and the bond has a nominal yield of 5%, it pays $50 a year, usually in two semiannual installments of $25. End of story. For investors on the secondary market, however, the story goes on in the form of **current yield**. That $50 per year the issuer pays would sure be a lot nicer if you could get it for $500 rather than for, say, $1,000, right? In fact, it would be exactly twice as nice. Getting (yielding) $50 from an investment of $1,000 represents a 5% current yield, but getting that same $50 from a $500 investment is a 10% current yield. Just do the math. See, current yield takes into account what you paid to get what you've gotten. Nominal yield's no mystery; pay 100 cents on the dollar for your bond, and your yield's printed right there on the paper. Pay 50 cents on the dollar, and your current yield is much higher. In fact, your current yield in that situation would be, as I said, twice as high. The price dropped by half, and so the yield doubled. Because, as always, when price drops, yield rises. And when price drops by half, yield.

Remember also that when the bond matures, it pays out $1,000. If you bought it for $1,000 and you get $1,000 at maturity, big deal. But, if you bought it for $500 and receive $1,000 at maturity, you gained $500, on top of all the nice interest/coupon payments you received. Now we're talking about **yield to maturity**, which is the yield an investor would receive in the form of all the interest payments plus (or minus) the difference between what they paid for the bond, and the par value the bond pays out at maturity. If you buy a bond for less than par, your yield to maturity is higher than the coupon rate and the current yield, because you get back more than you paid. If you buy a bond for more than par, your yield to maturity is lower than the coupon rate and the current yield, because you get back less than you paid. When interest rates rise, bond prices fall. That makes their current yield and yield to maturity go up above the nominal yield printed on the bond, if purchased on the secondary market.

One of your clients purchased a GE 5s debenture of '17 @96.375. What is the current yield?

Answer: of course you have to be able to read bond notation to answer this question. The "5s" means that the coupon rate is 5% or $50 per year. Divide that $50 of annual interest by the market price of $963.75, and you've got the current yield of about 5.2%.

For **yield to call**, just remember that a call can happen a whole lot sooner than the maturity date. So, for people who bought the bond at a discount from par, their yield to call is even better than current yield or yield to maturity, since they would end up making their gain sooner. But, for people who bought the bond at a premium to par, their yield to call is even worse, since they realize their loss a lot sooner. I don't know about you, but if I'm making money, I like to make it fast. And, if I'm going to lose money on a bond, let's make it a slow loss and give me lots of years to collect all those interest payments that would otherwise be lost to a call.

Right? So, the yields go in this order: nominal yield, current yield, yield to maturity, and yield to call. For a **discount bond**, they go UP in that order; for a **premium bond**, they go DOWN in that order. That is the bond see-saw covered in the discussion of debt securities, and it's also a way of measuring returns on bonds.

YIELD VS. TOTAL RETURN

NASAA is the organization of state securities regulators that we'll look at in the next chapter. For now, know that they have an adopted statement of policy on the sale of investment company shares (mutual funds, e.g.) that makes a very big deal out of the difference between yield and **total return** for a mutual fund, UIT, or closed-end fund investor. If you pay $10 for a mutual fund share and receive $1 in an income or dividend distribution, your yield is 10%. That's swell, but what if the fund share dropped $2 in the meantime? That's, like, bad! That's a drop of 20% in value! Suddenly, who cares about the 10% "yield?" Your "total return" is actually negative. If you go down 20% and the dividend (the yield) is only up 10%, your total return is −10%. So, when selling mutual fund products to your investors, be sure to explain how yield and total return are different, and don't quote one without quoting the other and explaining the difference.

If you get a $1 dividend on a $10 mutual fund share and the share price stays the same or goes up—appreciates—that's a good thing. Let's say you get the dividend of $1 and the share price appreciates $2. Now you're up in total (total return) $3. Three dollars on top of $10 is a 30% total return. When you read a mutual fund prospectus, one of the first displays you find is the bar chart showing the total return. This shows how much the fund has risen or fallen and how much it has returned to investors in the form of dividend and capital gains distributions.

Doesn't have to be a mutual fund, either. Any stock or bond would have a "total return" because there are exactly two ways that an investment can help you. Number one, it pays you some income and, number two, it goes up in price compared to what you paid for it. That's total return. It can be positive or negative depending on how things turn out for you. If the question gives you dividends, capital gains distributions (mutual funds), and share appreciation, factor in all three. Just ask yourself this question: "How much did the security go up and how much income did it produce, compared to where it started?"

XYZ common stock pays a quarterly dividend of 75 cents. One of your investors purchased the stock at $50 at the beginning of Q3. If the stock trades for $49 at the end of Q3, what is your investor's annualized rate of return?

Answer: see how the exam likes to combine concepts? This question is about both annualized return and total return. And, just to keep things fun, why not have one item be positive and one negative? See, the Series 65 takes what you know—or are supposed to—and spins it in some pretty interesting directions. Okay, how much money did the investor make over the quarter and what happened to the value of his investment? He took in 75¢, but the stock dropped $1. I'd say he's down 25¢ on a $50 investment, which is a return of negative ½%. Multiply the negative ½% by 4 to get a total annualized rate of return of **minus** 2%.

INFLATION-ADJUSTED OR "REAL" RETURN

There are definitely advantages to owning bonds. Number one, you are reasonably assured of receiving a dependable stream of income. For example, I noticed this morning that my investment in 100 shares of ORCL is up an impressive 110%. Trouble is, I bought those shares seven years ago, and the stock has only now started paying a dividend—a rather meager one at that. As we saw a few pages ago, making 110% over a seven-year period is an annualized return of about 15.7%. What was my yield on ORCL common stock? Right around zero percent. If I had purchased Oracle bonds, I would have been receiving interest checks on time over six years. That "stated rate of return" on the bond can buy a person a lot of sleep, while I do admit to losing a few winks when ORCL decided to get cute and drop down to five dollars a share a few years back.

So, a bond investor gets a stated rate of return and can usually depend on that like a landlord with a good tenant. Bond holders are higher up than shareholders in the pecking order if the company goes bankrupt. The market price of bonds is nowhere near as volatile as the market price for common stock.

But, if you're a fixed income investor, your income is fixed. As we said, if you buy a 5% bond, you get $50 per year, usually in two semiannual payments. What if inflation—the rising prices of stuff you want or need to buy—climbs by more than 5%?

That's a risk of being a bond investor, and you don't completely escape it in the stock market, either. When we factor in the effects of inflation, we are talking about something called either **inflation-**

adjusted return or **real return**. If you receive a 4% return from a bond, is that enough to help you pay bills when you're retired? Not if the price of everything you need to buy is rising by more than 4%, right? What if you're receiving 4%, but the price of everything is rising, say, 8%?

You're falling behind. So, if inflation is rising, you need to calculate whether the return on your investments is rising even higher and faster than the rate of inflation. The number that takes this into account is called the "inflation-adjusted return." But, since everything needs at least two names, we also refer to this as "real return." This one's easy. Just subtract the rate of inflation from a portfolio's return to get the inflation-adjusted/real return. If your investment returns 8% when inflation is 3%, you have an inflation-adjusted return of 5%. If your investment returns 3% when inflation is 8%, you have a nasty inflation-adjusted return of −5%. You may not be losing money on paper, but I guarantee you you're losing purchasing power.

Dale's investment depreciates 2% during a period in which the Consumer Price Index (CPI) decreases 3%. What is Dale's real rate of return?

Answer: as I said, this exam likes to mess with you. Clearly if the question says the investment drops, the return is negative, right? Right? Not so fast. Yes, the investment drops 2%, but prices are dropping even faster than that. The real rate of return is a positive 1%.

AFTER-TAX RETURN

Bond interest is often taxable, and if so, it's taxed at your ordinary income rate. Treasury securities are taxed at ordinary income rates by the federal government. Corporate bond interest is taxable by the federal, state, and local governments at your ordinary income rate. Clearly, when you have to cut a check for taxes, this reduces the returns on your investment. The return on your investment after tax is called your after-tax return, believe it or not.

When looking at municipal securities we took the corporate or US Treasury (taxable) bond yield and multiplied it by the percentage the investor actually keeps. If you're in the 28% federal tax bracket, you give up 28% of your return and keep 72%. So, if a bond pays you $100 a year, you keep 72% of that, or $72 per year.

Your after-tax yield on a bond paying 10% is 7.2%. Not as impressive when you factor in the taxes. The formula to calculate after-tax yield is:

*taxable yield * (100% − tax bracket)*

An investor purchasing a corporate bond yielding 9.5% would find that a tax-free bond yielding _____ would be equivalent? The investor is in the 25% marginal tax bracket.

Answer: simply take 9.5% (.095) and multiply that by the percentage the investor keeps, which is 75% or .75. What is .095 times .75? 7.125%. That is all the tax-free municipal bond would have to yield to put the same dollars in the investor's pocket.

TAX-EQUIVALENT YIELD

A municipal bond doesn't have to pay as much interest as a taxable bond, since investors don't pay federal income tax on the interest paid by most municipal bonds. As strange as it seems, someone in a 30% tax bracket would come out better with a 7% municipal bond than with a 9.5% corporate or Treasury bond. With the municipal bond, the investor would keep $70. With the taxable bond, she would keep 70% of 9.5%, which is only $66.50. To figure a municipal bond's **tax-equivalent yield,** take the yield the bond pays and divide by (100% minus tax bracket). In other words, in our example, take the 7% and divide it by 70% (100% minus 30%) to see that the municipal bond's 7% is equivalent to a 10% taxable yield for this investor.

Rather than have you calculate here, the exam might ask something like this, "What is the following formula used to calculate?"

tax-exempt yield / (100% − tax bracket)

If so, tell the exam that the formula is used to calculate "tax-equivalent yield."

An investor in a 30% marginal tax bracket would find that a General Obligation bond of the State of New York paying 4% would be equivalent to a taxable debenture paying…?

Answer: take the 4% and turn it into .04. Divide that by 70% (100% minus tax bracket), and that, my friend, is your answer. As your calculator informs you, this investor would find that a 4% tax-free yield is equivalent to a taxable yield of 5.7%.

RISK-ADJUSTED RETURN

Investors are generally **risk averse**, which means they don't like risk. Risk is measured by volatility or **standard deviation.** The more unpredictable the returns of an investment, the riskier that investment is. So, if your investment adviser/portfolio manager earns you an 11% total return for the year, you can then adjust that number for the risk it took to achieve it. As we saw, the **Sharpe ratio** is the most common form of **risk-adjusted return** measures. Using the Sharpe ratio, the portfolio manager only gets credit for the return he got above the **riskless rate of return.** If the account grew 11% when 3-month US Treasury Bills yielded 4%, we take the 11% minus the 4%, and we're down to 7%. We then divide that 7% by the standard deviation/risk over the period. If the standard deviation is high, the Sharpe ratio is weak; if the standard deviation is low, the Sharpe ratio is strong. The higher the Sharpe ratio, the better the risk-adjusted return of the portfolio.

Alpha is the risk-adjusted return of the portfolio compared to the benchmark. If the exam talks in terms of "positive alpha" or "negative alpha," it is referring to whether the portfolio manager is adding value (positive alpha) or not (negative alpha) with his active management. Because hedge funds try to extract big market returns in all environments, they are often marketed to investors with the phrase "alpha-driven results." How good is your portfolio manager? Alpha points to the answer of that important question. An investor who puts his money into index funds and lets it ride is on the opposite side of the chart from investors hoping their hedge fund manager can extract gains in bull, bear, or any other type of market. The best portfolio managers turn in results that exceed the expected return on a risk-adjusted basis—positive alpha. If the expected return is 8%, and the portfolio grows 9%, this represents positive alpha of 1%.

TIME-WEIGHTED, DOLLAR-WEIGHTED RETURN

Mutual fund prospectuses and sales literature show the total return of the fund both in bar charts and in statistical tables. While a mutual fund might have a 10% return over the past six years, the average investor in the fund might have a much different experience, depending on whether we're looking at the **time-weighted return** or the **dollar-weighted return** of the portfolio. See, when a mutual fund has a good run, the buzz attracts a lot of new investors and new money into the fund. What happens if the fund has an amazing run for two years, attracting lots of new money, but then the fund goes flat for the next four years? What happens is this: the time-weighted return still looks okay, while the dollar-weighted return looks pretty lousy. The time-weighted return figure tells the investor that the portfolio manager earned this percentage based on this time period. The dollar-weighted return figure tells the investor that based on the dollars invested, most of those dollars invested didn't do so good. Let's take a rather extreme example. Say a growth fund with $100 million of assets has an average annual return of 20% over a three-year period. That amazing performance attracts new assets of $1 billion. And, then, reality sets in, and the fund goes absolutely flat for the next three years. Well, the average return of the two three-year periods is still 10%, so that's the time-weighted return.

How did the average investor do? Not so well. Remember 10 times as much money was invested into the fund after the three-year winning streak, so most of the money in the fund has made absolutely nothing while a small percentage has made a decent return. The dollar-weighted return would be less than 2%, which is quite a different story. As always, when we're measuring returns it's like we're scientists using a wide array of microscopes. If we put the focus on this factor, we get this number. If we put the focus instead on this factor, we get this number. The actual dollars that an investor earns over a time period is what it is—or are what they are. How we then choose to measure that performance is really a separate matter.

By the way, I'm not re-posting what he provides on his blog, but I am using his math, so it would be in bad form not to credit Preet Banerjee at http://wheredoesallmymoneygo.com/time-weighted-vs-dollar-weighted-returns for the figures used in my example. I might have changed the numbers, but I have to admit that even my curiosity is at times over-satiated on some of the mathematics behind the exam concepts.

Outside of mutual funds, an individual investor who continues to make contributions to his account would need to figure his dollar-weighted return, since maybe only a small percentage of the account earned a high rate while most of the contributions then went in and got a relatively lousy rate of return. Similarly, the first $800 that I deposited into my SIMPLE IRA years ago has earned a much different rate of return than the $800 I just deposited a few months ago. Dollar-weighted return would account for the difference.

EXPECTED RETURN

Modern Portfolio Theorists analyze data and figure out likely outcomes based on probability. One example of this is called **expected return**. If we feel an investment will most likely return 8% and has a 75% probability of actually doing so, we can say the investment has an expected return of 6%. In other words 8% times the 75% probability of getting the 8% equals 6% (.75 x .08 = .06).

More likely, the exam would express three possible outcomes and say that that investment has a 75% chance of returning 8%, a 10% chance of returning 12%, and a 15% chance of returning −10%. What's the total expected return? Take 75% of 8% (6%), add it to 10% of 12% (1.2%), and add that to 15% of −10% (−1.5%). That's a total expected return of 5.7%.

What happens if we expect 5.7% and get −29.3%? That's why we don't guarantee results.

Rather than use numbers or calculations, the exam might just want you to define expected return as "possible return on an investment weighted by the likelihood of the outcomes."

Sometimes expected return and standard deviation are lumped together in order to make vague predictions about an investment's results. For example, the expected return for the stock market (S&P 500) is, say, 10%, but the standard deviation is 15. What does that tell us about next year's stock market results? Not much, unfortunately. All it can tell us is that about two-thirds of the time, the market returns are somewhere between +25% and −5%, since we add and subtract 15 from the expected return of 10. Ninety-five percent of the time, the market is somewhere between +40% and −20% (two standard deviations). We could do "three standard deviations," but most people get scared out of stocks as soon as they see that the market can end up doing just about anything any given year. Which is, of course, what makes investing in stocks so much fun in the first place.

PDQ common stock has a 40% chance of appreciating 10% and a 60% chance of appreciating 8%. Therefore, its expected return is…

Answer: just take 40% of 10 (4%) and add it to 60% of 8 (4.8%). The expected return is 8.8%. Just don't take out any loans on the street backed up by your expectations, please.

BENCHMARKS

For evaluation purposes, portfolio managers at mutual funds, pension funds, etc. often compare the performance of their portfolios to some **benchmark**, like the S&P 500 index. The most helpful comparisons compare a portfolio to a benchmark that most accurately reflects the makeup of the portfolio. In other words, if the mutual fund owns mostly technology stocks, why compare the portfolio to a pharmaceutical industry index? More accurately and more usefully, we would compare it to a technology index that more closely matches its own make-up. If my client invests in blue-chip companies in various industries, maybe I use a "blue chip index" such as the **Dow Jones Industrial Average**. If I manage a small-cap portfolio, I'm trying to beat the **Russell 2000**, or the S&P SmallCap 600. If I'm the manager of a mid-cap portfolio, I'm hoping to beat the S&P MidCap 400. If I'm a bond fund manager, I'm being matched up against various bond indexes. So, you might want to memorize the following indexes and be able to associate them with the proper portfolio composition.

- S&P 500 – overall market
- S&P 400 – mid-cap
- S&P 600, Russell 2,000 – small-cap
- Dow Jones Industrial Average – large-cap
- NASDAQ – technology

➤ Weighting

The exam might bring up the fact that indexes generally assign more weight to particular stocks inside the index, based either on the **market cap** of all the shares outstanding or the share price itself. The Dow Jones Industrial Average gives more weighting to stocks priced around $100 than to those priced at, say, $25. So, the exam could say that the DJIA is a "price-weighted index of 30 large, mostly industrial stocks." S&P doesn't use the share price in and of itself to weight their indices; instead, they use **market capitalization**. Market capitalization is simply the total value of a company's outstanding shares. Microsoft, for example, has just over 10 billion shares outstanding. If the shares close at $30 tomorrow, the market cap is 10 billion times $30, or $300 billion. So, Microsoft gets a lot more weighting in the S&P 500 than a stock whose market cap is only in the millions of dollars. In fact, Microsoft has maybe 10 times more impact on the overall S&P 500 than many other stocks within the index.

Of course, the concept of "weighting" is nothing new. In high school and college you might have taken courses that made your mid-term worth 30% of the final grade, the homework 10%, class participation 10%, and the final exam 50%. In that case, the final exam was heavily "weighted" at five times the importance of either the homework or the class participation.

POSSIBLE CALCULATIONS ON YOUR EXAM

MORTGAGE PAYMENTS

The exam might expect you to think like a financial planner the day you take it and ask you to calculate a mortgage payment for a hypothetical client. Maybe you'll get hit with something like this: Jennifer Myers is financing a $275,000 home with a 30-year fixed-rate mortgage of 6.5%. If she makes a down payment of 20%, her first monthly payment will be closest to which amount?

Okay, if Jennifer is putting down 20%, she's borrowing 80% of the purchase price. 80% of $275,000 is $220,000. The first year's interest payments will be 6.5% of $220,000 divided over 12 monthly payments. That's $14,300 in interest for the year, or about $1,191.66 per month. In interest. Is her mortgage an interest-only mortgage? If so, the answer is $1,191.66 per month. But, if it's a 30-year fixed-rate mortgage, there's no way to quickly figure how much principal is added to her payment in order to amortize/pay off the loan over a 30-year schedule. If the exam makes it a 30-year traditional mortgage, it must expect you to do the calculation we just enjoyed and then conclude that the payment is not all interest but is, rather, the interest plus a few hundred dollars of principal. Therefore, you eliminate $1,191.66 and any answer that is lower than that. On the other end, if an answer is too high, like, say, $2,945.52, eliminate that one. Why? You know the interest component of the monthly payment is about $1,200—no way is $1,700 or so on top of that going toward the principal. Some good false answer choices to this question would be $763.88 and $611.11. Why? Because if the test-taker divides $275,000 by 360 months, he gets $763.88. Is it fair to ding him for that calculation? Yes—his reasoning assumes there is no interest to be paid over 30 years. Here, buddy, take this house for $275,000 and just pay us back $275,000 over 30 years. Come on now, people. The other answer shows a little more thought because the test-taker does deduct the down payment but then, again, acts as if the remaining $220,000 is simply paid back over 30 years without interest at $611.11 per month. So, there will be some tough questions like this on the exam. But you'll notice that with a combination of problem solving and common sense, you can get even these things right. Or at least eliminate one or two answer choices to improve your odds.

Oh, by the way, the monthly payment (without taxes and insurance) would be closest to $1,390.55.

WITHDRAWAL RATES

Just as shocking, the test might expect you to calculate how long a retiree's money will last if his IRA account earns X percent while he, meanwhile, is withdrawing Y amount. So, we need to go back to our formula for future value (FV). In our examples, we were assuming that the investor would leave the money untouched so that if it compounds at 3% it's always the principal times 1.03. However, if the account is earning 3% while the account owner is withdrawing $12,000 a year, obviously, the account will be exhausted at some point. Which is, of course, sort of the point of having a retirement account. The trick is to die before you run out of money rather than the other way around. And, of course, you have to take withdrawals from a Traditional IRA at a required minimum rate, so this is a very common problem financial planners have to help their clients solve. I may never use an adviser to pick investments during my "accumulation period" of retirement savings, but I guarantee I'll consult my CPA—who is also now an IAR—before I set up a withdrawal plan from my retirement accounts.

Anyway, if the IRA is earning 3%, while the owner is withdrawing $12,000 a year from the account, how long before he runs out of retirement money? Let's say the IRA starts out at $100,000. The account grows 3% over the year, to $103,000. The client removes $12,000 at the end of the year, so the principal drops to $91,000. If that compounds at 3%, we get $93,700. The client removes $12,000, and now the account is down to $81,700. At this rate, the account will be exhausted in about 11 years.

Unfortunately, my assumptions there were extremely simple. In order to do a more realistic estimate of proper withdrawal rates, financial planners often use something called **Monte Carlo simulations** to estimate what would happen if inflation or interest rates went to this particular level, or if even the 3% I used might become unrealistic for short-term bonds if the Federal Reserve Board embarks on a long-term policy goal of keeping interest rates low. The Monte Carlo method is used in many different professions for decision making. The process uses multiple values for things like interest rates, stock market returns, inflation, etc. in order to come up with possible outcomes that should give the investor a more realistic plan for retirement.

TAX CONSIDERATIONS

Believe it or not, most of us pay income taxes at several different rates due to the graduated, progressive income tax system in the United States. Did you know that the first so much of your income is taxed at 10%, the next at 15%, then 25%? In other words, you don't pay 25% on all your income just because you reach that bracket; you pay 25% on the amount of money you make above a certain amount.

The 25% in that case would be your **marginal tax rate,** which is the highest rate at which you pay tax on your taxable income. If you start making decent money, the last dollars earned that year will be taxed at 28% or maybe 33%. And, if you're really making bank, some of your income (above approximately $400,000) will be taxed at the top rate, currently 39.6%.

The exam might ask, "What is an individual's 'marginal tax rate'?" You would choose an answer such as "the rate of tax paid on the last dollar of income earned."

Beyond the different tax brackets there are also different methods of filing income taxes, and these methods definitely affect the rate of taxes paid. For example, if you file as a single filer, you will get pushed into the 15% tax bracket and then the 25% bracket at a certain dollar amount, while a married couple filing jointly would get to make twice those amounts before being pushed into the 15% and then the 25% bracket. On the other hand, if they choose "married-filing-separately," the dollar amounts are different, and this explains why politicians are forever promising to "simplify the tax code" and why CPAs are still paid relatively well for their tax planning service. Turns out a married couple choosing to file separately can each earn as much as actual single people filing singly, until we get to those middle tax brackets and, suddenly, they get pushed into the 28% and 33% sooner than if they'd stayed unattached.

In other words, there definitely is a so-called "marriage penalty" built into these tax brackets. At the lower brackets, it makes perfect sense for two people to get married from a tax standpoint. They can choose married-filing-jointly and make exactly twice as much as they could make if living apart before being pushed into the next bracket. Or, they could choose married-filing-separately and get the same effect, while likely sharing expenses, too. But, at the next few brackets, married couples get pushed into the next higher rate at much lower dollar amounts of income than if they were to live apart. And that holds true whether they file jointly or separately. I suppose this could almost make sense, except that at the top bracket, once again a married couple can make exactly twice as much as a single filer before that bracket kicks in whether they file jointly or separately.

Bizarre. Not sure if Congress intended it that way, but the way I read the tax code, it makes sense for people to get married if they're either scraping by or killing it financially. All the folks making the low six figures—from a tax standpoint, it makes more sense to stay single.

There is another method of filing called "head of household." If the test question says that your client is now raising two children orphaned when her sister was killed in a car crash, that individual should file as "head of household" versus "single filer." For a "head-of-household" filer, the dollar amounts of income allowed before being pushed into the next tax bracket are much higher compared to a single filer.

Whatever the marginal tax bracket, what we're talking about here is **ordinary income**. Ordinary income is made up basically of wages, salaries, bonuses, commissions, some dividends, and bond interest. We'll talk later about investments held within retirement accounts, but for now, let's talk about the regular, old taxable brokerage account.

In a taxable account held at, say, Charles Schwab or TD Ameritrade, there are basically two types of taxes on investments:

- Taxes on income
- Taxes on capital gains

Let's start with income.

PORTFOLIO INCOME

Some investors focus on the market price of their stocks and bonds, while others focus more on the income that their stocks and bonds produce. Bonds pay interest on a regular basis, and many stocks pay consistent and increasing dividends. This income is a major component of a portfolio's total return. Unfortunately, it is also taxable.

➢ Dividends

Let's say you buy 1,000 shares of GE for $30 per share. Every three months you get a quarterly dividend check for 25 cents per share, or $250. Pretty neat, huh? Sure beats working for a living, even though this income—like the stuff you work for—is also going to be taxed. But, believe it or not, it's only taxed at a maximum rate of 15% in most cases nowadays. Before the big change to the tax code, those dividends were taxed at ordinary income rates. Many investors paying a 39% tax on dividends a few years ago are now paying no more than 15%. Imagine that. You're a wealthy individual receiving $200,000 in dividend income each year. You used to pay about $78,000 in taxes on that money; now you pay only $30,000. That's fiscal policy, and that's a lot of money left over to donate to the political party looking out for your interests as an investor.

But, of course, it's not as simple as saying, "Dividends are taxed at 15%." The dividends that get taxed at 15% are called **qualified dividends**. These would include dividends from GE, MSFT, or most any corporation. But there are still **ordinary dividends**, which we'll get to in just a second. First, however, why are dividends now taxed at just 15%? Believe it or not, this relates directly to our look at the corporate income statement. Remember, corporations like GE and MSFT pay dividends *after* they've already paid tax on their profit. Unlike bond interest, dividends don't get deducted from a company's income to reduce their tax burden. Since GE or MSFT already paid tax on the profits before giving you some of that profit in the form of a dividend check, why should you get fully taxed on that money?

Turns out you shouldn't, and you don't. We pointed out that C-corporations subject the owners to the double taxation of income, but at least, the taxation on dividends is reduced for most investors. If your marginal tax rate is 25%, 33%, or 35%, you pay only 15% on qualified dividends. But, check this out—if your tax bracket is lower than 25%, the tax you pay on qualified dividends is zero percent.

Zero. But, again, not all dividends are qualified and taxed at the kinder, gentler rates. The dividends that don't qualify for this tax treatment include "ordinary dividends," which are taxed at ordinary income rates. REITs, which kick out 90% of their earnings pre-tax to shareholders in order to act as a conduit to the investors, pay ordinary dividends that are taxed at ordinary income rates. Since the REIT already gets favorable tax treatment on the money it sends out to unit-holders, the unit-holder doesn't. Then there are royalty trusts. A royalty trust is simply an entity that owns the rights to, for example, oil and natural gas fields. After covering the administrative expenses of the trust (which are pretty minimal), most of the profits on sales of oil and natural gas are sent directly to the unit holders, usually every month. The distributions are nice, but they do not receive the 15% rate that qualified dividends enjoy.

But who cares? I happen to own about a thousand shares of a royalty trust that pays me a distribution every month. In fact, as oil and natural gas prices rise, so do the monthly distributions this thing pays out to me, and I'll gladly pay taxes on income I get for doing absolutely nothing.

In any case, when GE pays me a dividend, I get taxed at a rate of 15%. When HGT, the royalty trust, pays me a dividend, I pay my ordinary income rate on that. And my online broker, TD Ameritrade™, indicates whether each dividend is "ordinary," or "qualified," making my annual tax reporting a little easier.

There is actually some bad news for the folks who got pushed into the 39.6% marginal bracket. For these investors, qualified dividends and long-term capital gains are now taxed at 20%. I guess one could say that this is about half of what they pay on other ordinary income, but it is also 5 percentage points higher than they had been paying for about a decade.

Grrrr.

Finally, I am giving you the "real-world" tax rates on dividends. The exam will likely avoid the issue entirely and say something like, "*If* the tax on dividends is 20%, what is Joe's after-tax return?" The exam likes to keep things academic.

BOND INTEREST

Interest paid on corporate and government bonds is also taxable at ordinary income rates. This explains why wealthier investors often try to hold their corporate bonds in tax-advantaged accounts, which we'll discuss in a few pages. Corporate bonds are taxable at the federal, state, and local government levels, while US government bond interest is taxable "only" at the federal level. Of course, the federal level is the one that takes the biggest bite out of my wallet. Still, I would love to have $1 million in US Government bonds yielding, say, 5%. I'd get $50,000 a year in guaranteed interest payments, and would pay the same tax on that as if I'd had to get up every morning and work for the money.

Some people complain about paying up to 39.6% tax on this US government bond interest, but it's the same rate they pay on the income they earn by working, without the annoying payroll taxes. And this interest income is not taxable by the state or local governments, recall.

Corporate bond interest *is* taxable in states that have an income tax, and—believe it or not—even a few cities tax the corporate bond interest that their residents earn. GNMA, FNMA, and FHLMC are taxable at the federal, state, and local levels, also, just like corporate bonds.

> ➤ Taxation of municipal securities

The interest on general obligation bonds is going to be tax-exempt at the federal level, but your state could tax the interest if you buy a bond from an out-of-state issuer. If you live in Georgia and buy a bond issued by the State of Alabama, Georgia can tax that interest. Plus if you live in Atlanta, Georgia, and Atlanta has a tax on bond interest, your city could tax you as well.

How could you avoid being taxed by Georgia and the city of Atlanta? Buy a bond issued by Atlanta, Georgia. The state will give you a break, and so will Atlanta.

Finally, if you live in Atlanta and buy a bond issued by Valdosta, Georgia, the federal government will give you the tax break, and so will the State of Georgia, since both Valdosta and Atlanta are in that state. But, what about Atlanta—did you help them out? Not at all—so they can tax you. How do you get Atlanta off your back? Buy one of *their* municipal securities. You help us finance our schools, we'll help you deal with your little tax problem.

Nice and simple, the way the tax code always works.

SITUATION	FEDERAL	STATE	LOCAL
Resident of Topeka, KS, buys a Toledo, OH, municipal bond	EXEMPT	TAXABLE	TAXABLE
Resident of Topeka, KS, buys a Wichita, KS, municipal bond	EXEMPT	EXEMPT	TAXABLE
Resident of Topeka, KS, buys a Topeka, KS, municipal bond	EXEMPT	EXEMPT	EXEMPT

And if you thought that was confusing, check this out—not *all* municipal securities pay tax-free interest. The ones used for public purpose/essential services do, but if the IRS code says that the bond is a "private activity" bond, the interest is subject to **alternative minimum tax (AMT)**. Most municipal bond investors are subject to AMT, which would force them to add some of the interest received on a private activity bond back into their taxable income. For that reason **private activity bonds** usually offer higher yields (before tax). An example of a private activity bond would be a bond issued to finance a parking garage that will be operated by a private company, or bonds issued to build a sports stadium used by an NFL or NBA team. If the exam says your customer wants a municipal bond but is concerned about AMT, put her into a general obligation bond, such as a school bond. Or look for the concept of "essential, public purpose." And, if the exam really wants to hit hard, it might bring up the fact that some municipal bonds are simply taxable. For example, if a public university has already issued a certain amount of GO debt that is outstanding, additional bond issues could be taxable, requiring the issuer to offer much higher yields to investors.

So far, we have been discussing the income that securities provide to investors through interest and dividend payments.

CAPITAL GAINS

On the other hand, think of **capital gains** as the profit you take when you sell a stock, bond, or mutual fund for more than you bought it. Now, before you get all irked that you have to pay tax, remember what I just said: you sold an investment for more than you paid. That's known in the world of investing as a *good thing*. Of course, the IRS knows how to spot a good thing, too, and they'd like to share some of this good thing with you. In fact, even though we said that municipal bond interest is tax-exempt at the federal level, capital gains on municipal bonds are still taxed at capital gains rates, at both the federal and state level. If you own a municipal bond mutual fund in a regular taxable account, the dividends you receive will usually be tax-exempt, but the capital gains distributions will be taxable at capital gains rates, just to keep things nice and simple.

What is a capital gain, again? Let's go back to our GE example. You bought 1,000 shares @$30 each. Let's say you sell 100 shares for $40 in order to take a vacation. If you held GE for more than 1 year, you'd realize a long-term gain of $1,000, since $10 times 100 shares = $1,000 in capital gains. Go ahead and take your vacation, and at the end of the year, you'll owe Uncle Sam 15% of that $1,000, or $150. Your state may tax the gain as well. And, if you're in the top tax bracket of 39.6%, you actually get nailed with a 20% rate on long-term capital gains. Ouch.

If you had sold that stock within the space of a year, it would get taxed at your ordinary income rate since it's a "short-term" capital gain. If your ordinary income rate is 25%, you owe the IRS $250. If it's 35%, you only kept $650 of that capital gain when the dust settles.

Sorry about that. Don't eat out as much, maybe, or check out Priceline-dot-com first. But, either way, go on your vacation. It's not like you had to work for that money.

> ➤ Cost Basis

A capital gain is simply the difference between your **proceeds** (what you sell it for) and your **cost basis** (what you paid for it). Think of your "cost basis" as all the money that has gone into an investment after being taxed. When you buy GE for $30 a share, you don't get to deduct any of that from taxable income, so $30 a share is your cost basis. You also have to pay a commission in most cases, so you add that to your cost basis. When you bought 1,000 shares of GE @$30, you paid a $50 commission. So, while we used round numbers above to introduce the concept, your cost basis is really $3,050 divided by 1,000 shares, or $30.05 per share.

If an investor purchases shares of the same stock at different times and for different prices, there are different methods of determining the cost basis when he goes to sell the stock and turn it back into cash-money. For example, if he bought 100 shares for $50, 100 shares for $60, and 100 shares for $75 over the past several years, which 100 did he just sell? The IRS assumes the method used is **first in first out (FIFO)**. That means, he just sold the shares with the $50 cost basis, leading to a much larger taxable capital gain vs. using the shares purchased for $75. Could he use the $75 cost basis? Yes, but he and the broker-dealer would have to identify the shares with the **CUSIP number** when the sell order is placed. That method is called **share identification** and it's kind of a pain in the neck. The method I and many investors use is **average cost**, in which we just total up all the money we've spent on the shares and divide that by the current number of shares. Of course, we only have to do this stuff for a taxable brokerage account—and we can only do it when a broker-dealer or other custodian holds the shares on our behalf. Remember that in an IRA, for example, you can just buy and sell whenever you want without concerns for basis, proceeds, etc.—there are no capital gains in a retirement account. But that's true of *all* the taxation concerns we're discussing for securities investments. Just thought I'd point it out here.

Commissions are charged by broker-dealers when you buy and when you sell securities. So, when you buy shares of GE, you add the commission to the cost basis, and when you sell those shares of GE, you subtract the commission from your proceeds. If you sell 100 shares of GE @40 and pay a $50 commission, your proceeds would be $3,950, or $39.50 per share. On your tax returns for the year in which you sell the stock, you would report that your proceeds were $3,950, while your cost basis on those 100 shares was $3,005. The capital gain on that sale is $945.

➢ Holding Period

If you sell a security that you held for just one year or less, that is considered a short-term gain or loss. If it's a gain, it is taxed at your ordinary income/marginal rate. If you hold a security for more than one year, that is considered a long-term gain or loss. If it's a gain, it is taxed at the same 15% currently used for qualified dividends for most investors (0% for low-bracket, 20% for top-bracket investors). One advantage of a buy-and-hold investment strategy is that any gains will likely be taxed at the lower long-term capital gains rates. This helps portfolio performance. In fact, one reason that the efficient market theorists have so much evidence on their side is that any gains taken by the rare, gifted active trader are going to be taxed at the higher **short-term capital gains rates**.

Anyway, how do you count your **holding period**? Let's allow the IRS to tell us, which they do on their helpful website www.irs.gov, Publication 564:

To find out how long you have held your shares, begin counting on the day after the trade date on which you bought the shares. (Do not count the trade date itself.) The trade date on which you dispose of the shares is counted as part of your holding period. If you bought shares on May 6 of last year (trade date), and sold them on May 6 of this year (trade date), your holding period would not be more than 1 year. If you sold them on May 7 of this year, your holding period would be more than 1 year (12 months plus 1 day).

What a difference a day makes, huh? Imagine how miffed you'd be if you had sold those shares on May 6th, thinking you were going to be taxed at 15%, only to end up paying 25–35% on that gain. As the example explains, waiting to sell the stock on May 7th would drop the tax rate to the long-term capital gains rate of 15%. And, really, I'm not sure why you're in such a hurry to sell your winners, anyway. If it's a good stock, why not let it ride a few decades? Nothing worse than taking a 50% gain and then realizing that it would have been a 3,000% gain over 15 or 20 years.

As with qualified dividends, if the investor's marginal tax rate hits 25-35%, he pays no more than 15% tax on long-term capital gains, and if his marginal rate is lower than that, he could end up paying zero percent on capital gains. Zero percent.

CAPITAL LOSSES

You don't pay the tax on the day you sell the stock; you pay it with your income taxes. But you'll definitely want to keep track of the gain, because the IRS will want to know, and because when you sit down with your accountant at the end of the year, you might decide to sell some other stocks at a loss to balance out that gain. You took a $945 gain on GE. If you sell another stock at a $1,000 **capital loss**, you'd end up at zero capital gains for the year.

Congratulations, you made no money on your stocks this year. And, therefore, you have no capital gains taxes to pay. You could get really strategic and sell even more stock at a loss. If you lost, say, $10,000 for the year, you could use $3,000 of your total or net loss to offset (reduce) your adjusted gross income for the year. So, if your AGI was going to be $53,000, now it's only $50,000. That reduces your tax bill.

But you really did lose money. See the relationship? If you're paying no tax, it's because you're making no money. If you're paying taxes, it's because you're making money. Personally, I prefer the latter, but that's not the point, and many would argue that it's better to reduce your tax burden than to have the misfortune of making money in the stock market. Some will even purposely take a huge net loss for the year and continue to carry the excess that's over the $3,000 limit forward. I know a few part-time investors who have enough capital losses to last the rest of their lives, $3,000 at a time. They took about $100,000 in capital losses in 2002, and it's going to take quite some time to use that up at three grand a year.

Lucky devils.

➤ Offsetting Gains with Losses

In any case, if an investor only made a couple of sales during the year, figuring gains and losses would be extremely easy. An exam question, of course, could be anything but. Let's use possible exam questions to show you how to deal with the tricky process of matching up gains and losses to figure an investor's net gains and net losses.

1. Jarod Stevens had the following results on four stock sales last year:

$15,000 in long-term gains
$5,000 in long-term losses
$5,000 in short-term gains
$13,000 in short-term losses

Therefore, the tax implications were

A. short-term capital gain of $8,000

B. long-term capital gain of $2,000

C. short-term capital gain of $2,000

D. long-term capital gain of $15,000

Step one: line up the long-term gains and the long-term losses, then line up the short-term gains with the short-term losses. Matching up the long-term gain of $15,000 with the $5,000 long-term loss leaves Jarod with $10,000 in long-term capital gains. Subtract the $13,000 short-term loss from the $5,000 short-term gain, and Jarod has $8,000 in short-term losses. Now, here's the tricky part. You can take the $10,000 long-term gain and reduce it by the $8,000 short-term loss for a net long-term gain of $2,000.

Why is that $2,000 treated as a long-term capital gain? Because the IRS defines a net long-term capital gain as any long-term capital gain that remains after subtracting any short-term losses. Or think of it this way—it's the long-term net capital gain of $10,000 that triggered the capital gains tax. Regardless, the answer is…B. I know. I don't like taxation very much myself, but it could easily make the difference between a pass and a no-pass on the exam, so let's keep plodding through this.

2. Jarod Stevens had the following results on four stock sales this year:

$15,000 in long-term gains
$23,000 in long-term losses
$15,000 in short-term gains
$5,000 in short-term losses

[handwritten: (-8) LT Loss -10 ST gain]

Therefore, the tax implications are

A. short-term capital gain taxed at a maximum of 15%

B. no net gains or losses

C. short-term capital gain of $2,000 taxed at ordinary income rates

D. long-term capital loss of $8,000, short-term capital gain of $8,000

Line up the long-term with long-term, and the short-term with short-term. You end up with a net long-term loss of $8,000 and a net short-term gain of $10,000. The $8,000 in losses brings the total capital gain down to $2,000, which will be taxed as a short-term capital gain. Why a short-term capital gain? Because it was the short-term net gain that triggered the tax. The answer is…*C.*

One last time.

3. Jarod Stevens had the following results on four stock sales last year:

$15,000 in long-term gains
$5,000 in long-term losses
$5,000 in short-term gains
$17,000 in short-term losses

[handwritten: 10 LTG -12 STL]

Therefore, the tax implications will be

A. short-term capital gain of $2,000

B. long-term capital gain of $2,000

C. short-term capital gain of $5,000

D. short-term capital loss of $2,000, which offsets ordinary income

Match up long-term with long-term and short-term with short-term, then net out your results. There is a net long-term gain of $10,000 and a net short-term loss of $12,000. That makes it a net loss of $2,000, which can be used to offset ordinary income.

Too bad Jarod couldn't have lost another $1,000 on our stock picks to take full advantage of our services, huh? In any case, the answer is…*D.*

➢ Wash Sale Rules

So, the "benefit" of selling securities at a loss is that you can offset your ordinary income by up to $3,000 per year. But, in order to use that loss, *stay out of that stock for at least 30 days*. If you sell MSFT at a loss, don't buy any Microsoft stock for 30 days—and, you could not have purchased any 30 days *before* you made the sale, either. Also, don't get clever and buy warrants, convertible bonds, convertible preferred stock or call options that convert to Microsoft common stock. In short, don't get cute. Just take your little capital loss and stay out of Microsoft for 30 days both before and after the sale, and everything will be hunky-dory. What if you promise not to buy any Microsoft common stock over the next 30 days but simply can't stop yourself? First, I can recommend a good therapist and, second, you simply can't use the loss now to offset ordinary income on your taxes because of wash sale rules. Never fear, though, because if you took a $7-per-share loss on Microsoft, you would simply add $7 per share to your cost basis on the new purchase. If you were to repurchase MSFT @$40, your cost basis would actually be $47. In other words, you would eventually get the benefit of that loss you took, but not now. And, if you recall our discussion of the time value of money, now is always a better time to get those dollars rather than at some point in the future.

When you sell a bond at a loss, there is a similar rule. Either wait 30 days to buy a replacement, or, if you want to sell a GE bond at a loss and buy another GE bond, you'll need to substantially alter some features of the bond: interest rate, maturity, call feature, or some combination. Or, just buy a bond from a different issuer. The test might call this process a **bond swap** to make sure there is an endless list of vocabulary terms no human could anticipate, let alone memorize sufficiently.

A rather tricky issue concerning wash sales arises when the investor makes regular and frequent investments into a particular mutual fund. If he sells/redeems shares at a loss and then another automatic purchase occurs a few days later, that's going to be a problem. Remember, wait 30 days before repurchasing a security sold at a loss.

UNREALIZED CAPITAL GAINS

An **unrealized capital gain** is just an increase in value, a "paper gain," as some folks like to say. There is no tax to pay simply because your asset has become more valuable. As with your house, which could be worth twice what you paid for it at this point, you owe no capital gains tax on your securities just because they have gone up in value. Only if the investor has sold the security and realized a capital gain (profit) on the security would there be a capital gains tax to pay. So, don't let the test trick you on that. Again, I have given the current real-world tax rates for capital gains and qualified dividends, but that doesn't mean the exam will use those rates. An exam question might say, "If the taxation on dividends is 25% and long-term capital gains rates are 10%, what is the investor's after-tax return?" In other words, making sure you know the exact tax rates currently in use isn't the point. The point is to make sure you know how to apply taxation to dividends and capital gains. Why? The investments you put your clients into will be affected by different tax rates, and the regulators would be pleased as punch if investment professionals could explain that to their clients.

CAPITAL GAIN OR LOSS ON A PRIMARY RESIDENCE

Many readers are surprised to learn that if a homeowner owns and lives in a primary residence any two of the previous five years leading up to the sale of the property, any capital gain taken when he sells his house is tax-free up to $250,000 for individuals and up to $500,000 for married couples. He has to meet the "ownership and use tests" in order to claim up to those maximum amounts. But, even if he doesn't meet the two-year ownership and use tests, he may qualify for a reduced maximum amount if suffering a financial or health-related hardship.

I myself am looking forward to a modest tax-free capital gain under this beautiful section of the Internal Revenue Code, which could be taken in just a few months, actually. If two people jointly own a house, each could claim up to $250,000 on his or her separate return. A married couple claiming up to $500,000 as a tax-free capital gain is required to file jointly for the year they take advantage of this maneuver. For more information look up IRS Publication 523.

What about a capital loss on a primary residence? What if you put on a $100,000 addition to your house but end up selling for less than your cost basis? That is always painful. If you wanted to take a capital loss on your primary residence, you would first have to convert it to a rental property. If you rent it out to someone else, you can start taking depreciation on the property as we did under our look at partnerships. And, now, if you end up selling for less than your cost basis, you do get to claim a capital loss to offset taxable income for the year.

I happen to be utilizing this aspect of the tax code, as well. Once the lease expires and the tenants move out, I plan to sell the property. Though I would much prefer to make a profit, I will end up selling the place for far below my cost basis due to the realities of that real estate market. I should realize close to an $80,000 capital loss on that sale, which is why 2015 should be a good tax year for yours truly. Suddenly, the regrettable second-story addition I should have never put on will provide some benefit beyond an occasional hot, jetted-tub experience on annual visits to the city. For more information on gains and losses taken on rental properties, see IRS Publication 527.

But, really, if you're "taking a loss" under the tax code, it's because you really are—all due respect—losing. If you "harvest your losses" in the stock market it's because you really lost money on those stocks. I am happy to extract some benefit from this house I'm currently renting, but—as my CPA would concur—I would be much better off had I never put on the darned addition. When "harvesting tax losses," I think it's important to remember that you are, in fact, losing. It's just that the tax code lets you reap some sort of benefit from your losing experience. Turning lemons into lemonade, so to speak.

So, when investors utilize the tax code, it's not all gravy. Even my excitement over the tax-free capital gain on my primary residence is tempered with the fact that it's a struggle to meet the mortgage payments, and in order to make it a tax-free capital gain I'm adding at least one year of mortgage payments to my burden. As they say, there really is no free lunch in life. Certainly not in the world of investments.

MUTUAL FUND INCOME DISTRIBUTIONS

Remember that the owner of all the stocks and bonds inside a mutual fund is the investment company itself. The fund sells pieces of this big portfolio to investors in the form of common stock. So, like any common stockholder, you as a mutual fund holder will probably receive dividends from time to time. A stock mutual fund earns dividends (and maybe some interest payments) from the vast quantities of stocks (and maybe a few bonds) that they own. They pay expenses with that money and if there's a profit left over, they distribute it to the shareholders. The shareholders also get convenient **1099-DIV** statements that help keep track of this income, which will be taxable at some rate.

If it's a stock fund, the investor will be taxed at ordinary or qualified dividend rates, depending on the composition of the fund.

If it's a bond fund, income checks will be taxed just like bond interest, because that's where the income comes from. That means if it's a government bond fund, the interest is only taxable at the federal level. If it's a corporate bond fund, the interest is taxable at all levels. And if it's a municipal bond fund, the interest is tax-exempt at the federal level, but your state government often taxes the interest received on out-of-state municipal bonds, just to keep things nice and simple. For that reason, you'll find many state-specific municipal bond mutual funds for residents of high-tax states such as California, Virginia, and Maryland.

> Capital Gains in Mutual Funds

There are two ways that capital gains come into play for mutual funds, but before we get to that, remember that you have no control over when the investment adviser for the fund decides to sell a stock or bond. If he/she ends the year realizing more gains than losses, the fund realizes a net gain, whether that's inconvenient for your taxes this year or not. They can either distribute this to the shareholders or not. Either way, you'll get taxed on your proportional share of this capital gain that you may or may not actually get a check for. Sorry about that. That's the trouble with investing in funds that buy low and sell high. It's called a capital gain, and the **capital gains distribution** is taxed at your long-term capital gains rate.

Distributions to Shareholders

The first thing to remember is that a fund almost always makes sure that when it takes a capital gain, it's a long-term capital gain, since, as we saw, the difference to a high-tax-bracket investor could be significant. Assume it's a long-term gain on the exam. Could it be a short-term gain?

Sure, if the fund doesn't mind fielding a few million angry phone calls from frustrated high-bracket investors. They'd just take their stack of short-term gains, identify them as such, send out the tax info, and get ready for the switchboard to light up.

Now, things get a little tricky here. We've been saying that the interest on US Treasury securities is exempt from state and local taxation, and it is. Notice how we've deviously said nothing about capital gains until now. Yes, *capital gains* (not interest payments) on US Treasuries are taxable at the federal, state, and local levels.

And, on the tax-free front, even though the dividend checks you receive from your tax-exempt municipal bond fund are usually tax-exempt at the federal level, any capital gains distributions are treated as—get this—capital gains. That looks like a good test question, no matter which test you're taking. So, remember that the dividends received on a tax-exempt bond fund are tax-exempt at the federal level, but the capital gains distributions are taxable as capital gains at all levels.

Shareholder Sales

The second capital gain issue to be aware of with mutual funds is entirely within the investor's control, just as it is on a share of GE or MSFT. If she sells her mutual fund shares within a year, any gain is a short-term gain, taxed at her ordinary income rate. If she holds them for more than one year, it's a long-term gain, taxed at a maximum of 15% for most investors. The only thing that is different, then, between a share of GE and a mutual fund share is that there are two types of capital gains for fund shares: the ones that the fund takes and <u>distributes</u> to the shareholder, and the one the shareholder realizes only if and when she <u>sells/redeems</u> her shares. As opposed to a mutual fund share, the only way to take/realize a capital gain on GE or MSFT common stock would be to sell your shares. GE and MSFT pay dividends, but companies such as GE and MSFT do not distribute capital gains checks to investors. Only if the investor owns a pooled investment vehicle like an open-end mutual fund would he *receive* capital gains distributions.

> Unrealized Gains

If the test starts talking about an **unrealized gain**, it's probably trying to trick you. Remember if a mutual fund buys a stock at $10, and the stock now trades at $15, there is no tax to pay—not unless and until the portfolio manager realizes a gain by selling. Unrealized gains make the NAV of the fund go up, but that doesn't affect the investor unless or until A) the fund realizes a gain on the shares, or B) the investor does by redeeming some or all of his holdings at a higher value.

As I mentioned, many investors in funds choose not to take the income and capital gains distributions as checks. Rather, they put that money towards more shares of the fund, which they buy without a sales load (at the NAV). Since the distributions get taxed either way, the investor simply adds to her cost basis by the amount of the distribution.

Let's say she bought the ACE Equity Income Fund at $10 per share. Last year, she received $1 in dividends and $1 in capital gains distributions per share. If she reinvests the $2 per share, she pays tax on that amount, and her cost basis rises by that amount, too.

Every time you pay tax on a dividend or interest payment that you reinvest, you add to your cost basis by the amount that you reinvest. That's what "cost basis" means—the money within an investment holding that you've already paid tax on. The amount above that is subject to capital gains taxes, but not until you take the gain.

See, our culture is obsessed with tax deferral, but we've sort of forgotten that there was already a tax-deferred vehicle available long before IRAs came about. It's called *common stock*. If a common stock pays no dividends, you have absolutely nothing to pay tax on until you finally decide to sell it.

Seriously. If you bought 100 shares of XYZ for $10, and they're worth $90 fifteen years later, what's your tax bill? Zero. What if it's worth $100 five years later? Still no tax bill. Not until you sell it.

So common stocks that don't pay dividends are already tax-deferred. The ones that pay dividends do subject shareholders to taxation, but they also subject them to some very nice checks that the shareholders didn't have to lift a finger to "earn." And, we saw that the tax rate on most dividends is quite low compared to what those same investors pay on ordinary income.

Some investors will never pay a capital gains tax even on their biggest winners? That's because some investors will *never* sell. They just hang onto the stock and cash the dividend checks while they're alive, and when they die, they pass it on to their heirs, or maybe donate it to a charity.

Remember, nobody's forcing you to sell.

TAXATION OF ANNUITIES

➢ Accumulation Period

During the accumulation phase, the investment is growing tax-deferred. So, all the dividends and capital gains distributions from the subaccounts are being reinvested into more units, just like most people reinvest their distributions back into a mutual fund. If the individual dies, the death benefit is paid to the beneficiary. The death benefit is included in the annuitant's **estate** for estate tax purposes, and the beneficiary would have to pay ordinary income tax on anything above the cost basis. If the husband bought the annuity for $50,000, and it's now worth $60,000, she'll receive $60,000 and pay ordinary income rates on the $10,000 of earnings.

Sometimes people just can't stop themselves from cashing in their chips. Not that they haven't been given incentives not to. If they're under 59½ and don't have a qualifying exemption, they will not only pay ordinary income tax on the earnings, but also a 10% penalty tax, too. So, if it's a $60,000 annuity, and a 49-year-old surrenders the contract that he bought for $50,000, he'd pay his ordinary income rate on the $10,000 of earnings and also a 10% penalty of $1,000. You didn't think the IRS would, like, penalize him 10% and then take his ordinary income rate on what's left, did you? It's his ordinary income rate *and* 10% of the excess over his cost basis.

Notice how only the excess over cost basis is taxed and/or penalized on a non-qualified annuity. The after-tax cost basis is just the cost basis, which means the IRS taxed that money a long time ago and quickly lost interest in it. The earnings part—that part really intrigues them.

So, if you're not 59½ yet, the IRS is giving you all kinds of reasons not to surrender your contract. And, we already mentioned that the insurance company will keep a percentage on the back end if you surrender during the early years of the contract. So, you can have your money if you want to, but if you take it out too soon, you'll be penalized by the IRS and possibly the annuity/insurance company, too.

72(t) and Substantially Equal Periodic Payments

We've mentioned that the magic age for taking distributions is 59½ because, otherwise, the individual is hit with early withdrawal penalties. Remember that annuities are by nature retirement plans and are subject to the 10% penalty for early withdrawals made without a good excuse. One good excuse is to utilize IRS rule "**72(t)**." As with an IRA, an individual can avoid the 10% penalty if the withdrawal qualifies for an exemption. For example, if the individual has become disabled and can't work, or has certain medical expenses, money can be taken out penalty-free. Notice how I didn't say tax-free.

Basically, a reference to "72t" has to do with an individual taking a series of substantially equal periodic payments. Of course, the industry quickly turned that phrase into the acronym "SEPP." The IRS won't penalize the early withdrawal if the individual sets up a rigid schedule whereby he or she withdraws the money by any of several IRS-approved methods. Once you start your little SEPP program, stay on it. See, the IRS requires you to continue the SEPP program for five years or until you are the age of 59½, whichever comes last. So, if the individual is 45, she'll have to keep taking periodic payments until she's 59½. If the individual is 56 when she starts, she'll still have to continue for 5 years. Either that, or cut the IRS a check for the very penalties she was trying to avoid.

Loans

Some insurance companies allow contract owners to take a loan against the value of the annuity during the accumulation period. Usually, the interest charge is handled by reducing the number of accumulation units owned. If the owner pays back the loan in full, the number of units goes up again. Unlike a loan against a life insurance policy, however, a loan from an annuity is treated as a distribution. In other words, it is not tax-free.

1035 Exchanges

Both annuities and insurance policies allow people to exchange their contract for another without paying taxes. That's fine, just don't forget the surrender period. If somebody still has a 6% surrender fee (contingent deferred sales charge) in effect, and you push them to do a 1035 exchange, the IRS won't have a problem with it, but FINRA almost certainly will. Especially if you get caught.

Also, this isn't the same thing as a life insurance contract. With a life insurance policy, people often cash in part of their **cash value**. If they're only taking out what they put in—or less—the IRS treats it as part of their cost basis. In an annuity, however, if somebody does a **random withdrawal** for, say, $10,000, the IRS considers that to be part of the taxable earnings. So, if you get a test question where some dude put in $10,000 and with the annuity at $30,000 this dude takes out $10,000, remember that

that is *not* treated as his cost basis. The way the IRS sees things, the dude has $20,000 of earnings. So, whatever comes out is treated as part of that $20,000. So, the entire $10,000 random withdrawal is taxed as ordinary income. And, if he's not 59½ yet, the IRS will also penalize him $1,000.

Most annuities are **non-qualified**, which means that they are purchased with non-tax-deductible dollars. When you cut the check for, say, $50,000 for the annuity, you get no tax deduction from the IRS that year against adjusted gross income. In other words, that $50,000 was taxed that year, so the tax collectors won't tax that money again when you take it out someday. That $50,000 will be your **cost basis**. You will only pay taxes on the amount of earnings above that and only when you finally take out the money.

But, if the exam mentions a "tax-qualified variable annuity," you'll have to adjust your thinking. A "tax-qualified variable annuity" or "individual retirement annuity" is funded with pre-tax or tax-deductible contributions with the same maximums used for Traditional IRA accounts. Like the Traditional IRA—and unlike the <u>non</u>-qualified variable annuity—withdrawals from the IRA annuity account must begin at age 70½. The IRS refers to these plans as "individual retirement annuities," and they are basically just IRAs funded with an investment into a variable annuity. Why do that? Probably for the death benefit during the accumulation phase that guarantees your beneficiaries will receive at least the amount you contributed. Or, some people like the idea of an annuity payout that lasts as long as they live, perhaps longer, as we'll see. So, most questions—maybe all of them—will focus on non-qualified variable annuities funded with after-tax dollars. But, don't be shocked if you get a question or two about variable annuities funded with tax-deductible dollars.

➢ Annuity Period

When the annuitant begins receiving monthly checks, part of each check is considered taxable ordinary income, and part of it is considered to be part of the cost basis. Once the annuitant has received all of the cost basis back, each additional annuity payment will be fully taxable.

Also, if the beneficiary is receiving annuity payments through a "life with period certain" or a "joint with last survivor" settlement option, she will pay ordinary income tax on part of each monthly check, too—as always, on the "excess over cost basis."

TAXATION OF LIFE INSURANCE

When you pay your life insurance premiums, you don't get to take a deduction against income, so they are made after-tax. They usually grow tax-deferred, however, which is nice. When the insured dies, the beneficiary receives the death benefit free and clear of federal income taxes. But the death benefit will be added to the insured's estate to determine estate taxes. It's that simple when the beneficiary has the lump-sum settlement option, anyway. If we're talking about those periodic settlement options that generate interest, some of those payments could be taxed as interest income.

Rather than take a loan, the policyholder can also do a "partial surrender," whereby the policyholder takes out some of the cash value—not enough to make the policy lapse, of course. Depending on how much has been paid in premiums, taxes may be due on the amount withdrawn. Unlike for variable annuities, the IRS uses FIFO here, assuming that the first thing coming out is the cost basis, not the earnings. Only the part taken out above the premiums paid would be taxed.

If a loan is taken out, there are no immediate tax consequences.

TAXATION OF OPTIONS

Three things can happen once an option contract is opened:

- Expire
- Close
- Exercise

Let's see about the tax implications for each event.

> ### Expiration

Ordinary options expire within 9 months, so all gains and losses will be short-term. A short-term gain, as discussed in the Taxation chapter, is taxed at the investor's ordinary income rate. If you buy an option this November, and it expires next April, you lose all the money you paid. It will be a short-term loss that you claim for April's tax year, which is when you "realize" the loss. Back in November you were just putting down some money. Only in April of next year will you actually realize your loss. If you sell an option in November that expires the following April, you'll realize a **short-term capital gain** in April.

> ### Close

Options can be closed for either a gain or a loss. The investor/trader doesn't realize the gain or loss until both sides of the T-chart have been completed, so to speak. If she buys an option in November for $300 and sells it to close next April for $400, she realizes a $100 short-term capital gain in April. Obviously, if she only sells it for $200, she would realize a $100 **short-term capital loss** in April.

Same thing for the seller of the option. When they close with a "closing purchase," they realize either a short-term capital gain or loss when they do so.

> ### Exercise

It gets trickier when an option is exercised. The options premium will affect either the cost basis or the proceeds on the stock transaction. For example, when a call owner exercises her call, maybe she gets to buy the stock for $50 a share. If she paid $2 for the right to buy at $50, her cost basis on the stock acquired through exercise is really $52. Her proceeds will only come into play if and when she sells the stock.

The seller of that call took in her $2 a share. Upon assignment of the contract, the seller also sells the stock for $50, meaning he's taken in a total of $52 for selling that stock. Proceeds are what you take in when you sell.

So, the premium was added to the call buyer's cost basis on the stock. The premium was added to the call seller's proceeds on the stock.

Nice and simple, as always.

If you buy a put, you get the right to sell stock, so the premium will affect your proceeds. If you buy a Jun 50 put @2, you pay $2 for the right to sell stock at $50. If you exercise the put and actually sell the stock at $50, did you take in $50 per share? No, you only took in $48 per share, so $48 is your proceeds. Your cost basis is whatever you bought the stock for before putting it in somebody's reluctant face.

The reluctant face who sold you that put has the obligation to buy the stock at $50. So, the cost basis on the stock will be $50 per share, right?

No, since he took in your $2 first, the IRS says he really only has a cost basis of $48.

Position	Upon Exercise	Premium	Affects
Long Call	Buys stock	Add to strike price	Raises cost base
Short Call	Sells stock	Add to strike price	Raises proceeds
Long Put	Sells stock	Subtract from strike price	Lowers proceeds
Short Put	Buys stock	Subtract from strike price	Lowers cost base

> Leaps

Ordinary options expire in 9 months or sooner. Then, there are long-term options called LEAPS. Since the time value is, by definition, greater on these contracts that can go out over three years, LEAPS contracts trade at much higher premiums. The strategies are the same. You buy a call if you think the stock is going up—you simply pay more for a MSFT Oct 50 call expiring in 2 or 3 years versus the one expiring in 2 or 3 months.

The taxation is a little tricky. For the buyer of the contract, capital gains and losses are considered long-term. But a short seller never establishes a holding period, so any capital gains and losses for a seller of LEAPS contracts are considered short-term.

TRANSFERRED SECURITIES

We mentioned the transfer agent in earlier sections. The transfer agent keeps track of all the transfers of ownership among shareholders. Usually a transfer of ownership is the result of a sale, but there are of course other ways to transfer ownership of stock. Stock can be inherited when somebody dies, or received as a really nice gift, or received as a charitable donation.

> Inherited Securities

What if your grandmother bought stock in Harley-Davidson at $10 several decades ago and passed it to you through her will when she—you know. What's your cost basis? Whatever Harley-Davidson was worth on the day your grandma—you know. If it's worth $30 on the date of death, then that's your cost basis, $30. For a stock you inherit get to step up your cost basis to the fair market value on the date of death. Same for a mutual fund. And thank God for that. You don't have to figure out where Grandma kept all her trade confirmations over the decades, and you avoid paying tax on any capital appreciation over her holding period. If you sell the stock for $30 when your cost base is $30, you have a free capital gain on your hands.

Also—and you may not believe this though I swear it's true—if you sell that Harley stock for more than $30, the capital gain will be treated as *long term* no matter how long you actually held it. Most estates close out within a few months. If you liquidate the securities for more than the cost basis, there is a capital gain, but it's treated as long term, even though it looks as if you took it in six months, because you did.

In case the test gets a little deep, the heirs who inherit appreciated securities can either value them as of the date of death or six months after. Seriously. Estates typically close out within six months and would, therefore, find it easier to value the stocks and bonds as of the date they sell it in order to cut checks to all the beneficiaries named in Grandma's will and trigger no capital gains taxes. If they want to value the securities as of six months after the date of death, they'll need to value all of the assets as of that date. That means the estate may need to pay a real estate appraiser to value the house as of the same date the securities are valued. When the house is sold, the buyer might not be willing to pay the appraised value, or even if the house is sold for the appraised value, there are generally seller's expenses. In either case, the estate could end up showing a loss on the sale of the deceased's primary residence, or on the securities for that matter.

> Gifted Securities

What if Grandma decided to *give* you the stock while she's still alive? In that case you would take her original cost basis of $10. If the stock is worth $40 when you sell it, your gain is $30 a share. Not like when you inherited the shares. Then, your gain would have only been $10. Either way, you're making money when you sell some stock you never had to buy, so I hope you're not complaining too loudly. Also note that you would take over Grandma's holding period, and not necessarily have to hold it for 12 months plus one day to get the long-term capital gains treatment.

Still, because of the tax implications, you should probably find a nice way to tell Grandma it would be better for you if she died first.

> Tax-deductible Charitable Donations

What if Grandma decided to donate the stock to a charity instead of giving it to her grandkids? If she does that, she gets to deduct the fair market value of the stock on the date of the donation. If it's worth $50,000 when she donates it, she can deduct $50,000 from her taxable income that year. You, of course, would get squat in that case, so you might want to think about calling or sending a card once in a while.

A test question might ask what a client should do if he has a stock that has appreciated significantly and one that has gone down in value. A good tax move might be for him to donate the appreciated stock to a charity and sell the loser for a capital loss. This way he will avoid a capital gain on the appreciated stock while also getting the donation. And, he can use the capital loss to offset other gains or even some of his ordinary income. From there, he can donate the cash to a charity, or, of course, find other uses for it.

ESTATES

You have probably noticed how much the IRS enjoys taxing people while they're alive. Did you know they also enjoy taxing people when they die? Conservative politicians generally call this unfortunate reality the "death tax," while liberal politicians prefer the term "estate tax." But, whatever we call it, the fact is that when someone dies, the IRS and state tax collectors may end up taxing the value of assets (house, farmland, bank account, stock, life insurance, etc.) in the "estate. Just how is it that the IRS can tax a dead person?

They can't, actually. A dead person is not a person. The dead person's possessions become part of a **legal person** known as an **estate**. An estate is a legal entity in the same way that a trust, a corporation, or a partnership are legal entities. None of those entities is a human being, but all of those entities are "legal persons" in the eyes of the law. Think of it this way: Otis Redding is not a legal person. However, the Estate of Otis Redding *is* a legal person. The estate is a legally recognized entity. Like a corporation, it has an FEIN (federal employee identification number) and pays taxes on all those royalties received from songs like "Dock of the Bay," "R-E-S-P-E-C-T," and "Hard to Handle." Like a corporation, the assets of the estate are separate from the assets of the beneficiaries of the deceased person's will. So, if some bass player files a claim that Otis Redding still owes him $8,000,000, what happens if all of the estate assets are only worth $1,000,000?

Dude should have tried to collect sooner. Maybe he'll get every last dollar of that eight million bucks through the courts, but the children do not have to make up the difference. The estate is a separate legal entity, just like a corporation.

Again, an estate (like a corporation, partnership, limited liability company, etc.) is a separate legal entity from the person who died—the deceased. When Grandma dies, her checking and savings accounts, CDs, real estate, life insurance, etc., all go into a new legal entity called an estate. If you were named the executor of the estate, it's your job to get several death certificates and do all the paperwork required to transfer her checking and savings to a new bank account entitled, say, Jason Miller, Executor for the Estate of Maude L. Miller, Deceased. If Grandma owned stocks and bonds, they need to be re-titled in the name of the estate, as well. This will require affidavits, signature guarantees, stock powers, letters of office; the whole nine yards. When you effect these transfers of ownership, make sure you have plenty of original death certificates and that the court appointment/letters of office are no more than 60 days old.

You've probably heard the phrase that the only certainties in life are death and taxes. When we talk about estates, we're talking about both. When someone dies, the assets go into his/her estate and taxation is definitely a concern. We'll look at the strategy of establishing trusts to minimize estate taxes in a few minutes, but, first, let's make sure we understand how an estate is treated for the purposes of taxation.

Think of an estate account as a short-term account where safe, short-term debt securities are generally the only appropriate investments. T-Bills and other money market instruments are usually the right recommendation for an estate account. Debit put spreads—not so much. Assuming no huge tax or legal problems, the assets of the estate will soon be distributed to the heirs/beneficiaries. What happens if the stocks, bonds, CDs, etc., earn interest/dividends in the meantime? That income is taxable to the estate. Of course, the legal fees charged by the estate attorney may well cancel that income out, but if the estate earns $5,000 in dividend income when the legal bills are just $2,000, there is $3,000 of taxable income there. The estate will file a tax return (a 1041) for that income.

Will the value of the estate itself (not the income it generates) be taxed? First, we start with the gross estate—the value of the assets before we start taking deductions. The following are included in the value of the gross estate:

- house, farmland, savings account, checking account, investment accounts, clothing, oil paintings, Harley, etc.
- value of insurance and annuity contracts! (Don't forget these.)
- assets placed in revocable trusts
- does not include assets placed in irrevocable trusts (except certain property transferred within three years of death!)

So, we add up all of those values and then we start subtracting things to knock down the value of this estate. If we knock down the value enough, we might avoid paying any estate taxes. The following will reduce the value of the gross estate:

- Funeral and administrative expenses
- Debts owed at the time of death
- Any charitable gifts made after death
- The marital deduction

The "marital deduction" means that husbands and wives pass their property to one another at death without paying estate taxes, which seems fair enough. It's when the assets then go from the "second to die" to the heirs that things get dicey. So, after we've added up the value of all the assets (gross estate) and subtracted the first three bullet points above, maybe what's left is $1 million. Will we have to pay estate taxes?

No. Currently, there is a lifetime credit of $5 million for estates, indexed for inflation. Since the taxable estate is below that number, we avoid paying estate taxes on the estate itself, as an entity or "person."

How are the heirs taxed once they inherit Grandma's goodies? Remember that when Grandma died, we took the fair market value of her securities as our cost basis, which we enjoyed. When we sell the stocks and bonds for more than that fair market value, the excess is a *long-term capital gain*, even if we do it two or three months from now.

Also note that, generally, the state only goes after estate taxes when the estate is large enough to be taxed at the federal level.

GIFTS

What if several months ago Grandma had gone in for her regular checkup and found out from her doctor that she had maybe two months to live? To avoid estate taxes, couldn't she just start handing out big, fat envelopes of cash to all the kids and grandkids?

Sure. In fact, the IRS is cool with that. Well, they are to a point. See, the gifts that Grandma gives to individuals while she is alive are also taxable if they are over a certain amount. That number is forever changing but is currently $14,000. Whatever the amount is, there is an "annual gift-tax exclusion," which means that if Grandma gives anyone other than her husband a gift worth more than that amount, she has to start chipping away at her lifetime gift tax credit. The amount of the credit that was used up over her lifetime will reduce the amount of the credit you and the other beneficiaries can use when trying to reduce the size of the estate in order to avoid paying estate taxes.

Just to keep the tax code nice and simple, the way Congress and the IRS like it.

The IRS defines a **gift** as "transferring property to someone else and expecting nothing in return." The IRS also points out that the following can be considered gifts:

- selling something at less than its value
- making an interest-free or reduced-interest loan

Wait, so when Grandma sold Uncle Bill the back forty for $70,000 below market value, this could have been considered a "gift" to Uncle Bill?

Absolutely. So, when Grandma goes around giving people things worth more than the current annual exclusion, she files a return and tells the IRS that she's using part of her lifetime credit. What if the gift is worth no more than the current exclusion of $14,000?

Then nobody needs to know anything.

In the following cases, no gift taxes would be due and no returns would have to be filed:

- Gifts made to a spouse
- Gifts that do not exceed current exclusion amount
- Paying tuition costs for someone else—payable directly to educational institution
- Paying medical costs for someone else—payable directly to the care provider
- Political and charitable donations

> Gift Splitting

The IRS, believe it or not, is actually very clear on the topic of **gift splitting**, so let's use their Publication 950 from www.irs.gov to make the point:

Harold and his wife, Helen, agree to split the gifts that they made during the previous tax year. Harold gives his nephew, George, $24,000, and Helen gives her niece, Gina, $18,000. Although each gift is more than the annual exclusion ($14,000), by gift splitting they can make these gifts without making a taxable gift.

All that means is that half of $24,000 ($12,000) and half of $18,000 ($9,000) would be less than the annual exclusion of $14,000, so they can treat each gift as half from Harold and half from Helen. No gift taxes would be due and none of the lifetime credits would have to be used up, but the IRS would still require that they file a gift tax return.

TRUSTS

Like an estate or a corporation, a trust is also a separate legal entity with its own FEIN. The trust holds assets, just as a corporation or estate holds assets. The person who administers and oversees the investments of the trust is the "trustee." The one who grants the assets to the trust is called the "grantor." And the ones who benefit from the trust are called the "beneficiaries."

When an adult sets up an UTMA/UGMA account, the kid owns and controls the assets at the age of adulthood/majority, which is usually no later than age 21. If you set up a trust, on the other hand, you can specify all types of things in the trust agreement and, thereby, help to assure that your kids will be rich enough so that they can do pretty much anything, but not rich enough so that they can do absolutely nothing with the rest of their lives. The exam might point out other advantages of establishing trusts:

- Faster and less costly way to transfer property upon death, when compared to a will
- Avoids probate court process (time, expense), especially if property is owned in several different states
- Eliminates challenges to estate—just specifically disinherit anyone who poses a challenge to your wishes upon your death
- Keeps transfer of property private—probate can expose assets to prying eyes of the public
- Reduces amount of estate taxable to heirs

➤ Revocable, Irrevocable

As I said, reducing the amount of the taxable estate can come down to the difference between revocable and irrevocable trusts. In general, assets placed in an irrevocable trust do not count as part of the estate, while assets placed in a revocable trust do count. What's the difference? As always, let the words talk to you—if the trust is revocable, the person who set it up (grantor) can always take back (revoke) the assets. Therefore, not only are those assets still taxable to the grantor while he/she is alive, but when he/she dies, those assets do count towards the value of the estate, even if the assets were never actually "taken back." If a grantor sets up an irrevocable trust, by definition the assets cannot be revoked. This might sound like a lot of legal mumbo jumbo, but if you live in a rural area, chances are you know some farm folks who inherited farmland and found out they had to pay huge taxes on it, which generally isn't the sort of news folks like to get just after parents or grandparents pass away. I almost bought 10 acres of farmland myself from a guy I've known since grade school. He and his two siblings inherited over 1,000 acres of farmland a few years ago. Since their parents had no idea they were rich, they never moved the land into an irrevocable trust. So, when they passed on, those 1,000+ acres at about $12,000 per acre, they triggered estate taxes.

Ouch.

In order to hang onto the land, then, the three siblings started selling off 5- and 10-acre parcels to folks looking to build a house out in the country. Just to pay the estate taxes.

So, you can see how important estate planning can be. Remember that the assets placed in an irrevocable trust are no longer taxable to the grantor while he/she is alive, and when he/she dies, the assets do not count towards the value of the estate that the heirs are hoping to keep below the amount that triggers estate taxes.

Except when they do. Sorry about that, but even in an IR-revocable trust, certain property transferred within three years of death *does* count as part of the taxable estate. Basically, if the grantor maintains an interest in the property—for example, he still lives in the house he "transferred" to the trust—the value of the property would be included in the value of the estate even if the trust is irrevocable. And, if the irrevocable trust states that trust income is to be used or held for the benefit of the grantor or the grantor's spouse, the grantor will be subject to taxation while he/she is alive.

➤ Tax Liability

The irrevocable trust will either distribute income to the beneficiaries, or it won't. Either way, the interest, dividends, and capital gains generated are taxable. If the income is distributed to the beneficiaries, they include it on their own income tax forms. If the income is not distributed, it is taxable to the trust.

In a revocable trust, or even in an irrevocable trust where the grantor or grantor's spouse benefits from the income, the grantor is subject to taxation while he/she is still alive. In fact, because the IRS basically ignores the trust structure for revocable trusts, they are often called **grantor trusts,** because there is really no separation between the grantor and the trust at this point.

So, to sum up on the taxation of estates and trusts, when the estate earns income, that income is taxable to the estate. And, before the estate distributes property to the beneficiaries, the estate might—or might not—be taxed. Either way, the beneficiaries will pay capital gains taxes on stocks and bonds sold above cost basis. Some folks establish a trust to simplify the process and maybe avoid

247

the estate tax. If it's an irrevocable trust, generally, those assets don't get counted toward the estate for tax purposes.

Of course, now there is a trust to think about—the interest, dividends, and capital gains earned by this trust will either be taxable to the trust if it all remains in the trust, or taxable to the beneficiaries when distributed to them.

> ### Simple vs. Complex

If all income is to be distributed to the beneficiaries each year, that's a **simple trust**. If the trust retains some of the income to build up the principal or "corpus," that's a **complex trust**. Or, if the trust allows the trustee to sell assets and then make distributions to the beneficiaries "from corpus," that also pegs it as a complex trust. As we saw, income retained by the trust is taxable to the trust, while the income distributed to the beneficiaries is taxable to the beneficiaries.

Except when it isn't.

> ### Charitable Trusts

Many wealthy people reduce the size of their estate and also help out their favorite charitable causes by establishing **charitable trusts**. A charitable *remainder* trust is an irrevocable trust that first pays a beneficiary for a stated time frame and then donates the remainder to a designated charity. A charitable *lead* trust can be revocable or irrevocable. Some charitable lead trusts pay a portion of the income to a charity and then revert to the grantor (Grantor Lead Trust), while most pay a portion of the income to a charity for a stated time frame and then revert to the grantor's stated beneficiaries (Non-grantor Lead Trust). Either way, the charitable/501c3 organization receives a portion of the trust's income for the life of the charitable lead trust.

DISCLAIMING AN INHERITANCE

You could see a test question presenting a situation in which the wife of a recently deceased husband does not want or need the assets she is set to receive from the husband's will or trust agreement. If she wants the assets to bypass her and go to the next generation, she needs to formally disclaim the inheritance without ever touching or benefiting from the assets. This means she has to do it in writing and within 9 months of the death of the deceased individual. If she does it correctly according to federal and state law, the assets are treated as if she never touched them. However, the decision to disclaim the inheritance is irrevocable—if she loses a bunch of money on bad real estate or stock market investments in a few years, she cannot come back for a little help from the trust. Also, she does not get to designate who receives the assets—that is up to the probate court or the trust agreement.

If the test brings up the generation-skipping transfer tax, you are probably looking at one of the tougher questions that day—sorry about that. If the deceased leaves assets to his grandchildren or great-grandchildren through the will or trust, or to an unrelated person more than 37½ years younger than the deceased, there could be a tax on that transfer of assets depending on the size of the transfer. The tax rate and the exemption for the size of the transfer are the same as for the estate tax code. Unfortunately, this stuff all changes so much every year or so that mentioning precise numbers would be foolish. The exam—if it brings it up at all—will likely stick to the basic concepts. And, you can see how a wife disclaiming an inheritance could end up triggering a generation-skipping transfer tax if the assets end up going to the next generation in the family or an unrelated person more than 37½ years younger than the deceased.

AMT

If you're in a certain income bracket, you will be subject to an "Alternative Minimum Tax," or "AMT." That means that even though people say that municipal bonds pay tax-free interest, you will actually report *some* municipal bond interest on your AMT form as a "tax preference item." Generally, municipal bonds that are considered "private purpose" by the tax code subject investors to reporting income on their AMT forms. That's why many tax-exempt mutual funds also buy bonds that are not subject to AMT taxes.

The following comes IRS Publication 556 – Alternative Minimum Tax.

The tax laws give preferential treatment to certain kinds of income and allow special deductions and credits for certain kinds of expenses. The alternative minimum tax attempts to ensure that anyone who benefits from these tax advantages pays at least a minimum amount of tax. The alternative minimum tax is a separately figured tax that eliminates many deductions and credits, thus increasing tax liability for an individual who would otherwise pay less tax. The tentative minimum tax rates on ordinary income are percentages set by law. For capital gains, the capital gains rates for the regular tax are used. You may have to pay the alternative minimum tax if your taxable income for regular tax purposes plus any adjustments and preference items that apply to you are more than the exemption amount.

A test question might also bring up the fact that the owner of a limited partnership interest will need to consult the instructions to his K-1 and may have to add certain tax preference items such as "accelerated depreciation" to his AMT form. The test question might say that "straight-line depreciation" would not be a tax preference item. Try to stick some of this in your head and, when you say your prayers tonight, thank God for accountants.

PROGRESSIVE, REGRESSIVE

Progressive taxes include income, estate, and gift taxes. The bigger the income, estate, or gift, the higher the percentage rate the IRS charges. If you make a living, you pay 25% for ordinary income taxes. If you make a killing, you may pay up to 39.6%. That's progressive—as the income progresses up the scale, so does the rate of taxation.

Estates that are very large get taxed, too. So, when Bill Gates passes away, his heirs will receive a ton of money, but the IRS will take some first in the form of estate taxes. The bigger the estate, the higher the rate of taxation. Progressive.

And, if you should bump into Bill Gates on the red-eye to Seattle some night, maybe you'll impress him so much with your understanding of middleware in a non-Linux environment that he'll just *give you $100,000.* He'll have to keep track of that and pay gift tax on the excess above $14,000, which is another reason I don't think he'll be doing it, but you never know.

How much tax would he pay? It's progressive. The bigger the gift, the higher the rate.

A **regressive** tax is flat. A list of regressive taxes would include sales, gas, payroll, and excise taxes. Everybody pays the same rate there. When you check out your items at Walmart, the cashier doesn't ask you your marginal tax bracket before giving you your total, right? No, it's a flat tax. Just like gas taxes are applied equally to gallons of gas regardless of whether they're being pumped into a rusty, 1981 Monte Carlo, or a beautiful, 2013 Lexus. Equate "flat tax" with "regressive," because it isn't worth digressing into why they call it "regressive."

They just do.

TYPES OF INCOME

One type of income is the income you earn, so we go ahead and call it **earned income**. It includes salary, bonuses, tips, alimony, and any income derived from actively participating in a business. It doesn't include, for example, rental income you get from an apartment building. But it would include anything you actively worked for. Earned income is taxed as **ordinary income.**

The rental income from your rental property is called **passive income**. Yes, you meet the plumber over there on your lunch hour and lose some sleep over the rowdy new tenants, but you don't actively "work" for that rental income. You hold title to the property and you let the property work for you.

Passive income.

Direct participation programs (partnerships) give the limited partners passive income. We talked about this some. The LPs put in some money and then sit back and take a share of the income and expenses of the partnership, the business. If they have any passive losses, they can only deduct those against passive income from other partnerships or any rental properties they might own. They can't deduct passive losses against earned income or portfolio income, much as they'd like to. While mutual funds send you convenient 1099s for the dividends and capital gains, partnerships send the LPs K-1's, which are more complicated. Not too surprising, that if you want favorable tax treatment from a partnership, the IRS just might make getting that treatment a little bit complicated, right?

Portfolio income seems passive, but it's treated and labeled as, well, portfolio income. I've already discussed the rather complex tax treatment of dividends, interest and capital gains, so I'll spare you the details. Lord knows you've suffered enough at this point.

CORPORATE TAXES

Corporate profits are taxed at corporate tax rates. As we saw from the lemonade stand income statement in Chapter 1, and as we have mentioned elsewhere, bond (or any debt) interest is deducted pre-tax, while profits are taxed before any dividends are paid to shareholders. Corporate profits (net income after tax) are taxed at that corporation's tax rate.

On another note, some companies use the IRS's Subchapter M to set themselves up as a "**conduit**" to investors. REITs do this. Many mutual funds do it, too. If a mutual fund has $1,000,000 in net income, for example, they often send at least 90% of it (900K) to shareholders as a dividend or "income" distribution. That way, the mutual fund company only pays tax on the remaining $100,000. The shareholders pay tax on the money the fund sends them. The company has to send at least 90% of its net income to qualify for this tax treatment, and they can send more if they want.

When a corporation invests in the stocks of other companies, they receive dividends like any other investor. Unlike ordinary investors, though, the corporation receiving these fat dividend checks from other companies' stocks gets to exclude the first 70% from tax. Which means they only get taxed on 30% of what they receive. And, if they're really an owner of the other company because they own 20% or more of it, they can exclude 80% of the income from tax. Berkshire Hathaway purchases smaller companies outright—they typically receive preferred dividends from those acquired companies, and if the smaller entity is being taxed on the net income, why should the parent company be fully taxed, too?

Anyway, we're talking about dividends paid on stock. On the other hand, if a corporation holds the bonds of another corporation, they do NOT get to deduct any of the interest. That's because the company who paid the interest already deducted it from their taxable income, as you did when running your successful lemonade stand in Chapter 1. Municipal bond interest is tax-exempt to a corporate owner just as it is to any other owner.

PRACTICE

1. Which of the following statements is accurate?

    A. For securities received as a gift, the recipient takes the fair market value as her cost basis

    B. For inherited securities, the recipient takes the fair market value as her cost basis

    C. The fair market value of inherited securities is taxable as ordinary income to the recipient

    D. The fair market value of gifted securities is taxable as a long-term capital gain to the recipient

2. An investor in the 35% marginal tax bracket would likely find which of the following strategies the most tax-efficient?

    A. Buying corporate bonds

    B. Purchasing small-cap growth stocks for the long term

    C. Buying Treasury bonds

    D. Buying bank certificates of deposit under $250,000 in denomination

(ANSWERS)

1. **B,** step up the cost basis when securities are inherited.

2. **B,** small-cap growth stocks typically pay no dividends; if they appreciate, the capital gains do not have to be realized. Or, if the investor does sell, he enjoys the lower long-term capital gains rate.

RETIREMENT PLANS

We have already mentioned retirement plans in terms of their tax deferral. Now let's look at the details of the plans themselves. Some retirement plans are available through an employer; some are started by an individual. First, let's talk about the plans that an individual can open, as long as he has **earned income.** Remember that earned income includes salary, bonuses, tips, alimony, and any income derived from actively participating in a business. It does not include passive income such as rental income from an apartment building or portfolio income such as bond interest, dividends, or capital gains. In other words, retirement plans are for *working* people who need to save up for retirement. If somebody's sole source of income is rent checks or cash dividends, by definition, he doesn't need to save up for retirement. And, if he does, he'll just need to do it outside a retirement account.

INDIVIDUAL RETIREMENT PLANS
An **IRA** is an **Individual Retirement Account**, or an "Individual Retirement Arrangement."

> Traditional

To make a contribution to a **Traditional IRA** the individual must be younger than 70 ½ and have earned income for the year. What if the individual in the test question has an income consisting solely of dividends and bond interest? Then, he can't make an IRA contribution for that year. How much can an individual contribute if he does have earned income for the year? 100% of that earned income up to the current maximum. So, if the individual earns $1,800 waiting tables, $1,800 is her maximum IRA contribution. I guess she still lives at home or is still in college and is that rare 20-something who takes the money she gets from waiting tables and sticks it away in an account she can't touch for 40 years. Could happen—it must happen; otherwise, there wouldn't be a rule about it. Also, note that people 50 years and older can add a **catch-up contribution**. We aren't printing the maximum amounts here, as that leads to endless and needless updates. To download the current maximum contribution amounts, please click on www.irs.gov and look for IRA maximum contribution amounts.

Contributions into your IRA account are tax-deductible or made "pre-tax." That means if you contribute $6,000 to your IRA this year, that $6,000 no longer counts as taxable income for the year—if you were going to pay tax on $52,000, now it's only $46,000 of taxable income for the year. This is the opposite of how things work for the Roth IRA, which is coming right up, don't you worry.

Penalties

Over-funding an IRA results in a 6% penalty on the amount above the maximum contribution for the year and "any earnings associated with the excess contribution." If the individual in the test question realizes she has over-funded her IRA for the year, she can remove the excess by the tax filing deadline the following year, or re-characterize the excess as part of the following year's contributions. In other words, if it's March 17, 2016 when she realizes she has over-funded her IRA by $1,000 for 2015, she can remove the $1,000 to avoid a penalty or fill out a form to re-characterize it as part of her 2016 contributions. If she does nothing, she pays an annoying 6% penalty.

While you can always pull the money out of your Traditional IRA whenever you feel like it, if you take it out before age 59½, you'll pay a 10% penalty on top of the ordinary income tax that you always pay on money coming out of your IRA. Luckily, there are a few ways you can avoid the 10% penalty:

- Die
- Become permanently disabled
- Buy a first home for residential purposes (up to the current maximum amount)
- Take a series of substantially equal periodic payments under IRS Rule 72-t
- Use it for medical expenses
- Use it for higher education expenses

Note that while a parent or grandparent can withdraw money from her Traditional IRA prior to age 59 ½ without a *penalty* and help her daughter or granddaughter with education expenses, whenever money is withdrawn from the account, the withdrawal is subject to income tax.

So, an individual can't have the money until he's 59½ without paying a penalty unless he uses one of the exemptions above. That's on the front end. On the back end, he also has to start taking it out by the time he's 70½. If not, the IRS will slap a 50% "insufficient distribution penalty" on him. We're talking about "RMDs" here, or **required minimum distributions**. When somebody turns 70½, they have until April 1st of the following year to take out at least the required minimum distribution. If they don't, the IRS will help remind them by charging them a 50% penalty—50% of what they should have taken out at this point. Test questions often reach for the extreme, so we have to know the absolute latest date that an individual can take her first withdrawal from a Traditional IRA without penalty. Keep in mind that she *can* wait until April 1st of the year *following* her 70½th birthday, but if she does that, she has to take *two* distributions that year, which can push her into a higher tax bracket and make more of her social security benefits taxable. So, it's easier to take the first distribution in the year the individual turns 70½. Also note that, unlike the Roth IRA, no contributions can be made into the Traditional IRA after age 70½.

> Roth

The **Roth IRA** is funded with after-tax or non-deductible contributions into the account. That means you do not deduct the contributions made to the account when you file your income taxes for the year. However, the money comes out tax-free in retirement as long as the individual is 59½ years old <u>and</u> has had the account for at least 5 years. For the Roth IRA there is no requirement to start taking the money out at 70½. Since the IRS isn't going to tax that money, they couldn't care less when it starts coming out. In fact, <u>you can keep putting money in, as long as you have earned income</u>. So, a 72-year-old in a test question can refrain from taking Roth IRA withdrawals and can even keep on making contributions into the account if he/she has earned income. Neither option would be available, on the other hand, for her Traditional IRA account.

If the individual earns too much money, he cannot contribute to a Roth IRA. Period. So, get those Roth IRA accounts started while you're young and before you strike it rich, people. The money you contribute in your 20s and 30s can compound for decades, even if the IRS cuts off new contributions by age 40 based on your massive income.

If an individual has both a Traditional and a Roth IRA, the contribution limit would be the total allocated among the two accounts. Also, there is a funky thing about the Roth IRA that allows the individual to remove her "cost basis," or the amount she has contributed, after five years without a hassle. In other words, if you have contributed $25,000 into your Roth IRA and seven years later the account is worth $40,000, you could take the $25,000 out without a penalty and keep the remainder of $15,000 in the account. You could not put that $25,000 back in, however, and would not earn the tax-deferred and tax-free returns going forward.

But, as always, it's your money.

Converting a Traditional to a Roth IRA

Some individuals start out with a Traditional IRA and then decide to convert it to a Roth IRA. This requires the individual to pay tax on the entire amount going into the new Roth IRA, since Roth IRAs are funded with after-tax dollars. Even if the individual makes too much money to make a contribution to his Roth IRA, he can still convert a Traditional IRA to a Roth IRA.

Income Limits

In the "real world" there are income limits for investors in Roth IRAs, but I would not expect the exam to hit you with those. If it does, it's even more evil than I give it credit for. Chances are, someone in your office can tell you the point at which people are phased out of Roth eligibility. Or, if you ask three people, you can get three different sets of numbers. The IRS could tell you at www.irs.gov if you don't mind poking around a bit. Do remember, though, that there are really no income limits for the Traditional IRA, so in a test question referring to one of those, don't worry about how much money somebody makes or whether she's covered by an employer plan. All that would change is the amount she can deduct from her taxable income for her Traditional IRA. She can still have and fund a Traditional IRA.

See, nothing is simple. I'd like to say that all contributions to a Traditional IRA are made pre-tax, but if the individual is covered by an employer plan and makes what the IRS deems a high salary, she might only get to deduct some of her contribution, or even none of it.

So what? Either way, she can make her maximum contribution. And if she's pulling down seven figures, the loss of a $5,000 deduction probably won't keep her up nights. She'd just have to keep track of how much went in after-tax so she doesn't get taxed twice on that money when it comes out with everything else. In summary, it's a hassle, but if she has earned income, she can contribute to her Traditional IRA. She might not deduct 100% or even any percent of it, but it can still go in there and grow tax-deferred. Some of her distributions will represent a tax-free return of her after-tax cost basis and the rest will be fully taxable, and it will be kind of a pain to keep track of it, but it can happen.

Whether you deduct the contributions or not, the real beauty of these plans is that the earnings grow tax-deferred. As we've said before and intend to say again, a regular old investment account forces an individual in the 35% tax bracket to pay 35% taxes on bond interest. However, if the security is owned inside an IRA, there are no taxes to pay currently. That bond interest can buy more bonds that pay more interest that can be used to buy more bonds, and so on. Compounded returns—that's what tax deferral is all about. There is more money in the account working for the investor when we put off the taxation for a few decades. When she takes withdrawals later on, she'll pay taxes on the money withdrawn at her ordinary income rate, which should be lower when she retires.

> Investment Restrictions

I'm not sure why they do it, but some people like to use their Traditional IRA to invest in collectible items such as artwork, Persian rugs, antiques, coins, gems, stamps, etc. Money you take out of your IRA to buy this stuff is considered to be distributed to you, which means you'd have to pay ordinary income rates, plus a 10% penalty if you're not 59½.

US-minted gold or silver bullion coins are treated differently, should the exam actually hit that hard the day you take it. Municipal bonds typically make poor investments for a Traditional IRA. Municipal bonds pay tax-exempt interest, which is why their coupon payments are so low. *All* money coming out of the Traditional IRA is taxed, so the municipal bond's tax-advantage is destroyed and all the individual is left with is a lower coupon payment and a registered rep ducking his phone calls.

Check this out, though—not only can you write covered calls, these days, you can even buy calls and puts in your IRA. I'm not making that up, I swear. In fact, I've put it to the test in my own IRA.

Finally, don't let the test trick you into thinking you can't put REITs into your IRA. There is absolutely no reason why you couldn't—they're shares of stock, end of story. Tell the test that only cash and securities belong in an IRA. Not collectible items or commodities or tangible items of value such as rare oil paintings.

> Rollovers and Transfers

If you want to move your IRA from one custodian to another, your best bet is to do a **direct transfer**. Just have the custodian cut a check to the new custodian, nice and simple. You can do as many of these direct transfers as you want. If, however, you do a **rollover**, things get tricky. First, you can only do one per year, and, second, it must be completed within 60 days. Plus, the custodian withholds a % of the money, and that will become a huge hassle, so, if at all possible, do the transfer. In a rollover, the custodian cuts a reduced check in your name. You cash it and then send the money to the new custodian, but you have to make up the % that was withheld. Otherwise, you've got the 10% penalty thing plus ordinary income tax, plus much heartburn and lost sleep, etc. Imagine rolling over a $100,000 IRA, receiving a check for only $80,000, and then having to come up with an additional $20,000 within 60 days to avoid getting penalized and taxed.

No, thanks. Since the difference between a transfer and a rollover is so painful to the individual, this seems like fertile test question ground to me.

RETIREMENT PLANS OFFERED THROUGH AN EMPLOYER

> Defined Contribution Plans

Most plans offered by an employer these days are **defined contribution plans**. As their name implies, a defined contribution plan only defines the contributions the employer and/or you can make into the plan. The employer is not defining or promising any particular benefit at retirement. We'll talk about **defined benefit pension plans** in a bit, but let's focus first on the larger and more familiar category of defined *contribution* plans.

Maybe you've had a job where the human resources department gave you some paperwork to fill out concerning the **401(k) plan** sponsored by the employer as an employee benefit. Maybe you did or didn't see the big deal, but with any luck you did manage to fill it out, choose a few mutual funds, and tell the HR department to deduct X amount from your paycheck to go into the 401(k) account. This way, part of your salary goes straight into a retirement fund and is not taxable currently, just like the money that goes into a Traditional IRA. Pretty attractive, especially if the employer matches what you put in. Employers generally match all or part of an employee's contributions up to a certain level, as stipulated in their plan literature. But, they are not required to make matching contributions. Why might you still choose to participate in a 401(k) even if your company was not matching your contributions? Maybe you like the higher maximum contribution limit vs. the IRA or Roth IRA.

The advantage to a business owner setting up a 401(k) plan is that a **vesting schedule** can be laid out over several years, meaning that the employer's contributions don't actually belong to the employee until he/she is fully vested. However, 401(k) plans come with complicated **top-heavy** rules, which means the plan cannot provide benefits to just the key, highly compensated employees. A plan in which 60% of the benefits go to key employees is a plan that shows signs of being "top-heavy," and it will have to adjust things or deal with tax problems.

For-profit companies offer 401(k) plans to their employees. Non-profit organizations such as schools and hospitals offer **403(b) plans** to their employees. As with a 401(k) plan, the employee indicates how much of her paycheck should go into the 403(b) account, which simultaneously gives her a tax break now and helps her save up for retirement later. As with a 401(k) plan, the contributions go in pre-tax but come out fully taxable when the participant finally flips the switch and starts taking distributions out of the account. Basically, whenever the participant gets to deduct the contributions into the plan, the distributions from the plan later on will be taxed at ordinary income rates. Never capital gains rates. Remember that, along with everything else I'm telling you. While a 401(k) plan might offer participants the ability to purchase stocks and bonds a la carte, a 403(b) plan only offers annuities and mutual funds as investment vehicles. The 403(b) plans can also be referred to as **Tax-Sheltered Annuities** or **TSAs**, to make sure they have at least three names.

Some states and cities have begun to shift the burden of funding retirement benefits to their employees. These so-called **457 plans** are for state and local government employees, e.g., police and fire workers. Contributions are tax-deductible, and the plans use the same maximum contribution limits used by 401(k) and 403(b) plans.

Profit-sharing plans are also defined contribution plans, but the contributions can be very flexible. It's all based on corporate profits, so in a year of no profits, guess what? No sharing. But, if the company does make a contribution, it must be made for all eligible employees based on a predetermined formula. For example, maybe all workers receive up to 10% of their salaries when the company has a banner year. The profit-sharing plan uses much higher maximum annual contributions than the 401(k), 403(b) or Section 457 plans. Of course, that would only matter if you happened to work for a really profitable and really generous employer, but still.

A **money purchase plan** is not flexible the way a profit sharing plan is. The money purchase plan <u>requires</u> the employer to make a mandatory contribution to each employee's account, based on his/her salary, whether the company feels like it or not. The exam might say something like "in a money purchase plan, contributions are mandatory on the part of the employer and discretionary on the part of the employee." An actual human being might just say that in a money purchase plan, the employer has to contribute, while the employee doesn't have to.

Keogh plans are for individuals with self-employment income or for those working for a sole proprietorship with a Keogh plan in place. They're not for S-corps, C-corps, LLCs, etc.—only sole proprietors. If the individual in the test question has side income or is self-employed, he or she can have a Keogh. They can contribute a certain percentage of their self-employment income into the Keogh.

How much? A lot. As with the SEP-IRA, the business owner can put 20% of her compensation into a Keogh, and she can put in 25% of her employees' compensation. Some readers find it shocking that there may be employees at a "sole" proprietorship. But, trust me, there can be. A "sole proprietorship" is just a business with one owner, a guy doing business as himself. The number of employees he has? Anybody's guess. Also, to avoid confusion, remember we said that Keogh plans are for sole proprietorships only; we did not say that sole proprietorships can only have a Keogh plan. A SEP-IRA or SIMPLE IRA would also be available to a sole proprietor, for example.

A small business can establish a **SEP-IRA**, which stands for "Simplified Employee Pension" IRA. This allows the business owner to make pre-tax contributions for herself and any eligible employees. Twenty-five percent of wages can be contributed to an employee's SEP, up to the current maximum. SEP contributions are not mandatory on the part of the business owner. It's just that if the business makes any contributions, they have to be made to all eligible employees as stipulated in the plan agreement. Notice how the contributions are made by the business, not the employees. So, if you're self-employed, you can contribute to your own SEP-IRA, but if you're an employee at a company with a SEP-IRA, it's the company who will be making the contributions on your behalf, through the payroll as with a 401(k) plan. To establish a SEP, the employer uses a model agreement put out by the IRS (download it from www.irs.gov) that they and the employees sign. It does not have to be filed with the IRS, which does not issue an opinion or approval.

Keep in mind that even though a large contribution can be made to a SEP-IRA, that amount has to represent 25% of wages. In other words, we often focus on the maximum amounts that can be contributed, but to make contributions at all the small business owner has to be making a profit, and when contributing for employees, the contributions are 25% of wages. That means that the only way to put a lot of money into a SEP-IRA is to earn a lot of money—since 25% of a $33,000 salary is not going to make for a large contribution. A small business owner might not want to pay herself a huge salary—subject to self-employment taxes—just so she can put more money into her SEP-IRA. And she may be even less interested in paying her employees big salaries so she can max out her own contributions. In that case, maybe the small business owner decides to set up a **SIMPLE IRA** instead, which would actually allow for larger contributions at lower income levels. The SIMPLE IRA is for businesses with no more than 100 employees who have no other retirement plans in place. The SIMPLE IRA may allow participants to put more money away than the SEP. Of course, that depends on how much they earn. If they earn a lot, a SEP might be better. But if the participant made only, say, $15,000 annually, but wanted to sock a bunch of cash away for retirement, the SIMPLE would allow her to put in more. So, SEP-IRAs allow high earners to save more than they could save in a SIMPLE IRA, while SIMPLE IRAs allow lower-earning employees to save more than they would be able to put away in a SEP. Both provide for pre-tax contributions, meaning all the money will be taxable when it's distributed during the golden years.

In a SIMPLE plan, business owners must either match the employee's plan contributions up to 3% of compensation, or contribute 2% of the employee's compensation whether he contributes or not. There is also a funky thing about SIMPLE IRAs in the first two years. During that time, the participant can only roll the money into another SIMPLE IRA to avoid tax. During this phase, if she tried to roll it into a Traditional IRA, she'd get dinged with a 25% penalty (not 10%), plus ordinary income tax on all of it, plus it could be treated as an excess IRA contribution (6% penalty), so, all in all, not a real good idea.

Finally, if you're the business owner, remember that both of these plans are "IRAs." That means that as soon as you make the contribution into the employees' accounts, the money is theirs. They are "immediately vested," in other words. In a 401(k), the worker isn't entitled to all of your contributions until she is fully vested. That tends to motivate people to show up on time, be a little nicer, and maybe not send out so many resumes to your competitors. With the SIMPLE or the SEP, the contribution belongs to them immediately. So, while the plans are easy to set up, they also don't give you as much sway over your employees.

Many companies reward key employees by offering them **employee stock options**. These options do not trade among investors but are essentially free call options that allow employees to buy the company's stock at a set strike/exercise price. To keep the employee around a while, the company usually awards the options to buy the stock on a vesting schedule by which the employee gradually receives options as long as he shows up and does a really good job. An **ESOP** or **employee stock ownership plan** is pretty much what it sounds like. Through these plans the company allows all workers to purchase company stock at a discount and through a payroll deduction. The stock and the dividends/cap gains generated on it grow tax-deferred, like a 401(k) plan.

➢ Defined Benefit Plans

Defined benefit pension plans are the opposite of defined contribution plans. For a defined contribution plan, the employer puts in some money and then wishes you the best of luck with that whole retirement thing. For a defined <u>benefit</u> plan, the employer has to get sufficient returns on their investments to pay a defined benefit to retirees and their survivors. Maybe that defined benefit is 70% of your average salary figured over your last three years of service, paid out every year to you in retirement, plus maybe a benefit to your spouse or children if you die within a certain time frame. Sounds like a pretty generous and expensive benefit to be promising, doesn't it? That explains why most plans these days are defined contribution plans. So, plans either define how much they'll put in on your behalf (contribution), or how much you'll receive (benefit) when you retire. If they define the benefit, they bear the investment risk. If they only define the contribution, you bear the investment risk.

A defined benefit pension plan would be established as a trust and would not pay tax on the income it generates. In fact, the company gets to deduct the contributions it makes into the pension fund from taxable income. Not that they're, like, real willing to make those contributions. Corporations generally like to pay huge compensation to their officers and directors, and like to make big, fat profits, so the whole idea of putting some money aside for a rainy day—when, technically, the rain is only going to fall on *other people*, people they don't necessarily know or like—well, you can imagine that many defined benefit corporate pension plans are just a tad under-funded.

SPECIAL TYPES OF ACCOUNTS: SAVING FOR EDUCATION

Even though we're not talking about retirement any more, the educational savings plans are usually lumped in with retirement plans, since they offer tax deferral to help someone achieve a long-term goal. Another similarity is that, as with retirement planning, age is a key factor. The portfolio used for a one-year-old child will be more aggressive than the one used for a 16-year-old. As always, the closer you get to your target date, the more you shift your money into bonds and away from stocks.

529 SAVINGS PLAN

The **529 savings plan** allows investors to save/invest for education. Usually it would be a family member socking money away for a child's education, but, actually, the beneficiary does not have to be a child, or even a blood relative of the donor. In fact, an individual can even set up a 529 plan for him or herself. The person who opens the account is the owner; the beneficiary is the person who will use the money for education. For 529 savings plans, the owner controls the assets at all times.

Contributions are made after-tax (non-deductible), but the withdrawals used for qualified education expenses are tax-free at the federal level. Notice how I said "federal level." The plans are state-specific, so some states may tax the withdrawals. That means that if Grandma lives in New Jersey and buys a Wisconsin plan, New Jersey could end up taxing the money that the grandkids use for college. Then again, New Jersey might allow Grandma to deduct her contributions for purposes of state income taxes. So you don't want to buy into a 529 savings plan without first checking how it will be taxed by the state. And, even with the federal taxation, the withdrawals for education have to be qualified withdrawals that cover tuition, room & board, books, etc. The expenses need to be directly related to education; otherwise, you'll get hit on them just like you do for an early IRA distribution (10% penalty plus ordinary income tax). If the beneficiary decides he doesn't need the money, the account can name a second beneficiary without tax problems, as long as the second beneficiary is related to the first. And there's one area that can easily lead to confusion. Remember that when setting up a 529 plan it makes no difference whether the account owner is related to the beneficiary— I mean, the kid might just be the world's luckiest and most diligent paperboy. It's just that if you start a 529 plan for your paperboy and then discover that the kid has no intention of going to college or even technical school, then if you want to avoid tax implications, you can only change the beneficiary to a blood relative of the paperboy. If you want to change beneficiaries to someone not related to the paperboy, you'll have to deal with the 10% penalty and ordinary income tax. Just to keep things nice and simple.

Don't forget that when Grandma, for example, is putting money into a 529 savings plan on behalf of her granddaughter, she is basically making a gift. Gifts over a certain amount are taxable to the one making the gift. With a 529 savings plan, Grandma can contribute up to the gift tax exclusion without incurring gift taxes, and can even do a lump-sum contribution for the first five years without incurring gift tax hassles. In other words, if the annual gift tax exclusion is $14,000, she can put in $70,000 for the next five years. If she and Grandpa are married-filing-separately, they could put in twice that amount, or $140,000, without any gift tax hassles. Note that if somebody uses the five-year-up-front method, they can't make any more gifts to the beneficiary for the next five years without dealing with gift taxes.

The owner of the plan maintains control over the assets, deciding 529 when withdrawals will be made. The money can be withdrawn to cover higher education expenses, such as tuition, books, and room and board. Bear in mind that it doesn't have to be "college," necessarily—just any school higher than high school, basically. So if the exam asks if you can use the assets to go to heating & air-conditioning school, tell it that as long as the school is an accredited post-secondary institution eligible to participate in a student aid program, the answer is yes.

PREPAID TUITION

If you're pretty sure that Junior won't mind going to college in-state, you might want to lock him in as a future Boilermaker, Hoosier, or Sycamore through a plan whereby you pay for his tuition credits now for any public school in the fine state of Indiana. I didn't say you were locking him into being *accepted* at IU or Purdue, but he would get to go to a state school with a certain number of credits already paid for. Parents worried about the ever-rising cost of tuition, then, can pay today's prices and redeem the credits more than a decade into the future.

These tuition credits cover tuition and fees only. If the child gets a scholarship or doesn't need the money because of something tragic like death or disability, a refund is typically provided plus a modest rate of interest. The exam could refer to prepaid tuition plans as "defined benefit plans." You pay for the tuition credits now, and then you hope the state can afford to provide the benefit of education when your child needs it.

COVERDELL EDUCATION SAVINGS ACCOUNT

A **Coverdell Education Savings Account** (CESA) also allows for after-tax contributions (non-deductible), but the current maximum is only a few thousand dollars per year per child. While the 529 Plan is for higher education only, the Coverdell plan can be used for elementary, secondary, and higher education expenses. The distributions will be tax-free at the federal level if used according to the plan guidelines. As with the 529 plan, the Coverdell ESA account can be used for education expenses, including tuition, books, and room and board. In a Coverdell contributions must stop on the beneficiary's 18th birthday, and the assets must be used for education or distributed to him by age 30. Also, there are income limits on the donors of a CESA, similar to the limits placed on people trying to fund their Roth IRAs.

So, should you use a 529 plan or a CESA? Generally, it would come down to the amount of money you want to contribute. If you're going to contribute only a few thousand dollars, you might as well use the CESA. If you want to put large amounts of money away, you'll pretty much have to use the 529 plan. Either way, you'll get tax deferral and tax-free withdrawals at the federal level, assuming you do everything according to plan.

CALCULATING EDUCATIONAL FUNDING NEEDS

When a financial planner estimates the educational funding needs for a client, she uses the following five inputs:

- Current tuition cost per year
- Education inflation rate
- Number of years of college attendance
- Number of years before college begins
- Expected investment return

Because tuition has historically risen even faster than the general rate of inflation, the calculation uses a specific rate for education costs, above the rate of the CPI.

ERISA ISSUES

This federal securities act is enforced by the Department of Labor. It's a "securities law" in the sense that most retirement plans offered in the workplace do offer investments in securities to the participants. ERISA is shorthand for the federal government's Employee Retirement Income Security Act. ERISA was passed in 1974 and was designed to protect employees (and their beneficiaries) who depend on pension funds for their retirement security. A defined benefit pension plan promises to pay a predetermined amount of benefits to employees when they retire. The employer sets it up and takes on the awesome responsibility of figuring out how to deduct X amount of company dollars now and put them into the stock and bond markets wisely enough to pay out Y amount of pension fund dollars to retirees. Generally, the pension fund hires investment advisers to manage the fund's assets. Large pension funds typically dole out portions of the plan's assets to different money management/investment advisory firms. The investment committee hires various investment advisers to manage portions of the pension fund assets, and frequently even hires advisers to help them pick the other advisers.

The 401(k), defined benefit pension, profit sharing, and Keogh plan are all plans covered by ERISA. The SIMPLE and SEP-IRA, on the other hand, are informal plans between employer and employee. If you're a business owner, you may know that starting a 401(k) requires IRS approval, while starting a SIMPLE IRA requires you to print and fill out a form for your own records. Remember that ERISA does not require companies to have retirement plans. Rather, it establishes rules for companies who happen to have them.

FIDUCIARIES

A defined benefit pension plan is managed for the benefit of retirees. As the US Department of Labor explains:

Each pension plan has at least one fiduciary. The fiduciaries of a plan usually include:

- Trustee
- Investment advisers
- All individuals exercising discretion
- All members of the plan's administrative committee
- Those who select committee officials

The key to determining whether someone is a fiduciary is whether they are exercising discretion or control over the plan. Attorneys, accountants, and actuaries are generally not fiduciaries when acting in their professional roles.

The investment manager of a pension fund is using discretion/control to invest the plan assets; therefore, the investment manager is a "fiduciary" with huge obligations to the participants and beneficiaries of the plan. As ERISA makes clear:

- a fiduciary shall discharge his duties with respect to a plan solely in the interest of the participants and beneficiaries
- and for the exclusive purpose of: (i) providing benefits to participants and their beneficiaries; and (ii) defraying reasonable expenses of administering the plan
- with the care, skill, prudence, and diligence under the circumstances then prevailing that a prudent man acting in a like capacity and familiar with such matters would use in the conduct of an enterprise of a like character and with like aims
- by diversifying the investments of the plan so as to minimize the risk of large losses, unless under the circumstances it is clearly prudent not to do so; and
- in accordance with the documents and instruments governing the plan insofar as such documents and instruments are consistent with the provisions of this subchapter and subchapter III of this chapter.

The "documents and instruments governing the plan" might be referred to on the exam as an investment policy statement. If the policy statement says that no more than 40% of the plan assets are to be invested in equities, guess what? Don't put more than 40% into equities. Even if you ended up having a good year because of your renegade stock picks, you'd still be in trouble. The only time to override the policy statement is if it clearly violates ERISA. Also notice how diversification is presumed to be part of a prudent investment policy, "unless under the circumstances it is clearly prudent not to do so." This is a direct link to the Uniform Prudent Investor Act, which mentions ERISA many times throughout the text. In fact, all of those bullet points overlap with the Uniform Prudent Investor Act. It's just that the UPIA is talking more to the administrators of private trusts, while ERISA is concerned with the fiduciaries running pension trusts. Either way, if you're an investment adviser managing assets on behalf of either perpetual graduate students or company retirees, you need to use skill, prudence, and absolute honesty-above-reproach. You need to keep the costs of administering the plan reasonable. Why? Well, among other reasons, as the Department of Labor explains on a very helpful website, "Fiduciaries who do not follow the basic standards of conduct may be personally liable to restore any losses to the plan, or to restore any profits made through improper use of the plan's assets." The website goes on to suggest, "However, fiduciaries can limit their liability in certain situations. One way fiduciaries can demonstrate that they have carried out their responsibilities properly is by documenting the processes used to carry out their responsibilities." In other words, every time you make a decision, keep good notes and make a backup. This stock was purchased for this reason, these bonds were sold for that reason, we used this broker-dealer to execute the sale for these reasons, etc.

SAFE HARBOR, 404(C)
This heavy fiduciary duty implies that the plan is managing the assets on behalf of employees/participants/beneficiaries. Basically, we're talking about defined benefit plans in that case. If we're talking about a 401(k) or other defined contribution plan that lets the employee choose investments, now it's the employee's problem what happens in the big, scary stock and bond markets.

As an employer, you would probably rather match your employees' contributions into a plan in which they choose all their own investment options. That way, whatever happens in the market is their problem.

Well, in order to relieve yourself of the fiduciary duty over investment losses, your plan must make sure that participants actually have control, as defined by ERISA and the rules written under the Act. First, the plan needs to make a clear written statement to participants that it "intends to constitute a plan described in section 404(c) of ERISA, and that the fiduciaries of the plan may be relieved of liability for any losses which are the direct and necessary result of investment instructions given by the participant or beneficiary." Also, the plan must:

- Offer a selection of at least three investment choices with materially different risk and return characteristics
- Provide the ability to change investment allocations at least quarterly
- Provide sufficient education and information about the plan to allow participants to make informed investment decisions

In order to sail into these safe waters, the plan needs to provide the three bullet points above. Most plans provide at least three different investment choices, and participants can almost always change allocations among, say, the growth, income, and long-term bond funds quarterly, if not every single day. It's the third bullet point that is probably the hardest to satisfy. To make sure they have provided sufficient education in order to shield themselves from liability for the investment losses their employees may end up with, the company needs to make sure they have provided detailed information on the fees and expenses charged on investments, the risk/reward nature of all the investment options, the most recent prospectus for each investment option, the name of the investment manager/adviser for the investment options, and other important information.

Unfortunately, if the company gives too much advice of a personally targeted nature, they might cross into the territory of providing investment advice—yikes! That's the fiduciary relationship they're trying to avoid. So, many companies hire third-party investment advisers or other financial service providers to educate employees sufficiently to allow them to make informed investment decisions. Awkwardly, the act of hiring an investment adviser or a provider of investment education is itself a fiduciary action, so the folks they choose had better know what the heck they're doing. Otherwise, the company could be liable for the losses that result from incompetent or dishonest advice. Also note that advisers themselves are still fiduciaries when giving advice or managing assets for employees— when we're talking about relieving oneself of fiduciary duties, we're only talking about the employer, and even there we're only talking about relieving themselves of responsibility for investment losses that result from the participant's investment decisions. But, if the company provides a reputable investment adviser to participants, it is relieved of the fiduciary duty in terms of how well the investments pan out. The employer still has fiduciary duties connected to the 401(k) plan. For example, the employer has to make sure that when the employees make an investment into the plan, that money is deposited promptly. Sure, it would be more fun to let it all sit in the corporate money market account a few extra weeks earning interest, but that would not satisfy the fiduciary duty. Is it good for the company or for the participant? As a fiduciary, try to think about the participants first, even the ones you don't like.

Again, the employer has other fiduciary obligations to the people participating in the plan. It's just that the employer would prefer to pass the investment risk off to the employees. And since so many employers have already passed off the investment decisions and risks to employees, the industry you're in or are entering is looking like it's on a growth path for about 20–30 years. How do I know the employees might need your services some day? Research has shown that whatever the investment options are, employees will simply divide their money evenly among that number of funds. For example, if the company offers a stock fund and a balanced fund, most employees will choose to put half in each, thinking they have now "diversified." In fact, since the balanced fund usually holds about 60% stock, the employee is not nearly as "balanced" as she thinks and actually has a huge percentage of her retirement money in the stock market. Also, if there are 10 different stock funds, most employees put 10% in each one, regardless of how redundant or risky some of them are.

Anyway, you get the picture. You're in the right industry at the right time. The number of people aged 65 and over is expected to double to approximately 72 million over the next 25 years, and more and more of them will be responsible for their own retirement savings, which means they desperately need your help. All you have to do is pass your exams and stay on the right side of industry regulations. If you can do that, your own retirement should be quite solid, indeed.

COMPANY STOCK

If the company allows participants to invest in company stock, it should make sure that the following bulleted list is being followed:

- The company stock is publicly traded
- The company stock is traded with enough frequency and volume so participants' instructions to buy or sell can be executed promptly
- Participants are provided information given to shareholders of company stock generally
- Voting, tendering, and similar rights are passed through to participants
- The plan designates a fiduciary to ensure information regarding the purchase, sale, and holding of company stock, and the exercise of voting, tendering, and similar rights is maintained with procedures to keep it confidential
- An independent fiduciary is appointed to address any situations where the fiduciary responsible for confidentiality determines there is a potential for undue influence on a participant's decision to vote or tender shares

By the way, I copied that handy bulleted list from a handy checklist provided by Putnam at https://content.putnam.com/plan_sponsor/pdf/ERISA_section.pdf. Of course, URLs go bad on the Internet fairly often, so don't think the book is outdated if you can't find the document at that link. That link could be gone before I finish this paragraph. If so, do a Google search on "ERISA 404c," pour yourself a cold beverage, and have yourself as much fun as I'm having right now on a Friday night reading arcane passages of federal legislation.

A plan may not "acquire any employer security or real property, if immediately after such acquisition the aggregate fair market value of employer securities and employer real property held by the plan exceeds 10 percent of the fair market value of the assets of the plan." In other words, we don't want the pension fund for XYZ Corporation to invest more than 10% of the pension fund's assets into XYZ securities. It would be bad enough if XYZ goes down the tubes; no need to drag the pension fund down with it, right? We also don't want the plan to devote an inordinate amount of assets toward buying property that is then leased to the employing corporation. Again, if the plan put 90% of its assets into buying property that the suddenly deadbeat employer can't afford to make payment on, we'd have ourselves a real mess.

TRADING SECURITIES

On the primary market underwriters help corporations and governments raise capital by selling securities to investors. The investors would never buy those securities if they didn't have a **secondary market** where they could later turn the securities back into cash. An important testable point is that securities are issued on the primary market, where the issuer takes money from the investor. Securities are traded on the secondary market among investors—with no money going to the issuer. Broker-dealers not only perform underwriting/investment banking activities on the primary market, but also they execute trades for (and sometimes *with*) their customers on the secondary market. The broker-dealers trade the securities through various exchanges or electronic systems.

FIRST MARKET – NYSE AND REGIONAL EXCHANGES

Within the secondary market, there are four separate components. Let's start with the **first market**, the New York Stock Exchange. The exam will likely ask you to associate this with the phrase "**auction market**" or "**double auction market**." There are also regional exchanges in Chicago, Philadelphia, Boston, and San Francisco that are based on the NYSE. They tend to focus on regional stocks, but they still fill orders for NYSE-listed securities, such as GE, IBM, or KKD.

Big member firms have a **commission house broker** ready to fill orders on/through the exchange. He works for a <u>brokerage</u> <u>house</u> and fills their orders for a <u>commission</u>. Go figure. The more orders he can fill, the more money he can make. Firms that don't have a commission house broker on the floor often have orders executed by an individual known as a **two-dollar broker**. As with all brokers, a two-dollar broker earns a commission on transactions executed rather than taking a position in securities and dealing them. Then, there are **competitive floor traders** who try to buy low and sell high as much as possible through the trading session.

The NYSE now uses both a manual auction and an electronic trading model. That means that even though most trading throughout the day is done electronically, the exchange also uses manual auctions at the opening, at the closing, and during times of extreme volatility. The firms in charge of running those manual auctions are known as **Designated Market Makers** or **DMMs**. As the helpful video on the NYSE website explains, DMMs are kind of like commercial airline pilots. They have to be there for the take-off and the landing, and they have to step in whenever there is turbulence. During the rest of the flight, they participate, but not in such a dominant role.

Like other market participants, DMMs also trade electronically throughout the day using trading algorithms—computerized mathematical formulas designed to determine buying and selling opportunities. Replacing the old "specialist" model, Designated Market Makers are charged with the responsibility to maintain a fair and orderly market. Their job is to provide liquidity, especially during times of market volatility. In other words, to prevent panic, they step in ready to buy or sell securities to keep the flow of trading moving. They also have to quote at the National Best Bid or Offer (NBBO) a required percentage of the time. The NBBO is what it sounds like—the best prices for the particular security nationwide.

One of the main complaints over the former specialist system was that the specialist firms had a "book" of all stop and limit orders, allowing them to see what all the big players were willing to do and at which prices—kind of like a poker dealer who also gets to sit in and play the hand. That has been eliminated with the Designated Market Maker system. DMMs do not receive this "advanced look," meaning the cards are no longer marked in this game. We will explore stop and limit orders in great detail up ahead. For now, just know that a limit order to buy or sell names the number of shares and the price at which the party is willing to buy or sell. Rather than buying 1,000 shares of MSFT right now, some investors put in orders to buy 1,000 shares of MSFT when and only if they drop to a certain price.

Supplemental Liquidity Providers play a unique role in the trading of securities on the secondary market. Supplemental Liquidity Providers are market participants using sophisticated computerized trading strategies to create high volume on exchanges in order to add liquidity to the markets. As an incentive to provide liquidity, the exchange pays the Supplemental Liquidity Provider (SLP) a fee/rebate.

> Consolidated Tape

As we mentioned, if I place an electronic order to buy 1,000 shares of, say, GE, my order could be filled in New York, Philadelphia, Boston, San Francisco, or Chicago. In fact, that just happened the other day. As I was purchasing shares in several listed securities through my online broker, I noticed that some stocks were filled in Boston, most in New York, and one in Chicago. That's because they're all part of the "first market."

When an NYSE-listed security is sold, it doesn't matter whether it's sold in New York, Chicago, San Francisco, or Boston—the prices are all *consolidated* on the consolidated tape. That means that the seller has to report the price he just sold a certain number of shares within 30 seconds, whether it was sold in Philly, Boston, etc. If you've ever seen the data streaming endlessly across the bottom of the TV monitor, you've seen the prices being reported to the "tape." Yes, all that "10s GE 35.55" stuff actually means something. It means that somebody sold (and bought) 1,000 shares of GE for $35.55 per share. The number of round lots comes first, then the stock symbol, and then the price at which the transaction took place. Let's take a look at some more pretend stock trades as reported to the consolidated tape:

> *GE36.55...10s.IBM95.04... 99s.C.75.15...13,000s. GE.36.70*

The first thing we see is the stock symbol GE. If there is no number before the symbol, we know that one round lot (100 shares) of GE just traded for $36.55 per share. In the next case "10s" means 10 round lots, or 1,000 shares. So, 1,000 shares of IBM just traded at $95.04 per share. Next, we see that 99 round lots, or 9,900 shares of "C" (for Citigroup) just traded at $75.15 per share. But, when the number of shares gets up to 10,000 or more, they stop talking in round lots and just list the actual number of shares. In other words a trade for 10,000 shares would not be indicated as "100s." Rather, it would be "10,000s" just to keep things nice and simple. Therefore, we read the tape to indicate that 13,000 shares of GE just traded for $36.70 per share.

Also note that for stocks trading at $175 a share or higher, a round lot is now just one share. For these stocks, a transaction for less than 100 shares will no longer be reported as odd-lot transactions.

As usual, things get more complicated. What if you saw the following on your exam and were asked to interpret the report?

> *MCD12s35 .35*

That means 1200 shares of McDonald's traded at $35, followed by a trade for 100 shares at $35. Remember, if there's no number before the price, this means one round lot or 100 shares traded at that price. You also might be fortunate enough to be asked what the following means:

That means 100 shares of McDonald's traded at $35, followed by another round lot that traded at $35.15. Just to keep things nice and simple. In other words, there is a world of difference between "35.15" and "35 .15." In the first case, 100 shares sold at $35.15. In the second case, 100 shares sold at $35, followed by 100 shares at $35.15.

No wonder these traders are so uptight, huh?

For preferred stock, a round lot is just 10 shares, and they indicate that the only way possible, with an "s/s." Therefore, what does the following report mean?

ABC pr 7s/s.85.05

It means that 70 shares of ABC preferred traded for $85.05 per share.

And, just in case the exam is in an especially foul mood when you sit for it, also memorize the following abbreviations used on the consolidated tape:

- Halt: sometimes trading in a stock is halted, usually when big news is about to come out on it
- OPD: the first trade that happens after a delayed opening or a trading halt
- Pr: preferred stock (also look for the s/s thingie)
- R/T: somebody's trading rights
- W/S: somebody's trading warrants

> Trading Curbs, Halts

Sometimes trading gets a little chaotic, so the NYSE steps in to straighten things out. Many people trade through computer programs. If the stock goes to this price, sell 10,000 shares; if the stock goes to this price, buy 5,000 shares, etc. That's a lot of activity set on "auto-pilot," so if the market gets a little too volatile, the NYSE dictates that trading curbs be turned on. According to NYSE Rule 80A, when the Dow Jones Industrial Average (DJIA) changes by 2% from its previous day's close, trading **curbs** (restrictions) would be put into effect on program trading and index **arbitrage**, but not on all trading. The NYSE would also decide when program trading could begin again.

If the market gets extraordinarily volatile, the NYSE will **halt** trading in all stocks for a certain amount of time, as follows:

- When the DJIA declines by 10% from the previous close, trading halts for one hour.
- When the DJIA declines by 20% from the previous close, trading halts for two hours.
- When the DJIA declines by 30% from the previous close, everybody goes home.

Of course, if the Dow is currently in the range of 10,000, a drop of 10% would be a drop of about 1,000 points, which would make for one screaming headline, not to mention the mileage CNBC could get out of the Dow dropping 3,000 points in a single session. This is known as NYSE Rule 80B, in case the exam absolutely loses its mind the day you take it.

I have been teaching in this industry for about 15 years now. When I first started, distinguishing the NYSE/1st Market from the OTC/2nd Market was getting more complicated but not too bad. The NYSE was an **exchange** that used "open outcry" like all **auction markets** did at the time. Teaching the class in Chicago, I could usually get the students to relate to the idea of the funny-colored jackets, the bad, disheveled ties and hairstyles, and the arcane hand gestures used by swearing, snarling, spitting traders down in the pits at the options exchange, the mercantile exchange or the board of trade.

Well, your industry changes faster than most. Even though the NYSE is still an auction market and is still an exchange, much of the trading is done electronically. And, electronic trading is what we used to safely associate with the "OTC/2nd market," which we will discuss next.

Back in the day, we would routinely hit students with questions that neatly sorted the words "listed" and "exchange" over on one side with the NYSE/1st Market, and then the OTC/2nd Market safely on the other side, where securities were "traded" or "quoted" but never "listed" because even NASDAQ, the cream of the OTC crop, at that time was not a true "exchange." It always made for awkward moments with the smartest-guy-in-the-room when I had to explain how a NASDAQ stock could be threatened with a "de-listing," if no stocks were actually "listed" on NASDAQ to begin with. Luckily, I don't think you'll have to sweat it so much on your exam. NASDAQ has been an exchange for years now, and they have routinely used the terms "listed" and "de-listed" to describe the securities trading through their electronic trading facility. To end this discussion of minutiae, the term "listed" is usually thought of in terms of what it does *not* refer to. The term "listed" now accurately refers to NYSE securities and NASDAQ securities; however, the term should *not* be associated with securities trading over-the-counter but not on NASDAQ, e.g., the Over-the-Counter Bulletin Board, which we'll look at in a few pages.

Issuers who want to list their securities for trading on NYSE have to meet the exchange's rigid listing criteria. Understand that if your company lists its security on the NYSE (or NASDAQ), you will be monitored very closely by the exchange, and if you do not meet all of your obligations under exchange rules and SEC rules, your security will suddenly not be trading, which is not usually the sort of distraction any company needs.

For a company doing an IPO and getting authorized to list and trade on the NYSE, the total market value (market cap) for the outstanding shares has to be a minimum of $40 million and $100 million for other companies. We're still just talking about the shares of stock themselves. Remember that a company wanting to list and stay listed on the NYSE has to meet at least one of three financial tests. One is called the "earnings test" and is based on the profitability of the issuer, as its name implies. The next is the "valuation/revenue" test that is based both on the market value of the stock and the revenue of the company issuing it. And, there is an "assets/equity" test based on market valuation, assets, and stockholder's equity. No matter which test is being used, not that many companies can meet it for an initial listing, let alone maintain it to avoid the embarrassment of being de-listed and all the surrounding headlines no public company wants. Note that sometimes the issuing company itself will decide to de-list their security. If so, all that is required for a voluntary delisting is for the company's board of directors to approve it and for the issuer to then file a form with the SEC certifying the board's approval of the resolution.

I once had a young, argumentative finance major interrupt the flow of a Series 7 class in the fine state of Kentucky to insist that bonds do not trade on the New York Stock Exchange. If it's called the New York *Stock* Exchange, how could *bonds* trade there? Huh, Professor!?

I was clearly in a properly air-conditioned room at the time, because I refrained from responding with some snarky retort, like, "Oh no? Where do they trade, then, Billy Bob's Bond and Bait Shop?"

Despite all rumors to the contrary, companies do, in fact, also list their debt securities on the NYSE, as we see at http://www1.nyse.com/bonds/nysebonds/1095449059236.html. To meet the requirements here, the issue has to have a principal value of at least $5 million because any smaller than that, and the company can just become a contestant on The Shark Tank.

If the bond is convertible, it can only be listed if the underlying common stock is subject to real-time last sale reports in the US, and the par value has to be $10 million or larger. Even if the issue of debt securities meets those minimum sizes and requirements, the NYSE will only list the issue if it meets one of several criteria that basically require that the issuer have its stock listed on the NYSE, or that an issuer with stock listed on the exchange is either a majority owner or in common control with the other issuer, or that any NYSE-listed issuer has guaranteed the issue. There is also a criteria based on the credit rating of the issue being at least "B", which, as you probably remember or know, is a junk rating.

As the website for NYSE Bonds indicates:

> *NYSE Bonds operates the largest centralized corporate bond market in the U.S., providing an opportunity for participants to trade bonds in a fair, open environment. On NYSE Bonds, firm and executable orders entered by members or sponsored participants are displayed on the order book, and executed on a strict price/time priority.*

There are also specific NYSE requirements for special securities, including Real Estate Investment Trusts (REITs), closed-end investment companies, non-US companies, etc. But, we can only dig so deep into this information before it's time to keep moving.

OVER-THE-COUNTER

The over-the-counter market is sometimes called the **second market**. It's not a physical marketplace, but it's definitely a market, also known as a **negotiated market**. So, the first market is an "auction market," while the second or OTC market is "negotiated."

Since we don't all gather together on the floor of an exchange, we need big dealers to maintain inventories of over-the-counter stocks. We call these big buyers and sellers **market makers**, because they make a market in that security possible. A market maker is just a broker-dealer who carries an inventory of a particular security and stands ready to either buy or sell it throughout the day. They remind me of the vendors at a flea market all dealing in the same stuff—how about NFL sweatshirts? A savvy collector attending the flea market will sniff around trying to find out who will pay him the most if he wants to sell part of his collection and who will charge him the least if he wants to add to it today. Same thing here, only it all happens electronically. Morgan, Merrill, Goldman, etc., are all broker-dealers who deal in the same over-the-counter securities, with maybe a dozen or more such firms competitively buying and selling these securities through the trading day.

Investors are able to trade shares of MSFT, ORCL, and CSCO only because there are broker-dealers who "make a market" in those securities. What IS a market? It's a two-sided quote, allowing buyers to buy at the ask price and sellers to sell at the bid price. Without these two-sided quotes, how would we be able to buy or sell shares of MSFT, ORCL, or CSCO? Basically, we wouldn't. Again, liquidity is a big deal when it comes to securities—if you can't sell the thing, are you really prepared to hold it, no matter what?

Luckily, there are market makers who put out a **bid** and **ask** (or offer) price and stand ready to take either side of the trade, for at least one round lot. For stocks a round lot is 100 shares. So if a market maker says their quote is 20.00–20.11, they stand ready to buy 100 shares at $20.00 or sell 100 shares at $20.11. The difference between where they buy and where they sell is called the **spread**. Broker-dealers can act as **brokers**, whereby they charge commissions, or they can act as **principals** in the transaction by selling stock from their own inventory, or buying stock for their inventory. All of these terms (agent, broker, dealer, market maker, bid, ask, etc.) are testable, by the way, which is why I'm making this section much denser than you or I would probably prefer.

➤ NASDAQ

Over-the-counter stocks that can meet and maintain the stringent listing criteria trade on an electronic exchange known as **NASDAQ**, which stands for National Association of Securities Dealers Automated Quotation system.

NASDAQ has three tiers. The NASDAQ Global Market Companies is a group of over 1,450 companies that have applied for listing after meeting and continuing to meet stringent financial and liquidity requirements and agreeing to meet specific corporate governance standards. And, there is the NASDAQ Global Select Market, with even higher listing standards. The former "NASDAQ SmallCap Market" has been renamed the "NASDAQ Capital Market Companies." This group of stocks consists of over 550 companies that benefit from access to the capital markets in spite of their smaller size and less proven track records. These companies have to stay current in all their SEC filings but do not have to meet the same financial standards of the Global and Global Select Companies.

➤ Non-NASDAQ

Stocks that do not meet NASDAQ's financial and liquidity and corporate governance standards may be referred to on your exam as **Non-NASDAQ OTC Securities**. These securities trade on the OTC Bulletin Board and the Pink Sheets, where spreads are wider and stock prices generally more volatile. When a company no longer meets NASDAQ's listing requirements, the stock symbol changes, and the security begins to trade in the nether regions of the OTC market, where professional investors generally won't touch it with an 11-foot pole. At www.otcmarkets.com we see that the Pink Sheets are called "the speculative trading marketplace," which is the perfect description. If you want to acquire a huge position in a cheap stock, in a company you're convinced is going to go a lot farther than people yet realize, buy yourself some speculative stocks trading here. You'll notice at that website that some companies provide current information to investors and some don't. There is even a tier called "caveat emptor," which is Latin for "buyer beware." But, we can only have so much fun at one time so let's keep moving.

THIRD MARKET

The **third market** is just a term used when an **exchange-listed security** gets sold over-the-counter. Maybe an institutional buyer can get a better, negotiated price for an order of 10,000 IBM, a listed security, so they decide to buy it over-the-counter. When a listed security trades OTC, we refer to that situation as the "third market." The Consolidated Quotation System (CQS) displays quotations on all common stock, preferred stock, warrants, and rights that are registered on the American Stock Exchange or the New York Stock Exchange and trading in the OTC market (third market). Although executed in the over-the-counter market, these transactions must still be reported to the consolidated tape.

FOURTH MARKET

The **fourth market** involves direct trading between institutional investors, completely bypassing brokers by using **Electronic Communications Networks (ECNs)**. Institutional investors include insurance companies, mutual funds, pension funds, big trust departments, broker-dealers, etc. They're professionals with millions/billions of dollars flowing in and out of the market. Basically, ECNs work like an eBay for securities transactions by matching up buyers and sellers. Some broker-dealers use a market maker to execute client transactions during normal business hours and then use an ECN to execute orders after normal business hours (after 4 p.m.). Well-known electronic communications networks include INSTINET and NYSE ARCA. Here are some essential facts on ECNs:

- If the ECN system cannot match a buyer and seller, a client's order can have a limited ability to be executed
- Some ECNs will only accept certain types of orders, such as limit orders
- Electronic communications networks allow market participants themselves to display quotes and execute transactions
- Participants are referred to as *subscribers* and pay a fee to the ECN in order to trade electronically through the system
- ECNs allow subscribers to trade after-hours, quote and trade anonymously
- ECNs act in an agency capacity and do not buy or sell for their own account (not a market maker)

A term that probably won't show up on the test but is still lots of fun to say is **dark pools of liquidity**. At first, I thought this might be a term from one of the many Star Wars prequels I enjoyed missing, but, no, the term in fact refers to large institutional orders that are concealed from the public and executed on the fourth market usually. The phrase also has at least three synonyms, but I'm convinced you have already suffered enough at this point.

SELLING SHORT

You've probably heard that every investor should try to buy low and sell high, right? Well, some investors take that same principle and simply try to do it in reverse: they prefer selling high, then buying back low. We call these people "short sellers," because calling them high-risk lunatics wouldn't be polite.

It works like this. You go to your friend's house and see that she has a new mountain bike that she paid way too much money for. Mind if I borrow your mountain bike, you ask, to which your friend agrees. On the way home you run into another friend, who admires the bike very much. She likes it so much, in fact, that she offers you two thousand bucks for it.

Two thousand bucks? Sold! You take the two thousand bucks and put it in your pocket.

Wait a minute, that wasn't even your mountain bike! No problem. All you have to do is replace it with an identical machine. A few weeks later you go to the bike store to replace the borrowed bike, and—as predicted—the price has fallen to just $1,000. Perfect! You sold the bike for $2,000 and you can get out of your position by paying just $1,000, keeping the $1,000 difference as your profit. Just buy the bike for $1,000, wheel it over to your friend, and everybody's happy. Notice that you made money when the price went down. The exam would say that you were "bearish" on the price of mountain bikes, because the exam doesn't get out much.

Short sellers don't sell bikes or search engines short, but they can certainly sell the stock of the companies who make bikes or search engines short. If you think that Google is wildly overpriced and headed for a big drop, borrow the shares from your friendly broker-dealer and sell them at what you think is the top. Sell Google for $700 and, you hope, buy it back later for $30, keeping $670 per share as your profit.

However, many people tried that soon after Google went public (primary market) at $85. When it got to $100 many folks were convinced the stock would only go down from there, so they sold it short at $100. Expecting to buy it back or "cover their short positions" for less than $100, these poor souls must have been really embarrassed to see the stock soon climb up to $900 per share.

Hate it when that happens. Selling something for $100 and buying it back for $900 is not a particularly good business model. That's no different from buying something for $900 and then selling it for $100. It's just more dangerous. When you buy something, you've already lost all you could ever lose. But when you sell stock short, there is no limit to how much you'll have to spend to get out of your position. I mean, reality would tell us that Google was never going to hit $10,000 a share, but, hypothetically, it could have. Higher even.

So, short sellers are bearish. They profit when the stock goes down. But, they have limited upside and unlimited risk. If you short a stock for $5,000, $5,000 is the maximum you could make, and only if the stock went to zero. Your potential loss is unlimited, since no one can tell you for sure how high the stock could go up against you.

Stock is not the only thing that can be "sold short." Treasury securities are frequently sold short, as are corporate bonds, ETFs (exchange-traded funds), and closed-end funds. Writers of options are "short the option" and complete the trade when they buy it back to close.

➢ Regulation SHO

The SEC does not like it when short sellers abuse their chosen pastime by selling shares that don't actually exist. Allowing them to do so would distort the downward (bearish) pressure on a stock by distorting the laws of supply & demand that determine the stock's market price. Therefore, broker-dealers have to "locate" the shares their customers are selling short and document it before effecting the short sale—that means they reasonably believe the securities can be delivered by the settlement date (T + 3) as required. In olden days a short sale could only be executed at a price that was higher than the previous price for the security, or at the same price if the price before had been an "uptick." **Reg SHO** now requires that before executing a short sale, broker-dealers have to locate the securities so that the laws of supply and demand are not distorted by "naked short selling," in which people sell stock that doesn't even exist short, artificially depressing its price. If the broker-dealer executes a short sale without reasonably believing the shares can be delivered by the lender, they have violated the rule.

In May 2010 Reg SHO was updated to impose a temporary version of the old uptick rule that applies when a "circuit breaker" is tripped for a particular security. Starting in May of that year if a security dropped during the day by 10% or more below its most recent closing price, short sellers would not be able to sell short at or below the current best bid price for the security. In other words, people "selling long," which means selling the shares they own, will have priority and will be able to liquidate their holdings before short sellers can jump onto the pile. As the SEC states in their unique brand of English:

a targeted short sale price test restriction will apply the alternative uptick rule for the remainder of the day and the following day if the price of an individual security declines intra-day by 10% or more from the prior day's closing price for that security. By not allowing short sellers to sell at or below the current national best bid while the circuit breaker is in effect, the short sale price test restriction in Rule 201 will allow long sellers, who will be able to sell at the bid, to sell first in a declining market for a particular security. As the Commission has noted previously in connection with short sale price test restrictions, a goal of such restrictions is to allow long sellers to sell first in a declining market. In addition, by making such bids accessible only by long sellers when a security's price is undergoing significant downward price pressure, Rule 201 will help to facilitate and maintain stability in the markets and help ensure that they function efficiently. It will also help restore investor confidence during times of substantial uncertainty because, once the circuit breaker has been triggered for a particular security, long sellers will have preferred access to bids for the security, and the security's continued price decline will more likely be due to long selling and the underlying fundamentals of the issuer, rather than to other factors.

As we see from that passage, there is a big difference between a customer sell order marked "long" and a sell order marked "short." That is why Reg SHO requires all sell orders to be marked properly. As I write these words, FINRA happens to have an announcement that it just fined a member firm $12 million for improperly marking short sales as "long" and for failing to first locate the securities that were allegedly being sold short. It's a big deal because, again, if somebody is selling short when there are no actual shares connected to the trade, the markets are being distorted and manipulated, which is never a good thing. From the press release: Brad Bennett, FINRA Executive Vice President and Chief of Enforcement, said:

Firms must ensure their trading and supervisory systems are designed to prevent the release of short sale orders without valid locates, and properly mark sale orders, in order to prevent potentially abusive naked short selling. The duration, scope and volume of [the firm's] locate and order-marking violations created a potential for harm to the integrity of the market.

BOND TRADING

Corporate bonds traded over-the-counter are reported to FINRA's **TRACE** system, which stands for **Trade Reporting and Compliance Engine**. Brokerage firms are now required to report price and volume data on all corporate bond transactions to TRACE, within 15 minutes. FINRA publicly disseminates that transaction data immediately on virtually 100 percent of over-the-counter corporate bond activity (approximately 22,000 transactions and $18 billion in volume every day!). Recently, FINRA fined a firm $1.4 *million* for failing to report a huge percentage of their bond trades to TRACE. The whole purpose of the TRACE system is to provide transparency (what's going on) in the bond market, so by failing to report the trades, the firm deprived the market of the transparency it needs to remain effective. Several smaller fines have recently been levied for failing to report trades in "TRACE-eligible securities." FINRA insists that dealers provide the market with accurate and transparent data on securities transactions, and they are quite happy to remind them with disciplinary actions and fines.

The NYSE also provides a bond trading platform, and I'm simply going to let them tell you about it:

The NYSE Bonds trading platform provides a more efficient and transparent way to trade bonds. The platform incorporates the design of the current NYSE Arca all-electronic trading system. This system provides investors with the ability to readily obtain transparent pricing and trading information, enabling them to make better investment decisions. The system has also been expanded to include the bonds of all NYSE-listed companies and their subsidiaries without the companies having to list each bond issued. NYSE Bonds operates the largest centralized bond market of any US exchange or other self-regulatory organization. It offers investors a broad selection of bonds: corporate (including convertibles), agency and government bonds.

The majority of NYSE bond volume is in corporate debt, with some 94% in straight, or non-convertible bonds, and 6% in convertible debt issues. As of Monday, December 1, 2008 all NYSE Amex (formerly American Stock Exchange) listed bonds transferred to an electronic trading platform based on NYSE Bonds called NYSE Amex Bonds. Like NYSE Bonds, this electronic trading platform is based on the design of NYSE Arca's comprehensive matching technology allowing NYSE Members to enter orders to buy or sell bonds electronically.

MSRB Rule G-14 requires that transactions in municipal bonds be reported within 15 minutes of trade execution to the MSRB's Real-time Transaction Reporting System (RTRS). The MSRB disseminates trade data about all reported municipal securities transactions almost immediately at www.investinginbonds.com. You may have noticed that for both TRACE and RTRS, bond transactions are reported within 15 minutes, but when we're talking about stock transactions, the report is due within 30 *seconds*. Yet another indication of the increased volatility and faster pace of the stock—as opposed to the bond—market.

TYPES OF ORDERS

➢ Market Order

The exam will ask you to work with **market orders**, **limit orders**, **stop orders**, and even the dreaded **stop-limit** order. Market orders are easy. You want to buy 1,000 shares quickly, you place a market order. It will get filled as quickly as possible. We don't know exactly the price it will be filled at, but if we fill it fast enough it will probably be the same price we're looking at right now. *Now* is always the best time to fill a market order, which is also why those players down on the floor are running around like crazy people most of the day.

➢ Limit Order

Sometimes customers like to name their price. If a stock is at 43, maybe they're starting to get interested in selling it. They'd be a lot more interested if they could sell it for $45, so they enter a **sell limit** order above the current market price. Sell limit @45 means the investor will take 45 or better (*more* is better for a seller). If he can get 45 or 45.15, or even higher, he'll sell his stock. If the bid never rises that high, he won't sell it.

Another investor is interested in buying a stock currently trading at 30. He'd be a lot more interested in buying it at $25, so he places a **buy limit** order below the current price. That means he'll buy the stock if he can get it for $25 or better (*less* is better for a buyer). If the ask/offer price never drops to $25 or lower, he won't buy it.

Market orders guarantee a fill but not a price. Limit orders, on the other hand, guarantee a price, but they do not guarantee that the order will be filled. Many times the stock's price fails to perform like an investor wants it to. If it's entered as a day order, the limit order either gets executed that day or it goes away. If the investor is going on vacation for three weeks and doesn't want to look at his stocks while he's gone, he can leave the order open by entering it GTC, which stands for good 'til canceled. If the order doesn't get filled and the investor doesn't cancel it, the order remains open.

➢ Stop Order

Notice that when discussing limit orders I mentioned that a buy-limit order would be filled only if the ask/offer price dropped to the limit price or lower and a sell-limit order would be filled only if the bid price rose to the limit price or higher. Stop orders, on the other hand, are not based on the bid/ask—the prices that someone is *willing* to trade at. Stop orders are triggered only when an actual trade occurs between two other investors at the stop price or higher for a buy stop, or at the stop price or lower for a sell stop order. So, if the test question shows the stop price on the consolidated tape, understand that, by definition, that cannot be the customer's trade—that is the trade that put the customer's order in play. It is the "last sale" that activates the stop order.

Let's start with a **buy stop** order.

A technical analyst sees that a particular stock is trading in a narrow range, between 38 and 40. The technical analyst sees no reason to tie up his money in a stock that is stuck in a narrow trading range, known as **consolidation**. He decides if the stock can break through resistance (40), it will probably continue to rise, which is why he'd like to buy it on the way up. So he places a buy stop above the current market price. Buy stop @41 means that the market price first has to reach 41 or higher, at which point the order is triggered/activated. It will be executed at the next available price, whatever that is. Stop orders have a trigger price, at which point they become market orders. So if the ticker came in like this:

> *40.90, 40.95, 40.99, 41.00...*

his order would now be triggered or "activated" at 41.00. It would then be filled at the next available price, regardless of what that is. And, if the last two prices had been 40.099, 41.01, the order would have been triggered at 41.01, at which point the price has passed through the stop price of 41. Notice that stop orders don't guarantee a price for execution. The price named as the stop is just the price that triggers or activates the order. The order—now a market order—is filled at the next available price. Again, the stop price is not the exact price, either. A "buy stop at 41" is activated at 41 or any price higher than that. It's then filled as soon as possible.

On the other hand, let's say a day trader takes a large position in a high-risk security but then decides to play it safe and limit his loss. He buys 1,000 shares at $50 a share and immediately enters a **sell stop** order at 49. This means that as long as the stock stays above $49 he's in. As soon as it slips to 49 or lower, though, he's out. A sell stop at 49 would be activated as soon as the stock's price hit 49 or lower, at which point it would be sold at the next available price. The exam might tell you that a customer is bullish on a stock but fears a possible downturn in the short-term. What should she do?

Well, if she originally bought in at $20 and the stock is now at $50, you should tell her that selling for more than $50 would be great. At this point, however, she should make sure she doesn't lose too much of the $30 profit she has within her grasp. Many investors end up snatching defeat from the jaws of victory at this point, probably because they don't know how to use sell stops or "**stop loss**" orders. Not going to happen to us. We'll give up one dollar from here, you tell her, but if it falls to $49 or lower, she's selling and taking her profit. So, if it goes up, great, and if it goes down, she takes a profit, and you immediately put her into another stock…assuming it's suitable, of course.

If somebody wants to get really tricky, he can enter a **stop-limit** order. Now his stop order also names the most he will pay or the least he will accept for a particular stock. A buy stop @50, limit 50 would start out just like a buy-stop order. The stock has to hit 50 or higher before it's triggered. But, by adding the limit to the order the investor is saying he won't pay more than $50 for it, period.

On the other hand, a sell stop @30, limit 30 would be triggered if the stock hit 30 or lower, but the investor will not take less than $30 a share. If the order gets triggered and then the bid falls lower than 30, this sell order simply won't get executed, and the investor will end up holding a loser that would have otherwise been sold with a sell-stop (not a stop-limit) order. Or, our technical analyst who wants to buy stock on the way up might want to place a cap on how much he pays. If so, he enters a **buy stop-limit** order. In other words, a "buy stop @41" could be filled at whatever price—probably near $41—while a "buy stop @41, limit 41" could only be filled at $41 or lower. Neither order, however, will even get activated unless and until the stock first trades one time at $41 or higher.

> ➤ Further Details

At-the-open and at-the-close/market-on-close orders are filled, surprisingly enough, at the opening of the trading session and at the closing price, respectively. The customer's order is filled at the opening price (at-the-open) or the closing price (market-on-close), or as close to those prices as possible. MOC (market-on-close) orders can be placed by customers up to 20 minutes before the close of trading for the day.

Also, buy-limit orders and sell-stop orders are placed below the current market price of the stock. As we saw in our discussion of Equity Securities in Chapter 2, stock prices drop by the amount of the dividend on the ex-dividend date. So, both the buy-limit and the sell-stop order would be reduced by the amount of the dividend. Except when they wouldn't. If the customer wants the order marked **DNR (do not reduce)** then the price of the order would not be reduced because of a dividend. Would sell-limit and buy-stop orders be reduced? No, they're placed above the current market price, so they would not be triggered and/or filled due to the reduction of the stock's market price in response to a dividend.

PRACTICE

1. An investor originally purchased 100 shares of INTC at $20 a share. Now the stock is at $60. The investor is still bullish on the stock for the long-term but fears a possible downturn in the short-term. As her registered rep, you would tell her to place a:

   A. Market order to sell

   B. Sell limit order at $59

   C. Buy stop order at $61

   D. Sell stop order at $59

2. A sell stop order would be activated when:

   A. The stock price passes through the trigger price

   B. The stock price hits or passes through the trigger price

   C. The stock price hits the trigger price and conforms with the NYSE uptick rule

D. None of these choices

3. A sell stop at 45 would be triggered at all the following prices except:

    A. 44.00

    B. 44.37

    C. 44.87

    D. 46.00

(ANSWERS)

1. **D,** you had to eliminate any "buy" order, since the investor already owns the stock. If the investor only wants to sell if the stock drops, place a sell-stop.

2. **B,** it doesn't have to pass through the trigger price—if it hits the trigger price OR passes through, the order is elected.

3. **D,** at the trigger price or below. Not above the trigger price. That's for buy stops.

MARGIN

Investing "on **margin**" is a high-risk strategy that involves buying securities on credit, hoping to make more on the securities positions than the broker-dealer charges you in interest on the margin loans. Broker-dealers love **margin accounts** because they open up a whole new line of business—suddenly they're credit card companies, and they don't even have to issue the little plastic cards. Plus, credit card companies have no collateral from their customers—your VISA account is backed up solely by your tendency to repay. In a margin account, you pledge the assets you're buying on credit to the lender, the broker-dealer. If things turn south on you, they can sell the stock or bond to recover the money they lent you. So, the interest rate they charge is actually lower than what you'd pay on a credit card, since they have collateral backing the loan.

People talk about the "equity" in their houses (or used to). That means that maybe they bought the house for $200,000 and borrowed $180,000 to do that. If so, their account starts out like this:

$$\begin{array}{rl} \$200,000 & \text{Market Value} \\ - \quad \$180,000 & \text{Money Owed} \\ \hline \$20,000 & \text{Equity} \end{array}$$

Just remember that **equity** simply equals the difference between what somebody owns (assets) and owes (liabilities). Let's say that this home's value increased 15% for three years running—remember when that used to seem "normal"? Believe it or not, when an investment of that size compounds for just three years at 15%, it is suddenly worth $304,175. To check my math, just take $200,000 times 1.15, times 1.15, times 1.15. That's the formula for "future value" that you might wish to google for your own understanding (or not). Anyway, part of each monthly mortgage payment knocks down the principal that was borrowed, and maybe these homeowners diligently overpaid each month by a few hundred dollars. Suddenly, the value of their asset has risen while the amount owed has dropped. Their account now looks like this, maybe:

$$\begin{array}{rl} \$304,175 & \text{Market Value} \\ -\ \$170,000 & \text{Money Owed} \\ \hline \$134,175 & \text{Equity} \end{array}$$

What can these homeowners do with that equity? They can borrow against it—hey, you only go around once, right?

In a margin account, you aren't buying houses; you're buying stocks and bonds. If their market value rises, you win. What if their market value starts to drop? You have yourself a problem. This is, of course, where margin accounts get their bad name, but they're not all bad. I have one myself. My margin account entitles me to a cash advance of exactly $6,141.53 this morning. Or, I could buy $17,206.00 worth of stock completely on *credit*. But, nobody's holding a gun to my head either, so I just keep paying 100% in my so-called "margin account."

A "margin account" is simply a different type of account than a "cash account." In a **cash account**, you have to pay in full when you purchase securities, and you cannot sell short in a cash account. If your account is approved for margin trading, you can buy securities on credit and sell them short if you really like to party.

REG T

The Securities Exchange Act of 1934 gave the Federal Reserve Board the authority to regulate margin accounts. The "Fed" regulates credit, and one form of credit is the margin account, in which the broker-dealer fronts the customer half the purchase price. In the 1920s, too many customers were holding stock on margin without putting down enough money. When the prices of those stocks collapsed, they ended up owing money with nothing to show for it all. The Fed would sort of like to prevent another 1929-style market crash if at all possible. So, to purchase stock on margin, the broker-dealer follows **Regulation T (Reg T)**, which states that a listed stock can be pledged as collateral by the customer in exchange for a loan from the broker-dealer up to a maximum percentage of its value. Reg T tells broker-dealers how much credit they can extend to their customers—that percentage has been 50% for quite some time. The industry sometimes refers to the amount that a customer puts down as the "Fed call." For a test question, when a customer buys $200,000 of stock, he puts down ½ or $100,000. The other ½ or $100,000 is provided by the broker-dealer, who looks forward to charging interest on that $100,000 for just as long as the customer would like to go on owing them. The amount that the customer puts down is referred to as "the margin." **Margin** simply means "percent," but sounds more sophisticated somehow. The "margin" refers to the amount of money the investor has to deposit; the rest of the market value is extended on credit. That seems like a testable point, too, like everything else I'm telling you.

Regulation T requires 50% of the purchase price to be deposited by the customer within two business days after the settlement date of the transaction. Any market price change between the purchase of the security and the required payment would not affect the amount of the deposit the customer has to make. If the stock purchased on margin rises from, say, $50 to $60, or drops from, say, $50 to $40, the margin call is still based on $50 per share; it's figured at the time of purchase.

RUNNING THE NUMBERS

Say a customer bought 1,000 shares @40 and made the required Reg T deposit of half or $20,000. At that point the customer's account looks like this:

LMV	–	Dr	=	Equity	Reg T Deposit
$40,000	–	$20,000	=	$20,000	$20,000

LMV stands for "long market value." It could just be referred to as "market value" or "current market value," to make sure you have three names for the same darned thing. The "Dr" stands for "debit register," which can also be called the "debit balance." This is simply the amount the customer borrowed and still owes his broker-dealer, like the mortgage balance that the homeowner still owes the lender. So, the long market value of the stock he bought is $40,000. He made the required Reg T deposit of half—20K—so the broker-dealer fronted him the other half. Do you suppose the broker-dealer wants that money back?

You bet, so it's a debit (Dr) to the client's account until he pays it off.

He "owns" an asset worth 40K and he owes 20K to the lender. That's why his equity is $20,000. Just like if you owed $80,000 on your mortgage when your house was worth $100,000—the difference of $20,000 would be your equity.

So, the investor has $20,000 of equity. What happens if the stock rises, to, say, $50 a share? The account looks like this:

LMV	–	Dr	=	Equity
$50,000	–	$20,000	=	$30,000

The amount owed to the broker-dealer (Dr) didn't change. The long market value of the stock went up, increasing the equity dollar-for-dollar. Now, let's compare the equity of $30,000 to Reg T, which is 50% of the market value or "LMV." Reg T wants to see 50% equity in the account. Does this customer have at least half his "LMV" as equity? More, actually. Half of 50K is $25,000. The customer has $30,000 of equity. That's **excess equity** of $5,000. Like this:

LMV	–	Dr	=	Equity	–	Reg T	=	Excess Equity
$50,000	–	$20,000	=	$30,000	–	$25,000	=	$5,000

You know how a lot of homeowners used to borrow more money long before they really started to pay off their mortgage? Well, in a margin account you can do the same thing. Since this customer has excess equity of $5,000, we certainly wouldn't require him to do something crazy and, like, pay back the lender. Heck no. Instead, the customer has $5,000 credited to a special little line item called "SMA." SMA, which stands for **Special Memorandum Account,** is just a line of credit that the customer can tap. I mean he can withdraw $5,000 of his cash, like it's in a savings account, right? Not at all. The $5,000 is just a number—as with Social Security there's actually no money there. But, if the customer wants to borrow that *amount* of money, he can. And whenever he borrows from SMA, that amount is added to the debit balance/debit register. See why customers love margin accounts, especially when the markets are moving in the proper direction? The customer can just tell the broker-dealer to cut him a check for $5,000, which will be added to his tab, like this:

$$LMV - Dr = Equity$$

$$\$50,000 - \$25,000 = \$25,000$$

Borrowing the cash didn't affect the long market value of the securities. We added the amount borrowed to the debit balance, which reduced equity and wiped out the SMA. SMA can be used as a cash advance that will be repaid with interest. Or, SMA can be used as an initial margin requirement for the purchase of more stock. So, instead of borrowing the cash, the customer could have used the $5,000 SMA credit to purchase $10,000 of stock. If so, the account would have looked like this:

LMV	Dr	Equity	SMA
$60,000	$30,000	$30,000	$0

If the customer buys more stock, that definitely adds to the market value of securities held long in the account. Why did his Dr go up by $10,000? Because the $5,000 of SMA is not the customer's cash—it's just a line of credit. Funny money, no different from your line of credit on a credit card. You can use the credit, but since it isn't your money, it has to be paid back, with interest. The customer in our example used his line of credit (SMA) as his margin deposit, and the broker-dealer fronted him the other half, or $5,000, which is also added to the Dr along with the $5,000 he borrowed for the deposit from SMA. So, he borrowed $5,000 from his line of credit (SMA), plus $5,000 that the broker-dealer fronted him for the additional stock purchase. In other words, when the stock moves your way, you can end up using borrowed money in order to borrow more money. Also note that when dividends, interest, or capital gains distributions from mutual funds come into the account, that income is applied to/pays down the debit balance. Therefore, SMA is affected by such income being applied to the debit.

Reg T absolutely demands that a customer put up 50% of the long market value initially. After that, it really only sort of requests or prefers that the customer have 50% equity. What happens if the customer's equity dips below 50%?

Not much. Even though the account is called "restricted," there really aren't many restrictions. The customer has to put up ½ in order to buy more stock. If the customer sells stock, he can still withdraw/borrow ½ the proceeds. So the test question might show an account with less than 50% equity and ask you how much cash the customer can withdraw if he sells a certain amount of stock.

Half. The proceeds pay down the Dr; and half that amount is credited to SMA, where it can be promptly withdrawn. But, remember, no cash has been moved to SMA. Just a number. No different from a credit card issuer raising your line of credit.

Maybe we should take a look at the numbers there. The market value of the long position is $20,000, and the Dr is $13,000. That means the customer controls a $20,000 asset with not a lot of skin in the game. His equity or ownership is really only $7,000. Half of his long position would be $10,000, but his equity is below that. Therefore, we call this a "restricted account." Let's say he sells $5,000 of stock. The broker-dealer takes the $5,000 raised by selling the stock and pays down the debit by $5,000, since that debit is the money the customer owes them. So, the LMV becomes $15,000, and the Dr becomes $8,000. How much money can the customer borrow after making this sale? Half of the sale, or $2,500. And, if he did that, he'd end up with LMV of $15,000 and a Dr of $10,500. As we'll see, that's pushing it, since his equity is now just 30% of his long position. The **SROs** won't let the firm allow him to drop below 25% equity, so this guy is apparently a real party animal. Oh well. If the firm will allow him to control a position with just 30% equity, everything is just hunky-dory.

Also, check this out. <u>When the market value of a securities position drops, that does not affect SMA</u>. It certainly reduces the market value of the stock and, therefore, the equity, but SMA is just a line of credit. It does not get taken away. One of the best cheesy memory joggers I've ever heard comes from an instructor who would tell his students that excess equity is the water in the tub. When the excess equity rises, it makes a ring around the tub called "SMA." When the water drains away, the SMA is still here to stay.

SMA does not go away due to a drop in market value. The customer can always use SMA as long as using it does not take him below the minimum maintenance requirement, which we're about to look at right now.

MINIMUM MAINTENANCE

Reg T tells us what to put down on an initial transaction, and any excess above Reg T gives the customer "SMA." But, SMA and excess equity are, by definition, terms used when the market is cooperating with the margin customer. What happens when the market goes the wrong way? Suddenly, the customer's equity is deficient, and he either has to throw more cash on the fire or start liquidating securities. See, Reg T requirements apply initially and then help us figure if the customer has any SMA to play with. The customer's larger concern is the SRO 25% minimum maintenance requirement. The regulators say that a customer's equity can never go lower than 25% of the long market value. If it does, the customer gets a maintenance call to bring the equity up to the minimum 25%. If the customer can't deliver the cash, the firm sells/liquidates securities equal to four times the amount of the maintenance call. The following numbers should help to clarify the concept of the minimum maintenance requirement:

LMV	Dr	Equity	Minimum	Call	Liquidate
40,000	20,000	20,000	10,000	0	0

At this point, the customer has twice as much equity as the minimum (25% of long market value).

If the stock goes from 40K down to 30K, we're still okay:

LMV	Dr	Equity	Minimum	Call	Liquidate
30,000	20,000	10,000	7,500	0	0

But, if the long market value falls to 24K, we're in trouble:

LMV	Dr	Equity	Minimum	Call	Liquidate
24,000	20,000	4,000	6,000	2,000	8,000

The SROs demand $6,000 in equity, which is ¼ of $24,000, and the customer has only $4,000. So, the customer gets a maintenance call informing him that he needs to deliver $2,000. If the customer does that, the account looks like this:

LMV	Dr	Equity	Minimum	Call	Liquidate
24,000	18,000	6,000	6,000	0	0

He paid down the debit by $2,000 and now he has $6,000 in equity, the bare minimum of 25% of market value. If he didn't have the cash, the firm would have liquidated $8,000 worth of securities. If so, the account would have looked like this:

LMV	Dr	Equity	Minimum Maintenance
16,000	12,000	4,000	4,000

Whereas, it used to look like this:

LMV	Dr	Equity	Minimum Maintenance
24,000	20,000	4,000	6,000

Selling the $8,000 worth of securities reduced the LMV and the Dr by an equal amount, leaving the customer with exactly 25% equity. Remember, all we're doing here is selling $8,000 of stock and using the $8,000 to pay down the debit. By the way, since the firm might have to sell a customer's stock in a hurry, they hold the customer's securities in "street name." That means the securities are registered in the name of the firm for the beneficial ownership (FBO) of the customer, who hasn't exactly paid for them yet. Also, the 25% requirement is the *minimum* maintenance. That means the broker-dealer can be only that loose about things. Many broker-dealers require a higher minimum maintenance than just 25% to protect themselves from a bunch of dead-beat speculators. The regulators are just fine with that—they churn out *minimum* requirements; the firms are always encouraged to be more stringent if they so choose.

SHORT POSITIONS

Short accounts work a little different. Remember that when a customer sells short, he is selling borrowed securities in anticipation that he can buy them back to replace them at a lower price. So, if he wants to sell short $10,000 worth of securities, he has to deposit half that value, or $5,000 to meet the Reg T requirement. If he did so, his account would look like this:

Cr	$15,000
SMV	– $10,000
Equity	$5,000

The "Cr" stands for the "**credit**" and the "**SMV**" stands for "**short market value**," or, perhaps, we could just call it the "market value." In any case, when the customer sells short $10,000 worth of securities, that $10,000 is credited to the customer's account. Remember, he sold some stock—somebody paid him $10,000 for that stock. That somebody doesn't know or care that the seller is "short" the stock; he's just buying some stock from somebody he'll never meet.

So, our investor gets the proceeds from the sale and also deposits 50% of that to meet the Reg T requirement, which is added to the $10,000 he took in for selling the stock for a total credit of $15,000. For the exam questions "Cr" will remain unchanged; it's the "SMV" or "short market value" that fluctuates. Think about that for a second—which numbers move in a margin account? The ones with "MV" in their name, which stands for "market value." Market value is what changes in a margin account, whether long (LMV) or short (SMV). And, equity is always a percentage of market value or "MV."

If the "SMV" goes down, as the investor hopes, he'll end up with more equity. For example, if the SMV dropped to just $5,000, the customer's equity would increase by $5,000, like this:

Cr	$15,000
SMV	– $5,000
Equity	$10,000

Remember, the credit didn't change. He started with a credit of $15,000, and that's all the credit he's going to have. It's the market value (SMV) that changed, dropping in the desired direction for our short seller.

And if the market value of the securities sold short were to increase (ouch!), his equity would shrink, like this:

Cr	$15,000
SMV	– $11,000
Equity	$4,000

How high can the SMV go before a customer gets one of those nasty maintenance calls? For short accounts, customers need 30% of their SMV as equity. If the customer's SMV is $11,000, he needs at least $3,300 in equity. You can find the highest SMV at maintenance by taking the "Cr" and dividing it by 1.3. Since the customer has a credit of $15,000, just divide that by 1.3, and you see that the highest SMV without a maintenance call would be $11,538. As long as the securities' value doesn't exceed that number, his account will remain properly margined.

COMBINED EQUITY

Keep this simple. To find combined equity just find the equity for the long positions and add it to the equity for the short positions. You can also remember that the formula for combined equity would be:

$$LMV + Cr - Dr - SMV$$

Which is just another way of saying, "Add the two things that go on top and subtract the two things that go on the bottom." So if a customer had an LMV of $20,000, a Cr of $20,000, a Dr of $10,000, and SMV of $10,000, his combined equity would be $20,000:

$$LMV \quad + \quad Cr \quad - \quad Dr \quad - \quad SMV$$

$$20{,}000 + 20{,}000 - 10{,}000 - 10{,}000$$

In other words, he has $10,000 equity on the long positions, and $10,000 equity on the short positions. He has to have 25% equity for the long, and 30% for the short. This customer is okay on both fronts. Each day the markets are open, the margin department recalculates requirements by marking to the market. If market values have gone the wrong way, the customer might receive a margin call. If market values have gone the right way, the customer might see SMA increase.

MARGINABLE SECURITIES, ACCOUNTS

Not everything can be purchased "on margin," but that doesn't mean it can't be purchased within a margin account. A "margin account" is really just an account that has been approved for margin. I have one, myself. Luckily, I rarely use it to borrow money, much as I usually shred all those little pretend checks my credit card companies keep sending me. No thanks. Not interested in paying interest on purchases—I'm looking to make money, thank you. Well, if I really wanted to purchase securities "on margin," these are the securities I could buy by depositing half the market value, borrowing the rest through my friendly broker-dealer:

- NYSE, NASDAQ, AMEX stocks
- OTC securities on the FRB's approved list

The following can be purchased inside my margin account, but I'd have to pay for them in full:

- Non-NASDAQ OTC securities
- Options
- IPOs or any new issue for 30 days
- Mutual fund shares

Watch out re: the above bullet list. If the exam question asks if options can be purchased "on margin," the answer is no. If the question asks if options can be purchased "in a margin account," the answer is yes. Also, a retirement account cannot be set up as a margin account, since it would be rather crazy to let retirees lose money that quickly, losing perhaps more than they initially deposit into the account. UGMA/UTMA accounts also may not be established as margin accounts.

CHAPTER 3 QUIZ
40 questions

1. One of your clients wants to sell shares of stock only if they drop to or below a certain price. If your client does not wish to specify an execution price, he should place a:

    A. Sell-limit order

    B. Market order

    C. Sell-stop order

    D. Sell-stop limit order

2. An S-corporation is different from an LLC in which of the following ways?

    A. Annual shareholder meetings and minutes are required

    B. Owners are personally liable for debts incurred by the business

    C. Owners receive more protection from lawsuits against the business

    D. Owners are called "members"

3. A trust files federal income taxes on which of the following forms?

    A. 1040

    B. 1065

    C. 1041

    D. 1099

4. Which TWO of the following are accurate regarding a money purchase plan?

I. Contributions are discretionary on the part of the employer

II. Contributions are mandatory on the part of the employer

III. Contributions are discretionary on the part of the employee

IV. Contributions are mandatory on the part of the employee

    A. I, III

    B. II, III

    C. I, IV

    D. II, IV

5. Which of the following is typically the reason business owners choose to form general partnerships?

    A. Personal asset protection

    B. Flow-through of income and expenses

    C. Double taxation of dividends

    D. Unlimited liability

6. Which of the following proposes that expected return is equal to the riskless rate of return plus a risk premium?

A. Capital asset pricing model

$ER = rf +$

B. Beta

C. The Dow Theory

D. Sharpe ratio

7. Which of the following proposes that relatively uncorrelated investments can reduce the risk inherent in an investment account?

A. Modern Portfolio Theory

B. Sharpe ratio

C. CAPM

D. The Dow Theory

8. If an investor wants to buy a stock above the current market price, she should place a:

A. Buy-stop order

B. Buy-limit order

C. Market order

D. Short sale

9. Which of the following retirement plans allows the largest annual contribution?

A. SIMPLE IRA

B. 401(k)

C. Keogh

D. 403(b)

10. A value investor would most likely choose a stock trading:

A. At a low dividend yield

B. Near its 52-week high

C. At a high price-to-cash multiple

D. Near its book value

11. If a trader has purchased 1,000 shares of ABC, his safest risk modification technique would be to:

    A. Buy 10 ABC puts

    B. Sell 10 ABC calls

    C. Buy 8 ABC puts

    D. Sell 8 ABC puts

12. When a FINRA-member broker-dealer acts as a "market maker," the firm is involved with which of the following activities?

    A. Executing transactions in exchange-listed securities on an agency basis

    B. Executing transactions in OTC securities on a principal basis

    C. Bringing new issues of stock to public investors on the primary market

    D. Bringing new issues of stock to private investors on the secondary market

13. The CPI was −2% the past year. Suzanne's mutual fund had a total return of 1%. If GDP was +1%,  we can accurately conclude that:

    A. Suzanne's real rate of return was zero

    B. Suzanne's real rate of return was 1%

    C. Suzanne's real rate of return was 3%

    D. Suzanne's real rate of return was −1%

14. Mandi purchased a corporate bond with a 3% nominal yield. The bond is callable @102. If Mandi receives two interest payments with the bond being called at the end of one year, her total return is:

    A. 5%   100

    B. 8%   3

    C. 3%

    D. 7.7%

15. Melinda plans to backpack through Costa Rica in three years. She needs $7,000 at a minimum and has invested $1,900 with no further plans to invest in this account. As her investment adviser, you should first discuss which of the following with Melinda?

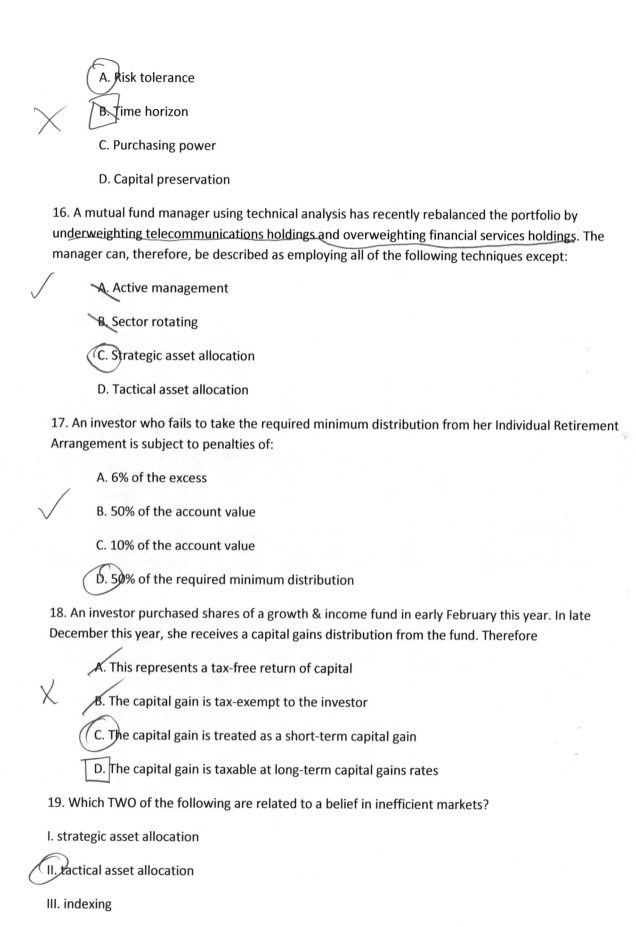

A. Risk tolerance

B. Time horizon

C. Purchasing power

D. Capital preservation

16. A mutual fund manager using technical analysis has recently rebalanced the portfolio by underweighting telecommunications holdings and overweighting financial services holdings. The manager can, therefore, be described as employing all of the following techniques except:

   A. Active management

   B. Sector rotating

   C. Strategic asset allocation

   D. Tactical asset allocation

17. An investor who fails to take the required minimum distribution from her Individual Retirement Arrangement is subject to penalties of:

   A. 6% of the excess

   B. 50% of the account value

   C. 10% of the account value

   D. 50% of the required minimum distribution

18. An investor purchased shares of a growth & income fund in early February this year. In late December this year, she receives a capital gains distribution from the fund. Therefore

   A. This represents a tax-free return of capital

   B. The capital gain is tax-exempt to the investor

   C. The capital gain is treated as a short-term capital gain

   D. The capital gain is taxable at long-term capital gains rates

19. Which TWO of the following are related to a belief in inefficient markets?

I. strategic asset allocation

II. tactical asset allocation

III. indexing

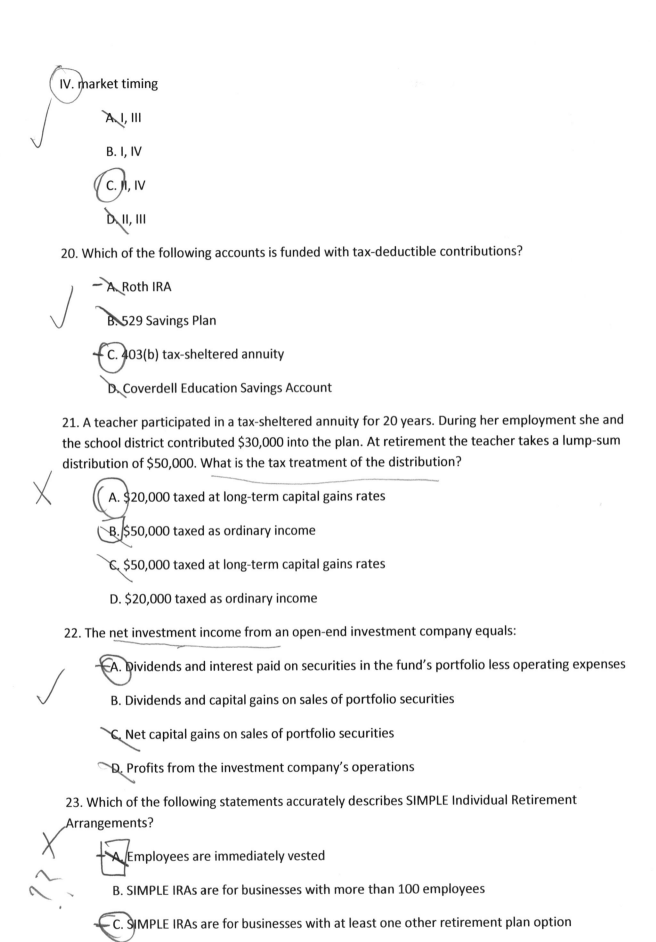

IV. market timing

    A. I, III

    B. I, IV

    C. II, IV

    D. II, III

20. Which of the following accounts is funded with tax-deductible contributions?

    A. Roth IRA

    B. 529 Savings Plan

    C. 403(b) tax-sheltered annuity

    D. Coverdell Education Savings Account

21. A teacher participated in a tax-sheltered annuity for 20 years. During her employment she and the school district contributed $30,000 into the plan. At retirement the teacher takes a lump-sum distribution of $50,000. What is the tax treatment of the distribution?

    A. $20,000 taxed at long-term capital gains rates

    B. $50,000 taxed as ordinary income

    C. $50,000 taxed at long-term capital gains rates

    D. $20,000 taxed as ordinary income

22. The net investment income from an open-end investment company equals:

    A. Dividends and interest paid on securities in the fund's portfolio less operating expenses

    B. Dividends and capital gains on sales of portfolio securities

    C. Net capital gains on sales of portfolio securities

    D. Profits from the investment company's operations

23. Which of the following statements accurately describes SIMPLE Individual Retirement Arrangements?

    A. Employees are immediately vested

    B. SIMPLE IRAs are for businesses with more than 100 employees

    C. SIMPLE IRAs are for businesses with at least one other retirement plan option

D. Contributions are non-tax-deductible

24. Jennifer originally invested $10,000 into an open-end fund. She has since reinvested dividend distributions of $1,000 and capital gains distributions of $500. If Jennifer currently holds 1,000 shares of the fund, her cost basis per-share is:

A. $10.00

B. $11.00

C. $11.50

D. $10.50

25. Doris contributed $60,000 into a non-qualified variable annuity at age 41. Nine years later Doris takes a random withdrawal of $15,000 with the account value at $85,000. Her tax liability on the withdrawal is:

A. Ordinary income tax on $15,000

B. Ordinary income tax on $15,000, plus a $1,500 penalty tax

C. None, as this represents a tax-free return of cost basis

— D. Ordinary income tax on $25,000

26. Which of the following statements accurately describe(s) the tax implications of insurance contracts?

A. Death benefits are not taxable to the beneficiary, but are includable in the insured's estate for purposes of estate taxes

B. Loans against the policy are charged interest, and both the principal and interest reduce the contract values

C. The policyholder may surrender the part of cash value representing net premiums paid into the contract tax-free

D. All choices listed

27. Which of the following is an accurate statement concerning 401(k) plans and Individual Retirement Arrangements?

A. The balance from a 401(k) plan may be transferred to a Roth IRA without tax implications

B. The balance from a 401(k) plan may be transferred to a Traditional IRA without tax consequences

C. The balance from a 401(k) plan may be transferred to an existing IRA only

D. The balance from a 401(k) plan may be transferred to a Traditional IRA provided the amount does not exceed the current maximum contribution limit for the IRA

28. A 1035 contract exchange may NOT take place in which of the following ways?

A. One annuity to another offered by a different company

B. One annuity to a life insurance policy issued by the same company

C. One insurance policy to another issued by a different company

D. One insurance policy to another issued by the same company

29. Julianne held 1,000 shares of ABC for 13 months before selling them for a loss of $1,000. If Julianne repurchases shares of ABC 23 days later, which of the following accurately describes the tax implications?

A. The loss is disallowed but is added to the cost basis of the new purchase

B. Julianne can be fined by the IRS

C. Julianne can be sued for tax fraud by the IRS

D. The loss is disallowed and regarded as having never taken place at all

30. If an investor wants to sell stock at a set price—or better—which of the following orders could be entered?

A. Sell-stop

B. Sell-stop-limit

C. Sell-limit

D. Short sale

31. A trust that may add part of Distributable Net Income (DNI) to the corpus is known as a:

A. Body trust

B. Complex trust

C. Simple trust

D. Unit trust

32. One of your investing clients is interested in building her net worth. Which of the following actions might help to achieve that goal?

     A. Paying off a credit card balance of $5,200 with a personal check

     B. Paying off a mortgage five years early

     C. Investing in growth & income mutual funds within a tax-deferred account

     D. All choices listed

33. Which of the following represents an inaccurate statement regarding Section 529 savings plans?

     A. Contributions are subject to gift tax limits

     B. The account owner can also be the beneficiary of the account

     C. They offer tax-deductible contributions for purposes of federal income tax

     D. Once every 12 months funds may be transferred to a different plan

34. Market timing is most closely related to:

     A. Tactical asset allocation

     B. Strategic asset allocation

     C. Growth investing

     D. Value investing

35. What is the Dow Jones Industrial Average?

     A. An electronic exchange similar to NASDAQ

     B. A large-cap value index

     C. A large-cap index

     D. A market-cap-weighted index of 50 stocks and bonds

36. Which of the following is an accurate statement of tax implications for various scenarios presented below?

     A. Inherited securities are taken over at the deceased's original cost basis if the market value has appreciated

     B. Gifted securities are taken over at the donor's original cost basis if the market value has appreciated

C. The recipient must claim receipt of any excess over the annual gift tax exclusion

D. An inherited security sold within 12 months leads to a short-term capital gain

37. A company with a 401(k) plan wants to be sure it successfully passes investment risk to the participants of the plan. In order to do so, which of the following would help the company?

A. Making sure the plan offers at least four equity portfolios

B. Making sure the plan offers at least three tax-exempt municipal bond portfolios

C. Assuring that all participants may purchase the company's stock for the plan

D. Making sure the plan offers at least three distinctly different portfolios

38. Your client is a single parent who wants to set up a tax-deferred account to fund her only son's education, but if the son decides not to go to school after high school graduation she does not want him to be able to receive the money at all. She should invest for this purpose through which of the following?

A. 529 plan

B. Mutual fund

C. Coverdell Education Savings Account

D. UTMA/UGMA account

39. As an agent of a broker-dealer, you know that one of your customers is a joint account with four account owners. You learn that one of the owners has died. Once proper paperwork is received, what will happen to the assets of this account if the account is held as "joint tenants in common"?

A. The deceased party's assets will revert equally to the other account owners

B. The deceased party's assets will revert to her estate

C. The deceased party's assets will revert to the other account owners as stipulated in the joint account agreement

D. The deceased party's assets will revert to her estate only if she died with a will in place

40. Which of the following is a true statement of margin accounts?

A. Options may not be purchased within margin accounts

B. Broker-dealers may require more than the initial Reg T requirement

C. Retirement accounts are typically established as margin accounts

D. Mutual funds may be purchased on margin

1. ANSWER: C

WHY: sell-stop orders are placed below the current market price for the security. A stop-limit order also names an execution price, while the stop (market) order simply is filled at the next available price.

2. ANSWER: A

WHY: owners are called members in an LLC, where no shareholder meetings are required—largely because there are no shareholders. Both forms of ownership provide protection to the owners.

3. ANSWER: C

WHY: the exam does ask a few questions that involve memorization. Individuals use Form 1040; trusts and estates use Form 1041; a corporation uses Form 1120; a partnership uses Form 1065.

4. ANSWER: B

WHY: the employer has to put a certain % into the employee's plan each year; the employee is also allowed to contribute.

5. ANSWER: B

WHY: the GP structure provides no protection against personal liability, and while it does leave owners with unlimited liability, that feature is not an advantage. Only the C-corporation leads to double taxation of dividends; partnerships, LLCs, sole proprietors, and S-corporations all enjoy "flow-through of income and expenses."

6. ANSWER: A

WHY: CAPM calculates expected return based on the fact that investors should expect both the riskless rate of return and a risk premium based on the beta of the stock.

7. ANSWER: A

WHY: rather than rule out any individual security, Modern Portfolio Theory tells us to manage the risk/reward of the portfolio as a whole. If securities are relatively uncorrelated, the portfolio should not experience huge drops in value across-the-board.

8. ANSWER: A

WHY: buy-stop orders are placed above the current market price; buy-limit orders are placed below the current market price.

9. ANSWER: C

WHY: the defined contribution plans allowing the largest annual contributions are: Keogh, Money Purchase, Profit Sharing, and the SEP-IRA.

10. ANSWER: D

WHY: value investors like stocks trading at low valuation ratios and high dividend yields. Value investors love to buy stocks trading at or below the book value—or even at a low multiple to the book value.

11. ANSWER: A

WHY: to protect against a drop in market value, this trader wants the right to sell the stock for a set price. Buying 8 puts would cover 800 shares; 10 puts would allow him to sell all 1,000 shares for the strike price.

12. ANSWER: B

WHY: a market maker buys from or sells to an investor—acting in a principal capacity. A firm acting in an agency capacity is arranging a trade as a broker for a commission. New issues involve investment banking, not market making.

13. ANSWER: C

WHY: even if the investment were flat, her purchasing power increased by 2 points when the CPI dropped by 2 points. Add the 1% gain on the investment, and she's up 3%.

14. ANSWER: A

WHY: she earns two interest payments of $15 each—$30 total. She makes $20 when the bond is called at $1,020. $50 divided by $1,000 equals a total return of 5%.

15. ANSWER: B

WHY: if we choose "risk tolerance," we're implying that we might actually go for that rate of return given an appropriate risk tolerance. No—we will not go for such an unrealistic rate of return. Rather, we'll explain that her time horizon is too short for such expectations.

16. ANSWER: C

WHY: he is actively managing the portfolio, which goes along with tactical asset allocation. He is rotating sectors. A passive manager using strategic asset allocation would only shift allocations based on the client, not the anticipated direction of the market.

17. ANSWER: D

WHY: taking ½ of the account would be a bit harsh, not that taking ½ of the RMD is especially pleasant. If the investor should have withdrawn $50,000, the penalty would be $25,000.

18. ANSWER: D

WHY: assume that capital gains distributions from mutual funds are long-term. If not, would every investor have an "initiation year" in which for them the gain is short-term? No—all shareholders get their share of the capital gains distribution, regardless of when they bought into the fund. If the investor buys shares in February and then sells shares in December—that would be a short-term capital gain.

19. ANSWER: C

WHY: if we believe markets are efficient, we don't try to time the markets—instead, we use indexing and passive management. If we are timing the markets and switching allocations based on predictions, we believe markets are not efficient and believe we can exploit these inefficiencies.

20. ANSWER: C

WHY: a non-qualified annuity purchased by an individual from an insurance/annuity company does not allow for deductions of the contributions into the account, but the workplace retirement plan called a Tax-Sheltered Annuity/403b plan does offer tax-deductible contributions…as does a 401(k) or 457 plan.

21. ANSWER: B

WHY: the money going into the plan was not taxed, so everything coming out of the account will be.

22. ANSWER: A

WHY: mutual funds generate dividends and interest payments used to cover all operating expenses. What's left is the net investment income that can be distributed to the shareholders. Capital gains would be far too unpredictable for purposes of making regular income distributions.

23. ANSWER: A

WHY: the plans are easy to set up, and the employer does not have to be especially generous, but any employer contributions immediately belong to the employee (immediate vesting). SIMPLE IRAs are for companies with no other retirement plan and no more than 100 employees. The contributions are tax-deductible.

24. ANSWER: C

WHY: her reinvestments are taxed, so she adds those amounts to her cost basis. She has invested $11,500 that has already been taxed, into 1,000 shares. $11.50 per share cost basis.

25. ANSWER: B

WHY: there are earnings of $25,000 here, and that is both taxable and subject to early withdrawal penalties. So, she is taxed on all of the $15,000 plus a 10% penalty on the withdrawal.

26. ANSWER: D

WHY: unlike with annuities, insurance policies don't get taxed on the first dollars coming out of the account automatically. The beneficiary receives the death benefit tax-free, but the value of the policy is included in the insured's estate.

27. ANSWER: B

WHY: the 401(k) money has to go to a pre-tax account, either an existing or newly created rollover IRA—not a Roth. The money transferred into the account has nothing to do with any contributions the individual might want to make for the year.

28. ANSWER: B

WHY: annuities can be switched for annuities. Life insurance can be switched for life insurance or an annuity. But an annuity cannot become a life insurance policy.

29. ANSWER: A

WHY: although the loss can't be used now, it is added to the cost basis of the new purchase. That way, it will be used when she sells the shares in the future.

30. ANSWER: C

WHY: if an investor wants to sell for a particular price—period—he enters a sell-limit order.

31. ANSWER: B

WHY: the simple trust pays out all DNI, while the complex trust can retain some income to add to the corpus/principal of the account.

32. ANSWER: C

WHY: removing a liability by removing an asset of equal value does not increase net worth. Net worth is increased when assets increase in value over time.

33. ANSWER: C

WHY: contributions to the plan are subject to gift tax limits, but the contributions are not deductible for purposes of federal income tax.

34. ANSWER: A

WHY: tactical asset allocation involves altering the percentages based on anticipated market moves.

35. ANSWER: C

WHY: the Dow would only be a "value index" if price-to-book or price-to-earnings ratios were taken into account. They are not—the index is just 30 stocks of very large companies including Microsoft, Walmart, Walt Disney, and American Express.

36. ANSWER: B

WHY: if the security has appreciated, the recipient only gets to step up the cost basis if the security was inherited—not received as a gift. The recipient does not have to claim anything when she receives a gift of stock—she just needs to record her cost basis for the day she ends up selling it. Inherited securities lead to long-term capital gains regardless of how soon they are sold.

37. ANSWER: D

WHY: the "safe harbor provisions" of ERISA 404c include a requirement that participants have at least three distinctly different investment options to choose from.

38. ANSWER: A

WHY: the 529 plan assets would remain under the client's control, not the son's. On the other hand, in a Coverdell the money must be distributed to the beneficiary by age 30, whether he goes to school or not. In an UTMA/UGMA account, the child would gain control at the age of adulthood or "majority." With a 529 plan, if the kid doesn't go to school, the parent could use the money, or she could just pay a 10% penalty plus ordinary income on any earnings above her contributions.

39. ANSWER: B

WHY: in a joint tenants with rights of survivorship account the assets would go equally to the other account owners, but with a joint tenants in common account the assets go to the deceased's estate. While it's better to die with a will in place, a probate judge can also appoint an administrator if the individual dies without one in place (intestate).

40. ANSWER: B

WHY: as with most rules, the initial Reg T requirement is a minimum. If the firm wants to require more than 50% down, that is just fine with the regulators. Options can be purchased within a margin account, but, as with mutual funds and IPO shares, they must be paid in full.

CHAPTER 4: Laws, Regulations, and Guidelines, Including Prohibition on Unethical Business Practices

These firms are **Broker-Dealers**:	These firms are **Investment Advisers**:
• Morgan Stanley	• Legg Mason Capital Management
• MetLife Securities	• Wells Capital Management
• Morgan Keegan	• Capital Research & Management Company
• Goldman Sachs	• Fidelity Capital Management
• Piper Jaffray	• Putnam Investment Management
• Charles Schwab	• Franklin Templeton
• TD Ameritrade	• Dreyfus Investment Advisors
• E*Trade Securities	• Barclays Capital
• NMIS	• Ariel Investments
• Northern Trust Securities	• Wellington Capital Management
• William Blair	
• American Funds Distributors	
• Janus Distributors	
• State Street Global Markets	

THE SECURITIES INDUSTRY

Many investors know the importance of investing but don't necessarily know how to approach it. Fortunately, there are financial services firms known as **investment advisers** out there who are happy to assist in exchange for a % of the client's account. The adviser might manage client accounts in exchange for, say, 1% of assets. Under that compensation arrangement if the client puts $1 million under the adviser's management, 1% would work out to be $10,000 a year to the adviser; more as the account value increases and/or the client adds more funds to the account.

That's a big difference from how the traditional stockbroker working for a broker-dealer gets paid. A stockbroker gets paid for generating activity. The broker/agent earns a commission when the customer buys a stock and then gets paid a commission when he sells the stock—regardless of whether the customer makes or loses money. But an investment adviser acting as a portfolio manager gets paid a percentage of the assets in the account. The client's $1 million account balance will pay the adviser $10,000 a year if they bill 1% of assets. But, if that account grows to $1.3 million, the adviser's fee rises to $13,000, and so on. On the other hand, if the adviser puts the client into a bunch of dogs and the account drops to $400,000, their paycheck drops right along with it, to $4,000. That's why many investors prefer to work with a fee-based investment adviser, knowing that their compensation is linked to the value of the investor's account rather than the number of trades executed in the account.

Most of the full-service financial firms can sign up clients either as brokerage customers or as advisory (fee-based) clients. If the client has a $10 million account and only likes to buy and sell a few times a year, she would almost certainly save money paying commissions in a brokerage account the few times she traded compared to 1% of $10 million every year—since that would be $100,000 a year in management fees. But, if the client believes in active portfolio management anyway, the advisory side could set him up with a **wrap account**, which bills a flat fee as a percentage of the account value for a professional to manage the account, and that might make more sense.

We'll dig deeper into these issues later. For now just understand that broker-dealers and the stockbrokers who work for them make money by executing buy and sell orders for securities. Investment advisers, on the other hand, don't get paid for executing securities transactions, and they don't sell securities to clients. Investment advisers are compensated for advising investors. It might seem strange that somebody actively trading the client's account is "advising" the client. I mean, isn't he doing a little more than just giving advice if he's buying and selling stocks as he sees fit? Yes, but "investment advice" is a legal definition that covers different types of business models, all of which have one thing in common—the professional's compensation comes from telling investors how to invest in securities or investing on their behalf.

So far, we've considered the advisers who manage client portfolios for a percentage of assets. Another type of investment adviser is the **financial planner**. A financial planner doesn't trade the investor's securities portfolio. Rather, the planner puts together detailed financial plans that may concern insurance needs, reducing taxes, estate planning, education funding, retirement planning—the whole financial picture. With this business model, the adviser would usually meet with the client once or maybe a few times a year, charging an hourly rate or a flat fee. $300 an hour would not be unheard of for a financial planner, or maybe $3,000 for a complete financial plan. Many planners earn certifications, but the only legal requirement is to register as an investment adviser before offering and delivering financial plans to investors. Usually registration requires passing the Series 65 or Series 66 exam, but financial planners with their CFP certification would simply have to register after receiving an exam waiver.

Quick question: did I just say that CFPs don't have to register as investment advisers or IARs? Not at all. They have to register. It's just that they usually receive a waiver from their state securities department to get out of taking the Series 65 exam.

The definition of investment adviser also includes professionals who issue reports/analyses on securities for compensation. Maybe you sell reports on technology stocks to portfolio managers that help them determine which securities to buy or when to buy and sell them. If so, you're probably an investment adviser, too.

In any case, you can probably guess that an **investment adviser representative** is an individual who represents an investment adviser. If he's a portfolio manager, or a salesman out wining and dining clients, he's probably an investment adviser representative (IAR) who needs to pass the exam and get registered. Do all individuals working for an investment adviser have to register? Not necessarily. But, if the individual working for an investment adviser helps to make recommendations to clients or sells the services of the firm, she has to register as an investment adviser representative. Or, if she supervises people who do that stuff, she has to be a registered investment adviser representative. On the other hand, the employees performing clerical work, what the law calls "ministerial" work, are not defined as "investment adviser representatives." So, the individual who makes the coffee, replaces the toner, and tells callers that Mr. Williams-is-at-lunch-would-you-like-to-go-to-voice-mail—that employee does not have to register.

Investment Adviser Representatives are registered employees of investment advisers who:

- manage accounts
- make recommendations
- determine recommendations
- sell services of firm
- supervise those who do any of the above

So, the investment adviser is the business that provides investment advisory services to its clients. It can be organized as a sole proprietor, an LLC, a corporation, etc. The individuals who represent investment advisers by bringing in or serving the firm's clients are called investment adviser representatives. Either way, investment advisers and investment adviser representatives are in the business of providing investment advice to their clients.

On the other hand, broker-dealers are in the securities transaction business. Besides helping people trade securities on the secondary market, broker-dealers also bring securities to investors for the first time on the primary market and raise money for their clients as investment bankers. You have probably heard the term "IPO" or "**initial public offering**." This is when investment bankers take a privately owned company and sell its shares to the public for the first time in order to raise millions or even billions of dollars for the issuer, and a few percentage points for the investment bankers as well.

Whether they're helping investors trade securities on the secondary market or raising capital for their clients on the primary market, broker-dealers are in the securities transaction business. They get paid because somebody wants to buy or sell securities. Their conduct is covered by the Securities Exchange Act of 1934, with its "know your customer" rule. Basically, as long as you are making suitable recommendations based on the information you have from the client, you are probably well within the rules of the brokerage business. Unlike investment advisers, broker-dealers don't have the **fiduciary duty** of loyalty spelled out in the Investment Advisers Act of 1940 and, therefore, don't have to provide as much disclosure of potential conflicts of interest.

If you're selling somebody a security, you're a salesperson/agent. If you're giving advice, you aren't selling products—you're investing the client's money on the client's behalf. And you therefore have a fiduciary/trustee relationship with that client, since, basically, they have opened up their purse to you.

How many people would you entrust with your life savings? Well, an investment adviser or IAR needs to be one of the few people to whom you would give that responsibility.

Broker-dealers can also help you invest, of course. You just need to understand that their motivation is to get you to buy and sell securities. Period. An investment adviser has to put the clients' needs ahead of their own, since they're investing the client's money in a way that is supposed to benefit only the client. Think of it this way—there is really no way to invest in securities without broker-dealers because these are the firms who can buy and sell securities and clear/settle the transactions involving bazillions of dollars every day the markets are open. Many investors find the broker-dealer model to be all they need. When it comes time to buy or sell securities, the investor pays some extra fees whether we call them commissions, sales charges, or markups. Broker-dealers sit across the table from the customer either pitching them investment products like mutual funds or talking them into buying or selling particular securities.

On the other hand, many investors want a professional to sit on the same side of the table with them and manage the portfolio on their behalf. Trades will still be executed by the broker-dealer with custody of the account, but the investment adviser will be entering them on the client's behalf, with the client's best interests in mind. To some folks this extra layer of investment advice is overkill, but to many others it is essential to have an experienced professional managing the account for a reasonable fee.

The large full-service firms often have a broker-dealer and an investment advisory business set up under the same parent company. That's fine, but the two entities are still separate from each other, with separate names, as well. Of course, whether the firm is an investment adviser or a broker-dealer, the securities regulators have the authority to crack down on those who violate securities laws and regulations. Let's start with the activities that can get the investment advisory side in hot water. Then, we'll examine the many things that can get the brokerage side of the business in trouble.

ETHICAL PRACTICES AND FIDUCIARY OBLIGATIONS

BUSINESS PRACTICES FOR INVESTMENT ADVISERS AND IARS

There are many ways that an investment adviser or investment adviser representative could end up losing their securities license. Operating as an IAR without bothering to pass the exam and register first, for example, would lead to regulatory problems. But the state securities regulators are primarily out to protect their residents from activities that are deceptive, manipulative, or dishonest in the securities industry. We will look in some detail at the model act known as "The Uniform Securities Act" throughout this chapter. This is how the model legislation announces its purpose from the start:

Relating to securities; prohibiting fraudulent practices in relation thereto; requiring the registration of broker-dealers, agents, investment advisers, and securities; and making uniform the law with reference thereto

So, we see that the Uniform *Securities* Act relates only to securities and that its first objective is to prohibit "fraudulent practices in relation to [securities]."

➢ Fraud

The people who pose a potential threat to the residents of any state include agents, broker-dealers, investment advisers, investment adviser representatives, plus all the entrepreneurs going around trying to raise money for their shaky little companies no one knows anything about. Whether registered in the industry or not, any person who is connected with the offer, sale, or purchase of any **security** is prohibited from making any misleading statements or leaving out important information in a way that is misleading. We're talking about the f-word here, people: **fraud**. Securities fraud is a financial crime in which someone misrepresents the truth in a way that takes advantage of the other side in connection to an investment in securities. For example, if an investment adviser inflated client account balances in order to overcharge them, this would be fraudulent. If an adviser sent out bogus account statements to conceal the fact that all client funds had long ago been converted to a fleet of Cadillac Escalades™, this would also operate as a fraud. Fraud can cause a person to end up losing their securities license (administrative action), getting sued (civil liability) and maybe even getting thrown in jail (criminal liability). The securities departments don't put the person in jail, but that's a technicality, since a court of law can always hand down a sentence including jail time and stiff monetary fines.

Let's take a look at a real-world example of an investment adviser who apparently defrauded investors in the "Garden State" of New Jersey and ended up looking at time in prison for her apparent misdeeds:

Office of The Attorney General, Anne Milgram, Attorney General

Division of Criminal Justice, Gregory Paw, Director

JACKSON WOMAN PLEADS GUILTY TO DEFRAUDING INVESTORS OF $641,000

TRENTON - Attorney General Anne Milgram and Criminal Justice Director Gregory A. Paw announced that an Ocean County woman pleaded guilty today to defrauding investors of more than $600,000 through a false investment scheme.

According to Director Paw, Zina A. Martin, 43, of Jackson, pleaded guilty today to second-degree securities fraud before Superior Court Judge James Den Uyl in Ocean County. Under the plea agreement, Martin faces a sentence of three to five years in state prison. In addition, Martin must pay restitution to her victims of $641,000.

During the plea hearing, Martin admitted that she represented to investors that their money would be placed within certain investment vehicles but, in fact, she used the funds for other purposes. An investigation by the New Jersey Bureau of Securities determined that Martin used the funds to pay business expenses, make payments to other investors, and pay personal expenses, including mortgage payments, monthly living expenses and the purchase of a Cadillac Escalade.

Martin solicited $641,000 from about 25 investors as sole owner and president of Kairos Financial Corporation, which had offices at 331 Newman Springs Road in Red Bank. The Bureau of Securities investigation determined that Martin distributed a brochure to investors describing six different investment funds called the "Kairos Funds," including average yearly returns for some of the funds. She also issued monthly statements informing investors of the amounts they purportedly held in each of the funds. In reality, the Kairos Funds were fictitious and investor monies were commingled in a brokerage account of Kairos Financial.

The case was investigated for the Bureau of Securities by Supervising Investigator Michael McElgunn, Investigator Richard Smullen and Chief of Enforcement Richard Barry. Deputy Attorney General Patrick Flor is prosecuting the case for the Division of Criminal Justice - Major Crimes Bureau and handled today's plea hearing.

In October 2007, the Bureau of Securities revoked the investment adviser registrations of both Martin and Kairos Financial.

You might have already assumed it's a violation to create pretend mutual funds in order to misappropriate money from investors. I mean, it's creative. It's just, you know, bad. It didn't involve guns or threats of violence, but people's property was wrongfully taken just the same. Then again, the securities regulators are not police officers. The regulators are administrative authorities concerned with granting, suspending, or revoking licenses in order to protect investors. When the activities go beyond unethical business practices and into the land of criminal offenses, the state securities regulators turn the case over to a criminal prosecutor. In the above press release, we see that the state securities department *also* took away this individual's license, but the larger story was that she was headed to prison after taking a plea bargain. That criminal case was handled by a different department than the one granting and revoking licenses to work in the securities investment industry.

And, I'm not implying that all acts of deception automatically lead to jail time. People in the brokerage and advisory industries make mistakes and suffer major lapses of judgment. Funds that were accidentally siphoned out of customer accounts by a rogue agent have been known to be promptly replaced by the employing broker-dealer, with that agent bounced from the business but nothing beyond that. In general, jail time is for those who make off with customer funds, leaving a mess too big for an employer to fix by settling with just one customer. And, when someone is creating little pretend securities as a ruse to take investors' money, prosecutors usually have mail fraud and wire fraud charges to file, as well, since false documents and statements would have been sent through the mail or over some electronic medium.

So, chances are you will make a few mistakes over your career. Chances also are that you will not decide to complete an IPO in a company that doesn't actually exist. Agents who make mutual fund recommendations that were a bit too aggressive are maybe suspended for a few weeks. Individuals who create schemes designed to wrongfully relieve investors of their property lose their licenses permanently, and then also may face criminal prosecution and lawsuits from those who were harmed.

> Conflicts of Interest

The most important thing to know about investment advisers and their IARs is that they are considered "fiduciaries" who must avoid or at least disclose all conflicts of interest to clients. The SEC lays it all out at their excellent website www.sec.gov, which describes the fiduciary obligation like so:

As an investment adviser, you are a "fiduciary" to your advisory clients. This means that you have a fundamental obligation to act in the best interests of your clients and to provide investment advice in your clients' best interests. You owe your clients a duty of undivided loyalty and utmost good faith. You should not engage in any activity in conflict with the interest of any client, and you should take steps reasonably necessary to fulfill your obligations. You must employ reasonable care to avoid misleading clients and you must provide full and fair disclosure of all material facts to your clients and prospective clients. Generally, facts are "material" if a reasonable investor would consider them to be important. You must eliminate, or at least disclose, all conflicts of interest that might incline you — consciously or unconsciously — to render advice that is not disinterested. If you do not avoid a conflict of interest that could impact the impartiality of your advice, you must make full and frank disclosure of the conflict. You cannot use your clients' assets for your own benefit or the benefit of other clients, at least without client consent. Departure from this fiduciary standard may constitute "fraud" upon your clients.

You may have noticed that regulators do enjoy double negatives such as the phrase, "to render advice that is not disinterested." As on the exam, you occasionally have to interpret such language back to a more natural form that you can work with. And this phrase is actually pretty simple. The advice needs to be disinterested, so anything that could make it "not disinterested" needs to be disclosed. If I'm buying a mutual fund for my advisory client because of the suitability and the excellent track record of performance and low expenses, I'm probably acting as a fiduciary. If I'm buying the mutual funds that pay me the best compensation as an agent or broker-dealer on the side without disclosing that to the client, my advice is "not disinterested," and I may be receiving some registered mail from the regulators very soon. Also notice the "consciously or unconsciously" phrase. An adviser may unconsciously favor advice and actions that benefit the adviser and must, therefore, be mindful of situations that may lead to that problem. He may be the most honest person in the world, but if he's getting a commission when putting his advisory clients' assets into particular securities, the advice is "not disinterested."

Some students in my classes seem to think they'll take care of such problems simply by continuing to be the same trustworthy, decent, hard-working sales professionals they've always been. No, the SEC is saying that you still have to consider, identify, and then disclose the potential conflict of interest, even if you think you're far too honest to stoop to such self-serving activities as overcharging clients or favoring mutual funds that pay the highest 12b-1 fees. Whether it is or not, you must tell your clients that this may be a conflict of interest or this could potentially lead to a conflict of interest. That is how advisers must communicate with their clients.

Clients of investment advisers have a right to expect all investment advice to be given objectively—the adviser doesn't stand to benefit when the client accepts the advice. Rather, the adviser is just giving the client the best advice they can and will charge the same amount whether the client buys a mutual fund, a stock, a bond, or even nothing at this time. We demand that investment advisers remain impartial, disinterested, objective advisers. They get compensated for doing just that. So, if a recommendation to a client would lead to a benefit to the adviser (on top of the advisory fee) if the client accepts it, we have a potential conflict of interest. The regulators and the courts have determined long ago that a failure to disclose any conflict of interest to an advisory client is a fraud/deceit, period. Therefore, the following conflicts must be carefully and clearly disclosed to advisory clients. Notice I didn't say the investment adviser can't *do* it; just that he has to clearly disclose the practice to his advisory clients. And that's why I'm presenting "conflicts of interest" as a separate but related section to "fraud" here rather than presenting the following actions as subheadings to "fraud," as if they are *automatically* fraudulent. They are not. The following actions are only fraudulent if you fail to properly disclose them to your advisory clients.

Acting as Principal

Full-service firms often have an investment advisory business and a broker-dealer business. So, when the investment advisory business is managing client accounts for a percentage of assets, should they just go ahead and buy the securities directly from the affiliated broker-dealer? Does that sound objective? Any chance that some of the trades this month might have been executed to help the affiliated broker-dealer more than it helped the advisory clients? Whose interests is the adviser looking out for here? In other words, the *interests* of the client are to be placed ahead of the adviser's, but, suddenly, the adviser's and the client's interests may be in *conflict.* Therefore, this conflict of interest must be disclosed.

In order to execute a **principal transaction** the adviser would have to disclose this fact and get the client's written consent before "completion of the transaction," which is settlement of the trade—when securities and cash have been formally exchanged between the buy and sell sides of the transaction. To act as a principal just means the adviser will either sell the security from the inventory of their related broker-dealer to the customer or buy it for inventory from the customer. It's okay to do it, as long as the potential conflict of interest is disclosed and the customer's written consent is given before the deal is completed.

Now, just in case the exam feels like turning up the heat, what I just told you only applies when the investment adviser is recommending the security. If this is an "unsolicited" order, then it was the client's idea, and now we have a completely different situation. It's when the investment adviser is recommending that you buy a security (or using discretion to buy it) that we need the disclosure. Also note that recommending a security and using discretion to purchase it on behalf of the client would be the same thing for the purposes of this rule.

Agency Cross Transaction

Another example of where the adviser will benefit as a result of the advice is called an **agency cross transaction**. Here, the firm is buying 1,000 shares of ABC for your account, and, as it turns out, their related/affiliated broker-dealer will act as a broker between you and the seller.

Excuse me? So, should you buy these 1,000 shares because they're a good investment, or because the adviser likes to help the affiliated broker-dealer pocket commissions in addition to the percentage-based advisory fee assessed on your account? That's what we mean by a "conflict of interest"—any situation where the adviser might be financially tempted to talk you into something that benefits the adviser, as opposed to giving objective advice. It might only be a potential conflict of interest, but the fact is that businesses like to make money, so there's just the slight chance that the advice to buy or sell the security might be tainted by the adviser's financial incentive to get the client to accept the advice. Now, the firm might not even charge the advisory client a commission, but if they're charging the other side (the brokerage client) a commission, that could be the incentive that makes their advice less than objective.

So, as usual, the adviser would need to disclose the potential conflict of interest in such a case, get the advisory client's written consent by completion/settlement of the trade, and at least once per year send a statement itemizing all the "agency cross transactions" effected on behalf of the client. And, the brokerage customer's transaction has to be unsolicited—the adviser and broker-dealer cannot convince the brokerage customer to buy or sell to the advisory client. It's just that the transaction is suitable for the advisory client's account, and there is a customer of the broker-dealer who wants to buy or sell that particular security.

Notice that even though broker-dealers and investment advisers are different business models, most well-known financial services firms are both advisers and broker-dealers. They charge some clients commissions and markups when they broker and deal securities. They act as investment advisers for others, charging a percentage of assets. So, for these first two examples of potential conflicts of interest, we are saying, basically, that your investment adviser would also like to work the broker-dealer side of the business. If they act as a dealer/principal on the transaction, they benefit by either selling you a security at a high price (markup) or buying one of yours at a low price (markdown). If they act as a broker on the transaction, they benefit by charging you a commission. Either way, the financial benefit they receive when you accept their advice might be tainting their objectivity. Did your adviser buy 1,000 shares of ABC for your account because it's a good investment, or because he'd like to make a commission or markup for the affiliated broker-dealer? Very possibly the former, but how can you decide if you don't have all the facts?

Full disclosure. That is probably the most important two-word phrase in all of the major securities Acts.

Additional Compensation for Directed Brokerage

If the investment adviser charging an asset-based fee is also a broker-dealer, they might want to act as a dealer/principal when the customer takes the advice to buy or sell a security, or they might want to act as an agent/broker when the customer takes the advice. Many advisers are not broker-dealers, though. Rather, they are very independent types who manage the accounts but let a completely unaffiliated broker-dealer hold the clients' assets and execute all the trades. Firms such as Charles Schwab and TD Ameritrade are two who reach out to such independent RIAs to provide custodial and clearing services. If I wanted to, I could take and pass the Series 65 again, then register as an investment adviser in Illinois or Colorado. If so, I would get my clients to grant me the authority to place trades in their account (discretion), but TD Ameritrade, the folks who currently have custody of my various IRAs and taxable accounts, would have custody of my client accounts, too. They would execute all the trades that I enter on my clients' behalf and would send account statements to the clients.

So, as a businessman, maybe I work out a deal with TD Ameritrade to provide some sort of economic benefit to me or my firm in exchange for letting them have custody of my client assets. Illegal? Hardly. But if the investment adviser is receiving any economic benefit from the broker-dealer in exchange for maintaining custody and/or executing securities transactions for the advisory clients, this needs to be disclosed to clients. As the SEC told us, "You cannot use your clients' assets for your own benefit or the benefit of other clients, at least without client consent." If anyone can imagine how "client consent" could be obtained without first providing disclosure, I'm not sure I follow. Right? If the client doesn't even know about it, there is no way he or she could have consented.

Even if the economic benefit is considered soft-dollar compensation that comes in the form of research services or computer software aiding the adviser, it would have to be disclosed to clients as a potential conflict of interest. Note that advisers can receive certain forms of soft-dollar compensation as long as they disclose the practice; however, the following forms of compensation are not allowed to be accepted by broker-dealers:

- Furniture and office equipment
- Salaries or overhead
- Vacations
- Cell phones

12b-1 Fees

Investment advisers and their IARs often also have a Series 6 or 7 license, allowing them to get compensated for selling mutual funds and variable annuities. If an adviser or an IAR is recommending mutual funds and annuities to their clients, they need to disclose the conflict of interest here—what conflict? Their advice is not objective if it leads to extra compensation, right? A 12b-1 fee is a form of regular compensation that the salesperson receives as long as the client stays invested in the mutual fund, and some funds pay upfront based on the sales charge on a front-end loaded fund (A-share). So, as NASAA indicates on their website, an investment adviser must disclose the fact that "the adviser is receiving transaction-based compensation, including 12b-1 or other marketing fees, related to securities recommended to its clients."

Again, did they recommend that you purchase this particular growth-and-income fund because it's an excellent investment opportunity, because it's an excellent opportunity for them to make 12b-1 fees, or maybe a little bit of both? See, when the adviser provides proper disclosure of potential conflicts of interest, the investor then has a chance to decide such important answers for herself.

Holds a Position in the Security Recommended

When a stock trades on the OTC market, it is called a NASDAQ stock if it's big and important enough to quote regularly over NASDAQ. The little, less important ones that aren't worth quoting all the time, trade on the "OTC Bulletin Board" or "Pink Sheets." These are often illiquid markets, which means that any large buy or sell order tends to shoot the stock price way up or way down. Therefore, if the investment adviser happens to own, say, 10,000 shares of some thinly traded Bulletin Board stock, they would benefit if they could get about 100 clients to put in buy orders. In fact, that might be the main reason they recommend the stock, which would be in direct conflict to their "fiduciary duty" to the client—to put the client's needs first. The stock recommended should be recommended only because it benefits the client. If the purchase of the stock would also benefit the adviser, that potential conflict of interest needs to be disclosed ahead of time. So investment advisers have to disclose that they may buy and sell the same securities that are bought and sold for client accounts. Personally, I would prefer that my adviser had some skin in the game before putting me into a large stock position, but that's just me. The regulators, as always, demand full and fair disclosure of all the important/material facts.

Just the way they roll.

Trade Allocations

Portfolio managers aren't generally buying different stocks for different clients. Generally, a portfolio manager has a portfolio model that all clients go into, and the adviser purchases what are called "bunched trades" and then allocates the big bunch of, say, ORCL or IBM shares to various accounts. As the SEC says, "An adviser may defraud its clients when it fails to use the average price paid when allocating securities to accounts participating in bunched trades and fails to adequately disclose its allocation policy. This practice violates the Advisers Act if securities that were purchased at the lowest price or sold at the highest price are allocated to favored clients without adequate disclosure." The SEC also says, "An adviser may defraud its clients by waiting to decide how to allocate a trade among its clients' accounts based on subsequent market movements. The concern is that the adviser could allocate the trade to favored clients if the price movement was favorable and allocate the trade to other accounts if the price movement was unfavorable. This practice is known as 'cherry-picking,' and violates the Advisers Act."

Also, there is nothing more exciting than an IPO of some company that most people are convinced is the new-new thing. But advisers need to make sure they have a policy on allocating IPO shares—especially "hot" ones, or those that are in great popular demand—and disclose any conflicts of interest here. As the SEC says, "An adviser may defraud its clients when it disproportionately allocates hot initial public offerings (IPOs) to favored accounts, and does not adequately disclose this practice to all clients. For example, allocations of IPOs may be inequitable when the following types of accounts are favored: proprietary accounts; accounts that pay performance-based fees; accounts that have relatively poor performance; and new investment companies (in order to boost performance to attract additional assets)."

Disclose or Abstain

Usually, disclosing potential conflicts of interest ahead of time and obtaining the client's consent will take care of the problem; however, sometimes the conflict is so great that the IA must simply abstain from action. What would be so bad that mere disclosure would not take care of the problem? How about if the portfolio manager manages the investment account (the proprietary accounts mentioned a few lines earlier) of the investment advisory business he works for? In this account there are 1 million shares of XYZ common stock. XYZ common stock has also been placed in many client accounts, based on the portfolio manager's discretion. Well, one morning the portfolio manager reads in *The Wall Street Journal* that XYZ's CEO is going to be indicted for fraud, and the company is also going to restate earnings for the past five years, so he unloads the 1 million shares the firm is holding before starting to sell the shares he's put in client portfolios.

Not a chance. Advisers are fiduciaries, who must put the needs of their clients first. This obvious conflict of interest is a no-no, and no amount of disclosure would make it okay. The adviser should have simply abstained from this self-serving activity. I mean, isn't the adviser the same genius who put XYZ stock in the client portfolios? Why should the captain of the ship get to be the one to bail out with the only lifeboat on board when the iceberg looms up out of the fog? You steered us into this mess, Captain, and you can go down with the rest of us.

Compensation Based on Capital Gains, Appreciation

Investment advisers performing "continuous, supervisory management services" get paid a flat fee. Maybe they charge 1% of the assets. That's a great incentive for the adviser. One percent of $150,000 is nice, but one percent of $200,000 is even nicer. So, the percentage stays flat and the adviser's compensation only grows if the customer's assets grow.

Sounds like a great way to compensate an investment adviser, right? Well, some advisers would prefer to just take a share of the paper gains or the actual profits made from trading. Every time the adviser buys at 10 and sells at 18, the adviser gets a piece of that capital gain. What about the rest of the stocks? Who cares? We had one big gain, and I, as your adviser, demand my cut. Those other stocks didn't work out the way we figured—what can I tell you?

See, if a client were to pay an adviser with a share of capital gains, the adviser could make a huge profit on one lucky stock pick even if the rest of the account goes down miserably. That might be hard to see, so let's drill down a bit. Say you invested $100,000 with an investment adviser who said he was not going to charge any ongoing fees; rather, he would just take half of any trading profits/capital gains. Sounds darned nice of him at first, but let's say he puts you into 10 stocks with $10,000 invested in each. One stock goes up from $10,000 to $18,000, and you sell it for an 80% profit. You make a short-term capital gain of $8,000, and the adviser takes $4,000. You get $4,000, which could be taxed somewhere between 25% and 39.6% at the federal level, plus a few more percentage points at the state level. Basically, your after-tax gain is going to be about $2,500. Now, the adviser tells you to just be patient, just wait until those 9 other stocks go up. Only, they never do. You wait and wait, and wait some more, but not only do the other stocks not begin to rise on cue, they also begin to spiral downward. The account drops from $90,000 to $60,000 in a hurry, then slowly drifts down to $36,000, at which point you tell him to sell everything and send you a check for what's left.

So, how did you do in this case? You put down $100,000 and are left with $36,000 plus an after-tax profit of about $2,500. You're down close to 62%! How did the adviser do? He made a fast profit of

$4,000 with absolutely no risk to himself. Maybe it's not such a great way to compensate your adviser after all.

Or, maybe dependable, blue chip growth and income stocks are perfectly suitable for a client's portfolio. Unfortunately, if the investment adviser gets paid on a share of capital gains/appreciation, why bother with the slow-and-steady stocks that might not go anywhere for a while? Regardless of the client's risk tolerance, why not pick 20 of the most speculative stocks trading on the OTC Bulletin Board? So, offering to share the gains or just the capital appreciation (paper gains) with an investment adviser entices the adviser to take on much bigger risks and often puts the adviser's interests in conflict with those of the client.

And that's why advisers cannot be compensated as a share of capital gains as a general rule. Advisers managing a portfolio, as a general rule, should be compensated as a percentage of assets over a specified time period. If the portfolio manager bills 1% of assets annually, then at the end of each financial quarter, the asset value is multiplied by .25% and that is billed to the account. But investment advisers generally cannot be compensated as a share of capital gains or capital appreciation, or receive a bonus for performance.

The Uniform Securities Act then clarifies that this rule "does not prohibit an investment advisory contract which provides for compensation based upon the total value of a fund averaged over a definite period, or as of definite dates or taken as of a definite date." Maybe "clarifies" was an overstatement. The lawyers who drafted that simply mean that while an adviser can't share the gains on individual stocks or take a percentage of the amount that the account "went up," the firm can bill the client based on the average account balance over a certain period of time or bill a percentage of assets as of, say, the end of each financial quarter, or on the last day the NYSE is open for the calendar year. Later, we'll see that this is the general rule, but that sophisticated clients actually can pay the adviser as a share of capital gains or pay a performance bonus to the adviser. But, let's save that for later.

Assignment of Contract

The prohibition against **assignment of contract** means that an adviser cannot sell or transfer a customer's contract to another party without the client's consent. Wouldn't you be ticked if you called up your advisory firm and found out that since your account balance fell below a certain minimum, they just sold it to a money manager in Missoula, Montana? That's why the contract between the investment adviser and the client can only be passed off or "assigned" to another party with the written consent of the client, and the contract must state that fact. Did you get that? Not only would the investment adviser get in trouble for assigning the contract to another party without the client's consent, but if their contract with the client forgot to stipulate that this is not allowed, that would also get them in trouble, even if they never assigned any contracts. The Uniform Securities Act states:

> "...that no assignment of the contract may be made by the investment adviser without the consent of the other party to the contract."

The Act also says:

> "...that the investment adviser, if a partnership, shall notify the other party to the contract of any change in the membership of the partnership within a reasonable time after the change."

Notification of Change in Partnership Structure

The point directly above means that if the advisory firm is organized as a partnership, whenever one of the partners withdraws or dies—or a new partner is admitted—the firm must inform all clients in a reasonable time frame that the partnership structure has changed. Why? Maybe you're a client because of Jenkins and never particularly cared for Williams or Sonoma, so if Jenkins leaves Williams, Jenkins, and Sonoma Wealth Management Partners, LP, maybe it's time for you to go, too. It doesn't matter in this case if the change was due to a partner with a majority or minority interest. Just disclose the change in ownership to clients promptly.

A related issue is "assignment of contract" as it relates to a change of ownership. If a minority partner is admitted, withdraws, or dies, even though the partnership must inform its clients of that fact in a timely manner, that is not considered to be an "assignment of contract." In other words, your investment adviser has not changed so drastically that the account is now being handled by another party. The contract didn't get assigned by ABC to XYZ, nor did ABC suddenly become XYZ. It's just that ABC has a slightly different partnership structure now. On the other hand, if the change in partners involves a majority owner being admitted or withdrawing, that would require the clients to sign new advisory contracts. If the firm didn't do that, they would have assigned the clients' contracts in violation of securities law. The same applies to an adviser owned as an LLC—a change in the managing members must be announced to clients promptly, but there would be no assignment unless a majority ownership stake were involved. Also, if an adviser organized as a corporation sells or even pledges a majority of the corporate stock to another party, that would also = assignment of contract. And, again, a client's advisory contract cannot be assigned; rather, a new contract would have to be executed between the client and the other adviser.

Before we move on, recall that both state and federal securities laws require advisory contracts to provide at least three things in writing:

- The adviser shall not be compensated for performance (except in certain cases)
- No assignment of contract is allowed without client consent
- If the adviser is a partnership, clients will be notified of any change in the partnership structure

➤ Custody of Client Assets

If fraud is the f-word, **custody** is the c-word. What's the big deal? Think "Bernie Madoff." How was he able to take clients' money? The clients, unfortunately, allowed him to maintain custody of their assets through an affiliated broker-dealer. Therefore, Bernie, the quote-unquote "investment adviser," was able to send out the account statements that showed his clients exactly what he felt they would believe, for years—even when it appears that no investing was actually taking place! So, it makes me nervous when the adviser, who gets paid as a percentage of client assets, can determine or report what those assets are worth without any independent oversight. Some states don't allow it, and good for them. Much of the fraud that takes place in the advisory business could be avoided if investors simply refused to give their investment adviser control of the account assets. I'm talking about small-time operators there, as opposed to large full-service financial firms that have a bank, a broker-dealer, an investment adviser, and maybe an insurance company all under the same roof. I'm saying, don't give your money to some guy you just met through a friend of a friend if you have any interest in getting the money back. On the other hand, if a large investment adviser is an affiliate of a large bank or broker-dealer, then custody would be a very natural thing for the adviser to have. Still, there would have to be an outside auditing firm providing that independent oversight I mentioned earlier, with a special report provided to the SEC.

So, custody is a very big deal. Most small advisers avoid taking custody of client assets, while the large firms connected to broker-dealers and/or banks do it, but with a lot of oversight. An investment adviser is considered to have custody of client assets if the adviser is either holding the funds/securities or has the ability to appropriate (get his hands on) them. If the adviser has the ability to automatically deduct money from the client's account or write checks out of the account, the adviser is considered to have custody of client assets. Or, if the adviser has an ownership stake in the broker-dealer who maintains custody, the adviser is also considered to have custody of client assets. Or, if the adviser is the general partner in a limited partnership or a managing member of an investment LLC, the adviser is considered to have custody. The Uniform Securities Act (state law) says that before taking custody, the adviser first has to check with the state securities Administrator to see if there is a rule prohibiting custody of client assets. If so, they don't take custody. If there's no rule against it, the adviser can take custody so long as they notify the Administrator in writing. So, what if there's no rule against taking custody, and the adviser, in fact, takes custody but fails to inform the Administrator?

The adviser screwed up.

Maintaining custody is an awesome responsibility, and it requires the adviser to maintain higher minimum net worth, to provide an audited balance sheet to the regulators and to clients, and the adviser even has to pay a CPA to come in and audit the books once a year in a surprise audit. If the CPA can't make sense of all the securities and cash positions on the "books and records," they have to notify the Administrator promptly in order to get the firm in trouble. So, the real point of "custody" is that most advisers avoid it like the plague. They're advisers, not banks, right?

The exam might ask what the adviser should do if he receives a check from a client payable to a third party and does not want to be considered to have custody of client assets. First, the "third party" had better truly be an independent party and not an affiliate of the adviser. Second, to avoid the adviser being deemed to have custody, the check must be forwarded to the third party within three business days of receipt, and the adviser must keep records of what happened. Also, if the adviser inadvertently receives client securities in the mail, they must be returned to the sender within three business days. As long as the adviser keeps records as to what happened with the check and/or the securities, they will avoid being deemed to have custody. Therefore, they don't need to maintain higher net worth, update their registration information (Form ADV), or have the annoying and expensive CPA audit.

Since few advisers want to keep books and records as accurate as a bank's, most use qualified custodians for their clients' funds and securities. If the exam asks about qualified custodians, remember this bullet-point list:

- Banks and Savings Associations
- Registered Broker-Dealers (Custodial Broker-Dealers)
- Registered Futures Commission Merchants

- Foreign Financial Institutions

And, if we're talking about mutual fund shares, the IA uses the transfer agent, which is the party holding custody of investors' mutual fund shares. That doesn't mean there are large stacks of paper certificates for all the shares of a large mutual fund, but the transfer agent has to keep the ownership records electronically, which is just as large a responsibility.

The NASAA website also states:

> NOTE: because the qualified custodian needs to be independent, there should not be any affiliation between the investment adviser and the qualified custodian through any direct or indirect common control relationship.

> When the investment adviser uses a qualified custodian, the adviser must notify the client immediately in writing of the qualified custodian's name, address, and manner in which the funds or securities are maintained when the account is opened. If the adviser opens accounts for a client with more than one custodian, the client must be notified of all qualified custodian locations. Prompt notification to the client in writing following any changes to the client's account information also is required.

And then continues with:

Advisers who automatically deduct management fees from the client account held by the custodian do have custody, but they can avoid maintaining higher net worth or having the CPA audit if they follow "certain safeguards." This means that the adviser must get the client's written authorization to bill the custodian directly, and the adviser must provide both the custodian and the client with a **billing statement** showing how they arrived at their fee. Do they have custody? Yes. Do they have to deal with the higher minimum financial requirements? No. Will the exam get this detailed? Maybe. Will I stop interviewing myself now? Yes.

If the exam asks about **account statements**, those will be sent from the custodian to the client and must be sent at least quarterly; however, it is still up to the investment adviser to send billing statements to the client. Account statements show the securities positions in the account and their most recent market values, plus any dividends and interest received, purchases and sales of securities, deposits and withdrawals of cash over the period. A billing statement, on the other hand, is just an invoice showing the adviser's management fee and how they arrived at it. Since the adviser has a fiduciary duty to the client to make sure that those account statements are being sent by the custodian, it's a good idea to ask the custodian to send a duplicate to the adviser.

For more information on custody, visit www.nasaa.org and read the Q & A as well as the NASAA Model Rule on Custody.

> ➤ Disclosing Identity, Affairs of Clients

If an advisory firm is trying to land new clients, it would probably be tempting to show prospects what the firm has done for existing clients, disclosing the identity, affairs, or investments of their clients, especially the rich and famous ones.

Yes, well, the existing clients—as well as the securities regulators—would probably have a problem with that. The only way the firm can disclose the identity or the financial matters of its clients is if the clients give permission, or if the firm is forced to turn over the information by court order or a subpoena from a securities regulator.

> ➤ Advertisements

An advertisement for an investment adviser is defined by the Securities and Exchange Commission as

any notice, circular, letter or other written communication addressed to more than one person, or any notice or other announcement in any publication or by radio or television, which offers (1) any analysis, report, or publication concerning securities, or which is to be used in making any determination as to when to buy or sell any security, or which security to buy or sell, or (2) any graph, chart, formula, or other device to be used in making any determination as to when to buy or sell any security, or which security to buy or sell, or (3) any other investment advisory service with regard to securities.

Basically, whatever the media he uses, an adviser is creating an advertisement if he addresses more than one person concerning his advisory services. Advertisements for investment advisers must be fair and accurate. An adviser may not use testimonials from satisfied clients. I guess they can't use testimonials from dissatisfied clients, either, though, of course, they wouldn't want to pay somebody big money to go on television and rip the heck out of them. The adviser can list past stock picks provided they don't imply that future results are somehow implied or guaranteed, and if the adviser lists past stock picks, they have to include ALL recommendations—winners and losers—over the same period, which must be at least one year. Because it would be misleading to talk about your 100% winners over the past week, right? Especially if you conveniently failed to bring up the 100% losers. If the actual picks aren't provided, it needs to be clear that a list will be provided upon written request without charge or obligation.

Also, if the adviser's stock picks are up 50%, how does that compare to the market in general? If the S&P gained 52% and this guy's stock picks gained 50%, I'd be better off knowing the whole story, right? If the recommendations listed pertain only to a select group of the adviser's clients, this needs to be made clear. It also needs to be clear whether the performance figures are including the IA's management fees (deducted from the returns, right?).

"If the advertisement claims that any graph, chart, formula or other device being offered will assist any person in making his own decisions, the advertisement must prominently disclose the limitations thereof and the difficulties with respect to its use." If the adviser offers "free services with no obligation," those services had better actually be free, with, sure enough, no obligation. In general, IA advertisements need to go to great lengths to avoid misleading prospects and clients. And, any performance claims made by the adviser need to be backed up by the "books and records" required to be kept by the firm.

Now, as exciting as this chapter and book have been up to now, I would like to raise the excitement level another notch by showing you that this stuff does not just exist in the so-called "test world." Most of what I'm telling you is as real-world as a heart attack. In fact, in my own fine state of Illinois, the securities Administrator recently cracked down on an investment adviser who was kind enough to exemplify many testable points that we just finished discussing. Let's take a look at how some of this regulatory stuff works out in the real world.

STATE OF ILLINOIS

SECRETARY OF STATE

SECURITIES DEPARTMENT

_____)

IN THE MATTER OF: ROBERT WILLIAM ESCH) No.

DBA WHITEMOUNTAIN FINANCIAL) 0300042

_____)

CONSENT ORDER

TO THE RESPONDENT: Robert William Esch

DBA WhiteMountain Financial

539 Troy Plaza

Troy, Illinois 62294

C/O Charles J. Northrup

Sorling, Northrup, Hanna,

Cullen & Cochran, Ltd

Attorneys at Law

607 East Adams Street, Suite 800

Springfield, Illinois 62705

WHEREAS, Robert William Esch DBA WhiteMountain Financial on January 12, 2005 executed a certain Stipulation To Entry Of Consent Order (the "Stipulation"), which hereby is incorporated by reference herein.

WHEREAS, by means of the Stipulation, the Respondent has admitted to the jurisdiction of the Secretary of State and service of the Notice of Hearing in this matter and the Respondent has consented to the entry of this Consent Order.

WHEREAS, the Secretary of State, by and through his designated representative, the Securities Director, has determined that the matter related to the aforesaid formal hearing may be dismissed without further proceeding.

WHEREAS, the Respondent has acknowledged that the allegations contained in paragraph seven (7) of the Stipulation shall be adopted as the Secretary of State's Findings of Fact as follows:

1. At all times relevant, the Respondent was an Illinois registered Investment Adviser and Investment Adviser Representative pursuant to Section 8 of the Illinois Securities Law of 1953, 815 ILCS 5/1 et seq. (the "Act").

2. That from on or about January 2003 to on or about July 15, 2004 the Respondent advertised, operated and managed an investment management system under the name of the Super T Asset Management System and had about 25 persons participating in the system including the Respondent and some of the Respondent's family members.

3. The Super T Asset Management System was advertised and described to clients and prospective clients ("clients") as an investment advisory program in which the client would invest a minimum of $25,000 to be managed by the Respondent for a management fee of .75% of assets under management or a minimum of $250 each half year. Additionally, clients were told that their investment would be invested all in cash or all in one stock of the Respondent's choice. In later contracts, the phrase "all one stock" was replaced with "all one security" or "all one investment."

4. As part of the Super T Asset Management System, clients entered into an investment advisory contract with the Respondent in which they agreed to open brokerage accounts with a third party discount brokerage firm and give authority to the Respondent to execute transactions in these accounts on their behalf. Pursuant to such authority the Respondent executed buy and sell transactions of the security SPY, an exchange traded fund in the form of a Unit Investment Trust listed on the American Stock Exchange.

5. The Respondent mailed, delivered or caused to be delivered to clients advertising material which included performance measurement figures and/or charts for the Super T Asset Management System.

6. The Respondent violated the Illinois Securities Act and its Rules and Regulations in the following matter.

7. The advertising material referenced in paragraph 5 above contained performance measurements without complying with United States Securities and Exchange Commission Rule 206(4)-1 of the Rules and Regulations Under the Investment Advisers Act of 1940.

8. Additionally, the advertising material was misleading or false because: (a) it did not disclose that the past performance measurements for the Super T Asset Management System were not based upon actual trades but were based solely upon hypothetical recommendations and transactions; (b) failed to disclose that the percentage returns quoted in the material were before any fees paid or transactions costs and that actual returns would be lower; (c) failed to disclose that a quoted annualized rate of return was hypothetical and based upon a projection of a rate of return from 3-4 months and not upon an actual annualized rate of return; and (d) falsely misrepresented that the Super T Asset Management System was a registered or trademarked system when in fact it was not.

9. Failed to disclose material information to clients by: (a) failing to disclose that management fees were negotiable and that some clients were paying a reduced fee or had their fees waived by the Respondent; (b) failing to disclose that the minimum investment amount of $25,000 in the Super T Asset Management System was negotiable and some clients had invested less; (c) failing to disclose that the security SPY was an Exchange Traded Fund and a Unit Investment Trust and not a stock; and (d) failing to disclose that some participants in the Super T Asset Management System were relatives of the Respondent and were not paying advisory fees and/or had invested less than the minimum investment amount of $25,000.

10. Respondent entered into some investment advisory contracts with clients which: (a) did not include terms stating that the contract could not be assigned without the consent of the other party; (b) did not reflect that the minimum investment amount had been modified by previous agreement of the parties; and/or (c) identified the incorrect name of the client/party to the contract.

11. For some clients, the Respondent was accepting fees of over $500 and six or more months in advance but was not complying with Illinois Securities Department Rule 844 and in one case the Respondent billed the client an incorrect fee amount resulting in an overcharge to the client of 2.5 times the correct amount.

12. The Respondent provided to clients forms which he requested the client to fill out which stated at the bottom of the forms that: a) "This form is required by the Illinois Securities Department. Thank you for your cooperation."; or (b) "The information requested on this form is required by the Illinois Securities Department. Your cooperation is appreciated." When in fact neither the form nor the information was required by the Illinois Securities Department.

13. Filing a Form ADV with the Department which contained misleading or inaccurate information or omitted material information.

14. That Rule 130.844 of the Rules and Regulations under the Illinois Securities Act, 14 Admin Code 130.100 et seq., provides, inter alia, that each registered investment adviser which accepts prepayment of fees in excess of $500.00 per client and six (6) or more months in advance shall file [with the Department] a statement of financial condition (balance sheet) and interim financial statement, in such detail as will disclose the nature and amounts of assets and liabilities and net worth of the investment adviser.

15. Section 8.E.1(b) of the Act provides, inter alia, that subject to the provisions of subsection F of Section 11 of the Act, the registration of an investment adviser or investment adviser representative may be suspended or revoked if the Secretary of State finds that the investment adviser or investment adviser representative has engaged in any unethical practice in the offer or sale of securities or in any fraudulent business practice.

16. Section 8.E.1(m) of the Act provides, inter alia, that subject to the provisions of subsection F of Section 11 of the Act, the registration of an investment adviser or investment adviser representative may be suspended or revoked if the Secretary of State finds that the investment adviser or investment adviser representative has conducted a continuing course of dealing of such nature as to demonstrate an inability to properly conduct the business of the dealer, limited Canadian dealer, salesperson, investment adviser or investment adviser representative.

17. Section 8.E.1(q) of the Act provides, inter alia, that subject to the provisions of subsection F of Section 11 of the Act, the registration of an investment adviser or investment adviser representative may be suspended or revoked if the Secretary of State finds that the investment adviser or investment adviser representative has failed to maintain the books and records required under this Act or regulations under this Act or under any requirements established by the Securities and Exchange Commission or self-regulatory organization.

WHEREAS, the Respondent has acknowledged that the allegation contained in paragraph eight (8) of the Stipulation shall be adopted as the Secretary of State's Conclusion of Law as follows: By virtue of the foregoing, the Respondent is subject to the entry of an Order which revokes his investment adviser and investment adviser representative registrations in the State of Illinois pursuant to the authority provided under Section 8.E.1(b), (m) or (q) of the Act.

NOW THEREFORE IT IS HEREBY ORDERED THAT:

1. The allegations contained in paragraphs seven (7) and eight (8) of the Stipulation shall be and are hereby adopted as the Secretary of State's Findings of Fact and Conclusion of Law;

2. The Respondent's Investment Adviser and Investment Adviser Representative registrations in Illinois are revoked as of the last date that the registrations were effective;

3. The Respondent, Robert William Esch, shall pay a fine of $15,000 payable to the Secretary of State by certified check or money order within thirty days of the entry of the order;

4. The Respondent shall deliver a copy of this consent order, along with a cover letter stating that if the recipient has any questions regarding the consent order to contact the Illinois Securities Department, to all of his current and former investment advisory clients within 10 business days of the entry of the consent order;

5. The Respondent shall not reapply for any registration under the Illinois Securities Act for two years from the date of entry of the consent order; and

6. The formal hearing scheduled on this matter is hereby dismissed without further proceeding.

ENTERED: This day of , 2005.

JESSE WHITE

Secretary of State

NOTICE: Failure to comply with the terms of this Order shall be a violation of Section 12.D of the Illinois Securities Law of 1953 [815 ILCS 5] (the "Act"). Any person or entity who fails to comply with the terms of this Order of the Secretary of State, having knowledge of the existence of this Order, shall be guilty of a Class 4 felony.

Attorney for the Secretary of State:

David Finnigan

Illinois Securities Department

Lincoln Tower, Suite 200

520 South Second Street

Springfield, Illinois 62701

Telephone: (217) 785-4947

So, first, it is not okay to enter into advisory contracts with clients that state that the minimum investment is $25,000 and the management fees are a set amount, when, in fact, some clients don't have to meet the minimum and don't have to pay any fee at all. If the minimum investment and the fees charged are actually negotiable, it is an unethical and fraudulent business practice to sign contracts with clients that state or imply otherwise. Speaking of the advisory contracts, we notice that the adviser accepted prepayment of fees in excess of $500 six or more months in advance but did not comply with the Administrator's rules governing this practice. Receiving that type of upfront fee creates custody, in other words, and he failed to comply with the requirements for investment advisers with custody of client assets. Also, his contracts failed to state that no assignment of contract was allowed without client consent. So, even though he didn't actually assign the contracts, he still got dinged for forgetting to insert that clause into the contract itself.

Okay, so his advisory contracts had problems, and he accidentally billed someone 2.5 times the correct amount. Stuff happens, right? What really caught my attention was his advertising. I mean, come on, all I have to do is find the 10 best performing stocks of last year and put out an advertisement claiming that I invested in them. If I didn't mind getting busted, that is. So, according to the order, not only did he not purchase the stocks he claimed to have picked, but the performance figures on the little pretend stock picks only covered a period of 3 or 4 months, which he then multiplied by 3 or 4 to get an annualized rate of return. Now, when we were calculating annualized rates of return in another section, we were partly just doing an academic exercise. No way can an investment adviser get a 10% return in one week and then advertise his 520% annualized rates of return. Remember that when an investment adviser puts out an advertisement listing stock picks, the period covered has to be at least one year. And, the regulators would be tickled to death if the adviser actually bought the stocks he claims to have bought and can back it all up with the "books and records required to be kept by the firm." I mean, if you say you picked all those stocks, what's the problem with pulling out the trade confirmations and account statements backing up your claims?

Finally, not only did he apparently not pick any of the stocks he claimed to have bought; not only did the period used for his little pretend stock picks not cover a full year; but also the performance figures he quoted on the stocks he never picked failed to clarify that if management fees and transaction costs had been included, the numbers would have been lower.

Did you also notice a few things at the end of the consent order? First, there is a mandatory two-year sabbatical. Next, he has to deliver a copy of this consent order to each current and former client with a cover letter encouraging the customer to contact the state regulator if they have any questions. Third, the order states that any "willful violation" of this order is considered a Class 4 felony in Illinois. And, the penalties for a Class 4 felony in Illinois are very close to what the Uniform Securities Act uses with its "three years in prison, $5,000 fine, or both."

In other words, try not to commit any willful violations if you can help it. And please know that I just happened to use an Illinois enforcement order. The exam is not concerned with the specifics of the Illinois Securities Act. It's just that the Illinois, California, Missouri, or Oregon securities laws would be very close to one another, since they all follow the template called the Uniform Securities Act. And, you can see hundreds of these enforcement orders at the state regulatory websites for yourself. Do a Google search on something like "State of California Securities" or "Oklahoma Securities Administrator." Or, assuming they don't change the website, you can quickly find any state regulator by going to www.nasaa.org and clicking on "contact your regulator," which pulls up a map of all the states and Canada.

There is one main reason I have not opened my own advisory business: I hate to sell. I hate making the phone calls, leaving the voice mails, and—most of all—I hate driving out to some godforsaken place and finding the client is not actually there for the appointment he just scheduled forty-five minutes ago. Since I don't want to sell, I could hire some licensed individuals as my investment adviser representatives. I'd send the state a U4 form with their information, pay an annoying little fee, and then turn them loose on investing prospects. Or, I could instead use the services of licensed individuals or firms on more of an independent contractor basis. Since the individual or firm would be going around soliciting new business, the regulators decided to call such people **solicitors**. Remember that to use a solicitor the adviser must be registered; there can be no outstanding order suspending, limiting, or barring the solicitor's activities; and there must be a written agreement between the solicitor and the adviser. Also, the following conditions must be met:

- The agreement between the adviser and the solicitor must describe the solicitation activities and the compensation arrangement.
- The solicitor must provide the client with the adviser's disclosure brochure and a separate solicitor disclosure document.
- The adviser must receive a signed acknowledgment from the client that he/she received both the IA's and the solicitor's disclosure documents.

As usual, the investment adviser has a lot of responsibility in this situation. Notice how the adviser needs a signed acknowledgment from the client that both disclosure brochures were received. Also, you can bet that if the solicitor were some shady character, the adviser would not be able to stand back shrugging off responsibility to the regulators.

The adviser would be expected to do some due diligence on the solicitors that they use, and if an adviser knew the individual was a convicted felon and hired him anyway, the adviser would be subject to regulatory action.

And, let's see how closely you're reading this material – does the solicitor have to be registered? I never actually said that, did I? The important point is that the adviser has to be registered, has to oversee the solicitor, and the solicitor cannot be someone ineligible for registration because of criminal or regulatory blemishes on his record. Most states would call a "solicitor" an "investment adviser representative" and make him register as such. But not all states feel that way.

➤ Use of Reports

If an adviser sells you a recommendation, plan, or analysis, you'd probably assume it was their work, right? To avoid misleading the client, then, if somebody else actually did the work, that would have to be disclosed by the adviser. However, if an adviser subscribes to a newsletter or buys reports that help them make recommendations to you, that's just fine and requires no disclosure. The adviser's disclosure brochure would already indicate in general what sources of information are used in determining recommendations (financial newspapers and magazines, research materials prepared by others, company press releases, annual reports filed with SEC, etc.). So, there's a big difference between passing off some other professional's work as the adviser's and using other professionals' work to help the IA make/render the investment advice to the client.

➤ Misleading Names

Regulators register securities professionals. They never certify or approve them. A securities professional might earn credentials such as "Chartered Financial Analyst" or "Certified Financial

Planner," but that means that an independent organization has decided to issue that designation. The securities regulators don't certify or approve the professionals. To indicate that you have been "certified" or "approved" by the securities regulators will get you into all kinds of trouble. Section 208 of the Investment Advisers Act of 1940 makes this very clear with the following statement:

Representations of sponsorship by United States or agency thereof. It shall be unlawful for any person registered under section 203 to represent or imply in any manner whatsoever that such person has been sponsored, recommended, or approved, or that his abilities or qualifications have in any respect been passed upon by the United States or any agency or any officer thereof.

The title **investment counsel** may only be used by those advisers deemed to be performing "supervisory services." In other words, to call yourself an "investment counsel," you have to be actively managing money/affairs for particular clients, not just writing newsletters to a group of subscribers or performing annual reviews of their financial plans.

And that same Section 208 of the Investment Advisers Act of 1940 makes this point quite clearly for us, as well, when it states:

Use of name "investment counsel" as descriptive of business. It shall be unlawful for any person registered under section 203 to represent that he is an investment counsel or to use the name "investment counsel" as descriptive of his business unless (1) his or its principal business consists of acting as investment adviser, and (2) a substantial part of his or its business consists of rendering investment supervisory services.

Securities regulators are currently making a coordinated effort to crack down on financial services professionals who use special designations to mislead senior citizens. While some of the credentials are legitimate, many make the regulators nervous, including the ever-popular "Certified Financial Gerontologist." Regulators recently performed a survey that showed that one-quarter of all senior investors were told that the financial professionals they were talking to were specially certified or qualified to help senior citizens, and half of those investors said they were more likely to listen to the advice because of that. Unfortunately, designations are often obtained simply by paying a fee to the organization that prints you up an official-looking certificate. NASAA has written a model rule for states trying to deal with this hot regulatory topic, and I recommend that you read it. You do plan to spend some serious time at the NASAA website, right? It is their exam, remember.

➤ Code of Ethics

Investment advisers are responsible for the activities of their employees and, therefore, the SEC requires that advisers "establish, maintain, and enforce a written code of ethics." If you are an investment adviser, your code of ethics needs to include:

- A standard of business conduct that you require of your supervised persons reflecting your fiduciary obligations and those of your supervised persons
- Provisions requiring your supervised persons to comply with applicable federal securities laws
- Provisions that require all of your access persons to report, and you to review, their personal securities transactions and holdings periodically
- Provisions requiring supervised persons to report any violations of your code of ethics promptly to your chief compliance officer

- Provisions requiring you to provide each of your supervised persons with a copy of your code of ethics and any amendments, and requiring your supervised persons to provide you with a written acknowledgment of their receipt of the code and any amendments

For purposes of this rule, the SEC uses the term "access persons" and then defines them as

any supervised person who has access to nonpublic information regarding any clients' purchase or sale of securities, or nonpublic information regarding the portfolio holdings of any reportable fund, or who is involved in making securities recommendations to clients, or who has access to such recommendations that are nonpublic.

In other words, if you are making recommendations to clients, managing their portfolios, or simply know what securities are inside those client portfolios, you are an access person. If your firm manages mutual funds, and you know what they're buying before the public does, you are clearly an "access person." Directors, officers, and partners are presumed to be access persons, as well. Under this code of ethics, the adviser needs to keep records of their access persons' securities holdings (what they own) and transactions (what they buy and sell). The holding reports must include:

- The title and type of security, and as applicable the exchange ticker symbol or CUSIP number, number of shares, and principal amount of each reportable security in which the access person has any direct or indirect beneficial ownership
- The name of any broker, dealer or bank with which the access person maintains an account in which any securities are held for the access person's direct or indirect benefit; and
- The date the access person submits the report

These reports must be filed with the chief compliance officer no later than 10 days after becoming an "access person," and once a year an updated report must be filed. The information must be accurate as of no more than 45 days prior to filing the report.

The transaction reports that "access persons" must file with the chief compliance officer have to include at a minimum:

- The date of the transaction, the title, and as applicable the exchange ticker symbol or CUSIP number, interest rate and maturity date, number of shares, and principal amount of each reportable security involved
- The nature of the transaction (e.g., purchase, sale or any other type of acquisition or disposition)
- The price of the security at which the transaction was effected
- The name of the broker, dealer or bank with or through which the transaction was effected; and
- The date the access person submits the report

These transaction reports need to be submitted for each financial quarter and no more than 30 days after the end of the quarter. The simplest way to comply with the code of ethics requirement is for the adviser to require their "access persons" to have copies of their brokerage statements and trade confirmations sent to the firm.

The rule also states that before an access person buys into an IPO or limited offering, he/she must receive pre-approval from the chief compliance officer. And, lest we think the SEC lacks a sense of humor, the rule actually states, "if you have only one access person (i.e., yourself), you are not required to submit reports to yourself or to obtain your own approval for investments in any security in an initial public offering or in a limited offering, if you maintain records of all of your holdings and transactions that this section would otherwise require you to report."

Since every rule has to have exceptions, an investment made through an "automatic investment plan" is not a transaction that has to be reported. In other words, if you are set up for a DRIP (dividend reinvestment program), in which your dividends regularly purchase more shares of stock, that is, by definition, not a suspicious purchase of securities since it's happening on autopilot. Or, if you're doing a systematic withdrawal plan out of a mutual fund, same deal. Finally, investments in the following are not reportable:

- Direct obligations of the government of the United States
- Banker's acceptances, bank certificates of deposit, commercial paper and high-quality short-term debt instruments, including repurchase agreements
- Shares issued by money market funds
- Shares issued by open-end funds other than reportable funds (you're not an adviser to this fund, and neither is the firm that controls you)
- Shares issued by unit investment trusts that are invested exclusively in one or more open-end funds, none of which are reportable funds

➢ NASAA Model Rule on Business Practices for Advisers

The organization of state and Canadian provincial securities regulators is called **NASAA**, which stands for the **North American Securities Administrators Association**. They're not a regulatory body themselves; they are the organization of state securities regulators that attempts to keep all the regulators on top of important issues and working from more or less the same page when writing and rewriting rules for their various states. NASAA is in charge of the Series 63, 65, and 66 exams, so you can maybe send them a thank-you note when you're done with your test. Either way, their model rules and statements of policy are expected to be tested heavily on everyone's trip to the exam center, so let's take a look at them in detail.

The following is the actual model rule telling investment advisers, investment adviser representatives, and federal covered advisers what's what. It is followed by my own plain-English translation of the legalese. These are among the most testable pages of material related to the exam.

```
Model Rule 102(a)(4)-1

Adopted 4/27/97, amended 4/18/04, 9/11/05

Rule 102(a)(4)-1 Unethical Business Practices Of Investment
Advisers, Investment Adviser Representatives, And Federal Covered
Advisers

[Introduction] A person who is an investment adviser, an
investment adviser representative or a federal covered adviser is
a fiduciary and has a duty to act primarily for the benefit of
```

its clients. The provisions of this subsection apply to federal covered advisers to the extent that the conduct alleged is fraudulent, deceptive, or as otherwise permitted by the National Securities Markets Improvement Act of 1996 (Pub. L. No. 104-290). While the extent and nature of this duty varies according to the nature of the relationship between an investment adviser or an investment adviser representative and its clients and the circumstances of each case, an investment adviser, an investment adviser representative or a federal covered adviser shall not engage in unethical business practices, including the following:

(a) Recommending to a client to whom investment supervisory, management or consulting services are provided the purchase, sale or exchange of any security without reasonable grounds to believe that the recommendation is suitable for the client on the basis of information furnished by the client after reasonable inquiry concerning the client's investment objectives, financial situation and needs, and any other information known by the investment adviser.

(b) Exercising any discretionary power in placing an order for the purchase or sale of securities for a client without obtaining written discretionary authority from the client within ten (10) business days after the date of the first transaction placed pursuant to oral discretionary authority, unless the discretionary power relates solely to the price at which, or the time when, an order involving a definite amount of a specified security shall be executed, or both.

(c) Inducing trading in a client's account that is excessive in size or frequency in view of the financial resources, investment objectives and character of the account in light of the fact that an investment adviser or an investment adviser representative in such situations can directly benefit from the number of securities transactions effected in a client's account. The rule appropriately forbids an excessive number of transaction orders to be induced by an adviser for a "customer's account."

(d) Placing an order to purchase or sell a security for the account of a client without authority to do so.

(e) Placing an order to purchase or sell a security for the account of a client upon instruction of a third party without first having obtained a written third-party trading authorization from the client.

(f) Borrowing money or securities from a client unless the client is a broker-dealer, an affiliate of the investment adviser, or a financial institution engaged in the business of loaning funds.

(g) Loaning money to a client unless the investment adviser is a financial institution engaged in the business of loaning funds or the client is an affiliate of the investment adviser.

(h) Misrepresenting to any advisory client, or prospective advisory client, the qualifications of the investment adviser or any employee of the investment adviser, or misrepresenting the nature of the advisory services being offered or fees to be charged for such service, or to omit to state a material fact necessary to make the statements made regarding qualifications, services or fees, in light of the circumstances under which they are made, not misleading.

(i) Providing a report or recommendation to any advisory client prepared by someone other than the adviser without disclosing that fact. (This prohibition does not apply to a situation where the adviser uses published research reports or statistical analyses to render advice or where an adviser orders such a report in the normal course of providing service.)

(j) Charging a client an unreasonable advisory fee.

(k) Failing to disclose to clients in writing before any advice is rendered any material conflict of interest relating to the adviser, or any of its employees which could reasonably be expected to impair the rendering of unbiased and objective advice including:

(1.) Compensation arrangements connected with advisory services to clients which are in addition to compensation from such clients for such services; and

(2.) Charging a client an advisory fee for rendering advice when a commission for executing securities transactions pursuant to such advice will be received by the adviser or its employees.

(l) Guaranteeing a client that a specific result will be achieved (gain or no loss) with advice which will be rendered.

(m) [Alternative 1] Publishing, circulating or distributing any advertisement which does not comply with Rule 206(4)-1 under the Investment Advisers Act of 1940.

(m) [Alternative 2] (1.) Except as otherwise provided in subsection (2.), it shall constitute a dishonest or unethical practice within the meaning of [Uniform Act Sec. 102(a)(4)] for any investment adviser or investment adviser representative, directly or indirectly, to use any advertisement that does any one of the following:

(i.) Refers to any testimonial of any kind concerning the investment adviser or investment adviser representative or

326

concerning any advice, analysis, report, or other service rendered by such investment adviser or investment adviser representative.

(ii.) Refers to past specific recommendations of the investment adviser or investment adviser representative that were or would have been profitable to any person; except that an investment adviser or investment adviser representative may furnish or offer to furnish a list of all recommendations made by the investment adviser or investment adviser representative within the immediately preceding period of not less than one year if the advertisement or list also includes both of the following:

(A) The name of each security recommended, the date and nature of each recommendation, the market price at that time, the price at which the recommendation was to be acted upon, and the most recently available market price of each such security.

(B) A legend on the first page in prominent print or type that states that the reader should not assume that recommendations made in the future will be profitable or will equal the performance of the securities in the list.

(iii.) Represents that any graph, chart, formula, or other device being offered can in and of itself be used to determine which securities to buy or sell, or when to buy or sell them; or which represents, directly or indirectly, that any graph, chart, formula, or other device being offered will assist any person in making that person's own decisions as to which securities to buy or sell, or when to buy or sell them, without prominently disclosing in such advertisement the limitations thereof and the difficulties with respect to its use.

(iv.) Represents that any report, analysis, or other service will be furnished for free or without charge, unless such report, analysis, or other service actually is or will be furnished entirely free and without any direct or indirect condition or obligation.

(v.) Represents that the [Administrator] has approved any advertisement.

(vi.) Contains any untrue statement of a material fact, or that is otherwise false or misleading.

(2.) With respect to federal covered advisers, the provisions of this section only apply to the extent permitted by Section 203A of the Investment Advisers Act of 1940.

(3.) For the purposes of this section, the term "advertisement" shall include any notice, circular, letter, or other written communication addressed to more than one person, or any notice or other announcement in any electronic or paper publication, by radio or television, or by any medium, that offers any one of the following:

(i.) Any analysis, report, or publication concerning securities.

(ii.) Any analysis, report, or publication that is to be used in making any determination as to when to buy or sell any security or which security to buy or sell.

(iii.) Any graph, chart, formula, or other device to be used in making any determination as to when to buy or sell any security, or which security to buy or sell.

(iv.) Any other investment advisory service with regard to securities.

(n) Disclosing the identity, affairs, or investments of any client unless required by law to do so, or unless consented to by the client.

(o) Taking any action, directly or indirectly, with respect to those securities or funds in which any client has any beneficial interest, where the investment adviser has custody or possession of such securities or funds when the advisor's action is subject to and does not comply with the requirements of Rule 102e(1)-1. and any subsequent amendments.

(p) Entering into, extending or renewing any investment advisory contract, unless such contract is in writing and discloses, in substance, the services to be provided, the term of the contract, the advisory fee, the formula for computing the fee, the amount of prepaid fee to be returned in the event of contract termination or non-performance, whether the contract grants discretionary power to the adviser and that no assignment of such contract shall be made by the investment adviser without the consent of the other party to the contract.

(q) Failing to establish, maintain, and enforce written policies and procedures reasonably designed to prevent the misuse of material nonpublic information contrary to the provisions of Section 204A of the Investment Advisers Act of 1940.

(r) Entering into, extending, or renewing any advisory contract contrary to the provisions of Section 205 of the Investment Advisers Act of 1940. This provision shall apply to all advisers and investment adviser representatives registered or required to be registered under this Act, notwithstanding whether such adviser or representative would be exempt from federal registration pursuant to Section 203(b) of the Investment Advisers Act of 1940.

(s) To indicate, in an advisory contract, any condition, stipulation, or provisions binding any person to waive compliance with any provision of this act or of the Investment Advisers Act of 1940, or any other practice contrary to the provisions of Section 215 of the Investment Advisers Act of 1940.

(t) Engaging in any act, practice, or course of business which is fraudulent, deceptive, or manipulative in contrary to the provisions of Section 206(4) of the Investment Advisers Act of 1940, notwithstanding the fact that such investment adviser or investment adviser representative is not registered or required to be registered under Section 203 of the Investment Advisers Act of 1940.

(u) Engaging in conduct or any act, indirectly or through or by any other person, which would be unlawful for such person to do directly under the provisions of this act or any rule or regulation thereunder. The conduct set forth above is not inclusive. Engaging in other conduct such as non-disclosure, incomplete disclosure, or deceptive practices shall be deemed an unethical business practice. The federal statutory and regulatory provisions referenced herein shall apply to investment advisers, investment adviser representatives and federal covered advisers to the extent permitted by the National Securities Markets Improvement Act of 1996 (Pub. L. No. 104-290).

Plain English Explanation

The first point this model rule makes is that an investment adviser, investment adviser representative, or federal covered adviser is a fiduciary and has a duty to act primarily for the benefit of its clients. Of course, we've already mentioned that, but notice how NASAA mentions it right off the bat in this model rule. It's that important. Also, by listing all three terms (investment adviser, investment adviser representative, federal covered adviser), the document reminds us that each term is related yet different. The investment adviser and federal covered adviser are business entities, while the investment adviser representative is the individual who represents one of those business entities. Also, there is a difference between an "investment adviser" and a "federal covered adviser." The difference is that the federal covered adviser is registered with the SEC, while the "investment adviser" is subject to the state's registration authority. Notice how the provisions laid out in this document (written by a group of state regulators) "apply to federal covered advisers to the extent that the conduct alleged is fraudulent, deceptive, or as otherwise permitted by [NSMIA]."

Okay, so that's the introduction. Let's now look at the specific items mentioned in the model rule. Item (a) reminds investment advisers not to recommend the purchase or sale of any security unless they have reasonable grounds to believe it's a suitable recommendation. Notice how the item specifically mentions clients "to whom supervisory, management or consulting services are provided." Another type of advisory service is called "impersonal advice," and this advice does not even purport/claim to be specific for the individual client. There is a world of difference between delivering the same advice to a group that is generally interested in, say, value investing, and providing "supervisory, management or consulting services" to a specific client. If I'm supervising your investment activities, actually managing your portfolio, or getting paid a big hourly rate as a consultant, the regulators would be tickled to death if I actually knew something about your situation before I start running my mouth or running the meter.

The second item is a little surprising to me. I would have figured the adviser needs written discretionary authority from the client before using discretionary power, but it turns out the client can give oral authorization to get the discretionary nature of the account going. The adviser then has 10 business days after the first discretionary order is placed to obtain written authorization.

Actually, this makes perfect sense. Broker-dealers need written discretionary authority before making any discretionary trades because they get compensated per transaction and the temptation to just start buying stuff on their client's behalf would be overwhelming, like asking my two cats to baby-sit your hamster for a couple of days. I mean, after a while, what are you going to do? It's a hamster—we're hungry predators with sharp claws. See the problem?

But an investment adviser gets compensated by charging a percentage of the assets, so if he makes some dumb purchases he'll not only not gain from it, but also his fee will start going down with the assets. One percent of $100,000 is better than 1% of $80,000, right? Whatever percent the client account drops, so drops the adviser's compensation, remember. They're not stockbrokers who collected a commission a long time ago and now have no skin in the game.

Discretion allows a broker-dealer or adviser to enter transactions on behalf of a client without first talking to the client. If they can choose which security is to be bought or sold and how many shares, they are using discretion. However, if the client knows he wants to buy 300 shares of ORCL today, that order does not require written discretionary authority. Choosing what time of day to enter a specific order does not make the regulators nervous, in other words. Choosing which security to buy or sell and how many shares to buy or sell—those are big decisions that the adviser can only make if granted discretionary authority by the client. While portfolio managers usually have discretion and do not talk to clients before placing trades, there could be financial planners out there who might otherwise over-step their authority by making decisions for clients without having that authority. If the financial planner wants to log into an online broker-dealer's trading platform and enter a trade where the customer fully named the important details, not a problem—even if the financial planner decided to wait until the close to place the trade that same day. But, a financial planner without discretionary authority can never fill in the important details of a trade or decide to place a trade without first discussing it with the client.

Item (c) says that advisers should not try to induce their clients to become frantic traders, especially if the adviser is getting compensated for those transactions. So, churning is always a bad idea, and an even worse idea if the adviser is also getting paid to broker the trades.

Item (d) reminds advisers and their reps not to purchase or sell securities when they have no authorization from the client to do so. I can't imagine trying to manage a client's portfolio unless I had the discretion to make trades as I saw fit, but that doesn't mean that all investment advisers have been granted that discretion. If the adviser or IAR is unauthorized to execute transactions without talking to the client, doing so would be a violation known, not surprisingly, as an "unauthorized transaction."

Item (e) is basically saying that if your client's husband calls up and says his wife wants you to sell 1,000 shares of MSFT, you can only do so if the client has given her husband written trading authorization and you have that on file. Otherwise, you have to talk to your customer, the wife. Don't take orders from anybody but your client, unless the third party has been granted written third-party trading authorization. This includes lawyers, accountants, insurance agents, and even the executor of someone's estate while the individual is still alive. Not one of those individuals has any inherent right to discuss the investor's account with your firm. Doing so would be a breach of your fiduciary duty, since—as we'll see—client confidentiality is part of that duty.

Items (f) and (g) address borrowing and lending. Borrowing money from clients is a practice that makes regulators really nervous. An investment adviser can only borrow money from a client if the client is a broker-dealer, an affiliate of the adviser, or a financial institution in the business of making loans (Bank, Savings & Loan, Thrift, etc.). So, don't borrow from customers unless the customer is in the business of loaning money. And, don't lend money to a customer unless your advisory firm is in the business of making loans, or the customer is an affiliate of your advisory firm. Examples of "affiliates" of an investment adviser include other business entities connected to the adviser, the owners/principals of the advisory firm, and the investment adviser representatives who have been with the firm at least one year. So, the regulators aren't going to stop the advisory business from getting capital from related entities and those who run the firm. What they won't do is let the adviser borrow money from any client who is not an institution in the business of lending money. And, if an IAR has a client who works as a mortgage broker, the IAR can definitely get a mortgage through that client's business. The IAR, however, had better not ask the client to personally lend him money.

Item (h) reminds us not to mislead prospects or clients about our qualifications, the qualifications of our employees, or the services we will provide through our contract with the client and the fees we will charge for performing those services. And, remember, the state regulators are convinced that advisers and their reps can commit fraud even when just soliciting clients, so lying about credentials would be a really bad idea.

Item (i) is a little tricky and, therefore, fertile ground for harvesting exam questions. If I provide a report or a recommendation to a client when, in fact, that report or recommendation was actually prepared by someone else, I have to disclose the fact and tell you who provided it. However, if I order prepared reports or use published research/statistical analyses to come up with my recommendations, that's different. No disclosure there. I'm just doing my homework to come up with a better plan for my customer. So, if you get a tricky question on this, try to determine if the adviser is trying to pass off somebody else's work as their own, or if they order reports and analyses to help them come up with better recommendations. I mean, I'd kind of like to think my adviser is constantly poring over published reports, just crunching data with his nose to the grindstone and shoulder to the wheel 10–12 hours a day, and I do not really care which websites or newsletters or reports he subscribes to. On the other hand, if he's paying another firm to come up with the recommendations for my portfolio, I want to know that rather than find out my adviser was just trying to make it look like he actually knew something about investing himself.

Item (j) prohibits advisers from gouging their clients. What would make the fee "unreasonable"? The regulators are indicating that you and your firm have two options here: 1) you can charge fees that are reasonable or 2) the state can schedule a disciplinary hearing.

The next item, (k), is saying that if the advice being given will also lead to the advisory firm or any of its employees receiving a commission or any other compensation should the client act on the advice, that potential conflict of interest must be disclosed in writing. In other words, wouldn't you feel better about paying for investment advice knowing that the advice is being given by a totally objective professional, rather than someone who will make a big commission check if you take the advice? For example, if the IAR or adviser receives 12b-1 fees on the mutual funds recommended or purchased for the client, this needs to be disclosed.

Item (l) is the very familiar prohibition against guarantees. Don't guarantee a profit. Don't guarantee against a loss. I have recently seen many instances at the state regulatory websites of representatives who have horribly dropped the ball and then tried to appease the client by cutting a personal check. You know, maybe after you accidentally sell 1,000 of the client's B-shares three years after purchase when you were sure they were A-shares, costing her $3,500 by your little gaffe, you invite her to lunch, slip her a check for $3,500, pick up the tab, and everybody's happy.

Not a good idea. In another instance, a shady operator sold an Illinois resident shares of stock in a company that was not even public yet, telling her that when the company did their IPO, she would make "a return at least equal to her original investment" and that by investing in said stock "she would become a millionaire." Of course, the stock never went public, the investor never made a return on her original investment, and can't seem to get a return of her original investment. Now, nobody said the word "guaranteed" can't be used. We're saying that investment advisers and IARs don't offer guarantees. The US Treasury guarantees the timely payment of interest and principal on a US T-Bond, and there are even guaranteed corporate bonds where a third party promises to pay if the issuer cannot. But, people in the securities industry do not guarantee investors against a loss or guarantee they will make a certain level of profit.

Item (m) probably threw you for a loop, what with the whole "[Alternative 1], [Alternative 2]" thing. Either way, the item is telling advisers to be careful about the advertisements they put out. If you have a photographic memory, perhaps you recalled that in that consent order against the adviser with the sloppy advertising the Illinois Administrator's office referred to the advertisement's not being in accordance with the rule under the Investment Advisers Act of 1940. Believe it or not, when I showed that consent order to a different state securities regulator, the folks at the table were a little baffled as to why anything about the Investment Advisers Act of 1940 had been referenced in a state regulatory action. In fact, they said they would not have written it that way themselves. In other words, there was a disagreement among lawyers, if you can believe such a thing. Well, NASAA is a group of lawyers, basically, and they know that some state regulators would rather not refer to the federal legislation, while some are quite comfortable not reinventing the wheel. I mean, if those high-energy types in Washington DC have already exhausted all kinds of time and effort laying out a set of perfectly good stipulations, why not use them? This way, we don't even have to go to the trouble of copying and pasting them into our own rules. Instead, we can just refer to the rule spelled out in the Investment Advisers Act of 1940 and call it a day.

In any case, whether we just point the adviser to the federal rule or kind of spell the same thing out for him in our own words, as state regulators we want advisers to know that their advertising had better not be misleading in any way. Of course, our buddy from Illinois provided a textbook definition of how not to do things. You can't list stock picks that you didn't actually pick. And when you do actually pick the stocks you claim to have picked, the period covered has to be at least one year, and all types of disclosures have to be provided, too. Also notice that testimonials from clients are not allowed.

Investment Advisers Act of 1940, Rule 206(4)-1…It shall constitute a fraudulent, deceptive, or manipulative act, practice, or course of business for any investment adviser to publish, circulate, or distribute any advertisement…which refers, directly or indirectly, to any testimonial of any kind concerning the investment adviser or concerning any advice, analysis, report or other service rendered by such investment adviser…

Item (n) has to do with client confidentiality. It says not to divulge the identity, affairs, or investments of your client to anyone else without the client's written permission or some sort of legal order to turn the information over to a court or the police. It might be tempting to show prospects what you've done for, say, Oprah Winfrey's account, but both Ms. Winfrey and the state securities Administrator would probably have a real problem with that. Note that you cannot divulge the financial affairs or the *identity* of your advisory clients unless you have the clients' written permission or a legal demand to turn over the information.

Item (o) basically boils down to, "Be real careful what you do with client funds/securities under custody." The Rule 102e(1)-1 referenced in this item is also currently viewable at the NASAA website and could easily help you snag a test question or two. We'll be looking at custody issues in more detail in a while. Try not to get too excited just yet.

Item (p) reminds us that all advisory contracts must be in writing and must stipulate all the terms of the contract: services provided, term of the contract, advisory fees, formula for computing the fees, the amount of prepaid fees that are refundable, whether the adviser has discretion, and that no assignment of contract can occur without client consent. Also note that even if the adviser did not end up assigning a client's contract to another party without consent, the fact that their contract with the client failed to state that provision could lead to problems with the regulators. So, before an advisory firm can sell a majority ownership position to a new entity, all client contracts would have to be re-executed with the new entity. Otherwise, the contracts would have been improperly "assigned" without client consent.

Item (q) is talking about the adviser's code of ethics policy. Any "access person" or individual at the firm who could easily see what the portfolio managers are up to is required to report his/her holdings to the advisory firm. We cover this in more detail elsewhere. Item (r) reminds us that state regulators often use SEC rules as their own—if the advisory firm has contracts that conflict with SEC rules under the "Act of 1940," the state Administrator has a real problem with that.

Item (s) reminds us that no waivers of any provision are allowed. So, if the adviser wants to charge a client in a way that's not allowed, he and the client cannot just draw up a waiver indicating that they both mutually agree to violate the laws and rules governing the industry. Any such "waiver of compliance" would be considered null and void in an Administrative or court proceeding, anyway, which means it would not be worth the paper it's printed on, much less the legal fees foolishly spent having the thing drawn up.

Item (t) points out that whether an adviser or IAR is subject to state registration, federal-only, or exempted from registration at the federal level, they can still get busted for fraudulent, deceptive practices by the state Administrator. Item (u) points out that beyond fraudulent/manipulative practices, an investment adviser or IAR can get in trouble for engaging in any conduct that is a violation of the securities laws of the state and the rules thereunder.

And the final blurb is very typical of these detailed lists. It reminds us that this list is "not inclusive," meaning this is just some of the stuff we felt like talking about in THIS particular publication. It does not represent ALL of the stuff that can get you in trouble.

So be on your best behavior.

UNIFORM PRUDENT INVESTOR ACT

The **Uniform Prudent Investor Act** is another piece of model legislation that provides guidance to trustees. While in earlier times a "prudent investor" was expected to avoid risk, as the Uniform Prudent Investor Act (UPIA) clarifies, the trustee's job is to consider the risk-reward nature of a portfolio so that a risky security here might be balanced out by an uncorrelated and safer security over there. For example, junk bonds might fit into an overall portfolio if balanced out by US Treasury Notes. Therefore, there is no list of prohibited investments. Rather, the trustee needs to read the trust documents and manage the risk/reward nature of the portfolio in a way that best meets the needs of the beneficiary or beneficiaries of the trust.

Diversification is considered a major part of any prudent investment strategy, and a trustee would only choose not to diversify if he had a good reason. For example, maybe he needs to wait until a short-term capital gain can be turned into a long-term capital gain before selling and rebalancing.

Some executors and trustees are just family members who have no training or experience in financial matters. While they would still be held liable for fraud or self-dealing at the expense of the beneficiaries, their level of skill and care would not be assumed to be as high as that of bank's trust department. So, the UPIA clarifies that amateur fiduciaries are not held to the same standard as professional fiduciaries in terms of exercising skill and care in financial matters. Again, though, a test question could have an amateur fiduciary spending the interest payments received on Treasury Bonds when that money should, instead, be going into the estate account and eventually distributed to the other beneficiaries. That would be a matter of self-dealing and "breach of fiduciary duty" regardless of her knowledge of the securities industry. If the executor decides to just move into the house of the deceased rather than get it sold for the benefit of the estate, this would also be a breach of fiduciary duty, no matter how often it probably happens in the day-to-day world.

In olden days, no responsibilities could be passed off, but the UPIA points out that a trustee could manage the investments of a pension trust while an insurance company handles payouts and actuarial calculations, for example.

BUSINESS PRACTICES – BROKER-DEALERS AND AGENTS

As we've mentioned, broker-dealers are in the business of "effecting transactions in securities for the account of others or for their own account." That means they can help somebody buy or sell securities and charge a commission, or they can take the other side of the trade with somebody and make a profit. In the first case, they act as a broker for the account of others. In the second case, they act as a dealer for their own account. We saw that investment advisers register with Form ADV. Not surprisingly, broker-dealers register with **Form BD**. On this form, the regulators request information on owners and executive officers of the firm, so if any of those individuals also wants to act as a securities agent, no separate registration is required. These individuals include the board of directors, the CEO, CFO, Chief Compliance Officer, and other executive officers, and also anyone who has a certain level of ownership in the firm.

A broker-dealer hires principals to supervise the firm's operations: the registered representatives, the communications, the written customer complaints, etc. It's important to know that if you're a registered representative/securities agent, you must consult with your principal on just about everything. Still, the principal doesn't have a magic pen that can make prohibited activities suddenly okay. If you get a test question that implies that violating the rules is somehow okay as long as you receive "prior principal approval," that could be a red flag. Yes, you do need prior principal approval to do many things in the industry, but getting a principal to sign off on something also doesn't make it automatically okay to do. Written customer complaints have to be forwarded immediately to a compliance principal, of course. A principal has to review and accept each new customer account. A principal has to review all the trade/order tickets placed by the firm that day. Sales literature, advertising, and public appearances all first have to be cleared by a compliance principal, as well.

While the broker-dealer (the firm) registers with Form BD, principals and agents are registered as "associated persons" of the firm through a **Form U4**. Depending on who's filling it out, Form U4 can be more unpleasant than an annual physical. Right at the beginning, Item #2 is talking about *fingerprint* information, for crying out loud. Pretty soon, it wants your residential history over the previous five years. Then, a detailed employment history over the previous 10 years. And then it wants to know about any felonies and certain misdemeanors—both charges and convictions. And, unlike with the 5-year residential and 10-year employment history, the form asks if the individual has <u>ever</u> been charged with any felony or any misdemeanor involving "investments or an investment-related business or any fraud, false statements or omissions, wrongful taking of property, bribery, perjury, forgery, counterfeiting, extortion, or a conspiracy to commit any of these offenses?"

Even if the individual has never been charged with, convicted of, or pled guilty to a crime, there are still annoying sections asking about any regulatory actions by any state or federal regulator of virtually any financially based industry, any civil actions in which a court handed down a penalty, or even arbitration awards to customers over a certain amount. U4 asks if the applicant has "ever voluntarily resigned, been discharged or permitted to resign after allegations were made that accused [him] of:

(1) violating investment-related statutes, regulations, rules, or industry standards of conduct?
(2) fraud or the wrongful taking of property?
(3) failure to supervise in connection with investment-related statutes, regulations, rules or industry standards of conduct?"

And, in case that wasn't enough probing, the form then asks about creditors and bankruptcies over the previous 10 years. The regulators aren't going to prevent someone from associating with a firm just because of a bankruptcy or short sale on a house, but they still want the information disclosed.

So, as you can see, there's the license exam phase of the registration process that takes out a certain percentage of applicants, but even after many applicants pass their exams, the U4 phase of the process can delay the registration and in many cases end it outright. For example, you could get a 90% on your exam, but if you also have a recent conviction for shoplifting, the regulators can prevent you from getting licensed. And a common problem is that the young, drunk, and stupid frequently get young, drunk and stupid enough one fateful weekend to get a felony charge that is then pled down to a misdemeanor. If the conviction/guilty plea were connected to theft of a barstool, for example, suddenly the applicant has real problems on his hands. If it was more than 10 years ago, and there is no other nonsense on the applicant's record, he (it's usually a he) will probably get in the business.

But if it happened recently, and/or there's a history of having a total lack of respect for other people's stuff, good luck getting registered in this industry.

Now before some readers panic, a misdemeanor involving the following would not be considered investment-related:

- Possession of a controlled substance
- Public intoxication
- DUI
- Assault, battery

If those charges were felonies, it could be a game-over situation, but if they were misdemeanors they would not even have to be disclosed on Form U4. Would the regulators even find out or hassle the applicant about them? Definitely, but the true game-over situations involve *any* felony at all, or any misdemeanor that happens to involve money or dishonesty.

While the state securities Administrator can establish minimum net capital requirements for broker-dealers, really, net capital requirements are set by the SEC and enforced by FINRA. So, the exam might want you to say something like, "The Administrator may establish minimum net capital requirements for broker-dealers subject to the limits of the Securities Exchange Act of 1934." And, they could make it a tough question by emphasizing that the broker-dealer has a principal office in State A and then another state has a higher net capital—what requirement does the BD have to meet? The answer would involve meeting the net capital established by the SEC under the Securities Exchange Act of 1934. If the principal of a broker-dealer fudges on the firm's financial reports with FINRA, he is, thereby, causing the firm to fail to comply with this super-important requirement from the "Exchange Act." Remember that broker-dealers typically hold customer assets, so, like a bank, their own balance sheet is really important. Un-invested customer cash is not wrapped up and placed in a vault—the broker-dealer parks it in an interest-bearing account and must be able to pay it out upon demand. Are they good for it? That's what minimum net capital requirements are all about. And the SEC has been establishing them since the passage of the Securities Exchange Act of 1934.

The state securities Administrator can perform routine inspections of broker-dealers doing business in the state, and they can inspect them subject to investor complaints or information that the securities laws are being violated. The Administrator can require books and records of broker-dealers, but, as a practical matter, they can just insist that the firms meet the requirements of FINRA, many of which are dictated by the SEC. Broker-dealers who have discretion over customer accounts or custody of customer assets are usually required to maintain a surety bond or meet a minimum net capital requirement. In other words, in case customers end up with claims of churning, unauthorized trading, or missing assets, there is something backing up the ability of the firm to make good.

This exam is controlled by NASAA, which is the North American Securities Administrators Association. NASAA is the organization of state regulators, and state regulators expect you to know the Uniform Securities Act as well as the statements of policy and model rules that NASAA has drafted to help keep the industry in check.

NASAA's Policy Statement for Broker-Dealers and Agents is fertile ground for test questions, so let's have a crack at it. First, we'll read it in the native legalese. Then, I'll break it down for you in a language you're likely more familiar with. English.

NASAA ADOPTED STATEMENT OF POLICY 5/23/1983
DISHONEST OR UNETHICAL BUSINESS PRACTICES OF BROKER-DEALERS AND
AGENTS

Each broker-dealer and agent shall observe high standards of commercial honor and just and equitable principles of trade in the conduct of their business. Acts and practices, including but not limited to the following, are considered contrary to such standards and may constitute grounds for denial, suspension or revocation of registration or such other action authorized by statute.

1. BROKER-DEALERS

a. Engaging in a pattern of unreasonable and unjustifiable delays in the delivery of securities purchased by any of its customers and/or in the payment upon request of free credit balances reflecting completed transactions of any of its customers;

b. Inducing trading in a customer's account which is excessive in size or frequency in view of the financial resources and character of the account;

c. Recommending to a customer the purchase, sale or exchange of any security without reasonable grounds to believe that such transaction or recommendation is suitable for the customer based upon reasonable inquiry concerning the customer's investment objectives, financial situation and needs, and any other relevant information known by the broker-dealer;

d. Executing a transaction on behalf of a customer without authorization to do so;

e. Exercising any discretionary power in effecting a transaction for a customer's account without first obtaining written discretionary authority from the customer, unless the discretionary power relates solely to the time and/or price for the executing of orders;

f. Executing any transaction in a margin account without securing from the customer a properly executed written margin agreement promptly after the initial transaction in the account;

g. Failing to segregate customers' free securities or securities held in safekeeping;

h. Hypothecating a customer's securities without having a lien thereon unless the broker-dealer secures from the customer a properly executed written consent promptly after the initial transaction, except as permitted by Rules of the Securities and Exchange Commission;

i. Entering into a transaction with or for a customer at a price not reasonably related to the current market price of the security or receiving an unreasonable commission or profit;

j. Failing to furnish to a customer purchasing securities in an offering, no later than the due date of confirmation of the transaction, either a final prospectus or a preliminary prospectus and an additional document, which together include all information set forth in the final prospectus;

k. Charging unreasonable and inequitable fees for services performed, including miscellaneous services such as collection of monies due for principal, dividends or interest, exchange or transfer of securities, appraisals, safekeeping, or custody of securities and other services related to its securities business;

l. Offering to buy from or sell to any person any security at a stated price unless such broker-dealer is prepared to purchase or sell, as the case may be, at such price and under such conditions as are stated at the time of such offer to buy or sell;

m. Representing that a security is being offered to a customer "at the market" or a price relevant to the market price unless such broker-dealer knows or has reasonable grounds to believe that a market for such security exists other than that made, created or controlled by such broker-dealer;

n. Effecting any transaction in, or inducing the purchase or sale of, any security by means of any manipulative, deceptive or fraudulent device, practice, plan, program, design or contrivance, which may include but not be limited to;

(1) Effecting any transaction in a security which involves no change in the beneficial ownership thereof;

(2) Entering an order or orders for the purchase or sale of any security with the knowledge that an order or orders of substantially the same size, at substantially the same time and substantially the same price, for the sale of any such security, has been or will be entered by or for the same or different parties for the purpose of creating a false or misleading appearance of active trading in the security or a false or misleading appearance with respect to the market for the security;

(3) Effecting, alone or with one or more other persons, a series of transactions in any security creating actual or apparent active trading in such security or raising or depressing the

price of such security, for the purpose of inducing the purchase or sale of such security by others;

o. Guaranteeing a customer against loss in any securities account of such customer carried by the broker-dealer or in any securities transaction effected by the broker-dealer or in any securities transaction effected by the broker-dealer with or for such customer;

p. Publishing or circulating, or causing to be published or circulated, any notice, circular, advertisement, newspaper article, investment service, or communication of any kind which purports to report any transaction as a purchase or sale of any security unless such broker-dealer believes that such transaction was a bona fide purchase or sale of such security; or which purports to quote the bid price or asked price for any security, unless such broker-dealer believes that such quotation represents a bona fide bid for, or offer of, such security;

q. Using any advertising or sales presentation in such a fashion as to be deceptive or misleading; or

r. Failing to disclose that the broker-dealer is controlled by, controlling, affiliated with or under common control with the issuer of any security before entering into any contract with or for a customer for the purchase or sale of such security, the existence of such control to such customer, and if such disclosure is not made in writing, it shall be supplemented by the giving or sending of written disclosure at or before the completion of the transaction;

s. Failing to make a bona fide public offering of all of the securities allotted to a broker-dealer for distribution, whether acquired as an underwriter, a selling group member, or from a member participating in the distribution as an underwriter or selling group member; or

t. Failure or refusal to furnish a customer, upon reasonable request, information to which he is entitled, or to respond to a formal written request or complaint.

2. AGENTS

a. Engaging in the practice of lending or borrowing money or securities from a customer, or acting as a custodian for money, securities or an executed stock power of a customer;

b. Effecting securities transactions not recorded on the regular books or records of the broker-dealer which the agent represents, unless the transactions are authorized in writing by the broker-dealer prior to execution of the transaction;

c. Establishing or maintaining an account containing fictitious information in order to execute transactions which would otherwise be prohibited;

d. Sharing directly or indirectly in profits or losses in the account of any customer without the written authorization of the customer and the broker-dealer which the agent represents;

e. Dividing or otherwise splitting the agent's commissions, profits or other compensation from the purchase or sale of securities with any person not also registered as an agent for the same broker-dealer, or for a broker-dealer under direct or indirect common control; or

f. Engaging in conduct specified in Subsection 1.b, c, d, e, f, i, j, n, o, p, or q.

[CONDUCT NOT INCLUSIVE.] The conduct set forth above is not inclusive. Engaging in other conduct such as forgery, embezzlement, nondisclosure, incomplete disclosure or misstatement of material facts, or manipulative or deceptive practices shall also be grounds for denial, suspension or revocation of registration.

Plain-English Explanation

As you saw, the policy statement starts with the conduct of broker-dealers and then moves on to the agents who represent them. Item A prohibits unreasonable and unjustifiable delays in delivering securities or in paying out a request from a customer's cash balance. Broker-dealers earn interest on their clients' un-invested cash, so they would probably prefer to sit on that client cash as long as possible. However, if the client has $2,000 of "cash" in her account, the firm has to pay her promptly upon request. Regular-way settlement is "T + 3," so once that trade is completed on the third business day, the customer can request a check for that amount. Also, stocks that pay dividends and bonds that pay interest will build up the cash balance in the investor's account. NASAA is just reminding broker-dealers that if their customers want their cash paid out to them, the firms cannot unreasonably delay these requests.

Item B is the legalistic definition for churning. Notice how churning involves excessive size as well as frequency of trading. Remember that suitability is the name of the game, and frequent trading is unsuitable for the vast majority of investors working with a registered representative. Of course, frequent trading does seem to help the registered rep's paycheck, and broker-dealers do know who their "big producers" are, but NASAA is reminding broker-dealers not to let registered reps encourage frequent trading or the trading of large positions relative to the account balance. Administrators in the real world frequently write orders to revoke a license that explain how a particular rep was engaging in a "turnover ratio" of, say, 15, or possibly higher. A "turnover rate/ratio of 15" would indicate that if the customer's average account balance is $20,000, the registered rep somehow talked the guy into executing $300,000 worth of trades over the year. Frequent trading might be suitable if the client is a former commodities trader and a multimillionaire who knows what he's doing, but given the character of the account, if the rep is encouraging trading that is too frequent, the Administrator can definitely move to suspend or revoke the license. Often, FINRA would catch it first and then just forward the information on over to the state—either way, regulators hate churning. It's an obvious way in which a registered rep can put the client's entire life savings at extreme risk while the registered rep faces no financial risk himself and, in fact, benefits on every trade whether the client wins or loses. That's okay for Vegas casinos, but broker-dealers are in a slightly different offshoot of the "financial services" industry.

Item C is a reminder that when the firm recommends the purchase, sale, or exchange of a security, they have to have reasonable grounds to make the recommendation based on an investigation of the client's situation. This brings up many important concepts. First, if the customer calls the firm to place an order, that's an unsolicited transaction in which the broker-dealer has no suitability requirements. But, if the broker-dealer recommends a transaction, they have to know that it's suitable. If the client is "unsophisticated," the firm has to know that the client understands the complexities or risks of products such as collateralized mortgage obligations, deferred variable annuities, or securitized viatical settlements.

Item D reminds the firm not to buy or sell securities for a customer if the customer hasn't authorized the broker-dealer to do so. You might be shocked to see how many firms seem to forget this idea, but if the customer hasn't talked to anyone about buying or selling securities, the customer should never end up seeing that purchases or sales have been taking place in the account, right?

If your roommate came home one night and said, "I bought you the nicest pair of shoes for $1,200— here's your credit card back," how would you feel? Would you be thankful that someone had the good sense to spend your money on something you didn't even know you needed? Of course not. That's why unauthorized transactions are a very serious violation. Spending clients' money without their knowledge has gotten many broker-dealers in hot water with the regulators, as it should. Broker-dealers make recommendations to clients, and as long as those recommendations are suitable, the broker-dealer isn't responsible for the outcome of the investment. However, if they're placing orders that no one actually gave, their license could certainly end up being suspended or revoked.

Item E is very closely related. Before a broker-dealer can choose to enter purchase or sale orders on behalf of a client, without first talking to the client and getting his okay, the customer must grant written discretionary authorization. So, if the firm does not have written discretionary authorization from the customer before making any of those choices, they've made a big mistake. A Series 65 question might ask what the broker-dealer can do once the client informs the firm that the discretionary authorization form is in the mail. Not much at this point—the broker-dealer needs it signed, in writing, on file, before they choose the asset, the activity, or the amount of shares. The time and price at which an order is executed is not considered such a major aspect, so the firm could take a market order from a customer and then have the "time and price discretion" to enter it later, when they're convinced the customer can get a better price—those are called "market not held" orders, by the way, in case you don't have enough to remember at this point. The firm does not need written discretionary authority to choose time/price for a customer order. So, to make sure we have a good grasp on this highly testable concept, if the customer says, "Buy 1,000 shares of a software company," the firm would need written discretionary authority to insert the name of a particular company into that order, e.g., Oracle, Microsoft, or Computer Associates. But, if the customer said, "Buy 1,000 shares of MSFT at a good price today," the broker-dealer does not need written discretionary authority to execute that as a "market not held" order that will be executed when they think they can get a better price. Also, remember that investment advisers can place trades that they feel are suitable, without first talking to the client, after receiving oral authorization from the client for 10 days before getting the authorization in writing. Broker-dealers need it in writing before placing any discretionary orders for the customer. Why? Broker-dealers get paid per transaction, regardless of how the trade works out for the client, while advisers have no such incentive to enter lots of trades.

Item F reminds the firm not to let a customer start trading on margin unless the firm gets a signed margin agreement promptly after the initial transaction. I would have expected the rule to require the agreement ahead of time, but nobody asked my opinion. And, you can see why the Series 65 has such a nasty reputation—you have to remember that the firm needs discretionary authorization signed before using discretion, but they can execute a margin transaction and then get the signed margin agreement. And, trust me, the Series 65 will try to trick you on these points—it could easily ask you which of the following four is a violation and make it look like the firm is screwing up by executing the margin transaction and then promptly getting the signed margin agreement. Most people who kind of half-studied will grab that answer choice as a violation and somehow overlook some obvious example of churning or unauthorized transactions.

Item G speaks to the bookkeeping requirements for broker-dealers holding customer securities, some of which have been pledged as collateral for the loan in a margin account. NASAA is reminding broker-dealers to keep the customers' fully paid securities separate from the firm's securities or securities pledged as collateral. Item H reminds broker-dealers not to pledge customer securities as collateral unless they have written authorization from the customer. In other words, in a margin account, the customer signs a hypothecation agreement, giving the broker-dealer the authority to pledge the securities as collateral. But, if a broker-dealer just started pledging the securities that customers thought were in "safekeeping" as collateral for loans to the firm, we would have a very ugly situation on our hands. It would be like finding out that a neighbor just borrowed $300,000 and put your house up as collateral. Even funnier, he can't repay the loan, so the bank is foreclosing on your property. To protect customer assets, broker-dealers need to keep their books stringently so that it's crystal clear that these shares belong to the firm's account, and those belong to the customers.

Item I is pretty straightforward. Let's say that a municipal bond issued by a small school district seldom trades. A customer comes in and wants to liquidate 100 of these bonds. There isn't much of a secondary market for these things, but if the firm knows that the most recent transactions occurred yesterday at $1,100 per bond, they can't give this guy $900 apiece for those same bonds. That's not reasonably related to the market price. The firm also can't charge commissions that are way out of line with the industry norms.

Item J requires underwriters to deliver a prospectus "no later than the due date for confirmation." Sometimes, rather than a final prospectus, a final statement is sent out that completes any information not already covered in the preliminary prospectus. Either way, NASAA is reminding firms to deliver a prospectus in a new offering. Why wouldn't a firm always want to deliver a prospectus? Because those things lay out a lot of gloom-and-doom scenarios that can easily scare an investor away from the table. One minute the investor is ready to buy an additional offering of Starbucks common stock, the next minute she's reading about the risk of a "global pandemic" or "possible negative health effects associated with the company's products" and padlocking her purse. Oh, well. Investors have to be fully informed of all the important risks—otherwise, the broker-dealer would be selling securities fraudulently.

Item K reminds firms not to charge unreasonable or inequitable fees for services performed, including a host of various services that broker-dealers provide. The regulators don't spell out maximum fees, but they expect firms to keep their charges reasonable and fair among their various customers. If not, the Administrator can always schedule a hearing at the firm's earliest convenience.

Point L is talking about a violation called "backing away." If a broker-dealer puts out a firm quote, they had better be prepared to trade at the price they indicate. Point M is admonishing broker-dealers not to mislead customers by saying that a security is being offered "at the market" if there is really no secondary market out there for the security. I have seen several examples of investors getting duped into buying "preferred stock" in some shaky company and then finding out later that the stock isn't listed or traded anywhere. Maybe one of those investors wants to liquidate and get some of her money back—the broker-dealer can't say that they're offering to buy those shares "at the market" unless they know an actual secondary market for the security exists. If they're the only firm willing or crazy enough to buy that preferred stock, they need to be clear about that.

Item N goes into great detail in explaining that market manipulation will get you into all kinds of trouble. We can't just get together with another firm and buy a huge block of thinly traded stock, then start creating the illusion of an active market for it, so that we can later dump our stock at a much higher price, all based on our deception and manipulation of the market.

Item O reminds the firm not to guarantee the customer against a loss. Broker-dealers make suitable recommendations, but they don't protect customers from market losses. If the word "guaranteed" is used, it has to be explained clearly to the investor to avoid misleading him. A US Treasury security is definitely guaranteed as to interest and principal by the US Treasury, but it still has interest rate and market risk. A corporate bond could be "guaranteed" if a third party promised to pay interest and/or principal in the event of a default, but that also needs to be explained clearly to an investor. A broker-dealer could sell someone a "put-able bond" or a bond with a "put option" that gives the investor the right to sell the bond back for a set price in exchange for some kind of premium. In this case, there would be a written agreement, and it would be clear what the customer paid and what the customer would get. But a broker-dealer doesn't tell a customer that if the trade they're recommending goes sour, the broker-dealer will eat the losses for them. They're not insurance companies accepting premiums in exchange for protection against market loss. And, if they tell an investor her money is "guaranteed" when, in fact, it isn't, that would be a very serious violation. If they told her that a Fannie Mae mortgage-backed security is guaranteed by the US Treasury—which it isn't—the firm would be in big trouble, no matter how safe the security might be or how close Fannie and Freddie really are to being guaranteed. "Close" doesn't count—the regulators want full disclosure of all material facts.

Item P reminds broker-dealers not to publish that a transaction has occurred unless they actually know it occurred. Otherwise the firm might be engaging in market manipulation, trying to make it appear that a stock's price is moving a certain way when it's all based on fictitious transactions.

Item Q reminds the firm not to circulate material that is misleading or deceptive. For example, it might be tempting to put out a flyer that shows how much Company XYZ would be worth if over the next 6 months they simply eliminated $5 billion in debt, increased revenues 10,000%, and slashed costs 89% without resorting to layoffs or pay cuts. You could even show graphs of this wonderful turnaround effort. Trouble is, it's all based on wild conjecture, is so improbable as to be nearly impossible and, therefore, should not be circulated at all. It is "nonfactual," misleading, and probably deceptive.

Don't do that.

If the broker-dealer is owned by the issuer of the stock that the firm is selling to investors, that's kind of an important detail that should be disclosed, as Point R reminds us. Right? The broker-dealer is recommending that you buy stock, bonds, or commercial paper in the parent company? Doesn't that sort of directly benefit the broker-dealer even beyond the typical commissions earned? Item S reminds underwriters not to get greedy when they realize that the stock they're bringing to the primary market is likely to take off like a rocket ship. Might be tempting to hang onto the stock for their own accounts and cancel all the indications of interest, but that would be "failure to make a bona fide offering" and would get the firm into all kinds of trouble.

Item T is a very clear reminder to give customers the information they are entitled to. Customers are certainly entitled to trade confirmations, account statements, mutual fund prospectuses, etc. They are even entitled to independent research on companies generated by other firms. Broker-dealers have to respond to written customer complaints, as well. And, they have to keep detailed records on how the complaint was handled.

And then the policy statement addresses agents specifically.

Item A reminds agents not to borrow money from customers unless the customer happens to be a lending institution: bank, savings & loan, thrift, credit union, building & loan, etc. An agent cannot "act as a custodian for" customer money or securities because generally once the client's money goes into the agent's bank or brokerage account, it has no chance of ever coming out again.

Item B warns against executing transactions not recorded on the books and records of your firm unless you have written authorization from the firm to do so, and it's slightly hard to picture how you'd get that. An official order to deny an agent's license in the State of Washington told the sad story of an agent who got an elderly investor to cut him three personal checks for $50,000, all of which ended up in his brokerage account. So, right there, he has "acted as a custodian for client money" and "commingled client funds with his own," which is, to say the least, ill-advised. But then when he started executing trades, the Administrator could also add item B to the list of allegations, since those transactions were certainly not recorded on the regular books or records of the broker-dealer, who knew nothing about the little scheme. If an agent is approaching investors without his employer's knowledge, he is committing the violation of "selling away," which is short for "selling away from the firm." The rules are clear her, people—don't offer or sell any securities investments without your firm's knowledge, approval, and oversight.

Item C is pretty clear. If there is an offering of stock open only to accredited investors, and your customer isn't close to meeting the net worth and income requirements, would it be okay to indicate a higher net worth and income on the required paperwork in order to allow him to buy the limited offering?

No. Opening accounts based on fictitious information is a bad idea.

Item D reminds us that, basically, you shouldn't be sharing profits and/or losses with a customer. The only exception is when you're in a joint account with the customer and you've received the customer's authorization as well as your broker-dealer's.

Item E makes it clear that you can only split commissions with registered agents at your firm or a firm directly related to your firm—such as a subsidiary, for example. So, you can split commissions, as long as the agent is registered and works for your firm directly or indirectly. Many agents' assistants get their licenses in order to take client orders and share commissions with their agents. That's fine.

But it wouldn't be fine for an agent to tell 20 of his friends that he'll split commissions with them in exchange for referrals. Don't share commissions with unregistered persons.

The policy statement then tells the agent not to do most of the things it told broker-dealers not to do. And then the policy statement ends with a reminder that these prohibited activities are not inclusive, meaning there's still plenty of other stuff that could get you in hot water with the regulators. They just felt like pointing out some of the things not to do in this policy statement.

MORE NASAA CONCERNS

➤ Research Reports

First, it is a major violation for broker-dealers to compensate their research analysts, who publish reports on the merits of particular stocks, based on the amount of investment banking they can drum up by making certain companies happy with said research reports. In other words, a broker-dealer can't offer a bonus to the research analyst who just wrote a positive report on, say, GE when GE then hires the firm to help with a merger/acquisition as a thank-you for helping to push the price of the stock up, that inflated stock now being used to acquire the target company. I know that concept is a little hard to follow, and that's the nature of most industry violations—the average Joe and Joann don't even understand what the heck the firms are doing or why that would be, like, bad. Well, in the situation we're explaining here, the average Joe and Joann are being defrauded—how? They're being sent research reports to help guide their investment selection…only these "research reports" are not objective in the least. Rather, they are tools used to inflate the market price of the stock just so the firm can make money helping the issuer do some investment banking down the road—that issuer often using the inflated stock price as the currency used to buy the other company. Talk about an unholy mess!

So, there had better not be any funny business going on between the broker-dealer's research analysts and their investment bankers. The investment banking division cannot set the compensation of research analysts, and there can be no link between the research analysts and the investment banking division. If you look at a research report these days, you'll see lots of disclosure on the front cover that the broker-dealer may do underwriting business for the issuers whose stock they are promoting— I mean, researching. Due to a settlement with the New York State Attorney General's office, the disclosure also mentions that readers should consult other sources before making decisions and can request free independent research reports from the broker-dealer.

➤ Using the Internet

NASAA has a policy statement on the use of the internet for "general dissemination of information on products and services." Basically, it comes down to this: if you're putting up a website discussing your services and products, anyone with a web connection can see it, which might include people in states where you and the broker-dealer are not registered. If you are deemed to be transacting securities business in a state where you're not registered, well, your life is going to become very complicated. So, NASAA is putting out the uniform idea for state regulators that an agent or broker-dealer using a website is not considered to be transacting business in states where they're not registered if the following bullet points are taken into account:

- The Internet Communication contains a legend in which it is clearly stated that the broker-dealer, investment adviser, BD agent or IA rep in question may only transact business in this state if first registered, excluded or exempted from registration requirements, and follow-up, individualized responses to persons in this state that involve either the effecting or attempting to effect transactions in securities, or the rendering of personalized investment advice for compensation, will not be made absent compliance with state registration requirements, or an applicable exemption or exclusion

In other words, your website needs some text clearly explaining that you're not trying to offer securities or investment advice through the website and would only do so if registered or excused from registration in the web visitor's state.

Also:

- The Internet Communication does not involve either effecting or attempting to effect transactions in securities, or the rendering of personalized investment advice for compensation in this state over the Internet, but is limited to the dissemination of general information on products and services

That means that the website had better not involve effecting or attempting to effect purchases/sales of securities or the delivery of personalized investment advice for compensation.

Now, when this statement of policy first went out, not that many agents had the time or technical savvy to build an actual "website." But nowadays, with Facebook, Twitter, blogs, etc. imagine how easy it is for a securities agent to open up Facebook and accidentally post something about the benefits of variable annuities or the superiority of the mutual funds she sells. As many readers have already been told by a supervisor or two, be very careful what you post on Facebook and other social media. You might think it's "just your opinion" or that you're speaking your mind "on your own time," but that's not the case. Whatever you post concerning securities would have to first be cleared by a compliance principal as advertising. Most firms are probably telling their agents and IARs right now something like the following: don't talk about securities or your practice on Facebook or other social media, and only post what we give you to post.

I shudder to think how many agents will end up getting fired and regulated right out of the business due to an inability to keep their opinions in check, but I predict that by the time this book goes to press we will be seeing the first round of let's-make-an-example-out-of-these-clowns disciplinary actions by the securities regulators. So, just to make sure you don't end up in that crowd, let's clarify that I, the guy who writes the textbook, can say whatever the heck I want on my Facebook wall and my company's fan page. You, the person with the securities license, you can't say squat on Facebook about securities, your firm, or your practice, unless your firm says it's okay.

This NASAA policy statement applies to state-registered investment advisers and investment adviser representatives, whether working for a federal covered or state-registered advisory firm.

> Holding Seminars

Whenever the regulators hear that financial services professionals are holding seminars, their ears perk up just like my cat's do at the sound of an electric can opener. Holding seminars, are we? Senior citizens? Oh, they get a free hot lunch, and there's no pressure to invest. Tell us more. No, we insist.

There is just something at least mildly dangerous about combining the following words in any order:

- Senior citizens
- Investment seminar
- Free hot lunch

In other words, things might turn out okay here, but we certainly do want to take a much closer look. For example, are you holding yourself out as being an objective adviser when, in fact, you're just trying to scare these senior citizens out of perfectly safe bank accounts and into some fixed annuity products that pay you HUGE commissions? The State of Massachusetts had a recent action against some folks doing exactly that, and it would be hard to find any state that wasn't showing increased concern over the increased use of senior seminars and annuity sales. Not that annuities are inherently evil (they aren't), but if they carry a long surrender period and a big surrender charge, that would make them almost inherently unsuitable for senior citizens. And if the seminar somehow failed to disclose such facts, we'd be talking about securities fraud.

Also, the seminar might be perfectly legitimate and otherwise compliant except for one problem—the agent forgot to tell his compliance principal about the seminar and forgot to show him the invitations, handouts, and PowerPoint slides. That would be a violation of industry rules and when FINRA finds out, they'll fine and suspend/bar the agent and then send notice to the state regulators.

REGISTRATION OF PERSONS - INVESTMENT ADVISERS AND IARS

The first thing an investment adviser registering with the regulators sees on Form ADV is this:

> WARNING! Complete this form truthfully. False statements or omissions may result in denial of your application, revocation of your registration, or criminal prosecution.

Then, right after that, he sees the four different ways that an adviser could use the same form:

- Submit an initial application to register as an investment adviser with the SEC.
- Submit an initial application to register as an investment adviser with one or more states.
- Submit an annual updating amendment to your registration for your fiscal year ended _____.
- Submit an other-than-annual amendment to your registration.

Whether the adviser registers with the SEC or with one or more state regulators, Form ADV is filed electronically through a system called the **Investment Adviser Registration Depository** (IARD). Setting up an IARD account is the first step in the registration process. Once an adviser establishes an IARD account, the adviser can access Form ADV (Part I) on IARD, complete this part of Form ADV, and submit it electronically to the SEC.

To register with the SEC, the adviser has to check at least one box showing the SEC why they're eligible. For example, if the assets under management are at least $100 million, or if the adviser manages registered investment company portfolios, they are eligible for federal registration. Within 45 days, the SEC will either grant the registration or—in rare, unfortunate cases—start proceedings to determine if maybe the registration should be denied. Maybe there are regulatory histories that give the regulators pause, or maybe the balance sheet looks about as reliable as an Enron balance sheet. In most cases, assuming the form is filled out correctly and the payment clears, the adviser will be granted a registration.

So, one use of Form ADV is to file an initial application with the SEC. Another use is to update the registration on an annual basis. Within 90 days after the end of each fiscal year, the adviser must file what the SEC calls an "annual updating amendment" in order to renew the registration. They must update their responses to all items on Form ADV Part I when they do this. And—as always—they must pay a fee. You're dealing with the federal government; they like fees.

A third use of Form ADV would be the "other-than-annual updating amendment" mentioned on Page 1 of the form. That means that if something major changes at the firm—they move to a different state, their business structure changes, or management changes hands—they must file a new Form ADV to inform the SEC of the change promptly (within 30 days of the change). See the difference? You update your ADV part I every year, period, with the annual updating amendment. And, if something major changes at your firm, you go ahead and update promptly, whenever this change occurs. Since the latter is used for a purpose other than the purpose of updating annually, it is called, very cleverly, an "other-than-annual updating amendment."

Form ADV contains two parts. Part 1 contains the following information:

- the name and form of organization under which the investment adviser engages or intends to engage in business; the name of the state or other sovereign power under which such investment adviser is organized; the location of his or its principal business office and branch offices, if any; the names and addresses of his or its partners, officers, directors, and persons performing similar functions or, if such an investment adviser be an individual, of such individual; and the number of his or its employees;
- the education, the business affiliations for the past ten years, and the present business affiliations of such investment adviser and of his or its partners, officers, directors, and persons performing similar functions and of any controlling person thereof;
- the nature of the business of such investment adviser, including the manner of giving advice and rendering analyses or reports;
- the nature and scope of the authority of such investment adviser with respect to clients' funds and accounts;
- the basis or bases upon which such investment adviser is compensated;
- whether such investment adviser, or any person associated with such investment adviser, is subject to any disqualification which would be a basis for denial, suspension, or revocation of registration of such investment adviser under the provisions of subsection (e) of this section; and
- a statement as to whether the principal business of such investment adviser consists or is to consist of acting as investment adviser and a statement as to whether a substantial part of the business of such investment adviser consists or is to consist of rendering investment supervisory services

All the list is really saying is that the regulators would like to know some basic information about your investment advisory firm. What's the address? Is this a business address or a makeshift office above your garage? Yes, an adviser could be a sole proprietor. He could also work from home in his pajamas all day long. I would assume he would shower, shave, and dress for any regulatory inspections, but I'll leave that to the individual. In any case, the regulators want to know if this advisory business is a sole proprietorship, a partnership, a corporation, an LLC, etc. If it's a corporation, where is it incorporated? Tell us a little bit about the partners, officers, and directors of the firm—who knows, maybe some of their mug shots will pop up when we do a criminal background search, and won't that be fun? What is the education and business background of these big shots at the firm? How many employees do you have? What kind of services do you offer your clients? How many and what types of clients do you serve? How are you compensated? Do you have discretion over the accounts, or custody over client assets? Do you act as a principal in client transactions? Do you get compensated from broker-dealers that have custody of your client accounts? Et cetera, et cetera. Basically, it's the information you would expect the regulators to want to know in order to protect investors from advisers who have no business being in the business.

> FEDERAL COVERED ADVISERS

Okay, so which advisers are eligible to register with the SEC? Here we go with the bullet points:

- Adviser with at least $100 million of assets under management
- Adviser to a registered investment company
- Mid-sized adviser ($25–100 million assets under management) to a business development company
- Pension consultants providing advice to employee benefit plans with assets of at least $200 million
- Adviser that would be required to register in 15 or more states
- Internet investment advisers
- Affiliates of federally registered adviser if the principal office and place of business of the affiliate is the same as that of the SEC-registered adviser
- Newly formed advisers that reasonably believe that they will become eligible for federal registration within 120 days
- Adviser with their principal place of business in the US Virgin Islands or Wyoming
- Adviser with their principal place of business outside the United States

Remember that an adviser with over $110 million of assets under management must register with the SEC, as must an adviser managing investment company assets or a mid-sized adviser managing business development company assets. The others (including advisers with between $100 and $110 million in assets under management) are eligible to register with the SEC. Why would they even want to register with the SEC? Well, if you were an internet adviser in Colorado with clients in Montana, California, Oregon, and Washington, you might get tired of dealing with five different regulators; therefore, it would be easier to just register with the SEC.

Notice Filings

On Form ADV the SEC asks which states need to receive a copy of the form. See, even though the investment advisory firm is registering with the SEC, they also need to make a **notice filing** with a state if they have a place of business in the state or have six or more clients in that state, regardless of their place of business. Since the federal covered adviser would be filing notice with various states, the regulators go ahead and call this process a notice filing. For the privilege of having the SEC file a duplicate of the form with various state regulators, the adviser pays a notice-filing fee. So, even though the firm is federal covered, they still would perform a notice filing in the state(s) where they maintain an office. And, they would still be subject to the state's anti-fraud authority. It was NSMIA (National Securities Markets Improvement Act) that created this concept of "federal covered advisers," but NSMIA made it clear that the state regulators still have the authority to require and collect a fee for a notice filing, and still have the authority to legally pursue even a federal covered adviser if they're misleading and defrauding the heck out of investors in the state. Not that the SEC wouldn't jump right on the pile once the state regulators got things rolling.

If the adviser wants to withdraw their registration, they file a Form **ADV-W**. They don't just stop showing up at the office, in other words. I suppose the IA might just be getting out of the business. More likely, they're switching from federal to state-level registration. Why? Maybe they're lousy stock pickers, who just turned $105 million of assets into $60 million. Hate it when that happens. Or, maybe they're just a bunch of rude, arrogant jerks and all of their big customers have left. In any case, the IA would file their annual updating amendment reporting that they are no longer registering with the big dogs because of the level of assets under management. They would then file an ADV-W ("w" for "withdrawal") within 180 days after the close of their fiscal year. During this period while they are registered with both the Commission and one or more state securities authorities, the Investment Advisers Act of 1940 and applicable state laws will apply to their advisory activities.

Although this next scenario is not a withdrawal, it makes sense to talk about the opposite case here, where the IA is moving up from state-level registration to federal (SEC) registration. Why? Maybe their assets under management have grown to over $100 million, or they now advise registered investment companies. In this case, the IA must apply for SEC registration within 90 days of filing an annual updating amendment to Form ADV that showed why they're suddenly eligible to play with the big kids.

Also know that even if a firm has withdrawn its registration with the SEC, they can still end up getting in trouble with the feds. In fact, although the ADV-W is considered effective when it's filed, the registration actually continues for 60 days just in case the SEC finds out they need to take regulatory action against a firm that is suddenly in a big hurry to flee from their watchful eyes. Up to and during this 60-day period, the SEC can decide to suspend a firm's registration. A suspension is a definite strike against the firm, and the SEC can suspend a firm for as long as 12 months, which is bad for a firm's business. Why would the SEC cop such an attitude against an investment adviser? Perhaps the person (individual or firm):

- Willfully made or caused to be made any false or misleading report or application regarding a material fact, or omitted a material fact
- Has been convicted within the previous 10 years of any felony or any securities-related misdemeanor
- Is enjoined by court order
- Has willfully violated any provision of federal securities law
- Has willfully aided another person's violation of federal securities law or has failed to supervise a person who commits a violation
- Is subject to an order of the SEC barring or suspending the person from being associated with an investment adviser

➢ Disclosure Brochure

Most prospects and customers must also be given a **disclosure brochure**, which is usually a copy of **Form ADV Part 2**. The test might ask you when the brochure must be delivered to a prospect. The answer for a state-registered adviser is within 48 hours (before) of signing the contract, or at the time of signing the contract if the client has five days to cancel without penalty. A federal covered adviser—operating under SEC rules—can deliver the brochure before or at the time the client signs the advisory agreement.

If an investment adviser provides substantially different types of advisory services to different clients, any information required in the disclosure brochure may be omitted for a particular client if that information does not apply to that particular client. For example, if a particular client is not being charged performance bonuses, there would be no need to provide a detailed explanation of how performance bonuses are calculated. Similarly, only wrap-fee clients would need to receive the wrap fee brochure.

The adviser's disclosure brochure must either contain substantially the same information as—or be an actual copy of—ADV Part 2. This part of the form tells customers the essential information on their investment adviser, such as:

- Types of securities about which advice is rendered and the types of analyses used to make such recommendations
- Services provided, fees charged
- Education and business background of all officers of the firm and any employee that determines advice
- Any compensation incentives to the adviser for placing trades through particular broker-dealers/affiliations with other securities professionals
- A balance sheet if the adviser has custody or requires prepayment of fees of >$500 six or more months in advance
- Criminal and regulatory disclosure (if any is required) over previous 10 years

But, not *all* Investment Advisers have to deliver this brochure. If the client is an investment company or a business development company defined under the Investment Company Act of 1940, we don't need to deliver a brochure. For example, an investment adviser such as Janus Capital Management has a contract with the board of directors of the Janus Funds. The adviser does not need to send a disclosure brochure to every shareholder who buys into the mutual funds. Rather, those investors receive a prospectus or other disclosure document before buying into the fund, under the Securities Act of 1933.

Also, if the advice is considered "impersonal," meaning it isn't tailored to specific client situations and costs less than $500 per year, we don't need a brochure. The opposite of "impersonal" advice would be "supervisory services," where the IA purports to tailor advice to each client, rather than directing advice to a whole group of clients—retirees, teachers, day traders, small-cap value investors. And this can get a little tricky, so let's take a minute to make sure you understand what's happening here. We are *not* saying that if someone charges less than $500 per year and doesn't meet regularly with investors he escapes the definition of "investment adviser." The amount of money never determines whether someone is or is not an investment adviser. The activities performed by the professional determine this under the three-pronged approach used by the SEC. For example, I subscribe to a newsletter on value stocks in which regular recommendations are made to buy, hold, and occasionally sell particular stocks. Why do I read and pay for this monthly newsletter? Because it is written by people who know what they're doing—actual investment advisers. Do they have to deliver their ADV Part 2 to me and the thousands of other subscribers?

No, they never purport to have looked at our situations and tailored their recommendations based on their analysis. The advice is impersonal because of that and because the annual subscription is well south of $500. Are they investment advisers? Yes—they have managed other people's money for years as registered IAs or IARs. If not, why would I read, let alone act upon, their advice?

On the other hand, when the SEC is using the three-pronged approach to determine if a newsletter writer is an investment adviser, they ask if he is providing advice based on the individual situations of the readers. If not, it doesn't matter what he charges; this guy is not an investment adviser, *if that is all he does.* Now, before anyone shouts, "No fair—why doesn't he have to register!" ask who would read, let alone pay for, some guy's advice if he has never been and is not currently an investment adviser? If some creative writer wants to publish a blog and entertain his readers while discussing securities investing, he is really just exercising his First Amendment rights under the US Constitution. As long as he doesn't engage in fraud by, perhaps, taking money from OTC equity securities issuers to pump up their stock price, he's good to go.

Though, again, how he gets people to pay for investment advice without having any "street cred," I have no idea.

In any case, things are always changing in this industry, and just in case your exam wants to bring up some recent changes to Form ADV Part 2, let's be ready for it. In the past Form ADV 2 has been presented in a check-box format. Now the SEC requires advisers to drop the check-box format and use a narrative, "Plain English" style when creating the disclosure brochure. As the SEC explains, advisers must now:

- Use Plain English.
- Use a narrative form as opposed to the former check-box approach.
- Add a table of contents with the disclosure items listed in the same order as the items in the form.
- Provide a supplement (ADV Part 2B) about advisory personnel on whom clients rely for investment advice.
- Provide a copy of the current (updated) brochure annually to existing clients that includes or is accompanied by the summary of material changes; or provide existing clients a summary of material changes that includes an offer to provide a copy of the current brochure.
- Attach a cover page to the adviser's brochure (ADV Part 2) that states that the brochure has not been approved by the Commission or any state securities authority. Also, if an adviser refers to itself as a "registered investment adviser," it also must include a disclaimer that registration does not imply a certain level of skill or training.

Concerning the New ADV Part 2B, let's just let the SEC tell us what's what in their own words:

Rule 204-3 also requires that each firm brochure be accompanied by brochure supplements providing information about the advisory personnel on whom the particular client receiving the brochure relies for investment advice. Among other things, the brochure supplements will contain information about the educational background, business experience, and disciplinary history (if any) of the supervised persons who provide advisory services to the client. The brochure supplement thus includes information that would not necessarily be included in the firm brochure about supervised persons of the adviser who actually provide the investment advice and interact with the client. We are requiring as proposed that a client be given a brochure supplement for each supervised person who: (i) formulates investment advice for that client and has direct client contact; or (ii) makes discretionary investment decisions for that client's assets, even if the supervised person has no direct client contact. We believe that clients are most interested in learning about the background and experience of these individuals from whom they receive investment advice. We are adopting as proposed, the requirement that advisers deliver an updated supplement to clients only when there is new disclosure of a disciplinary event, or a material change to disciplinary information already disclosed.

For existing clients, a federal covered adviser must deliver annually (within 120 days after the end of their fiscal year and without charge) either the brochure or a summary of all material changes since their last annual updating amendment. Advisers now file ADV Part 2A (not the supplement) electronically with the SEC. They create it in Adobe PDF format, and then upload it electronically.

➢ Wrap-Fee Programs

We've discussed the differences between broker-dealers and investment advisers. One of the inherent problems with a brokerage account is that the client always wonders if the broker-dealer is executing trades simply to make commissions. Some clients prefer to pay a portfolio manager whose compensation is tied to the value of the account, while also knowing that there are no extra charges for large numbers of trades. The solution for these clients is the **wrap account**. A wrap account is an advisory account where portfolio management services, custody, and brokerage transactions are "wrapped" together into one flat fee called a **wrap fee**. Investment advisers sponsor these programs by getting custodial broker-dealers on board to charge a flat fee for all trades entered by the adviser's portfolio managers. This way the client receives portfolio management and pays nothing extra even if a large number of trades are executed on his behalf. This eliminates the concern for churning. If the adviser sponsors a wrap fee program, the adviser must deliver a written disclosure statement (**wrap fee brochure**) of how these wrap fees work, pointing out that the client may pay more this way than if the services were purchased separately. Generally, clients who are comfortable with frequent trading do better under wrap-fee programs, while those who are more buy-and-hold types would probably save money paying for each transaction if/when it occurs.

Also note that if one adviser refers the client to another adviser who will provide the client with a wrap-fee brochure, the first adviser does not need to do so.

➢ State Registration

In general, the large firms register with the SEC (federal), while the smaller firms register with the states. If the firm has not been excluded from the definition of investment adviser and not granted an exemption (excuse) from state registration, they'll have to register in the states where they have a place of business. The investment adviser would file an application with the state securities Administrator, and this is usually the same Form ADV used for SEC registration. The state securities Administrator might also require the applicant to publish an announcement in one or more specified newspapers published in the state. The initial application is accompanied by a consent to service of process, which you can see at www.nasaa.org under "uniform forms." This authorizes the Administrator to receive court papers (service of process) on the applicant's behalf in any non-criminal legal complaint, meaning that I wouldn't have to chase down the suddenly hard-to-locate adviser; instead, I'd just serve process on the Administrator, which would have the same validity of serving them on the party who doesn't seem to be returning voice mails all of a sudden. Remember this consent to service of process thing—it is filed with the initial application for advisers, adviser reps, broker-dealers, agents, and securities subject to state registration. The consent to service of process is filed only initially; it does not have to be filed with every renewal application. Fees must also be paid to the state when the applicant registers. No big surprise there.

We'll be looking at the Uniform Securities Act, which is a model for state securities laws, in a moment. For now, let's look at this stipulation from the Uniform Securities Act:

With respect to investment advisers, the [Administrator] may require that certain information be furnished or disseminated as necessary or appropriate in the public interest or for the protection of investors and advisory clients. To the extent determined by the [Administrator] in his discretion, information furnished to clients or prospective clients of an investment adviser that would be in compliance with the Investment Advisers Act of 1940 and the rules thereunder may be used in whole or partial satisfaction of this requirement.

And that's why the state securities regulators typically write rules that require investment advisers to do X, Y, and Z in compliance with SEC rules made under the Investment Advisers Act of 1940. Those federal regulators in Washington, DC, do a fine job churning out rules for advisers, so why should the states waste time reinventing the wheel? Whether the Administrator writes his/their own requirements or just requires the firms to comply with the federal regulations, the Administrator not only wants the books and records preserved; he may want to have himself a look someday.

NASAA has a model rule that declares the minimum net capital for an adviser based on certain activities:

- Adviser with custody: $35,000
- Adviser with discretion but not custody: $10,000
- Adviser accepting prepayment > $500 six + months in advance: positive net worth

Because maintaining custody leads to higher net capital requirements and the responsibility to have the books audited, most advisers try to avoid maintaining custody and use a qualified custodian instead. Also note that if the adviser has custody or accepts prepayment as indicated above, the adviser must submit an audited balance sheet to both the Administrator and the client. And, of course, an accounting firm has to be paid to audit that balance sheet and sign off on it.

State regulators may not require an adviser properly registered in its home state and meeting that state's net capital requirements to maintain a higher requirement. Federal covered advisers who provide notice filings in the state, though, will be subject to the SEC net capital requirements. The states could not make the adviser comply with a higher requirement than what's covered under the Investment Advisers Act of 1940, should the exam decide to go there. Similarly, the Administrator can't require a higher net capital for broker-dealers than what is required under the Securities Exchange Act of 1934.

Record Keeping

Investment advisers have to keep all kinds of books and records on their business, such as:

- Receipts and Disbursements Journals (money and/or securities)
- General Ledger

- Order Memoranda
- Bank Records (for the firm)
- Bills and Statements (for the firm)
- Financial Statements (for the firm)
- Originals of all written communications received and copies of all written communications sent by the investment adviser relating to (A) recommendations/advice, (B) any receipt, disbursement or delivery of funds or securities, or (C) the placing or execution of any securities transaction
- List of Discretionary Accounts
- Advertising
- Personal Transactions of Representatives and Principals
- Powers Granted by Clients
- Disclosure Statements
- Solicitors' Disclosure Statements
- Performance Claims
- Customer Information Forms and Suitability Information
- Written Supervisory Procedures

If the adviser has custody of client funds or securities, the IA must keep the following records:

- Journals of Securities Transactions and Movements
- Separate Client Ledgers
- Copies of Confirmations
- Record by Security Showing Each Client's Interest and Location Thereof

Notice above that the adviser needs two separate and related lists: one is a list of each client and which securities he holds in his account, another list is by each security, e.g., MSFT common stock, and how many shares each advisory client owns of that total. You can imagine how those cross-referenced lists could help spot any discrepancies.

If the IA actively manages client assets, the firm must maintain the following records:

- Client Purchases and Sales History
- Current Client Securities Positions

These records (the two above bullet points) are required to be maintained in an easily accessible place for a period of five years from the end of the fiscal year during which the last entry was made and, for the first two years, the records must be maintained in the adviser's principal office. Electronic records are okay, as long as the firm can verify that the records are accurate and complete and could not have been easily altered. Maybe a test question will want you to say that a "read-only" file would work, since it would not allow anyone to make alterations to the records. In other words, electronic records have to give the regulators confidence that certain transactions have not been accidentally deleted or altered to conceal some sort of violations. Remember that record-keeping is a big responsibility and that deficient records lead to fines and sanctions by the state regulators all the time. Every year NASAA publishes data on the results of state securities regulatory examinations of advisers, and every year the main problem is a lack of record keeping. If the adviser has discretion but doesn't keep sufficient records on the transactions made using that discretion, it's a problem. If the adviser puts out advertising touting their stock picks, but can't seem to back it up with trade confirmations and account statements, it's a problem. If the adviser seems to have five or six more investment adviser reps working at the firm than they've indicated on Form ADV, well, you get the idea.

Finally, if a firm is deemed to have custody of client funds and securities, what sort of questions would the state regulators be trying to answer? Luckily, NASAA saw fit to tell us. As NASAA states on their website (www.nasaa.org):

If an adviser has direct or indirect access to client funds or securities, it is considered to have custody of client funds and is subject to additional scrutiny. State regulators will want to see how you handle those assets by asking the following:

- Has the adviser complied with the rules relating to safeguarding client assets in the adviser's custody?
- Does the Form ADV reflect that the adviser has custody?
- Are these assets maintained in segregated accounts?
- Does the adviser maintain the required records of client assets in its custody?
- Does the client get an itemized statement at least every three months showing the assets in the adviser's custody and the activity in the account?
- Has a surprise audit of client assets been conducted at least annually by an independent accountant?
- If the adviser has discretionary authority over the client's account, is there any evidence of excessive trading, self-dealing, preferential treatment, unsuitable recommendations, unauthorized transactions, or incomplete disclosure?

➢ Investment Adviser Exclusions

Here is the verbatim, legalistic definition of "Investment Adviser" under the Uniform Securities Act:

"Investment adviser" means any person who, for compensation, engages in the business of advising others, either directly or through publications or writings, as to the value of securities or as to the advisability of investing in, purchasing, or selling securities, or who, for compensation and as a part of a regular business, issues or promulgates analyses or reports concerning securities. "Investment adviser" also includes financial planners and other persons who, as an integral component of other financially related services, provide the foregoing investment advisory services to others for compensation and as part of a business or who hold themselves out as providing the foregoing investment advisory services to others for compensation.

In a second we'll see who does and does not fit within that rather complicated definition above by applying the so-called "three-pronged test." But first let's see who is excluded outright from the definition of "investment adviser" by the Uniform Securities Act:

"Investment adviser" does not include (1) an investment adviser representative;(2) a bank, savings institution, or trust company; (3) a lawyer, accountant, engineer, or teacher whose performance of these services is solely incidental to the practice of his profession; (4) a broker-dealer or its agent whose performance of these services is solely incidental to the conduct of its business as a broker-dealer and who receives no special compensation for them; (5) a publisher of any bona fide newspaper, news column, newsletter, news magazine, or business or financial publication or service, whether communicated in hard copy form, or by electronic means, or otherwise, that does not consist of the rendering of advice on the basis of the specific investment situation of each client; (6) any person that is a federal covered adviser; or (7) such other persons not within the intent of this subsection as the [Administrator] may by rule or order designate.

First, an investment adviser is not an investment adviser representative and vice versa. One is the firm, the other represents the firm. We saw the same relationship between the broker-dealer firm and the agent who represents it. Some states go so far with this separation that they require an investment adviser set up as a sole proprietor or single-member LLC to register as both the investment adviser and the investment adviser representative. And then that leads to rather bizarre and comical statements from the regulators such as, "If you are both the adviser and the adviser representative, you are not required to file a report of securities holdings with yourself or receive authorization from yourself."

Anyway, the RIA and the IAR are two different entities.

As with the definition of broker-dealer, the following entities are also excluded from the definition of investment adviser: banks, savings institutions, and trust companies. They may be related to the investment adviser, with the same parent company and everything, but the investment adviser is not the bank or the savings & loan and vice versa. If a bank or other savings institution wants to get into the managed funds business, they set up a separate entity and register that entity as an investment adviser, just as they have to do if they want to set up a broker-dealership. Since I own a few shares of Wells Fargo common stock, I decided to look up the Form ADV information on their investment adviser. As their registration information indicates, Wells Capital Management is the investment advisory subsidiary of Wells Fargo Bank. The bank is not an adviser. The adviser is not a bank. Related, sure. But separate entities.

Lawyers, accountants, teachers, and engineers could all end up talking about securities or the value of securities, or having conversations with investment implications. Lawyers could be doing estate planning and trying to determine the value of some oil & gas partnership that nobody knew anything about. An accountant could be "advising" somebody to make a maximum 401(k) contribution. A teacher could be teaching about the value of IBM stock. And an engineer or geologist could be rendering his opinion that there is, in fact, oil or natural gas on a particular patch of ground with that opinion attached to a securities offering, but in none of those cases is the professional acting as an investment adviser. For example, making your maximum 401(k) contribution could help your tax situation; as long as the accountant isn't charging you to help you select the investments for that contribution into your 401(k), she's just acting as an accountant. So, if their advice is "solely incidental" to their profession, they escape the definition of "investment adviser." Be careful how you read the test question, though—if the lawyer or accountant (teacher or engineer) is clearly providing investment advice for compensation, then they are acting as investment advisers. It's just that their professions might require them to deal with securities' values to some extent. But as long as it's within the scope of their profession, they're not acting as investment advisers.

Broker-dealers and their agents definitely do advise clients on how to invest. But, as the above language states, as long as they don't get compensated for the advice itself, and only get paid by commissions or markups/markdowns on the sale of securities, then they are still just acting as broker-dealers and/or agents. Now, that doesn't mean that because somebody is an agent he is automatically not an investment adviser. If a securities agent starts providing financial planning services on the side, he would be an investment adviser who needs to register and let the broker-dealer know what the heck he's up to. So, basically, just ask yourself if the agent is trying to get compensated for selling securities or for providing investment advice. He's only registered to do the former; to do the latter, he'd need a separate registration.

The Wall Street Journal and *Forbes* pass out all kinds of general investment advice in exchange for the subscription or newsstand price. That doesn't make them an investment adviser. You'd have to be rendering specific advice based on a specific situation and getting compensation for it before anyone would accuse you of being an investment adviser. This point of distinction could lead to confusion, unfortunately. A publication of general and regular circulation does not meet the definition, but what if the circulation is irregular, based on market movements or market signals? In that case, the regulators usually consider the newsletter writer to fit the definition of "investment adviser." There is a big difference between, on the one hand, writing general articles on investing and, on the other, charging people money to tell them when to buy and sell stock through email or text messaging, or even targeted mailings based on market conditions. The definition of investment adviser includes this phrase: any person who, for compensation, engages in the business of advising others, either directly or through publications or writings, as to the value of securities or as to the advisability of investing in, purchasing, or selling securities. That means that if you have, say, 30 clients and rather than meet with them face-to-face you, instead, send them written recommendations, you are definitely acting as their investment adviser. When the advice is specific to the client's needs, you're an adviser.

If you're writing a newsletter, newspaper, magazine, etc., that goes to a general audience on a regular publication schedule, you're not an adviser. Notice it's not the terminology we use that makes us an adviser or not. It's not whether or not you call the publication a "newsletter" that determines if you're an investment adviser. It's the function of that "newsletter" or "financial publication" or of your written recommendations that determines things. Are you publishing information on small-cap stocks in general to a general audience who receives the publication regularly? Or, are you dressing something up as a "newsletter" when, in fact, you're just charging people to tell them which securities to buy and sell and when to buy and sell them? You don't have to meet with someone to "advise" them, remember. If your sophisticated website takes the financial data that visitors enter and delivers a personalized investment recommendation, you are an investment adviser if you get any sort of compensation as a result of this "self-serve" website. But, again, if you're just writing articles about investing, chances are you do not meet the definition of an investment adviser.

A federal covered adviser is defined as an adviser under the federal Investment Advisers Act of 1940 and, therefore, not defined under the state securities law as an investment adviser. Finally, the Administrator also has the authority to name other individuals and entities that he considers outside the scope of regulation as an "investment adviser."

➢ Investment Adviser Exemptions

So those folks are excluded from the definition of "investment adviser." Whatever an investment adviser may—or may not—be able to do doesn't apply to them. They are NOT investment advisers.

If you are granted an "exemption," on the other hand, that basically means that you are an adviser, but you get an exemption (you're excused) from having to go through the process of registration. Bottom line is, whether you're excluded or exempted, it means you don't have to register. But, you might have to tell the exam that an adviser who is excluded from the definition of "investment adviser" under the Investment Advisers Act of 1940 is also excluded at the state level. However, the fact that someone gets an SEC exemption does not mean that the person necessarily gets a free hall pass at the state level.

358

I'm not convinced that the exam is all that concerned about SEC exemptions, but since there would be no way for you to, like, guess at the testing center if I'm wrong, I sort of have to include them. Sorry about that. I've decided in this version of the book to only mention the new exemptions that the SEC has come up with. Here we go. Advisers to private funds (private equity, hedge funds) with less than $150 million of assets under management are now exempt from registration, but are considered to be "exempt reporting advisers," meaning they must submit reports to the SEC and maintain certain scaled-down books and records, even though they don't have to register. Advisers to private funds (private equity, hedge funds) with $150 million of assets under management or more will be required to register with the SEC and will notice file with the states in which they have a place of business. Finally, advisers to VC (venture capital) funds are exempt, and here is how the SEC defines a "venture capital fund." First, an adviser claiming this exemption can advise only "venture capital funds," which the SEC defines like so:

a private fund that: (i) Holds no more than 20 percent of the fund's capital commitments in non-qualifying investments (other than short-term holdings) ("qualifying investments" generally consist of equity securities of "qualifying portfolio companies" that are directly acquired by the fund); (ii) does not borrow or otherwise incur leverage, other than limited short-term borrowing; (iii) does not offer its investors redemption or other similar liquidity rights except in extraordinary circumstances; (iv) represents itself as pursuing a venture capital strategy to its investors and prospective investors; and (v) is not registered under the Investment Company Act and has not elected to be treated as a business development company ("BDC").

So, if the investment adviser advises only venture capital funds—funds that meet the definition above—the adviser qualifies for an SEC exemption. The state regulators will likely also play along, not that they have to.

More important, let's focus on the exemptions under the Uniform Securities Act. The following persons might be investment advisers, but they don't have to register in the state:

- person who has *no place of business in this state* if his only clients in this state are other investment advisers, broker-dealers, banks, savings institutions, trust companies, insurance companies, investment companies as defined in the Investment Company Act of 1940, pension or profit-sharing trusts, or other financial institutions or institutional buyers
- person who has *no place of business in this state* if during any period of twelve consecutive months he does not direct business communications into this state to more than 5 clients other than those specified above

Again, notice how I put the phrase "no place of business in this state" in italics. If the firm has a place of business in the state, the firm will always have to register in the state.

Except when it doesn't.

NSMIA

The **National Securities Markets Improvement Act of 1996** decided that certain advisers should be "federal covered." That means that these folks register with the SEC. So, if you had an office in Albany, New York, you would not register with the State of New York if you were a federal covered adviser. You would, instead, register with the SEC. Either way, you'd fill out Form ADV, but you would indicate on it that you were registering with the SEC, who will provide a notice filing to the

State of New York. But a **notice filing** is simply a filing of notice that sounds much more official when we say it backwards.

Remember that federal covered advisers are still subject to the state's power to enforce anti-fraud regulations. But as long as they don't plan on defrauding investors, they can have an office in the state without registering with the state. The firm just needs to have the SEC send the state regulators a copy of Form ADV and all required schedules and pay a notice filing fee. This is done, by the way, through the convenient **IARD** system. The state can also demand a "consent to service of process."

What about the investment adviser representatives working for a federal covered adviser? Those individuals still register with the states. The investment advisory firm registers with the SEC if they're federal covered, but the individuals register with the states where they maintain a place of business. Just to keep everything nice and simple. Again, I suggest you take a look at the flow charts for investment adviser and investment adviser representative registration.

Also remember that the officers, partners, and directors of the adviser are automatically registered as investment adviser representatives when the firm registers with Form ADV. This is similar to the fact that partners, officers, and directors of a broker-dealer who will act as agents are automatically registered as agents when the broker-dealer registers.

SEC RELEASE IA-1092

Some readers would probably think that after the regulators went to the trouble of spelling out all those details, it's now crystal clear who is and is not an investment adviser and who does and does not have to register. Unfortunately, that is not the case. In fact, it is so unclear that the SEC is frequently responding to letters from attorneys of various clients trying to figure out if it's okay to do what they're proposing to do without actually registering as an investment adviser. In case the exam asks, those requests are called "requests for **no-action relief**." That means that the attorney for the client is seeking verification from the SEC or the securities Administrator that his client is okay to do what he proposes to do without registration, and the regulators will take no action. Sometimes the regulator can grant "no-action relief," sometimes they can't.

What kind of facts would the regulators use to determine if somebody is acting as an investment adviser? All relevant facts, actually, but there are three "prongs" that we need to look at, which help the regulators determine if somebody meets the definition of "investment adviser" or not.

Why is it so hard to make such a determination? Well, some professionals provide investment advice in connection with other financial services, and maybe they don't think of the advice as being an important part of the business. For example, a financial planner who focuses almost exclusively on insurance products could still be considered to provide investment advice if he told clients to sell their mutual funds in order to buy his fixed annuity. Many sports and entertainment agents are attorneys who negotiate contracts for star athletes and performers. They also end up telling clients how to invest their money. A sports agent might not give out a detailed report on stocks, but if tells his client to put 1/3 in real estate, 1/3 in insurance, and 1/3 in mutual funds, he is giving investment advice. Many pension fund consultants are hired by pension funds to help select all the investment advisers for the fund; are those people investment advisers or not? Usually, they are.

Since it's not always clear if a professional meets the definition of "investment adviser," the SEC put out a release back in 1987 that attempts to help explain their thought process when determining if somebody is or is not an investment adviser. This release made clear that the "three-pronged" test to determine if someone is an investment adviser involves the following:

- Does the professional provide investment advice?
- Is he/she in the business of providing advice?
- Do they receive compensation for this advice?

If the answer to all three questions is "yes," then the person is an investment adviser and must register unless he/they can claim a specific excuse known as an exemption. So, first, does the professional provide investment advice? Generally, if someone is helping someone decide on whether to invest in securities or how to allocate a portfolio based on the client's particular needs, that person is providing investment advice. The advice in this case doesn't have to be on a specific security. If a financial planner or sports agent is helping clients pick investments in securities in general as an alternative to an investment in real estate or insurance-based products, then he/she IS an investment adviser. In fact, if we rewrote that sentence in the other direction—the professional is helping clients pick insurance-based products or real estate as an alternative to investing in securities—same deal.

Pension consultants who help pension plans decide on either which securities to invest in or whether to invest in securities over some other asset are advisers. The consultants who help the funds determine which investment advisers to hire or retain are as well.

What does it mean to "be in the business of providing advice"? The SEC and NASAA determined that a person is in the business of providing advice if he or she gives advice on a regular basis and that advice "constitutes a business activity conducted with some regularity." The frequency is a factor, but it's not the only factor in determining if the person is "in the business" or not. In other words, the regulators can take it all on a case-by-case basis. What are the relevant factors in the case of this particular adviser who claims they don't have to register? Does it look like something that's part of a regular business or not? Providing advice doesn't have to be the main activity of the person, either. You could be a CPA doing tax work and only provide investment advice if a client asks for it. That's close enough for the regulators; you're an adviser. If the person "holds himself out to the public" as one who provides investment advice—via business cards, Yellow Page® ads, billboards, letterhead, office signage, etc.—then he/she is in the business and is an adviser.

What about the compensation question, the third prong? Some folks would like to think they're not advisers because they don't receive money for their advice. But regulators wouldn't leave a loophole that big. They use the broader term "compensation" to determine who is and isn't an investment adviser. Compensation is any economic benefit, not necessarily just money. Surprisingly, even if the compensation is paid by someone other than the client, you're still an investment adviser. For example, if you advise Coca-Cola's employees on how to allocate their 401(k) investment dollars, and you bill the company, you're an adviser.

Some securities agents with a Series 6 or 7 actually function as financial planners, even if they don't call themselves that. Many of these planners figure that they can just put together a financial plan for free and only get paid off any resulting commissions to avoid being defined as investment advisers. Unfortunately, Release IA-1092 says they would likely be considered "investment advisers" because they receive an economic benefit as a result of their advice. The compensation might come directly or indirectly as the result of providing specific investment advice to clients. However it comes, the regulators will probably require such people to get registered.

Notice it's not about the language one uses; it doesn't matter whether the compensation is called a "commission" or a "fee." The compensation doesn't have to be listed as a separate item. The regulators, as always, look at how things function to determine if the activity meets a particular definition. If it were based on terminology, the folks who wanted to escape registration could just use different terms.

Compensation can come in the form of "soft dollars," such as receiving goodies from broker-dealers when you direct clients to put trades through the firm or maintain custody of assets. Goodies such as research reports, custodial and clearing (trade processing) services, and special software aiding in research are considered soft-dollar compensation, so if you receive anything like that from a broker-dealer because of your advisory clients, you must disclose this relationship to your clients.

Most soft-dollar compensation is allowable, though it must be disclosed to clients. On the other hand, the regulators won't let investment advisers receive the following soft-dollar compensation arrangements at all, even with disclosure: furniture and office equipment, salaries or overhead, vacations, cell phones, etc. In other words, the only form of soft-dollar compensation that is allowed is a service that helps the clients of the adviser. Paying the advisory firm's overhead or sending them on lavish vacations, on the other hand, cannot be said to benefit clients.

Allowable:

- Research reports
- Custodial and clearing (trade processing) services
- Special software aiding in research

Non-allowable:

- Furniture and office equipment
- Salaries or overhead
- Vacations
- Cell phones

FLOW CHARTS

Some people learn best by reading; many people prefer pictures, and still others prefer both. Whatever the case, it might help to look at some flow charts that summarize exemptions/exclusions for broker-dealer and investment advisory businesses.

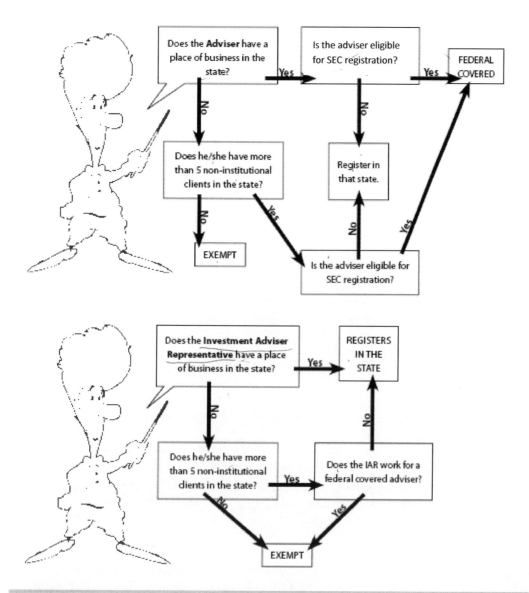

COMMENT:

So, if the test question says that the IAR working for a federal covered adviser meets with clients "only once a month" in State B, make sure the IAR gets registered in State B because he/she has a "place of business" in State B. Also notice how meticulously the regulations are worded—because the above passage is so carefully crafted, whether the IAR actually meets with clients regularly at that office or merely makes it known that the office is a location where advisory services are provided or solicited, he has a "place of business" in that state and needs to be registered. Remember that there is a big difference between having an office in State A, with 5 or fewer clients who reside in State B, and actually having a "place of business" in State B. In the first case, no registration is required in State B; in the second case, registration is required. As always, read the exam questions very carefully.

BROKER-DEALER AND AGENT REGISTRATION REQUIREMENTS

As we've seen, broker-dealers and their agents, as well as investment advisers and their representatives, generally have to be registered with the Administrator so he can keep tabs on them.

These professionals can be firms or individuals; either way they are persons. A person may include an individual, but the definition of "person" is not limited to that. Microsoft is a legal person. A Unit Investment Trust is a legal person. The estate of a dead person is a person, for crying out loud. Since the definition of "person" includes corporations, partnerships, etc., when the regulators want to refer to an individual, they usually call him a natural person. When they simply use the word "person" or "any person," they're referring to any individual, partnership, corporation, etc. These are all "legal persons."

The list of who is a person is too long to complete in just one lifetime, but I can tell you who is not a person. A person is not:

- Dead
- Declared mentally incompetent
- A minor child

Remember, if they're not dead, declared mentally incompetent, or a child, they're a person who can manage his/her own affairs, sign binding contracts, etc. A broker-dealer or investment adviser could be organized as either a sole proprietorship or a corporation; either way, he/it would be considered a person.

We said that broker-dealers are in the transaction business, not the advice business. The Uniform Securities Act defines a broker-dealer like this:

A broker-dealer is any person engaged in the business of effecting transactions in securities for the account of others or for its own account.

So, of course, the investment in question would have to be a "security" as defined by law, not a fixed annuity, bank deposit, etc. But if any "person" is effecting transactions for the accounts of others in securities, they fit the definition of "broker-dealer." And, if the state finds out they're doing it without a license, they sort of have a real problem with that.

As the Uniform Securities Act says, "It is unlawful for any person to transact business in this state as a broker-dealer or agent unless he is registered under this act." The next sentence of the Uniform Securities Act says, "It is unlawful for any broker-dealer or issuer to employ an agent unless the agent is registered. The registration of an agent is not effective during any period when he is not associated with a particular broker-dealer registered under this act or a particular issuer. When an agent begins or terminates a connection with a broker-dealer or issuer, the agent as well as the broker-dealer or issuer shall promptly notify the [Administrator]."

I can picture at least a handful of test questions based on these concepts. For example, if a broker-dealer's license is suspended/revoked by the Administrator, what's the deal with their agents' licenses?

Well, they're not currently in effect, since they are no longer "associated with a particular broker-dealer registered under this act," right? I'm not saying the agents' licenses are suspended/revoked because the folks in charge of the firm screwed up. I'm saying that it's time for the agents to find a new job. Another concept is that if a broker-dealer employs somebody to help clients buy or sell securities, that somebody had better be registered as an agent. Otherwise, the firm is in big trouble. A pretty common test question asks what needs to happen when an agent terminates employment with one broker-dealer and signs up with another broker-dealer. Answer: both broker-dealers and the agent must notify the Administrator promptly. In practical terms, that means that the one firm completes the U5 to terminate the agent's employment, and the other firm completes the U4 to hire the agent. The agent is also filling out the information, so "both broker-dealers and the agent" are informing the Administrator. One of the Administrative orders at www.nasaa.org mentions that a firm had moved without informing the Administrator, which the Administrator felt was rather impolite. See, the Administrator wants "persons" to register and to keep all their registration information current with the Administrator. The Administrator will do unannounced inspections from time to time, and if they come in for an inspection and find a hair & nail salon at the address they have for a broker-dealer, well, that's not cool, no matter what the current condition of their cuticles may, in fact, be.

➤ Registration Procedure

The Uniform Securities Act gives the Administrator the power to decide by rule what is required of a broker-dealer, agent, investment adviser, and investment adviser representative for purposes of registration. The Act says, "The application shall contain whatever information the Administrator by rule requires concerning such matters as:"

- Applicant's form and place of organization
- Applicant's proposed method of doing business
- Qualifications and business history of the applicant
- For broker-dealers and investment advisers—qualifications and business history of any partner, officer, or director
- Any injunction or administrative order or conviction of a misdemeanor involving a security or any aspect of the securities business, and any conviction of a felony
- Applicant's financial condition and history

Even if that seems like dense legalese, all it's really saying is that before you start doing business in the securities industry within a state, you need to apply for a license, on which you tell the state about your background and how you propose to do business. Is the broker-dealer a partnership or a corporation? If a corporation, where is it incorporated and can we please see a copy of the articles of incorporation and the bylaws? Does a court or another state Administrator sort of have a problem with you? Are you financially sound, or teetering on the verge of bankruptcy?

That sort of thing. After you register, assuming the state sees no problem with the information provided, your license will be granted no later than noon of the 30th day after filing. Of course, if you indicated that the State of Alabama recently revoked your license, it's probably going to take more than 30 days to grant your registration in this state if, against all odds, they decide to grant one at all. If while reviewing your application they see that you indicated an arbitration award you had to pay to a client in New Jersey, they may need you to file an amendment to your application, which could slow things down a bit. Nevertheless, your registration will be granted by noon of the 30th day, except in the rare cases when it isn't.

When filing your initial application as a broker-dealer, agent, IA, or IAR, you need to attach a form called a consent to service of process. This document gives the Administrator the authority to receive "service of process" in any non-criminal suit against the applicant. In other words, should another state need to serve papers on an out-of-control investment adviser, they don't have to chase them around and around. Instead, they can just serve the papers on the Administrator, which is the same thing as serving them on the person who has already signed his consent to let the Administrator receive the process on his behalf.

You wouldn't let a carpet cleaning company into your house unless they were "bonded and insured," right? What if their equipment or chemicals destroy $10,000 worth of carpeting—are they able to cover that damage? Similarly, a firm with custody over client assets or an agent with discretion over an account could cause huge damages; therefore, there usually needs to be a **surety bond** in place to cover potential losses to client accounts. Broker-dealers, investment advisers, and IARs and agents with discretion may be required to maintain surety bonds in amounts up to $10,000. The test question may point out that this surety bond can be obtained by a cash deposit or a deposit of securities. While the Administrator can rule which type of securities can be used as a deposit, he cannot rule that the deposit has to be cash. And, if an individual or a firm has or ends up with a criminal conviction, he/they may find that no insurance company will issue a bond to back them up in the future. In which case, it's usually time for a new career.

> Record Keeping Requirements

The Uniform Securities Act's "Post-Registration Provisions" state that:

> *Every registered broker-dealer and investment adviser shall make and keep such accounts, correspondence, memoranda, papers, books, and other records as the Administrator by rule prescribes.*

The Administrator generally just requires that a broker-dealer keep the books and records required by the SEC under the Securities Exchange Act of 1934, with those requirements enforced by our friends at FINRA.

If you poke around the state regulatory websites long enough, you'll probably find instances where some hard-nosed broker-dealer or investment adviser told the state they couldn't see client communications that were "protected by attorney-client privilege." And, once they've finished wiping the tears of laughter away, the Administrator and his or her staff will then prepare a notice of an opportunity for a hearing to determine why they shouldn't, in fact, just go ahead and revoke the firm's registration at their earliest convenience. For the hard-nosed firms who thought they could deny access to records, y'all must have forgot to read the following section of the Uniform Securities Act:

All the records referred to are subject at any time or from time to time to such reasonable periodic, special, or other examinations by representatives of the Administrator, within or without the state, as the Administrator deems necessary or appropriate in the public interest or for the protection of investors.

The word "books" still conjures an image of paper, but the "books and records" required by broker-dealers and investment advisers are typically kept electronically these days. Of course, that immediately brings up concerns about the ability to alter the records, lose them, or give access to them to people who shouldn't have it. NASAA published a model rule on recordkeeping requirements, which made the following major points:

In the case of records created or maintained on electronic storage media, the investment adviser must establish and maintain procedures:

(A) To maintain and preserve the records, so as to reasonably safeguard them from loss, alteration, or destruction;

(B) To limit access to the records to properly authorized personnel and the [Administrator] (including its examiners and other representatives); and

(C) To reasonably ensure that any reproduction of a non-electronic original record on electronic storage media is complete, true, and legible when retrieved.

➢ Net Capital Requirements

The Administrator may require a minimum net capital for a broker-dealer or investment adviser applying for or renewing their license. That means that, depending on their activities, the Administrator can rule that the firm's balance sheet must show a net worth of at least this amount. Remember here that agents/IARs don't have minimum net capital requirements, but broker-dealers and investment advisers have to file financial reports as required by the Administrator (balance sheets, trial balance sheets, etc.) to show that they're meeting the net capital requirements. "If the information contained in any document filed with the Administrator becomes inaccurate or incomplete in any material respect, the registrant shall promptly file a correcting amendment," says the Uniform Securities Act. Seems reasonable enough. If the firm's net capital drops from, say, $5 million to $5,000, the Administrator might just want to know about that. Broker-dealer net capital requirements would be based on the types of activities the firm is involved with—the riskier the activities, the greater the minimum net capital requirement. The Administrator requires that broker-dealers meet a certain minimum financial requirement, but, really, it's the Securities and Exchange Commission that establishes broker-dealer net capital requirements.

➢ Renewals and Other Registration Specifics

Not only must persons in the securities industry file an initial registration, but also they must renew their license every year. When do registrations/licenses of persons expire? On December 31st, unless properly renewed. How do you renew your license? Same way you renew your vehicle registration—by paying the required fee.

So, the Uniform Securities Act and the exam want you to understand that broker-dealers, agents, investment advisers, and investment adviser representatives need to apply for a license, need to renew that license every year, and need to keep whatever records the Administrator requires. The Administrator has the power to take a look at the required records whenever it's necessary or appropriate in the public interest or for the protection of investors. And, if you try to prevent the Administrator from inspecting the required records, you just violated the Act right there and will soon be signing for some registered mail.

You may see a test question about a broker-dealer registering also as an investment adviser. First, know that this is very common. Many firms are both broker-dealers and advisers. The exam requirements are different and the business models/forms of compensation are different, but, still, many firms perform both activities. The exam may point out something from the Uniform Securities Act, which states:

When the Administrator finds that an applicant for initial or renewal registration as a broker-dealer is not qualified as an investment adviser, he may by order condition the applicant's registration as a broker-dealer upon his not transacting business in this state as an investment adviser.

What the law is trying to say is this: if you're a broker-dealer who also wants to be an investment adviser, the state may say, "No. You can be a broker-dealer as long as you don't try to stretch and hurt yourself acting as an investment adviser, which you, apparently, have no business trying to do." In other words, they don't lose their broker-dealer license just because they also wanted to transact business as an adviser. They simply have to promise not to act as an adviser if they want to keep their broker-dealer license.

The Uniform Securities Act also points out that when the Administrator is determining the qualifications of broker-dealers and investment advisers, they can base their decision only on the firm and the agents themselves…not on the receptionist or the file clerk, for example. Or on the limited partners who simply invested in the firm and have nothing to do with its day-to-day operations. You might also see a question about partners, officers, and directors of a broker-dealer or investment adviser. If so, tell the exam that those people are already considered to be registered as agents of the broker-dealer and investment adviser representatives of the adviser when the firm itself registers with Form BD and Form ADV respectively.

If you get a question about the registration of a successor firm, first of all, your luck is running dangerously low, and, second, remember this passage from the Uniform Securities Act:

A registered broker-dealer or investment adviser may file an application for registration of a successor, whether or not the successor is then in existence, for the unexpired portion of the year. There shall be no filing fee.

In other words, if Able-Brooks Broker Dealers, LLC, is going to become Able-Brooks, Inc., in early spring, they can go ahead and register the new entity, which can use the rest of the year's registration without paying a fee.

DEFINING OUR TERMS

The other day I was visiting several state securities websites and came across an enforcement action taken by a large Midwestern state starting with the letter "M." To save time, I'll summarize the case for us rather than wading through 37 pages of legalese. Seems there was a successful insurance agent with a successful practice writing a whole lot of whole life insurance business and a whole lot of indexed annuity business. He was a guy in his mid-50s who saw no reason to be securities licensed—he was only selling insurance products, after all.

The guy held dozens of free hot lunch seminars primarily for retired investors. He got all his marketing materials from an organization based out of Portland, Oregon, which was lucky since he would not have been willing or able to create even one PowerPoint slide, let alone an entire presentation, himself. The marketing organization also issued a certificate attesting to his ethics and clean background, which looked like a pretty good deal for just $150 plus an annual $50 renewal. So, the guy would pull in 20 or 30 affluent retirees, feed them a nice catered lunch, and then dim the lights for his PowerPoint presentation. As the state securities Administrator pointed out, some of the titles of the slides included:

- Why your $ isn't safe in the bank!
- FDIC's credit rating is D–
- Earn up to 25%, guaranteed!
- Heads you win—tails you win!

Who knows how over-the-top the graphics were, but, clearly the message worked its magic by scaring several dozen investors into liquidating their savings accounts and fixed-income mutual funds in order to buy the indexed annuity product this guy was pitching. All told, he pulled in something like $14 million in annuity investments that year pocketing something like $725,000 in commissions. So far, some readers are probably thinking, good for him! Who wouldn't want to earn $725,000 helping retired investors protect their savings with an indexed annuity backed up by a solid insurance company?

Well, not so fast. Here were just some of the problems that the state securities Administrator had with the whole thing:

- The respondent held himself out as an objective, impartial investment adviser when, in fact, he was an annuity salesman.
- The respondent held himself out as an investment adviser without being registered as such or shown to be exempt from registration.
- The respondent failed to disclose the 10-year surrender period on the annuity product that contradicted his many assurances to investors that the product provided "excellent liquidity."
- Several investors have faced financial emergencies leading to losses of up to 10% of their invested principal despite assurances from the respondent that this was a "can't-lose investment opportunity."
- The respondent's sales materials were deceptive and misleading.
- The respondent presented credentials issued by an organization with no objective criteria for certification other than payment of a fee.
- The respondent used high-pressure and misleading sales practices to intimidate and convince senior investors to sell securities in order to purchase his annuity product.

The state securities Administrator was stating all this in the notice of hearing, where they have to explain what the guy did and which sections of state law or securities rules he violated. The hearing would be held at the Administrator's office to determine if the state should issue an order preventing the respondent from ever applying for any type of securities license or offering/selling securities in the state. Also, they were considering filing a petition with the courts to order that restitution be paid to any investor who wanted his/her money back.

So did the guy, like, end up going to jail? Whoa, easy now! This is just a state securities Administrator here. And, the guy did not cash the investors' checks and buy a fleet of Ferraris or anything. He just used some distasteful methods to move their money from perfectly safe bank accounts and fixed-income mutual funds into fixed annuities with steep surrender charges that were never explained.

But, the situation is not cut and dried, either. Securities regulators are lawyers, but the respondent can bring in as much legal talent as he can afford, too…and $725,000 in commission checks should have left this guy with enough cash to cover a legal emergency. The respondent's lawyers are going to attack and twist every definition involved with the case. The Uniform Securities Act's anti-fraud statute says that it's unlawful for any person "connected with the offer, sale, or purchase of any security" to mislead or deceive the investor. But, we contend that our client did not, in fact, make an offer or sale of any security; therefore, no fraud occurred. Maybe the state counters that the respondent in effect was connected to the sale of various bond and money market mutual funds—which are securities—which were required to free up money for investors to purchase his annuity products. But, his attorneys counter that he never advised them on any aspect of the sale, that it's not his problem where investors get the money to buy his insurance product. On another note, the state is contending that the respondent acted as an "investment adviser." They say he was deceptively holding himself out as an objective investment adviser, which is fraudulent, and that he was actually unregistered and not exempt from registration. Then again, the respondent's attorneys argue that since the product he offered and sold is not a security, he cannot be defined as an "investment adviser."

I know this kind of stuff drives a lot of readers crazy. But to pass the exam, candidates usually have to step outside their comfort zone and start thinking along much different lines than they're used to. If you're a salesperson with decades of experience, you're used to attending sales kickoffs where a speaker might cover all of three simple bullet points in 90 minutes. Now suddenly, you're expected to deal with 10 bullet points just on a moderately testable topic like American Depository Receipts, and you also have to deal with a bunch of mumbo-jumbo churned out by a bunch of wishy-washy lawyers.

It isn't easy, but it has to be done. So, we'll just have to take our time.

Up to now we've been talking about the different "persons" in the securities industry: broker-dealers, agents, investment advisers, and investment adviser representatives. Now we have to drill down much deeper into these definitions, focusing on all the people who either do not meet the definition of broker-dealer, agent, investment adviser, or investment adviser representative or are excused from having to register as such.

EXCLUSIONS AND EXEMPTIONS FOR PERSONS

Nobody wants to register. Registration usually requires somebody to study for at least one difficult exam, fill out a bunch of cumbersome paperwork, pay a bunch of fees, keep a bunch of records, and hope the state regulators never cop an attitude against them. So, let's talk about the folks lucky enough to avoid the hassles of registration. As we've said a few times already, a "broker-dealer" is defined by the Uniform Securities Act as "any person engaged in the business of effecting transactions in securities for the account of others or for his own account."

> ➤ Not a Broker-Dealer

The Uniform Securities Act then states that:

"Broker-dealer" does not include:

- agent
- issuer
- bank, savings institution, or trust company

That simply means that agents, issuers, banks, savings institutions, and trust companies do not meet the definition of "broker-dealer." They are excluded from the definition. And that would be similar to saying that in baseball the shortstop, pitcher, and third baseman are excluded from the definition of "outfielder." When the baseball regulators write rules for outfielders, they aren't talking to shortstops, pitchers, or third basemen. Why not? Because those people are not outfielders.

So, if the question is looking for "broker-dealers," skip over any answer choice that's talking about agents, issuers, banks, savings institutions, or trust companies.

Why?

They're not broker-dealers.

Okay, but why are the regulators pointing this out? I mean, who thought that a bank or savings institution might be a broker-dealer in the first darned place? Think of it this way: banks, broker-dealers, and investment advisers are all in the financial services industry. Many large firms have divisions that cover all the bases; the securities laws are simply trying to keep all those divisions separate. When your grandmother used to go to the bank as a young woman, she would have never seen any signs about IRAs or mutual fund investing. But these days we all see information on investing in securities while waiting for a teller or an open ATM. That's because the bank and the broker-dealer are related entities. They probably have the same parent company. But the securities regulators are pointing out that if a bank wants to get into the broker-dealer business, they need to establish a separate entity and register it as a broker-dealer. Later we'll see that these full-service financial firms probably also have a registered investment adviser. In that case, there would probably be a public company in which we could own stock and underneath that public company we'd find a bank, a broker-dealer, and an investment adviser. It's like three children of the same parent—they're related but still separate entities. For example, there is a public company that trades under the stock symbol WFC. That's "Wells Fargo" for short. Under that **bank holding company** we would also find a bank, a broker-dealer, and an investment adviser with similar but slightly different names.

➤ Exemptions

The folks above simply are not broker-dealers. Now let's talk about broker-dealers who are excused from registration requirements. A broker-dealer with no place of business in the state might not have to register. Please don't forget the italicized phrase there though—no place of business in the state. Why? Because if they DO have a place of business in the state, they'll have to register with the state. We're talking about firms with no place of business in the state. See, if I'm the state securities Administrator, I'm registering the broker-dealers who have offices in my state. If I'm the Colorado Administrator, I don't care about the broker-dealers with offices in Nebraska.

Well, not until they start doing securities business with residents of Colorado, anyway. I'm out to protect my residents from fraud and other shenanigans, so if you want to do business with my residents, you'll have to register here. However, the out-of-state broker-dealer may only want to do business with my "big kids," known as "institutional investors." If so, I'm not worried about making the firm register. If they try to take advantage of my kids, I'll come after them with everything I've got, but as long as they mind their p's and q's, I'll let them do business exclusively with the following investors in my state without requiring the firm to register:

- issuers of the securities involved in the transactions
- other broker-dealers
- banks, savings institutions, trust companies, insurance companies
- investment companies as defined in the Investment Company Act of 1940
- pension or profit-sharing trusts
- other financial institutions or institutional buyers

So, if the firm has a place of business in my state, they register in my state. If they want to do business with individuals, they'll also have to register, whether they have an office in my state or not. But, if they don't have an office in my state, they will not have to register if their only clients are those in the bulleted list above. Also, a broker-dealer is not required to register in a state if they're dealing with an existing customer who just happens to be visiting the other state temporarily. They can't solicit for new clients in that other state, but the broker-dealer and the agent can definitely do securities business with an existing customer temporarily in another state. That means that if the existing customer stays so long he becomes a resident of that other state, then the broker-dealer and agent would have to register in that state.

> Agents

As we saw earlier, the Uniform Securities Act defines an "agent" as "any individual other than a broker-dealer who represents a broker-dealer or issuer in effecting or attempting to effect purchases or sales of securities." The Uniform Securities Act also points out that if the individual represents the ISSUER of the securities involved, he would not be an agent if:

- the security is exempt (for specific exempt securities only!)
- the transaction is exempt

What this means is that if you represent the US Treasury selling T-Bonds, you are not an agent. Or, if you represent the issuer of commercial paper in a direct sale to a pension fund, you are also not an agent. You aren't being called in from Morgan Stanley to help the issuer do a private placement in exchange for a commission. Rather, you are probably an officer of the issuing company and would otherwise have no connection to securities offerings. This is just a transaction between your firm and a pension fund buying your commercial paper. You don't look and walk like an agent—you're not an agent.

The Uniform Securities Act also says that an individual can effect transactions with the issuer's employees, partners, or directors if no commission or other remuneration is paid. Maybe you work in the human resources department and help employees buy their employer's stock for the 401(k) plan. As long as you don't get a commission for the transactions, you're not an agent. But, clearly, if your company offered you, say, $50 for every sale of stock, you might just start pestering and pressuring the employees to buy stock, and that would be a different situation.

But the fact that the individual is representing the issuer of the securities is not the be-all and end-all. There are only five specific types of exempt securities that afford an exemption for the individual, and if the transaction does not qualify for an exemption, that individual is an agent of the issuer and must register. I've seen many enforcement actions involving unregistered agents selling securities issued by fly-by-night companies that qualify for no exemption imaginable. Of course, the unregistered agent selling the unregistered, non-exempt securities always manages to mislead investors, who then inform the state securities regulators.

Some of you readers own your own firms. If that describes you, you almost certainly cannot hire somebody to go around rounding up investors in exchange for 10% of the money raised, unless the individual is registered as an agent of the issuer—your firm. At that point the state will want to see a Form U4 registration to make sure the individual is not a bad-boy they would prefer to keep out of the securities industry.

Finally, the Uniform Securities Act says, "A partner, officer, or director of a broker-dealer or issuer, or a person occupying a similar status or performing similar functions, is an agent only if he otherwise comes within this definition."

In other words, if he's not functioning as an agent, he's not an agent. If the individual is on the board of directors for a broker-dealer, is he automatically an agent? No. Not unless he wants to start offering/selling securities. If he just wants to sit on the board, he's a board member. If he wants to act like an agent, he's an agent. And, if this person will act as an agent, his registration is effective when the firm's registration is effective; there is no need to register him or her as an agent separately.

Notice how the whole idea of squirming out of the requirement to register as an agent is predicated on the fact that the individual represents the ISSUER. And, the issuer has to be issuing exempt securities or issuing securities through an exempt transaction, with the individual representing the issuer as an employee or officer/director receiving no extra compensation for selling the securities. What if the individual represents a broker-dealer? Then, he will have to register if:

- he and/or the broker-dealer have a place of business in the state
- the investors are individuals (not institutions)

Remember that an agent who sells municipal securities of a broker-dealer has to get either a Series 52 or a Series 7, even though he, by definition, is offering and selling exempt securities. The municipal bonds don't have to be registered; the agent offering and selling them on behalf of a broker-dealer does.

Exemptions

Just like for the broker-dealer he represents, if the agent has no place of business in the state, and the customers are all institutional investors, he does not have to register in that state. He is exempt from registration, we could say. Also, the agent can do business with an existing customer who is not a resident of the state without having to register. If you're an agent in Nebraska, one of your existing customers might go on vacation in Florida. If so, you can contact your customer without having to register in Florida. Same way you could drive your rental car in Florida without having to get licensed. Of course, if your customer becomes a Florida resident, that's completely different. And, just like with the rental car, even though you don't have to be licensed, if you break the law, Florida can bust you. Florida has authority over any offer or sale of a security that is directed into or accepted in their state. So, while you don't have to register when talking to your existing customer who's just visiting the Sunshine State, watch what you do and say, okay?

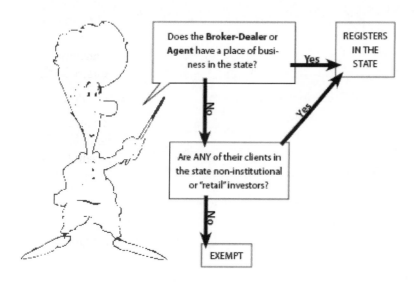

STATE AND FEDERAL SECURITIES ACTS

The Financial Industry Regulatory Authority (FINRA) is a self-regulatory organization (SRO) with authority over member broker-dealers and their associated persons. They are registered under the Securities Exchange Act of 1934 with the Securities and Exchange Commission. This is how FINRA explains themselves to the public at their website link http://www.finra.org/AboutFINRA/.

ABOUT THE FINANCIAL INDUSTRY REGULATORY AUTHORITY

The Financial Industry Regulatory Authority (FINRA) is the largest independent regulator for all securities firms doing business in the United States. FINRA's mission is to protect America's investors by making sure the securities industry operates fairly and honestly. All told, FINRA oversees nearly 4,540 brokerage firms, about 163,675 branch offices and approximately 631,725 registered securities representatives.

FINRA touches virtually every aspect of the securities business—from registering and educating industry participants to examining securities firms; writing rules; enforcing those rules and the federal securities laws; informing and educating the investing public; providing trade reporting and other industry utilities; and administering the largest dispute resolution forum for investors and registered firms. We also perform market regulation under contract for the major US stock markets, including the New York Stock Exchange, NYSE Arca, NYSE Amex, The NASDAQ Stock Market and the International Securities Exchange.

FINRA has approximately 3,000 employees and operates from Washington, DC, and New York, NY, with 20 regional offices around the country.

So, those 4,500 brokerage firms, with their 163,000 branch offices and over 630,000 registered representatives, are all regulated by FINRA. FINRA handles violations of the member conduct rules through their Code of Procedure. For example, if a broker-dealer is not delivering mutual fund prospectuses to their investing customers, FINRA can fine the firm and make them promise to improve their supervisory system. If an agent is churning accounts or making unsuitable recommendations, they can suspend him (temporarily) or even bar him (permanently). What is the maximum monetary fine that FINRA can impose?

Trick question—they've never set a maximum. They simply have the authority to set fines that seem to fit the violation. What if you were barred from associating with any member firm and fined $250,000? If you didn't pay the fine, would they come after your house and other possessions? No, but unless you paid that fine they would never let you back into the brokerage industry. They're not a court of law; they're just a self-regulatory organization with lots of power over broker-dealers and their associated persons. If an agent, a principal, or the firm itself gets in hot water with FINRA, they do get a chance to tell their side. But if FINRA still thinks a disciplinary action is in order, they can suspend or expel a member firm, and they can suspend or bar an individual from associating with his member firm or any member firm for x-amount of time. Monetary fines, as we mentioned, are also frequently used to get people's attention. For a highly educational and surprisingly interesting read, go to the FINRA website sometime at www.finra.org and look up recent disciplinary actions. They usually have them for the month and/or the financial quarter. You will see quickly that people in the brokerage business find many, many ways to run afoul of FINRA regulations and securities law.

FINRA doesn't want member firms and their associated persons suing each other all the time. To avoid the time-consuming and costly process of civil court, FINRA insists that virtually all disputes in the industry are handled by their Code of Arbitration. If one broker-dealer says another broker-dealer owes them money, they can't sue them endlessly in civil court. Rather, they submit the claim to arbitration, and an arbitration panel makes a final decision to resolve the matter. Period. No appeals.

Customers of a broker-dealer are only forced to use arbitration if and when they sign an arbitration agreement. The arbitration agreement has to be very clear what the process is and what it involves. Customers need to understand that arbitrators often come from the industry, that there are generally no appeals to their decisions, and that the arbitration panel does not have to explain how they reached their decision. As we mention elsewhere, when an individual wants to associate with a broker-dealer as a registered representative, the firm and he complete a Form U4. If there are any arbitration awards above a certain amount of money, they must be disclosed here. Also, when an agent/registered representative leaves the firm, the firm files a Form U5. Here, they have to list the reason for the agent's termination. Often, the agent is terminated for violating firm policies, breaking industry rules, and/or having to pay out an arbitration award to some very upset former customers. If so, that's all disclosed on Form U5.

FINRA is then nice enough to make the relevant sections of an agent's U4 and U5 information open to the public through a handy service called "BrokerCheck." For fun, go to www.finra.org and find this part of the site. You can then type in the name of your firm, your principal, your coworkers, etc., to see if they've all actually passed their exams and if anybody has gotten into hot water before. It's all public information, just the way FINRA likes it.

The system that broker-dealers use to register themselves and their employees is called the Central Registration Depository (CRD), by the way. FINRA opens up the regulatory and disclosure reporting sections to the public through "BrokerCheck," so that investors can say no-thanks to certain bad boys out there and also feel more confident about the good guys after doing a quick background check. After all, if you saw that the guy planning to come to your house to sell you a mutual fund had been busted for signing customer signatures to documents, wouldn't you cancel that appointment? Or at least ask him to explain what the heck he was thinking at the time before cutting a check and handing it to him.

Broker-dealers, principals, and agents are regulated by FINRA, then, and also the SEC. You have a place of business in at least one state, so you will also have to register with at least one state securities Administrator. Therefore, the brokerage side of the industry is regulated by the state securities Administrators, the SRO known as FINRA, and also the SEC or Securities and Exchange Commission.

The investment advisory business, on the other hand, does not have an SRO. Why not? Unlike broker-dealers, who are trading partners with one another and work together as syndicates bringing securities to the primary market, investment advisers do not work cooperatively. They manage their clients' portfolios, period. No cooperation required between one adviser and another.

Investment advisers—the firms—are either registered with the state securities Administrators or with the SEC (Securities and Exchange Commission). While the firm might be registered with the SEC, all investment adviser representatives are subject to state registration only.

UNIFORM SECURITIES ACT

So let's now look in great detail at one of the most important areas of your exam, the **Uniform Securities Act,** which grants much authority to the state securities Administrators. When you go on vacation, maybe you rent a car and drive it in a state where you're not licensed. Why is that okay?

Because you have a valid license issued by your home state, and the rules of the road are fairly uniform from one state to the next. Luckily, the securities laws among the states are also fairly uniform, since they use a template called the Uniform Securities Act. The Uniform Securities Act announces its purpose as follows:

Relating to securities; prohibiting fraudulent practices in relation thereto; requiring the registration of broker-dealers, agents, investment advisers, and securities; and making uniform the law with reference thereto.

And, that is what it's all about. The state securities regulators want to make the securities laws uniform from state to state, and they want to protect investors by requiring persons in the securities industry and the securities themselves to be registered. The states end up tweaking things, but, overall, the state securities laws all sound pretty much the same when they're defining key terms such as: agent, security, investment adviser, broker-dealer, offer, sale, fraud, etc. Some might call their state regulator the "Securities Commissioner," and others might refer to them as "The Division of Securities," but they all take their cue from the Uniform Securities Act and appoint an agency to "provide necessary protection" to investors.

So, if you get a bizarre test question asking if the Uniform Securities Act is the law in a particular state, the answer is, "No. It's the template or model act upon which state laws are based." It's the reason that most rules and definitions look pretty much the same whether you're reading the specific laws of Massachusetts, Ohio, Michigan, Arizona, what have you.

➤ Administrative Provisions

The Uniform Securities Act calls the official in charge of securities regulation the [**Administrator**] and puts the term in brackets, encouraging each state to insert the appropriate title. Often the Secretary of State is the Administrator, with a specific "Division" or "Department of Securities" enforcing the state's securities act. For example, here in Illinois I would apply for a driver' license with the same office with which I would file Form ADV for my advisory firm. Is that office actually called "The Administrator?" No. But that office is an administrative authority with the power to grant, deny, suspend, or revoke licenses in order to protect residents of this state. We don't want dangerous, unlicensed drivers on the roads making things unsafe for everyone else. Similarly, we don't want dangerous people out there taking money from unsuspecting investors. So, in general, people have to get licensed before driving a car or getting a license to work as a nurse, a dental hygienist, or an investment adviser representative. Whatever that office is actually called in a particular state, the Uniform Securities Act calls it "the Administrator." They are an administrative authority empowered by the state legislature to enforce the securities law of the state in order to provide necessary protection to securities investors. Under the Uniform Securities Act, in order to "provide necessary protection to investors," the Administrator can:

- Issue rules and orders
- Issue subpoenas to obtain evidence and testimony
- Issue subpoenas at the request of other regulators
- Cooperate with other regulators
- Apply to a court of law to issue a court order to compel persons to comply with subpoenas
- Administer oaths, take testimony
- Investigate both in and outside the state

- Publish results of investigations, actions

An Administrative rule would be, for example, a requirement to file Form ADV with the state if you're an investment adviser. An order is issued if somebody breaks that rule by not bothering to register but going ahead with the whole rendering of investment advice thing, anyway. If somebody is violating the securities laws of the state, the Administrator can issue an order to suspend or revoke their license to sell securities or provide investment advice. Or, if the person is not currently registered/licensed, the Administrator can fire a formal warning shot, called a cease and desist order. Maybe the Administrator finds out that a local farmer is about to issue certificates that give 4% ownership stakes in his soybean farm to investors. Wait—stop! Those securities must be registered before they are even offered (let alone sold) to investors. So, maybe the Administrator issues a "cease and desist" order, telling the farmer not to do a darned thing until the securities are registered and the folks offering/selling them are properly registered or properly excused from being registered.

How did the Administrator find out about it? Investors who lose a bunch of money tend to find out which office of the state they can talk to. State securities Administrators provide handy investor complaint forms, and they have investigators on staff who talk to investors and gather evidence.

What if a resident of, say, Louisiana is swindled by an agent and/or broker-dealer with an office in, say, Nevada? No problem. The Louisiana Securities Administrator can investigate both in and outside his state in order to provide necessary protection to his investors. You mess with just one Louisiana investor, and the State of Louisiana has the authority to make life really difficult for you. Now, maybe you're thinking, "Big deal, so they'll lose their license in Louisiana—they can still sell in the other 49 states."

Au contraire! If you get your license suspended or revoked by one state, all other states can use that as a reason to suspend or revoke your license in their states. And, often, the states find out about an agent's or broker-dealer's activities when FINRA informs them of a disciplinary action they recently took.

A subpoena is a demand for information. If the Administrator issues a subpoena, and the affected party fails to respond or cooperate, that is known as contumacy. The Administrator would then have to apply to a court—or get the Attorney General's office to do it—and seek an injunction/restraining order from the court. If the affected party blows off a court order, he/they could be held in contempt of court, and that can lead to fines and even jail time. In the bullet list above we saw that the Administrator of one state can issue a subpoena at the request of the Administrator of another state. The test might even go so far as to point out that this can happen, even if the violation leading to the subpoena did not happen in the Administrator's state, as long as it would have been a violation of that Administrator's state's securities law/regulations. How they expect people to know that kind of stuff, I have no idea. I mean, I nailed the question on my exam, but how much information can we fit into a customer's head before the whole system just overheats and shuts down?

Probably a lot more, so let's keep going. With so much power at their disposal, it's easier to talk about what the Administrator can't do. The Administrator cannot:

- Issue Judicial Injunctions
- Sentence people to prison or impose criminal penalties
- Make arrests

Why not? Because the Administrator is not a court of law. They can petition a court to issue a judicial injunction or have somebody fined and thrown in jail for fraud. But they have to ask first. In other words, while an unruly agent can definitely have a court injunction/restraining order slapped on him or have himself fined and thrown in jail, it's not the Administrator who just snaps his fingers and makes it happen. It takes a court ruling, not just an Administrative order. Unfortunately, if the court/judge does issue an injunction, the Administrator can then use that as a reason to take away or deny the person's license, or prevent him from ever getting one.

Administrative Orders

When the Administrator finds out that an agent or adviser is misleading investors and taking advantage of them, he can issue an order against the person running afoul of regulations. But, usually, he gives the person a heads-up and shows the reasons for the state's sudden hostility.

> Punitive Orders

If it's an order to deny, suspend, or revoke a license, the Administrator will provide the affected parties with:

- Prior notice
- Opportunity for a hearing
- Written findings of fact, conclusions of law

They're usually nice enough to do that even before issuing a cease and desist order, but they don't have to be. It depends, of course, on what's going on. There are plenty of emergency cease and desist orders issued because what's happening or what's about to happen is so out of control that they need to take action right now. But your exam may ask you to say that before issuing a "stop" order (deny, suspend, revoke), the Administrator will provide the three bullet points above.

After receiving the notice of hearing from the Administrator, the respondent usually has to file an answer in writing by a certain deadline. If there is to be a hearing, it is open to the public, and the affected party can be represented by an attorney and can present evidence and witnesses in his favor. But this is not a trial. This is an Administrative hearing to determine if somebody's license should be suspended, revoked, denied, etc. The standard of proof is just "a preponderance of the evidence"— none of that fancy "beyond a reasonable doubt" stuff here. The Administrator's office sends one of their attorneys to present their findings to the hearing officer, and the respondent's attorney—if he can afford one—puts on a defense. The hearing officer is like an arbitrator, a disinterested third party who listens to the testimony, examines the evidence, and can recommend that the person have his license denied, suspended, or revoked. Let's hope that this whole experience I'm describing is only something you read about for your exam—you do not want to be referred to as the respondent in any documents or proceedings with the Administrator of your state, or any other state.

So, if the respondent has his little hearing and—like most people—loses, he can file an appeal of the Administrator's order in a court of law if he does so within 60 days. The Administrator's order to suspend or revoke the license is in effect until—against all odds—the court is convinced and compelled to overturn the Administrative order.

Why would the Administrator want to issue a deny/suspend/revoke order, anyway? First, the order has to be "in the public interest, providing necessary protection to investors," and, then, somebody:

- has filed a false or misleading application

- has willfully violated or willfully failed to comply with any provision of this act
- was convicted within last 10 years of any securities-related misdemeanor or any felony
- is enjoined by any court from engaging in the securities business
- is the subject of an order of the Administrator denying, suspending, or revoking registration as a broker-dealer, agent, or investment adviser
- is the subject of an order entered within the past 5 years by the securities administrator of any other state or by the SEC denying or revoking registration as a broker-dealer, agent, or investment adviser
- is the subject of an order of the SEC suspending or expelling him from a national securities exchange or national securities association registered under the Securities Exchange Act of 1934
- has engaged in dishonest or unethical practices in the securities business
- is insolvent
- isn't qualified because they lack training, experience, and knowledge [Lack of experience isn't enough if the applicant does have training and knowledge]
- has failed reasonably to supervise his agents if he is a broker-dealer or his employees if he is an investment adviser
- has failed to pay the proper filing fee (denial only, and the order is vacated as soon as the fee is paid)

That might look like an intimidating list, but, really, it comes down to a few important concepts. Like, if any other regulator already has a problem with you, we have a problem with you. If you're already misleading us on your application, we don't want to see how much you'll try to mislead your investors. If you're a firm that isn't supervising a bunch of rowdy, out-of-control, cold-calling-cowboy agents, we can revoke your license. And—not surprisingly—if you're a convicted felon, or convicted of a misdemeanor concerning nonsense such as forgery, counterfeiting, embezzlement, perjury, fraud, etc., we don't have to give you a license, and we can take the one we granted you right back. After letting you tell your side of the story, of course. And letting you spend a fortune on attorney fees.

Speaking of attorney fees, please don't be confused—an Administrative hearing over a license is not a trial in either a civil or criminal court, but you do generally pay a good attorney to present your case and maybe convince the state to cut you some slack. Or, if you know your situation to be hopeless, you can be like many folks and just not show up for the hearing, which the state takes as an admission of all their findings of fact. That's called a default decision, by the way. Again, the Administrator doesn't have any authority to hand down criminal convictions, but if you have been charged with or convicted of a felony or a securities-related misdemeanor, that would seem like a really good reason to deny, suspend, or revoke your license to sell securities or provide investment advice, right? In other words, the following line just doesn't work somehow: "So, Steve, I hear your portfolio manager was just paroled—is he taking on new clients?"

Notice how a felony is a felony, but the misdemeanors that will get you in trouble with the securities regulators have to do with mishandling money, forging your client's signature, counterfeiting, etc. See how those particular misdemeanors directly relate to the issue of whether you should be allowed to get investors' bank routing numbers, social security numbers, FEINs, etc.? Heck, I don't want a convicted felon even knowing the ages of my children or the name of my wife, let alone my sensitive financial information. What happens if his commissions dry up? Is he going to start shaking me down, sending two of his buddies by the office to collect a little juice every Friday afternoon? Of course, I'm from Chicago, so maybe my perception is a little warped, but you get the idea. I'm just saying that extortion would—and should—be one of those misdemeanors that would tend to keep a guy out of the business.

Remember that although regulators usually only hold felonies and securities-related misdemeanors against an individual for 10 years, Form U4 asks if you have ever been convicted of, pled guilty or no contest to, or even been charged with any felony or securities-related misdemeanor. So, if you get a question about an applicant who answers "no" to the disclosure questions because a felony conviction occurred 12 years ago, remember that this will give FINRA and the state regulators grounds to deny or take away his license. On the other hand, if he had simply told the truth, there would have been no such action taken.

Now, you may even be required to know that the Administrator can actually take two specific actions even without being nice enough to first give notice and an opportunity for a hearing. The "cease & desist" order can be issued without prior notice, because sometimes the thing that somebody is doing or is planning to do is so outrageous that the state has to at least try to stop him in his tracks. Also, the Administrator can "summarily suspend a registration pending final determination" of the matter. That means that until the hearing has been held and the decision has been reached, your license is "summarily suspended." Sorry about that.

So, the Administrator can never issue an order to deny, suspend or revoke a license without prior notice, opportunity for a hearing, and written findings of fact and conclusions of law. On the other hand, a cease & desist or a summary suspension could be issued, with a hearing soon to follow.

> Non-punitive Orders

Denial, suspension, and revocation orders are all considered "punitive orders," because they provide a form of "punishment" considered necessary in order to protect investors. On the other hand, there are two orders that are non-punitive: withdrawal and cancellation. If the firm or agent decides they no longer want a license in, say, the State of Tennessee, they can withdraw rather than pay a renewal fee. Fine. Of course, if they think they can withdraw to avoid a suspension/revocation, I've got news for them. The Administrator can actually initiate a suspension or revocation proceeding for up to a year after their departure if he finds out that there was actually a reason they were in such a hurry to leave the state. And, as we said, that strike against them can knock the dominos over across all other states.

But a withdrawal in and of itself has nothing to do with punishment. The applicant or the registrant simply says thanks, but no thanks. As long as they haven't done anything wrong, the Administrator simply accepts the withdrawal. Or, as we saw during our discussion of federal covered advisers, some years the firm might send Form ADV to the SEC and, other years, they might go back to state-level registration. If you go from state-registered to federally registered, you would file a Form ADV-W with your state in order to withdraw your registration.

So that's a withdrawal.

A cancellation order happens because the party dies, goes out of business, is declared mentally incompetent, or simply can't be located. Canceled. The person, apparently, no longer needs the license, so it's canceled.

Similar to a driver's license, if the individual dies, the state cancels his securities license as opposed to revoking it. A revocation of a license is a punitive action taken when the individual becomes a danger to the residents of the state. A cancellation occurs because the person is no longer in need of the license.

➢ Criminal Penalties

Your exam may ask what the criminal penalties are for willful violations under the Uniform Securities Act. The penalties are three years in prison, a $5,000 fine, or both, per violation. As the exam might say, "criminal liability attaches" when the person knew what he was doing—was not mentally incompetent—and did it anyway. Doesn't mean the guy had to know that what he was doing was against the law—he just had to be aware of what he was doing. For example, he knew that his firm had custody of client assets but refused to indicate that on Form ADV. Did he or the firm actually read the particular rule prohibiting that? Doesn't matter. He knew the truth, and he put down a different answer, anyway. That's a willful violation. It's not as serious as printing up bogus stock certificates or a family of little pretend mutual funds, but it could still lead to criminal prosecution.

Of course, the criminal prosecutors at the district attorney or attorney general's office have to come after an offender within 5 years of the alleged misdeed. Otherwise, the statute of limitations runs out in their favor. Not that they're ever going to work in the securities industry again, but at least they won't be spending any time in prison, which is something.

Normally, you'd think ignorance of the law is no excuse. However, under the Uniform Securities Act, in the case of a false/misleading document being filed with the Administrator, if the respondent can prove that they did not mean to make a misleading filing, they cannot be imprisoned. They can be fined in this case, but not imprisoned. In a criminal case, the burden of proof is almost always on the prosecutors representing the state, but in this situation, the burden of proof would shift to the respondent who's claiming ignorance.

Not that it really matters, but we're talking about the criminal penalties under the Uniform Securities Act only. There are other state and federal laws that somebody can be tried under. I mean, if you break into one of your investing clients' homes and steal $500,000 from the wall safe, I think we can place all issues concerning your securities license at the bottom of your priority list. You're going to prison for breaking and entering, burglary/home invasion, maybe getting a mandatory minimum sentence of 20 years if you were also crazy enough to be carrying a loaded gun, etc. The fact that you'll lose your license as an agent is a foregone conclusion once you get convicted of a felony. The fact that it involved "misappropriation" of large sums of cash means that even if you plead it down to a misdemeanor, it's the type of misdemeanor that regulators use to revoke licenses.

The Uniform Securities Act makes this all pretty clear when it states:

The Administrator may refer such evidence as is available concerning violations of this act or of any rule or order hereunder to the attorney general or the proper district attorney, who may institute the appropriate criminal proceedings under this act.

Nothing in this act limits the power of the state to punish any person for any conduct which constitutes a crime by statute or at common law.

➢ Civil Liabilities

The civil liabilities under the Uniform Securities Act are pretty scary, as well. If you sold me shares of bogus stock in a non-existent company, what would happen when my $500,000 investment becomes worthless? Assuming you're still alive, I could sue to make you return my $500,000 plus interest, plus court costs/attorneys' fees.

Under the Uniform Securities Act the plaintiff (victim) can sue for and recover:

- Price paid for the security and/or advice
- Plus interest
- Plus court costs/attorneys' fees
- Minus any income received on the security

That last item is a little jarring—but if the transaction violated securities law, still the seller can deduct the dividend or interest payment the security provided before the whole thing went up in flames. And, we're not talking about "pain and suffering" here. Just give the investor her money back, plus interest, basically. And try not to screw up again if you can help it.

If it's discovered that the security sold wasn't registered, or that the agent wasn't registered, or some type of deception took place, the buyer can sue if he initiates action within two years.

Sometimes the seller will realize that the security sold was unregistered. If so, he screwed up, but he can make the buyer a formal offer of rescission. This is a legal "do-over," where he offers to buy back the security plus interest. The buyer now has 30 days to accept the offer. If they just sit on it for more than 30 days, it's too late.

One of my favorite orders found at various state regulatory websites shows that even though the person who defrauded the heck out of people over some oil-drilling "opportunities" has died, his estate can—and will—be sued by those affected. Similarly, if the investor has passed away, her children or grandchildren could still file suit on an agent who defrauded her. The Uniform Securities Act, in its proverbially punchy prose, points out that:

Every cause of action under this statute survives the death of any person who might have been a plaintiff or defendant.

➢ Securities

You probably noticed that the definitions of investment adviser, broker-dealer, and agent all included the word "securities." That means if the investment does not meet the definition of a "security," the Uniform Securities Act has nothing to say about it. I mean, even the anti-fraud statute does not apply. A security involves an investment of money, but not every investment of money is a security. A security is not an insurance product, a bank account, or a commodity. That means that the following are not securities and are not being regulated by the Uniform Securities Act:

- Fixed annuity
- Whole life insurance, term life insurance, universal life insurance, endowment policy
- Commodity futures contract

That means that you could not possibly commit securities fraud selling those things deceptively. Why not? Because they aren't securities. Similarly, baseball umpires don't get to call many clipping violations. Two different sports subject to different regulations. So insurance, banking, and commodities investments are in different sports, each with its own set of rules and officials. We're talking about the sport called "securities" on this exam and in the Uniform Securities Act.

That lays the groundwork for one of the few easy questions on the exam. If the test asks, "Which of the following is not a security?" look for one of the bulleted items above. Or maybe they'll make you stretch a bit further and ask you, "Which of the following is least likely to be an investment adviser?" If so, remember that if the advice is on one of the bulleted items, we're not talking about an investment adviser. Why? Investment advisers give advice on securities.

Like the federal Securities Act of 1933 and the Securities Exchange Act of 1934, the Uniform Securities Act is kind enough to list examples of securities:

- note
- stock
- treasury stock
- bond
- debenture
- evidence of indebtedness
- certificate of interest or participation in any profit-sharing agreement
- collateral-trust certificate
- pre-organization certificate or subscription
- transferable share
- option on commodity/futures contract
- investment contract
- voting-trust certificate
- certificate of deposit for a security
- certificate of interest or participation in an oil, gas, or mining title or lease or in payments out of production under such a title or lease
- in general, any interest or instrument commonly known as a "security"
- warrant, right, or option for a security
- variable annuity or variable life insurance policy

So, of course, the exam may try to mess with you about commodity futures contracts. While the commodity futures contract is not a security, the option to buy or sell that contract is a security. So the "December wheat" or "November corn" futures contract is not a security, but the puts and calls traded on those commodities futures contracts are securities. Also, watch out for this: a "single stock futures contract" is considered a security. Oy!

If you've been reading through any enforcement actions through "contact your regulator" at www.nasaa.org, you have surely seen phrases such as, "The stock referenced in paragraph 6 is a 'security' as that term is defined" in some specific section of the state securities law. The regulators first explain that the investment fits the definition of "security" so that they can at least enforce the anti-fraud statute. Then, since it is a security, it therefore needs to be registered unless shown to be exempt, as do the people offering and selling it.

Did you happen to notice the bulleted item identified as "in general, any interest or instrument commonly known as a 'security'"? That casts a wide net, doesn't it? Just means that if court cases and/or securities regulators have already deemed something to be a security, guess what—it's a security. You may also have noticed investment contract above. That was what the **Howey Decision** defined for us. The Howey Decision says that an "investment contract" is:

- investment of money due to
- an expectation of profits arising from
- a common enterprise
- which depends solely on the efforts of a promoter or third party

So, the SEC uses a three-pronged approach to determine if somebody is an investment adviser. The SEC and other state securities regulators use the Supreme Court's four-pronged approach to determine if something is a security. The "depends solely on the efforts of a promoter or third party" above means that this person is providing money, not labor, to the enterprise. The fact that the seller had no pre-existing relationship with the buyer would factor in, as well. For example, if you have been a trusted farm hand for many years and the farmer then sells you a part-ownership of his dairy farming operation, you could just be a managing member of the LLC. But, if a farmer is rounding up investors and offering them 10% ownership certificates in which they provide money in exchange for a share of the farm's profits, now that is a security and you are simply an investor, not a farm hand. It fits all four prongs above, right? It's an investment of money in a common enterprise in which the investor would expect to profit solely through the efforts of others. Since the thing being offered is a "security," the farmer could end up committing securities fraud, whether he's in the securities industry or not. If he, for example, gave you an offering document representing that he owns 300 head of cattle, when it's really only 100 that he keeps shuffling around when your back is turned, that would be misleading. Same thing if he gives you an income statement or balance sheet full of bogus numbers. Or fails to disclose a large bill for fuel and fertilizer he can't possibly pay, etc.

And, since this thing fits the definition of a "security," it probably needs to be registered. Remember the very first phrase in the Uniform Securities Act, which explains that the whole thing is designed to prevent fraud and to make securities get registered before they're offered and sold to investors.

Registering Securities

Not all securities have to be registered at the state level, but we haven't messed with that yet. Don't worry, it's coming up. We're still talking about the securities that do have to be registered. If the security has to be registered with the state, this is what the state wants from the person filing the registration statement:

- Filing fee (big surprise)
- Total amount of the offering
- Amount of securities offered in their state
- Names of other states where securities will be offered (not the amount offered in each state)
- Any adverse order, judgment, or decree entered by a court, the securities agency or Administrator in any state, or the Securities and Exchange Commission in connection with the offering.

Also, know that:

- Registrations are effective for one year
- Securities offered by coordination or qualification may require an escrow account whose proceeds are impounded by the Administrator and not released to the issuer/underwriters until they have raised the specified amount

- Securities offered by coordination or qualification may need to be sold through a specified form as stipulated by the Administrator
- The securities registration statement must include consent to service of process
- Underwriters can file the registration on behalf of the issuer

At www.nasaa.org, you can take a look at a uniform securities registration form, which will show you pretty much what I just listed above. Do note that securities registrations are effective for one year going forward from the effective date. See, if an agent gets registered on August 15th, her license is still going to expire on December 31st unless properly renewed. But if a security's registration is declared effective on August 15th, it will be effective for one full year going forward. Also, issuers often apply for a "shelf offering," in which they register the securities now and then sell them gradually over two years, or maybe longer.

> Administrative Stop Orders

So, as long as you fill out your securities registration statement and pay your filing fee, you'll get to issue your securities, right?

Maybe, maybe not. The Administrator gets really nervous when some little company decides it wants to sell securities to people who don't know any better. When an issuer registers a security, the state is going to want to see all the sales literature and advertising to be used in connection with the offering. They'll probably want to see a specimen of the security and, of course, all the offering documents. They'll want to know if the security has been registered with the SEC and if any other regulator—including the courts—might have a problem with it. They'll want to see a copy of the agreement between the issuer and the underwriters, as well as the agreement among the underwriters. That point seems to shock many students, but, trust me, the regulators want to know if the underwriters and/or promoters of the whole scheme are simply planning to get rich taking money for nothing while everybody else is left holding some high-risk security not worth the paper it's printed on.

If so, no dice.

Yes, that's right. Just as he can do with the registration/application of an agent, broker-dealer, or investment adviser, the Administrator can prevent a security from getting registered. Why would he do a thing like that?

Because it's in the public interest and:

- The registration statement contains any statement that is incomplete, misleading, or false
- Any provision of the Uniform Securities Act, or any rule or order by the Administrator, has been willfully violated in connection with the offering
- The security registered or sought to be registered is the subject of an administrative stop order or a court injunction entered under any other federal or state act applicable to the offering
- The issuer's enterprise includes or would include activities which are illegal where performed
- The offering has worked or tended to work a fraud upon purchasers (or would so operate)
- The offering has been or would be made with unreasonable underwriter compensation or excessive promoters' profits, or unreasonable amounts or kinds of options
- A security seeking to be registered by filing is not eligible for such registration

- A security seeking to be registered by coordination has failed to comply with the requirements of that process
- The proper filing fee has not been paid (but only a denial order can be entered and shall be vacated once the fee is paid)

As with registrations of persons, before a deny, suspend, or revoke order is entered, the issuer would get a prior notice of an opportunity for a hearing and all the written findings of fact and conclusions of law. Of course, as before, there are emergency cease & desist orders and there are also "summary suspensions pending final determination of a proceeding." It'd be interesting to see what kind of nonsense a would-be issuer would be up to that would make the Administrator go and do a thing like that.

Also, did you notice the thing about illegal operations? That means that if Crystal MethCorp decides to do an IPO, they'll probably run into some serious snags with the Administrator.

Methods of Registration

There are three different ways to register securities with the state securities Administrator. Let's start with Registration by Coordination.

> Coordination

Why would they call this method "registration by coordination"? Because the issuer has to first register the securities with the SEC under the Securities Act of 1933, and then they can coordinate the process with the states where the securities will be offered for sale. What if the issuer is not going to register with the SEC? Then they can't use this method. Also, the securities can generally not already be declared effective by the SEC. Actually, the Administrator could allow that to happen, but the greater the interval between the SEC declaration of effectiveness and the filing with the state, the more likely the Administrator will deny the registration.

Typically, the test question would indicate that the company is doing an interstate IPO. The prefix "inter" means "between" or "among." Since these securities are being sold among many states, this is interstate commerce, which the federal government typically feels is their business. You have probably noticed that some of the road signs in your state indicate the name of your state, but if you're driving on I-80, I-57, I-10, I-95, etc., the signs are suddenly red, white, and blue. Why? Those are interstate highways, the domain of Uncle Sam.

So, the issuer of an interstate offering is subject to registration with the SEC under the Securities Act of 1933, and, since the issuer is not big enough to be granted a break at the state level, they also have to register with the states.

That's the deal with registration by coordination. As the Uniform Securities Act indicates, "A registration statement under this section shall contain the following information and be accompanied by the following documents in addition to the [requirements of all registrations] and a consent to service of process."

And those documents are:

- Three copies of the prospectus and all amendments filed with the SEC under the Securities Act of 1933

- If the Administrator requires it, a copy of the articles of incorporation and bylaws currently in effect, a copy of any agreements with or among underwriters, a copy of any indenture, and a specimen/copy of the security

So, as you can see, the issuer and its underwriters are really sweating it out with the SEC and also showing the state regulators what they've shown the federal regulators. The state wants to see what the stock or bond actually looks like, and they'd like to see how much the underwriters are going to make by selling securities in their state. The effective or release date, which is the day that the underwriters can sell to investors, will be declared by the SEC. Just means that as long as you meet the following conditions, your effective/release date at the state level will be whatever day the federal regulators (SEC) declare:

- No stop order is in effect and no proceeding is pending (deny, suspend, revoke)
- The registration statement has been on file with the Administrator for at least 10 days
- A statement of the maximum and minimum proposed offering prices and the maximum underwriting discounts/commissions has been on file for two full business days

> Registration by Filing

Securities registered under this method also must be registered with the SEC, as with registration by coordination. As long as the issuer and any predecessors have been in continuous operation for at least five years, registration by filing for their additional offering is available if:

- There has been no default during the current fiscal year or within the three preceding fiscal years in the payment of principal, interest, or preferred dividend
- The issuer and any predecessors during the past three fiscal years have had average net earnings, in accordance with generally accepted accounting practices (GAAP), of 5% of either the maximum offering price or the market price within 30 days of filing, whichever is higher

By the way, what if the issuer's securities meet the requirements for both coordination and filing/notification? The issuer uses its discretion, meaning they can choose the method to use.

As the Uniform Securities Act says, a registration statement under this section shall contain the following information and be accompanied by the following documents in addition to the [general requirements for all securities] and the consent to service of process:

- A statement demonstrating eligibility to use this method
- Name, address, form of organization, the state or foreign jurisdiction where the issuer is organized and the date of organization, and the general character and location of its business
- If some/all of the securities are being sold by someone other than the issuer (non-issuer distribution), the name and address of the person, the amount of securities held by him as of the date of filing, and a statement of his reasons for making the offering
- A description of the security being registered
- If the issuer has not been in business continuously for five years—a balance sheet as of a date within four months prior to filing and a summary of earnings for each of the two fiscal years preceding the date of the balance sheet

If no stop order is in effect and no proceeding is pending, a registration statement under this section automatically becomes effective at 3 o'clock Eastern Time in the afternoon of the second full business day after filing the registration statement or the last amendment, or at such earlier time as the Administrator determines.

> Qualification

As the Uniform Securities Act declares, any security may be registered by qualification, but, as we'll see, this is the most arduous method of registering securities at the state level. And, it requires that the issuer await a specific response from the Administrator, while the other forms have the issuer waiting just for the SEC to give the release date. In addition to the requirements for securities registration in general, a registration statement under qualification must contain the following amazingly dense bulleted list:

- The following information on the issuer: name, address, form of organization, state/foreign jurisdiction where organized and date of organization, description of physical properties and equipment, and a statement of the general competitive conditions in the industry in which it is or will be engaged
- With respect to every director and officer of the issuer: name, address, principal occupation for the past five years, amount of securities of the issuer held by him as of a specified date within 30 days of filing, the amount of the securities covered by the registration statement to which he has indicated his intention to subscribe
- Remuneration paid during the past 12 months and estimated to be paid during the next 12 months by the issuer to the directors and officers mentioned above
- For the folks who own 10%+ of the issuer's securities, indicate the amount of securities of the issuer held by them as of a specified date within 30 days of filing and the amount of the securities covered by the registration statement to which they have indicated their intention to subscribe
- If anyone is doing a non-issuer distribution connected to this offering, give the same information asked for under registration by filing/notification
- Capitalization and long-term debt of the issuer
- Kind and amount of securities to be offered, proposed offering price, estimated underwriter compensation and finders' fees to be paid
- Estimated cash proceeds to be received by the issuer, purposes for which the proceeds will be used and the amounts to be used for each purpose, source of any proceeds to also be used to achieve the purposes listed
- Description of any stock options outstanding or to be created in connection with the offering together with the amount held or to be held by every person required to be listed above (officer, director, 10%+ owners)
- Copy of any prospectus, pamphlet, circular, form letter, advertisement, or other sales literature to be used
- Specimen/copy of the security being registered, copy of articles of incorporation and bylaws, and copy of the indenture if applicable
- Signed statement of a legal opinion
- Balance sheet as of a date within four months prior to filing, income statement for each of the three fiscal years preceding the date of the balance sheet, and if any part of the

proceeds of the offering will be used to purchase another business, the same financial statements on that business

- Small, brown bag of cash left surreptitiously near a locked emergency exit of the offices of the Administrator

A test question might ask, "Which of the following methods requires a specific response from the Administrator?" The answer would be "registration by qualification." The other two methods—coordination and filing—lead to a release/effective date determined by the SEC.

Exempt Securities

Exempt means excused. So, if a security is an exempt security, it is excused from the filing/registration requirements we just had a lot of fun discussing. If the security is "non-exempt," it is not excused from the filing/registration requirements.

Okay, so which securities have to be registered with the state? Well, certainly not the exempt ones. The only securities that have to be registered are the non-exempt ones. Why do non-exempt securities have to be registered? Because they are not excused from registration requirements.

The following exempt securities are still securities (subject to anti-fraud), but they are excused from registering under the Uniform Securities Act:

- any security issued/guaranteed by US Treasury/US Government
- municipal securities
- any security issued by ANY Canadian government
- any security issued by a foreign government with diplomatic relations (national/federal only…except Canada, eh?)
- bank, savings institution, trust company security (not bank holding company)
- savings & loan, building & loan securities, credit union securities
- debt securities issued by an insurance company
- securities issued by railroad or other common carrier, public utility, or holding company subject to Interstate Commerce Commission, or the Public Utility Holding Co. Act of 1935
- a federal covered security
- non-profit securities (e.g., religious, educational, fraternal, charitable, social, or trade/professional associations)
- promissory note maturing in 9 months/270 days or less, issued with denominations of $50,000+, and rated in top 3 credit tiers by a nationally recognized statistical rating agency
- investment contract issued in connection with pension/employee benefit program

Two of those securities could actually lose their exemption if they aren't careful. Those two would be:

- investment contract issued in connection with pension/employee benefit program
- non-profit securities (e.g., religious, educational, fraternal, charitable, social, or trade/professional associations)

Why are the securities above exempt in the first place? Because the Uniform Securities Act says so. And, if you look at the list, you find a lot of government securities, right? They're either the direct obligation of a federal government, or covered by some federal act like the Public Utility Holding Company Act of 1935, or covered by some federal agency such as the now-defunct Interstate Commerce Commission, which had jurisdiction to set rates for services provided by railroads, trucking companies, bus lines, freight forwarders, water carriers, oil pipelines, transportation brokers, and express agencies. Fine, the state regulators have enough trouble trying to stop all the shady characters trying to sell shares of 17% preferred stock that trades on exactly zero secondary markets and has as much likelihood of paying out as a lottery ticket. Let the federal regulators deal with federal government securities and securities covered by various federal laws. We'll deal with the little companies nobody's ever heard of. See, those "federal covered securities" are more easily regulated by the SEC, but the weird little promissory notes that pop up in Slapout, Alabama, are better spotted and regulated by the state regulators in Alabama. That's really the securities that have to be registered with the states—the ones that are not trading on a national exchange or issued by a government, a bank, savings & loan, credit union, or insurance company.

Federal Covered Securities

So, all securities will have to be registered at the state level, except for all the securities that don't have to be registered at the state level. If the Uniform Securities Act declares a security to be exempt, that means it does not have to be registered and is not subject to the filing of advertising materials, sales literature, the prospectus, etc. The security and the offer and sale of it are still subject to anti-fraud rules, of course, but not subject to registration requirements. We saw above that one type of exempt security is a "federal covered security." Like a federal covered investment adviser, federal covered securities don't have to be registered with the states. As their name suggests, these securities are covered at the federal level. The National Securities Markets Improvement Act of 1996 (NSMIA) is what created this special class of security. This Act also reminds us that while the SEC plays the very important role of providing necessary protection to investors, they also play the important roles of promoting capital formation and encouraging efficiency and competition in the securities markets. See, the SEC exists because of the "commerce clause" of the US Constitution. They have the power to oversee interstate commerce, and since the securities markets function through interstate commerce and affect the banking system, the economic health of the nation, and even the amount of tax receipts the federal government takes in, the federal government saw a need to regulate the securities markets. Are they out to protect the investor per se? Probably not. They're out to protect the securities markets from getting so corrupt that nobody wants to play anymore. They want investors to feel confident enough in the integrity of the markets that they will keep putting up money for stocks and bonds that allow companies to expand, which keeps the economy, banking system, and federal tax rolls healthy as well. So, whenever they make rules, they try to balance the need to provide investor protection with the need to help issuers raise capital and the need to make the markets as efficient and competitive as possible. With this in mind, the federal regulators decided that investors would be plenty protected and the markets would become more efficient if certain securities registered only with the SEC. So, registration of the following federal covered securities is covered at the federal level only:

- Securities listed, or authorized for listing, on the New York Stock Exchange or the American Stock Exchange, or listed on the Nasdaq Stock Market (or any successor to such entities)

- Securities listed, or authorized for listing, on a national securities exchange that has listing standards that the Commission determines are substantially similar to the listing standards applicable to securities described in subparagraph (A); or
- Securities of the same issuer that are equal in seniority or that are a senior security to a security described in subparagraph (A) or (B)
- Securities issued by an investment company that is registered, or that has filed a registration statement, under the Investment Company Act of 1940
- SALES TO QUALIFIED PURCHASERS—A security is a covered security with respect to the offer or sale of the security to qualified purchasers, as defined by the Commission by rule. In prescribing such rule, the Commission may define the term 'qualified purchaser' differently with respect to different categories of securities, consistent with the public interest and the protection of investors.

Why should these securities automatically be on the federal government's turf? Well, if the security is trading on a national exchange, first, we're talking about interstate commerce, which is the federal government's domain. Just as there are state highways and also federal interstate highways, some securities are on the state's turf and some are on the federal government's turf. Second, the security has to provide lots of disclosure and meet all kinds of rigid criteria just to be trading on this national exchange—notice the phrase "has listing standards that the Commission determines are substantially similar to the listing standards applicable to securities described in subparagraph (A)." The "Commission" (SEC) also reserves the right to determine that exchanges created in the future have similar criteria. If so, those securities are federal covered, too. And, if your common stock is federal covered, so is your preferred stock and so are your bonds (senior securities). Investment company securities include open- and closed-end funds, UITs, ETFs, and variable contracts. Those are federal covered. They might do a notice filing, but that's just a filing of notice with the states. Note that there is a uniform notice filing for investment company shares at www.nasaa.org.

So, nobody said that a federal covered security doesn't have to be registered. What we're saying is that a federal covered security doesn't have to be registered with the states. All these issuers have to worry about is the Securities and Exchange Commission (SEC), which is plenty to worry about, as it turns out.

Now, let's apply the concept. Since these securities such as IBM, Microsoft, or variable annuities are federal covered, the states, therefore, have no power to enforce anti-fraud regulations on any offer or sale, right?

Right? Well, how does the fraud definition go again? Does it say that it's unlawful to employ any device, scheme, or artifice to defraud in connection with any security that has to be registered with the state?

No, remember that it says "any security." IBM doesn't have to register with the states—so what? If anybody makes a fraudulent offer or sale of IBM, the states can still enforce anti-fraud regulations. IBM is still a "security."

Just like a fixed annuity, right? No—a fixed annuity is not a security. If the thing is not a "security," it's not subject to anything under the Uniform Securities Act. But, if the investment of money is a security, it is always subject to at least the anti-fraud statutes. So, whether the security has to be registered or not is one concern. If the issuers can claim an exemption, the issuers are happy about avoiding paperwork, fees, and public disclosure of their business. But registration has nothing to do with the f-word, fraud. If the thing fits the definition of a "security," the anti-fraud statutes apply. And, if the thing isn't even a security, then the Uniform Securities Act has nothing to say about it.

Okay, so we can now draw three very clear conclusions:

1. If it is a security, it is subject to anti-fraud regulations
2. If it is a security, it has to be registered
3. Unless it doesn't

Federal covered securities are exempt from state-level registration. Other exempt securities such as bank securities and religious organization securities are excused from the requirements to register and file sales and advertising materials with the regulators. So, if it is an exempt security, it is a security that does not have to be registered. If anybody sells it fraudulently at any time, that's a whole different issue. It would be fraud because the thing in question would be a security, whether it's exempt or not. But exempt securities do not have to be registered.

On the other hand, non-exempt securities always have to be registered. Except when they don't. Just like federal law, the Uniform Securities Act lists securities that are exempt from registration requirements and calls them "exempt securities." Then, the Uniform Securities Act lists transactions that make the security exempt from registration and calls them **exempt transactions**. Why don't these non-exempt securities have to be registered? Because they're being offered and sold in an exempt transaction, such as:

- any sale or offer to a bank, savings institution, trust company, insurance company, investment company, pension or profit-sharing trust, or other financial or institutional buyer, or to a broker-dealer
- private placements

  > No more than 10 non-institutional buyers in the state per 12-month period

  > Seller believes that all non-institutional buyers hold for "investment purposes"

  > No commissions paid for soliciting any non-institutional buyer

- transactions between issuers and their underwriters
- transactions by fiduciaries: executors, administrators, sheriffs, marshals, receivers/trustees
- pledges
- unsolicited non-issuer transactions effected through a broker-dealer
- isolated non-issuer transactions
- any transaction to existing security holders of the issuer, if no commission is paid for soliciting buyers
- offerings of pre-organization certificates

  > No more than 10 buyers, period

  > No commissions paid for soliciting any buyer

  > No payment made by any subscriber

- any offer (but not a sale) of a security for which a registration statement has been filed under the Uniform Securities Act and the Securities Act of 1933 if no stop order is in effect. Sales may only take place after registration is effective
- any transaction in a bond secured by a real mortgage or deed of trust provided that the entire mortgage or deed of trust, together with the bonds, are offered and sold as a unit
- non-issuer transactions in securities subject to reporting requirements of the Exchange Act of 1934, or in securities registered under the Investment Company Act of 1940, or in securities where the issuer has filed with the Administrator information substantially the same as that required for registered issuers by the Securities Exchange Act of 1934 for a period of at least 180 days prior to the transaction

If we dig below the surface, we can see the logic to most of these exemptions. For example, we can easily see why the transactions by fiduciaries—executors, administrators, sheriffs, marshals of the court, receivers/trustees in a bankruptcy liquidation of assets—qualify for a more relaxed treatment by the Administrator. They're all being supervised by the courts, whether it's an executor disposing of the estate assets or an accounting firm liquidating the assets of a deadbeat company. A receiver placed in charge of a bankrupt entity's assets might liquidate those assets, some of which could be unregistered, non-exempt securities. Oh, well, it's not like this receiver/trustee/marshal in a bankruptcy is a securities dealer trying to skirt the registration requirements.

Not so long ago, I actually heard of an investment advisory firm getting a call from a Texas broker-dealer, who said, "By the way, one of your managers bought a stock that was never blue-skied in Texas." What this rather cryptic remark meant was that a portfolio manager with discretion over an account bought stock in a really small company for a "microcap" portfolio. But, since nobody called up and solicited the client, it was an "unsolicited, non-issuer transaction effected through a broker-dealer." The word "non-issuer" means it was not part of an IPO or other offering where the issuer is raising money.

So, the broker-dealer had the customer sign the unsolicited order acknowledgment, and they had themselves an exempt transaction. And I had myself an amusing story that, so far, has been extremely difficult to work into conversation.

But, there you have it. By the way, tell the test that "non-issuer" and "secondary" both mean that the transaction is "not for the benefit of the issuer."

These exemptions would be claimed when a security is sold from one investor to another. The security was never registered in the state; then again, no issuer is skirting registration requirements in order to funnel capital to its operations. On the other hand, there are not many transactional exemptions available to an issuer of a security. If my own company, Pass the Test, Inc., wanted to offer some of the 1,000 shares our charter authorizes us to issue to investors, we could get around registration requirements if we offered only to institutional investors, e.g., insurance companies and broker-dealers. Or, we could offer to up to 10 individuals who live in the state and call that a private placement. In both cases the Administrator would want a notice that the transaction occurred, but we could file it after the fact and would not have to make our financials public. Rather, we could provide our financial disclosure just to the small group of carefully selected investors.

And, if you think about it, that would mean we had a much different situation on our hands, which is why it would be treated differently than a general public offering of securities. If you want to put up a website or publish a full-page ad in a magazine soliciting investors for your company, the regulators had better find a registration statement on file for this offering. On the other hand, if your company is talking to a handful of institutional investors, the state securities department does not have to put up a wall of protection in that case. The regulators always have the anti-fraud statutes to use if the institutional investors end up being defrauded, and, chances are, that won't happen nearly as often as it happens among the Average Joe investor.

Another exemption is for an offer of a security that is in the process of registration. Here we're talking about "indications of interest." As long as the issuer has filed the registration statement, they can take the indications of interest, providing investors with a preliminary prospectus. They just can't make a sale until the effective date. And, they can't start making offers before that registration statement is on file.

Offers and Sales

As the Uniform Securities Act states:

> *"Offer" or "offer to sell" includes every attempt or offer to dispose of, or solicitation of an offer to buy, a security or interest in a security for value.*

An offer is an attempt to sell somebody a security, or an attempt to entice them to offer to buy a security.

A sale is defined this way:

> *"Sale" or "sell" includes every contract of sale of, contract to sell, or disposition of, a security or interest in a security for value.*

Why are these definitions important? Because the most important part of the Uniform Securities Act is the very beginning. In the beginning, the Uniform Securities Act created the fraud statute, which states:

It is unlawful for any person, in connection with the offer, sale, or purchase of any security…to employ any device, scheme, or artifice to defraud.

So, the guy who is the subject of an Administrative action might hire an attorney to argue that the conduct in question did not fit the definition of "offer" or "sale." Because, if the conduct in question does fit the definition of an offer and/or a sale of securities, it is subject to the anti-fraud statutes and might require some people to get registered.

Not Offers

Now we get to look at some examples of things that are not offers of securities, which means they would not be subject to registration requirements. As the Uniform Securities Act states, the following are not considered to be offers of securities:

- any bona fide pledge or loan of a security
- any stock dividend if nothing of value is given by stockholders for the dividend

- any act incident to a class vote by stockholders…on a merger, consolidation, reclassification of securities, or sale of corporate assets in consideration of the issuance of securities of another corporation
- any act incident to a judicially approved reorganization in which a security is issued in exchange for one or more outstanding securities, claims, or property interests

First, if you're pledging securities as collateral, you are not making an offer to sell securities. So, you can pledge a security as collateral even if the security isn't registered. A stock dividend is really a non-event. The issuer used to cut the big earnings pie into 10 million slices; now they're going to give everybody more slices by cutting the pie into 15 million smaller slices and having everybody pretend they've gained something. That is not an offer—just a way of pushing down the market price for the stock to entice investors to buy more of it. When a corporation merges with another corporation, the acquiring company is not really offering their securities to the other shareholders—the two companies are simply going to become one. And the last bullet point has to do with a bankruptcy proceeding. The bankruptcy judge will approve the plan to wipe out the current shareholders and give the stiffed bondholders shares in the newly organized entity. So, that's a way of dealing with some mighty ticked-off creditors, not an offer of securities.

For extra credit google "tombstone ad images" and open up a few tombstone announcements. Notice the text at the very top stating that this is just an announcement and neither an offer to sell nor a solicitation of an offer to buy the securities being announced. All offers, the caveat clarifies, are made by prospectus. So, yes, if you send someone a prospectus, you are offering to sell those securities.

D-O-A

So, the next question is, "When has an offer been made in a particular state?" Luckily the Uniform Securities Act tells us that:

> *…an offer to sell is made in this state when the offer originates from this state, or is directed by the offeror to this state.*

If you get a test question stating that an agent in State A calls an investor in State B trying to interest the investor in some securities, tell the exam that an offer to sell a security has been made in both states. The Uniform Securities Act also gives the Administrator authority when an offer has been accepted in the state. An offer to sell "is accepted in this state when acceptance is communicated to the offeror in this state and has not previously been communicated to the offeror outside this state." That communication could be by phone, text message, email, fax, etc., by the way.

As usual, this is much simpler than it first appears. If an agent in North Dakota calls a customer vacationing in South Dakota and asks if she'd like to buy a variable annuity, an offer to sell a security has been made in both states. If the buyer isn't sure, maybe she calls back a few days later while visiting her Aunt Lorraine in Lincoln, Nebraska. "Sure," she says, "I'd like to communicate my acceptance of said variable annuity to you, the offeror." Now the offer has been accepted in Nebraska. Using our nifty little "D-O-A" mnemonic device thing, you can get the test question right. The offer was D-directed into South Dakota, O-originated in North Dakota, and A-accepted in Nebraska. Who's got jurisdiction if the agent is scamming the customer? Could be any or all of the three states involved.

What if the investor cuts a check while kickin' it up in Branson, Missouri? Nobody cares where the check is cut. It's all about where the offeror and offeree were when they were communicating. Also, if the agent had been offering shares of General Electric, headquartered in New York, that would not imply that the New York Administrator is somehow involved. GE almost certainly has nothing to do with this North Dakota agent.

Please remember that in another section we'll be saying that the North Dakota agent can call an existing customer who's just visiting the state of South Dakota without having to register as an agent in South Dakota. Fine. The agent could also get into his pickup truck and drive to the other state without getting a South Dakota driver's license. But, in either case, if the dude starts violating the law, the State of South Dakota can nail him. What if the agent doesn't like that fact?

Tell him to stay the heck out of South Dakota.

FEDERAL SECURITIES ACTS

The securities markets are regulated by a handful of highly detailed federal securities Acts of the United States Congress. The Securities and Exchange Commission (SEC) also makes ("promulgates") rules under these federal securities acts. The exam is expected to touch on just the fundamentals of each law, but even that requires us to do some homework. And if you REALLY like to study, take a look at the full text of the federal securities acts, the rules under them, and even the forms used to comply with the various securities acts and rules. The link is currently http://www.sec.gov/about/laws.shtml.

➤ Securities Act of 1933

As the SEC explains on their website:

Often referred to as the "truth in securities" law, the Securities Act of 1933 has two basic objectives:

- require that investors receive financial and other significant information concerning securities being offered for public sale; and
- prohibit deceit, misrepresentations, and other fraud in the sale of securities.

The scope of this securities law is narrower than the more far-reaching Securities Exchange Act of 1934. The Securities Act of 1933 focuses solely on the offering of securities to public investors for the very first time. The Act requires issuers to register an offering of securities with the SEC before the issuer is allowed to sell or "issue" their securities to the public. Because of this securities law an investor must be provided with a prospectus that discloses everything he might need to know about the company issuing the security *before* the issuer or underwriters take his money and close the deal. Investors can read about the issuer's history, its board of directors, its products and services, its chances for success, and its chances for failure. They can look at the balance sheet and the income statement. They'll still be taking a risk if they buy—because all securities carry risk—but at least they'll be able to make an informed decision because of this full and fair disclosure.

When a corporation wants to raise capital (money) by selling securities, they get a group of underwriters together and fill out paperwork for the federal government in the form of a registration statement. Part of this registration statement will become the prospectus, which is the disclosure brochure that investors will be provided with. An "underwriter" is just a broker-dealer that likes to take companies public, remember. Another name for an underwriter is investment banker, but they don't act like a traditional bank. No deposits or checking offered here. They're just salesmen who like to play a high-risk game known as securities underwriting or investment banking. Part of the reason they like it is because it can pay very well.

Once the underwriters file the registration statement on behalf of the issuer, the process goes into a cooling-off period, which will last a minimum of 20 days. This process can drag on and on as the SEC reviews the paperwork, but no matter how long it takes, the issuer and underwriters can only do certain things during this "cooling-off" period. Number one, they can't sell anything. They can't do any general advertising of the securities offering. They *can* announce that a sale is going to take place by publishing a tombstone ad in the financial press, because a tombstone ad is just a boring rectangle with some text. It announces that a sale of securities will take place at a particular offering price (or yield) and informs the reader how he/she can obtain a prospectus. But it is neither an offer nor a solicitation to buy the securities. The underwriters can find out if anyone wants to give an "indication of interest," but those aren't sales. Just names on a list. If someone gives an indication of interest, they have to receive a preliminary prospectus, which contains everything that the final prospectus will contain except for the effective date and the final/public offering price or "POP." The registered rep may NOT send a research report along with the preliminary prospectus and may not highlight or alter it in any way. A research report is considered sales literature and, remember, during the cooling-off period no sales or advertising is allowed. As you may know, the preliminary prospectus is also referred to as a "red herring," due to the red-text warning that information may be added or altered. The release date and the final public offering price are two pieces of information yet to be added to what's in the red herring in order to make it a final prospectus. But, the preliminary prospectus has virtually all the material information a potential investor would need before deciding to invest or not.

The issuer and the underwriters attend a due diligence meeting toward the end of the cooling-off period to try and make sure they provided the SEC and the public with accurate and full disclosure. Nothing gets sold until the SEC "releases" the security on the release date/effective date. Starting on that date, the prospectus will have to be delivered to all buyers of these new securities for a certain length of time.

And, even though the SEC makes issuers jump through all kinds of hoops, once it's all done, the SEC pretty much washes its hands of the whole affair. The SEC doesn't approve or disapprove of the security. They don't guarantee accuracy or adequacy of the information provided by the issuer and its underwriters. In other words, if this whole thing goes horribly wrong, the liability still rests squarely on the shoulders of the issuers and underwriters, not on the SEC. For that reason, there has to be a disclaimer saying basically that on the prospectus. It usually looks like this:

The Securities and Exchange Commission has not approved or disapproved of these securities. Further, it has not determined that this prospectus is accurate or complete. Any representation to the contrary is a criminal offense.

So, how does the SEC feel about the investment merits of the security? No opinion whatsoever. They just want to make sure you receive full and fair disclosure in order to make an informed decision to invest or to take a pass.

Exempt Securities

The Securities Act of 1933 is a piece of federal legislation, so it's not surprising that the folks who passed it gave themselves an exemption from the rule. That's right; US government securities are exempt from this act. They don't have to be registered in this way. Neither do municipal securities. Charitable organization securities, such as church bonds, are exempt from the act. So are bank securities, which are already regulated by bank regulators. Securities that mature in 270 days or less—commercial paper, bankers' acceptances—are also exempt from this arduous registration process. An exempt security is excused from the registration requirement, but it's still a security. So, if anybody offers or sells it deceptively, that is considered securities fraud, which is always a bad idea. People can get sued and thrown in jail for fraudulent offers/sales of securities, and registered representatives have been known to lose their registration. Whether a security had to be registered or not has nothing to do with whether securities fraud transpired. Securities fraud can happen with *any* security, whether it's common stock or an exempt US Treasury Bond. If the seller gets the buyer's money through lies, tricks, and deceit, we're talking about securities fraud, people.

Exempt Transactions

There are exempt securities, and there are also transactions that qualify for exemptions. Believe it or not, the transactions that qualify for exemptions are called exempt transactions. In other words, there's absolutely nothing special about the security being offered here—it's the way it's being offered and sold that makes it exempt from the typical registration process. Under a Reg A exemption, an issuer can sell a small offering of securities without going through the full registration process. Or, if the issuer agrees to sell the stock to residents of only one state, they will qualify for a Rule 147 exemption. This only works if the issuer's main business is located in that state and 80% of its assets are located there. Also, the buyers can't sell the security to a non-resident for 9 months after the close of the offering period. The issuer registers with the state, rather than the SEC, since it's all taking place in that one state. IntrAstate. All in A state. When we get down to the state (Uniform Securities Act) level, we see that the issuer would most likely use "registration by qualification" to do the intra-state IPO. The SEC is federal, in charge of INTERstate commerce. So if it's all within a state, it's that state's concern.

Sometimes issuers offer their shares primarily to "accredited investors." These are sophisticated investors, often with millions of dollars at their disposal. If the individual has a certain amount of net worth or income, he/she is accredited, and presumed to be able to look after him- or herself. So, an issuer can place their securities under a Reg D transaction with as many of these folks as they want. This "private placement" is, by definition, not being offered to the general public, so the SEC eases up a bit—as much as the SEC ever eases up, anyway. Besides wealthy individuals, the issuer can place these unregistered securities with as many institutional investors—mutual funds, pension plans, insurance companies—as they want, again on the assumption that they can tell a loser from a winner. They can also sell to insiders of the corporation, which would include officers, directors, and large shareholders. So, a Reg D/private placement transaction is exempt from the Act of 1933 because it is offered to an exclusive group of investors. No more than 35 non-accredited investors can buy these securities, and everybody has to hold the stock for the first year before selling it. That's a restriction—having to hold the stock fully paid for at least one year—so they often call stock purchased in a private placement "restricted stock." There is a legend printed on the certificates indicating when the shares may be transferred, and the transfer agent won't allow the transfer to happen until that date. Because of the little legend, the securities are sometimes referred to as "legend stock."

Seriously. I'm not saying it's likely you'll have to recall the phrase "legend stock," or even "restricted stock," but I am saying it could show up.

SECURITIES EXCHANGE ACT OF 1934

As I mentioned, the Securities Exchange Act of 1934 is broader in scope. As the SEC explains on the same page of their website:

With this Act, Congress created the Securities and Exchange Commission. The Act empowers the SEC with broad authority over all aspects of the securities industry. This includes the power to register, regulate, and oversee brokerage firms, transfer agents, and clearing agencies as well as the nation's securities self regulatory organizations (SROs). The various securities exchanges, such as the New York Stock Exchange, the NASDAQ Stock Market, and the Chicago Board of Options are SROs. The Financial Industry Regulatory Authority (FINRA) is also an SRO.

The Act also identifies and prohibits certain types of conduct in the markets and provides the Commission with disciplinary powers over regulated entities and persons associated with them.

The Act also empowers the SEC to require periodic reporting of information by companies with publicly traded securities.

The Securities Exchange Act of 1934 gave the SEC broad powers over the securities markets. The Act gave the Federal Reserve Board the power to regulate margin. It also requires public companies to file quarterly and annual reports with the SEC. If a material event occurs before the next regular report is due, the issuer files an 8-K. There are reports filed when the officers and members of the board sell their shares. Mergers and acquisitions have to be announced through various filings. You get the idea.

The Securities Exchange Act of 1934 talked about insider trading, warning investors not to pass around or use non-public information. If you knew that your sister's company was going to be purchased by Google, it would be very tempting to buy a bunch of calls on her company's stock and tell your clients to do the same. Unfortunately, the SEC would sue you for "treble damages," meaning they would try to extract three times the amount of your benefit in civil court.

The Securities Exchange Act of 1934 gives federal prosecutors the authority to prosecute criminal violations. So, if the insider trading activity is handled in civil court, the SEC will try to extract three times your benefit. If they turn it over to the US Attorney's office for criminal prosecution, God help you.

Finally, the exam could mention that the "Exchange Act" also wrote rules on short sales in an attempt to prevent short sellers from piling onto a dying stock. The "plus tick rule" or "uptick rule" based on this has actually been rewritten again as "regulation SHO," which we discussed under "Trading Securities."

TRUST INDENTURE ACT OF 1939

Again, the SEC appears to be on a roll here, so let's them announce this federal securities law as well:

This Act applies to debt securities such as bonds, debentures, and notes that are offered for public sale. Even though such securities may be registered under the Securities Act, they may not be offered for sale to the public unless a formal agreement between the issuer of bonds and the bondholder, known as the trust indenture, conforms to the standards of this Act.

As we see above, the Trust Indenture Act of 1939 is all about protecting bondholders. If a corporation wants to sell $5,000,000 or more worth of bonds that mature outside of one year, they have to do it under a contract or indenture with a trustee, who will enforce the terms of the indenture to the benefit of the bondholders. In other words, if the issuer stiffs the bondholders, the trustee can get a bankruptcy court to sell off the assets of the company so that bondholders can recover some of their hard-earned money. Sometimes corporations secure the bonds with specific assets like airplanes, securities, or real estate. If so, they pledge title of the assets to the trustee, who just might end up selling them off if the issuer gets behind on its interest payments. So just remember that an indenture is a contract with a trustee, who looks out for the bondholders.

INVESTMENT COMPANY ACT OF 1940

The SEC summarizes this federal securities law like so:

> This Act regulates the organization of companies, including mutual funds, that engage primarily in investing, reinvesting, and trading in securities, and whose own securities are offered to the investing public. The regulation is designed to minimize conflicts of interest that arise in these complex operations. The Act requires these companies to disclose their financial condition and investment policies to investors when stock is initially sold and, subsequently, on a regular basis. The focus of this Act is on disclosure to the investing public of information about the fund and its investment objectives, as well as on investment company structure and operations. It is important to remember that the Act does not permit the SEC to directly supervise the investment decisions or activities of these companies or judge the merits of their investments.

So, mutual funds have to register their securities and provide a prospectus to all investors under the Securities Act of 1933. The Investment Company Act of 1940 requires the investment company itself to register and then lays out an exhaustive array of dos and don'ts for their operations. The Investment Company Act of 1940 classified investment companies as face amount certificate companies, unit investment trusts, or management companies. As we saw in an earlier chapter, the management companies are either open-end or closed-end funds. The distinguishing factor is that the open-end funds are redeemable, while the closed-end shares trade on the secondary market among investors. The unit investment trust has no investment adviser managing the portfolio and is sometimes linked with "having no board of directors." Note that the separate account for a variable annuity is registered under this Act, too, either as an open-end fund or as a UIT.

To fit the definition of "investment company," the shares must be able to easily be sold and the number of shareholders must exceed 100. Hedge funds go the other way to avoid fitting the definition of "investment company." That is, they don't let people sell their investment freely and they keep the number of investors under 100, because if you can escape the definition of "investment company," you can escape the hassle of registering the investments and providing lots of disclosure to the SEC and the public markets. As usual, under the Act of 1940 the average investor is protected more than the sophisticated investor. Mutual funds and variable annuities are for the average investor; therefore, they need to be registered and watched closely by the SEC. Hedge funds are for the sophisticated investor primarily, so maybe things don't need to be watched so closely with them.

INVESTMENT ADVISERS ACT OF 1940

The SEC is *way* into the Investment Advisers Act of 1940, so let's let them explain it in their own words:

> This law regulates investment advisers. With certain exceptions, this Act requires that firms or sole practitioners compensated for advising others about securities investments must register with the SEC and conform to regulations designed to protect investors. Since the Act was amended in 1996 and 2010, generally only advisers who have at least $100 million of assets under management or advise a registered investment company must register with the Commission.

If you want to give people your expert advice on their specific investment situation and receive compensation for doing so, you have to register under the Investment Advisers Act of 1940 or under your state securities law. Portfolio managers, financial planners, pension fund consultants, and even many sports and entertainment agents end up having to register in order to give investment advice to their clients. All open- and closed-end funds are managed by registered investment advisers, and pension funds typically farm out their assets to many different investment advisory firms. Because the role they play is so important and so potentially dangerous, all investment advisers have to be registered unless they can qualify for some type of exemption.

Federal covered advisers (federally registered advisers) are subject to the provisions of the Investment Advisers Act of 1940. That's why we saw that the Administrator of a state cannot impose a higher net capital requirement on investment advisers in the state than what is established by the SEC under the Investment Advisers Act of 1940. A federal covered investment adviser with offices in various states only complies with the recordkeeping requirements and the net capital requirements set by the SEC.

The SEC makes/promulgates rules under the Investment Advisers Act of 1940, and we saw that the state regulators will often write their own rules in reference to the rules the SEC has already made. For example, the SEC is very specific on the dos and don'ts for investment advisers putting out advertisements. Most states will just tell advisers not to do anything that would violate that particular SEC rule.

The SEC doesn't care whether an investment adviser is subject to registration or not—either way, if the person fits the definition of "investment adviser," he is at least subject to the anti-fraud section of the Investment Advisers Act of 1940. If the investment adviser qualifies for an exemption, he may get to skip various filing requirements, but he would still be subject to the anti-fraud provisions of the Act. That also means that if the person is not an investment adviser, he is not subject to the Investment Advisers Act of 1940, period. I doubt the exam would go there, but this represents a major difference between federal and state securities law. The Uniform Securities Act doesn't look to see if someone is or is not an investment adviser per se. Rather, it looks at the activity, as we see from this passage: "It is unlawful for any person who receives, directly or indirectly, any consideration from another person for advising the other person as to the value of securities or their purchase or sale..." Again, that would seem like an unlikely test question, but one never knows. Either way, remember that an investment adviser with an exemption is excused from some or all registration requirements; however, anyone who is an investment adviser or is acting like one is subject to the anti-fraud sections of federal and state securities law.

The SEC can discipline federal covered investment advisers through administrative hearings to determine if a license is to be denied, suspended or revoked. They can also represent the US Government in federal court and ask a judge to issue an injunction/restraining order against an investment adviser violating various sections of the "Advisers Act." As we saw, the SEC does this even more often against insider trading violators under the Securities Exchange Act of 1934. Either way, they're a busy bunch the SEC, believe you me.

INSIDER TRADING & SECURITIES FRAUD ENFORCEMENT ACT OF 1988 (ITSFEA)

Although the Act of 1934 talked about insider trading, apparently it didn't quite get the message across. So in 1988 Congress passed the **Insider Trading & Securities Fraud Enforcement Act** of 1988 and raised the penalties for insider trading, making it a criminal offense with stiff civil penalties as well. If your brother-in-law happens to be the Chief Financial Officer of a public company and over a few too many martinis lets it slip that his company is going to miss earnings estimates badly this quarter, just pretend like you didn't hear it. Tell your principal and no one else. If you start passing out that information, or if you—God forbid—buy a bunch of puts on the stock, you could go to federal prison. More likely, the SEC would just sue the heck out of you in federal court and try to extract a civil penalty of three times the amount of the profit made or loss avoided.

How would they ever catch me, though?

Interestingly enough, those words have been carved into many federal prison cell walls since they passed the Insider Trading and Securities Fraud Enforcement Act of 1988. As we mentioned earlier, the SEC offers bounties of up to 10% of the amount they get out of the inside traders. Any material information the public doesn't have, that's inside information. Don't pass it around, don't use it. People who violate the act can be held liable to what they call "contemporaneous traders." That means that if you're dumping your shares based on an inside tip, and that hurts me, we might need to have a little talk with our attorneys.

The investment banking arm of a broker-dealer has access to all kinds of material non-public information. To prevent that sensitive information from flowing to other areas of the firm, the broker-dealer is required to create a **Chinese Wall** around departments that obtain such information. No, they don't build an actual wall. They just try to prevent the investment bankers working on a merger from revealing some good trading tips to the registered representatives working the telephones.

CHAPTER 4 QUIZ
40 questions

1. Which federal securities act requires that public companies report to the SEC and shareholders through 10-K and 10-Q filings?

   A. ERISA

   B. NSMIA

   C. Securities Exchange Act of 1934

   D. Securities Act of 1933

2. A securities agent is registered in State A. She sells an unregistered exempt security issued by State B to a customer who is a resident of State A. This activity:

A. Is prohibited

B. Is fraudulent, unethical and prohibited

C. Is not prohibited

D. Is prohibited if the order is not, in fact, unsolicited

3. Which of the following is an accurate statement addressing fraudulent, unethical, or prohibited practices in the securities industry?

A. All fraudulent practices are also prohibited

B. All prohibited practices are also fraudulent

C. Fraud occurs only if the state can prove beyond a reasonable doubt that the violator knew he was misleading the other side of the transaction

D. Fraudulent sales practices are unethical but not inherently prohibited by law

4. Under the Uniform Securities Act, which of the following must register as a broker-dealer in the state of South Dakota?

A. A firm properly registered in North Dakota effecting transactions in securities exclusively with large pension funds located in South Dakota

B. A firm properly registered in North Dakota effecting transactions in securities exclusively with banks, S&Ls, and trust companies located in South Dakota

C. A financial planner with an office in South Dakota

D. A firm with a place of business in South Dakota effecting transactions in securities exclusively with banks, S&Ls, and trust companies located in South Dakota

5. Which of the following would allow a security to be sold in a state without registration?

A. The selling agents represent the issuer of the securities

B. The security is common stock trading on the non-NASDAQ OTC market

C. The firm selling the security is excluded from the definition of a broker-dealer

D. The security is sold in a private placement

6. Under the Uniform Securities Act unregistered, non-exempt securities may be sold

A. Under no circumstances

B. To accredited investors

C. Through exempt transactions

D. Provided the broker-dealer and agents are properly registered

7. According to NASAA model rules, an investment adviser would not be deemed to have custody of client assets in which of the following cases?

A. An adviser places client assets in custody of a financial institution in which he is merely a limited partner

B. An adviser automatically deducts management fees, sending a billing statement to the custodian and the client

C. An adviser accepts client securities from a client in the adviser's office and promptly forwards them to the custodian

D. An adviser inadvertently receives client securities in the mail and returns them to the sender 2 days later

8. Which of the following accurately addresses an investment adviser's business practices in connection to mutual fund 12b-1 fees?

A. A conflict of interest is inherent if the adviser receives 12b-1 fees based on client recommendations

B. As long as the 12b-1 fee does not exceed .25%, there is no duty to disclose the fact that the adviser receives such 12b-1 fees on investor purchases

C. 12b-1 fees are considered soft-dollar compensation

D. Investment advisers and IARs may receive 12b-1 fees whether Series 6- or 7-registered or not

9. Which of the following Administrative orders is most severe?

A. Cancellation

B. Cease & Desist

C. Revocation

D. Suspension

10. Which of the following is an example of the violation known as frontrunning?

A. A registered representative purchases shares for his son's UTMA account before placing a large customer buy order

B. A registered representative sells a mutual fund investment based on an upcoming dividend

C. A registered representative fails to disclose a breakpoint to a mutual fund investor

D. A registered representative asks his firm's investment bankers for stock tips based on upcoming unannounced mergers

11. A firm with a place of business in the state charges corporations to advise on mergers and acquisitions and to help structure and sell initial equity offerings. The firm must register as a(n):

A. Investment adviser

B. Broker-dealer

C. Investment adviser and broker-dealer

D. Primary analyst

12. A broker-dealer needs written discretionary authorization over an account before accepting which of the following orders from a customer?

A. Purchase 155 shares of a technology stock today

B. Purchase 100 shares of ABC this afternoon

C. Purchase 100 shares of ABC today

D. Sell 100 shares of ABC at a good price today

13. Which of the following investments are subject to anti-fraud rules under the Uniform Securities Act?

A. Variable life insurance

B. Commodity futures

C. Whole life insurance

D. All of these choices

14. Which of the following accurately describes the organization FINRA?

A. A regulatory body with authority to enforce rules and impose fines and sanctions of members and associated persons

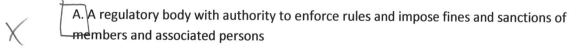

B. An industry-funded trade association advocating for the rights of member broker-dealers

C. A government-sponsored enterprise empowered and funded by tax dollars

D. A regulatory body with authority over broker-dealers, agents, investment advisers and IARs

15. Which of the following activities is not a violation?

A. Selling away

B. Selling dividends

C. Breakpoint selling

D. Selling short without first buying the stock

16. Regulations for Broker-Dealers and Investment Advisers are most similar in which of the following areas?

A. Obligation to disclose conflicts of interest

B. Discretionary authorization procedure

C. Record keeping requirements

D. Obligation to disclose material facts

17. Regulations for agents of broker-dealers and investment adviser representatives are most similar in which of the following areas?

A. Duty to disclose potential conflicts of interest to clients and prospects

B. Duty to provide a copy of the firm's ADV 2

C. Obligation to disclose affiliation with their employer in any internet-based communications involving securities

D. Pre-license exam requirements

18. What does the term "hypothecation" have to do with?

A. An equity deficiency in a long margin account

B. Pledging securities as collateral in a margin account

C. Publishing an offering memorandum for a private placement

D. Amortizing the premium on a tax-exempt security

19. According to NASAA policy statements, which of the following accurately explains a broker-dealer's responsibilities when it comes to customer securities?

A. The broker-dealer may pledge customer fully paid securities to secure a short-term loan to the firm

B. The broker-dealer may pledge customer securities held in safekeeping in an amount not to exceed 50% of any loan made directly to the firm

C. The broker-dealer may pledge only customer securities for which it holds a proper lien

D. Broker-dealers are no longer allowed to maintain control or possession of customer securities

20. Based on the Howey Decision, which TWO of the following investments are most likely considered to be "securities"?

I. A prize-winning racehorse

II. Interests in dairy cattle

III. Rare oil paintings from the 17th century

IV. A share of profits derived from the managerial efforts of others

A. I, II

B. I, III

C. II, III

D. II, IV

21. Under the Uniform Securities Act if a securities agent passes her exam and registers just after Thanksgiving, she will be required to:

A. Pay the full year's registration fee now and renew by December 31st for the following year by paying next year's fee at that point.

B. Register now but make payment by December 31st for the following year only.

C. Pay only a pro-rated portion of this year's fee but make full payment for the following year by December 31st.

D. Wait to register until December 31st, and for the following year only.

22. When an investment adviser representative working for a federal covered investment adviser leaves her place of employment to take a position with a state-registered investment adviser, which

of the following accurately describes the requirement to notify the state securities Administrator of these facts?

A. There are no such requirements as a result of NSMIA (National Securities Markets Improvement Act)

B. The federal covered adviser must notify the Administrator of the termination, and the state-registered firm must notify the Administrator of the new hire

C. The IAR must notify the Administrator of the termination, and the state-registered firm must notify the Administrator of the new hire

D. The federal covered adviser and the IAR must notify the Administrator of the termination, and both the IAR and the state-registered firm most notify the Administrator of the new hire

23. If Wanda terminates her position as an agent of a broker-dealer registered in the state and takes a position with another broker-dealer registered in the state, who must notify the Administrator of these facts?

A. There is no requirement to notify the Administrator, as FINRA will provide such notification to the states

B. Both broker-dealers and Wanda must notify the Administrator when terminating or hiring Wanda as an agent

C. Only Wanda need notify the Administrator of the termination, but both she and the hiring broker-dealer must notify the Administrator of the new hire

D. Both Wanda and the terminating broker-dealer must notify the Administrator, but only the hiring firm need notify the Administrator of the new hire

24. Under the Uniform Securities Act, once a security's registration has been declared effective, which of the following facts stated in the registration statement may be altered?

A. The type of security to be issued

B. The terms at which additional securities are to be issued to promoters and underwriters

C. The number of shares to be issued at the same terms stated in the registration statement

D. No facts may be altered once a registration statement has been declared effective

25. A Unit Investment Trust would be MOST closely associated with which of the following federal securities acts?

A. Securities Act of 1933

B. Securities Exchange Act of 1934

C. Investment Advisers Act of 1940

D. Investment Company Act of 1940

26. A securities agent sells a 78-year-old customer a deferred variable annuity, telling her if she wants to access the funds at any time she may do so. However, he fails to add that withdrawals during the next 10 years may be subject to surrender charges as high as 9%. A disciplinary action taken by the state securities Administrator would, therefore, be based on all of the following EXCEPT:

A. Suitability requirements

B. Fraud

C. Failure to maintain high standards of commercial honor

D. Churning

27. The Administrator may take disciplinary actions against registrants for many reasons. Which of the following activities would probably be considered the most serious violation that an Administrator would use to take such an action?

A. An agent fails to inform her employing broker-dealer that she is moonlighting two nights a week at a local factory.

B. An agent enters an unauthorized transaction and marks the order ticket "unsolicited."

C. An agent makes an unsuitable recommendation.

D. All industry violations are deemed equally serious under state securities law.

28. A public company's 10-Q or quarterly report is associated with which of the following federal securities acts?

A. The Securities Act of 1933

B. The Securities Exchange Act of 1934

C. Sarbanes-Oxley

D. National Securities Markets Improvement Act

29. According to NASAA's Model Rule on unethical business practices for the investment advisory industry, which of the following is accurate concerning an adviser's advertising practices?

A. An adviser's compliance with FINRA standards is dispositive that the adviser is in compliance with any and all advertising requirements

B. Client testimonials may be provided only with written permission from clients

C. No unrealistic performance projections of any kind may be used, even with supporting documentation

D. Performance figures may be cited in advertisements provided the period covered does not exceed 1 year

30. Under the Uniform Securities Act, a broker-dealer registered in the state agrees to comply with all requirements related to an administrative or civil proceeding by filing which of the following?

    A. A fidelity bond

    B. A consent to service of process

    C. A Form ADV

    D. A notice filing

31. Jason is a securities agent for Williams, Smith, and Parker, LLC, a broker-dealer registered in the state. Occasionally on his lunch hour Jason monitors the accounts of two former college friends held at another broker-dealer and sometimes enters online orders to buy or sell securities. Jason accepts no compensation for his efforts; therefore, which of the following best addresses this situation?

    A. There is no violation because Jason accepts no remuneration for services rendered.

    B. Provided the trades entered meet suitability requirements, no violation has occurred.

    C. Jason is likely guilty of the sales practice violation known as "frontrunning."

    D. Jason is improperly entering transactions in securities not recorded on the regular books and records of his employer.

32. In which of the following cases was an offer of securities made under the Uniform Securities Act?

    A. An advertisement appears in a newspaper published in the state, with 75% of its circulation in neighboring states

    B. An individual makes a gift of assessable stock to a close personal friend

    C. A themed restaurant chain offers to purchase a chain of bakeries by giving shareholders .77 shares of the restaurant company's stock for each share of the bakery chain currently held

    D. The board of directors for ABC declares a 15% stock dividend

33. John Johnson has just had his firm's registration accepted as a registered investment adviser in the state. This means that the securities Administrator of the state has authorized John and his firm to engage in which of the following activities?

   A. Executing transactions in securities for compensation

   B. Raising capital for corporate clients on the primary market for securities

   C. Providing and selling reports and analyses on securities and investment strategies

   D. Selling mutual funds and annuities to clients for compensation

34. Jessica is a securities agent who just finalized a long and painful divorce with her husband, who ran up large amounts of credit card debt and raided various savings accounts without Jessica's knowledge. In order to finalize the divorce Jessica was forced to do a "short sale" on the house, resulting in a sale that was $37,000 under what was owed. Therefore, which of the following best addresses this situation?

   A. Jessica must report the short sale on Form U4 promptly.

   B. Jessica need not report this event, as the disposition of the matter was accepted by the lender.

   C. A short sale would be reported on an initial application only.

   D. If the amount of the loss/deficiency exceeds $50,000, the event is reportable on Form U4.

35. Which of the following is an accurate statement concerning investment advisers and custody?

   A. Advisers with custody must undergo regular, scheduled audits by a CPA of the Administrator's choosing

   B. Advisers with custody now have minimum net capital requirements waived as a result of Dodd-Frank

   C. Advisers with custody must inform the Administrator by close-of-business on the day following the discovery of any deficiency in net capital

   D. Advisers may avoid being deemed to have custody by using only affiliated broker-dealers

36. Under the Uniform Securities Act, the Administrator may issue which TWO of the following?

I. Cease and desist orders in advance of a hearing

II. Subpoenas

III. Injunctions

IV. Arrest warrants for violations of securities law only

   A. I, II

   B. II, III

   C. II, IV

   D. I, IV

37. If an investing customer asks her securities agent what the significance of an "exempt" security is, the agent could accurately reply with which of the following statements?

   A. Exempt securities are generally safer securities of "investment quality"

   B. Exempt securities are not subject to typical registration requirements

   C. Exempt securities are granted an exemption based on passing a merit test with the Securities and Exchange Commission

   D. Exempt securities and government securities are synonymous

38. Under the Uniform Securities Act, which of the following represents an acceptable method of compensation for a registered investment adviser?

   A. A percentage of the increase the account experiences either quarterly or annually

   B. A percentage of capital gains, but not capital appreciation, over any financial quarter

   C. A percentage of capital appreciation, but not capital gains, over any financial quarter

   D. A percentage of the account value averaged over four consecutive financial quarters

39. Assuming there is no disciplinary proceeding in place, an individual who applies as an agent with the Administrator will be granted her license to sell securities in the state:

   A. As soon as FINRA declares her registration effective

   B. By noon of the 30th day, if not sooner

   C. As soon as she is bonded

   D. As soon as she passes her exams and presents the results to the Administrator

40. According to the Uniform Securities Act, a registration statement for an offer of securities must stipulate all of the following EXCEPT:

   A. All states in which the security is to be offered

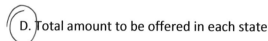

B. Total amount of the securities offering

C. Amount of the securities to be offered in the Administrator's state

D. Total amount to be offered in each state

(ANSWERS TO CHAPTER 4 QUIZ)
1. ANSWER: C

WHY: the Securities Act of 1933 is all about new issues of securities. Public companies keep investors informed going forward with reports filed under the Securities Exchange Act of 1934

2. ANSWER: C

WHY: the question is designed to make it appear something wrong is taking place—actually, the security does not have to be registered, and the agent is properly registered in the investor's state.

3. ANSWER: A

WHY: fraud is definitely unlawful, and is definitely a prohibited practice. But, fraud involves deceit/trickery/manipulation. On the other hand, many prohibited practices have nothing to do with fraud—e.g., an agent working outside the broker-dealer without their knowledge. Proving that the violator knew he was misleading the other side is important only if the state is making a criminal case. Fraud occurs whenever the other side is deprived of the knowledge needed to make an informed decision.

4. ANSWER: D

WHY: it's easy to get distracted by a question like this, but there are only two firms with a place of business in South Dakota, and one of them is a financial planner/investment adviser.

5. ANSWER: D

WHY: the only way to sell a non-exempt security without registration is to do so through an exempt transaction, e.g., a private placement, or an offer to institutional investors.

6. ANSWER: C

WHY: if the security is not exempt, it must either be registered or offered/sold through an exempt transaction.

7. ANSWER: D

WHY: if the adviser accepts the securities, custody has occurred right then and there, but if the adviser inadvertently receives them in the mail, the firm just needs to keep records of what happened and return them within 3 business days to the sender. Although an adviser deducting management fees can avoid the minimum financial requirements, they still are considered to have custody by the state regulators. And, if the adviser is an owner of the institution holding custody, then the adviser by definition has custody of client assets.

8. ANSWER: A

WHY: any time an adviser gets additional benefit from client transactions, a conflict of interest arises. 12b-1 fees are not "soft dollars" but are actual dollars that must be disclosed to advisory clients. To receive sales compensation, an adviser would also have to be licensed as a securities salesperson.

9. ANSWER: C

WHY: a revocation of a license is the stiffest penalty the Administrator can issue, and only after a hearing, of course. A cancellation occurs when the registrant goes out of business, dies, can't be located, etc. A suspension is a temporary disciplinary order. A cease & desist order is a formal warning to refrain from further violations of the Uniform Securities Act.

10. ANSWER: A

WHY: taking advantage of a customer order that is about to be placed = frontrunning, a major violation. The other activities here are also violations, in this order: selling dividends, breakpoint sales, and insider trading.

11. ANSWER: B

WHY: don't assume the firm is an investment adviser solely because the word "advise" is used in the question. Is the firm helping clients invest their capital in securities? No? Then, the firm is not an investment adviser. The firm is also not a "primary analyst." No, the firm is a broker-dealer acting as an investment banker.

12. ANSWER: A

WHY: the firm needs to have written discretionary authorization over the account before choosing which security is to be bought or sold. In the other cases, the firm would merely be entering a particular order the customer has given at, perhaps, a later time during the day and at, maybe, a better price.

13. ANSWER: A

WHY: remember, it has to be a SECURITY to be subject to ANY part of the Uniform SECURITIES Act.

14. ANSWER: A

WHY: FINRA is not a government body; it is a Self-Regulatory Organization (SRO) registered with the SEC (federal government) under the Securities Exchange Act of 1934. FINRA regulates member broker-dealers, their principals, and their agents; it has no authority over the investment advisory industry.

15. ANSWER: D

WHY: Choice D simply states how short selling takes place—the shares are borrowed and sold, with the obligation to replace them in the future. Selling away occurs when a registered representative offers investments without his firm's knowledge or permission. Selling dividends is a fraudulent practice where an agent tries to hurry an investor into buying a stock just for an upcoming dividend—the investor could just as well wait for the stock to drop by the amount of the dividend and avoid the tax. Breakpoint selling occurs when a customer is not informed of quantity discounts on mutual fund purchases.

16. ANSWER: D

WHY: all material facts must be disclosed to investors. However, investment advisers have a higher obligation to disclose conflicts of interest than broker-dealers. Also, the record keeping requirements and the process for discretionary authorization are quite different for the two types of firms.

17. ANSWER: C

WHY: both IARs and agents must prominently disclose their affiliation with their employing firms in any internet communications involving securities—assuming their employer even allows such nonsense. The first two choices apply to IARs, not securities agents. The exams required of each are also different.

18. ANSWER: B

WHY: customers pledge/hypothecate their securities as collateral to the broker-dealer to secure the loan in a margin account.

19. ANSWER: C

WHY: unless the broker-dealer has the customer's written permission to pledge securities as collateral in a margin account, the firm had better not be pledging customer securities as collateral to secure a loan, right?

20. ANSWER: D

WHY: a thing of value is not a security, but an INTEREST in things of value could be. Choice "IV" is one of the prongs of the Howey Decision, and an interest in dairy cattle would likely be a share of profits derived from the efforts of others.

21. ANSWER: A

WHY: it doesn't matter when she registers; she has to pay the full year's fee, and she has to renew for the following year by December 31st of this year.

22. ANSWER: C

WHY: the process is much different for the advisory than for the brokerage industry. For broker-dealers and agents both the firm and the agent always notify the Administrator of any change in registration status. However, for the advisory side, it's an either-or situation. If the firm is federal covered only the IAR notifies the Administrator; however, if the firm is state-registered only the firm notifies the Administrator. Seriously.

23. ANSWER: B

WHY: it's simple for the broker-dealer side—the firm and the agent must notify the Administrator when the agent is hired or when she leaves the firm. Period. A U5 is used to notify of the termination, while a U4 is used to notify of the new hire.

24. ANSWER: C

WHY: as long as the terms of the offering are not being altered, the number of shares may be increased due to heavy demand. But the Administrator will freak out if suddenly a bunch of shares are transferred to promoters or underwriters on more favorable terms than those offered to investors and stated in the registration statement.

25. ANSWER: D

WHY: the only act that UITs have nothing to do with is the Investment Advisers Act of 1940, since there is no investment adviser managing the portfolio. The securities offering would be registered under the Securities Act of 1933, and all securities are subject to the Exchange Act's anti-fraud statutes at a minimum. But, since a UIT is an investment company, it is most closely associated with and regulated under the Investment Company Act of 1940.

26. ANSWER: D

WHY: there is no churning going on here, but that is, unfortunately, about the only positive thing I can think of to mention. The recommendation is unsuitable even if the agent had decided to tell the whole truth. By telling her that she can access her money any time but leaving out the part about losing maybe 9% of it, the agent has committed fraud, which is not a good way to maintain "high standards of commercial honor."

27. ANSWER: B

WHY: spending a customer's money without bothering to talk to him is a VERY serious violation, especially when the agent then enters a false record implying the customer called the order in. Failing to inform the employing broker-dealer of outside employment is a violation of FINRA rules, and so if FINRA makes a stink, the state could also use that as a reason to go after him. An unsuitable recommendation is, first of all, a little bit of a subjective call and, secondly, more of a mistake than the outright fraud involved with an unauthorized transaction—and, a principal would have signed off on an inappropriate recommendation whereas an unauthorized transaction involves faking out the principal as well.

28. ANSWER: B

WHY: the Securities Act of 1933 is involved with new offerings of securities, e.g., IPOs. Going forward, public companies file 10-Q, 10-K, 8-K, and other reports under the Securities Exchange Act of 1934.

29. ANSWER: C

WHY: projections/predictions of performance are a big no-no, whether backed up by supporting documentation or not, especially when the predictions are unrealistic. Testimonials are not allowed, and if past performance is touted, the period covered must be a minimum of 1 year.

30. ANSWER: B

WHY: persons registered under the Uniform Securities Act are required to file a formal "consent to service of process," binding them to play along with all the rules involved in any administrative or civil proceeding against the person. This is also a requirement for a registered offer of securities.

31. ANSWER: D

WHY: NASAA's model rule on unethical business practices for broker-dealers and agents points out that it is a violation to execute securities transactions not recorded on the regular books and records of the broker-dealer, unless the firm gives written notification that it's okay.

32. ANSWER: B

WHY: assessable stock comes with a catch—the owner may be assessed fees in the future. So, to prevent some scoundrel from "giving" the loaded stock to someone, the Uniform Securities Act treats even a gift of assessable stock as an offer and sale. If the newspaper's publication is more than 2/3 outside the state, no offer to sell has been made in the state. A merger—even in an all-stock deal—is excluded from the definition of an offer to sell securities, as is a stock dividend.

33. ANSWER: C

WHY: investment advisers are not in the business of selling securities or being paid to execute transactions in securities. Nor are they investment bankers (broker-dealers) raising capital on the primary market. They are compensated for telling people how to invest or investing on their behalf.

34. ANSWER: A

WHY: compromises with creditors must be promptly reported on U4—failure to do so leads to disciplinary action.

35. ANSWER: C

WHY: investment advisers with custody are in a position to inflate client account balances for the purpose of over-billing them, or—worse—they could actually be lying about the existence of cash and securities with each bogus account statement they or their affiliated broker-dealer send to clients. If custody is allowed in the state, the adviser would have to contract with a CPA firm to come in annually at irregular and unannounced times to audit the books and records pertaining to client assets. This is expensive, and is why many advisers avoid being deemed to have custody.

36. ANSWER: A

WHY: only a judge can issue an injunction or an arrest warrant. The Administrator does not issue a denial, suspension, or revocation order without granting a hearing, but a cease and desist can be issued before any hearing is granted.

37. ANSWER: B

WHY: some exempt securities happen to be safe; many do not. For example, US Treasury Bonds are definitely "safe" in terms of having no default risk, but a bank or insurance company stock could be the shakiest thing on the market. The only thing we can conclude is that an exempt security is excused from having to register.

38. ANSWER: D

WHY: typically, investment advisers cannot be compensated as a percentage of the increase on a particular security or the account itself. An hourly rate is fine, as is a percentage of the account value itself—not a share of its increase. To figure the % of assets, many advisers take ¼ of their annual fee times the account balance at the end of each financial quarter. Some might take the account balances at the end of each financial quarter, average that out, and take the annual fee as a percentage of this figure. Either way suits the regulators just fine.

39. ANSWER: B

WHY: unless there is a problem with the U4, the agent will get her license granted no later than in 30 days. The Uniform Securities Act says "by noon of the thirtieth day."

40. ANSWER: D

WHY: the Administrator of a state needs to know the names of the other states, the total amount of the offering, and how much is to be offered in his state. The state-by-state totals would be unnecessary.

Glossary

3-Pronged Approach: Test used by SEC to determine if an entity meets the definition of an investment adviser. Does the person provide "investment advice" relating to securities and based on the client's situation? Does the person receive compensation as a result of providing investment advice? Is the person in the business of providing investment advice?

8-K: SEC report required by the Securities Exchange Act of 1934 of public companies announcing unusual material events.

10-K: SEC report required by the Securities Exchange Act of 1934 annually of public companies.

10- Q: SEC report required by the Securities Exchange Act of 1934 quarterly of public companies.

12b-1 fee: Fee deducted from a mutual fund's assets to cover distribution costs, e.g., selling, mailing, printing, advertising. An operating expense, unlike the sales charge that is deducted from the investor's check.

72-t: Section of the tax code allowing individuals to make withdrawals prior to age 59 ½ from a Traditional IRA or variable annuity without penalty based on taking a series of substantially equal payments over a number of years.

75-5-10 Rule: Diversification formula for a fund advertising itself as "diversified." 75% of the portfolio must have no more than 5% of assets invested in any one security, and no more than 10% of a company's outstanding shares may be owned.

200-day Moving Average: Average closing price over the previous 200 days for a stock or an index.

401(k) Plan: Qualified defined contribution plan offering employer-matched contributions.

403(b): Qualified plan for tax-exempt, non-profit organizations.

404(c): Safe-harbor provisions allowing employers to pass off risk to participants of defined contribution plans.

457 Plan: Tax-advantaged retirement account for state and municipal government employees. AKA "Section 457 Plan."

529 Plans: Education savings plans offering tax-deferred growth and tax-free distributions at the federal level for qualified educational expenses.

1035 Contract Exchange: Tax-free exchange of one annuity contract for another, one life insurance policy for another, or one life insurance policy for an annuity. The contracts do not have to be issued by the same company.

1040: Tax form used by individuals and sole proprietors.

1041: Tax form used by trusts and estates.

1065: Tax form used by partnerships.

1099-DIV: Tax form sent to investors showing dividends and capital gains distributions from a mutual fund for the tax year.

1099-INT: Tax form sent to investors showing interest payments for the tax year.

1099-OID: Tax form used to pay annual accretion on a zero coupon or any taxable original issue discount (OID) bond.

1120: Tax form used by corporations.

A

A-Shares: Mutual fund shares sold with a front-end sales load/charge. Lower annual expenses than B- and C-shares.

Account at Maintenance: The point at which a customer's equity in a margin account is just high enough to avoid a margin call.

Account Freeze: Temporary restrictions placed on a customer account for violations of Regulation T.

Accounts Payable: What a company owes its vendors in the short-term, a current liability.

Accounts Receivable: What customers owe a company in the short-term, a current asset.

Account Statement: Document sent to a broker-dealer customer showing the recent value of all cash and securities, plus all recent activity in the account.

Accredited Investors: Large institutional investors, and individuals meeting certain income or net worth requirements allowing them to participate in, for example, a private placement under Reg D of the Securities Act of 1933, or hedge funds.

Accretion: Increasing the cost basis of a discount bond for tax purposes.

Accrued Interest: The interest that the buyer of a debt security owes the seller. Bond interest is payable only twice a year, and the buyer will receive the next full interest payment. Therefore, the buyer owes the seller for every day of interest since the last payment up to the day before the transaction settles.

Accrued Taxes: Taxes that are owed by a company over the short-term, a current liability.

Accrued Wages: Wages that are owed by a company over the short-term, a current liability.

Accumulation Stage/Period: Period during which contributions are made to an annuity, during which the investor holds "accumulation units."

Accumulation Units: What the purchaser of an annuity receives in exchange for his purchase payments during the accumulation phase, an accounting measure representing a proportional share of the separate account.

Active Investor: Investor who feels markets are not perfectly efficient and, therefore, selects particular investments.

Ad Valorem: Property tax, relating to general obligation municipal bonds.

Additional Takedown: The piece of the spread that goes to the various members of the syndicate when the bonds they've been allotted are sold.

Adjustable Rate Preferred Stock: Preferred stock whose dividend is tied to another rate, often the rate paid on T-bills.

Adjusted Gross Income (AGI): Earned income plus passive income, portfolio income, and capital gains. The amount upon which we pay income tax.

Adjustment Bond: Another name for an "income bond," on which the issuer may miss interest payments without going into default.

Administrator: (1) The securities regulator of a particular state; (2) A person authorized by the courts to oversee and liquidate an estate.

ADR/ADS: Abbreviation for an American Depository Receipt/Share. A foreign stock on a domestic market. Toyota and Nokia are two examples of foreign companies whose ADRs trade on American stock markets denominated in dollars.

Advance Refunding/Pre-refunding: Issuing new bonds and depositing part of the proceeds in escrow ahead of the first legal call date on the existing bond issue.

Advance/Decline Ratio: The number of stocks whose market prices increased versus the number of stocks whose market prices decreased during a trading session.

Advertising: For investment advisers, any written communication delivered to more than one person.

Affiliated Investor, Person: Person who is an officer or director of the issuer, or a 10%+ owner of its common stock.

Age-Based Portfolio: A mutual fund or other portfolio adjusting asset allocation to match the needs of a beneficiary in a 529 Plan or an adult in a retirement account. AKA "lifecycle" or "target" funds.

Agency Cross Transaction: A potential conflict of interest arising when an investment adviser enters a trade for a client that is filled by matching the order with an order placed by one of the affiliated broker-dealer's customers. Requires disclosure.

Agency Issue (Agency Bond): Debt security issued by an agency authorized by the federal government but not directly backed by the federal government.

Agent: Individual representing a broker-dealer or issuer in effecting/completing transactions in securities for compensation.

Aggressive Growth: Equity investments that face a higher risk of loss but also a higher potential return, e.g. emerging market or sector funds.

Aggressive Investor: An investor willing to risk a large loss of principal in order to earn potentially large returns.

Agreement Among Underwriters: Document used by an underwriting syndicate bringing an issue of securities to the primary market. This document sets forth the terms under which each member of the syndicate will participate and details the duties and responsibilities of the syndicate manager.

AIR: Assumed Interest Rate. Rate used to determine the value of annuity units and death benefits for variable contracts.

All or None: Type of underwriting in which the syndicate will cancel the offering if a sufficient dollar amount is not raised as opposed to being responsible for the unsold shares (as in a "firm commitment"). Also a type of order on the secondary market in which the investor wants the order to be canceled if the broker cannot acquire the full number of shares on one attempt.

Alternative Investment: An investment generally open only to sophisticated investors and providing limited or no liquidity, e.g. direct participation programs or hedge funds.

AM Best: Entity that rates the credit strength of insurance companies, a key to evaluating fixed annuities and other pure insurance products backed by the claims paying ability of the insurance company.

American Style: An option that can be exercised at any time up to expiration, as opposed to "European style."

Amortization: Spreading the cost of an intangible item, e.g., a patent or trademark, over its useful life.

Amortized: Intangible assets that have been written down over the estimated useful life of the assets.

AMT (Alternative Minimum Tax): Tax computation that adds certain "tax preference items" back into adjusted gross income. Some municipal bond interest is treated as a "tax preference item" that can raise the investor's tax liability through the AMT.

Annualized Return: The rate of return adjusted for increments of one year. For example, a 5% return over 1 month represents a 60% annualized rate of return, while a 15% return over three years represents a 5% annualized rate of return.

Annual Shareholder Report: Formal statement issued by a corporation to the SEC and shareholders discussing the company's results of operations, challenges/risks facing the company, any lawsuits against the company, etc. Required by the Securities Exchange Act of 1934. Form 10K.

Annual Updating Amendment: Process of annually updating all answers to an investment adviser's Form ADV-1 filing.

Annuitant: The person who receives an annuity contract's payments.

Annuitize: Process of converting an annuity contract's value to a series of payments to the annuitant.

Annuity: Contract between an individual and an insurance company that provides income for the rest of the individual's life in return for a lump-sum or periodic payment to the insurance company.

Annuity Units: What the annuitant holds during the pay-out phase, with the value tied to AIR.

Anticipation Notes: Short-term debt obligations of a municipality, often held by tax-exempt money market mutual funds.

Anti-Fraud Statutes: Key sections of federal and state securities law designed to protect investors from fraudulent, deceptive, or manipulative activities in the securities industry.

Appreciation: The increase in an asset's value that is not subject to tax until realized.

Arbitrage: A trading tactic that involves taking advantage of the disparity of two things. If you think GE will buy a small company, you can make a bet that GE will temporarily drop and the small company's stock will skyrocket. Or, you can trade on the disparity between a convertible bond and its underlying common stock.

Arbitration: Settling a dispute without going to an actual court of law.

Arbitration Award: The decision rendered through FINRA Arbitration.

Ask, Asked: The higher price in a quote representing what the customer would have to pay/what the dealer is asking the customer to pay. Ask/asked is also called "offer/offered."

Assessed Value: The percentage of market value used to calculate property taxes owed.

Asset Allocation: Maintaining a percentage mix of equity, debt, and money market investments, based either on the investor's age (strategic) or market expectations (tactical).

Assets: Something that a corporation or individual owns, e.g., cash, investments, accounts receivable, inventory, etc.

Asset Coverage: A measure of how strong a company's balance sheet is relative to its obligations to bond holders

Assignment of Contract: Transferring an investment advisory client's contract to another party by any means; not allowed without client consent.

Associated Person: A registered representative or principal of a FINRA member broker-dealer.

Assumed Interest Rate: The full name for AIR, used to calculate payments in a variable annuity.

At-The-Money: An option whose strike price is equal to the market price of the underlying instrument.

Auction Market: The NYSE, for example, where buyers and sellers simultaneously enter competitive prices. Sometimes called a "double auction" market because buying and selling occur at the same time.

Auction Rate Securities: Debt securities with a variable rate of interest or preferred stock with a variable dividend rate that is re-set at regular auctions.

Authorized Stock: The number of shares a company is allowed to issue by its corporate charter. Can be changed by a majority vote of the outstanding shares.

Automated Client Account Transfer (ACAT): System that provides instructions among broker-dealers for transfer and delivery of customer assets among firms.

Automatic Reinvestment: Feature offered by mutual funds allowing investors to automatically reinvest dividend and capital gains distributions into more shares of the fund, without paying a sales charge.

Average Cost Basis: Method of figuring cost basis on securities for purposes of reporting capital gains and/or losses. The investor averages the cost for all purchases made in the stock, as opposed to identifying particular shares to the IRS when selling.

B

B-Shares: Mutual fund shares charging a load only when the investor redeems/sells the shares. Associated with "contingent deferred sales charges." B-shares have higher operating expenses than A-shares.

Backdating: Pre-dating a letter of intent (LOI) for a mutual fund in order to include a prior purchase in the total amount stated in the letter of intent. LOIs may be backdated up to 90 calendar days.

Back-end Load: Commission/sales charge added when mutual fund or variable contracts are redeemed. The back-end load declines gradually, as described in the prospectus. Associated with "B-shares."

Backing Away: Violation in which a market maker fails to honor a published firm quote to buy or sell a security at a stated price.

Backup Withholding: Required withholding from an investment account that results when the customer refuses/fails to provide a tax identification number.

Balanced Fund: Mutual fund that maintains a mix of stocks and bonds at all times. Related term "core fund."

Balance of Payments: The total inflow or outflow of capital for imports/exports and investments/financial products.

Balance of Trade: The difference between a nation's imports and exports. See trade surplus, trade deficit.

Balance Sheet: Financial statement of a corporation or individual showing financial condition (assets vs. liabilities) at a particular moment in time.

Balance Sheet Equation: Assets – Liabilities = Shareholders' Equity, or Assets = Liabilities + Shareholders' Equity. Forms the "foundation for all of accounting."

Bankers' Acceptance (BA): Money-market security that facilitates importing/exporting. Issued at a discount from face-value. A secured loan.

Bank Holding Company: Company that owns banks and often other financial services firms including broker-dealers and investment advisers.

Bar: The most severe sanction that FINRA can impose on an individual, effectively ending his/her career.

Basis: Synonym for yield. Or, reference to cost basis for tax purposes.

Basis Points: A way of measuring bond yields or other percentages in the financial industry. Each basis point is 1% of 1%. Example: 2% = .0200 = 200 basis points. 20 basis points = .2% or 2/10ths of 1%.

Basis Quote: The price at which a debt security can be bought or sold, based on the yield. A bond purchased at a "5.50 basis" is trading at a price that makes the yield 5.5%.

Bear, Bearish: Investor who takes a position based on the belief that the market or a particular security will fall. Short sellers and buyers of puts are "bearish." They profit when stocks go down. Seriously.

Bear Market: A trading market for stock or bonds in which prices are falling and/or expected to fall. Characterized by a series of lower highs and lower lows.

Bear Spread: A call or put spread in which the investor benefits if the underlying instrument's value drops. For example, an investor who buys the ABC Aug 50 call and sells the ABC Aug 45 call establishes a bear spread. The spread would also happen to be a "credit spread" in this case.

Bearer Bond: An unregistered bond that pays principal to the bearer at maturity. Bonds have not been issued in this way for over two decades, but they still exist on the secondary market.

Benchmark: The index to which an investment manager's results are compared.

Beneficiary: The one who benefits. An insurance policy pays a benefit to the named beneficiary. IRAs and other retirement plans, including annuities, allow the owner to name a beneficiary who will receive the account value when the owner dies.

Best Efforts: Type of underwriting leaving the syndicate at no risk for unsold shares, and allowing them to keep the proceeds on the shares that were sold/subscribed to. Underwriters act as "agents," not principals, in a best efforts underwriting.

Best Execution: SEC requirement for advisers and broker-dealers to execute customer transactions at the best available market price.

Beta Coefficient: Another way of referring to "beta."

Beta: Risk measurement that compares the volatility of a security or portfolio to the volatility of the overall market. A beta of more than 1 is associated with an investment or portfolio that is more volatile than the overall market. A beta of less than 1 is associated with an investment or portfolio that is less volatile than the overall market.

Bid: What a dealer is willing to pay to a customer who wants to sell. Customers sell at the bid, buy at the ask.

Billing Statement: The document an investment adviser delivers in connection with an advisory fee deduction explaining how the fee was computed.

Blank Check Company: A company with a specific business plan.

Blend Fund: A fund that does not stick to just growth or just value stocks.

Blind Pool Offering: A direct participation program in which the sponsor does not identify the assets of the partnership.

Blue Chip: Stock in a well-established company with proven ability to pay dividends in good economic times and bad. Lower risk/reward ratio than other common stock.

Blue Sky: State securities law.

Board of Directors: The group elected by shareholders to run a mutual fund or a public company and establish corporate management policies.

Bond: A debt security issued by a corporation or governmental entity that promises to repay principal and pay interest either regularly or at maturity.

Bond Anticipation Note (BAN): A short-term municipal debt security backed by the proceeds of an upcoming bond issue. Often found in tax-exempt money market funds.

Bond Counsel: Law firm advising a municipal issuer on the legality and tax treatment of a bond issue.

Bond Fund: Mutual fund with an objective of providing income while minimizing capital risk through a portfolio of bonds.

Bond Point: 1% of a bond's par value. 1 bond point = $10.

Bond Rating: Evaluation of a bond issue's chance of default published by companies such as Moody's, S&P, and Fitch.

Bond Ratio: A measure of an issuer's long-term solvency, found by comparing long-term debt to total capitalization (long-term debt plus shareholder's equity).

Bond Resolution: Document that legally authorizes the process of issuing municipal bonds for a specific purpose.

Bond Swap or Tax Swap: Taking a loss on a bond and replacing it with a substantially different bond to avoid tax problems.

Bonus Annuities: Annuities with special riders/features attached.

Book Entry: A security maintained as a computer record rather than a physical certificate. All US Treasuries and m mutual funds are issued in this manner.

Book Value or **Book Value Per-Share:** The hard, tangible asset value associated with each share of common stock. Calculated by taking stockholder's equity minus preferred shares, divided by the number of shares outstanding.

Brady Bonds: Debt securities issued primarily by Latin American government and collateralized by US Treasuries.

Branch Office: Any location identified by any means to the public or customers as a location at which the member conducts an investment banking or securities business. The small Charles Schwab or E-Trade office at the nearby mall or office complex is a "branch office."

Bottom-Up Analysis: A type of fundamental analysis involving a look at particular companies rather than the overall economy.

Breakeven: The price at which the underlying security is above or below the strike price of the option by the amount of the premium paid or received. For example, an ABC Aug 50 call @2 has a "breakeven" of $52 for both the buyer and the seller.

Breaking the Buck: Jargon used for the extremely rare case in which a money market mutual fund is unable to maintain the NAV-per-share at $1.

Breakpoint: A discounted sales charge or "volume discount" on mutual fund purchases offered on A-shares at various levels of investment.

Breakpoint Selling: Preventing an investor from achieving a breakpoint. A violation.

Broad-Based Index: An index such as the S&P 500 or the Value Line Composite Index that represents many companies from many industries.

Broker: An individual or firm that charges a commission to execute securities buy and sell orders submitted by another individual or firm.

Broker Call Loan Rate: An interest rate relating to margin accounts.

Broker-Dealer: A person/firm in the business of completing transactions in securities for the accounts of others (broker) or its own account (dealer).

Broker's Broker: A municipal securities firm acting as a broker for other firms who are not active in the municipal securities market in order to obtain pricing superior to what the firm could obtain itself.

BrokerCheck: Public disclosure database provided by FINRA allowing the public to check the qualifications and disciplinary history of member firms, principals, and agents.

Bull, Bullish: An investor who takes a position based on the belief that the market or a particular security will rise. Buyers of stock and call options are bullish.

Bull Market: A trading environment for stocks or bonds in which prices are rising and/or expected to rise.

Bulletin Board: OTC stocks too volatile and low-priced for NASDAQ.

Business Cycle: A progression of expansions, peaks, contractions, troughs, and recoveries for the overall (macro) economy.

Business Risk: The risk that the company whose stock or bond you own will not be successful as a business. Competition, poor management, obsolete products/services are all examples of business risk.

Buy and Hold: Investment approach that involves holding securities long-term in order to reduce transaction costs and based on a belief that good companies, in general, rise in value over time.

Buy-Limit: An order to buy a security at a price below the current market price, executable at a specified price or lower/better.

Buy-Stop: An order to buy a security at a price above the current market price triggered only if the market price hits or passes through the stop price.

Buy-To-Cover: The trade entered by a trader who has sold short in order to buy and replace the securities borrowed.

C

C-Shares: A type of mutual fund share often called "level load" because of the high 12b-1 fee. Appropriate for shorter-term investing only.

Call (n.): A contract that gives the holder the right to buy something at a stated exercise price.

Call (v.): To redeem a bond or preferred stock prior to the redemption date.

Callable: A security that may be purchased by the issuer as of a certain date, e.g., callable preferred stock, callable bonds.

Call Premium: The price paid and received on a call option. Or, the amount above the par value paid by the issuer to call/retire a bond.

Call Protection: Period during which a security may not be called or bought by the issuer, usually lasting 5+ years.

Call Provision: The agreement between the issuer and the bondholders or preferred stockholders that gives the issuer the ability to repurchase the bonds or preferred stock on a specified date or dates before maturity.

Call Risk: The risk that a callable bond or preferred stock will be forcibly called when interest rates fall.

Call Spread: Buying and selling a call on the same underlying instrument where the strike price, the expiration, or both are different.

Capital Appreciation: The rise in an asset's market price. The objective of a "growth investor."

Capital Gain: The amount by which the proceeds on the sale of a stock or bond exceed your cost basis. If you sell a stock for $22 and have a cost basis of $10, the capital gain or profit is $12.

Capital Gains Distribution: Distribution from fund to investor based on net capital gains realized by the fund portfolio. Holding period determined by the fund and assumed to be long-term.

Capital Loss: Loss incurred when selling an asset for less than the purchase price. Capital losses offset an investor's capital gains and can offset ordinary income to a certain amount.

Capital Risk: The risk that an investor could lose some or all of her investment principal. For securities investors avoided only by purchasing US Treasury Securities *and* holding to maturity.

Capital Structure: The make-up of a corporation's financing through equity (stock) and debt (bonds) securities.

CAPM or Capital Asset Pricing Model: Method of calculating expected return based on the riskless rate, expected market return, and beta. Based on idea that equity investors expect the time value of money *plus* a risk premium to compensate for the risk taken by investing in the stock market.

Capping: A form of market manipulation. A violation.

Cash Account: An investment account in which the investor must pay for all purchases no later than 2 business days following regular way settlement. Not a margin account.

Cash Dividend: Money paid to shareholders from an issuer's current earnings or accumulated profits.

Cash Equivalent: A security that can readily be converted to cash, e.g., T-bills, CDs, and money market funds.

Cash Flow: Net income plus depreciation/amortization. Or, "cash flow from operations" as shown on the company's statement of cash flows.

Cash Flows from Financing Activities: Cash provided/used through issuing securities, paying interest/dividends, redeeming bonds, or repurchasing stock.

Cash Flows from Investing Activities: Cash provided/used by selling or purchasing assets.

Cash Flows from Operating Activities: Cash provided/used by running the business.

Cash Settlement: Same-day settlement of a trade requiring prior broker-dealer approval. Not the "regular way" of doing things.

Cash Value: The value of an insurance policy that may be "tapped" by the policyholder through a loan or a surrender.

Catastrophe Call Provision: A provision for a municipal revenue bond providing for a mandatory call of the bonds due to unforeseen circumstances, e.g. a weather disaster, or the bonds losing their tax-exempt status.

Catch-Up Contribution: The increased amount that a person 50+ can make to a retirement account.

CDO or Collateralized Debt Obligation: A complex security like a CMO only rather than underlying mortgages, the debt securities are backed by a variety of other debt securities/loans.

CEO: Chief Executive Officer. Individual ultimately responsible for a corporation's results.

Certificate of Deposit or CD: A longer-term bank deposit offering higher yields than savings accounts.

Certificate of Limited Partnership: Document filed by the general partner of a direct participation program with a state disclosing who the partnership is and what it does.

CFO: Chief Financial Officer. Individual in charge of a corporation's financial activities.

Charitable Trust: A trust established to minimize tax liability.

Chart: Graphical representation of a stock's price and volume information.

Chartist: A technical analyst making trading decisions based on stock charts and patterns.

Check-writing Privileges: A privilege offered by mutual funds, especially money market funds, by which investors can automatically redeem shares by writing checks.

Chicago Board Options Exchange Market Volatility Index: VIX, a key measure of market expectations of near-term volatility conveyed by S&P 500 stock index option prices.

Chinese Wall: The separation that is supposed to exist between the investment banking department and the traders and registered representatives in order to prevent insider trading violations.

Churning: Excessive trading in terms of frequency and size of transactions designed to generate commissions without regard for the customer.

Clearance: Post-trade processing done by clearing agencies such as the NSCC.

Clearing Agency: An entity such as the NSCC that performs post-trade processing for the clearing and settlement of securities transactions.

Clearing Rate: The interest rate established by auction in connection with auction rate securities.

Closed-end Fund: An investment company that offers a fixed number of shares that are not redeemable. Shares are traded on the secondary market at a price that could be higher or lower than NAV (or even the same as NAV). Also "closed-end management company."

CMO or **Collateralized Mortgage Obligation**: A complicated debt security based on a pool of mortgages or a pool of mortgage-backed securities. Pays interest monthly but returns principal to one tranche at a time.

Code of Arbitration: FINRA method of resolving disputes (usually money) in the securities business. All decisions are final and binding on all parties.

Code of Procedure: FINRA system for enforcing member conduct rules.

Coincident Indicator: Economic indicator used to determine where the economy is currently, e.g. personal income, manufacturing & trade sales.

Collateral: Assets pledged to a lender to support the loan, e.g. the house in a mortgage loan.

Collateral Trust Certificate: A bond secured by a pledge of securities as collateral.

Collection Ratio: The amount of taxes collected by a municipality divided by the amount of taxes assessed.

Combination: A multiple options position that is neither a straddle nor a spread. For example, if an investor buys an ABC Aug 45 call and sells an ABC Aug 50 put, he has established a combination. AKA "Combo."

Combination Privilege: Feature that allows investors to combine purchases of many funds within the mutual fund family to reach a breakpoint/reduced sales charge.

Combined Equity: In a margin account with both long and short positions combined equity is found by adding the Credit and the Long Market Value and subtracting the Short Market Value and the Debit Balance.

Combined Offering: An offering of securities in which both the issuer and other large shareholders will be selling to the public.

Commercial Paper: Short-term unsecured loan. Issued at a discount from the face value. A money market security.

Commission House Broker: A broker who works for a particular member of the exchange filling orders for the firm and receiving a commission per-order.

Commissions: A service charge an agent earns for executing a security purchase or sale.

Commodity: A basic raw material used to produce value-added products. For example, wheat, corn oil, sugar, and salt are commodities used to make the value-added product known as bread.

Commodity Future: Futures contract in which the underlying instrument is a commodity such as corn, wheat, soy beans, crude oil, live cattle, etc.

Common Stock: An equity or ownership position that allows the owner to vote on major corporate issues such as stock splits, mergers, acquisitions, authorizing more shares, etc.

Competitive Floor Traders: Members of the NYSE who buy and sell exchange-listed securities for their own account.

Competitive, Sealed Bids: Process used for most general obligation bonds in which the underwriting business is awarded to the syndicate that turns in the lowest cost of borrowing to the issuer.

Compliance Department: The principals and supervisors of a broker-dealer responsible for making sure the firm adheres to SEC, exchange, and SRO rules.

Compound Interest: An interest rate applied to an ever-increasing principal to which interest is continuously added, e.g. the rate offered on a bank CD. As opposed to "simple interest," which is applied to a flat principal, e.g. a long-term bond.

Compound Returns: What investors hope to achieve by reinvesting interest and dividends.

Concession: The amount that the seller of a new issue of municipal bonds receives, whether a syndicate member or a selling group member.

Conduct Rules: An SRO's rules for member conduct that, if violated, may lead to sanctions and fines.

Conduit Theory (Tax Treatment): A favorable tax treatment achieved if a company (REIT, mutual fund) distributes 90%+ of net income to the shareholders.

Confirmation: Document stating the trade date, settlement date, and money due/owed for a securities purchase or sale. Delivered on or before the settlement date.

Conflict of Interest: Primarily a concern for investment advisers and officers/directors of public companies, who may find their own interests at odds with those of clients or shareholders to whom they owe a fiduciary duty.

Consolidated Tape: The reporting "ticker" showing last-sale information for NYSE-listed securities, wherever they are traded.

Consolidated Quotation System (CQS): System used for trading in the third market.

Consolidation: A stock trading in a narrow price range. Sometimes called "accumulation."

Constant Dollar Plan: A defensive investment strategy in which an investor tries to maintain a constant dollar amount in the account, meaning that securities are sold if the account value rises and purchased if it goes down.

Constructive Receipt: The date that the IRS considers an investor to have put his grubby little hands on a dividend, interest payment, retirement plan distribution, etc. For example, IRA funds are not taxable until "constructive receipt," which usually starts somewhere between age 59½ and 70½.

Consumer Price Index (CPI): A measure of inflation/deflation for basic consumer goods and services. A rising CPI represents the greatest risk to most fixed-income investors.

Consumer: For purposes of Regulation S-P, a consumer is someone considering a financial relationship with a firm.

Contemporaneous Trader: Any investor harmed by another's manipulative/deceptive actions in the securities markets, especially in insider trading cases.

Contingency Offer: An offer of securities that will be canceled if a minimum amount is not raised, with all investor payments placed in escrow.

Contingent Deferred Sales Charge or CDSC: Associated with B-shares, the sales charge is deducted from the investor's check when she redeems/sells her shares. The charge is deferred until she sells and is contingent upon when she sells—the sales charges decline over time, eventually disappearing after 7 years, at which point the B-shares become A-shares.

Continuing Commissions: The accepted practice of paying retired registered representatives and principals commissions on business written while still employed with the firm, e.g., 12b-1 fees on mutual funds and annuities.

Contraction: Phase of the business cycle associated with general economic decline, recession or depression.

Contribution: The money put into a retirement plan subject to the limits imposed by the plan.

Control Relationship: A situation in which the broker-dealer is related to the issuer of the securities involved in a transaction, requiring disclosure.

Conversion Ratio: The number of shares of common stock that the holder of a convertible bond or preferred stock would receive upon conversion. A bond "convertible at $50" has a conversion ratio of 20 (20 shares of stock per $1,000 par value).

Conversion/Exchange Privilege: A feature offered by many mutual funds whereby the investor may sell shares of one fund in the family and use the proceeds to buy another fund in the family at the NAV (avoiding the sales load). All gains/losses are recognized on the date of sale/conversion for tax purposes.

Convertible: A preferred stock or corporate bond allowing the investor to use the par value to "buy" shares of the company's common stock at a set price.

Cooling-off Period: A minimum 20-day period that starts after the registration statement is filed with the SEC. No sales or advertising allowed during this period, which lasts until the effective or release date.

Core Fund: Mutual fund that combines growth and value investing, or both stock and bond investing to provide a solid, "core" holding for a conservative investor.

Core Inflation: The CPI after food and energy costs are excluded. Core inflation removes the more weather-related and volatile pricing associated with food, oil, natural gas, etc. when measuring the overall rise or drop in pricing.

Corporation: The most common form of business organization, in which the business's total value is divided among shares of stock, each representing an ownership interest or share of profits.

Cost Basis: The amount that has gone into an investment and has been taxed already. For stock, includes the price paid plus commissions. For a variable annuity, equals the after-tax contributions into the account. Investors pay tax only on amounts above their cost basis, and only when they sell or take "constructive receipt."

Cost Of Goods Sold of **COGS:** The cost of materials and direct labor going into the production of a company's products or delivery of its services, as opposed to general operating expenses and other costs/expenses listed on the income statement. A company subtracts COGS from revenue to arrive at its gross margin.

Coterminous: Municipal issuers who overlap, e.g., a village and a school district.

Counterparty Risk: The risk faced by parties to a forward contract that the other side will default.

Coupon Rate: a.k.a. "nominal yield." The interest rate stated on a bond representing the percentage of the par value received by the investor each year. For example, a bond with a 5% "coupon rate" or "nominal yield" pays $50 per bond to the holder per year. Period.

Covered Call: A position in which an investor generates premium income by selling the right to buy stock the investor already owns, and at a set price.

CPI or **Consumer Price Index**: Measure of inflation/deflation for basic consumer goods and services. A rising CPI represents the greatest risk to most fixed-income investors.

CRD or **Central Registration Depository:** An automated database used by FINRA to store and maintain registration records of former and current associated persons of member firms.

Credit: In a margin account, the amount of the proceeds from the short sale plus the initial Reg T deposit. For example, a short sale of $20,000 of ABC creates a credit of that $20,000 plus $10,000 or $30,000 in total.

Credit Agreement: Document that must be signed by a margin customer in which all finance charges are explained in connection to the margin account.

Credit Risk: a.k.a. "default" or "financial" risk. The risk that the issuer's credit rating will be downgraded, or that the issuer will default on a debt security.

Credit Spread: Selling a more valuable call/put and simultaneously buying a less valuable call/put on the same underlying instrument.

Crossover Point: The point at which a limited partnership has exhausted the tax shelter and is now beginning to show a profit.

Cumulative Preferred Stock: Preferred stock where missed dividends go into arrears and must be paid before the issuer may pay dividends to other preferred stock and/or common stock.

Cumulative Voting: Method of voting whereby the shareholder may take the total votes and split them up any way he chooses. Said to benefit minority over majority shareholders. Total votes are found by multiplying the number of shares owned by the number of seats up for election to the Board of Directors.

Currency Exchange Risk: The risk that the value of the US dollar versus another currency will have a negative impact on businesses and investors.

Currency Transaction Report (CTR): Report submitted to the US Treasury by a broker-dealer when a customer deposits more than $10,000 cash.

Current Account: The difference between a nation's imports and exports. A "current account deficit" is synonymous with a "trade deficit."

Current Asset: Cash or something to be converted to cash in the short-term, e.g. accounts receivable, inventory.

Current Liability: A debt to be paid in the short-term, usually one year or sooner.

Current Ratio: Short-term measure of a corporation's liquidity found by dividing current assets by current liabilities; the higher the number, the more liquid the corporation.

Current Yield: Annual interest divided by market price of the bond. For example, an 8% bond purchased at $800 has a CY of 10%. $80/$800 = 10%.

CUSIP Number: An identification code for a security. Lost securities may be re-issued by the transfer agent if the CUSIP numbers are available, among other required proof of ownership.

Custodial Account: Investment account in which a custodian enters trades on behalf of the beneficial owner, who is usually a minor child.

Custodian: Party that maintains custody of a mutual fund's securities and cash. Performs payable/receivable functions for portfolio purchases and sales. In an UGMA, the custodian is the adult named on the account who is responsible for the investment decisions and tax reporting.

Custody: Having possession/control of an investor's assets, or the ability to appropriate them.

Customer: A person who opens an investment account with a broker-dealer.

Customer Complaint: Defined by FINRA as "any grievance by a customer or any person authorized to act on behalf of the customer involving the activities of the member or a person associated with the member in connection with the solicitation or execution of any transaction or the disposition of securities or funds of that customer."

Cyclical Industry: An industry sensitive to the business cycle, e.g., steel, automobiles, and construction equipment.

D

Dated Date: The date on which interest begins to accrue on a new issue of municipal bonds.

Day Order: A limit or stop order that will be canceled if not executed on the day it is placed. As opposed to "GTC."

Day-trading: Purchasing and selling—or selling and purchasing—the same security on the same day in a margin account.

Dealer: A person who buys or sells securities for his/its own account, taking the other side of the trade.

Death Benefit: The amount payable to the beneficiary of a life insurance (or annuity) contract, minus any outstanding loans and/or unpaid premiums.

Debenture: An unsecured bond backed by the issuer's ability to pay. No collateral.

Debit Balance: The amount that a margin customer owes the broker-dealer in a margin account.

Debit Spread: Buying a more expensive call/put and selling a less expensive call/put on the same underlying instrument.

Debt Limit: A self-imposed restriction on the total amount of general obligation debt that an issuer may have outstanding at any one time.

Debt per Capita: A measure that shows a bond analyst how much general obligation debt is outstanding divided by the number of residents of the municipality.

Debt Ratio: Measure of a company's long-term solvency found by comparing total liabilities to total assets. The higher the percentage, the more leveraged the company.

Debt Security: A security representing a loan from an investor to an issuer. Offers a particular interest rate in return for the loan, not an ownership position.

Debt Service: The schedule for repayment of interest and principal on a debt security.

Debt Service Coverage: The projected ability of a project built with revenue bond proceeds to cover the debt service.

Debt Statement: A statement in which a municipal issuer lists all of its outstanding debts.

Debt-To-Equity Ratio: Measure of long-term solvency found by dividing a company's total liabilities by shareholder equity. The higher the ratio, the more leveraged the company.

Declaration Date: The date the Board declares a dividend.

Default: When the issuer of the bond is unable to pay interest and/or principal.

Default Hearing: A disciplinary hearing held by FINRA or a state regulator when the respondent fails to cooperate and in the respondent's absence after proper notice has been served.

Default Risk: The risk that the issuer of the bond will stiff you. Measured by S&P and Moody's.

Defensive: An industry or a company that can perform well even during bad economic times. For example, food and basic clothing represent two products purchased through both good and bad economic times; therefore, stocks of food and basic clothing companies would be "defensive" investments.

Deferred Annuity: An annuity that delays payments of income, installments, or a lump sum until the investor elects to receive it. Usually subject to surrender charges during the deferral period.

Deferred Compensation Plan: A non-qualified business plan that defers some of the employee's compensation until retirement. Usually for highly compensated employees.

Deficiency Letter: SEC notification of additions or corrections that an issuer must make to a registration statement before the offering can be cleared for distribution.

Defined Benefit Pension Plan: Qualified corporate pension plan that, literally, defines the benefit payable to the retiree.

Defined Contribution Plan: Qualified corporate plan that defines the contribution made on behalf of the employee, e.g., profit sharing, 401(k).

Deflation: A general drop in demand and the level of prices across the economy, usually connected to an economic slump.

Delivery: The change in ownership of a security that takes place when the transaction settles. The seller delivers the securities purchased to the buyer or to the clearing agency.

Demand Deposit: Any deposit at a bank where the funds may be withdrawn at any time, e.g. checking and savings accounts.

Department of Enforcement: FINRA enforcers of the member conduct rules.

Depreciation: A non-cash expense on the income statement listed in order to spread the cost of a fixed asset over its useful life. Depreciation is also shown on the balance sheet, usually as "accumulated depreciation" next to fixed or long-term assets.

Depreciation Recapture: A tax collected when an investor sells an asset that was providing depreciation.

Depression: A prolonged economic slump lasting six quarters (18 months) or longer.

Derivative: An investment that derives its value from some other instrument, includes options, futures, and forwards.

Designated Examining Authority: Another name for an SRO or Self-Regulatory Organization, e.g., CBOE or FINRA.

Designated Market Maker: NYSE market participant charged with maintaining a fair and orderly market in the stocks they quote. DMMs must quote at the national best-bid-or-offer (NBBO) a specified percentage of the time, and facilitate price discovery throughout the day as well as at the open, close and in periods of significant imbalances and high volatility.

Developed Market: An economy with mature financial systems and infrastructures, as opposed to an "emerging market."

Developmental Program: An oil or gas drilling program in an area in which reserves are known to exist.

Diluted Earnings per Share: A company's EPS calculated as if all convertible securities have been converted to shares of common stock.

Dilution of Equity: A reduction in the earnings per share of common stock, often due to convertible bonds or preferred stock being converted to common stock.

Direct Debt: The general obligation debt of a municipal issuer for which it is solely responsible.

Direct Participation Program (DPP): A limited partnership or similar pass-through entity in which the investor receives a share of income and expenses.

Direct Transfer: The easiest method of moving funds from a qualified retirement account to a Traditional IRA, or among such accounts. In a direct transfer the existing custodian sends assets to the new custodian, bypassing the account owner.

Disclaim an inheritance: To give up all claims on an inheritance so that it passes to other heirs.

Disclosure Brochure: Required information of an investment adviser provided to prospects and offered to clients; either a copy of ADV-2 or a document containing the same information.

Discount (n.): The difference between the (lower) market price for a bond and the par value.

Discount (v.): To calculate the present value of future cash flows by some rate known as the "discount rate."

Discount Bond: A bond trading below par value.

Discounted Cash Flow Analysis: A method of valuing a company or income-producing security based on the net present value of all expected cash flows.

Discount Rate: Interest rate charged by the 12 Federal Reserve Banks to member banks who borrow from the FRB. Or, the rate used when performing "discounted cash flow analysis." See textbook for explanation on discounted cash flow analysis.

Discretion: Authority given to someone other than the account owner to make trading decisions for the account.

Discretionary Income: What an investor has to invest after all expenses are met.

Disintermediation: A situation in which money is being withdrawn from banks and savings & loans by depositors in order to reinvest the funds into higher yielding money market instruments (Treasury bills, certificates of deposit, money market funds).

Distribution Stage (Annuity): Period during which an individual receives payments from an annuity.

Distribution Expenses: The cost of distributing/marketing a mutual fund, including selling, printing prospectuses and sales literature, advertising, and mailing prospectuses to new/potential clients. Covered by sales charges/12b-1fees.

Distribution: The money taken out of a retirement plan or annuity.

Distributor: A FINRA member firm that bears distribution costs of a fund, profiting from the sales charges paid by the investors; a.k.a. "sponsor," "underwriter," "wholesaler."

Diversification: Purchasing securities from many different issuers, or industries, or geographic regions, to reduce "nonsystematic risk."

Diversifiable Risk: Another name for an un-systematic risk, e.g. regulatory or business risk.

Diversified Mutual Fund: A fund that complies with an SEC rule so that no more than 5% of assets are invested in a particular stock or bond and so that the fund does not own more than 10% of any issuer's outstanding stock. Associated with the "75-5-10 rule."

Dividend: Money paid from profits to holders of common and preferred stock if and when the Board of Directors declares.

Dividend Payout Ratio: The amount of dividends paid divided by the earnings per share. Stocks with high dividend payout ratios are typically found in "equity income" funds.

Dividend Reinvestment Plan or DRIP: A program allowing investors to automatically reinvest cash dividends into more shares of fractional shares.

Dividend Yield: Annual dividends divided by market price of the stock. Equivalent to current yield for a debt security.

Dividend/Income Distributions: Distributions from a fund to the investors made from net investment income. Typically, may be reinvested at the NAV to avoid sales charge.

DK Notice: A notice sent to the other broker-dealer when a firm does not recognize a transaction.

Do Not Reduce (DNR): A buy-limit or sell-stop order that will not be reduced for the payment of a cash dividend.

Dollar Cost Averaging: Investing fixed dollar amounts regularly, regardless of share price. Usually results in a lower average cost compared to average of share prices, as investors' dollars buy majority of shares at lower prices. Also a way of figuring cost basis for income tax purposes, usually called "Average Cost Basis."

Dollar Weighted Return: The rate of return weighted by the dollars invested rather than taking a simple average of annual returns (time-weighted return).

Domestic Equity Fund: A mutual fund that focuses on stocks of American companies.

Donor: Person who makes a gift of money or securities to another.

Double Barreled: A municipal bond backed by both the issuer's full faith and credit and revenues.

Dow Jones Industrial Average (DJIA): An index comprised of 30 large-cap companies.

DRP or Disclosure Reporting Page: Disclosure provided on a Form U4, Form U5, or Form ADV of prior bad acts relevant to the securities industry.

Dual-Purpose Fund: A closed-end fund with two classes of stock: income shares and capital shares. The income shares receive dividends and interest, while the capital shares receive capital gains distributions.

Due Bill: Document sent by a broker-dealer when a dividend payment was sent to the wrong party and belongs to the broker-dealer's customer.

Due Diligence: Meeting between issuer and underwriters with the purpose of verifying information contained in a registration statement/prospectus.

Duration: The weighted average of a bond's cash flows; a bond's price sensitivity to a small change in interest rates.

DVP: A form of settlement in which payment will be made when the securities involved in the transaction are delivered and accepted. AKA "Delivery Versus Payment."

E

Earned Income: Income derived from active participation in a business, including wages, salary, tips, commissions, and bonuses. Alimony received is also considered earned income. Earned income can be used toward an IRA contribution.

Earnings Available to Common: Net income minus any preferred stock dividends. Dividing this amount by the shares outstanding arrives at the EPS for the company's common stock.

Earnings per Share (EPS): The amount of earnings or "net income" available for each share of common stock. A major driver of the stock's price on the secondary market. Found by taking "earnings available to common" divided by the shares outstanding.

Eastern/Undivided Account: A syndicate account in which participants are responsible for a percentage of all bonds, even if they sell their allotment.

EBIT: Earnings Before Interest and Taxes. The profit that would be shown before interest and taxes are subtracted from revenue on the income statement.

EBITDA: Earnings Before Interest, Taxes, Depreciation and Amortization. The profit that would be shown before interest, taxes, depreciation and amortization are subtracted from revenue on the income statement. Or, revenue minus COGS and general operating expenses only,

Economic Indicator: Data providing economists with important information about the current state and possible future direction of the economy and various sectors of the economy.

EDGAR: Section of the SEC's website where various required filings are made by reporting companies and accessible by the public. To pull up a prospectus, 10Q, or 10K, for example, go to the "EDGAR" section of www.sec.gov. EDGAR is an acronym for "Electronic Data Gathering, Analysis, and Retrieval."

Education IRA: Another name for the Coverdell Education Savings Account in which after-tax contributions may be made to pay qualified education expenses for the beneficiary.

Effective Date: Date established by SEC as to when the underwriters may sell new securities to investors; a.k.a. "release date."

Efficient Frontier: Graph showing expected return on the vertical axis and standard deviation on the horizontal axis, with a curve known as the efficient frontier upon whose line optimal portfolios are constructed to balance maximum returns with any risk taken. Portfolios behind the line are inefficient, and portfolios above the line are not possible.

Efficient Market Hypothesis: Investing approach that assumes markets are efficient with information immediately priced into securities. See textbook for "weak, semi-strong, and strong-form" of this hypothesis.

Electronic Communications Networks (ECNs): Electronic trading platforms that allow institutional investors to buy and sell securities directly. AKA "Fourth market."

Emerging Market: The financial markets of a developing country. Generally, a small market with a short operating history, not as efficient or stable as developed markets. For example, Brazil, China, India.

Employment Indicators: Economic indicators relating to employment, e.g., weekly unemployment claims, non-farm payroll.

Equipment Leasing Program: A direct participation program that leases computers, mining equipment, etc. Depreciation is a major tax-advantage of such a program.

Equipment Trust Certificate: Bond secured by a pledge of equipment, e.g., airplanes, railroad cars.

Equity: Ownership, e.g., common and preferred stock in a public company.

Equity Funds: Mutual funds that primarily invest in equity securities.

Equity Income Fund: A mutual fund that purchases common stocks whose issuers pay consistent and, perhaps, increasing dividends. The fund has less volatility than an equity fund with "growth" as an objective.

Equity-Indexed Annuity: An insurance product offering a minimum guaranteed rate and the opportunity to participate in some of the gains of a particular index, usually the S&P 500. AKA "indexed annuity."

Equity Options: Standardized derivatives giving the holder the right to buy or sell the underlying stock at a set price (strike/exercise price).

Equity REIT: A Real Estate Investment Trust that owns and operates a portfolio of real properties.

ERISA: The Employee Retirement Income Security Act of 1974 that governs the operation of most corporate pension and benefit plans.

Estate: A legal entity/person that represents all assets held by a deceased person before he died.

Estate Tax: A tax on estates over a certain amount, currently $5 million indexed for inflation.

ETF or **Exchange-Traded Fund**: A fund that trades on an exchange, typically an index fund tracking the S&P 500, the Dow Jones Industrial Average, etc. Unlike an open-end index fund, the ETF allows investors to sell short, trade throughout the day, and even purchase shares on margin.

European Style: An option that may be exercised at expiration only.

Excess Equity: The amount of equity above the Reg T requirement in a margin account.

Exchange-Listed Security: A security that has met listing requirements to trade on a particular exchange such as NYSE, or NASDAQ. Also a "federal covered security" by definition.

Exchange Rate: The relative value of two currencies, e.g. US dollars to Yen or Euro, impacting exports and imports.

Exchanges: Any electronic or physical marketplace where investors can buy and sell securities. For example, NASDAQ, NYSE.

Exclusion Ratio: Method of determining which part of an annuity payment is taxable, and which part represents the tax-free return of the annuitant's after-tax cost basis.

Ex-Date or **Ex-Dividend Date:** The date upon which the buyer is not entitled to the upcoming dividend.

Executor: The party charged with administering an estate.

Exempt: Not subject to registration requirements of a particular securities law or rule/regulation.

Exempt Security: A security not required to be registered under the Securities Act of 1933. Still subject to anti-fraud rules; not subject to registration requirements, e.g., municipal bonds and bank stock.

Exempt Transaction: A transactional exemption from registration requirements based on the manner in which the security is offered and sold, e.g., private placements or offers to institutional investors only.

Exercise: The act of using an option to buy or sell the underlying instrument.

Exercise Price: The price at which the underlying security can be bought (call) or (sold) in an options contract. AKA "strike price."

Existing Properties: A direct participation program that purchases operating real estate.

Expansion: Phase of the business cycle associated with increased activity.

Expected Return: A calculation of the return hoped for based on probabilities of outcomes or the CAPM formula.

Expense Ratio: A fund's operating expenses divided by/compared to average net assets. Represents operating efficiency of a mutual fund, where the lower the number the more efficient the fund.

Expiration Date: The date after which an options contract ceases to exist.

Exploratory Programs: A direct participation program that drills for oil or natural gas.

Extension Risk: The risk that interest rates will rise, and the holder of a CMO or mortgage-backed security will have to wait longer than expected to receive principal.

F

Face-Amount Certificate: A debt security bought in a lump-sum or through installments that promises to pay out the stated face amount, which is higher than the investor's purchase price.

Face-Amount Certificate Company: One of the three types of investment companies under the Investment Company Act of 1940. Issues face-amount certificates. Not a UIT or "management company."

Fair and Orderly Market: What the DMMs (Designated Market Makers) at the NYSE are charged with maintaining.

FDIC (Federal Deposit Insurance Corporation): Federal government agency that provides deposit insurance for member banks and prevents bank and "thrift" failures. Bank deposits are currently insured up to $250,000.

Feasibility Study: A study put together by a consulting firm analyzing the economic merits of a facility to be financed by municipal revenue bonds.

Fed Funds Rate: Interest rate charged on bank-to-bank loans. Subject to daily fluctuation.

Federal Covered: A security or an investment adviser whose registration is handled exclusively by the federal government (SEC).

Federal Farm Credit System: Organization of privately owned banks providing credit to farmers and mortgages on farm property.

Federal Open Market Committee (FOMC): Council of Federal Reserve officials that sets monetary policy based on economic data. The money supply is tightened to fight inflation, loosened to provide stimulus to a faltering economy.

Federal Reserve Board: Seven-member board directing the operations of the Federal Reserve System.

Federal Reserve System: The central bank system of the United States, with a primary responsibility to manage the flow of money and credit in this country.

FEIN or Federal Employer Identification Number: A tax ID number assigned to an entity such as a corporation, trust, or estate.

FHLMC or Freddie Mac: Like Fannie Mae, a special purpose enterprise structured as a public company that purchases mortgages from lenders and sells mortgage-backed securities to investors. Stock is listed on NYSE.

Fiduciary: Someone responsible for the financial affairs of someone else, e.g., investment adviser, trustee, who owes the beneficiary a duty of loyalty and a duty of good faith.

FIFO or First-In-First-Out: First-in-first-out. An accounting method for valuing a company's inventory or for determining the capital gain/loss for an investor. Using FIFO, an investor indicates that, for example, the 100 shares of ABC that were sold at $55 are the first 100 shares that he purchased.

Filing Date: The date that an issuer files a registration statement with the SEC for a new issue of securities.

Final Prospectus: Disclosure document delivered with final confirmation of a new issue of securities detailing the price, delivery date, and underwriting spread.

Financial Future: Futures contract where the underlying instrument is a stock index, interest rate, etc.

Financial Planner: Professional who provides total financial strategies to clients involving insurance needs, retirement needs, estate planning, investing, tax reduction, etc. Usually required to register as an investment adviser, unless securities are never part of any plan.

Financial Risk: Another name for "credit risk," or the risk that the issuer of a bond could default.

Financial Statement: A balance sheet, income statement, statement of cash flows, or other document showing various aspects of a business's financial condition or results. Found in the 10K and other required reports of public companies.

FinCEN: US Treasury's "Financial Crimes Enforcement Network." Suspicious Activity Reports must be provided to FinCEN if a broker-dealer notices activity in accounts that appears suspicious or possibly related to fraud or money laundering activities.

FINRA (Financial Industry Regulatory Authority): The Self-Regulatory Organization formed when the NASD and the NYSE regulators merged.

Firm Commitment: An underwriting commitment in which the underwriters agree to purchase all securities from an issuer, even the ones they failed to sell to investors. Involves acting in a "principal" capacity, unlike in "best efforts," "all or none," and "mini-max" offerings.

Firm Quote: A quote by a dealer representing a price at which the dealer is prepared to trade.

First Market: Another name for the exchange market, where the NYSE is the model.

Fiscal Policy: The process of taxation and spending done by the US Congress.

Fixed Annuity: An insurance product in which the annuitant receives fixed payments, usually for the rest of his or her life.

Fixed Assets: Long-term assets that generate revenue but are not intended to be sold. For example, a printing press.

Fixed Exchange Rate: A system in which a nation ties the value of its currency to a commodity such as gold or to another currency, e.g. the former system of fixing the exchange rate between Swiss Francs and Euro.

Fixed-Income: Type of investor who seeks a stream of income, usually from bonds, but also from preferred stock.

Flexible Premium: A premium that may be changed as time goes on, a characteristic of "universal" insurance.

Floating-Rate Currency: A system allowing the value of a nation's currency to rise and fall due to supply and demand.

Flow of Funds Statement: A statement connected to a revenue bond showing how revenues are to be allocated in terms of operations and maintenance, reserve account deposits, debt service, etc.

FNMA or **Fannie Mae**: Like little brother Freddie Mac, Fannie buys mortgages from lenders and sells mortgage-backed securities to investors. A quasi-agency, a public company listed for trading on the NYSE.

FOMC: The Federal Reserve Board's Federal Open Market Committee. Sets short-term interest rates by setting discount rate, reserve requirement and buying/selling T-bills to/from primary dealers.

Footnotes: Explanatory notes provided to explain financial statements more clearly. For example, accounting methods for inventory or one-time expenses might require further explanation after the numbers are presented in the company's 10K.

Foreign Currency Options: Standardized options in which the underlying instrument is a foreign currency, e.g., the yen, the euro, etc.

Foreign Exchange Risk: The risk to an American ADR holder that the American dollar will strengthen versus the currency used by the foreign corporation. For example, an American holding the Toyota ADR is at risk that the US dollar will strengthen versus the yen. AKA "currency exchange risk."

Form ADV: Registration form for an investment adviser.

Form ADV-2: The disclosure document for an investment adviser.

Form BD: Registration form for a broker-dealer.

Form N-1A: SEC form filed by an investment company to register under the Investment Company of 1940 and to register its securities under the Securities Act of 1933.

Form U4: Registration form for a securities agent or principal of a broker-dealer, or an investment adviser representative.

Form U5: The form filed when an IAR or agent/principal terminate employment for any reason.

Forward: An unregulated derivative security.

Forward Pricing: The method of valuing mutual fund shares, whereby a purchase or redemption order is executed at the next calculated price. Mutual fund shares are bought and sold at the next computed price, not yesterday's stale prices.

Fourth Market: Electronic Communications Networks used by institutional investors to trade directly through an electronic alternative display facility.

Fractional Share: A portion of a whole share of stock. Mutual fund shares typically are issued as whole and fractional shares, e.g., 101.45 shares.

Fraud: Using deceit or manipulation to wrongfully take money/property from someone under false pretenses.

Free Credit Balance: The cash in a customer account that can be withdrawn.

Free-Look: Period during which a contract or policyholder may cancel and receive all sales charges paid.

Freeriding: Under Regulation T, freeriding occurs when a customer buys stock and then uses the sales proceeds rather than sending funds to pay for the buy side. Leads to an account freeze.

Freeriding & Withholding: A violation in which underwriters fail to distribute all shares allocated in an offering of a "hot issue."

Front-end Load: A mutual fund commission or sales fee charged when shares are purchased (A-shares). The amount of the load is added to the NAV to determine the public offering price (POP).

Front-running: The violation of taking advantage of a customer order by purchasing securities before entering a customer's buy order or selling securities before entering a customer's sell order.

Frozen Account: Account in which purchase orders will be accepted only if the cash is in the account due to the customer's failure to comply with Reg T.

Full Faith and Credit: A phrase used to denote that there are no specific assets backing a bond issue, only the issuer's ability to repay the loan.

Fully Registered Bonds: Bonds whose principal and interest payments are tracked/registered for purposes of taxation. A physical certificate with the owner's name, and interest payable automatically by the paying agent (no coupons).

Fundamental Analysis: Studying companies in terms of their competitive position and financial strength to determine the advisability of investing in their securities.

Funded Debt: Another term for corporate bonds backed by a sinking fund as opposed to collateral.

Futures Contract: A derivative contract where the underlying instrument is a commodity or a financial index.

Future Value: The amount to which an investment will grow by a future date given a compounded rate of return.

G

GDP: Total of goods and services being produced by the economy; economic output regardless of the nationality of the workers.

GTC or **Good-Til-Canceled:** A limit or stop order that is to remain open until executed or canceled by the investor, as opposed to a "day order."

General Account: Where an insurance company invests net premiums in order to fund guaranteed, fixed payouts.

General Obligation Bond: Municipal bond backed by the issuer's full faith and credit or full taxing authority.

General Partner: The owner of a General Partnership or the manager of a limited partnership with unlimited liability and a fiduciary obligation to the limited partners.

General Partnership: A pass-through entity that provides no protection to the owners against debts and lawsuits.

Generic Advertising: Investment company communications with the public that promote securities as investments but not particular securities.

Gift Splitting: Claiming a gift among both husband-and-wife to avoid exceeding the annual gift tax exclusion.

Gift Tax: A tax paid when a gift exceeds the current exclusion limit.

Global Fund: A mutual fund investing in companies located and doing business all across the globe, including the US.

GNMA or **Government National Mortgage Association**: A government agency (not a public company) that buys insured mortgages from lenders, selling pass-through certificates to investors. Monthly payments to investors pay interest and also pass through principal from a pool of mortgages.

GNP: The economic output of a nation's citizens, wherever they are located.

Good Faith Deposit: Deposit required by a municipal issuer for all syndicates submitting bids for an issue of bonds. Typically 1–2% of par value.

Goodwill: Intangible asset representing the price paid to acquire a company above its hard, tangible value.

Grantor: The party funding a trust with a transfer of assets.

Grantor Trust: Trust where the grantor receives an economic benefit and, therefore, is responsible for taxation of the trust.

Green Shoe Clause: Agreement allowing the underwriters to sell additional shares if demand is high for an offering of securities.

Gross Domestic Product: See GDP.

Gross Margin: Gross profit divided *into* revenue. For example, a company with $100 million in revenue and cost-of-goods-sold of $70 million has a gross margin of 30%.

Gross National Product: See GNP.

Gross Profit: A company's revenues minus their "cost of goods sold." For example, a company with $100 million in revenue and cost-of-goods-sold of $70 million has a gross profit of $30 million.

Gross Revenue Pledge: Less common method used by revenue bond issuers in which debt service is paid even before operations & maintenance.

Growth: Investment objective that seeks "capital appreciation." Achieved through common stock, primarily.

Growth & Income: A fund that purchases stocks for growth potential and also for dividend income. Less volatile than pure growth funds due to the income that calms investors down when the ride becomes turbulent. Or, the investment objective of an investor seeking both growth and income.

Growth Funds: Mutual funds investing in stocks expected to grow faster than the overall market and trading at high price-to-earnings multiples.

Growth Stock: A stock in a company expected to outperform the market and trading at a high valuation ratio, e.g. P/E.

GSE or **Government-Sponsored Enterprise:** A privately held financial services company created by the US Congress, e.g. FNMA.

Guaranteed Bond: A bond that is issued with a promise by a party other than the issuer to maintain payments of interest and principal if the issuer cannot.

Guardian: A fiduciary who manages the financial affairs of a minor or a person declared mentally incompetent.

H

Head and Shoulders: Chart pattern used by technical analysts to determine that a bull or bear trend is about to reverse.

Hedge, Hedging: To modify the risk taken on a stock position by buying or selling options, e.g., a covered call.

Hedge Fund: Private investment partnership open to accredited investors only. Illiquid investments that generally must be held one or two years before selling. Typically charge a management fee plus the first 20% of capital gains in most cases.

High-Yield: Investment whose income stream is very high relative to its low market price. A high-yield bond is either issued by a shaky company or municipal government forced to offer high nominal yields, or it begins to trade at lower and lower prices on the secondary market as the credit quality or perceived credit strength of the issuer deteriorates.

Holding Company: Company organized to invest in other corporations, e.g., Berkshire-Hathaway, which holds large stakes in other companies such as Coca-Cola, See's Candy, Dairy Queen, and Wells Fargo.

Holding Period: Period during which a security was held for purposes of determining whether a capital gain or loss is long- or short-term.

Howey Decision: US Supreme Court decision that defined an "investment contract" as "an investment of money in a common enterprise where the investor will profit solely through the efforts of others."

HR-10: A reference to a Keogh plan.

Hybrid REIT: A REIT that owns and operates a portfolio of real estate as well as provides financing for real estate projects.

Hypothecate: To pledge securities purchased in a margin account as collateral to secure the loan.

Hypothecation Agreement: Document that gives a broker-dealer the legal authority to pledge a margin customer's securities as collateral to secure the margin loan.

I

IARD or Investment Adviser Registration Depository: Defined by the SEC as "an electronic filing system that facilitates investment adviser registration, exempt reporting adviser filing, regulatory review, and the public disclosure information of investment adviser firms." Serves a similar purpose for the advisory industry served by CRD for the brokerage industry.

IDR or Industrial Development Revenue Bond: A municipal revenue bond that builds a facility that the issuing municipality leases to a corporation. The lease payments from the corporation back the interest and principal payments on the bonds.

Immediate Annuity: Insurance contract purchased with a single purchase payment that starts to pay the annuitant immediately.

Immediate or Cancel Order: Order to buy or sell securities in which the customer will accept any part of the order that becomes available at a certain price, with the remainder of shares to be canceled.

Income: Investment objective that seeks current income, found by investing in fixed-income securities, e.g., bonds, money market, preferred stock.

Income Bond: A bond that will pay interest only if the issuer earns sufficient income and the board of directors declares the payment; a.k.a. "adjustment bond."

Income Program: A direct participation program that invests in existing producing oil and/or natural gas wells.

Income Statement: A financial statement showing a corporation's results of operations over the quarter or year. Shows revenue, all expenses/costs, and the profit or loss the company showed over the period.

Indenture: A contract that spells out the responsibilities and rights of an issuer in connection with a bond issue.

Index: A theoretical grouping of stocks, bonds, etc. The Consumer Price Index is a theoretical grouping or "basket" of things that consumers buy, used to track inflation. The Dow Jones Industrial Average is a theoretical grouping of 30 large-company stocks that analysts use to track the stock market.

Indexed Annuity: Insurance product offering a minimum guaranteed rate of return and some participation in an underlying index, usually the S&P 500.

Index Option: A call or put option based on the value of a particular index, e.g., the Dow Jones Industrial Average or the S&P 500.

Indication of Interest: An investor's expression of interest in purchasing a new issue of securities after reading the preliminary prospectus; not a commitment to buy.

Inflation: A loss of purchasing power as measured by the Consumer Price Index (CPI).

Inflation-Adjusted Return: An investment's return after the rate of inflation/deflation has been factored in. AKA "real rate of return."

Inflation Risk: Also called "constant dollar risk" or "purchasing power risk," it is the risk that inflation will erode the value of a fixed-income stream from a bond or preferred stock.

Initial Public Offering (IPO): A corporation's first sale of stock to public investors. By definition, a primary market transaction in which the issuer receives the proceeds.

Inside Information: Material information about a corporation that has not yet been released to the public and would likely affect the price of the corporation's stock and/or bonds. Inside information may not be "disseminated" or acted upon.

Insider: For purpose of insider trading rules, an "insider" is anyone who has or has access to material non-public information. Officers (CEO ,CFO), members of the board of directors, and investors owning > 10% of the company's outstanding shares are assumed to possess and have access to inside information. As fiduciaries to the shareholders, insiders may not use inside information to their benefit.

Insider Trading and Securities Fraud Enforcement Act (ITSFEA) of 1988: An Act of Congress that addresses insider trading and lists the penalties for violations of the Act. Insider traders may be penalized up to three times the amount of their profit or their loss avoided by using inside information.

Institutional Investor: Not an individual, but, for example, a pension fund, insurance company, or mutual fund.

Insurance: Protection against loss of income due to death, disability, long-term care needs, etc.

Insurance Covenant: Promise by a revenue bond issuer to keep the facility properly insured.

Intangible Asset: An asset not easily valued or converted to cash, e.g. goodwill.

Integration: The final stage in the money laundering process.

Interest Rate: The charge for borrowing money. In a loan, the borrower pays some rate against the principal amount borrowed until the loan is retired. That rate is the interest rate on the loan.

Interest Rate Options: Options based on the price or yield of US Treasury securities.

Interest Rate Risk: The risk that interest rates will rise, pushing the market value of a fixed-income security down.

Interest Rate: The cost of borrowing money. In order to borrow money, borrowers pay a rate called an interest rate on top of the principal they will return at the end of the term.

Internal Rate of Return: In discounted cash flow analysis, the rate of return that makes the net present value of cash flows expected from a project equal to zero. AKA "discount rate."

Internal Revenue Code (IRC): Tax laws for the US written by Congress with all blame passed off conveniently to the IRS.

Internal Revenue Service (IRS): Agency for the federal government responsible for collecting federal taxes for the US Treasury and for administering tax rules and regulations.

International Fund: A mutual fund investing in companies established outside the US.

Inter-positioning: Unnecessarily inserting another party between the broker-dealer and the customer. A violation.

Interstate Offering: An offering of securities in several states, requiring registration with the SEC.

In-the-money: A call option allowing an investor to buy the underlying stock for less than it is worth or a put option allowing an investor to sell the underlying stock for more than it is worth. For example, if ABC trades @50, both the ABC Oct 45 calls and the ABC Oct 55 puts are "in-the-money."

Intrastate Offering: An offering of securities completed in the issuer's home state with investors who reside in that state, and, therefore, eligible for the Rule 147 Exemption to registration with the SEC. Intrastate offerings generally register with the state Administrator—registration by qualification.

Intrinsic Value: The amount by which an option is in-the-money. For example, if ABC trades @50, an ABC Oct 45 call has $5 of intrinsic value, regardless of what the premium might be.

Inventory: Finished goods that have not yet been sold by a corporation. A current asset that is included in the current ratio but excluded in the quick ratio.

Inventory Levels: Economic indicator showing finished goods not yet sold, a lagging indicator.

Inventory Turnover Ratio: A measure of how effectively a company deploys its capital, found by taking cost of goods sold from the income statement and dividing that amount by the average inventory over the period.

Inverse Relationship: When one goes up, the other goes down, and vice versa. Interest Rates and Yields are inversely related to Bond Prices. Your rate of speed is inversely related to your travel time to and from the office.

Inverted Head-and-Shoulders: AKA "head-and-shoulders bottom," a reversal of a down trend.

Investment Adviser: A business or professional compensated for advising others as to the value of or advisability of investing in securities.

Investment Banker: A firm that raises capital for issuers on the primary market. AKA "underwriter."

Investment Banking: The business of helping companies with mergers and acquisitions, performing IPOs and additional offerings. Investment bankers raise capital for issuers not by loaning money (like a traditional bank) but by finding investors willing to contribute to the cause.

Investment Company: A company engaged in the business of pooling investors' money and trading in securities on their behalf. Examples include unit investment trusts (UITs), face-amount certificate companies, and management companies.

Investment Company Act of 1940: The federal securities legislation that classified Investment Companies and set rules for registration and operation.

Investment Company Products: Packaged investment products in which the pooled capital of many investors is managed by an investment adviser according to stated objectives and policies. For example, mutual funds and UITs.

Investment Contract: An example of a "security," defined by the Supreme Court's Howey Decision.

Investment Counsel: Term that may be used by investment advisers providing continuous, supervisory management services only (not impersonal advice).

Investment Grade: A bond rated at least BBB by S&P or Baa by Moody's. The bond does not have severe default risk, so it is said to be appropriate for investors, as opposed to the speculators who buy non-investment grade bonds.

Investment Objective: Any goal that an investor has including current income, capital appreciation (growth), capital preservation (safety), or speculation.

Investment Risk: Potential factors that can have a negative effect on the value of an investment or the income it produces.

Investment Style: An approach to investing, such as active, passive, or buy-and-hold.

IRA or **Individual Retirement Account**: A retirement account/arrangement for an individual with earned income and no older than 70 ½. The Traditional IRA offers tax-deductible contributions while the Roth IRA is funded with non-deductible contributions.

Issued Shares: The number of shares that have been issued by a corporation, a number usually lower than the number of shares authorized by the charter.

Issuer: An individual or entity who issues or proposes to issue any security. For example, the issuer of Google common stock is Google.

Issuing Securities: Raising capital by offering securities to investors on the primary market.

J

Joint Account: Investment account owned by more than one individual.

JTIC or **Joint Tenants In Common**: Account where the assets of the deceased party pass to the deceased's estate, not the other account owner(s).

JTWROS or **Joint Tenants with Rights of Survivorship**: Account where the assets of the deceased party pass to the other account owner(s).

Jumbo: A bank CD of large denominations that can be traded on a secondary market though not usually backed by FDIC insurance.

Junk Bond: A bond backed by an issuer experiencing financial difficulties. AKA "high-yield" or "high-income" bond.

K

K-1: Tax form required of people who own direct participation interests (limited partnership, S-corp).

Keogh: Qualified retirement plan available to sole proprietorships. AKA "Qualified Plan for the Self-Employed."

Keynesian Economics: Economic school of thought that advocates government intervention through fiscal policy as a way to stimulate demand for goods and services.

L

Lagging Indicator: Economic indicator used to confirm a recent trend, e.g. duration of unemployment, inventory.

Large Cap: A stock where the total value of the outstanding shares is large, generally greater than $10 billion. For example, SBUX, MSFT, ORCL.

Last-In-First-Out (LIFO): Accounting method used for random withdrawals from an annuity. The IRS assumes that all withdrawals represent part of the taxable "excess over cost basis" first.

Layering: The phase of money laundering in which the first attempt at disguising the source of the ownership of the funds is made by creating complex layers of transactions.

Leading Indicator: Economic indicator used to predict future developments in the economy, e.g. new claims for unemployment, building permits.

LEAPS: A long-term standardized option.

Legal Opinion: The opinion of the bond counsel attesting to the municipality's legal authority to issue the bonds as well as the tax status of the bonds.

Legal Person: An entity rather than a human being/natural person. For example, a trust, estate, or corporation.

Legislative Risk: The risk to an investor that laws will change and have a negative impact on an investment. For example, if municipal bonds lose their tax-exempt interest, their value would plummet. AKA "regulatory risk."

Letter of Intent or **LOI:** Feature of many mutual funds whereby an investor may submit a letter or form expressing the intent to invest enough money over 13 months to achieve a breakpoint.

Level Load: Ongoing asset-based sales charge (12b-1 fee) associated with mutual fund C-shares.

Leverage: Using borrowed money to increase returns. Debt securities and margin accounts are associated with "leverage."

Liabilities: What an individual or a company owes, e.g., credit card debt, bonds, mortgage balance, accounts payable.

Life Insurance: Protection against a sudden loss of income due to the death of the "insured."

Life Only/Life Annuity: Payout option whereby the insurance/annuity company promises to make payments only for the rest of the annuitant's life.

Life with Joint and Last Survivor: Payout option whereby the insurance/annuity company promises to make payments to the annuitant for the rest of his life, then to the survivor for the rest of her life.

Life With Period Certain: Payout option whereby the insurance/annuity company promises to make payments to the annuitant for the rest of his life or a certain period of time, whichever is greater.

Life With Unit Refund: Payout option whereby the insurance/annuity company promises to make at least a certain number of payments to the annuitant or beneficiary.

Lifecycle Fund: An age-based or target portfolio automatically adjusting asset allocation to match the investor's needs based on the age of the beneficiary or retiree, for example.

Limit Orders: Orders to buy or sell a security at a specified price or better.

Limited Liability: An investor's ability to limit losses to no more than the amount invested. Holders of common stock and limited partnership interests enjoy "limited liability," which means they can only lose 100% of what they invest.

Limited Liability Company or LLC: Form of business ownership in which the owners, called members, receive their share of income/loss and receive protection against personal liability.

Limited Partner: A person who owns a limited partnership interest. Has no managerial responsibility and is shielded from debts of—and lawsuits against—the partnership.

Limited Partnership: Form of business ownership in which income and expenses flow through directly to the partners rather than to a separate business entity.

Limited Representative: what one would be after passing the Series 6 and getting registered to represent one's broker-dealer. One would be a "general securities representative" once one passes the Series 7 exam.

Limited Tax Bonds: General obligation bonds backed by a tax whose rate may not be increased above a certain limit.

Limited Trading Authorization: Authorization for someone other than the account owner to enter purchase and sale orders but make no withdrawals of cash or securities.

Liquidation Priority: The priority of claims on a bankrupt entity's assets that places creditors (bondholders) ahead of stockholders and preferred stockholders ahead of common stockholders.

Liquid Net Worth: Net worth figured without including hard-to-sell assets such as real estate or art work.

Liquidity: Ability to quickly convert an investment to cash and get a fair price.

Liquidity Risk: The risk of being unable to sell a security quickly for a fair price; a.k.a. "marketability risk."

Listed: Refers to a security trading on NYSE, Nasdaq, or any nationally-recognized exchange that monitors the issuers who list for trading there.

Loan Consent: Document giving the broker-dealer permission to lend a customer's securities to short sellers.

Long: To buy or own. To begin a securities transaction by making a purchase.

Long-Term Gain: Profit realized when selling stock held for at least 12 months plus 1 day. Subject to lower capital gains tax rates than short-term gains.

Long-Term Liability: A debt to be repaid in the long-run, e.g., the principal value of an outstanding bond issue.

Long-Term Loss: A loss realized when selling stock held for at least 12 months plus 1 day. Used to offset long-term capital gains.

Lump Sum Payment: A settlement/payout option for annuities or insurance where the annuitant or beneficiary receives one payment as opposed to a series of payments.

M

Maintenance Covenant: A promise of a revenue bond issuer to keep the facility properly maintained.

Maloney Act: Amendment to the Securities Exchange Act of 1934 creating the NASD as the self-regulatory organization (SRO) for the over-the-counter (OTC) market.

Management Company: One of the three types of Investment Companies, including both open-end and closed-end funds.

Management Fee: The % of assets charged to a mutual fund portfolio to cover the cost of portfolio management services provided by the investment adviser to the fund.

Manager's Fee: Typically the smallest piece of the spread, paid to the managing underwriter for every share sold by the syndicate.

Managing Underwriter: The broker-dealer who negotiates the underwriting with the issuer and manages the syndicate during the offering.

Margin: Amount of equity contributed by a customer as a percentage of the current market value of the securities held in a margin account.

Margin Account: As opposed to a cash account, allows investors to engage in short sales and investing borrowed money.

Marginal Tax Bracket: The range of adjusted gross incomes subject to a particular marginal tax rate.

Marginal Tax Rate: The tax rate applied to the last dollar of income earned.

Markdown: Difference between the highest bid price for a security and the price that a particular dealer pays an investor for her security.

Marketability: The ease or difficulty an investor has when trying to sell a security for cash without losing his shirt. More often called "liquidity."

Marketability Risk: Usually called "liquidity risk," the risk that a thinly-traded security cannot be converted to cash without experiencing a loss of principal.

Market Cap: The total value of an issuer's outstanding shares.

Market Maker: A dealer maintaining an inventory of a particular security and a firm Bid and Ask price good for a minimum of 100 shares. Acts as a "principal" on transactions, buying and selling for its/their own account.

Market Manipulation: The illegal process of using deception to move securities prices in favor of the conspirators. Includes terms such as "painting the tape" or "pegging."

Market Order: An order to buy or sell a security at the best available market price.

Market Risk: A type of "systematic risk," the risk inherent to the entire market rather than a specific security. The risk that the stock market may suffer violent upheavals due to unpredictable events including natural disaster, war, disease, famine, credit crises, etc.

Marking to the Market: Process of calculating margin requirements based on the most current market values for the securities in a margin account.

Markup: The difference between the lowest ask/offer price for a security and the price that a particular dealer charges.

Material Information: A fact that could reasonably affect an investor's decision to buy, sell, or hold a security. For example, profits and losses at the company, product liability lawsuits, the loss of key clients, etc.

Maturity Date: The date that a bond pays out the principal, and interest payments cease. Also called "redemption."

Mean: A measure of central tendency, the average of a set of numbers.

Median: The middle value in a set of numbers.

Member Firm: A broker-dealer and/or underwriting firm that belongs to FINRA or other securities association (MSRB, CBOE).

Millage Rate: The property tax rate used to calculate a property owner's tax bill. The assessed value times the millage rate is the property tax owed, before any exemptions or other factors are included.

Mini-Max: A type of best efforts underwriting where the syndicate must sell a minimum amount and may sell up to a higher, maximum amount.

Minimum Death Benefit: The minimum death benefit payable to the insured, regardless of how lousy the separate account returns are in a variable policy.

Minimum Maintenance Requirement: The minimum amount of equity that a margin customer must maintain on either a short or a long position.

Mode: The number in a data set occurring most frequently.

Model Rule: Publication by NASAA stating accepted regulatory approaches to certain aspects of the securities industry faced by state and provincial regulators.

Modern Portfolio Theory: Investment approach using optimal portfolios to maximize returns for a given level of risk. Based on belief that uncorrelated investments can reduce the overall risk of a portfolio. Associated with "efficient frontier."

Monetarists: Those who advocate and/or implement monetary policy, e.g. The Federal Reserve.

Monetary Policy: What the FRB implements through the discount rate, reserve requirement, and FOMC open market operations. Monetary policy tightens or loosens credit in order to affect short-term interest rates and, therefore, the economy.

Money Laundering: The process of turning profits from illegal enterprises into seemingly legitimate assets, e.g. Saul Goodman of "Breaking Bad."

Money Market Mutual Fund: A highly liquid holding place for cash. Sometimes called "stable value" funds, as the share price is generally maintained at $1. The mutual funds invest in—surprisingly—money market securities.

Money Market Security: A short-term debt obligation, e.g., commercial paper, bankers' acceptance, T-Bill.

Money Purchase Plan: A retirement plan in which the employer must contribute a set percentage of the employee's salary, regardless of profitability.

Monte Carlo: Simulations used to predict the effects of various factors, e.g. bear markets, inflation, high interest rates, etc., often used to assist with estimating withdrawal rates from a retirement account.

Moody's Investors Service: One of the top three credit rating agencies for corporate and municipal bonds as well as stocks.

Moral Obligation Bond: Type of revenue bond with a provision to seek emergency funding from the state legislature should the issuer run into financial problems.

Mortality & Expense Risk Fees: Extra charges in addition to charges for investment services for variable contracts.

Mortality Guarantee: A promise from an insurance company to pay out no matter how soon the insured dies, or to pay an annuitant no matter how long he lives.

Mortgage-Backed Security: A security in which the interest and principal payments are backed by a pool of mortgages.

Mortgage Bond: A corporate bond secured by a pledge of real estate as collateral.

Mortgage REIT: A Real Estate Investment Trust that buys and/or makes loans for real estate projects.

MSRB (Municipal Securities Rulemaking Board): The self-regulatory organization overseeing municipal securities dealers.

Municipal Bond: A bond issued by a state, county, city, school district, etc., in order to build roads, schools, hospitals, etc., or simply to keep the government running long enough to hold another election.

Municipal Bond Fund: A mutual fund that invests in municipal bonds with an objective to maximize federally tax-exempt income.

Municipal Note: A short-term obligation of a city, state, school district, etc., backed by the anticipation of funds from revenues, taxes, or upcoming bond issues, e.g., TAN, RAN, BAN.

Mutual Fund: An investment company offering equity stakes in a portfolio that is usually managed actively and that always charges management fees and other expenses.

N

Narrow-based Index: Index focusing on a particular industry or geographic region, e.g., a transportation index.

NASD (National Association of Securities Dealers): Former name of the SRO empowered with the passage of the Maloney Act of 1938. Regulates its own members and enforces SEC rules and regulations. Now called FINRA after a merger with the regulators from the NYSE.

NASDAQ: National Association of Securities Dealers Automated Quotation system. The main component of the OTC market. Stocks that meet certain criteria are quoted throughout the day on NASDAQ, e.g., MSFT, ORCL, and INTC.

NASAA or North American Securities Administrators Association: Organization of state and Canadian provincial securities regulators responsible for the Series 65, Series 66, and Series 63 exams.

National Adjudicatory Council: NAC, the first level of appeal for a party sanctioned by the DOE under FINRA's Code of Procedure.

Natural Event Risk: Risk that a weather-related event could have a negative effect on securities or securities markets.

NAV or Net Asset Value: The net asset value of a mutual fund share. Assets – Liabilities/Outstanding Shares.

Needs Analysis: The process of determining how much insurance an individual should buy based on mortgage and other debts, income, final expenses, etc.

Negotiable: The characteristic of a security that allows an investor to sell or transfer ownership to another party. For example, savings bonds are not negotiable, while Treasury Bills are negotiable.

Negotiable CD: A bank CD that can be traded on a secondary market, usually of large denominations.

Negotiated Market: Another name for the "second" or "over-the-counter" market.

Negotiated Underwriting: A municipal bond—usually a revenue bond—underwritten without a competitive, sealed bid.

Net Asset Value: NAV, the value of one share of a mutual fund or unit of a UIT.

Net Asset Value per Bond: A measure of an issuer's long-term solvency, found by dividing the net tangible assets of the company (not goodwill and other intangible assets) by the number of bonds issued.

Net Income After Tax: Revenue minus all expenses. Also known as a "profit" or a "loss," depending on whether it's a positive or negative number.

Net Interest Cost: A measure of a municipal issuer's total cost of borrowing money by issuing bonds.

Net Investment Income: The source of an investment company's dividend distributions to shareholders. It is calculated by taking the fund's dividends and interest collected on portfolio securities, minus the operating expenses. Funds using the "conduit tax theory" distribute at least 90% of net investment income to avoid paying taxes on the amount distributed to shareholders.

Net Overall Debt: A municipal issuer's direct debt plus their overlapping debt.

Net Present Value: The present value of a project's expected cash flows minus the costs associated with acquiring the asset.

Net Profit: Another name for net income after tax.

Net Profit Margin, Net Margin: A company's net income after tax divided by revenue, showing the percentage of each dollar of revenue making its way to the bottom line.

Net Revenue: Another name for revenue, accounting for any returns, refunds or discounting. AKA "net operating revenue" or "net sales."

Net Revenue Pledge: The more common method used by the issuer of a revenue bond in which operations & maintenance are covered before debt service.

Net Sales: AKA, "net revenue."

Networking Arrangement: A broker-dealer operating on the premises of a bank where retail deposits are taken.

Net Worth: The difference between assets and liabilities.

New Construction: A type of DPP in which the partnership builds and then sells housing units.

New Issue Market: The primary market, where securities are issued to investors with the proceeds going to the issuer of the securities. Initial public offerings (IPOs), for example, take place on the "new issue market."

NHA – New Housing Authority (bonds): Revenue bonds issued by a municipal government but ultimately backed by the United States Government, who guarantees rental payments for the residents of the housing project.

No-Action Relief: Letter to a securities regulator verifying that a particular action or course of business would require no registration and lead to no regulatory action on their part if performed as stated in the request.

Nolo Contendere: A Latin phrase used when the defendant does not contest the charges, a problem when completing Form U4 or Form ADV.

No-load Fund: Mutual fund sold without a sales charge, but one which may charge an ongoing 12b-1fee or "asset-based sales charge" up to .25% of net assets.

Nominal Quote: A quote in which a dealer is giving an estimate rather than a firm price at which he is ready to trade. Must be clearly identified as nominal to avoid backing away.

Nominal Yield: Interest rate paid by a bond or preferred stock. The investor receives this % of the par value each year, regardless of what the bond or preferred stock is trading for on the secondary market.

Non-accredited Purchaser: Investor who does not meet various SEC net worth and/or income requirements. For a Reg D private placement, accredited investors may participate, but only a limited number of non-accredited investors may purchase the issue.

Non-cumulative Preferred Stock: Preferred stock that does not have to pay missed dividends (dividends in arrears).

Nondiscrimination Covenant: A promise by a municipal revenue bond issuer that all users of a facility must pay to use it, including VIPs of the municipality.

Non-diversified Fund: A fund that doesn't meet the 75-5-10 rule, preferring to concentrate more heavily in certain issues.

Non-equity Options: Standardized options based on things other than equity securities, e.g., indexes or foreign currency options.

Non-NASDAQ OTC Securities: Over-the-counter securities that do not meet the requirements of NASDAQ. For example, Pink Market or OTCBB securities. By definition, "unlisted" securities.

Non-systematic Risk: The risk of holding any one particular stock or bond. Diversification spreads this risk among different issuers and different industries in order to minimize the impact of a bankruptcy or unexpected collapse of any one issuer.

Non-Qualified Plan: Tax-deferred, employer-sponsored retirement plan that falls outside the guidelines of ERISA, e.g., a non-qualified deferred compensation plan.

Not Held (Order): AKA "market not held." A market order in which the customer allows the broker-dealer to enter the trade when they feel the price is right, as opposed to a market order, which is filled as soon as possible.

Note: A short-term debt security.

Notice Filing: A requirement under NSMIA for a federal covered adviser to notify any state securities regulator where it maintains a place of business, or for investment companies to notify the states where there shares are offered and sold.

Numbered Account: Account identified with a number rather than a name. Allowed if the owner files a statement with the broker-dealer attesting to ownership.

NYSE: New York Stock Exchange, an auction market where buyers and sellers shout out competitive bid and asked/offered prices throughout the day.

NSMIA or National Securities Markets Improvement Act: Legislation creating a class of securities to be registered exclusively with the SEC.

O

Obsolescence Risk: The unsystematic risk that an issuer's products/services will become obsolete or no longer in demand due to changing times, technologies, and consumer behaviors.

Odd Lot: Order for less than the usual trading unit for a security, e.g. fewer than 100 shares of common stock.

Odd Lot Theory: Investment approach that does the opposite of what odd-lot investors are doing.

Offer: Another name for "ask," or the price an investor must pay if he wants to buy a security from a dealer/market maker.

Offer of Settlement: A respondent's offer to the disciplinary committee of FINRA to settle his or her recent rule violations.

Officers: High-level executives at a public corporation, e.g., the Chief Executive Officer (CEO), Chief Financial Officer (CFO), and the Chief Operating Officer (COO).

Official Notice of Sale: Advertisement in the Bond Buyer in which a municipal issuer hopes to attract potential underwriters.

Official Statement: Document that discloses detailed information about a municipal bond issuer's financial condition.

OID or Original Issue Discount: A bond purchased for less than the par value on the primary market, e.g., a STRIP.

Omitting Prospectus: Advertisement for a mutual fund that typically shows performance figures without providing (omitting) the full disclosure contained in the prospectus. Therefore, it must present caveats and encourage readers to read the prospectus and consider all the risks before investing in the fund.

Open-end Fund: Investment company that sells an unlimited number of shares to an unlimited number of investors on a continuous basis. Shares are redeemed by the company rather than traded among investors.

Open Market Operations: What the FOMC engages in when buying or selling US Treasuries to achieve targets for short-term interest rates.

Operating Agreement: Document governing the structure and operation of an LLC.

Operating Expenses: Expenses that a mutual fund deducts from the assets of the fund, including board of director salaries, custodial and transfer agent services, management fees, 12b-1 fees, etc. More generally, operating expenses are shown on a company's income statement to indicate expenses beyond COGS, e.g. administrative salaries, office supplies, office rent.

Operating Income, Operating Profit: Measurement from a company's income statement, revenue minus COGS, operating expenses, and depreciation.

Operating Margin: Operating income divided by revenue.

Opportunity Cost: The return on an investment given up in order to pursue another opportunity.

Option: A derivative giving the holder the right to buy or sell something for a stated price up to expiration of the contract. Puts and calls.

Order Room: The department of a broker-dealer that places trades. AKA "wire room."

Order Ticket/Trade Ticket: Information filled out by a registered representative when placing an order to buy or sell securities.

Ordinary Dividend: A dividend payment that does not receive qualified-dividend tax treatment but is, rather, treated as ordinary income.

Ordinary Income: Most income received by a taxpayer, including salary, wages, bonuses, bond interest, ordinary dividends, etc.

Ordinary Income Rate: Tax rate paid on earned income and some forms of investment income.

OTC/Over-the-Counter: Not traded on NYSE, but through NASDAQ and also Bulletin Board and Pink Market stocks.

Out-of-The-Money: An option that gives the holder no benefit because it has no intrinsic value.

Outstanding Shares: Number of shares a corporation has outstanding. Used to calculate EPS.

Overbought: A technical analysis/chartist term for a security trading near resistance.

Oversold: A technical analysis/chartist term for a security trading near support.

Overlapping Debt: The debt that a municipal issuer is responsible for along with a coterminous issuer.

P

PAC or Planned Amortization Class: Type of CMO (collateralized mortgage obligation) that provides more protection against extension risk vs. a TAC.

Paid-In Surplus: Amount above the par value that investors paid when purchasing the company's initial public offering.

Painting the Tape: Form of market manipulation in which bogus trades are reported in order to affect the market price of a security. A violation.

Par: The face amount of a bond payable at maturity. Also, the face amount of a preferred stock. Preferred = $100, Bond = $1,000. AKA "principal."

Parity: When a convertible bond's or convertible preferred stock's market price is exactly equal to the value of the shares to which it converts.

Partial Surrender: When a life insurance policyholder cashes in part of the cash value. Excess over premiums is taxable.

Participating Preferred Stock: Preferred stock whose dividend is often raised above the stated rate.

Participation: Provision of ERISA requiring that all employees in a qualified retirement plan be covered within a reasonable length of time after being hired.

Participation Rate: The percentage of the index's increase credited to the value of an indexed annuity.

Partnership: A flow-through business entity established as either a general or limited partnership, in which the owners—not the business itself—are taxed on their share of any net income.

Partnership Agreement: Agreement governing the operation of a general or limited partnership.

Partnership Democracy: Term referring to a limited partner's right to vote in certain matters of major importance.

Passive Income: As opposed to "earned income," the income derived from rental properties, limited partnerships, or other enterprises in which the individual is not actively involved.

Passive Investor: Investor who feels markets are efficient and, therefore, does not actively select/trade investments. Associated with the exclusive use of index funds based on the goals of the investor rather than on anticipated market movements.

Passive Loss: A loss derived from rental properties, limited partnerships, or other enterprises in which the individual is not actively involved.

Pass-Through Certificate: A mortgage-backed security (usually GNMA) that takes a pool of mortgages and passes through interest and principal monthly to an investor.

Payable (or Payment) Date: Date that a dividend check is paid to investors.

Payroll Deduction: Non-qualified retirement plan offered by some businesses.

P/E Ratio: The market price of a stock compared to the earnings per share. Stocks trading at high P/E ratios are "growth stocks," while those trading at low P/E ratios are "value stocks." See "price-to-earnings ratio."

Peak: Phase of the business cycle between expansion (good times) and contraction (bad times).

Pegging: A form of market manipulation. A violation.

Penny Stock: An OTC equity security trading below $5 per share.

Penny Stock Cold Calling Rules: Rules to protect consumers receiving telemarketing pitches to buy risky stocks trading below $5 a share. Rules require special disclosure and investor signatures when selling penny stocks.

Pension Plan: Contract between an individual and an employer that provides for the distribution of benefits at retirement.

Per Capita: For an inheritance, per capita means if a beneficiary dies, his share is split by the other named beneficiaries.

Performance Figures: Total return for a mutual fund over 1, 5, and 10 years, and/or "life of fund." Only past performance may be indicated, and there must be a caveat that past performance does not guarantee future results.

Period Certain: A payout option on an annuity promising payments for a minimum number of years.

Periodic-Payment Deferred Annuity: Method of purchasing an annuity whereby the contract holder makes periodic payments into the contract. The pay-out phase must be deferred for all periodic payment plans.

Permanent Insurance: Life insurance other than "term."

Per Stirpes: For an inheritance, per stirpes means if a beneficiary dies, his share passes to his heirs and not the other named beneficiaries.

Pink Markets: A virtually unregulated part of the OTC market where thinly traded, volatile stocks change hands.

Placement: The first stage in the cycle of money laundering in which illegally generated funds are placed into the financial system or are smuggled out of the country.

Placement Ratio: A statistic published in the Bond Buyer showing the dollar amount of municipal securities sold on the primary market out of the dollar amount offered the previous week; a.k.a. the "acceptance ratio."

Policy Owner, Policy Holder: The person who owns a life insurance policy. Often, though not necessarily, also the insured

Political Risk: The risk that a country's government will radically change policies or that the political climate will become hostile or counterproductive to business and financial markets. Faced especially by emerging market investors.

POP or Public Offering Price: The price paid by an investor purchasing a new offering of securities. For an IPO, this includes the spread to the underwriters. For a mutual fund, this includes any sales loads that go to the underwriter/distributor.

Portfolio: A batch of stocks, bonds, money market securities, or any combination thereof that an investor owns.

Portfolio Income: Income earned through investing in securities; not to be used toward IRA contributions and not off-settable with passive income.

Portfolio Optimization: Using the efficient frontier to match an investor's risk tolerance and objectives with the most efficient portfolio possible on a risk-adjusted basis.

Position Limit: Maximum number of options contracts that a trader can have on the same side of the market (bull/bear) and/or may exercise over a five day period.

Power of Substitution: Document that when signed by the security owner authorizes transfer of the certificate to another party.

PPI or Producer Price Index: A measure of costs to sellers/producers, as opposed to CPI, which measures the cost to consumers.

Pre-dispute Arbitration Agreement: Agreement signed by the customer of a broker-dealer in which the customer agrees to use arbitration rather than civil court to settle disputes.

Pre-emptive Right: The right of common stockholders to maintain their proportional ownership if the company offers more shares of stock.

Preferred Stock: A fixed-income equity security whose stated dividends must be paid before common stock can receive any dividend payment. Also gets preference ahead of common stock in a liquidation (but behind all bonds and general creditors).

Preliminary Official Statement: The official statement for a municipal bond issue subject to further additions and changes.

Preliminary Prospectus: A prospectus that lacks the POP and the effective date; a.k.a. "red herring." Used to solicit indications of interest.

Premium: 1) The amount by which a bond's price exceeds the par value. 2), the amount paid to acquire an options contract. 3), the amount paid to maintain an insurance contract.

Premium Bond: A bond purchased for more than the par value, usually due to a drop in interest rates.

Prepayment Risk: The risk that the mortgages underlying a mortgage-backed security/pass-through will be paid off sooner than expected due to a drop in interest rates. Investors reinvest the principal at a lower rate going forward.

Present Value: The value today of an amount of money in the future, discounted by some compounded rate of return.

Preservation of Capital: Investment objective placing the emphasis on making sure the principal is not lost.

Pre-Tax Contribution: A contribution made to a tax-advantaged plan for which the individual receives a current deduction for income tax purposes, e.g. contributions to a Traditional IRA or 401(k) plan.

Pre-Tax Margin: A company's pre-tax profit divided by revenue.

Pre-Tax Profit: A measure of profitability from a company's income statement accounting for all expenses other than taxes.

Price-To-Book Ratio: The market price of a common stock compared to the book value per share.

Price-To-Cash Ratio: The market price of a common stock compared to the cash flow per share.

Price-To-Earnings Ratio: The market price of a common stock compared to the EPS of that stock. AKA "P/E ratio."

Price-To-Sales Ratio: The market price of a common stock compared to the revenue per share.

Primary Market: Where securities are issued to raise capital for the issuer. AKA "new-issue market."

Primary Offering: Offering of securities in which the proceeds go to the issuer, e.g., an IPO.

Prime Rate: Interest rate charged to corporations with high credit ratings for unsecured loans.

Principal: A word that can mean many different things in the securities industry. 1) The amount to be received upon maturity for a bond, 2) A supervisor of a broker-dealer or investment adviser, 3) To buy or sell from or to a customer in a securities transaction, 4) The amount borrowed when taking out a mortgage, against which an interest rate is to be charged.

Principal-Protected Fund: A mutual fund for people who want their principal protected. Involves holding the investment for several years, at which point the fund guarantees that the value of the investment will be equal to at least what the investor put in.

Principal Transaction: A potential conflict of interest arising when the investment adviser enters a transaction to buy or sell a security on behalf of a client with the transaction done on a principal basis by the affiliated broker-dealer. Requires disclosure and client consent.

Private Activity Bond: A municipal bond subjecting investors to AMT because the issuer does not qualify under the Internal Revenue Code as a municipal issuer. For example, a parking garage built with the proceeds of a revenue bond may benefit a corporate entity as opposed to a city government or subdivision.

Private Equity Fund: An alternative investment fund open to sophisticated investors only and specializing in buying out companies both public and private.

Private Placement: Exempt transaction under Reg D (Rule 506) of the Securities Act of 1933, allowing issuers to sell securities without registration to accredited investors, who agree to hold them for a required period that is subject to change by the SEC before selling them through Rule 144. Or, an exempt transaction under state securities law in which the security is offered to no more than 10 persons in the state.

Private Securities Transaction: Offering an investment opportunity not sponsored by the firm. Requires permission from the firm and any disclosure demanded; otherwise, a violation called "selling away."

Probate: The process of "proving" a will through the submission of various legal documents used to gather the assets of the deceased, pay off debts, and distribute assets to any named beneficiaries.

Proceeds: The amount an investor receives when selling a capital asset, less any commissions or fees to execute the sale.

Proceeds Transaction: Using the proceeds from a sale of securities to buy other securities on the same day.

Producer Price Index: An index measuring price changes at the wholesale or producer level. AKA "PPI."

Profit: The bottom line of a company's income statement, revenue minus all expenses. AKA "net income."

Profit-Sharing Arrangement: A security involving a share of profits from any source.

Profit Sharing Plan: A defined contribution plan whereby the company shares any profits with employees in the form of contributions to a retirement account.

Progressive Tax: A tax that increases as a percentage as the thing being taxed increases, including gift, estate, and income taxes. Not a flat tax.

Prospectus: Disclosure document that details a company's plans, history, officers, and risks of investment. It's the red herring plus the POP and the effective date.

Protective Covenants: Promises from the issuer of a revenue bond to the bondholders designed to protect the bondholders against default.

Proxy: A form granting the power to vote according to a shareholder's instructions when the shareholder will not attend the meeting.

Prudent Investor Standards: Guidance provided to fiduciaries investing on behalf of a third party, e.g., trustees or custodians of UTMA accounts.

Public Housing Authority (PHA) Bonds: Revenue bonds backed by guaranteed rental payments from the US Treasury. See "NHA/New Housing Authority Bonds."

PSA Model: Method of estimating the speed of prepayments on a CMO investment.

Public Offering: The sale of an issue of common stock, either an IPO or an additional offer of shares.

Public Offering Price (POP): The price an investor pays for a mutual fund or an initial public offering. For a mutual fund, POP = NAV + the sales charge.

Purchase Payment: What an annuitant pays into the annuity contract.

Purchasing Power: The ability of a dollar to buy the things one needs on an inflation-adjusted basis. Inflation erodes the purchasing power of the dollar, which is why investors allocate funds to equity investments, the best inflation-adjusted investment vehicle historically.

Purchasing Power Risk: The risk that a fixed payment will not be sufficient to keep up with rising inflation (as measured through the CPI). AKA "inflation risk," "constant-dollar risk."

Put (n.): A contract giving the owner the right to sell something at a stated exercise price.

Put (v.): To sell.

Q

Qualification: A method of registering a securities offering with the Administrator when not registering with the SEC and performing—usually—an intra-state offering only.

Qualified Dividend: A dividend that qualifies for a lower tax rate vs. ordinary income.

Qualified Institutional Buyers: Investors meeting certain SEC criteria allowing them to participate in certain investment opportunities not open to the general public.

Qualified Opinion: Opinion by the bond counsel for a municipal issuer in which some doubt or reservations are expressed.

Qualified Plan: Retirement plan that qualifies for deductible contributions on behalf of employers and/or employees and covered by ERISA. For example, 401(k), defined benefit, Keogh.

Quick Assets: Current assets that are easily liquidated; cash & equivalents and accounts receivable *minus* inventory. Quick assets are used to calculate the company's quick ratio from the balance sheet.

Quick Ratio: More stringent measure of liquidity than the current ratio. Inventory is excluded from current assets before comparing them to the company's current liabilities.

Quote, Quotation: A price that a dealer is willing to pay or accept for a security. A two-sided quote has both a bid and an asked/offer price.

R

Random Withdrawals: Settlement option in an annuity whereby the annuitant takes the value of the subaccounts in two or more withdrawals, rather than one lump sum.

Range: In a set of numbers, the difference between the largest and smallest value.

Rate Covenant: Promise that the issuer of a revenue bond will raise rates if necessary to cover the debt service.

Rating Service: Company that assigns credit ratings to corporate and municipal bonds, e.g., Moody's and S&P.

Raw Land: Unimproved real estate providing no cash flow and no depreciation. A speculative investment in land.

Realized Gain: Amount of the "profit" an investor earns when selling a security.

Real Rate of Return: An investment's return after inflation/deflation has been factored in. AKA "inflation-adjusted return."

Rebalance: To sell securities in order to return to the stated percentages/goals of a portfolio. Associated with strategic asset allocation.

Recession: Two quarters (6 months) or more of economic decline. Associated with rising unemployment, falling interest rates, and falling gross domestic product.

Reclamation: Document sent by a broker-dealer when delivery of securities is apparently in error.

Record Date: Date determined by the Board of Directors on which the investor must be the holder "of record" in order to receive the upcoming dividend. Settlement of a trade must occur by the record date for the buyer to receive the dividend.

Recourse Note: Obligation of a limited partnership for which a limited partner is responsible personally beyond any collateral pledged to secure the loan.

Red Herring: Disclosure document containing essentially the same information that the final prospectus will contain, minus the POP and effective date. AKA "preliminary prospectus."

Redeemable Security: Security that may be presented to the issuer for payment, e.g., open-end funds.

Redemption: For mutual funds, redemption involves the sale of mutual fund shares back to the fund at the NAV (less any redemption fees, back-end loads). For bonds, the date that principal is returned to the investor.

Redemption Fee: A charge to a mutual fund investor who sells her shares back to the fund within a certain time frame.

Refunding: Replacing an outstanding bond issue by issuing new bonds at a lower interest rate. Also known as "calling" a bond issue.

Reg A: An exempt transaction under the Securities Act of 1933 for small offerings of securities.

Reg D: An exempt transaction under the Securities Act of 1933 for private placements.

Reg FD: Legislation requiring that any material non-public information disclosed by a public corporation to analysts or other investors must be made public.

Reg SHO: Rules requiring broker-dealers to locate securities before executing short sales.

Reg T: Federal Reserve Board requirements for cash and margin accounts.

Reg U: Federal Reserve Board requirements for credit extended by banks to broker-dealers for margin accounts.

Registered as to Principal Only: Bond with only the principal registered. Interest coupons must be presented for payment.

Registered Representative: Associated person of an investment banker or broker-dealer who effects transactions in securities for compensation.

Registered Secondary: Offering of securities by persons other than the issuer. For example, the former CEO of a corporation may offer a large block of restricted (unregistered) stock to the public through a broker-dealer.

Registrar: Party that audits the transfer agent to make sure the number of authorized shares is never exceeded.

Registration by Coordination: Method of registering a securities offering with the states where they are to be offered, in addition to required SEC registration.

Registration by Filing: Method of registering a securities offering with the states where they are to be offered in an additional offering that is also registered with the SEC.

Registration by Qualification: Method of registering a securities offering with only the state securities Administrator.

Registration Statement: Legal document disclosing material information concerning an offering of a security and its issuer. Submitted to SEC under Securities Act of 1933.

Regressive Tax: A flat tax, e.g., gasoline, sales, excise taxes.

Regular Way Settlement: The typical time frame for purchasing and settling securities transactions, e.g. T +3 for common stock trades or T + 1 for trades in US Treasury securities.

Regulated Investment Company: An investment company using the conduit tax theory by distributing 90% or more of net investment income to shareholders.

Regulatory Risk: The unsystematic risk that changes to legislation/regulations will have a negative impact on an issuer's business. AKA "legislative risk."

Reinstatement Privilege: A feature of some mutual funds allowing investors to make withdrawals and then reinstate the money without paying another sales charge.

Reinvestment Risk: The risk that a fixed-income investor will not be able to reinvest interest payments or the par value at attractive interest rates. Happens when rates are falling.

REIT (Real Estate Investment Trust): A corporation or trust that uses the pooled capital of investors to invest in ownership of either income property or mortgage loans. 90% of net income is paid out to shareholders.

Release Date: Date established by the SEC as to when the underwriters may sell new securities to the buyers; a.k.a. "effective date."

Repurchase Agreement: Agreement in which one party sells something to the other and agrees to repurchase it for a higher price over the short-term.

Required Minimum Distribution (RMD): The required minimum amount that must be taken from a retirement plan to avoid IRS penalties. Usually must occur by April 1st of the year following the individual's 70½th birthday.

Reserve Requirement: Amount of money a bank must lock up in reserve, established by the FRB.

Residual Claim: The right of common stockholders to claim assets after the claims of all creditors and preferred stockholders have been satisfied.

Respondent: The party named in a disciplinary proceeding or arbitration.

Restricted Person: Person who is ineligible to purchase an equity IPO, including members of the brokerage industry and their immediate family members.

Restricted Stock: Stock whose transfer is subject to restrictions, e.g., a holding period. Stock purchased in private placements is an example of restricted stock.

Retained Earnings: A balance sheet account showing accumulated net income, from which any dividends are first declared. Can be thought of as all the profits of the business that have not been paid out as dividends but, rather, reinvested into the business as reflected by other balance sheet accounts, e.g. capital equipment, new stores, etc.

Return on Equity: A measure showing how much in profits each dollar of common stockholder's equity generates for the company, net income / shareholder equity.

Revenue: The proceeds a company receives when selling products and services, the top line of the income statement. AKA "sales."

Revenue Anticipation Note (RAN): A short-term debt obligation of a municipal issuer backed by upcoming revenues.

Revenue Bond: Municipal bond whose interest and principal payments are backed by the revenues generated from the project being built by the proceeds of the bonds. Toll roads, for example, are usually built with revenue bonds backed by the tolls collected.

Reverse Repurchase Agreements: Repurchase agreement initiated by a buyer, who then resells the securities to the other side of the transaction at the agreed-upon price.

Rights: Short-term equity securities that allow the holder to buy new shares below the current market price.

Rights of Accumulation: Feature of many mutual funds whereby a rise in account value is counted the same as new money for purposes of achieving a breakpoint.

Rights Offering: Additional offer of stock accompanied by the opportunity for each shareholder to maintain his/her proportionate ownership in the company.

Risk: The variability/volatility involved with investing, typically measured by standard deviation.

Risk-Adjusted Return: Returns adjusted for risk, most commonly through the Sharpe ratio.

Riskless Principal Transaction: Transaction in which a broker-dealer chooses to act as a principal when they could have acted as an agent for the customer.

Risk Modification Techniques: Using options and other strategies to reduce the risks presented by current holdings, e.g. buying a put to protect against a large loss on a particular stock holding.

Risk Tolerance: The ability to withstand fluctuations in principal value due to the investor's time horizon, financial stability, etc.

Rollover: Moving retirement funds from a 401(k) to an IRA, or from one IRA to another. In a "60-day rollover," the check is cut to the individual, who must then send a check to the new custodian within 60 days to avoid early distribution penalties.

Roll-up Transaction: The combination of business units with, for example, a DPP investment.

Roth IRA: Individual retirement account funded with non-deductible (after-tax) contributions. All distributions are tax-free provided the individual is 59½ and has had the account at least five years.

Round Lot: The usual or normal unit of trading. 100 shares for common stock.

R-Squared: A risk measure showing how closely the movement of a portfolio is due to the movement of the benchmark index.

RTRS: Trade reporting system used for transactions in municipal securities on the secondary market. AKA "Real-Time Transaction Reporting System."

Rule of 72: Not a regulation but, rather, a shortcut for figuring compounded returns. For example, if the compounded rate is 8%, 8 divided into 72 tells us the investment will double in approximately 9 years.

Rule (and Form) 144: Regulates the sale of "control stock" by requiring board members, officers, and large shareholders to report sales of their corporation's stock and to adhere to volume limits. The form is filed as often as quarterly—no later than concurrently with the sale.

Rule 144a: Rule that allows restricted securities to be re-sold to institutional investors including banks, insurance companies, broke5r-dealers, investment advisers, pension plans, and investment companies without violating holding period requirements.

Rule 145: Rule that requires corporations in a proposed merger/acquisition to solicit the vote of the shareholders of both the purchasing and the acquired corporation.

Rule 147: Transactional exemption under the Securities Act of 1933 for intra-state offerings of securities.

Russell 2,000: A small-cap index.

RVP: Receipt versus payment, a method of settlement whereby payment on the transaction is made when delivery of the securities is received and accepted.

S

Safety: Investment objective that seeks to avoid loss of principal first and foremost. Bank CDs, Treasury securities, and fixed annuities are generally suitable. AKA "capital preservation."

SAI: Detailed and long-form disclosure document for a mutual fund. AKA "Statement of Additional Information."

Sale, Sell: To dispose of a security for something of value.

Sales: The top line of the income statement, usually called "revenue."

Sales Charge, Sales Load: One-time deduction from an investor's check that goes to the distributors/sellers of the fund. Deducted from investor's check, either when she buys (A-shares) or sells (B-shares).

Savings Bond: US Government debt security that is not "negotiable," meaning it can't be traded or pledged as collateral for a loan. Includes series I, EE and HH bonds.

Scheduled Premium: Life insurance with established, scheduled premium payments, e.g., whole life, variable life. As opposed to "universal" insurance, which is "flexible premium."

S-Corporation or S-Corp: A form of business ownership with a maximum # of shareholders who receive a share of income/loss and also protection of personal assets.

SEC Release IA-1092: Document explaining the SEC's approach to defining investment advisers based on a so-called "three-pronged approach."

Secondary Market: Where investors trade securities among themselves and proceeds do not go to the issuer.

Secondary Offering/Distribution: Distribution of securities owned by major stockholders—not the issuer of the securities. Not the same as an additional primary offer of securities.

Sector Fund: Fund that concentrates heavily in a particular industry, e.g., the "Technology Fund." Higher risk/reward than funds invested in many industries.

Sector Rotating: Portfolio management technique that involves selling or underweighting securities of companies in certain areas of the economy and buying or overweighting securities in other areas. For example, reducing holdings in pharmaceutical stocks in order to buy more stocks in the telecommunications sector.

Secured Bond: Corporate bond secured by collateral, e.g., mortgage bond, collateral trust certificate, equipment trust certificate.

Securities Act of 1933: Securities legislation requiring non-exempt issuers to register securities and provide full disclosure.

Securities and Exchange Commission or SEC: Federal government regulator of broad aspects of securities markets, empowered by passage of Securities Exchange Act of 1934.

Securities Exchange Act of 1934: Legislation that prevents fraud in the securities markets. No person and no security exempt from anti-fraud regulations. Created/empowered the SEC. Requires broker-dealers, exchanges and securities associations to register with SEC. Requires public companies to report quarterly and annually to SEC.

Security: An investment of money subject to fluctuation in value and negotiable/marketable to other investors. Other than an insurance policy or fixed annuity, a security is any piece of securitized "paper" that can be traded for value.

Self-Regulatory Organization: SRO, e.g., FINRA. An organization given the power to regulate its members. Not government bodies like the SEC, which oversees the SROs.

Sell Limit: Order to sell placed above the current market price that may be executed only if the bid price rises to the limit price or higher.

Sell Stop: Order to sell placed below the current market price, activated only if the market price hits or passes below the stop price.

Selling Away: Violation that occurs when a registered representative offers investment opportunities not sponsored by the firm.

Selling Concession: Typically, the largest piece of the underwriting spread going to the firm credited with making the sale.

Selling Dividends: Violation where an investor is deceived into thinking that she needs to purchase a stock in order to receive an upcoming dividend.

Selling Group: Certain broker-dealers with an agreement to act as selling agents for the syndicate (underwriters) with no capital at risk.

Selling, General, and Administrative: General operating expenses listed on the company's income statement. Expenses not directly related to the production of the company's product or delivery of its services. AKA "operating expenses."

Semi-Annual: Twice per year, or "at the half year," literally. Bond interest is paid semi-annually, for example.

Senior Security: Security that grants the holder a higher claim on the issuer's assets in the event of a liquidation/bankruptcy.

Separate Account: Account maintained by an insurance/annuity company that is separate from the company's general account. Used to invest clients' money for variable annuities and variable insurance contracts. Registered as an investment company under Investment Company Act of 1940.

SEP-IRA: Pre-tax retirement plan available to small businesses. Favors high-income employees (compared to SIMPLE). Only employ-er contributes.

Series EE Bond: Nonmarketable, interest-bearing US Government savings bond issued at a discount from the par value. Interest is exempt from state and local taxation.

Series HH Bond: Nonmarketable, interest-bearing US Government savings bond issued at par and purchased only by trading in Series EE bonds at maturity. Interest is exempt from state and local taxation.

Series I Bond: Savings bond issued by the US Treasury that protects investors from inflation or purchasing power risk.

Settlement: Final completion of a securities transaction wherein payment has been made by the buyer and delivery of the securities has been made by the seller.

Settlement Options: Payout options on annuities and life insurance including life-only, life with period certain, and joint and last survivorship.

Share Identification: Method of calculating capital gains and losses by which the investor identifies which shares were sold, as opposed to using FIFO or average cost.

Sharpe Ratio: The most commonly used method of calculating risk-adjusted return.

Shelf Registration: Registering securities that will be sold gradually on the primary market.

Short: To begin a securities transaction by selling.

Short Interest Theory: Theory that a high level of short sales is a bullish indicator, as it creates potential buying pressure on a particular security.

Short Sale: Method of attempting to profit from a security whose price is expected to fall. Trader borrows certificates through a broker-dealer and sells them, with the obligation to replace them at a later date, hopefully at a lower price. Bearish position.

Short-Term Capital Gain: Profit realized on a security held for 12 months or less.

Short-Term Capital Loss: Loss realized on a security held for 12 months or less, deductible against Short-Term Capital Gains.

Signature Guarantee: Official stamp/medallion that officers of a bank affix to a stock power to attest to its validity.

SIMPLE IRA: Retirement plan for businesses with no more than 100 employees that have no other retirement plan in place. Pre-tax contributions, fully taxable distributions. Both employer and employees may contribute.

Simple Trust: Trust that accumulates income and distributes it to the beneficiaries annually.

Simplified Arbitration: FIINRA method of resolving disputes involving a small amount of money (currently $50,000).

Single-Payment Deferred Annuity: Annuity purchased with a single payment wherein the individual defers the payout or "annuity" phase of the contract.

Single-Payment Immediate Annuity: Annuity purchased with a single payment wherein the individual goes immediately into the payout or "annuity" phase of the contract.

Sinking Fund: Account established by an issuing corporation or municipality to provide funds required to redeem a bond issue.

SIPC: Stands for the Securities Investor Protection Corporation, a non-profit, non-government, industry-funded insurance corporation protecting investors against broker-dealer failure.

SMA: A line of credit in a margin account. AKA "Special Memorandum Account."

Small Cap: A stock where the total value of all outstanding shares is considered "small," typically between $50 million and $2 billion.

Soft-Dollar Compensation: Economic benefits provided to an investment adviser by a broker-dealer in exchange for using the broker-dealer's custodial and/or execution services.

Sole Proprietor: A business owned as a natural person.

Solicitor: An individual or entity who does not provide investment advice but, rather, sells the services of an investment adviser in exchange for compensation. In most states requires registration as an IAR.

Solvency: Ability of a corporation or municipality to meet its obligations as they come due.

Sovereign Debt: Bonds issued by a national government payable in a foreign currency.

Special Assessment Bond: Revenue bond backed by an assessment on only those properties benefiting from the project.

Special Memorandum Account (SMA): Line of credit in a margin account.

Special Tax: A tax on gasoline, hotel and motel, liquor, tobacco, etc.

Special Tax Bond: A revenue bond backed by taxes on gasoline, hotel and motel, liquor, tobacco, etc.

Specialized Fund: A type of mutual fund devoted to a particular strategy or tactic, e.g. sector funds, asset allocation funds.

Specified Program: Direct participation program in which the assets of the partnership are identified.

Speculation: High-risk investment objective for investors willing to bet on a large price-change in an asset, irrespective of any income it might produce. Short-term speculators trade options and futures, while long-term speculation is evidenced by holding warrants or raw land.

Sponsor: The party who puts together a direct participation program.

Spousal Account: IRA established for a non-working spouse.

Spread: Generally, the difference between a dealer's purchase price and selling price, both for new offerings (underwriting spread) and secondary market quotes. For underwritings the spread is the difference between the proceeds to the issuer and the POP.

Stabilizing/Stabilization: Surprising practice by which an underwriting syndicate bids up the price of an IPO whose price is dropping in the secondary market.

Standby Underwriting: Commitment by an underwriter to purchase any shares that are not subscribed to in a rights offering.

Standard Deviation: The dispersion of results from their mean, the standard unit of risk.

Statute of Limitations: A time limit that, once reached, prevents criminal or civil action from being filed.

Statutory Disqualification: Prohibiting a person from associating with an SRO due to disciplinary or criminal actions within the past 10 years, or due to filing a false or misleading application or report with a regulator.

Statutory Prospectus: The prospectus for a mutual fund, as opposed to just the summary prospectus.

Statutory Voting: Method of voting whereby the shareholder may cast no more than the number of shares owned per candidate/item.

Stock: Ownership or equity position in a public company whose value is tied to the company's profits (if any) and dividend payouts (if any).

Stock Dividend: Payment of a dividend in the form of more shares of stock; not a taxable event.

Stockholders' Equity: The difference between a company's assets and liabilities. AKA "net worth."

Stock Power: Document used to transfer ownership of a stock.

Stock Split: A change in the number of outstanding shares designed to change the price-per-share; not a taxable event.

Stop Loss: Another name for a sell-stop order. So named because an investor's losses are stopped once the stock trades at a certain price or lower.

Stop Order: A securities buy or sell order that is activated only if the market price hits or passes through the stop price. Does not name a price for execution. Or, a disciplinary order by the Administrator of denial, suspension, or revocation.

Stop-limit Order: A stop order that once triggered must be filled at an exact price (or better).

Straddle: Buying a call and a put on the same underlying instrument with the same strike price and expiration…or selling a call and a put on the same underlying instrument with the same strike price and expiration.

Straight Life Annuity: Settlement option in which the annuity company pays the annuitant only as long as he or she is alive. Also called "straight life" or "life only."

Straight Preferred Stock: Preferred stock whose missed dividends do not go into arrears, a.k.a. "non-cumulative preferred."

Strategic Asset Allocation: Allocating a portfolio according to the needs of the investor rather than on the expected direction of the stock and bond markets, e.g. any age-based portfolio for retirement or educational funding.

Street Name: Securities held in the name of a broker-dealer on behalf of customers.

Strike Price: Price at which a call or put option allows the holder to buy or sell the underlying security. AKA "exercise price."

STRIPS: Acronym for "Separate Trading of Registered Interest and Principal of Securities." A zero coupon bond issued by the US Treasury in which all interest income is received at maturity in the form of a higher (accreted) principal value. Avoids "reinvestment risk."

Student Loan Marketing Association or **Sallie Mae:** A government-sponsored enterprise providing liquidity to institutions making student loans.

Subaccount: Investment options available within the separate account for variable contract holders. Basically, these are mutual funds that grow tax-deferred.

Subchapter M: Section of the Internal Revenue Code providing the "conduit tax treatment" used by REITs and mutual funds distributing 90% or more of net income to shareholders. A mutual fund using this method is technically a Regulated Investment Company under IRC Subchapter M.

Subject Quotes: Quotes in which the dealer/market maker is sharing information and not yet ready to trade at those prices.

Subordinated Debenture: Corporate bond with a claim that is subordinated or "junior" to a debenture and/or general creditor.

Subscription Agreement: Document signed by a potential limited partner in a DPP.

Subscription Price: Price that all buyers of a new issue will pay to buy the security being offered on the primary market.

Suitability: Determination by a registered representative that a security matches a customer's stated objectives and financial situation.

Summary Prospectus: The most concise disclosure document used to offer and sell mutual fund shares.

Supervision: System implemented by a broker-dealer to ensure that its employees and associated persons comply with federal and state securities law, and the rules and regulations of the SEC, exchanges, and SROs.

Surrender: To cash out an annuity or life insurance policy for its surrender value.

Surrender Charge: The percentage of the contract value retained by the insurance company when an annuity is cashed in during the surrender period.

Surrender Period: The period during which surrender charges apply in a deferred annuity.

Surety Bond: Insurance providing protection to a broker-dealer, investment adviser, or agent against actions related to losses in client accounts.

Syndicate: Group of underwriters bringing a new issue to the primary market.

Syndicate Letter: Another name for the agreement among underwriters. The document detailing the terms of operation for an underwriting syndicate.

Systematic Risk: Another name for "market risk," or the risk that an investment's value could plummet due to an overall market panic or collapse. Other "systematic risks" include inflation, interest rate, and natural event risk.

T

T + 3: Trade date plus three business days.

TAC – Targeted Amortization Class: Type of CMO (collateralized mortgage obligation) that leaves the investor with greater extension risk as compared to a PAC (planned amortization class).

Tactical Asset Allocation: Changing the allocation of a portfolio based on anticipated market movements. Associated with active management and market timing.

Target Fund: An age-based mutual fund that shifts asset allocation in line with the retirement target date of the investors in the fund. AKA "lifecycle" or "age-based" fund.

Tax and Revenue Anticipation Note (TRAN): Short-term debt obligation of a municipal issuer backed by future tax and revenue receipts.

Tax Anticipation Note (TAN): Short-term debt obligation of a municipal issuer backed by future tax receipts.

Tax Credit: Amount that can be subtracted from the amount of taxes owed.

Tax-Deferral: The ability to delay taxation on investment income within a tax-deferred account until constructive receipt.

Tax-Deferred: Account where all earnings remain untaxed until "constructive receipt."

Tax-Equivalent Yield: Rate of return that a taxable bond must offer to equal the tax-exempt yield on a municipal bond. To calculate, take the municipal yield and divide that by (100% – investor's tax bracket).

Tax-Exempt Bonds: Municipal bonds whose interest is not subject to taxation by the federal government.

Tax Preference Item: Certain items that must be added back to an investor's income for purposes of AMT, including interest on certain municipal bonds.

Tax-Sheltered Annuity (TSA): Annuity funded with pre-tax (tax-deductible) contributions. Available to employees of non-profit organizations such as schools, hospitals, and church organizations. a.k.a. "403(b) Plan."

T-Bills: Direct obligation of US Government. Sold at discount, mature at face amount. Maximum maturity is 1 year.

T-Bonds: Direct obligation of US Government. Pay semi-annual interest. Quoted as % of par value plus 32nds. 10–30-year maturities.

Technical Analysts: Stock traders who rely on market data to spot buying and selling opportunities rather than information on the companies who issue stocks.

Telemarketing: To market by telephone, assuming you can get past the caller ID.

Telephone Consumer Protection Act of 1991: Federal legislation restricting the activities of telemarketers, who generally may only call prospects between 8 a.m. and 9 p.m. in the prospect's time zone and must maintain a do-not-call list, also checking the national registry.

Tenants in Common: Joint account wherein the interest of the deceased owner reverts to his/her estate. AKA "joint tenants in common" or "JTIC."

Tender Offer: Offer to purchase the securities currently held by investors if the investors care to "tender" their securities for payment.

Term Life Insurance: Temporary insurance that builds no cash value and must be renewed at a higher premium at the end of the term. Renting rather than buying insurance.

The Insured: The person upon whose death a life insurance policy will pay out. Though usually also the policy owner, the insured could be a business partner whose death would require the other partners to do a buyout and, therefore, need the death benefit payable to the business.

Third Market: NYSE exchange-listed stock traded OTC primarily by institutional investors.

Third-party Account: Account managed on behalf of a third party, e.g., trust or UGMA.

Time Horizon: The anticipated holding period for an investment.

Times Interest Earned: Measurement from the income statement showing an issuer's ability to pay bond interest, EBIT divided by interest.

Time Value: The value of an option above its intrinsic value. For example, if XYZ trades @50, an XYZ Oct 50 call @1 has no intrinsic value but has $1 of time value.

Time Value of Money: The fact that a sum of money is worth more now than at some point in the future due to its earning potential.

Time Weighted Return: The average of returns over the time period.

Timing Risk: The risk of purchasing an investment at a peak price not likely to be sustained or seen again. Timing risk can be reduced through dollar cost averaging, rather than investing in a stock with one purchase.

Tippee: The guy who listened to the insider information.

Tipper: The guy who told him.

T-Notes: Direct obligation of US Government. Pay semi-annual interest. Quoted as % of par value plus 32nds. 2–10-year maturities.

Tombstone: Communication allowed during the cooling-off period to announce an offer of securities, listing the issuer, the type of security, the underwriters, and directions for obtaining a prospectus.

Top-Down Analysis: A type of fundamental analysis starting with overall economic trends and then moving down to industry sectors and particular companies.

Top-Heavy: A tax problem incurred by 401(k) plans providing too much benefit to key employees.

Total Assets: Current assets plus fixed assets plus intangible assets.

Total Liabilities: Current liabilities plus long-term liabilities.

Total Return: Measuring growth in share price plus dividend and capital gains distributions.

Total Takedown: The additional takedown plus the concession.

Trade Confirmation: Document containing details of a securities transaction, e.g., price of the security, commissions, stock symbol, number of shares, registered rep code, trade date and settlement date, etc.

Trade Date: Date that a trade is executed.

Trade Deficit: Excess of imports over exports in a nation's balance of trade with a trading partner.

Trade Reporting and Compliance Engine (TRACE): System used to report corporate bond transactions in the secondary market.

Trade Surplus: Excess of exports over imports in a nation's balance of trade with a trading partner.

Trading Authorization: Form granting another individual the authority to trade on behalf of the account owner.

Traditional IRA: Individual retirement account funded typically with tax-deductible contributions.

Tranche: Class of CMO. Principal is returned to one tranche at a time in a CMO.

Transfer Agent: Party that maintains an issuer's shareholder records.

Transfer and Hold in Safekeeping: Buy order for securities in which securities are bought and transferred to the customer's name, but held by the broker-dealer.

Transfer and Ship: Buy order for securities in which securities are purchased and transferred to the customer's name, with the certificates sent to the customer.

Transfer on Death (TOD): Individual account with a named beneficiary—assets transferred directly to the named beneficiary upon death of the account holder.

Treasury Bill: see T-Bills.

Treasury Bond: see T-Bonds.

Treasury Note: see T-Notes.

Treasury Receipts: Zero coupon bonds created by broker-dealers backed by Treasury securities held in escrow. Not a direct obligation of US Government.

Treasury Securities: Securities guaranteed by US Treasury, including T-bills, T-notes, T-bonds, and STRIPS.

Treasury Stock: Shares that have been issued and repurchased by the corporation. Has nothing to do with the US Treasury.

Trendline: The overall upward, downward, or sideways pricing trend of a stock or index as revealed by a chart.

Trough: Phase of the business cycle representing the "bottoming out" of a contraction, just before the next expansion/recovery.

True Interest Cost: Measure of a municipal issuer's total cost of borrowing money by issuing bonds. Unlike net interest cost, true interest cost factors in the time value of money.

Trust Indenture: Written agreement between an issuer and creditors wherein the terms of a debt security issue are set forth, e.g., interest rate, means of payment, maturity date, name of the trustee, etc.

Trust Indenture Act of 1939: Federal legislation requiring that corporate bond issues in excess of $5 million with maturities greater than 1 year must be issued with an indenture.

Trustee: Person legally appointed to act on a beneficiary's behalf.

Turnover Ratio: The frequency of trading that a mutual fund portfolio engages in.

TSA: Tax-sheltered annuity. A retirement vehicle for 403(b) and 501c3 organizations.

Two-dollar Broker: Independent broker on the floor of the NYSE.

U

UGMA or Uniform Gifts to Minors Act: Account set up for the benefit of a minor, managed by a custodian.

UIT or Unit Investment Trust: Type of investment company where investments are selected, not traded/managed. No management fee is charged. Shares are redeemable.

Underwriter: Broker-dealer that distributes shares on the primary market. AKA "investment banker."

Underwriting Spread: The profit to the syndicate. The difference between the proceeds to the issuer and the POP.

Unearned Income: Income derived from investments and other sources not related to employment, e.g., savings account interest, dividends from stock, capital gains, and rental income. Not eligible for an IRA contribution.

Unfunded Pension Liabilities: Obligations to retiring municipal workers that outweigh the funds set aside to actually pay them. A negative factor when analyzing general obligation municipal bonds.

Uniform Prudent Investor Act: A model Act providing guidance to fiduciaries interested in avoiding lawsuits for breach of fiduciary duty in terms of suitability/prudence in investment selection.

Uniform Securities Act: Model act that state securities laws are based on. Designed to prevent fraud and maintain faith in capital markets through registration of securities, agents, broker-dealers, and investment advisers. Main purpose is to provide necessary protection to investors.

Unit of Beneficial Interest: What an investor in a Unit Investment Trust (UIT) owns.

Universal Life Insurance: Form of permanent insurance that offers flexibility in death benefit and both the amount of, and method of paying, premiums.

Unlisted Security: A security that does not meet the listing requirements of a nationally recognized exchange such as NYSE or NASDAQ.

Unrealized Gain: The increase in the value of a security that has not yet been sold. Unrealized gains are not taxable.

Unsecured Bond: A bond issued without specific collateral. AKA "debenture."

Unsolicited: A transaction placed by the investor at no prompting from an agent/broker-dealer.

Unsystematic Risk: A risk that affects only a particular issuer or industry space, e.g. regulatory risk.

User Fee: Source of revenue used to retire a revenue bond, e.g., park entrance fees, tolls, skybox rentals, etc.

UTMA or Uniform Transfers to Minors Act: A custodial account, like an UGMA. Some states allow the transfer to happen as late as age 25, while in most states this occurs at age 21.

V

Valuation Ratio: A comparison of a stock's market price to the EPS, book value, cash flow, or revenue associated with one share of that stock.

Value Funds: Mutual funds investing in stocks currently out of favor with investors trading at low multiples.

Value Stock: As opposed to a "growth stock," a value stock trades at a low P/E or price-to-book ratio.

Variable Annuity: Annuity whose payment varies. Investments allocated to separate account as instructed by annuitant. Similar to investing in mutual funds, except that annuities offer tax deferral. No taxation until excess over cost basis is withdrawn.

Variable Life Insurance: Form of insurance where death benefit and cash value fluctuate according to fluctuations of the separate account.

Variable Universal Life Insurance: Flexible-premium insurance with cash value and death benefit tied to the performance of the separate account.

Vesting Schedule: A time-table for determining at what point the employer's contributions become the property of the employee in a pension plan.

Viatical Settlement: The sale and purchase of a life insurance policy wherein the investor buys the death benefit at a discount and profits when the insured dies. AKA "life settlement."

Visible Supply: Total par value of municipal bonds to be issued over the next 30 days, published in the Bond Buyer.

VIX: a key measure of market expectations of near-term volatility conveyed by S&P 500 stock index option prices. There are both options and futures contracts based on the VIX or "fear index."

Volatility: Up and down movements of an investment that make investors dizzy and occasionally nauseated.

Volume: Total number of shares traded over a given period (daily, weekly, etc.).

Voluntary Accumulation Plan: Mutual fund account into which the investor commits to depositing amounts of money on a regular basis.

Voter Approval: Process of approving the issuance of a general obligation bond by referendum.

VRDO – Variable Rate Demand Obligation: Debt security whose interest rate is regularly re-set and which can be "put" or sold back to the issuer or a designated third party for the par value plus accrued interest.

W

Warrant: Long-term equity security giving the owner the right to purchase stock at a set price. Often attached as a "sweetener" that makes the other security more attractive.

Wash Sale: Selling a security at a loss but then messing up by repurchasing it within 30 days and, therefore, not being able to use it to offset capital gains for that year.

Western/Divided Account: Syndicate account in which each participant is responsible for their share of the bonds only.

When-issued Confirmations: Confirmations of a purchase on the primary market delivered before the bonds have been issued.

Whole Life Insurance: Form of permanent insurance with a guaranteed death benefit and minimum guaranteed cash value.

Withdrawal Plan: Feature of most mutual funds that allows investors to liquidate their accounts over a fixed time period, or using a fixed-share or fixed-dollar amount.

Working Capital: Difference between a company's current assets and current liabilities measuring short-term liquidity. Related term "current ratio."

Wrap Account or Wrap Fee Program: Account in which the customer pays one fee to cover the costs of investment advisory services, execution of transactions, etc.

Wrap Fee: Fee charged in a wrap account covering execution, custodial, and portfolio management services.

Wrap Fee Brochure: Required supplement to an investment adviser's ADV 2 if sponsoring a wrap program.

Y

Yield: The income a security produces.

Yield Curve: A graph representing the yield of debt securities of similar credit quality across various maturities.

Yield Spread: The difference in yields between two types of debt securities, e.g. junk bonds vs. investment-grade, or junk bonds vs. US Treasury's.

Yield to Call: The yield received on a bond if held to the date it is called.

454

Yield to Maturity: Calculation of all interest payments plus/minus gain/loss on a bond if held to maturity. Or, the discount rate at which the sum of all future cash flows from the bond is equal to the price of the bond.

Z

Zero Coupon Bond: Bond sold at a deep discount to its gradually increasing par value.

Z-Tranche: The last tranche to receive principal in a CMO.

42244354R00253

Made in the USA
Lexington, KY
13 June 2015